Cisco Firepower Defense (FTD)

Configuration and Troubleshooting Best Practices for the Next-Generation Firewall (NGFW), Next-Generation Intrusion Prevention System (NGIPS), and Advanced Malware Protection (AMP)

Nazmul Rajib

Cisco Press

800 East 96th Street

Indianapolis, Indiana 46240 USA

Cisco Firepower Threat Defense (FTD)

Configuration and Troubleshooting Best Practices for the Next-Generation Firewall (NGFW), Next-Generation Intrusion Prevention System (NGIPS), and Advanced Malware Protection (AMP)

Nazmul Rajib

Copyright © 2018 Cisco Systems, Inc.

Published by:
Cisco Press
800 East 96th Street
Indianapolis, IN 46240 USA

Printed in the United States of America

1   17

Library of Congress Control Number: 2017953843

ISBN-13: 978-1-58714-480-6

ISBN-10: 1-58714-480-8

Warning and Disclaimer

This book is designed to provide advanced information about the Next-Generation Firewall (NGFW), Next-Generation Intrusion Prevention System (NGIPS), and Advanced Malware Protection (AMP) system using the Cisco Firepower technologies. Every effort has been made to make this book as complete and as accurate as possible, but no warranty or fitness is implied.

The information is provided on an "as is" basis. The authors, Cisco Press, and Cisco Systems, Inc. shall have neither liability nor responsibility to any person or entity with respect to any loss or damages arising from the information contained in this book or from the use of the discs or programs that may accompany it.

The opinions expressed in this book belong to the author and are not necessarily those of Cisco Systems, Inc.

Trademark Acknowledgments

All terms mentioned in this book that are known to be trademarks or service marks have been appropriately capitalized. Cisco Press or Cisco Systems, Inc., cannot attest to the accuracy of this information. Use of a term in this book should not be regarded as affecting the validity of any trademark or service mark.

Special Sales

For information about buying this title in bulk quantities, or for special sales opportunities (which may include electronic versions; custom cover designs; and content particular to your business, training goals, marketing focus, or branding interests), please contact our corporate sales department at corpsales@pearsoned.com or (800) 382-3419.

For government sales inquiries, please contact governmentsales@pearsoned.com.

For questions about sales outside the U.S., please contact intlcs@pearson.com.

Feedback Information

At Cisco Press, our goal is to create in-depth technical books of the highest quality and value. Each book is crafted with care and precision, undergoing rigorous development that involves the unique expertise of members from the professional technical community.

Readers' feedback is a natural continuation of this process. If you have any comments regarding how we could improve the quality of this book, or otherwise alter it to better suit your needs, you can contact us through email at feedback@ciscopress.com. Please make sure to include the book title and ISBN in your message.

We greatly appreciate your assistance.

Editor-in-Chief: Mark Taub	**Copy Editor:** Kitty Wilson
Alliances Manager, Cisco Press: Ron Fligge	**Technical Editors:** John Groetzinger, Foster Lipkey
Product Line Manager: Brett Bartow	**Editorial Assistant:** Vanessa Evans
Executive Editor: Mary Beth Ray	**Cover Designer:** Chuti Prasertsith
Managing Editor: Sandra Schroeder	**Composition:** codeMantra
Development Editor: Ellie C. Bru	**Indexer:** Erika Millen
Senior Project Editor: Tonya Simpson	**Proofreader:** Larry Sulky

CISCO

About the Author

Nazmul Rajib is a senior engineer and leader of the Cisco Global Technical Services organization focusing on next-generation security technologies. He leads cybersecurity training initiatives, develops internal training programs, and trains the current generation of Cisco engineers who support Cisco security solutions around the world. He also reviews design specifications, tests security software, and provides solutions to business-critical networking issues. Nazmul has authored numerous technical publications at Cisco.com and in the Cisco support community.

Nazmul is a veteran engineer of Sourcefire, Inc., which developed Snort—the most popular open-source intrusion prevention system in the world. He created and managed the global knowledge base for Sourcefire and designed Sourcefire security certifications for partner enablement. Nazmul trained security engineers from many managed security service providers (MSSP) in the United States. He supported the networks of numerous Fortune 500 companies and U.S. government agencies.

Nazmul has a master of science degree in internetworking. He also holds many certifications in the areas of cybersecurity, information technology, and technical communication. He is a Sourcefire Certified Expert (SFCE) and Sourcefire Certified Security Engineer (SFCSE).

About the Technical Reviewers

John Groetzinger is a member of the Global TAC Security Technical Leadership team, supporting Firepower, AMP for Endpoints, Threat Grid, and third-party integrations. He has been a leader in developing tools and procedures for supporting the Cisco Firepower and AMP security software platforms. He has worked closely with the various engineering teams in the Cisco security space to improve quality and serviceability. He holds a bachelor's degree in mechanical engineering with a minor in computer science. John's primary areas of interest are enterprise security, open source software, API development/integration, and automation.

Foster Lipkey is a member of the Global TAC Security Technical Leadership team. He has been supporting Firepower technologies since 2012. He is responsible for many automated tools leveraged by the Global Technical Assistance Center (TAC). Prior to working for Sourcefire and Cisco, he was an application solution specialist for the National Cancer Institute (NCI), supporting Java Enterprise applications for the NCI Center for Biomedical Informatics and Information Technology (CBIIT). Foster's primary areas of interest are enterprise security and security automation. He was a technical editor of *Cisco Next-Generation Security Solutions: All-in-One Cisco ASA FirePOWER Services, NGIPS, and AMP*.

Dedication

I am me, because of…

My grandparent's blessings

My mom's inspiration

My dad's support

My wife's devotion

My children's love

My teacher's advice

This book is dedicated to all of them,

with my sincere gratitude.

Acknowledgments

Thank you, God, for giving me the ability to write this book.

I am grateful to two technical support managers of the Cisco Global Technical Services team, Andrew Firman and Maurice Spencer, for their encouragement and support throughout the process of authoring this book.

I am thankful to the technical leaders of the Cisco Firepower technology, John Groetzinger and Foster Lipkey, who are also the technical editors of this book. Their commitment and thorough reviews have been indispensable to this book.

I appreciate the time Principal Engineer Gonzalo Salgueiro took to review the draft proposal for this book. Many thanks to Senior Vice President Tom Berghoff and Senior Director Marc Holloman for sending me their words of appreciation for writing this book.

I would also like to acknowledge the daily cooperation of my colleagues in the Research Triangle Park (RTP), North Carolina. Shout-out to all of my fellows, students and readers in Fulton, Richardson, San Jose, Mexico City, Krakow, Sofia, Bangalore, Sydney, Beijing, Tokyo (and many other cities), for providing me feedback on my internal training and publications.

Finally, I recognize all of the editors at Pearson Education and Cisco Press for working with me diligently and keeping me on track to get this book published.

Contents at a Glance

Appendixes

Contents

Reader Services

Register your copy at www.ciscopress.com/title/9781587144806 for convenient access to downloads, updates, and corrections as they become available. To start the registration process, go to www.ciscopress.com/register and log in or create an account*. Enter the product ISBN 9781587144806 and click Submit. When the process is complete, you will find any available bonus content under Registered Products.

*Be sure to check the box that you would like to hear from us to receive exclusive discounts on future editions of this product.

Icons Used in This Book

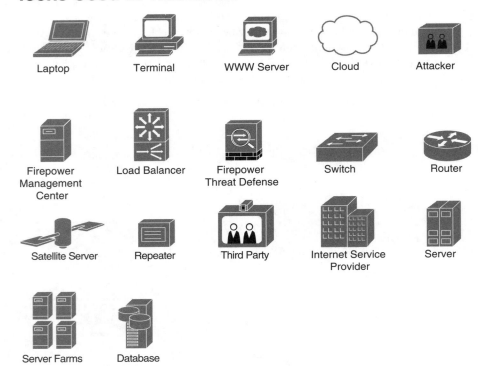

Command Syntax Conventions

The conventions used to present command syntax in this book are the same conventions used in the IOS Command Reference. The Command Reference describes these conventions as follows:

■ **Boldface** indicates commands and keywords that are entered literally as shown. In actual configuration examples and output (not general command syntax), boldface indicates commands that are manually input by the user (such as a **show** command).

■ *Italic* indicates arguments for which you supply actual values.

■ Vertical bars (|) separate alternative, mutually exclusive elements.

■ Square brackets ([ ]) indicate an optional element.

■ Braces ({ }) indicate a required choice.

■ Braces within brackets ([{ }]) indicate a required choice within an optional element.

Introduction

Cisco introduces next-generation security technologies in the unified Firepower Threat Defense (FTD) software. It offers the Next-Generation Firewall (NGFW), Next-Generation Intrusion Prevention System (NGIPS), Advanced Malware Protection (AMP), and many more features—all in a single software image.

This book provides best practices, demonstrates configurations, analyzes debugs, and illustrates GUI screenshots from real-world deployment scenarios. It empowers you to configure your own Firepower system with confidence. The book summarizes complex operations in a simple flowchart, and presents many diagnostic tools that allow you to investigate any potential technical issues by yourself. In other words, it could serve you as a "personal technical support engineer."

Who Should Read This Book?

Any network engineer, security engineer, security analyst, firewall specialist, or system administrator who wants to configure and manage a Cisco Firepower System should read this book. Any technical support engineers, advanced services engineers, professional services engineers, field engineers, network consulting engineers, sales engineers, and security engineers who would like to diagnose any technical issues by their own will find this book very useful.

This book is an important resource to channel partners and managed security service providers (MSSPs) who want to provide technical support to their own customers.

This book is invaluable to the administrators of classified environments, such as U.S. government agencies, who are not allowed to share troubleshooting data due to security restriction, and therefore want to troubleshoot their own issues.

Any students or candidates who want to take a Cisco security certification exam will find valuable information in this book. This book covers Firepower next-generation security-related topics that are included in the CCNA Security, CCNP Security, and CCIE Security exam curricula.

This book is not a replacement for an official Cisco Firepower publication, such as a user guide or an installation guide. It is, rather, a supplement to the official publications.

How This Book Is Organized

- **Chapter 1, "Introduction to the Cisco Firepower Technology":** The book begins with the history and evolution of the Cisco Firepower technology. This chapter introduces various software components that may be installed on a Firepower system. It also provides a quick overview of the hardware that supports the Cisco Firepower Threat Defense (FTD) technology.

- **Chapter 2, "FTD on ASA 5500-X Series Hardware":** This chapter describes the differences between various software images that may be installed on ASA 5500-X Series hardware. It demonstrates the detailed process of reimaging ASA 5500-X Series hardware to the FTD software. In addition, this chapter provides the command-line tools you can use to verify the status of the hardware and software.

- **Chapter 3, "FTD on the Firepower eXtensible Operating System (FXOS)":** This chapter describes the architecture, implementation, and installation of FTD on a Firepower security appliance running Firepower eXtensible Operating System (FXOS). It demonstrates several command-line tools you can use to determine the status of various components of the appliance.

- **Chapter 4, "Firepower Management Center (FMC) Hardware":** This chapter discusses and compares various hardware platforms for the FMC. It illustrates the complete reimaging process (also known as System Restore) and describes the best practices for doing it. You can also learn many different command-line tools to determine any issues with FMC hardware.

- **Chapter 5, "Firepower System Virtual on VMware":** This chapter describes various aspects of the Firepower virtual appliance, such as how to deploy a virtual appliance, how to tune the resources for optimal performance, and how to investigate issues with a new deployment.

- **Chapter 6, "The Firepower Management Network":** This chapter describes the best practices for designing and configuring a management network for the Firepower System. It also discusses the tools you can use to verify any communication issues between the management interfaces of the FMC and FTD. Before you begin the registration process, which is described in Chapter 7, you must ensure that the FMC and FTD are successfully connected through your network.

- **Chapter 7, "Firepower Licensing and Registration":** This chapter discusses licensing and registration—two important initial tasks in a Firepower system deployment. It describes the capabilities of different Firepower licenses and the steps involved in registering the FMC with a Smart License Server. It also demonstrates the registration process and the tools to investigate any communication issues.

- **Chapter 8, "Firepower Deployment in Routed Mode":** This chapter explains Routed Mode, which is a widely deployed firewall mode. It describes the steps involved in configuring the routed interfaces with static IP addresses as well as dynamic IP addresses. In addition, this chapter discusses various command-line tools you can use to determine any potential interface-related issues.

- **Chapter 9, "Firepower Deployment in Transparent Mode":** This chapter discusses another mode, Transparent Mode, including how to configure the physical and virtual interfaces, and how to use various command-line tools to investigate any potential configuration issues.

- **Chapter 10, "Capturing Traffic for Advanced Analysis":** This chapter describes the processes involved in capturing live traffic on an FTD device by using the system-provided capturing tool. To demonstrate the benefit of the tool, this chapter shows how to use various **tcpdump** options and BPF syntaxes to filter and manage packet capture.

- **Chapter 11, "Blocking Traffic Using Inline Interface Mode":** This chapter demonstrates how to configure an FTD device in Inline Mode, how to enable fault tolerance features on an inline set, and how to trace a packet in order to analyze the root cause of a drop. This chapter also describes various command-line tools that you can use to verify the status of an interface, an inline pair, and an inline set.

- **Chapter 12, "Inspecting Traffic Without Blocking It":** This chapter explains the configuration and operation of various detection-only modes of an FTD device, such as Passive Mode, Inline Tap Mode, and Inline Mode with the Drop When Inline option disabled. It also provides various command-line tools that you can use to determine the status of interfaces and traffic.

- **Chapter 13, "Handling Encapsulated Traffic":** This chapter shows you how to analyze and block traffic that is encapsulated with the GRE protocol. This chapter also demonstrates the steps to bypass an inspection when the traffic is transferred over a tunnel. Besides showing configurations, this chapter also shows various tools to analyze an action applied by the Prefilter and Access Control policy of an FTD device.

- **Chapter 14, "Bypassing Inspection and Trusting Traffic":** This chapter discusses the techniques to bypass an inspection. It provides the steps to configure different methods. The chapter also analyzes the flows of bypassed packets to demonstrate how an FTD device acts during different bypassing options. You will learn how to use various debugging tools to determine whether the bypass process is working as designed.

- **Chapter 15, "Rate Limiting Traffic":** This chapter goes through the steps to configure QoS policy on an FTD device. It also provides an overview to the common rate-limiting mechanisms and the QoS implementation on an FTD device. This chapter also provides the command-line tools to verify the operation of QoS policy in an FTD device.

- **Chapter 16, "Blacklisting Suspicious Addresses by Using Security Intelligence":** This chapter illustrates the detection of a malicious address by using the Security Intelligence feature. It describes how to configure an FTD device to block, monitor, or whitelist an address when there is a match. This chapter also discusses the backend file systems for the Security Intelligence feature. You can apply this knowledge to troubleshoot an issue with Security Intelligence.

- **Chapter 17, "Blocking a Domain Name System (DNS) Query":** This chapter demonstrates various techniques to administer DNS queries using a Firepower DNS policy. Besides using traditional access control rules, an FTD device can incorporate the Cisco Intelligence Feed and dynamically blacklist suspicious domains. This chapter shows various ways to configure and deploy a DNS policy. This chapter also demonstrates several command-line tools you can run to verify, analyze, and troubleshoot issues with DNS policy.

- **Chapter 18, "Filtering URLs Based on Category, Risk, and Reputation":** This chapter describes techniques to filter traffic based on the category and reputation of a URL. It illustrates how a Firepower system performs a URL lookup and how an FTD device takes action based on the query result. This chapter explains the connection to a URL through debugging messages, which is critical for troubleshooting.

- **Chapter 19, "Discovering Network Applications and Controlling Application Traffic":** This chapter shows how a Firepower system can make you aware of the applications running on your network and empowers you to control access to any unwanted applications. It also shows the techniques to verify whether an FTD device can identify an application properly.

- **Chapter 20, "Controlling File Transfer and Blocking the Spread of Malware":** Cisco integrates the Advanced Malware Protection (AMP) technology with the Firepower technology. This chapter explains how the technologies work together to help you detect and block the spread of infected files across your network. In this chapter, you will learn the configurations and operations of a file policy on a Firepower system. This chapter also demonstrates various logs and debugging messages, which are useful for determining issues with cloud lookup and file disposition.

- **Chapter 21, "Preventing Cyber Attacks by Blocking Intrusion Attempts":** This chapter describes the well-known feature of a Firepower system: the Snort-based next-generation intrusion prevention system (NGIPS). In this chapter, you will learn how to configure an NGIPS, how to apply any associated policies, and how to drill down into intrusion events for advanced analysis. This chapter discusses the Firepower Recommendations feature and demonstrates how the recommended ruleset can reduce system overhead by incorporating discovery data.

- **Chapter 22, "Masquerading the Original IP Address of an Internal Network Host":** This chapter discusses various types of NAT on an FTD device. It shows the steps to configure a NAT rule and demonstrates how FTD can leverage NAT technology to masquerade internal IP addresses in a real-world scenario.

Chapter 1

Introduction to the Cisco Firepower Technology

This book describes various components of next-generation security solutions. Each chapter walks you through a unique feature of the Cisco Firepower security technologies. Before diving into the technical details, this chapter helps you become familiar with the Firepower technologies by providing an overview.

History of Sourcefire

Cisco acquired Sourcefire in 2013. At that time, Sourcefire was one of the top leaders in the cybersecurity industry for its intrusion detection system (IDS), intrusion prevention system (IPS), and next-generation firewall (NGFW) solutions. The Sourcefire IPS was based on Snort, an open source network intrusion detection and prevention system. In fact, Martin Roesch, the creator of Snort, founded Sourcefire in 2001.

Since acquiring Sourcefire, Cisco has leveraged its technologies on various existing Cisco appliances, such as ASA 5500-X Series and Integrated Services Router (ISR) devices. Cisco has also released new hardware platforms, such as the Firepower 2100 Series, 4100 Series, and 9300 Series, which also implement the Sourcefire technologies. Integration of the Sourcefire technologies has made Cisco one of the leaders in the Gartner Magic Quadrant for IDS and IPS. Gartner is an advisory company that performs research on various branches of information technology and publishes numerous research papers every year.

Figure 1-1 shows the Cisco leadership position in the IDS and IPS spaces since the Sourcefire acquisition. This graphic was published by Gartner, Inc. as part of a larger research document and should be evaluated in the context of the entire document. The Gartner document is available upon request from Cisco. Go to cisco.com/go/ngips.

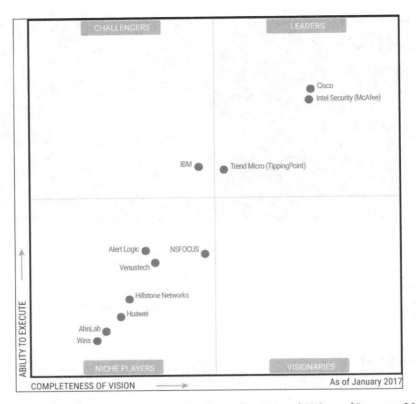

Figure 1-1   *Gartner's Magic Quadrant for IDS and IPS as of January 2017*

> **Note**   Gartner does not endorse any vendor, product, or service depicted in its research publications, and does not advise technology users to select only those vendors with the highest ratings or other designation. Gartner research publications consist of the opinions of Gartner's research organization and should not be construed as statements of fact. Gartner disclaims all warranties, expressed or implied, with respect to this research, including any warranties of merchantability or fitness for a particular purpose.

Evolution of Firepower

A Firepower System deployment primarily consists of two types of appliances: a management appliance and a sensor. Basically, a sensor inspects network traffic and sends any events to its management appliance. A management appliance, as the name implies, manages all kinds of security policies for a sensor.

Figure 1-2 shows the workflow of a Firepower System deployment.

Sourcefire originally had two different software trains—Version 4.x (primarily for IPS) and Version 5.x (with NGFW functionalities). Depending on the software train, the management appliance had two different names. In Version 4.x, it was known as Sourcefire Defense Center. In Version 5.x, it was known as FireSIGHT System or FireSIGHT Management Center (FMC). Similarly, a sensor was known as a 3D sensor in Version 4.x and a FirePOWER appliance in Version 5.x. Therefore, it would be correct to say that, in Version 4.x, the Sourcefire Defense Center manages the 3D sensors, whereas in Version 5.x, the FireSIGHT Management Center manages the FirePOWER appliances.

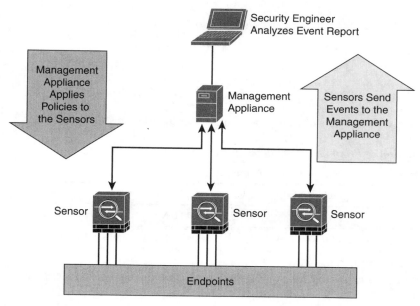

Figure 1-2 *Block Diagram of a Firepower System Deployment*

FirePOWER Versus Firepower

In the previous section, did you notice that different words, FireSIGHT and FirePOWER, are used to refer to different types of appliances in different versions? Did you notice the word POWER with all uppercase letters?

To make the nomenclature simple as well as to maintain brand reputation, Cisco rebranded the Sourcefire technologies with one simple word, Firepower. (Cisco did not retrospectively change the names of the legacy Sourcefire software and hardware from FirePOWER to Firepower; only hardware and software released since the Cisco acquisition use the new nomenclature.) Figure 1-3 shows the evolution of the Firepower Threat Defense (FTD) technology from the pre-acquisition period to post-integration.

Some examples of new Firepower products are the Cisco Firepower 9300 appliance hardware and the Cisco FTD software. Similarly, Cisco FirePOWER 8000 Series appliances have been available since the pre-acquisition period.

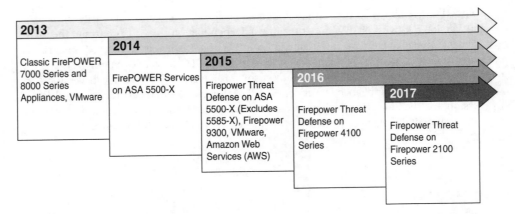

Figure 1-3 *Evolution of FTD Technology*

Table 1-1 shows various names of management appliances in different software versions.

Table 1-1 *Evolution of Firepower Management Center*

Software Version	Management Appliance
Version 4.x	Defense Center (DC)
Version 5.x	FireSIGHT System or FireSIGHT Management Center (FMC)
Version 6.x	Firepower System or Firepower Management Center (FMC)

Figure 1-4 shows the login page for a management appliance running Version 5.x. This page displays the legacy name FireSIGHT and the Sourcefire Support contact information.

Figure 1-5 shows the login page of a management appliance running Version 6.x. As you can see, this version displays the name Firepower and does not provide the legacy Sourcefire Support contact information.

Despite the differences already mentioned, the login pages for Version 5.x and 6.x look almost identical. As you can see in Figure 1-6, the Defense Center login page for Version 4.x is totally different from the login pages for Version 5.x or 6.x.

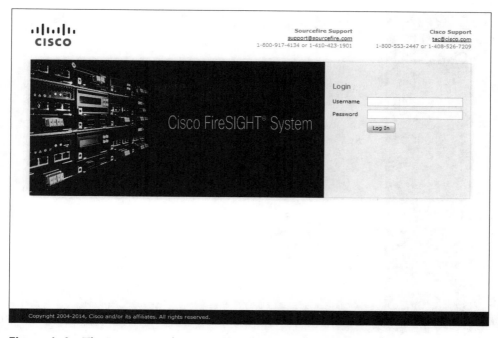

Figure 1-4 *The Login Page for FireSIGHT Management Center Running Version 5.x*

Figure 1-5 *The Login Page for Firepower Management Center Running Version 6.x*

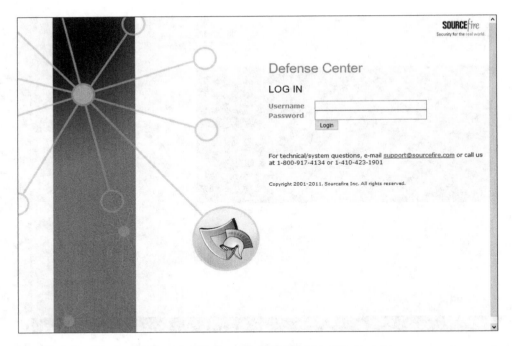

Figure 1-6   *The Login Page for Defense Center Running Version 4.x*

Firepower Threat Defense (FTD)

Now is the time to learn about the FTD. Before we dig into the software components and hardware platforms, let's try to identify the difference between the FirePOWER Services and Firepower Threat Defense (FTD).

FirePOWER Service Versus Firepower Threat Defense (FTD)

As you might have guessed, FirePOWER Services refers to features that are similar to the pre-acquisition period software releases, such as Next-Generation Intrusion Prevention System Virtual (NGIPSv). In FTD, Cisco converges all the Sourcefire FirePOWER features, ASA firewall features, and some additional new features into one single unified software image.

Figure 1-7 illustrates the convergence of Cisco ASA software with Sourcefire FirePOWER software into the FTD code. Due to this convergence, FirePOWER Services no longer runs as a separate service module, which reduces overhead and increases efficiency.

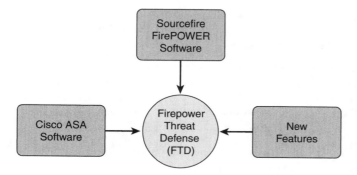

Figure 1-7 *Logical Representation of the FTD Software*

Note This book is written based on Firepower Version 6.1 running on FTD. Although this book uses the ASA 5500-X Series hardware, managed using the Firepower Management Center (FMC), you can still apply this knowledge on other platforms running Firepower technologies.

Firepower System Software Components

The Firepower System offers lot of security features. Unlike with traditional Cisco ASA firewall software, the security features of the Firepower System are delivered as multiple software components:

- **Firepower core software:** The core part of the software includes the Snort engine for intrusion detection and prevention, a web server for the graphical user interface (GUI), a database to store events, firmware for the hardware, and so on. The core software image for the Firepower System depends on the hardware platform you are using.

- **Software patches and hotfixes:** Cisco releases software patches periodically to address any security vulnerabilities and to fix any defects with the Firepower System. When an issue demands resolution earlier than a scheduled maintenance update, Cisco may release a hotfix for it, on case-by-case basis.

- **Snort/Sourcefire rules:** The Snort engine uses a special ruleset to detect and prevent intrusion attempts. Each rule considers certain conditions. When a packet goes through a sensor and matches a condition in a Snort rule, the Snort engine takes the appropriate action.

- **Vulnerability database (VDB):** A VDB stores vulnerability information and fingerprints of various applications, services, and operating systems (OSs). The Firepower

System uses the fingerprints to discover the application, service, and OS running on a network host, and then it correlates the application and network discovery data with the vulnerability information on a VDB.

- **Geolocation database (GeoDB):** A GeoDB stores geographical information and associated IP addresses. For example, when the Firepower System displays an intrusion event in the GUI, you can view the name and flag of the country that originated that intrusion attempt. This information allows you to make decisions quickly, without performing reverse lookups for IP addresses.

Figure 1-8 illustrates the various software components installed on the Firepower System. All these software components are explained in later chapters of this book.

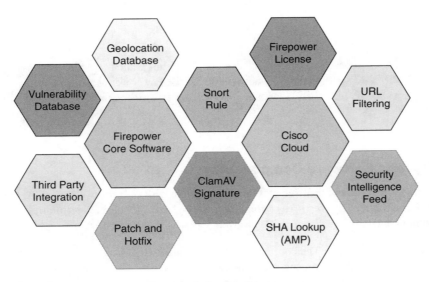

Figure 1-8   *Firepower System Software Components*

- **URL filtering database:** The Firepower System can categorize websites based on their targeted audiences or business purposes. To give you more granular control, the system also enables you to control access to a certain type of website, based on its reputation or known risk level. All this information is stored in the URL filtering database. Unlike with Firepower software components, any updates for the URL filtering database are provided directly through the Cisco cloud, so your FMC must be connected to the Internet.

- **Security Intelligence Feed:** Talos, the Cisco threat intelligence team, is continuously researching the Internet to identify potential malicious IP addresses, domain names, and URLs. For Firepower System users, Talos shares intelligence data through the Security Intelligence Feed. The FMC can download the feed directly from the cloud.

■ **Local malware detection:** With a malware license, FTD can detect viruses in your files. This allows you to block the spread of malware across your network. FTD uses the ClamAV engine to analyze files locally. The FMC obtains the signatures of the latest viruses through the local malware detection updates.

■ **Integration:** You can integrate the Firepower System with various products and technologies, such as Cisco Identity Services Engine (ISE), Microsoft Windows Active Directory Server, Event Streamer (eStreamer), and Syslog Server. This empowers you with unlimited opportunities to monitor and secure your network. (This book focuses on core Firepower technologies, and features related to integration are beyond the scope of this book. Please read the official Firepower user guide to learn more about integration.)

Firepower System Hardware Platforms

FTD Version 6.1 is available on a wide variety of hardware platforms. The internal architecture of each platform is different. There are, of course, differences in form factor, throughput, and price. Later in this book, you will learn more about the architectures and operations of the Firepower System.

Table 1-2 summarizes the hardware platforms (available as of this writing) that support FTD software. All of the following platforms support Version 6.1, except Firepower 2100 Series (Version 6.2.1 or greater) and Microsoft Azure (Version 6.2 or greater).

Table 1-2 *Hardware Platforms That Support FTD Software*

Hardware Category	Platform Name/Model Number
Cisco ASA 5500-X Series	ASA5506-X, 5506H-X, 5506W-X, 5508-X, 5516-X, 5512-X, 5515-X, 5525-X, 5545-X, 5555-X
Firepower 2100 Series	Firepower 2110, 2120, 2130, 2140
Firepower 4100 Series	Firepower 4110, 4120, 4140, 4150
Firepower 9000 Series	Firepower 9300
Virtual	VMWare ESXi/vSphere, Kernel-Based Virtual Machine (KVM), Amazon Web Services (AWS) Microsoft Azure

Figure 1-9 illustrates the placement of various ASA and Firepower platforms in different types of networking environments. The throughput of appliances varies significantly depending on the number of enabled features, such as firewall (FW) only, firewall along with Cisco Application Visibility and Control (AVC), next-generation intrusion prevention system (NGIPS), URL filtering, SSL decryption, and so on.

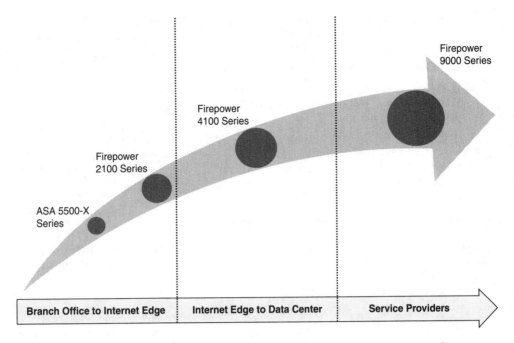

Figure 1-9   *Placement of ASA and Firepower Appliances in Various Networking Environments with Different Needs*

Note   To find out what hardware models support FTD and the throughput of each hardware model, please check the Cisco Firepower NGFW data sheet at cisco.com or contact your account representative.

Firepower Accessories

When you open a brand-new Firepower appliance box, you will find various accessories along with the actual appliance. The accessories are necessary to configure the initial setup and obtain a license. Figure 1-10 shows an example of the accessories that come with a Cisco ASA 5506-X appliance:

- The ASA 5506-X appliance (see #1 in Figure 1-10)
- A DB-9 to RJ-45 console cable (see #2)
- Envelope with the product activation key (PAK) (see #3)
- Power adapter (see #4)
- Power cord to connect with the power adapter (see #5)

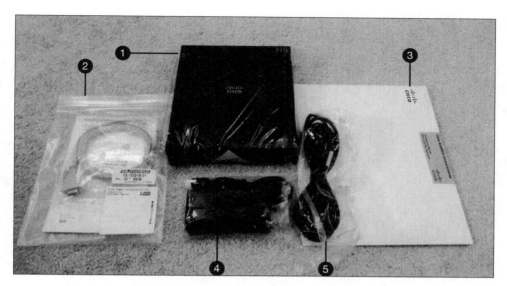

Figure 1-10   *Cisco ASA 5506-X Appliance Accessories Example*

Note   The accessories in a box are subject to change, depending on various factors. In your box, you may receive more or fewer items than are shown in this example.

Tip   Read the Installation Guide for your appliance model (available at cisco.com) to learn how to install it into a rack and power it up.

Summary

This chapter discusses the history and evolution of the Cisco Firepower technology. It introduces various software components that may be installed on the Firepower System. This chapter also provides a quick overview of the supported hardware for the Cisco Firepower Threat Defense (FTD) technology.

The next few chapters demonstrate how to install the FTD software on various hardware platforms. You also learn how to identify hardware-related issues before taking on a more advanced configuration.

Chapter 2

FTD on ASA 5500-X Series Hardware

If your ASA is currently running FirePOWER Services as a separate module and you want to deploy Firepower Threat Defense (FTD), you must reimage your ASA with the unified FTD image. This chapter discusses the steps required to reimage and troubleshoot any Cisco ASA 5500-X Series hardware.

ASA Reimaging Essentials

To reimage ASA hardware with FTD, you need to use more than one type of image on the same hardware. This section describes the purposes of those images.

Figure 2-1 shows the subsets of a Firepower Threat Defense software image that you install or upgrade on the Cisco ASA 5500-X Series hardware platforms during the FTD reimaging process:

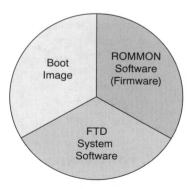

Figure 2-1 *Subsets of a Firepower Threat Defense Software Image*

- **ROMMON software:** The ROMMON software is the firmware of an ASA. In an ASA, you enter the ROMMON mode to perform all the necessary tasks to copy a boot image from an external server. If you are reimaging one of the low-end ASA hardware platforms, such as ASA 5506-X, 5506W-X, 5506H-X, 5508-X, or 5516-X, you must update the firmware to Release 1.1.8 or greater. If you are running one of the midrange ASA hardware platforms, such as 5512-X, 5515-X, 5525-X, 5545-X, or 5555-X, and want to reimage it to the FTD software, you do not need to update the default firmware.

- **Boot image:** The FTD boot image is a subset of the FTD system software. After you load your ASA with an FTD boot image, you can use the CLI of the boot image to prepare your ASA for downloading the FTD system software and beginning the setup.

- **System software:** All the features of FTD are packaged in a system software image. You begin the FTD system software installation from the CLI prompt of the boot image. This is the last step of a basic reimaging process.

Table 2-1 summarizes various types of software that you might have to install to complete the FTD reimaging process.

Table 2-1   *Software Images Required to Complete an FTD Reimage*

	ROMMON Software	Boot Image	System Software
Purpose	To update the firmware of an ASA.	To load an ASA with the network config, download the system software, and begin setup.	To install the features of the FTD system.
Low-end ASA (5506-X, 5508-X, 5516-X)	Firmware release 1.1.8 or greater is required. Use the *.SPA file to upgrade firmware.	Use a *.lfbff file to load a low-end ASA with the FTD boot image.	Use a *.pkg file to install the FTD system software package. You can use the same system software package on any low-end and midrange ASA hardware models.
Midrange ASA (5512-X, 5515-X, 5525-X, 5545-X, 5555-X)	Not necessary to update the default firmware version.	Use a *.cdisk file to load a midrange ASA with the FTD boot image.	

Best Practices for FTD Installation on ASA Hardware

Consider the following best practices before reimaging ASA 5500-X Series hardware:

- If you have just received a new ASA 5500-X, it might already have the FTD software preinstalled. In this case, you just need to update the FTD to the latest release and complete the configurations. However, reimaging is necessary when the hardware has traditional ASA software installed or when FirePOWER Services is running as a separate module.

■ You should perform reimaging during a maintenance window because the process interrupts the network traffic.

■ Prior to the maintenance window when you plan to do the reimaging, make sure you are able to access the software.cisco.com website and can download all the FTD software. If needed, register for a Cisco account. If after the self-registration process you cannot download any of the desired software, you might need to get further assistance from your Cisco channel partner or the Cisco Technical Assistance Center (TAC).

■ The reimaging process may take about an hour, depending on the hardware model. However, you should plan for additional time to fulfill any prerequisites.

■ After you download any software from software.cisco.com, always verify the MD5 or SHA512 checksum of the files you have downloaded to confirm that the file is not corrupt and has not been modified during download. Figure 2-2 shows how the MD5 and SHA512 checksum values are displayed at software.cisco.com when you hover your mouse over a filename.

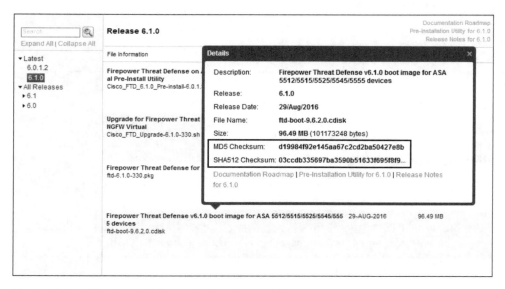

Figure 2-2   *Checksum Values of a Boot Image File*

■ Reimaging an ASA with FTD software wipes out all the previous configurations, so make a backup of the existing configurations before you start the reimaging.

■ Never power off, shut down, or reboot ASA hardware when reimaging is in progress. A login prompt appears after all the reimaging processes are complete.

■ Read the release notes to determine any known issues and any special requirements or instructions.

Installing and Configuring FTD

In this section, you learn the detailed steps involved in installing the FTD software on ASA 5500-X Series hardware. Before you install anything on an ASA, there are some prerequisites. Once you fulfill them, you can perform the remaining tasks of the reimaging process.

Figure 2-3 summarizes the steps involved in reimaging ASA 5500-X hardware to the FTD system software.

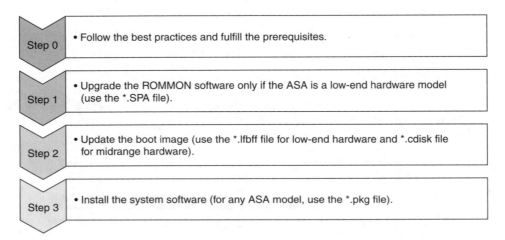

Step 0
- Follow the best practices and fulfill the prerequisites.

Step 1
- Upgrade the ROMMON software only if the ASA is a low-end hardware model (use the *.SPA file).

Step 2
- Update the boot image (use the *.lfbff file for low-end hardware and *.cdisk file for midrange hardware).

Step 3
- Install the system software (for any ASA model, use the *.pkg file).

Figure 2-3 *Major Steps in Reimaging ASA 5500-X Series Hardware*

Fulfilling Prerequisites

You must fulfill storage and connectivity requirements before you begin reimaging. The following are the storage prerequisites:

- To install FTD software, an ASA requires at least 3 GB free space plus additional space to store an FTD boot image (which is usually about 100 MB). See the "Verification and Troubleshooting Tools" section, later in this chapter, to learn how to determine how much free disk space an ASA has.

- Make sure the ASA has a solid state drive (SSD) installed. See the "Verification and Troubleshooting Tools" section, later in this chapter, to learn how to determine whether an SSD is installed in an ASA.

Caution   If you have installed an SSD for the first time or replaced an SSD in midrange ASA hardware, you must reload your ASA and then reimage or reinstall any software.

The following are the connectivity prerequisites:

- Using a console cable, connect your computer to the console port of the ASA that you want to reimage.

- Ensure that you have access to TFTP and HTTP servers. You use the TFTP server to copy the firmware and boot image files to the ASA during the reimaging process. You copy the FTD system software from the HTTP server to the ASA. You can use an FTP server in lieu of an HTTP server, but you might find that a basic HTTP server is easier to set up.

Figure 2-4 shows a topology in which the management network is segregated from the data traffic, according to security best practice. An administrator computer is directly connected to an ASA through a console cable, and it also has access to the management network.

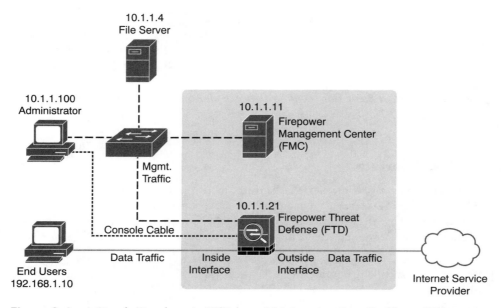

Figure 2-4 *A Simple Topology in Which an ASA Inspects Data Traffic and Keeps Management Traffic Isolated*

Figure 2-5 shows the simplest topology that provides both console and IP connectivity between an ASA and a computer and allows an administrator to perform reimaging and basic configuration.

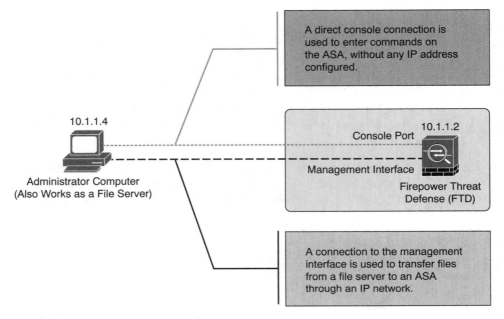

Figure 2-5   *The Most Basic Connectivity Between an ASA and a Server for Performing Reimaging and Basic Setup*

Upgrading Firmware

If you plan to reimage a low-end ASA hardware model, such as 5506-X, 5508-X, or 5516-X, to the FTD software, you must make sure that the firmware version of the ASA is 1.1.8 or greater. See the "Verification and Troubleshooting Tools" section, later in this chapter, to learn how to determine the firmware version.

Note   You do not need to upgrade the default firmware of any midrange ASA hardware models, such as 5512-X, 5515-X, 5525-X, 5545-X, and 5555-X. Therefore, you can skip this section if you are running a midrange ASA model.

Follow these steps to upgrade the firmware (ROMMON software) of a low-end ASA model:

Step 1.   Download the ROMMON software from software.cisco.com and store it to your TFTP server. Figure 2-6 shows the ROMMON software file asa5500-firmware-1108.SPA that you use to upgrade the firmware of low-end ASA 5500-X Series hardware before you begin the reimaging process.

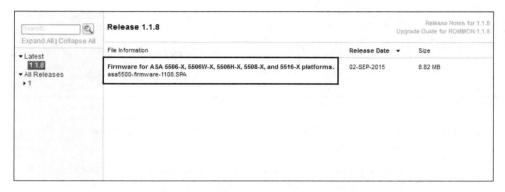

Figure 2-6 *The ROMMON Software File Information*

Step 2.   Copy the file from your TFTP server to your ASA storage. To copy a file from a TFTP server to an ASA, run the following command:

```
ciscoasa# copy tftp://TFTP_server_address/filename disk0:
```

Example 2-1 shows that the ROMMON software file asa5500-firmware-1108.SPA is successfully copied from a TFTP server (IP address 10.1.1.4, for example) to the storage of ASA 5506-X hardware.

Example 2-1   *Copying a File from a TFTP Server to ASA Hardware*

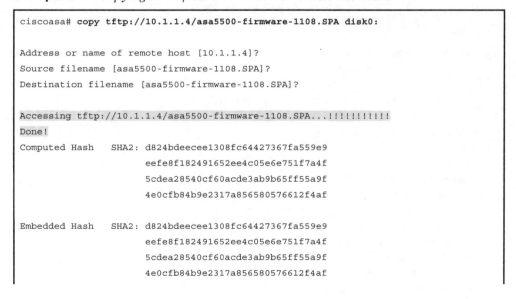

```
Digital signature successfully validated
Writing file disk0:/asa5500-firmware-1108.SPA...
!!!!!!!!!
9241408 bytes copied in 8.230 secs (1155176 bytes/sec)
ciscoasa#
```

Step 3.   Once the file is copied successfully, begin the upgrade by running the following command:

```
ciscoasa# upgrade rommon disk0:/asa5500-firmware-1108.SPA
```

Example 2-2 shows the command to upgrade the firmware of ASA hardware. After the ROMMON software file is verified, the ASA prompts for a confirmation to reload.

Example 2-2   *Running the Command to Begin the ROMMON Upgrade*

```
ciscoasa# upgrade rommon disk0:/asa5500-firmware-1108.SPA

Verifying file integrity of disk0:/asa5500-firmware-1108.SPA

Computed Hash    SHA2: d824bdeecee1308fc64427367fa559e9
                       eefe8f182491652ee4c05e6e751f7a4f
                       5cdea28540cf60acde3ab9b65ff55a9f
                       4e0cfb84b9e2317a856580576612f4af

Embedded Hash    SHA2: d824bdeecee1308fc64427367fa559e9
                       eefe8f182491652ee4c05e6e751f7a4f
                       5cdea28540cf60acde3ab9b65ff55a9f
                       4e0cfb84b9e2317a856580576612f4af

Digital signature successfully validated
File Name                     : disk0:/asa5500-firmware-1108.SPA
Image type                    : Release
    Signer Information
        Common Name           : abraxas
        Organization Unit     : NCS_Kenton_ASA
        Organization Name     : CiscoSystems
    Certificate Serial Number : 55831CF6
    Hash Algorithm            : SHA2 512
    Signature Algorithm       : 2048-bit RSA
    Key Version               : A
Verification successful.
Proceed with reload? [confirm]
```

Step 4. Press the Enter key to confirm. Example 2-3 shows the reloading of the ASA
hardware after the firmware upgrade starts.

Example 2-3 *Reloading ASA Hardware After an Upgrade Starts*

```
***
*** --- START GRACEFUL SHUTDOWN ---
***
*** Message to all terminals:
***
***    Performing upgrade on rom-monitor.
Shutting down isakmp
Shutting down webvpn
Shutting down sw-module
Shutting down License Controller
Shutting down File system
***
*** --- SHUTDOWN NOW ---
***
*** Message to all terminals:
***
***    Performing upgrade on rom-monitor.
Process shutdown finished
Rebooting... (status 0x9)
..
INIT: Sending processes the TERM signal
Stopping OpenBSD Secure Shell server: sshdno /usr/sbin/sshd found; none killed
Deconfiguring network interfaces... done.
Sending all processes the TERM signal...
Sending all processes the KILL signal...
Deactivating swap...
Unmounting local filesystems...
Rebooting...
```

During the firmware upgrade process, the ASA reboots automatically a few
times. Example 2-4 shows the ASA completing the first two steps of the
ROMMON upgrade process. The system reloads every time it completes a step.

Note Do not reboot an ASA manually while the ROMMON or firmware upgrade is in
progress.

Example 2-4   *Upgrading the ROMMON Software*

```
Rom image verified correctly
Cisco Systems ROMMON, Version 1.1.01, RELEASE SOFTWARE
Copyright (c) 1994-2014  by Cisco Systems, Inc.
Compiled Mon 10/20/2014 15:59:12.05 by builder


Current image running: Boot ROM0
Last reset cause: PowerCycleRequest
DIMM Slot 0 : Present
INFO: Rommon upgrade state: ROMMON_UPG_START (1)
INFO: Reset code: 0x00002000
Firmware upgrade step 1...
Looking for file 'disk0:/asa5500-firmware-1108.SPA'
Located 'asa5500-firmware-1108.SPA' @ cluster 1608398.
###############################################################################
  ###
############################################################
Image base 0x77014018, size 9241408
LFBFF signature verified.
Objtype: lfbff_object_rommon (0x800000 bytes @ 0x77014238)
Objtype: lfbff_object_fpga (0xd0100 bytes @ 0x77814258)
INFO: FPGA version in upgrade image: 0x0202
INFO: FPGA version currently active: 0x0202
INFO: The FPGA image is up-to-date.
INFO: Rommon version currently active: 1.1.01.
INFO: Rommon version in upgrade image: 1.1.08.
Active ROMMON: Preferred 0, selected 0, booted 0
Switching SPI access to standby rommon 1.
Please DO NOT reboot the unit, updating ROMMON......
INFO: Duplicating machine state......
Reloading now as step 1 of the rommon upgrade process...


Toggling power on system board...
Rom image verified correctly


Cisco Systems ROMMON, Version 1.1.01, RELEASE SOFTWARE
Copyright (c) 1994-2014  by Cisco Systems, Inc.
Compiled Mon 10/20/2014 15:59:12.05 by builder
Current image running: Boot ROM0
Last reset cause: RP-Reset
DIMM Slot 0 : Present
INFO: Rommon upgrade state: ROMMON_UPG_START (1)
```

```
INFO: Reset code: 0x00000008
Active ROMMON: Preferred 0, selected 0, booted 0
Firmware upgrade step 2...
Detected current rommon upgrade is available, continue rommon upgrade process
Rommon upgrade reset 0 in progress
Reloading now as step 2 of the rommon upgrade process...
```

Step 5.   After Step 1 and Step 2 of the upgrade process, when the ASA reloads, the
ROMMON version shows 1.1.8 (see Example 2-5). The process, however, is
still in progress. When the ASA prompts for a manual or automatic reboot,
just wait a few seconds and let the system reboot itself.

Example 2-5   *The Last Stage of the ROMMON Upgrade Process*

```
Rom image verified correctly
Cisco Systems ROMMON, Version 1.1.8, RELEASE SOFTWARE
Copyright (c) 1994-2015  by Cisco Systems, Inc.
Compiled Thu 06/18/2015 12:15:56.43 by builders


Current image running: *Upgrade in progress* Boot ROM1
Last reset cause: BootRomUpgrade
DIMM Slot 0 : Present
INFO: Rommon upgrade state: ROMMON_UPG_START (1)
INFO: Reset code: 0x00000010
PROM B: stopping boot timer
Active ROMMON: Preferred 0, selected 0, booted 1
INFO: Rommon upgrade state: ROMMON_UPG_TEST


!!!!!!!!!!!!!!!!!!!!!!!!!!!!!!!!!!!!!!!!!!!!!!!!!!!!!!!!!!!!!!!!!!!!!!!!!!
!! Please manually or auto boot ASAOS now to complete firmware upgrade !!
!!!!!!!!!!!!!!!!!!!!!!!!!!!!!!!!!!!!!!!!!!!!!!!!!!!!!!!!!!!!!!!!!!!!!!!!!!


Platform ASA5506 with 4096 Mbytes of main memory
MAC Address: a4:6c:2a:e4:6b:bf
Using default Management Ethernet Port: 0


Use BREAK or ESC to interrupt boot.
Use SPACE to begin boot immediately.
Boot in 5 seconds.
```

Example 2-6 shows the confirmation message you get for a successful
ROMMON upgrade, after the final reboot. At this stage, the ROMMON
software is fully upgraded, and you are ready to begin the next step of the
reimage process.

Example 2-6 *Completion of a Successful Upgrade*

```
Located '.boot_string' @ cluster 1607965.


#
Attempt autoboot: "boot disk0:/asa961-50-lfbff-k8.spa"
Located 'asa961-50-lfbff-k8.spa' @ cluster 10.


################################################################################
  ##############################################################################
  ##############################################################################
  ###########################################################
LFBFF signature verified.
INIT: version 2.88 booting
Starting udev
Configuring network interfaces... done.
Populating dev cache
dosfsck 2.11, 12 Mar 2005, FAT32, LFN
There are differences between boot sector and its backup.
Differences: (offset:original/backup)
  65:01/00
  Not automatically fixing this.
Starting check/repair pass.
Starting verification pass.
/dev/sdb1: 104 files, 811482/1918808 clusters
dosfsck(/dev/sdb1) returned 0
Mounting /dev/sdb1
Setting the offload CPU count to 0
IO Memory Nodes: 1
IO Memory Per Node: 205520896 bytes


Global Reserve Memory Per Node: 314572800 bytes Nodes=1


LCMB: got 205520896 bytes on numa-id=0, phys=0x10d400000, virt=0x2aaaab000000
LCMB: HEAP-CACHE POOL got 314572800 bytes on numa-id=0, virt=0x7fedbc200000
Processor memory:    1502270072


Compiled on Fri 04-Mar-16 10:50 PST by builders
Total NICs found: 14
i354 rev03 Gigabit Ethernet @ irq255 dev 20 index 08 MAC: a46c.2ae4.6bbf
ivshmem rev03 Backplane Data Interface     @ index 09 MAC: 0000.0001.0002
en_vtun rev00 Backplane Control Interface  @ index 10 MAC: 0000.0001.0001
en_vtun rev00 Backplane Int-Mgmt Interface     @ index 11 MAC: 0000.0001.0003
en_vtun rev00 Backplane Ext-Mgmt Interface     @ index 12 MAC: 0000.0000.0000
en_vtun rev00 Backplane Tap Interface      @ index 13 MAC: 0000.0100.0001
```

```
Rom-monitor was successfully upgraded.
Verify the activation-key, it might take a while...
.
.
! Licensing and legal information are omitted for brevity
.
.
                Cisco Systems, Inc.
                170 West Tasman Drive
                San Jose, California 95134-1706


Reading from flash...
!.
Cryptochecksum (unchanged): 868f669d 9e09ca8b e91c32de 4ee8fd7f

INFO: Power-On Self-Test in process.
.....................
INFO: Power-On Self-Test complete.
INFO: Starting HW-DRBG health test...
INFO: HW-DRBG health test passed.

INFO: Starting SW-DRBG health test...
INFO: SW-DRBG health test passed.
Type help or '?' for a list of available commands.
ciscoasa>
```

When an ASA is running, you can also manually check its ROMMON software version, as discussed in the "Verification and Troubleshooting Tools" section, later in this chapter. Example 2-7 shows that the current firmware version is upgraded to 1.1.8.

Example 2-7 *The Upgraded Firmware Version*

```
ciscoasa> enable
Password: *****
ciscoasa# show module


Mod  Card Type                                           Model              Serial No.
---- --------------------------------------------------- ------------------ -----------
   1 ASA 5506-X with FirePOWER services, 8GE, AC, ASA5506              JAD191100HG
 sfr Unknown                                             N/A                JAD191100HG


Mod  MAC Address Range                   Hw Version  Fw Version  Sw Version
---- ----------------------------------- ----------- ----------- ---------------
   1 a46c.2ae4.6bbf to a46c.2ae4.6bc8  1.0         1.1.8       9.6(1)50
 sfr a46c.2ae4.6bbe to a46c.2ae4.6bbe  N/A         N/A
```

```
Mod   SSM Application Name              Status             SSM Application Version
----  ------------------------------   ----------------   --------------------------


Mod   Status                  Data Plane Status     Compatibility
----  -----------------       --------------------  -------------
   1  Up Sys                  Not Applicable
 sfr  Unresponsive            Not Applicable


ciscoasa#
```

Installing the Boot Image

You begin the setup of the FTD software from the command line interface (CLI) of a boot image. To access the CLI of the boot image, you need to reload the ASA with the FTD boot. This section discusses the steps that are necessary to reload an ASA with an appropriate boot image on any ASA 5500-X Series hardware:

Step 1.   Download the appropriate boot image for your ASA hardware:

  ■ For low-end ASA hardware, use the *.lfbff file.

  ■ For midrange hardware, use the *.cdisk file.

Figure 2-7 shows the boot image file ftd-boot-9.6.2.0.lfbff that you use during the reimaging of ASA 5506-X, 5508-X, or 5516-X hardware.

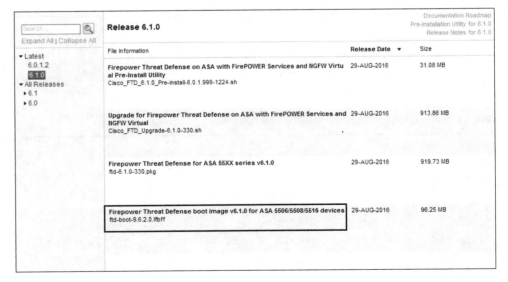

Figure 2-7   *The *.lfbff Boot Image File for Low-End ASA 5500-X Series Hardware*

Figure 2-8 shows the boot image file ftd-boot-9.6.2.0.cdisk that you use during the reimaging of ASA 5512-X, 5515-X, 5525-X, 5545-X, or 5555-X hardware.

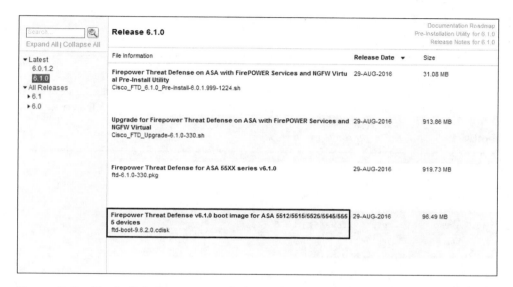

Figure 2-8   *The *.cdisk Boot Image File for Midrange ASA 5500-X Series Hardware*

Step 2.   Reload the ASA. As shown in Example 2-8, the ASA shuts down all its processes before it gracefully reboots.

Example 2-8   *Reloading ASA Hardware*

```
ciscoasa# reload
Proceed with reload? [confirm]
ciscoasa#
***
*** --- START GRACEFUL SHUTDOWN ---
Shutting down isakmp
Shutting down webvpn
Shutting down sw-module
Shutting down License Controller
Shutting down File system
***
*** --- SHUTDOWN NOW ---
Process shutdown finished
Rebooting... (status 0x9)
..
INIT: Sending processes the TERM signal
Stopping OpenBSD Secure Shell server: sshdno /usr/sbin/sshd found; none killed
```

```
Deconfiguring network interfaces... done.
Sending all processes the TERM signal...
Sending all processes the KILL signal...
Deactivating swap...
Unmounting local filesystems...
Rebooting...
```

Step 3.   Interrupt the bootup process by pressing the Esc key. Example 2-9 shows that the bootup process is interrupted and the ASA enters ROMMON mode.

Example 2-9   *Interrupting the Bootup Process*

```
Rom image verified correctly

Cisco Systems ROMMON, Version 1.1.8, RELEASE SOFTWARE
Copyright (c) 1994-2015  by Cisco Systems, Inc.
Compiled Thu 06/18/2015 12:15:56.43 by builders

Current image running: Boot ROM1
Last reset cause: PowerCycleRequest
DIMM Slot 0 : Present

Platform ASA5506 with 4096 Mbytes of main memory
MAC Address: a4:6c:2a:e4:6b:bf
Using default Management Ethernet Port: 0

Use BREAK or ESC to interrupt boot.
Use SPACE to begin boot immediately.
Boot in 7 seconds.
Boot interrupted.
rommon 1 >
```

Step 4.   To see the ROMMON configuration mode's limited command options, run the **help** command. Example 2-10 shows the available commands in the ROMMON configuration mode, with the commands used to install the boot image highlighted.

Example 2-10   *Available Commands in the ROMMON Configuration Mode*

```
rommon 1 > help
?                  Display this help menu
address            Set the local IP address
boot               Boot an application program
confreg            Configuration register contents display and management
console            Console BAUD rate display and configuration
```

```
dev                    Display a list of available file system devices
dir                    File directory display command
erase                  erase the specified file system
file                   Set the application image file path/name to be TFTPed
gateway                Set the default gateway IP address
help                   "help" for this menu
                       "help <command>" for specific command information
history                Show the command line history
netmask                Set the IP subnet mask value
ping                   Test network connectivity with ping commands
server                 Set the TFTP server IP address
show                   Display system device and status information
tftpdnld               Download and run the image defined by "FILE"
reboot                 Reboot the system
reload                 Reboot the system
repeat                 Repeat a CLI command
reset                  Reboot the system
set                    Display the configured environment variables
sync                   Save the environment variables to persistent storage
unset                  Clear a configured environment variable
```

Step 5.   Configure the network by using the commands shown in Example 2-11. You must configure these options to ensure successful network communication between the ASA, FMC, and other servers.

Example 2-11   *Commands to Configure the Network Settings in ROMMON Mode*

```
rommon 2 > address 10.1.1.21
rommon 3 > netmask 255.255.255.0
rommon 4 > gateway 10.1.1.1
rommon 5 > server 10.1.1.4
```

Note   The IP addresses in the configuration shown in Example 2-11 are based on the topology shown in Figure 2-4. Here, the ASA, FMC, and all other servers are in the same switching network, which means their IP addresses are in the same subnet. If the ASA, FMC, and servers are in different subnets, the ingress interface of the router (where the ASA is deployed) becomes the gateway for the ASA.

Step 6.   Test the connectivity from the ASA to the TFTP server where the image files are stored, as shown in Example 2-12. You get confirmation that the ASA can communicate with the TFTP server.

Example 2-12   *A Successful* **ping** *Test from the ASA to the TFTP Server*

```
rommon 6 > ping 10.1.1.4
Sending 10, 32-byte ICMP Echoes to 10.1.1.4 timeout is 4 seconds
!!!!!!!!!!
Success rate is 100 percent (10/10)
```

Step 7.   Once connectivity is established, provide the name of the boot image file you want to download from the TFTP server, save the changes, and begin the download. Example 2-13 shows that the ASA 5506-X has successfully downloaded the boot image file ftd-boot-9.6.2.0.lfbff from a TFTP server.

Caution   If you are reimaging midrange ASA hardware, such as 5512-X, 5515-X, 5525-X, 5545-X, or 5555-X, you must use the ftd-boot-9.6.2.0.cdisk file instead of the ftd-boot-9.6.2.0.lfbff file.

Example 2-13   *Commands to Select and Download a File from a TFTP Server to ASA Hardware*

```
rommon 7 > file ftd-boot-9.6.2.0.lfbff
rommon 8 > sync
rommon 9 > tftpdnld
            ADDRESS: 10.1.1.21
            NETMASK: 255.255.255.0
            GATEWAY: 10.1.1.1
             SERVER: 10.1.1.4
              IMAGE: ftd-boot-9.6.2.0.lfbff
            MACADDR: a4:6c:2a:e4:6b:bf
          VERBOSITY: Progress
              RETRY: 20
         PKTTIMEOUT: 60
            BLKSIZE: 1460
           CHECKSUM: Yes
               PORT: GbE/1
            PHYMODE: Auto Detect


Receiving ftd-boot-9.6.2.0.lfbff from 10.1.1.4!!!!!!!!!!!!!!!!!!!!!!!!!!!!!!!!!!!!!!!!!
   !!!!!!!!!!!!!!!!!!!!!!!!!!!!!!!!!!!!!!!!!!!!!!!!!!!!!!!!!!!!!!!!!!!!!!!!!!!!!!!!!!!!!!
   !!!!!!!!!!!!!!!!!!!!!!!!!!!!!!!!!!!!!!!!!!!!!!!!!!!!!!!!!!!!!!!!!!!!!!!!!!!!!!!!!!!!!!
   !!!!!!!!!!!!!!!!!!!!!!!!!!!!!!!!!!!!!!!!!!!!!!!!!!!!!!!!!!!!!!!!!!!!!!!!!!!!!!!!!!!!!!
   !!!!!!!!!!!!!!!!!!!!!!!!!!!!!!!!!!!!!!!!!!!!!!!!!!!!!!!!!!!!!!!!!!!!!!!!!!!!!!!!!!!!!!
   !!!!!!!!!!!!!!!!!!!!!!!!!!!!!!!!!!!!!!
File reception completed.
```

The ASA boots up automatically with the FTD boot CLI, as shown in
Example 2-14.

Example 2-14 *Bootup Process of ASA Hardware with an FTD Boot Image*

```
Boot buffer bigbuf=348bd018
Boot image size = 100921600 (0x603f100) bytes
[image size]        100921600
[MD5 signature]       0264697f6f1942b9bf80f820fb209ad5
LFBFF signature verified.
INIT: version 2.88 booting
Starting udev
Configuring network interfaces... done.
Populating dev cache
Detected PID ASA5506.
Found device serial number JAD191100HG.
Found USB flash drive /dev/sdb
Found hard drive(s):  /dev/sda
fsck from util-linux 2.23.2
dosfsck 2.11, 12 Mar 2005, FAT32, LFN
There are differences between boot sector and its backup.
Differences: (offset:original/backup)
  65:01/00
  Not automatically fixing this.
/dev/sdb1: 52 files, 811482/1918808 clusters
Launching boot CLI ...
Configuring network interface using static IP
Bringing up network interface.
Depending on your network, this might take a couple of minutes when using DHCP...
ifup: interface lo already configured
Using IPv4 address: 10.1.1.21
INIT: Starting system message bus: dbus.
Starting OpenBSD Secure Shell server: sshd
  generating ssh RSA key...
  generating ssh ECDSA key...
  generating ssh DSA key...
done.
Starting Advanced Configuration and Power Interface daemon: acpid.
acpid: starting up
acpid: 1 rule loaded
acpid: waiting for events: event logging is off
Starting ntpd: done
Starting syslog-ng:[2016-09-19T19:43:24.781411] Connection failed; fd='15',
  server='AF_INET(127.128.254.1:514)', local='AF_INET(0.0.0.0:0)', error='Network is
  unreachable (101)'
```

```
[2016-09-19T19:43:24.781508] Initiating connection failed, reconnecting;
  time_reopen='60'
.
Starting crond: OK


              Cisco FTD Boot 6.0.0 (9.6.2.)
              Type ? for list of commands
ciscoasa-boot>
```

Step 8.   Optionally press the ? key to see the list of the available commands on the
FTD boot CLI, as shown in Example 2-15. (In the next section of this chapter,
you will see the commands highlighted in this example used to install an FTD
software system image.)

Example 2-15   *The Command Options on the FTD Boot CLI*

```
ciscoasa-boot> ?
    show            => Display system information. Enter show ? for options
    system          => Control system operation
    setup           => System Setup Wizard
    support         => Support information for TAC
    delete          => Delete files
    ping            => Ping a host to check reachability
    traceroute      => Trace the route to a remote host
    exit            => Exit the session
    help            => Get help on command syntax
ciscoasa-boot>
```

Installing the System Software

Installing the FTD software is the last step of the reimaging process. This section
describes the steps to install the FTD system software on any ASA 5500-X series
hardware:

Step 1.   Download the FTD system software package file from software.cisco.com
and copy it to an HTTP or FTP server. Figure 2-9 shows the FTD system
software package ftd-6.1.0-330.pkg that you install on any low-end or
midrange ASA 5500-X Series hardware during the reimaging process.

Note   This book uses an HTTP server in lieu of an FTP server. You can use either one,
though. You may find that the setup of an HTTP server is easier than the setup of an
FTP server.

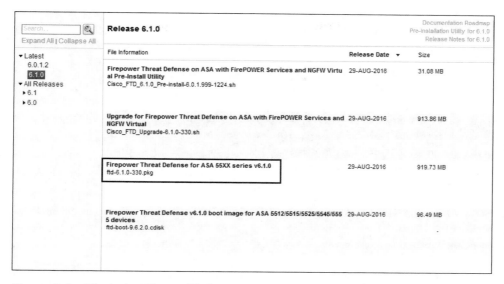

Figure 2-9 *The *.pkg File Installed on Any Low-End or Midrange ASA Hardware Models*

Step 2. As shown in Example 2-16, run the **setup** command to configure or update the network settings so that the ASA can download the FTD system software package from the HTTP server. During the installation of the boot image, you configured the network settings. Now you either verify the existing configuration or provide any missing information that was not entered before.

Tip When a default value (shown in square brackets, [ ]) is acceptable, press Enter to keep the settings unchanged.

Example 2-16 *A Complete Walk-through of the Network Setup Process*

```
ciscoasa-boot> setup

              Welcome to Cisco FTD Setup
                [hit Ctrl-C to abort]
              Default values are inside []


Enter a hostname [ciscoasa]:
Do you want to configure IPv4 address on management interface?(y/n) [Y]:
Do you want to enable DHCP for IPv4 address assignment on management interface?(y/n)
    [N]:
```

```
Enter an IPv4 address [10.1.1.21]:
Enter the netmask [255.255.255.0]:
Enter the gateway [10.1.1.1]:
Do you want to configure static IPv6 address on management interface?(y/n) [N]:
Stateless autoconfiguration will be enabled for IPv6 addresses.
Enter the primary DNS server IP address: 10.1.1.8
Do you want to configure Secondary DNS Server? (y/n) [n]:
Do you want to configure Local Domain Name? (y/n) [n]:
Do you want to configure Search domains? (y/n) [n]:
Do you want to enable the NTP service? [Y]:
Enter the NTP servers separated by commas: 10.1.1.9


Please review the final configuration:
Hostname:               ciscoasa
Management Interface Configuration

IPv4 Configuration:     static
        IP Address:     10.1.1.21
        Netmask:        255.255.255.0
        Gateway:        10.1.1.1

IPv6 Configuration:     Stateless autoconfiguration

DNS Configuration:
        DNS Server:     10.1.1.8

NTP configuration:      10.1.1.9

CAUTION:
You have selected IPv6 stateless autoconfiguration, which assigns a global address
based on network prefix and a device identifier. Although this address is unlikely
to change, if it does change, the system will stop functioning correctly.
We suggest you use static addressing instead.
Apply the changes?(y,n) [Y]:
Configuration saved successfully!
Applying...
Restarting network services...
Done.
Press ENTER to continue...
ciscoasa-boot>
```

Step 3.   Test the connectivity, as shown in Example 2-17. This example also shows that
the ASA can successfully **ping** from the FTD boot CLI to the HTTP server.

Example 2-17   ping *Test Between the ASA and the HTTP Server*

```
ciscoasa-boot> ping 10.1.1.4
PING 10.1.1.4 (10.1.1.4) 56(84) bytes of data.
64 bytes from 10.1.1.4: icmp_seq=1 ttl=64 time=0.364 ms
64 bytes from 10.1.1.4: icmp_seq=2 ttl=64 time=0.352 ms
64 bytes from 10.1.1.4: icmp_seq=3 ttl=64 time=0.326 ms
64 bytes from 10.1.1.4: icmp_seq=4 ttl=64 time=0.313 ms
^C
--- 10.1.1.4 ping statistics ---
4 packets transmitted, 4 received, 0% packet loss, time 2997ms
rtt min/avg/max/mdev = 0.313/0.338/0.364/0.030 ms

ciscoasa-boot>
```

Step 4.   Download the FTD system software package from the HTTP server, as shown in Example 2-18. After a successful download, the file is extracted automatically.

Example 2-18   *Downloading the FTD System Software*

```
ciscoasa-boot> system install http://10.1.1.4/ftd-6.1.0-330.pkg

######################## WARNING ############################
# The content of disk0: will be erased during installation! #
#############################################################

Do you want to continue? [y/N] Y
Erasing disk0 ...
Verifying
Downloading...
```

Step 5.   When prompted, press Y to start the upgrade process. Example 2-19 shows the extraction of the FTD system software package ftd-6.1.0-330.pkg and the beginning of the upgrade process.

Caution   Extracting the FTD system software package can take approximately 10 minutes. In addition, the system takes 6 minutes to populate the system image. ASA hardware does not show any progress status while it is extracting or populating a file. Be patient and do not interrupt the process or reboot the ASA. Doing so might make your ASA unstable.

Example 2-19   *Starting the Upgrade Process*

```
Extracting.....
Package Detail
        Description:                    Cisco ASA-FTD 6.1.0-330 System Install
        Requires reboot:               Yes


Do you want to continue with upgrade? [y]:
Warning: Please do not interrupt the process or turn off the system.
Doing so might leave system in unusable state.


Starting upgrade process ...
Populating new system image..
```

Step 6.   When the image is populated and the system prompts you to reboot the
system, press Enter to reboot. Example 2-20 shows the ASA hardware
rebooting after the image is populated.

Example 2-20   *Rebooting the ASA Hardware to Complete the Upgrade*

```
Reboot is required to complete the upgrade. Press 'Enter' to reboot the system.

Broadcast mStopping OpenBSD Secure Shell server: sshdstopped /usr/sbin/sshd (pid 1723)
.
Stopping Advanced Configuration and Power Interface daemon: stopped /usr/sbin/acpid
  (pid 1727)
acpid: exiting

acpid.
Stopping system message bus: dbus.
Stopping ntpd: stopped process in pidfile '/var/run/ntp.pid' (pid 1893)
done
Stopping crond: OKs
Deconfiguring network interfaces... done.
Sending all processes the TERM signal...
Sending all processes the KILL signal...
Deactivating swap...
Unmounting local filesystems...
Rebooting...


Rom image verified correctly


Cisco Systems ROMMON, Version 1.1.8, RELEASE SOFTWARE
```

```
Copyright (c) 1994-2015  by Cisco Systems, Inc.
Compiled Thu 06/18/2015 12:15:56.43 by builders

Current image running: Boot ROM1
Last reset cause: PowerCycleRequest
DIMM Slot 0 : Present

Platform ASA5506 with 4096 Mbytes of main memory
MAC Address: a4:6c:2a:e4:6b:bf
Using default Management Ethernet Port: 0

Use BREAK or ESC to interrupt boot.
Use SPACE to begin boot immediately.
Boot in 5 seconds.


Located '.boot_string' @ cluster 260097.
#
Attempt autoboot: "boot disk0:os.img"
Located 'os.img' @ cluster 235457.


#################################################################################
   ##############################################################################
   ##############################################################################
   ##############################################################################
   ##############################################################################
   ##############################################################################
   ###########
LFBFF signature verified.
INIT: version 2.88 booting
Starting udev
Configuring network interfaces... done.
Populating dev cache
Detected PID ASA5506.
Found device serial number JAD191100HG.
Found USB flash drive /dev/sdb
Found hard drive(s):  /dev/sda
fsck from util-linux 2.23.2
dosfsck 2.11, 12 Mar 2005, FAT32, LFN
/dev/sdb1: 7 files, 24683/1919063 clusters
```

After bootup, the initialization of the FTD software begins automatically. Example 2-21 shows the launch of FTD software and the execution of various scripts throughout the installation process.

Caution Depending on the ASA hardware model, initialization may take about an hour to complete. At a certain point, you might think the process is hung, but it is not. The system does not display progress status, but be patient. Do not interrupt the process or reboot the ASA. Doing so might make your ASA unstable. Once the FTD is completely installed, a login prompt appears.

Example 2-21 *The FTD Initialization Process*

```
Use ESC to interrupt boot and launch boot CLI.
Use SPACE to launch Cisco FTD immediately.
Cisco FTD launch in 21 seconds ...


Cisco FTD launch in 0 seconds ...
Running on kenton
Mounting disk partitions ...
Initializing Threat Defense ...                                  [  OK  ]
Starting system log daemon...                                    [  OK  ]
Stopping mysql...
Sep 19 20:29:33 ciscoasa SF-IMS[2303]: [2303] pmtool:pmtool [ERROR] Unable to connect
  to UNIX socket at /ngfw/var/sf/run/PM_Control.sock: No such file or directory
Starting mysql...
Sep 19 20:29:33 ciscoasa SF-IMS[2304]: [2304] pmtool:pmtool [ERROR] Unable to connect
  to UNIX socket at /ngfw/var/sf/run/PM_Control.sock: No such file or directory
Flushing all current IPv4 rules and user defined chains: ...success
Clearing all current IPv4 rules and user defined chains: ...success
Applying iptables firewall rules:
Flushing chain 'PREROUTING'
.
! Omitted the messages related to iptables flushing for brevity
.
Flushing chain 'OUTPUT'
Applying rules successed
Starting nscd...
mkdir: created directory '/var/run/nscd'                         [  OK  ]
Starting , please wait...grep: /ngfw/etc/motd: No such file or directory
...complete.
Firstboot detected, executing scripts
Executing S01reset_failopen_if                                   [  OK  ]
Executing S01virtual-machine-reconfigure                         [  OK  ]
Executing S02aws-pull-cfg                                        [  OK  ]
Executing S02configure_onbox                                     [  OK  ]
Executing S04fix-httpd.sh                                        [  OK  ]
Executing S05set-mgmnt-port                                      [  OK  ]
```

```
Executing S06addusers                                    [  OK  ]
Executing S07uuid-init                                   [  OK  ]
Executing S08configure_mysql                             [  OK  ]


************ Attention *********


   Initializing the configuration database.  Depending on available
   system resources (CPU, memory, and disk), this may take 30 minutes
   or more to complete.


************ Attention *********


Executing S09database-init                               [  OK  ]
Executing S11database-populate                           [  OK  ]
Executing S12install_infodb                              [  OK  ]
Executing S15set-locale.sh                               [  OK  ]
Executing S16update-sensor.pl                            [  OK  ]
Executing S19cert-tun-init                               [  OK  ]
Executing S20cert-init                                   [  OK  ]
Executing S21disable_estreamer                           [  OK  ]
Executing S25create_default_des.pl                       [  OK  ]
Executing S30init_lights_out_mgmt.pl                     [  OK  ]
Executing S40install_default_filters.pl                  [  OK  ]
Executing S42install_default_dashboards.pl               [  OK  ]
Executing S43install_default_report_templates.pl         [  OK  ]
Executing S44install_default_app_filters.pl              [  OK  ]
Executing S45install_default_realms.pl                   [  OK  ]
Executing S47install_default_sandbox_EO.pl               [  OK  ]
Executing S50install-remediation-modules                 [  OK  ]
Executing S51install_health_policy.pl                    [  OK  ]
Executing S52install_system_policy.pl                    [  OK  ]
Executing S53change_reconciliation_baseline.pl           [  OK  ]
Executing S70remove_casuser.pl                           [  OK  ]
Executing S70update_sensor_objects.sh                    [  OK  ]
Executing S85patch_history-init                          [  OK  ]
Executing S90banner-init                                 [  OK  ]
Executing S95copy-crontab                                [  OK  ]
Executing S96grow_var.sh                                 [  OK  ]
Executing S96install_vmware_tools.pl                     [  OK  ]


********** Attention **********


   Initializing the system's localization settings.  Depending on available
   system resources (CPU, memory, and disk), this may take 10 minutes
   or more to complete.
```

```
********** Attention **********
Executing S96localize-templates                              [  OK  ]
Executing S96ovf-data.pl                                     [  OK  ]
Executing S97compress-client-resources                       [  OK  ]
Executing S97create_platinum_forms.pl                        [  OK  ]
Executing S97install_cas                                     [  OK  ]
Executing S97install_cloud_support.pl                        [  OK  ]
Executing S97install_geolocation.pl                          [  OK  ]
Executing S97install_ssl_inspection.pl                       [  OK  ]
Executing S97update_modprobe.pl                              [  OK  ]
Executing S98check-db-integrity.sh                           [  OK  ]
Executing S98htaccess-init                                   [  OK  ]
Executing S98is-sru-finished.sh                              [  OK  ]
Executing S99correct_ipmi.pl                                 [  OK  ]
Executing S99start-system                                    [  OK  ]
Executing S99z_db_restore                                    [  OK  ]
Executing S99_z_cc-integrity.sh                              [  OK  ]
Firstboot scripts finished.
Configuring NTP...                                           [  OK  ]
fatattr: can't open '/mnt/disk0/.private2': No such file or directory
fatattr: can't open '/mnt/disk0/.ngfw': No such file or directory
Model reconfigure detected, executing scripts
Pinging mysql
Found mysql is running
Executing 45update-sensor.pl                                 [  OK  ]
Executing 55recalculate_arc.pl                               [  OK  ]
Starting xinetd:
Mon Sep 19 20:59:07 UTC 2016
Starting MySQL...
Pinging mysql
Pinging mysql, try 1
Pinging mysql, try 2
Found mysql is running
Running initializeObjects...
Stopping MySQL...
Killing mysqld with pid 22285
Wait for mysqld to exit\c
 done
Mon Sep 19 20:59:32 UTC 2016

Starting sfifd...                                            [  OK  ]
Starting Cisco ASA5506-X Threat Defense, please wait...No PM running!
...started.
INIT: Starting system message bus: dbus.
Starting OpenBSD Secure Shell server: sshd
```

```
  generating ssh RSA key...
  generating ssh ECDSA key...
  generating ssh DSA key...
done.
Starting Advanced Configuration and Power Interface daemon: acpid.
Starting crond: OK
Sep 19 20:59:42 ciscoasa SF-IMS[22997]: [22997] init script:system [INFO] pmmon
  Setting affinity to 0-3...
pid 22993's current affinity list: 0-3
pid 22993's new affinity list: 0-3
Sep 19 20:59:42 ciscoasa SF-IMS[22999]: [22999] init script:system [INFO] pmmon The
  Process Manager is not running...
Sep 19 20:59:42 ciscoasa SF-IMS[23000]: [23000] init script:system [INFO] pmmon
  Starting the Process Manager...
Sep 19 20:59:42 ciscoasa SF-IMS[23001]: [23001] pm:pm [INFO] Using model number 75J

IO Memory Nodes: 1
IO Memory Per Node: 205520896 bytes

Global Reserve Memory Per Node: 314572800 bytes Nodes=1

LCMB: got 205520896 bytes on numa-id=0, phys=0x2400000, virt=0x2aaaac200000
LCMB: HEAP-CACHE POOL got 314572800 bytes on numa-id=0, virt=0x7fa17d600000
Processor memory:    1583098718

Compiled on Tue 23-Aug-16 19:42 PDT by builders

Total NICs found: 14
.
! Omitted the MAC addresses, licensing and legal messages for brevity
.
                Cisco Systems, Inc.
                170 West Tasman Drive
                San Jose, California 95134-1706

Reading from flash...
!
Cryptochecksum (changed): f410387e 8aab8a4e f71eb8a9 f8b37ef9

INFO: Power-On Self-Test in process.
...........................................................................
INFO: Power-On Self-Test complete.

INFO: Starting HW-DRBG health test...
```

```
INFO: HW-DRBG health test passed.

INFO: Starting SW-DRBG health test...
INFO: SW-DRBG health test passed.
Type help o '?' for a list
Cisco ASA5506-X Threat Defense v6.1.0 (build 330)
firepower login:
```

Step 7.   At the Firepower login prompt, which indicates that the installation is complete, enter the default login credentials (username admin and password Admin123), as shown in Example 2-22.

Example 2-22   *Entering the Default Login Credentials*

```
firepower login: admin
Password: Admin123
```

Step 8.   When prompted to accept the End User License Agreement (EULA), press Enter to display the agreement and to accept it. Example 2-23 shows the system prompts for the EULA. The detailed legal messages are omitted from this example for brevity.

Tip   To exit the EULA at any time, press q.

Example 2-23   *Agreeing to the EULA*

```
You must accept the EULA to continue.
Press <ENTER> to display the EULA:
END USER LICENSE AGREEMENT
.
.
!The EULA messages are omitted for brevity
.
.
.Please enter 'YES' or press <ENTER> to AGREE to the EULA:
```

Step 9.   As the system initialization process begins, change the password for the admin user and set up the network by pressing Enter to accept the default values in brackets ([ ]). Example 2-24 illustrates the configuration of the password and network settings.

Example 2-24 *Configuring the Network After the First Login to FTD*

```
System initialization in progress.  Please stand by.
You must change the password for 'admin' to continue.
Enter new password:
Confirm new password:
You must configure the network to continue.
You must configure at least one of IPv4 or IPv6.
Do you want to configure IPv4? (y/n) [y]:
Do you want to configure IPv6? (y/n) [n]:
Configure IPv4 via DHCP or manually? (dhcp/manual) [manual]:
Enter an IPv4 address for the management interface [192.168.45.45]: 10.1.1.21
Enter an IPv4 netmask for the management interface [255.255.255.0]:
Enter the IPv4 default gateway for the management interface [192.168.45.1]: 10.1.1.1
Enter a fully qualified hostname for this system [firepower]:
Enter a comma-separated list of DNS servers or 'none' []:
Enter a comma-separated list of search domains or 'none' []:
If your networking information has changed, you will need to reconnect.
For HTTP Proxy configuration, run 'configure network http-proxy'
```

Step 10.   When the question about local management (also known as *on-box management*) appears, enter **no**.

Note   The option for FTD local management enables a built-in Firepower Device Manager (FDM) application, which can be used to manage only a single FTD system—itself. This book uses a standalone version of a manager, known as Firepower Management Center (FMC), which can manage multiple FTD systems that might be deployed in different geographical locations.

Example 2-25 shows the configurations related to how to manage this FTD and how to deploy it in the network. In this example, the system is configured to be managed by a dedicated management appliance (the FMC) and is deployed in routed mode.

Example 2-25 *Configuring the Deployment Type and Modes*

```
Manage the device locally? (yes/no) [yes]: no
Configure firewall mode? (routed/transparent) [routed]:
Configuring firewall mode ...
Update policy deployment information
    - add device configuration
    - add network discovery
    - add system policy
```

```
You can register the sensor to a Firepower Management Center and use the
Firepower Management Center to manage it. Note that registering the sensor
to a Firepower Management Center disables on-sensor Firepower Services
management capabilities.

When registering the sensor to a Firepower Management Center, a unique
alphanumeric registration key is always required.  In most cases, to register
a sensor to a Firepower Management Center, you must provide the hostname or
the IP address along with the registration key.
'configure manager add [hostname | ip address ] [registration key ]'

However, if the sensor and the Firepower Management Center are separated by a
NAT device, you must enter a unique NAT ID, along with the unique registration
key.
'configure manager add DONTRESOLVE [registration key ] [ NAT ID ]'

Later, using the web interface on the Firepower Management Center, you must
use the same registration key and, if necessary, the same NAT ID when you add
this sensor to the Firepower Management Center.

>
```

The > prompt at the end of Example 2-25 confirms that the initial network configuration is complete. The next step is to verify network connectivity on the management interface and then begin the registration process. (Chapter 6: "The Firepower Management Network," explains the management connection, and Chapter 7, "Firepower Licensing and Registration," describes the registration process.)

Verification and Troubleshooting Tools

This section describes the commands you can use to verify the status of ASA hardware before and after the FTD software is installed.

Navigating to the FTD CLI

After a reboot following a successful installation of FTD software, your ASA hardware should automatically display the > prompt. This prompt is different from the traditional prompt ciscoasa> that you see on classic software running on ASA hardware. Furthermore, when ASA hardware runs the FTD software, you can enter various consoles or shells, including the following:

■ **FTD default shell:** You can configure most of the necessary items and view their status by using this shell.

- **ASA console:** This console allows you to perform advanced commands for diagnostic purposes.

- **Firepower Linux shell:** This shell lets you enter the back end of the operating system and is used by Cisco for advanced troubleshooting.

Figure 2-10 shows different types of consoles and command prompts of an ASA running the FTD software.

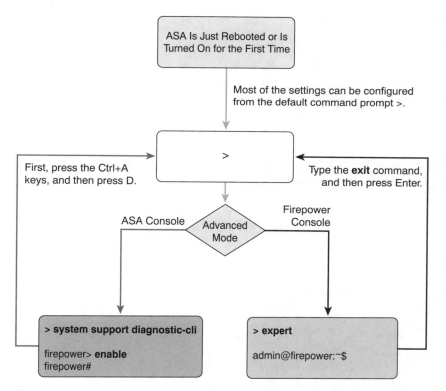

Figure 2-10   *Command Prompts on ASA Hardware Running FTD Software*

Example 2-26 shows the commands that allow you to navigate various modes of an FTD CLI.

Example 2-26   *Commands to Connect to the Various Shells of the FTD CLI*

```
>

! The > prompt confirms that you are on the FTD default shell. Run the following
  command to connect to the ASA console:

> system support diagnostic-cli
```

```
Attaching to ASA console ... Press 'Ctrl+a then d' to detach.
Type help or '?' for a list of available commands.

firepower>

! Now you have entered the ASA console. Run the enable command to enter the privi-
  lege exec mode.

firepower> enable
Password:
firepower# exit

Logoff
Type help or '?' for a list of available commands.

firepower>

! If you want to quit from the ASA console, the exit command logs you off from the
  ASA console, but does not let you return to the FTD default shell. To disconnect
  from the ASA console, press the Ctrl+a keys together, then press d separately.

firepower>

Console connection detached.
>

! To connect to the Firepower Linux shell, run the expert command. To return to the
  FTD default shell, run the exit command.

>  expert
admin@firepower:~$ exit
logout
>
```

Determining the Version of Installed Software

From the default command prompt > in FTD, you can determine what FTD software version is running on ASA hardware.

Example 2-27 shows ASA 5506-X hardware running FTD Version 6.1.0.

Example 2-27   *Finding the Software Version Running on an ASA After a Fresh FTD Installation*

```
> show version


------------------[ firepower ]-------------------
Model                      : Cisco ASA5506-X Threat Defense (75) Version 6.1.0
  (Build 330)
UUID                       : c84ceb32-7ea7-11e6-a7ad-94bcd8f36790
Rules update version       : 2016-03-28-001-vrt
VDB version                : 270
--------------------------------------------------


>
```

Tip   The Model field for the **show version** command output must show "Cisco ASA55XX-X Threat Defense Version 6.1.0". If the Model field shows "ASA55XX Version 6.1.0"—without the "Threat Defense" keyword—it means the ASA is running Firepower Version 6.1 as a separate service, not in a unified image.

Determining the Free Disk Space on ASA Hardware

Before you install FTD on ASA hardware, you must check whether the currently available space is sufficient. To do so, you can run one of the following commands on your ASA software in privileged exec mode:

```
ciscoasa# dir
ciscoasa# show flash:
```

Example 2-28 shows the amount of free space on the same ASA hardware from two different command outputs. The shaded portion of the example shows that the ASA hardware has free space of 4544851968 bytes, which is equal to 4438332 KB, or 4334.3 MB, or 4.23 GB. The first command output uses disk0: to indicate internal flash memory. If there were external flash memory, it would be denoted by disk1:.

Example 2-28   *Finding the Amount of Free Space on ASA Hardware*

```
ciscoasa# dir


Directory of disk0:/


88      -rwx   91290240     11:04:08 May 12 2016   asa961-50-lfbff-k8.spa
89      -rwx   63           16:25:14 Sep 19 2016   .boot_string
11      drwx   4096         12:14:22 May 12 2016   log
```

```
19     drwx   4096          12:15:12 May 12 2016   crypto_archive
20     drwx   4096          12:15:16 May 12 2016   coredumpinfo


7859437568 bytes total (4544851968 bytes free)


ciscoasa#


ciscoasa# show flash:


--#--  --length--  -----date/time------   path
   88  91290240    May 12 2016 11:04:08   asa961-50-lfbff-k8.spa
   89  63          Sep 19 2016 16:25:14   .boot_string
   11  4096        May 12 2016 12:14:22   log
   13  0           May 12 2016 12:14:22   log/asa-appagent.log
   19  4096        May 12 2016 12:15:12   crypto_archive
   20  4096        May 12 2016 12:15:16   coredumpinfo
   21  59          May 12 2016 12:15:16   coredumpinfo/coredump.cfg


7859437568 bytes total (4544851968 bytes free)


ciscoasa#
```

Deleting a File from a Storage Device

When you want to delete a file to free up disk space, run the following command in the privileged exec mode:

```
ciscoasa# delete flash:/filename
```

Example 2-29 shows the command to delete a file named output.txt.

Example 2-29 *Deleting a File from ASA Hardware*

```
ciscoasa# delete flash:/output.txt
```

Determining the Availability of Any Storage Device or SSD

From the CLI, you can determine the type of a storage device that is installed on an ASA. Example 2-30 shows that the ASA 5506-X hardware has one SSD installed.

Example 2-30   *Viewing the Storage Device Information on ASA 5500-X Series Hardware*

```
ciscoasa# show inventory
Name: "Chassis", DESCR: "ASA 5506-X with FirePOWER services, 8GE, AC, DES"
PID: ASA5506          , VID: V01      , SN: JMX1916Z07V


Name: "Storage Device 1", DESCR: "ASA 5506-X SSD"
PID: ASA5506-SSD      , VID: N/A      , SN: MSA190600NE


ciscoasa#
```

Example 2-31 shows ASA 5545-X hardware with two storage devices.

Example 2-31   *Determining the List of Storage Devices on ASA 5500-X Series Hardware*

```
ciscoasa# show inventory
Name: "Chassis", DESCR: "ASA 5545-X with SW, 8 GE Data, 1 GE Mgmt"
PID: ASA5545          , VID: V02      , SN: FTX1841119Z


Name: "power supply 0", DESCR: "ASA 5545-X/5555-X AC Power Supply"
PID: ASA-PWR-AC       , VID: N/A      , SN: 47K1E0

Name: "Storage Device 1", DESCR: "Model Number: Micron_M550_MTFDDAK128MAY"
PID: N/A              , VID: N/A      , SN: MXA183502EG


Name: "Storage Device 2", DESCR: "Model Number: Micron_M550_MTFDDAK128MAY"
PID: N/A              , VID: N/A      , SN: MXA183502FW


ciscoasa#
```

Table 2-2 summarizes the default availability of SSDs in various ASA 5500-X Series hardware. It also shows whether an SSD is hot-swappable on a particular model in case of a failure.

Table 2-2 *Availability and Replacement of SSD on ASA 5500-X Series Hardware*

ASA 5500-X Series Models	Availability of SSD	Hot-Swappable?
5506-X, 5506W-X, 5506H-X	Comes with an SSD.	No.
5508-X, 5516-X	Comes with an SSD.	Yes, requires a screwdriver.
5512-X, 5515-X, 5525-X	Might not come with an SSD, if not ordered separately. You can install one Cisco SSD.	Yes, easy to hot-swap. A button is available to push and release the locking lever.
5545-X, 5555-X	Might not come with an SSD, if not ordered separately. You can install up to two Cisco SSDs with RAID 1.	

Determining the Version of the ROMMON Software or Firmware

The version information for the ROMMON software (also known as firmware) is displayed during the bootup process for ASA 5500-X hardware. Example 2-32 shows the initial messages that appear after ASA 5506-X hardware is turned on. It shows that the ROMMON version is 1.1.01.

Example 2-32 *Messages That Appear During the Bootup Process*

```
Cisco Systems ROMMON, Version 1.1.01, RELEASE SOFTWARE
Copyright (c) 1994-2014  by Cisco Systems, Inc.
Compiled Mon 10/20/2014 15:59:12.05 by builder

Current image running: Boot ROM0
Last reset cause: PowerCycleRequest
DIMM Slot 0 : Present

Platform ASA5506 with 4096 Mbytes of main memory
MAC Address: a4:6c:2a:e4:6b:bf
Using default Management Ethernet Port: 0

Use BREAK or ESC to interrupt boot.
Use SPACE to begin boot immediately.

Located '.boot_string' @ cluster 1607965.
#
Attempt autoboot: "boot disk0:/asa961-50-lfbff-k8.spa"
Located 'asa961-50-lfbff-k8.spa' @ cluster 10.
```

```
######################################################################
######################################################################
######################################################################
#######################################

LFBFF signature verified.
INIT: version 2.88 booting
Starting udev
Configuring network interfaces... done.
```

If ASA hardware is running in a production environment, and you do not want to reboot it, you can still determine the version of the ROMMON software by running the **show module** command. Example 2-33 shows that the ROMMON version of the ASA 5506-X hardware is 1.1.01.

Example 2-33 *Command That Displays the ROMMON Software Version of an ASA*

```
ciscoasa# show module

Mod  Card Type                                        Model              Serial No.
---- ------------------------------------------------ ------------------ -----------
   1 ASA 5506-X with FirePOWER services, 8GE, AC,     ASA5506            JAD191100HG
 sfr Unknown                                          N/A                JAD191100HG

Mod  MAC Address Range                Hw Version   Fw Version   Sw Version
---- -------------------------------- ------------ ------------ ---------------
   1 a46c.2ae4.6bbf to a46c.2ae4.6bc8 1.0          1.1.1        9.6(1)50
 sfr a46c.2ae4.6bbe to a46c.2ae4.6bbe N/A          N/A

Mod  SSM Application Name           Status            SSM Application Version
---- ------------------------------ ----------------- --------------------------


Mod  Status             Data Plane Status    Compatibility
---- ------------------ -------------------- -------------
   1 Up Sys             Not Applicable
 sfr Init               Not Applicable

ciscoasa#
```

Summary

This chapter describes the differences between various images that may be installed on ASA 5500-X hardware. It demonstrates the detailed process of reimaging ASA 5500-X Series hardware to the FTD software. In addition, this chapter shows the command-line tools you can use to verify the status of the hardware and software.

After installation, the next step in deploying FTD in a network is to register it with an FMC. Part II of this book describes that.

Quiz

1. What would be the correct workflow for reimaging ASA 5506-X hardware to FTD?
   i. Upgrade the ROMMON software.
   ii. Reload the ASA hardware with a boot image.
   iii. Install the FTD system software.
   iv. Copy the image files to a server.

   a. ii > i > iii > iv
   b. iv > ii > iii
   c. ii > iii
   d. iv > i > ii > iii

2. What would be the correct workflow for reimaging ASA 5545-X hardware to FTD?
   i. Upgrade the ROMMON software.
   ii. Reload the ASA hardware with a boot image.
   iii. Install the FTD system software.
   iv. Copy the image files to a server.

   a. ii > i > iii > iv
   b. iv > ii > iii
   c. iii > ii
   d. iv > i > ii > iii

3. When reimaging ASA 5516-X hardware to FTD, which type of file is not necessary?
   a. *.spa
   b. *.lfbff
   c. *.cdisk
   d. *.pkg

4. What kind of server should you use to transfer a boot image file to ASA hardware?
   a. TFTP server
   b. FTP server
   c. Web server
   d. Secure copy server

5. Which protocol is used in this chapter to transfer the system software image to ASA hardware?

    a. HTTP

    b. TFTP

    c. FTP

    d. SCP

6. Which command do you run to confirm whether an SSD is installed on ASA hardware?

    a. show flash

    b. show inventory

    c. show run

    d. show module

7. Which command displays the firmware version of an ASA?

    a. show firmware

    b. show rommon

    c. show module

    d. show inventory

8. Which of the following is the default command prompt in the FTD software?

    a. ciscoasa#

    b. ciscoasa-boot>

    c. firepower>

    d. >

Chapter 3

FTD on the Firepower eXtensible Operating System (FXOS)

Within the ASA 5500-X Series models, the ASA 5585-X hardware is designed for a data center network. However, an ASA 5585-X device does not support the Firepower Threat Defense (FTD) software. To meet the needs of a service provider network, Cisco introduced a new career-class Firepower hardware platform that runs FTD on top of a supervisor. The supervisor runs on an independent operating system called the Firepower eXtensible Operating System (FXOS). This chapter discusses the deployment of the FTD software on FXOS.

Firepower 9300 and 4100 Series Essentials

Cisco introduced the Firepower 9300 Series and the Firepower 4100 Series hardware models in 2015 and 2016, respectively. In 2017, it added the Firepower 2100 Series hardware models to the Firepower hardware family. The new Firepower hardware platforms are designed to deliver better performance than the traditional ASA 5500-X hardware. While the architecture of every Firepower hardware series is unique, every model in this family runs FTD on FXOS.

Note This book uses FTD Version 6.1 as the baseline; however, the Firepower 2100 Series hardware supports FTD Version 6.2.1 or greater. Therefore, the configuration examples in this chapter focus on the Firepower 9300 and 4100 Series models, which support Version 6.1. However, the command-line tools described in this chapter are useful for any Firepower hardware series running FTD software on FXOS.

Table 3-1 shows the hardware specifications of the Firepower 4100 Series and the Firepower 9300 Series platforms.

Table 3-1   *Specifications of the Firepower 4100 and 9300 Hardware*

	4100 Series	**9300 Series**
CPU	Single 12-core (4110)	
	Dual 12-core (4120)	Dual 12-core (Module 24)
	Dual 18-core (4140)	Dual 18-core (Module 36)
	Dual 22-core (4150)	Dual 22-core (Module 44)
Memory	64 GB (4110)	256 GB of memory per security module
	128 GB (4120)	
	256 GB (4140, 4150)	
Storage	200 GB (4110, 4120)	800 GB of solid state drive (SSD) storage per security module (RAID-1 set up with two SSDs)
	400 GB (4140, 4150)	
	(The SSD slot 2 is used to install the optional Malware Storage Pack)	
Security module	1 (embedded)	3 (online insertion and removal supported)
Form factor	1 rack unit	3 rack units

Figure 3-1 shows various modules on a Cisco Firepower 9300 Series chassis.

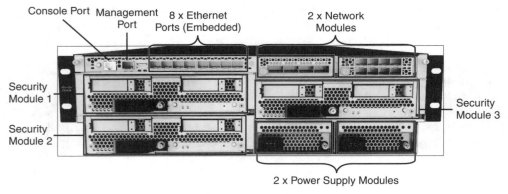

Figure 3-1   *Front Panel of a Cisco Firepower 9300 Series Chassis*

Figure 3-2 shows the console, management, and other network ports on a Cisco Firepower 4100 Series chassis.

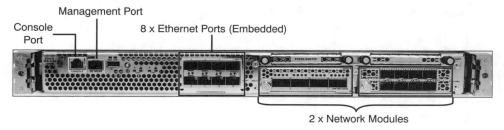

Figure 3-2   *Front Panel of a Cisco Firepower 4100 Series Chassis*

Architecture

The Cisco Firepower 9300 Series and 4100 Series chassis use modular hardware components. You can leverage the modular architecture to upgrade, troubleshoot, or replace any particular modules without replacing an entire Firepower chassis.

A Firepower security appliance has various modules (for example, network module, security module, power supply module, fan module). All these modules interact with two major components—the supervisor and the security module:

- **Supervisor:** A supervisor uses FXOS to manage the configuration of network modules, security modules, and chassis. It also monitors all the hardware components, such as power supplies, fans, and so on.

- **Security module:** A security module runs the security application, such as the FTD software. The adapters on a security module receive traffic from the external network modules through a switch fabric and send them to the FTD for any necessary actions.

> **Note**   For ease of understanding, you can compare a security module with a blade server. The Firepower Chassis Manager of the 9300 Series and of the 4100 Series use two different terms to refer to this blade server: *security module* (9300 Series) and *security engine* (4100 Series).

Figure 3-3 shows the architecture of a Firepower 9300 Series appliance and demonstrates the connections between the supervisor and a security module. In Firepower 4100 Series hardware, the number of security engines is one.

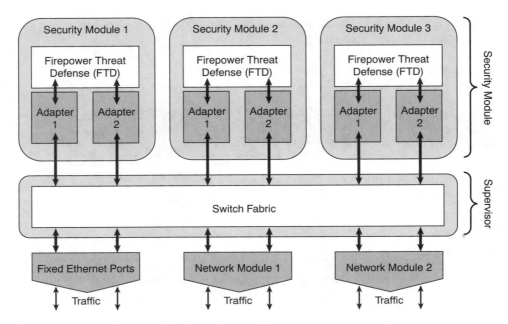

Figure 3-3 *Architecture of a Cisco Firepower 9300 Security Appliance*

Note The Firepower 2100 Series hardware introduces an additional processor, called the *network processing unit* (NPU). The NPU is designed to process any traffic that is not intended for advanced inspection. The other x86 CPU processes traffic that matches an advanced next-generation security policy.

Software Images

At software.cisco.com, you can find a variety of software for a Firepower security appliance. For a core FTD deployment on a Firepower appliance, you need only two types of software:

- FXOS
- FTD software

Figure 3-4 highlights the software images that are necessary to install FTD on FXOS. The screenshot displays the software that you can download from the Cisco support site for a Firepower 9300 Series appliance. A 4100 Series appliance supports all of them except the third-party software Radware Virtual Defense Pro (as of this writing).

Figure 3-4 *Types of Software for a Firepower Security Appliance*

Firepower Extensible Operating System (FXOS)

The FXOS software, also known as the *platform bundle*, contains software for the supervisor and the hardware components on a Firepower security appliance. The bundle includes the essential components of the FXOS except for any security applications.

Figure 3-5 shows the fxos-k9.2.0.1.86.SPA file, which is a platform bundle for a Firepower security appliance. It installs FXOS Release 2.0.1.

Release 2.0.1		
File Information	Release Date	Size
FX-OS image for Firepower fxos-k9.2.0.1.37.SPA	23-JUN-2016	715.15 MB
FX-OS image for Firepower fxos-k9.2.0.1.68.SPA	16-AUG-2016	715.17 MB
FX-OS image for Firepower fxos-k9.2.0.1.86.SPA	27-OCT-2016	715.23 MB
MIBS zip for Firepower FX-OS image firepower-mibs.2.0.1.37.zip	23-JUN-2016	0.73 MB
MIBS zip for Firepower FX-OS image firepower-mibs.2.0.1.68.zip	16-AUG-2016	0.73 MB
MIBS zip for Firepower FX-OS image firepower-mibs.2.0.1.86.zip	27-OCT-2016	0.73 MB

Figure 3-5 *The Platform Bundle for a Firepower Security Appliance*

FTD Software

The FTD software, also called the *application package*, is one of the security applications that you can install on a security module of a Firepower appliance. Once the FTD software is installed and registered with the Firepower Management Center (FMC), you can manage the security policies of an FTD through the FMC.

Figure 3-6 shows the cisco-ftd.6.1.0.330.SPA.csp file, which is an application package for the FTD. When you upload a .csp file to a Firepower appliance, it is stored on the supervisor, but when you install a .csp file, it is deployed on a security module.

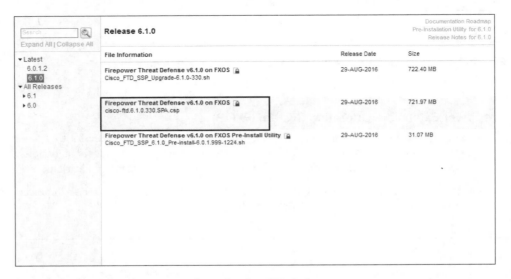

Figure 3-6   *An Application Package for the FTD Software*

Firmware

Cisco also occasionally releases firmware images for Firepower appliances. Upgrading the firmware is not a mandatory requirement for FTD software installation. It is, however, necessary when you want to enable any enhanced or new hardware features. For example, to enable the Firepower two-port 100 GB network module double-wide, you need to upgrade the firmware to Version 1.0.10 or greater.

Note   Read the official FXOS guides, published at cisco.com, to learn when and how to install firmware on a Firepower security appliance.

Web User Interfaces

The Firepower 9300 Series and 4100 Series security appliances have their own web interface, called *Firepower Chassis Manager*. To install, upgrade, or downgrade any security application on a Firepower appliance, you can either log in to the Firepower Chassis Manager or access the CLI of the Firepower appliance through Secure Shell (SSH) or a console connection.

To access the web interface, enter the management IP address of the Firepower security appliance in a supported browser, like this:

```
https://IP_Address_of_Management_Interface
```

Figure 3-7 shows the login page that appears when you enter the Firepower Chassis Manager management IP address in a browser.

Figure 3-7 *Login Page of the Firepower Chassis Manager*

Note If you are running Firepower 2100 Series hardware with FTD Version 6.2.1 or higher, you can choose one of the two web user interfaces to configure and manage FTD: You can register it with a standalone Firepower Management Center (FMC) and manage it through the FMC, or you can enable local management capability and manage the FTD directly via an on-box manager called *Firepower Device Manager* (FDM).

Best Practices for FTD Installation on Firepower Hardware

Consider the following best practices when you install the FTD software on a Firepower security appliance running FXOS:

- Perform the installation tasks during a maintenance window so that any network interruption does not impact your business. You should also plan for additional time to complete any post-installation setup.

- Prior to the maintenance window when you plan to do the installation, make sure you are able to access the cisco.com website and can download all the necessary FXOS and FTD images. If needed, register for a Cisco account. If after the self-registration process you cannot download any of the desired software, you might need to get further assistance from your Cisco channel partner or the Cisco Technical Assistance Center (TAC).

- After you download any software from cisco.com, always verify the MD5 or SHA512 checksum of the files you have downloaded to confirm that the file is not corrupt and has not been modified during download. Figure 3-8 shows how the MD5 and SHA512 checksum values are displayed at cisco.com when you hover your mouse over a filename.

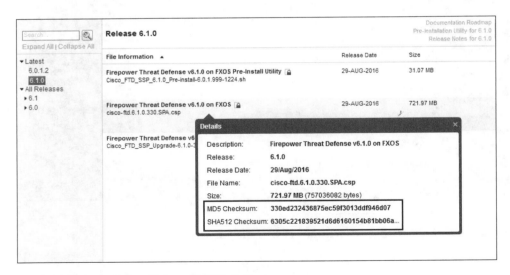

Figure 3-8   *Checksum Values of FTD Software*

- If your Firepower chassis is already running with a good configuration, make a backup of the existing configuration before you make any changes. Go to **System > Configuration > Export** on the Firepower Chassis Manager to export the configuration. Figure 3-9 shows the options to export the configuration of a Firepower security appliance.

Caution   The export of a configuration is stored in XML file format. Do not alter the contents of an XML file, or it may fail an import attempt.

Figure 3-9   *Configuration Export Page in Firepower Chassis Manager*

■ During an import, the software version of FXOS must match with the version when a configuration (XML file) was exported. Similarly, any detail of the hardware, such as platform model and network module installed (including the slot number), must be the same during export and import.

Caution   A configuration export using Firepower Chassis Manager includes the configuration settings of FXOS. It does not include any configurations from the FTD software.

■ Do not power off, shut down, reboot, or reinitialize a Firepower chassis or a security module when the FTD installation is in progress.

■ If you need to power down a Firepower chassis that has FTD software already installed, you must gracefully shut down the FTD application beforehand. An ungraceful power-down of a Firepower chassis can corrupt the FTD data and file system.

■ Some of the modules on a Firepower appliance support the Online Insertion and Removal (OIR) feature (for example, the security module, power supply module, and fan module). However, to replace a network module that does not support OIR (as of this writing), you must gracefully shut down the FTD software and then power down the Firepower chassis.

■ Before you deploy FTD on a Firepower chassis, read the hardware installation guide to learn the latest information about any hardware features.

Installing and Configuring FTD

In this section, you will learn the detailed steps involved in installing the FTD system software on Cisco Firepower 9300 Series hardware. The process is identical for Firepower 4100 Series hardware.

Fulfilling Prerequisites

Before you install the FTD application, you must fulfill any prerequisites. For example, be sure to delete any existing logical devices from FXOS, upgrade the FXOS software version, and enable necessary interfaces. The following sections elaborate on these prerequisites.

Deleting Any Existing Logical Devices

If your Firepower appliance is currently running any logical devices with different types of software, such as any ASA software or an earlier version of FTD software, you need to delete them. The installation of multiple types of software on a single Firepower appliance is not supported (as of this writing). To delete a logical device, follow these steps:

Step 1.   Go to the Logical Devices tab in Firepower Chassis Manager. Figure 3-10 shows that the ASA security application is running as a logical device on a Firepower 9300 appliance.

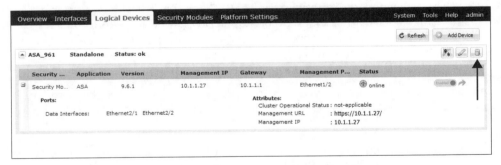

Figure 3-10   *Logical Devices Page on a Firepower Appliance*

Step 2.   Click the recycle bin icon next to a logical device to delete it.

Step 3.   In the confirmation window that appears, click **Yes** to delete the logical device.

Step 4.   Click **Yes** once again when the system asks whether you want to delete its application configuration (see Figure 3-11).

Figure 3-11   *Confirmation Window During Deletion of a Logical Device*

When all the logical devices are deleted, Firepower Chassis Manager displays the message "No logical devices available. Click on Add Device to add a new logical device." (See Figure 3-12.) You see this message in a brand-new system or when you delete all the existing logical devices.

Figure 3-12   *Confirmation of the Deletion of All the Logical Devices*

Upgrading the FXOS Software

To install FTD Version 6.1, a Firepower appliance must be running FXOS Version 2.0.1 or greater. If your appliance runs an earlier release, follow these steps to upgrade the FXOS software:

Step 1.   Download an appropriate FXOS platform bundle from the Cisco support site.

Step 2.   Log in to Firepower Chassis Manager and go to **System > Updates**.

Step 3.   Click the **Upload Image** button, and then click **Browse** to find the FXOS platform bundle image. Select an image and click the **Upload** button to begin the upload process (see Figure 3-13).

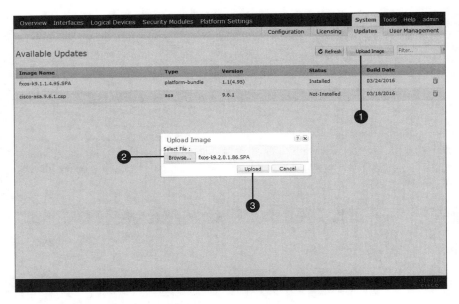

Figure 3-13   *Uploading an Image*

Step 4.   In the confirmation window that appears after a successful upload, click **OK** to close the window (see Figure 3-14).

Figure 3-14   *Confirmation of a Successful Upload*

Step 5.   In the System > Updates page, click the Upgrade icon next to the image you have just uploaded (see Figure 3-15).

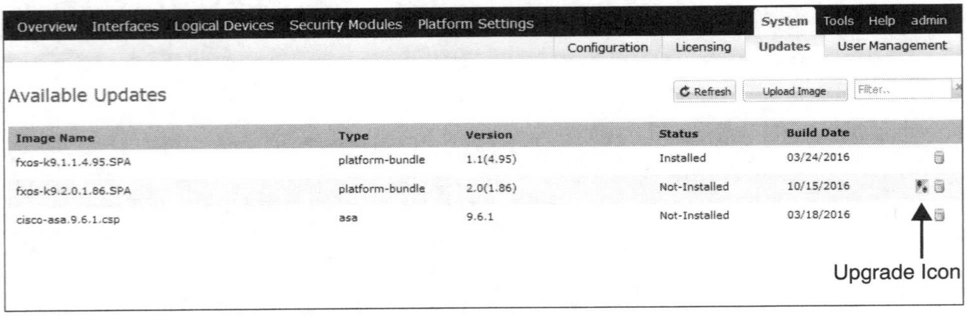

Image Name	Type	Version	Status	Build Date	
fxos-k9.1.1.4.95.SPA	platform-bundle	1.1(4.95)	Installed	03/24/2016	
fxos-k9.2.0.1.86.SPA	platform-bundle	2.0(1.86)	Not-Installed	10/15/2016	
cisco-asa.9.6.1.csp	asa	9.6.1	Not-Installed	03/18/2016	

Upgrade Icon

Figure 3-15   *Icon for the FXOS Platform Bundle Upgrade*

Step 6.   Click **Yes** when a confirmation window appears, asking if you want to proceed (see Figure 3-16).

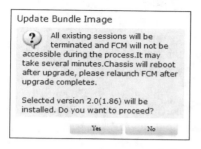

Figure 3-16   *Update Bundle Image Confirmation Window*

After the upgrade begins, the web interface does not show any progress status, and the connection to the GUI is lost for some time. When it comes back, the status of the new software is *Installed* (see Figure 3-17).

Overview	Interfaces	Logical Devices	Security Modules	Platform Settings		System	Tools	Help	admin

			Configuration	Licensing	Updates	User Management

Available Updates   C Refresh   Upload Image   Filter..

Image Name	Type	Version	Status	Build Date	
fxos-k9.1.1.4.95.SPA	platform-bundle	1.1(4.95)	Not-Installed	03/24/2016	📋 🗑
fxos-k9.2.0.1.86.SPA	platform-bundle	2.0(1.86)	Installed	10/15/2016	🗑
cisco-asa.9.6.1.csp	asa	9.6.1	Not-Installed	03/18/2016	🗑

Figure 3-17   *The System Updates Page with a List of Available Update Files*

Tip   During an upgrade, you can access the console terminal to determine the upgrade status. See the "Verification and Troubleshooting Tools" section, later in this chapter, to learn the CLI commands for it.

Enabling Interfaces

Before installing FTD software, you must enable the network interfaces on your Firepower appliance (the physical chassis) that will be used by the FTD (a logical device) to transfer traffic. The options to configure interfaces can be categorized into two types—mandatory and optional:

- **Mandatory configurations:** When you enable an interface, you must define whether the interface will be used to transfer management traffic or data traffic.

The interfaces on a Firepower appliance carry only one type of traffic at a time. A Firepower appliance does not share the same data interface between two logical devices, but it can share a management interface between multiple logical devices.

■ **Optional configurations:** You can, optionally, use the built-in FTD features to segregate or aggregate traffic. For example, you can enable an interface with the Firepower-eventing option to segregate events from the management traffic, which means you can use an interface exclusively to transfer events.

You can also bundle multiple physical interfaces and aggregate their traffic into a single logical port, known as a port channel or an EtherChannel. The FXOS software uses Link Aggregation Control Protocol (LACP) to bundle up to 16 interfaces.

Enabling the Management and Data Interfaces

To enable an interface with an existing configuration, go to the Interfaces page of Firepower Chassis Manager. By default, you should be at the All Interfaces tab. Here, you can just click on the **Disabled** button in the Admin State column (see Figure 3-18).

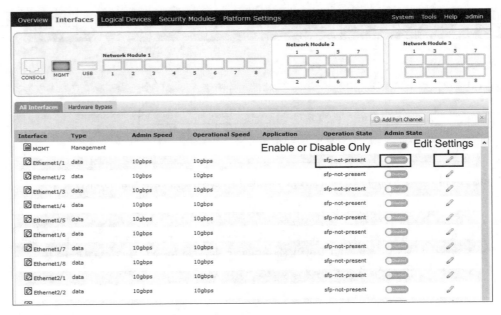

Figure 3-18 *Options to Change the Settings of an Interface*

If, however, you want to modify any existing settings, such as changing the type from data traffic to management traffic or vice versa, follow these steps:

Step 1.   Navigate to the Interfaces page of Firepower Chassis Manager.

Installing and Configuring FTD 69

Step 2. On the All Interfaces tab, click the pencil icon for the interface you want to modify. The Edit Interface dialog appears. Figure 3-19 shows the Ethernet1/1 interface enabled and configured with the management (mgmt) type traffic.

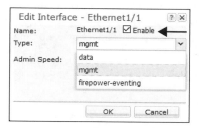

Figure 3-19 *The Configurable Options for an Interface*

Step 3. From the Type drop-down, select the type of traffic you want the interface to carry. Optionally, you can also modify the speed.

Step 4. Select the **Enable** check box if you want to enable this interface immediately with the updated settings.

Step 5. Click the **OK** button to save the changes. The Interfaces page reflects the changes you have just made.

Figure 3-20 shows that the Operation State is Up and the Admin State is Enabled after the Ethernet1/1 interface is configured and enabled. The first port on Network Module 1 also becomes green.

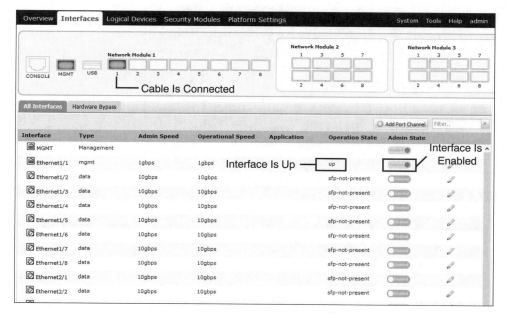

Figure 3-20 *Changes to the User Interface After an Interface Is Enabled*

Adding a Port Channel or an EtherChannel

A port channel or an EtherChannel is a logical group of up to 16 physical ports. It can aggregate traffic from individual interfaces into a logical port so that the appliance can have an aggregated higher bandwidth. It is also fault-tolerant: When one of the links in a logical group fails, the remaining links in the group stay up. The Firepower security appliance natively supports port channels. You can configure a port channel by following these steps:

Step 1.   On the Interfaces page, click the **Add Port Channel** button. The Add Port Channel configuration window appears.

Step 2.   Assign a number in the Port Channel ID box. The valid values range from 1 to 47.

Step 3.   Select the **Enable** check box if you want to activate the port channel as soon as the configuration is saved.

Figure 3-21 shows Ethernet2/1 and Ethernet2/2 being grouped together in a port channel (ID = 20) to carry data traffic.

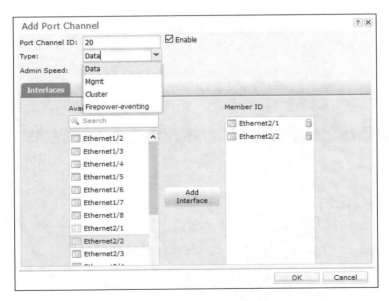

Figure 3-21   *Configuring a Port Channel*

Step 4.   Define the purpose of the channel by selecting an appropriate option from the Type dropdown: Data, Mgmt, Cluster, or Firepower-eventing.

> **Note**   The Cluster type is used exclusively by clustered devices as a cluster control link. You can cluster multiple security modules of a Firepower 9300 appliance to gain higher throughput and redundancy.

Step 5.   Select the interfaces that you want to bundle together in a channel and click the **Add Interface** button after each one. The selected interfaces move to the Member ID box. You can bundle up to 16 interfaces in one port channel.

Step 6.   Click the **OK** button to save your configuration. On the Interfaces page, you can view the status of the port channel you have just created, along with its member interfaces. For example, Figure 3-22 shows port channel 20 with two member interfaces, Ethernet2/1 and Ethernet2/2.

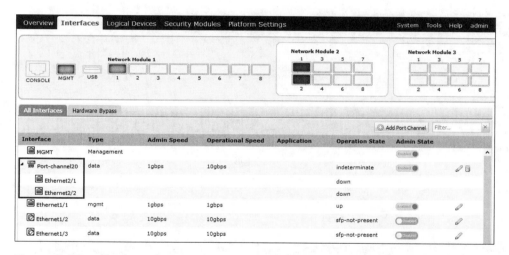

Figure 3-22   *Checking the Status of a Port Channel on the Interfaces Page*

> **Note**   This section describes the process of creating a port channel for demonstration purposes only. The examples in the remainder of this chapter do not use any port channels. To learn more about port channels and additional Firepower hardware-specific features, please read the "Cisco FXOS Firepower Chassis Manager Configuration Guide."

Installing FTD

Once your Firepower appliance runs FXOS Version 2.0.1 or later and the necessary interfaces are enabled, you are ready to install FTD Version 6.1. The following sections describe the FTD installation process:

Uploading the FTD Software Image

Follow these steps to upload the FTD software image:

Step 1.   Download FTD Version 6.1 from the Cisco support site.

Step 2.   Log in to Firepower Chassis Manager and go to **System > Updates**.

Step 3.   Click the **Upload Image** button, and then click **Browse** and find the FTD software image. Select an image and click the **Upload** button to begin the upload process (see Figure 3-23).

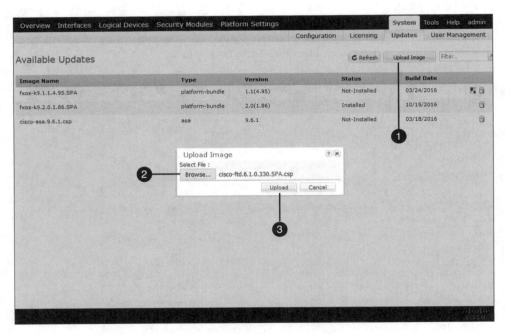

Figure 3-23   *Uploading an FTD Software Image*

Step 4.   Accept the End User License Agreement (EULA) window that appears after a successful upload and click **Ok** (see Figure 3-24). The FTD software image is now stored on the appliance but is not yet installed.

Figure 3-24 *The Appearance of the EULA Message Indicates a Successful Upload*

Adding a Logical Device for FTD

If you have completed all the steps described in the previous sections, you are now ready to add a logical device for FTD. While you're adding a logical device, FTD Version 6.1 is installed on FXOS Release 2.0.1. Here is the process, step by step:

Step 1.   In Firepower Chassis Manager, navigate to the Logical Devices page and click the **Add Device** button. The Add Device window appears.

Step 2.   Provide a name for the logical device you are going to deploy on FXOS and select the FTD template and the image version 6.1.x. Figure 3-25 shows a new FTD logical device called FTD_610 being added.

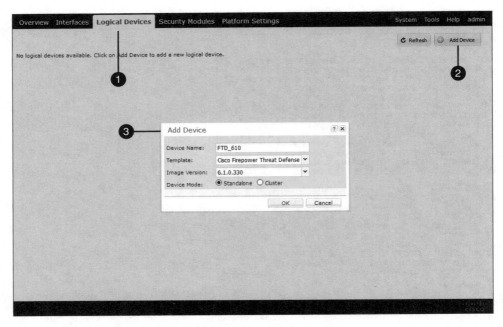

Figure 3-25 *Navigating to the Add Device Window*

Step 3.   Choose the **Standalone** device mode and click **OK**. A configuration page appears, where you provision the standalone FTD logical device.

> **Note** Standalone mode enables you to create a unique logical device on each security module, whereas Cluster mode enables you to bundle multiple security modules into one logical device.

Figure 3-26 shows the three major steps to provision an FTD logical device.

Step 4.   On the right-hand side, click the FTD icon. A configuration window appears.

Step 5.   In the General Information section of the configuration window, select a security module where you want to install the FTD software and configure the management network, as shown in Figure 3-27. When you are finished, click **OK** to return to the provisioning page. Figure 3-27 indicates that security module 1 (SM 1) is selected for the FTD installation, and Ethernet1/1 is configured as the management interface for the FTD.

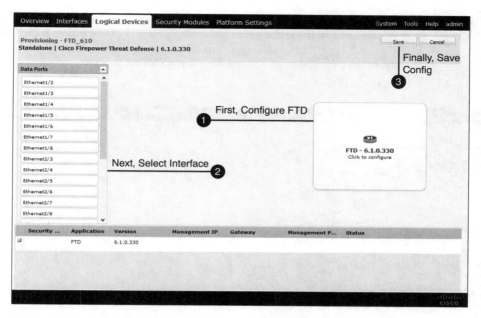

Figure 3-26   *Workflow for Provisioning an FTD Logical Device*

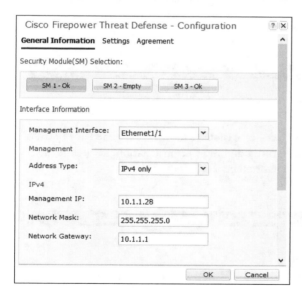

Figure 3-27   *Configuring the FTD Management Network*

Tip   This example skips the configurable items in the Settings and Agreement sections for now; they reappear on the CLI of the FTD, during the initialization process. You can configure them at that time through the CLI.

Step 6.   On the provisioning page, as shown in Figure 3-28, select the interfaces or port channels that will be transferring data traffic to and from FTD. In Figure 3-28, the Ethernet2/3 and Ethernet2/4 interfaces of the Firepower chassis are selected as the data interfaces, and the Ethernet1/1 interface is configured as a management interface.

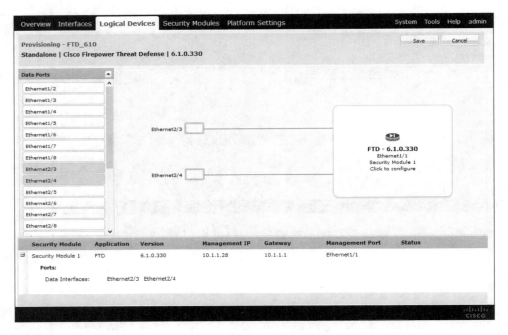

Figure 3-28   *Graphical Representation of an FTD Logical Device*

Step 7.   When you are finished with the provisioning settings, click the **Save** button. The Logical Devices page returns, and the FTD installation process begins. As shown in Figure 3-29, the installing status indicates that the FTD installation is in progress.

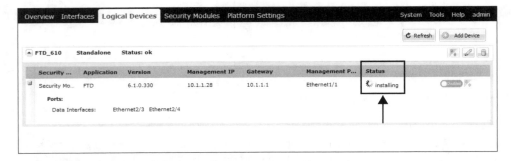

Figure 3-29   *The FTD Installation Process in Progress*

Figure 3-30 shows the FTD software installation complete and online. From the time the FTD installation begins, the system takes about 5 to 10 minutes to get to the online state.

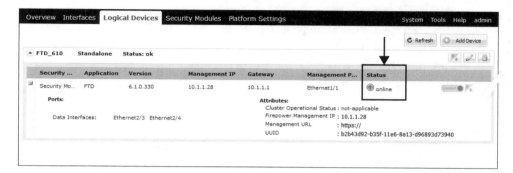

Figure 3-30 *The Fully Complete FTD Installation Process*

Completing the Initialization of FTD

After the installation is complete, the FTD logical device begins initialization by itself and applies the settings you configured in the FTD provisioning page. Using the CLI, you can now view the progress of initialization and configure any additional settings, such as the password for the admin user.

To access the CLI of the FTD, first you have to access the CLI via Secure Shell (SSH) or the console terminal. Then you can connect to the security module where FTD is installed and then complete any necessary steps.

Example 3-1 shows an example of the process of accessing the CLI of the FTD software from the CLI of the FXOS and completing the system initialization.

Example 3-1 *Accessing the FTD CLI for the First Time*

```
! Run the following command on the CLI of the FXOS


Firepower-9300# connect module 1 console
Telnet escape character is '~'.
Trying 127.5.1.1...
Connected to 127.5.1.1.
Escape character is '~'.
CISCO Serial Over LAN:
Close Network Connection to Exit
Firepower-module1>


! Now, run the following command to connect to the CLI of the FTD:


Firepower-module1> connect ftd
Connecting to ftd console... enter exit to return to bootCLI
```

```
! The following network settings should auto-populate, if you configured them in the
  FTD provisioning page. In such case, no action necessary. Please be patient.

You must configure the network to continue.
You must configure at least one of IPv4 or IPv6.
Do you want to configure IPv4? (y/n) [y]: y
Do you want to configure IPv6? (y/n) [n]: n
Configure IPv4 via DHCP or manually? (dhcp/manual) [manual]: manual
Enter an IPv4 address for the management interface [10.1.1.28]: 10.1.1.28
Enter an IPv4 netmask for the management interface [255.255.255.0]: 255.255.255.0
Enter the IPv4 default gateway for the management interface [10.1.1.1]: 10.1.1.1
Enter a fully qualified hostname for this system [Firepower-module1]: Firepower-module1
Enter a comma-separated list of DNS servers or 'none' [none]: none
Enter a comma-separated list of search domains or 'none' [none]: none
If your networking information has changed, you will need to reconnect.
For HTTP Proxy configuration, run 'configure network http-proxy'

Configure firewall mode? (routed/transparent) [routed]: routed
Configuring firewall mode ...


Update policy deployment information
    - add device configuration
    - add network discovery
    - add system policy

You can register the sensor to a Firepower Management Center and use the
Firepower Management Center to manage it. Note that registering the sensor
to a Firepower Management Center disables on-sensor Firepower Services
management capabilities.

When registering the sensor to a Firepower Management Center, a unique
alphanumeric registration key is always required.  In most cases, to register
a sensor to a Firepower Management Center, you must provide the hostname or
the IP address along with the registration key.
'configure manager add [hostname | ip address ] [registration key ]'

However, if the sensor and the Firepower Management Center are separated by a
NAT device, you must enter a unique NAT ID, along with the unique registration
key.
'configure manager add DONTRESOLVE [registration key ] [ NAT ID ]'

Later, using the web interface on the Firepower Management Center, you must
use the same registration key and, if necessary, the same NAT ID when you add
this sensor to the Firepower Management Center.
>
```

The > prompt at the end of Example 3-1 confirms that the installation is complete. The next step is to verify the network connectivity on the management interface, and then you can begin the registration process.

Verification and Troubleshooting Tools

This section describes the commands you can run to verify the status of Firepower hardware before and after an FTD logical device is added.

Navigating to the FTD CLI

To determine the status of various hardware and software components, you need to know how to go back and forth between the FXOS CLI and FTD CLI. Figure 3-31 shows how to access various levels of the FTD CLI from the FXOS CLI.

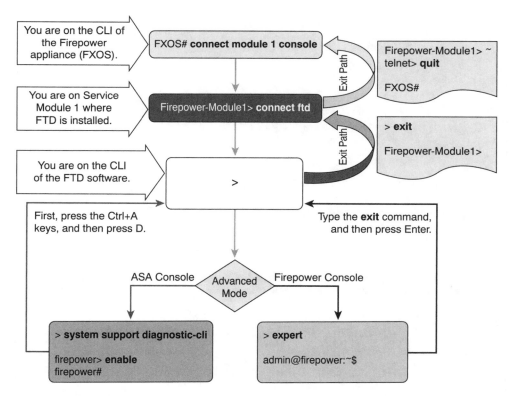

Figure 3-31 *FTD CLI Navigation*

Example 3-2 demonstrates the use of the commands to connect to the FTD software and then return to the FXOS software.

Example 3-2   *Entering and Exiting the CLI of FTD and FXOS*

```
! Assuming you are on the CLI of FXOS, first run the following command to connect to
  the Security Module (SM 1) where FTD software is installed.

Firepower-9300# connect module 1 console
Telnet escape character is '~'.
Trying 127.5.1.1...
Connected to 127.5.1.1.
Escape character is '~'.
CISCO Serial Over LAN:
Close Network Connection to Exit

Firepower-module1>

! Now, you are on the CLI of the Security Module 1 (SM 1). Run the following command
  to connect to the CLI of the FTD:

Firepower-module1> connect ftd
Connecting to ftd console... enter exit to return to bootCLI

>

! Now, you are on the CLI of the FTD software where you perform most of the FTD
  related tasks. If you want to ASA console, run the following command on the CLI of
  the FTD:

> system support diagnostic-cli
Attaching to ASA console ... Press 'Ctrl+a then d' to detach.
Type help or '?' for a list of available commands.

firepower>

! Now, you are on the CLI of the ASA software. Run the following command to access
  the privileged mode. Press the enter key when you are prompted for a password.

firepower> enable
Password:
firepower#

! To exit from the ASA console, press 'Ctrl+a then d' to detach.

firepower#
Console connection detached.
>
```

```
! You are now back to the CLI of FTD. To exit from the FTD CLI, run the following
  command:

> exit
Firepower-module1>

! You have now returned to the Service Module CLI. To exit, press the escape
  character '~', run the 'quit' command.

Firepower-module1> ~
telnet> quit
Connection closed.

Firepower-9300#

! You are now back to the CLI of the FXOS software.
```

Verifying the FXOS Software

By using the CLI of the FXOS, you can verify the version, settings, and status of various software components, such as firmware, host operating system, guest operating system, and so on. You can also enter the modular components of the Firepower hardware independently by changing the modes on the CLI. The command to change the current mode is **scope**. To find the available modes and their descriptions, type **?** after the **scope** command. A mode (scope) can also have a submode—a child mode within a parent mode.

Example 3-3 shows that the Firepower security appliance is running Version 1.0.10 of the firmware.

Example 3-3   *Verifying the Firmware Version and Its Status*

```
Firepower-9300# scope chassis 1
Firepower-9300 /chassis # show sup version detail
SUP FIRMWARE:
    ROMMON:
        Running-Vers: 1.0.10
        Package-Vers: 1.0.10
        Activate-Status: Ready
        Upgrade Status: SUCCESS
    FPGA:
        Running-Vers: 1.05
        Package-Vers: 1.0.10
        Activate-Status: Ready

Firepower-9300 /chassis #
```

Example 3-4 shows Firepower Chassis Manager running FXOS Release 2.0.1. However, the FXOS software on Security Module 3 is currently being upgraded from Release 1.1.4 to Release 2.0.1.

Example 3-4   *Determining the Status of the FXOS Software*

```
Firepower-9300# scope system
Firepower-9300 /system # show firmware monitor
FPRM:
    Package-Vers: 2.0(1.86)
    Upgrade-Status: Ready

Fabric Interconnect A:
    Package-Vers: 2.0(1.86)
    Upgrade-Status: Ready

Chassis 1:
    Server 1:
        Package-Vers: 2.0(1.86)
        Upgrade-Status: Ready
    Server 3:
        Package-Vers: 2.0(1.86),1.1(4.95)
        Upgrade-Status: Upgrading

Firepower-9300 /system #
```

Verifying the Status of a Security Application

When you add an FTD logical device on a Firepower appliance, it installs the FTD software as an application. If you suspect that there is an issue with the FTD software operation, you need to check the status of the application.

Example 3-5 shows the status of the FTD_610 logical device. As you can see, the device is operational and running on Security Module 1 (slot ID 1) on a Firepower 9300 appliance.

Example 3-5   *Verifying the Status of the Logical Device*

```
Firepower-9300 /ssa # show logical-device

Logical Device:
    Name        Description  Slot ID    Mode        Operational State     Template Name
    ----------  -----------  ---------- ----------  --------------------  -------------
    FTD_610                  1          Standalone Ok                     ftd

Firepower-9300 /ssa #
```

Example 3-6 shows the status of an FTD application. The output first confirms that the application is being installed. The output then shows when the FTD installation is complete and the application comes online.

Example 3-6   *Verifying the Status of the FTD Application Instance*

```
! The following output confirms that FTD application is being installed.

Firepower-9300# scope ssa
Firepower-9300 /ssa # show app-instance detail

    Application Name: ftd
    Slot ID: 1
    Admin State: Disabled
    Operational State: Installing
    Running Version:
    Startup Version: 6.1.0.330
    Cluster Oper State: Not Applicable
    Current Job Type: Install
    Current Job Progress: 0
    Current Job State: Queued
    Clear Log Data: Available
    Error Msg:
    Hotfixes:
    Externally Upgraded: No

Firepower-9300 /ssa #

! The following output proves that the FTD application is up and running.

Firepower-9300# scope ssa
Firepower-9300 /ssa # show app-instance detail

    Application Name: ftd
    Slot ID: 1
    Admin State: Enabled
    Operational State: Online
    Running Version: 6.1.0.330
    Startup Version: 6.1.0.330
    Cluster Oper State: Not Applicable
    Current Job Type: Start
    Current Job Progress: 100
    Current Job State: Succeeded
    Clear Log Data: Available
    Error Msg:
    Hotfixes:
    Externally Upgraded: No

Firepower-9300 /ssa #
```

Verifying the Security Modules, Adapters, and Switch Fabric

FTD software is installed on a security module. If you experience an issue with the FTD, you should check the status of the security module where the FTD software is installed.

> **Note**   As noted earlier in this chapter, the terms *security module* and *security engine* refer to the same hardware component but are used on two different platforms—Firepower 9300 and 4100, respectively.

You can verify the status of a security module from the Firepower Chassis Manager as follows:

- On a Firepower 9300 Series appliance, go to the Security Modules page.

- On a Firepower 4100 Series appliance, go to the Security Engine page.

Figure 3-32 shows three security modules on a Firepower 9300 appliance. If you run a Firepower 4100 Series appliance, you see only one security engine. For demonstration purposes, the icons for the security modules are highlighted in this figure.

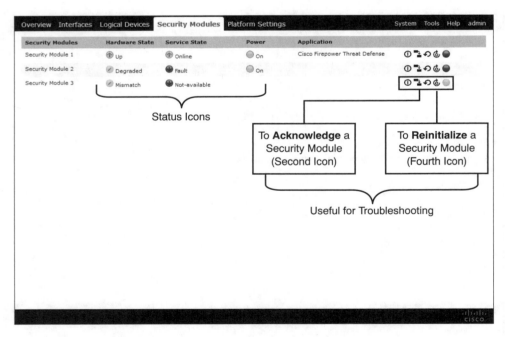

Figure 3-32   *Different Hardware and Service States of the Service Modules*

> **Tip**   Read the "Cisco FXOS Firepower Chassis Manager Configuration Guide" to learn more about the possible hardware and service states.

To determine the status of a service module from the CLI, you can run the **show server** command.

Example 3-7 shows that Service Modules 1 and 2 are equipped, but only Service Module 1 is up and Service Module 2 is faulty. Service Module 3 is mismatched, which means this module is decommissioned, unacknowledged, or newly installed.

Example 3-7   *Verifying the Overall Status of the Security Modules*

```
Firepower-9300# show server status
Server   Slot Status                        Overall Status         Discovery
-------  -------------------------------    --------------------   ---------
1/1      Equipped                           Ok                     Complete
1/2      Equipped                           Degraded               Complete
1/3      Mismatch
Firepower-9300#
```

Table 3-2 describes various scenarios for a security module and the action you should take to bring the module into an operational state.

Table 3-2   *Operating a Security Module in Various States*

Scenario	Action
Security module is new and installed into a slot.	Acknowledge the security module.
Security module has existing data, but you want to place it in a new or different slot.	Reinitialize the security module before you deploy a logical device on it.
Security module is decommissioned in order to discontinue its use temporarily.	Acknowledge the security module.
Error in a security module.	Try restarting the security module.
Security module shows "mismatch" or "token mismatch" status.	Acknowledge the security module. If it is not fixed, reinitialize the security module.

Example 3-8 shows that Security Modules 1 and 3 are operable, which means they are in good health. Security Module 1 is running, and Security Module 3 is booting up (config state). However, Security Module 2 is inoperable.

Example 3-8   *Determining the Health of a Security Module*

```
Firepower-9300# show server environment
Server 1/1:
    Overall Status: Ok
    Operability: Operable
    Oper Power: On

Server 1/2:
    Overall Status: Degraded
    Operability: Inoperable
    Oper Power: On

Server 1/3:
    Overall Status: Config
    Operability: Operable
    Oper Power: On
Firepower-9300#
```

In the architectural diagram of a Firepower appliance (refer to Figure 3-3), you can see that each security module is connected to two adapters, which are connected to a switch fabric. When you are troubleshooting, it is also important to determine whether the adapter and the switch fabric are operational.

Example 3-9 shows two adapters on each security module. All the adapters are in good health.

Example 3-9   *Finding Overall Status of the Adapters*

```
Firepower-9300# show server adapter
Server 1/1:
    Adapter PID               Vendor            Serial        Overall Status
    ------- ----------        ----------------  ------------  --------------
          1 FPR-C9300-MP      Cisco Systems Inc XXXXXXXXXXX   Operable
          2 FPR-C9300-MP-MEZZ Cisco Systems Inc XXXXXXXXXXX   Operable

Server 1/3:
    Adapter PID               Vendor            Serial        Overall Status
    ------- ----------        ----------------  ------------  --------------
          1 FPR-C9300-MP      Cisco Systems Inc XXXXXXXXXXX   Operable
          2 FPR-C9300-MP-MEZZ Cisco Systems Inc XXXXXXXXXXX   Operable

Firepower-9300#
```

Example 3-10 shows that the switch fabric Interconnect A is operable.

Example 3-10 *Determining the Operability of the Switch Fabric*

```
Firepower-9300# show fabric-interconnect environment
Fabric Interconnect A:
    Operability: Operable

    Fabric Card 1:
        Threshold Status: N/A
        Overall Status: Operable
        Operability: Operable
        Power State: Online
        Thermal Status: N/A
        Voltage Status: N/A
    .
    .
<Output_Omitted>

Firepower-9300#
```

Verifying the Hardware Chassis

You can determine the FXOS software versions of a Firepower appliance by selecting **Help > About**. Alternatively, you can select **System > Updates** to see any software installed on a system. However, the Firepower Chassis Manager web interface does not show the details of the Firepower hardware. To find more detailed information about hardware components, run the **show chassis detail** command, as shown in Example 3-11.

Example 3-11 shows the detailed hardware information of a Firepower 4110 appliance. It also shows an operable condition of the appliance.

Example 3-11 *Verifying the Hardware of a Firepower Security Appliance*

```
Firepower-4110# show chassis detail

Chassis:
    Chassis: 1
    User Label:
    Overall Status: Operable
    Oper qualifier: N/A
    Operability: Operable
    Conf State: Ok
    Admin State: Acknowledged
    Conn Path: A
    Conn Status: A
    Managing Instance: A
  Product Name: Cisco Firepower 4110 Security Appliance
    PID: FPR-4110-K9
    VID: V00
    Part Number: XX-XXXXXX-XX
```

```
   Vendor: Cisco Systems Inc
   Model: FPR-4110-K9
   Serial (SN): XXXXXXXXXXX
   HW Revision: 0
   Mfg Date: 2015-12-05T00:00:00.000
   Power State: Ok
   Thermal Status: Ok
   SEEPROM operability status: Operable
   Dynamic Reallocation: Chassis
   Reserved Power Budget (W): 600
   PSU Capacity (W): 0
   PSU Line Mode: Lower Line
   PSU State: Ok
   Current Task:

Firepower-4110#
```

You can view a summary of the hardware operations on the Overview page of Firepower Chassis Manager. This page displays any hardware errors, along with severity level, description, cause, occurrence, and time of each incident.

Figure 3-33 shows the Overview page for a Firepower 9300 appliance. While the top of the page shows an overall operational state, below this you can see more detailed information.

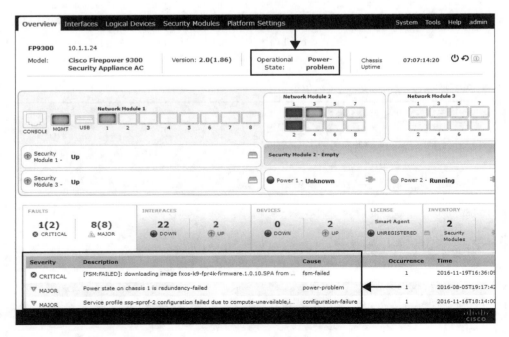

Figure 3-33 *Identifying Hardware Errors in Firepower Chassis Manager*

Similarly, if you choose to use the CLI, you can run multiple commands to determine whether there has been a failure of any major hardware components on a Firepower appliance.

Example 3-12 shows the same errors you just saw in the web interface in Figure 3-33.

Example 3-12 *Identifying Hardware Errors from the CLI of FXOS*

```
Firepower-9300# show fault

Severity   Code      Last Transition Time      ID        Description
---------  --------  ----------------------  --------  -----------
Critical   F999690   2016-11-19T16:36:09.980  15304334 [FSM:FAILED]: downloading image
   fxos-k9-fpr4k-firmware.1.0.10.SPA from (FSM:sam:dme:FirmwareDownloaderDownload)
Major      F0327     2016-11-16T18:14:00.622  15234559 Service profile ssp-sprof-2
   configuration failed due to compute-unavailable,insufficient-resources
Warning    F0528     2016-08-05T19:17:42.663    44431 Power supply 1 in chassis 1
   power: off


Firepower-9300#
```

You can also view the system event log (SEL) of a Firepower appliance from the CLI. The **show sel** command on FXOS provides output similar to what you can see with the **ipmitool** command on a Linux system.

Example 3-13 shows events from the Cisco Integrated Management Controller (CIMC) and basic input/output system (BIOS). The **1/1** parameter with the **show sel** command represents chassis1/module1.

Example 3-13 *Viewing the SEL of a Firepower Security Appliance*

```
Firepower-9300# show sel 1/1
1 | 12/22/2016 00:03:52 | CIMC | Drive slot(Bay) LED_BLADE_STATUS #0xa6 | Drive
Presence | Asserted
2 | 12/22/2016 00:03:55 | CIMC | Voltage P2V63_VPP_EF #0x1c | Lower critical - going
low | Asserted | Reading 2.48 <= Threshold 2.48 Volts
3 | 12/22/2016 00:03:55 | CIMC | Platform alert LED_SYS_ACT #0xa4 | LED color is
amber | Asserted
4 | 12/22/2016 00:04:29 | BIOS | System Event #0x00 | Timestamp clock synch | SEL
timestamp clock updated, event is first of pair | Asserted
5 | 12/22/2016 00:05:53 | BIOS | System Event #0x83 | OEM System Boot Event |  |
Asserted
6 | 12/22/2016 00:18:26 | CIMC | Entity presence MAIN_POWER_PRS #0x55 | Device
Absent | Asserted
7 | 12/22/2016 00:37:15 | CIMC | Temperature GPU1_TEMP_SENS #0x59 | Upper
Non-critical - going high | Asserted | Reading 136 >= Threshold 136 degrees C
```

```
8 | 12/22/2016 00:37:35 | CIMC | Temperature GPU1_TEMP_SENS #0x59 | Upper
  Non-critical - going high | Deasserted | Reading 134 <= Threshold 136 degrees C
.
.
.
<Output_Omitted>

Firepower-9300#
```

Verifying the Power Supply Unit (PSU) Modules

You can find an issue with a power supply unit (PSU) from the Overview page of Firepower Chassis Manager. In addition, you can run several commands on the CLI to investigate power-related issues.

Example 3-14 uses the **show fault** command to confirm that one of the PSUs is not turned on.

Example 3-14   *Determining the Overall Operational Status of a Firepower Appliance*

```
Firepower-9300# show fault
Severity   Code      Last Transition Time      ID        Description
---------  --------  -----------------------   --------  -----------
Warning    F0528     2016-08-05T19:17:42.663   44431     Power supply 1 in chassis 1
  power: off
Major      F0408     2016-08-05T19:17:42.662   44430     Power state on chassis 1 is
  redundancy-failed

Firepower-9300#
```

Example 3-15 uses the **show chassis environment** command to show whether there is a power problem. In this case, there is a power problem: The Firepower 9300 appliance has a power redundancy failure.

Example 3-15   *Determining the Overall Operational Status of a Firepower Security Appliance*

```
Firepower-9300# show chassis environment
Chassis 1:
    Overall Status: Power Problem
    Operability: Operable
    Power State: Redundancy Failed
    Thermal Status: Ok

Firepower-9300#
```

Example 3-16 shows filtered output of the **show sel** command. It shows events with the **power** keyword only. The events in this example were generated when the main power was disconnected and then reconnected.

Example 3-16   *Viewing the SEL of a Firepower Appliance*

```
Firepower-9300# show sel 1/1 | egrep ignore-case power
1 | 12/13/2016 16:37:52 | CIMC | Entity presence MAIN_POWER_PRS #0x55 | Device
  Absent | Asserted
2 | 12/13/2016 16:39:23 | CIMC | Entity presence MAIN_POWER_PRS #0x55 | Device
  Present | Asserted

Firepower-9300#
```

Example 3-17 confirms that the Firepower appliance is equipped with two power supply units, but PSU 1 has no power.

Example 3-17   *Viewing the Details of Two PSUs*

```
Firepower-9300# show chassis psu detail

PSU:
    PSU: 1
    Overall Status: N/A
    Operability: N/A
    Threshold Status: N/A
    Power State: Off
    Presence: Equipped
    Thermal Status: OK
    Voltage Status: N/A
    Product Name: Cisco Firepower 9000 Series AC Power Supply
    PID: FPR9K-PS-AC
    VID: V01
    Part Number: 341-0723-01
    Vendor: Cisco Systems Inc
    Serial (SN): ART1918F298
    HW Revision: 0
    Firmware Version: N/A
    Type: Unknown
    Wattage (W): 0
    Input Source: Unknown

    PSU: 2
    Overall Status: Operable
    Operability: Operable
    Threshold Status: OK
```

```
Power State: On
Presence: Equipped
Thermal Status: OK
Voltage Status: OK
Product Name: Cisco Firepower 9000 Series AC Power Supply
PID: FPR9K-PS-AC
VID: V01
Part Number: 341-0723-01
Vendor: Cisco Systems Inc
Serial (SN): ART1918F28X
HW Revision: 0
Firmware Version: N/A
Type: Unknown
Wattage (W): 2500
Input Source: Unknown

Firepower-9300#
```

Verifying the Fan Modules

A Firepower 9300 Series appliance has four fan modules, and a 4100 Series appliance has six fan modules. There are a few ways to determine the status of any fan modules on a Firepower security appliance:

- You can look at the LED on a fan module. If the color of the LED is amber, you know there has been a failure.

- In Firepower Chassis Manager, you can go to the Overview page to identify the status of the fans.

- You can run several commands at the CLI to investigate any fan-related issues.

Example 3-18 shows a warning for a missing fan module. One of the fan modules was removed to demonstrate this alert.

Example 3-18   *Warning Message When a Fan Module Is Missing or Inoperable*

```
Firepower-9300 /chassis # show fault
Severity  Code    Last Transition Time      ID        Description
--------- ------- ------------------------- -------- -----------
Warning   F0377   2016-12-02T18:06:24.196   15575670 Fan module 1-2 in chassis 1
  presence: missing
.

.
<Output_Omitted>


Firepower-9300 /chassis #
```

Example 3-19 shows the overall status of the fan modules on a Firepower 9300 appliance. If you were to run the same command on a 4100 Series appliance, you would find six modules in the output.

Example 3-19 *Determining the Overall Health Status of the Fan Modules on a Firepower 9300 Appliance*

```
Firepower-9300 /chassis # show fan-module

Fan Module:
    Tray        Module      Overall Status
    ----------  ----------  --------------
        1           1       Operable
        1           2       Removed
        1           3       Operable
        1           4       Operable

Firepower-9300 /chassis #
```

Example 3-20 shows detailed information about the fan modules on a Firepower 9300 appliance. The first module is equipped and operational, and the second module is missing.

Example 3-20 *Viewing Detailed Information About the Fan Modules*

```
Firepower-9300 /chassis # show fan-module detail

Fan Module:
    Tray: 1
    Module: 1
    Overall Status: Operable
    Operability: Operable
    Threshold Status: OK
    Power State: On
    Presence: Equipped
    Thermal Status: OK
    Product Name: Cisco Firepower 9000 Series Fan
    PID: FPR9K-FAN
    VID: 01
    Part Number: XX-XXXXX-XX
    Vendor: Cisco Systems Inc
    Serial (SN): XXXXXXXXXXX
    HW Revision: 0
    Mfg Date: 2015-05-28T00:00:00.000
```

```
      Tray: 1
      Module: 2
      Overall Status: Removed
      Operability: N/A
      Threshold Status: N/A
      Power State: Off
      Presence: Missing
      Thermal Status: N/A
      Product Name:
      PID:
      VID: 01
      Part Number: XX-XXXXX-XX
      Vendor:
      Serial (SN):
      HW Revision: 0
      Mfg Date: 2015-05-28T00:00:00.000

  .
  .
<Output_Omitted>

Firepower-9300 /chassis #
```

Summary

This chapter describes the architecture, implementation, and installation of FTD on a Firepower security appliance running FXOS. It demonstrates several command-line tools you can use to determine the status of various components of the appliance.

After installation, the next step in deploying an FTD in a network is to register it with a Firepower Management Center. Part II of this book describes that.

Quiz

1. A Firepower 4100 Series security appliance has various hardware components. In which component is FTD software installed?

    a. Switch fabric

    b. Security engine

    c. Supervisor

    d. Adapter

2. The "mismatch" status of a security module indicates
   a. that the module has been decommissioned.
   b. that the module was recently installed.
   c. that the module has prior data that does not match.
   d. all of the above.

3. Which command can you run at the CLI to see any hardware errors that you could also view on the Overview page of Firepower Chassis Manager?
   a. **show environment**
   b. **show fault**
   c. **show status**
   d. **show chassis**

4. Which command is necessary to access the ASA console if you are currently on the FXOS CLI?
   a. **connect module 1 console**
   b. **connect ftd**
   c. **system support diagnostic-cli**
   d. All of the above

5. A Firepower 9300 appliance is currently running FXOS Release 1.1.4. If you want to install FTD Version 6.1 on it, what is the correct order of action?
   a. Install firmware Version 1.1.10 and then install FTD Version 6.1.
   b. Install FXOS Release 2.0.1 and then install FTD Version 6.1.
   c. Install FTD Version 6.0 and then upgrade to Version 6.1.
   d. Install FTD Version 6.1 only.

Chapter 4

Firepower Management Center (FMC) Hardware

In the previous chapters, you have learned how to install Firepower Threat Defense (FTD) on various hardware platforms. You cannot, however, define and apply any security policies for your network without assistance from a manager. This chapter discusses different options for deploying managers for FTD. It describes the process of reimaging a manager with the FTD software and describes various tools used for troubleshooting hardware.

FMC Component Essentials

To manage FTD, you need a manager. Depending on the deployment scenario and hardware model, you can choose either an on-box manager or an off-box manager (see Table 4-1). This section provides an overview of both types of Firepower managers. Table 4-1 shows the key differences between the two available options for managing FTD and provides reasons for choosing an off-box manager over an on-box solution.

Table 4-1 *Major Differences Between an On-Box Manager and an Off-Box Manager*

	On-Box	Off-Box
GUI software	Firepower Device Manager (FDM)	Firepower Management Center (FMC)
Management capability	1 FTD system	Depending on the model, can manage hundreds of FTD systems
Supported FTD platform	Low-end and midrange ASA 5500-X Series hardware	Any platforms that support FTD software
Deployment	Small to medium business (SMB)	Large enterprise network

	On-Box	Off-Box
Cost	Free; no additional hardware necessary	Need to purchase additional hardware or a license for a virtual appliance
Policy configuration	Limited functionality	Full functionality
Number of stored events	Can store only few hundred events	Can store millions of events
API integration	Does not support third-party integration	Fully supports integration with various APIs

Note This book uses the user interface of an off-box manager to demonstrate advanced configurations. The user interface of an on-box manager, which is different from the interface of an off-box manager, is beyond the scope of this book.

In addition, in this section, you will learn about some of the key hardware components of a Firepower manager, such as the Cisco Integrated Management Controller (CIMC) and internal storage for system restoration. This section also introduces you to the different types of user interfaces in Firepower manager hardware.

On-Box Managers

The FTD software introduces a new user interface, called the Firepower Device Manager (FDM), that you can run from a web browser, without any requirement for a third-party client. As of this writing, the FDM supports the ASA 5500-X Series (low-end and mid-range platforms), Firepower 2100 Series hardware, and FTD Virtual (on VMware platform). However, it does not support the Firepower 4100 Series, or the 9300 Series.

Tip To determine whether a new Firepower feature is supported on your Cisco hardware, you can read the "Cisco Firepower Compatibility Guide."

The FDM can manage one FTD at a time. If you have more than one FTD system, you cannot use the FDM to manage all the FTD systems. Therefore, using the FDM is a good solution for small to medium business (SMB) networks but is not a scalable solution for large enterprise networks. The FDM is designed to be simple and intuitive, and its use is targeted to users who are not experts on the Firepower System.

Figure 4-1 shows a simple topology in which FTD could be managed by an on-box manager such as the FDM.

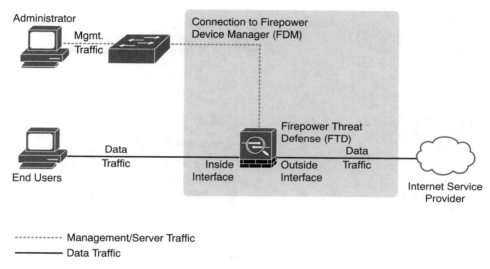

**Firepower Threat Defense
On-Box Management**

(Management Traffic Is Out of Band
While Data Traffic Is Being Inspected)

------------ Management/Server Traffic
——————— Data Traffic

Figure 4-1 *FTD Managed by an FDM*

Off-Box Managers

An off-box manager, as the name implies, is located outside an FTD appliance. It is designed to configure, monitor, and administer multiple FTD systems using just a single user interface. The Firepower Management Center (FMC) is an off-box manager, a dedicated standalone appliance.

The FMC is available as physical hardware or as a virtual appliance. You may find that a virtual FMC is easier and cheaper to deploy because it allows you to use your existing virtual machine's infrastructure. On the other hand, although a physical FMC requires you to purchase and deploy additional hardware for your network, it is able to manage more FTD systems, process additional hosts and users in a network, and store more events.

Figure 4-2 shows a typical topology in which multiple FTD appliances from different geographical locations are managed by one off-box manager—the FMC.

Table 4-2 shows the specifications for various FMC hardware. It compares the two latest FMC models that are based on the Cisco UCS C220 M3 chassis, with an FMC virtual appliance.

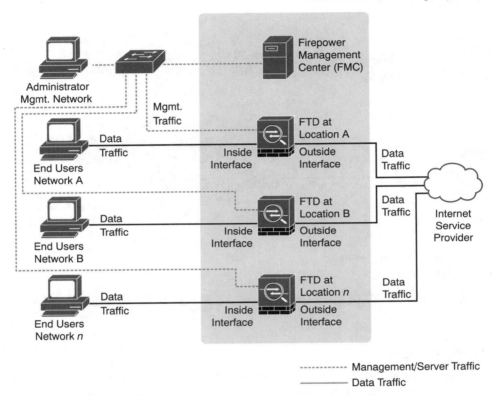

Figure 4-2   *Multiple FTD Appliances Managed by the FMC*

Table 4-2   *Hardware Specifications of Various FMC Appliances*

Specification	FMC 2000	FMC 4000	Virtual
Processor	Intel Xeon CPU E5-2630 v2 @ 2.60 GHz	Intel Xeon CPU E5-2660 v2 @ 2.20 GHz	64-bit with virtualization support
Thread/core × Core/ socket × Socket	24 (2×6×2)	40 (2×10×2)	4 to 8 virtual CPUs
Memory	64 GB	128 GB	8 GB (minimum)
Storage	4 × 600 GB SAS	6 × 960 GB SSD	250 GB

Table 4-3 shows the differences in performance for various FMC appliances. The differences are based on the hardware resources available in each appliance.

Table 4-3 *Performance of Various FMC Appliances*

Maximum...	FMC 2000	FMC 4000	Virtual
Managed FTD	250	300	2, 10, 25
Event storage	1.8 TB	3.2 TB	250 GB
Hosts	150,000	600,000	50,000
Users	150,000	600,000	50,000
IPS events	60 million	300 million	10 million
Flow rate	12,000 fps	20,000 fps	Resource dependent
Support for high availability	Yes	Yes	No

Note   As of this writing, Cisco supports additional FMC models. For example, prior to FMC 2000 and FMC 4000 models, the FMC 750, FMC 1500, and FMC 3500 models were released, supporting any trains of Version 6.x. After the FMC 2000 and FMC 4000 models, Cisco introduced the FMC 1000, FMC 2500, and FMC 4500 models, which support Version 6.2 or later. While new hardware models and software versions are continuously being developed, you can apply the knowledge you learn from this book to any FMC hardware models running Firepower Version 6.1 or later.

Cisco Integrated Management Controller (CIMC)

The two latest FMC models, FMC 2000 and FMC 4000, are based on the Cisco Unified Communication System (UCS) C220 M3 chassis. One of the hardware components of a UCS C220 server is the CIMC. CIMC uses the Intelligent Platform Management Interface (IPMI) to monitor a UCS server. One of the advantages of CIMC is that it runs on a separate chip. Therefore, if a UCS server fails, you should still be able to connect to the CIMC to troubleshoot any hardware issues.

Figure 4-3 shows an architectural overview of the CIMC. It shows how the hardware-related information is exchanged with the IPMI and is viewed through the syslog, SNMP, or XML API.

You can access the CIMC Configuration Utility by pressing F8 during the power-on self-test (POST) operation. Using the Configuration Utility, you can assign an IP address for the CIMC interface. You can either use a web browser to access the CIMC GUI or a Secure Shell (SSH) client to connect to the CIMC CLI.

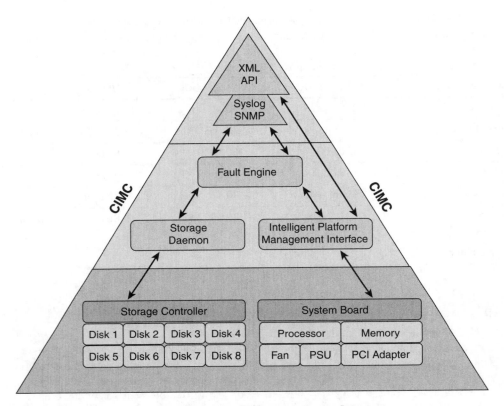

Figure 4-3   *Interaction of the CIMC with Various Server Components*

Figure 4-4 shows the IP address 10.1.1.12 assigned to the CIMC interface. In the Additional Settings page (which you access by pressing F1), you can change the default login password of the CIMC interface.

One of the useful features of the CIMC is the keyboard, video, and mouse (KVM) console. Using the KVM console, you can directly connect to the console of the FMC, without the need for dedicated KVM-based hardware.

Figure 4-5 shows the KVM Console option in the CIMC GUI. To access this GUI, use the default username/password (admin/password), or reset these default credentials from the CIMC Configuration Utility.

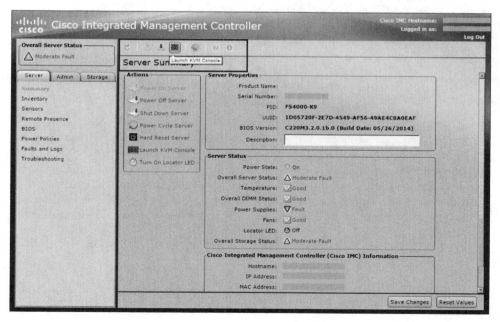

```
Cisco IMC Configuration Utility Version 2.0, Cisco Systems, Inc.
**************************************************************************
NIC Properties
  NIC mode                                  NIC redundancy
  Dedicated:       [X]                       None:              [X]
  Shared LOM:      [ ]                        Active-standby:    [ ]
  Cisco Card:      [ ]                        Active-active:     [ ]
  Shared LOM Ext:  [ ]
IP (Basic)
  IPV4:            [X]        IPV6:  [ ]
  DHCP enabled     [ ]
  CIMC IP:         10.1.1.12
  Prefix/Subnet:   255.255.255.0
  Gateway:         10.1.1.1
  Pref DNS Server: 0.0.0.0
VLAN (Advanced)
  VLAN enabled:    [ ]
  VLAN ID:         1
  Priority:        0
**************************************************************************
<Up/Down>Selection   <F10>Save   <Space>Enable/Disable   <F5>Refresh   <ESC>Exit
<F1>Additional settings
```

Figure 4-4 *The CIMC Configuration Utility*

Figure 4-5 *Launching the KVM Console Option in the CIMC GUI*

Internal USB Storage for the System_Restore Image

The UCS C-Series server has internal USB storage that is used to store an image for the system restoration. You can select the System_Restore image from the LILO boot menu.

> **Note**   Linux Loader (LILO) is one of the most popular default boot loaders for Linux. A boot loader is a small program that loads an operating system when you turn on a computer system.

Figure 4-6 shows the System_Restore image in the LILO boot menu.

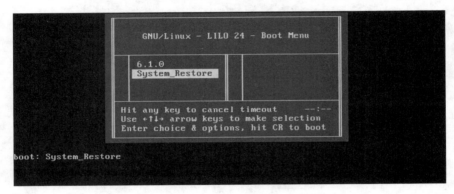

Figure 4-6   *Selecting the System_Restore Image in the LILO Boot Menu*

User Interfaces

After you power on any computer system, you need an interface that allows you to interact with the system. This is the case with the FMC. In fact, the FMC has many different types of user interfaces, depending on what you want to do. For example, you can use the GUI to apply security policy and monitor events, you can use the CLI for advanced troubleshooting, and you can use the text-based user interface (TUI) to configure any specific components when the actual operating system is not loaded or installed. Figure 4-7 illustrates different types of user interfaces for the FMC. Each dark box represents a unique type of interface.

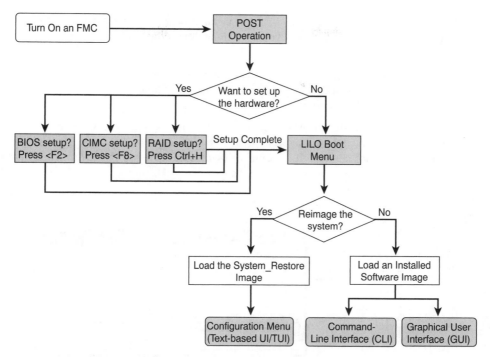

Figure 4-7 *Different Types of User Interfaces for the FMC*

Best Practices for FMC Reimage

This section discusses some of the best practices you should follow when you reimage the FMC to Version 6.1. It also provides you with a list of items you should verify on the FMC hardware after reimaging is complete.

Pre-installation Best Practices

If your FTD system is running Version 6.1, the FMC must be running Version 6.1 or later. Consider the following best practices when you reimage the FMC to Version 6.1:

- Prior to the maintenance window when you plan to do a reimaging or a fresh installation, make sure you are able to access the cisco.com website and can download any necessary software. If needed, register for a Cisco account. If after the self-registration process you cannot download any of the desired software, you might need to get further assistance from your Cisco channel partner or the Cisco Technical Assistance Center (TAC).

- Depending on the appliance model, a fresh installation or system restoration process can take about an hour. However, you should plan for additional time to fulfill any prerequisites.

- Do not rename any files after you download them from the cisco.com. For FMC 2000 and FMC 4000 models, the name of the ISO file is Sourcefire_Defense_ Center_S3-6.1.0-330-Restore.iso.

- After you download any software from cisco.com, always verify the MD5 or SHA512 checksum of the files you have downloaded to confirm that the file is not corrupt and has not been modified during download. Figure 4-8 shows how the MD5 and SHA512 checksum values are displayed at cisco.com when you hover your mouse over a filename.

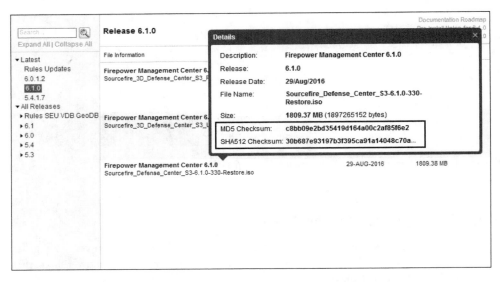

Figure 4-8   *Checksum Values of an ISO Image File Displayed in a Popup Box*

- Before you reimage currently operational FMC hardware or redeploy a virtual machine, you should prepare a backup plan. Make a backup of the existing events and configurations. During a backup, take a note of the detailed software versions and hardware models of the FMC because they must match during restore. After a backup, make sure you copy the backup file to external storage because a reimage erases backup files along with any other data on an FMC. Figure 4-9 illustrates the backup management page in the FMC. It is located at **System > Tools > Backup/ Restore**.

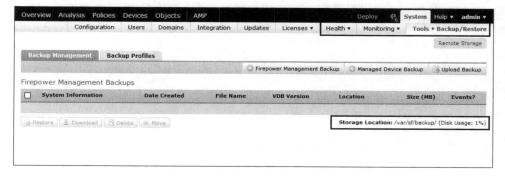

Figure 4-9   *The Backup Management Page*

- You can use the Import/Export tool to copy any policies running on your FMC. During an import, the versions of a restored system must match with the FMC from where any policies are originally exported. Therefore, when you export, you must remember the software and rule update version information of the original FMC. Figure 4-10 shows the Import/Export page, which is located at **System > Tools > Import/Export**.

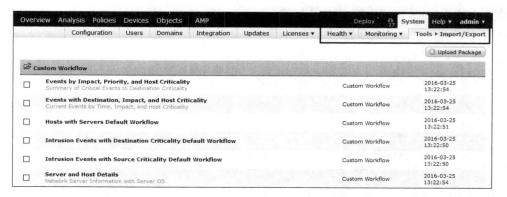

Figure 4-10   *The Import/Export Page*

- If the FMC was previously licensed through the Cisco Smart Software Manager, deregister the FMC gracefully from the user interface of the FMC. Otherwise, periodic communication attempts from the Cisco License Authority may trigger alerts for the Out-of-Compliance state. Figure 4-11 shows a red octagonal icon in the Smart License Status page, which is located at **System > Licenses > Smart Licenses**. This icon deregisters an FMC from the Smart License cloud.

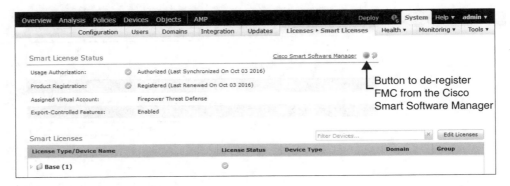

Figure 4-11 *The Smart License Management Page*

- Never power off, shut down, or reboot the FMC when reimaging is in progress. A login prompt appears after all the reimaging processes are complete.

- Read the release notes to determine any known issues and any special requirements or instructions before you begin reimaging or performing system restoration.

Post-installation Best Practices

After the software is installed, take some time to perform the following tests:

- Determine the status of the RAID battery.
- Verify the status of the power supply units.
- Identify the status of the fans.
- Check for any errors with the IPMI.
- Access the GUI. You must use a supported browser. The list of supported browsers for a particular version is available in the release notes.

Performing these tests will help you determine whether there are any hardware issues before you deploy the FMC in a production environment and hence will help you avoid any potential downtime.

Tip   To learn the commands and tools that allow you to perform these tests, see the "Verification and Troubleshooting Tools" section, later in this chapter.

Installing and Configuring the FMC

In this section, you will learn how to restore or reimage the FMC.

Fulfilling Prerequisites

You must fulfill the following requirements before you begin a new installation:

- Upload the necessary software image to an HTTP server from where the FMC downloads it during reimaging. You can use an SCP or FTP server in lieu of an HTTP server. However, you might find that an HTTP server is easier to set up and use to host files.

- If you choose to use an IP-based KVM console to connect to the FMC you want to reimage, do not use any KVM with USB storage because the FMC may assume that the USB storage is a boot device. Please read the official Hardware Installation Guide to find out about any hardware-specific limitations.

> **Tip** Although you can, you do not need to obtain a dedicated KVM switch for the FMC because the CIMC of an FMC provides built-in KVM console functionality. See the section "Cisco Integrated Management Controller (CIMC)," earlier in this chapter, to learn more.

- For reimaging purposes, if you want to connect your computer directly to the management interface (eth0) of the FMC with an RJ-45 cable, make sure the computer is disconnected from the Internet (after you have downloaded any necessary software from cisco.com) and has the following network settings:

  - **IP address:** 192.168.45.2

  - **Subnet/netmask:** 255.255.255.0

  - **Default gateway:** 192.168.45.1

- You need to be able to access the System_Restore image of the FMC to perform reimaging. If the image is missing in the LILO boot menu or the LILO boot menu itself does not appear, you will not be able to begin reimaging. Follow these steps to access the System_Restore image:

  Step 1.   Reboot the FMC.

  Step 2.   During the POST operation, press the F6 key to enter the boot menu.

  Step 3.   When the boot selection window appears, select **HV**. The hypervisor (HV) partition stores the System_Restore image. If you are running an older FMC model, you may see a different option, such as USB DISK MODULE.

  Figure 4-12 shows HV as an option in the boot menu of the FMC. You can enter this boot menu by pressing the F6 key during the POST operation.

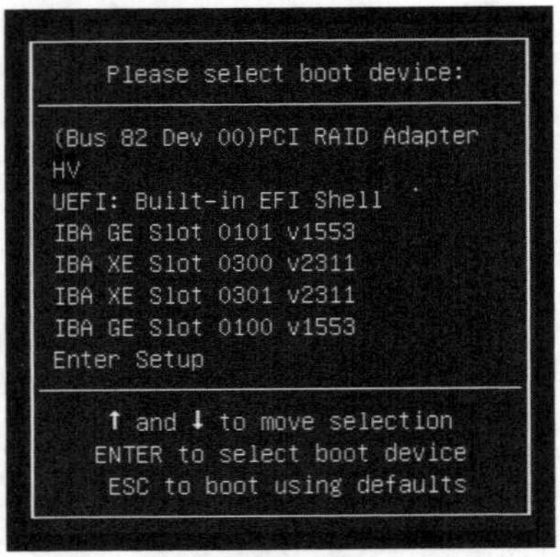

```
     Please select boot device:

(Bus 82 Dev 00)PCI RAID Adapter
HV
UEFI: Built-in EFI Shell
IBA GE Slot 0101 v1553
IBA XE Slot 0300 v2311
IBA XE Slot 0301 v2311
IBA GE Slot 0100 v1553
Enter Setup

   ↑ and ↓ to move selection
  ENTER to select boot device
   ESC to boot using defaults
```

Figure 4-12   *Hypervisor (HV)—The Internal Storage Option in the Boot Menu*

Step 4.   Press Enter to boot the FMC with HV. The FMC should now load the System_Restore image.

Configuration Steps

To reimage or restore the FMC with a Firepower software image, you must complete the following key steps:

Step 1.   Load the System_Restore image.

Step 2.   Configure the network settings.

Step 3.   Choose a transport protocol.

Step 4.   Download and mount the ISO file.

Step 5.   Run the installation.

Step 6.   Reboot the system to initialize.

Figure 4-13 shows the steps to restore or reimage the FMC with a Firepower software release. The following sections provide more details about these steps.

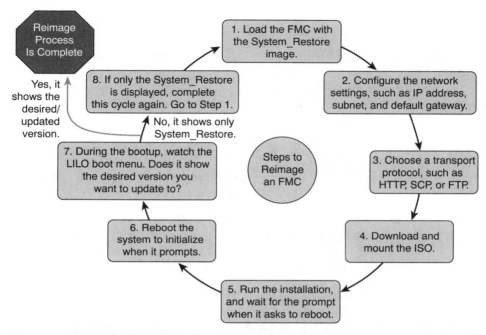

Figure 4-13 *Restoring the FMC to Factory Default Software*

Step 1: Load the System_Restore Image

Follow these steps to load the System_Restore image:

Step 1. Download an appropriate ISO image for your FMC hardware model and store it in a server from where the FMC will download the image. The example in this chapter uses an HTTP server.

Step 2. Turn on the FMC. If the FMC is already running, reboot it. Example 4-1 shows that if you enter the **reboot** command with **sudo** (with root privilege), you are prompted for the root password.

Example 4-1 *Rebooting the FMC from the CLI*

```
admin@FMC4000:~$ sudo reboot

We trust you have received the usual lecture from the local System
Administrator. It usually boils down to these three things:

    #1) Respect the privacy of others.
    #2) Think before you type.
    #3) With great power comes great responsibility.
```

```
Password:

The system is going down for reboot NOW!
INIT: Switching to runlevel: 6
INIT: Sending processes the TERM signal
Stopping Sourcefire Defense Center 4000......ok
 .
 .
 .
<command output>
```

Step 3.   During the initial bootup, BIOS displays several options, such as setup, boot menu, and diagnostic. Unless you want to configure a hardware component, do not press any key. The system displays the LILO boot menu in red. Figure 4-14 shows the System_Restore image selected as the boot option. If you do not select the System_Restore image within three seconds, the system, by default, loads the pre-installed software image 6.1.0.

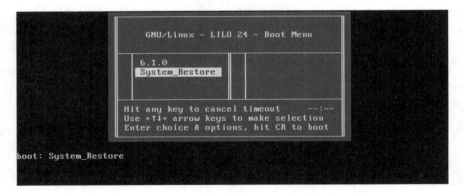

Figure 4-14   *The LILO Boot Menu with the System_Restore Image Selection*

Step 4.   When the LILO boot menu appears, select the **System_Restore** option by using an arrow key, then press the Enter key.

Step 5.   Choose an appropriate display mode to boot. Example 4-2 shows the welcome message for the Sourcefire Linux operating system. This is what you see after the System_Restore image is loaded. The example in this chapter uses option 0—Load with standard console—as the display mode. Select option **0** for a keyboard and monitor connection. Option 1 is used for serial, Serial over LAN (SOL), or Lights Out Management (LOM) connections.

Example 4-2   *Choosing a Console Type*

```
boot: System_Restore
Loading System_Restore


SYSLINUX 3.35 2007-01-28 EBIOS Copyright (C) 1994-2007 H. Peter Anvin


Welcome to the Sourcefire Linux Operating System


0. Load with standard console
1. Load with serial console

Please select a display mode to boot. If no option is selected after
a timeout of 30 seconds, the default will be display mode 0 (Load with
standard console). Press any key to cancel the timeout


boot: 0
```

Step 6.   A text-based user interface (TUI) starts and shows a copyright notice. Select
OK and press the Enter key to continue. The Cisco Firepower Appliance
Configuration Menu appears. Figure 4-15 shows a TUI for the Cisco
Firepower Appliance configuration menu.

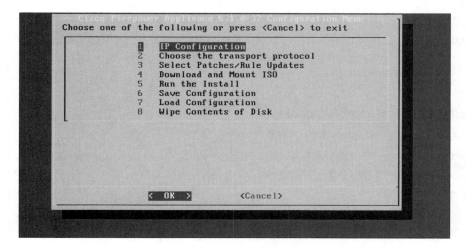

Figure 4-15   *The Cisco Firepower Appliance Configuration Menu*

Step 2: Configure the Network Settings

Follow these steps to configure the network settings:

Step 1.   Select **IP Configuration** and press the Enter key. The Pick Device window appears.

Figure 4-16 shows the eth0 interface selected as the management interface.

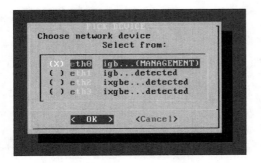

Figure 4-16   *Selection of a Management Interface*

Step 2.   Use the Spacebar to select **eth0** as the management interface and press Enter. The IP Configuration window appears.

Step 3.   Select IP information, such as **IPv4** or **IPv6, Static** or **DHCP**, and so on. (The example in this chapter uses the IPv4 and Static options.)

Step 4.   Enter an IP address, a netmask, and a default gateway for the FMC. At the end of the IP configurations, when a verification window appears, press the Enter key to return to the main configuration menu.

Step 3: Choose a Transport Protocol

Follow these steps to choose a transport protocol:

Step 1.   Enter the **Choose the Transport Protocol** option from the main configuration menu (see Figure 4-17) to define a file transfer method.

Step 2.   Select **HTTP** as the transport protocol (see Figure 4-18). You could select FTP or SCP instead, but you may find that an HTTP server is easier to build.

Step 3.   Input the IP address of the HTTP server and press the Enter key.

Step 4.   Enter the path on the HTTP server and press the Enter key. Keep it blank if you stored the ISO file in the default directory of your web server.

Step 5.   Use the Spacebar to select an ISO that you want to download and load into your FMC. Figure 4-19 shows two ISO images. Both images are downloaded from the cisco.com to the HTTP server. Select the Sourcefire_Defense_ Center_S3-6.1.0-330-Restore.iso image for FMC hardware.

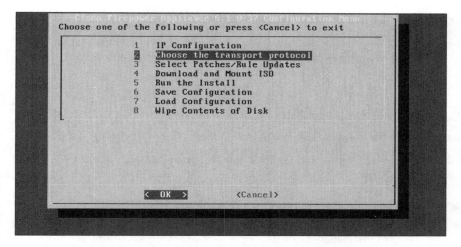

Figure 4-17   *Selecting the Choose the Transport Protocol Option*

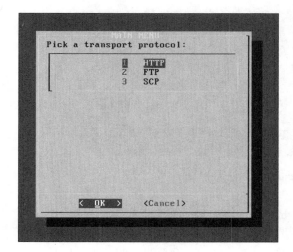

Figure 4-18   *Three Available Protocols for an ISO File Transfer*

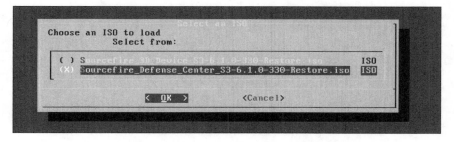

Figure 4-19   *Selecting an ISO Image During the Reimaging Process*

Step 6.   Select **OK** and press the Enter key.

Step 7.   In the window that prompts to confirm the HTTP configuration, select **Yes** if everything looks good, and you will be returned to the main configuration menu.

Step 4: Download and Mount an ISO File

Follow these steps to download and mount an ISO file:

Step 1.   In the main configuration menu, select the **Download and Mount ISO** option (see Figure 4-20).

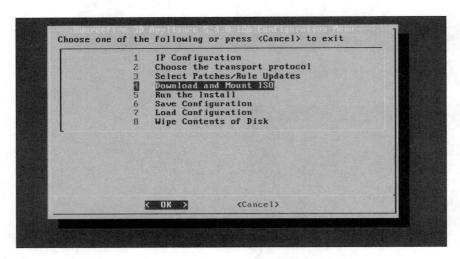

Figure 4-20   *Selecting the Download and Mount ISO Option*

Step 2.   Select **Yes** in the message that warns you that all existing data will be destroyed (see Figure 4-21).

Step 3.   Press the Enter key to continue. The ISO file is downloaded from the HTTP server, and the main configuration menu reappears.

Figure 4-21   *The Repartition Process in Progress*

Step 5: Run the Installation

Follow these steps to run the installation:

Step 1.   Select the **Run the Install** option from the main configuration menu (see Figure 4-22). The FMC begins the installation process.

Depending on the state of the internal USB storage (that is, the System_Restore image), output at this stage could be one of the following:

■ A prompt to press Enter to restart

■ A prompt to confirm the restore (Yes/No)

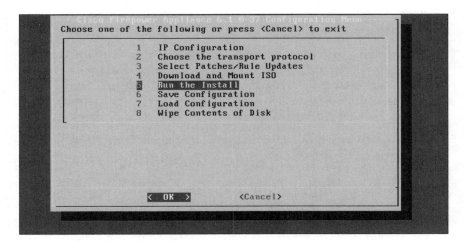

Figure 4-22   *Selecting the Run the Install Option*

If the system does not ask for a confirmation to restore but instead prompts you to press the Enter key to reboot the FMC from the internal USB, this indicates that you have imaged just the internal storage, not the hard drive, with the latest version of the System_Restore software.

Example 4-3 shows a confirmation message indicating that the USB device, not the hard drive, is imaged. It also instructs you to reboot the FMC from the USB device to continue installation.

Example 4-3   *Confirmation Message for a Successful Image of the Internal USB*

```
Restore CD     Sourcefire Fire Linux OS 6.1.0-37 x86_64
               Sourcefire Defense Center S3 6.1.0-330


     Checking Hardware


The USB device was successfully imaged. Reboot from the USB device to continue
  installation...
####################################
######
The system will restart after you press enter.
```

This happens when the FMC has been running an older version than the version you are trying to reimage to. If the internal storage of the FMC does not have a System_Restore image from the same software version you are trying to reimage to, the FMC reimages the internal storage, and then it reloads the FMC with the upgraded System_Restore image.

Step 2.   Select **System_Restore** and repeat all the steps one more time. That is, redownload and remount the ISO file from your server, rerun the installation on the FMC, and so on.

Step 3.   If the system prompts for your confirmation to restore, type **yes** and press the Enter key to continue.

Step 4.   After you press the Enter key, let the system know if you want to preserve the existing license and network settings. If you want to redeploy the FMC in exactly the same network and want to reuse the previously used license and network settings, enter **no**. If you plan to deploy the FMC in a completely new environment and want to wipe out the previous settings, enter **yes**.

Step 5.   Enter **yes** when the final confirmation message appears. The software installation begins.

Caution   If you choose to delete the previous license and network settings, make sure you have a copy of the licenses or that you are able to regenerate the licenses from cisco.com.

Example 4-4 shows the questionnaire before the installation begins. The system warns you about the permanent data loss and provides an option to keep the already configured license and network.

Example 4-4 *Questionnaire Before an Installation Begins*

```
     Restore CD      Sourcefire Fire Linux OS 6.1.0-37 x86_64
               Sourcefire Defense Center S3 6.1.0-330


        Checking Hardware


####
This CD will restore your Defense Center S3
to its original factory state. All data will be destroyed
on the appliance.

Restore the system? (yes/no): yes

During the restore process, the license file and basic
network settings are preserved. These files can also be
reset to factory settings

Delete license and network settings? (yes/no): no
**********************************************************************
THIS IS YOUR FINAL WARNING. ANSWERING YES WILL REMOVE ALL FILES
FROM THIS DEFENSE CENTER S3.
**********************************************************************


Are you sure? (yes/no): yes
```

Example 4-5 shows the beginning of an installation.

Caution   Do not reboot or power off a system while the installation is in progress.

Example 4-5 *The Software Installation Has Begun*

```
   Restore CD      Sourcefire Fire Linux OS 6.1.0-37 x86_64
               Sourcefire Defense Center S3 6.1.0-330


       (1) Preparing Disk


###############

       (2) Installing System


####
```

Step 6.   When the system confirms that the installation is complete and prompts you to reboot, press the Enter key to reboot the system.

Step 6: Initialize the System

Follow these steps to initialize the system:

Step 1.   After the reboot, the FMC should display the LILO boot menu and should load the 6.1.0 image automatically. Figure 4-23 shows that Firepower Version 6.1.0, which has just been installed, is loaded automatically after a three-second timeout.

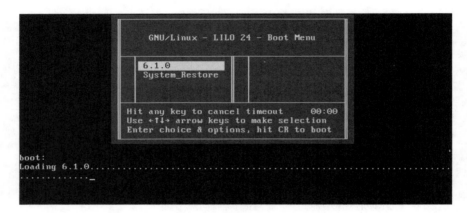

Figure 4-23   *Loading the Firepower Version 6.1.0*

> **Tip**   If the LILO boot menu does not show an option for Version 6.1.0 and only shows an entry for System_Restore, reload the FMC with the upgraded System_Restore image and repeat all the earlier steps one more time.

Step 2.   The system automatically begins the initialization process, which takes some time. Be patient.

> **Caution**   Do not reboot or power off a system while the initialization is in progress.

Example 4-6 shows many scripts executing during the initialization process. The process may take more than 30 minutes to complete.

Example 4-6   *Initialization of the Firepower Software*

```
<command output>
.


.


.

********** Attention **********

    Initializing the configuration database. Depending on available
    system resources (CPU, memory, and disk), this may take 30 minutes
    or more to complete.

********** Attention **********

Executing S09database-init                     [ OK ]
Executing S10_001_install_symmetric.pl         [ OK ]
Executing S11database-populate                 [ OK ]
<command output>
.


.


.

<command output>
Executing S50install-remediation-modules       [ OK ]
Executing S51install_health_policy.pl          [ OK ]
Executing S52install_system_policy.pl          [ OK ]
Executing S53change_reconciliation_baseline.pl [ OK ]
Executing S53createcsds.pl                     [ OK ]
Executing S85patch_history-init                [ OK ]
Executing S90banner-init                       [ OK ]
Executing S95copy-crontab                      [ OK ]
Executing S96grow_var.sh                       [ OK ]
Executing S96install_sf_whitelist              [ OK ]
Executing S96install_vmware_tools.pl           [ OK ]

********** Attention **********

    Initializing the system's localization settings. Depending on available
    system resources (CPU, memory, and disk), this may take 10 minutes
    or more to complete.

********** Attention **********
Executing S96localize-templates                [ OK ]
Executing S96ovf-data.pl                       [ OK ]
Executing S97compress-client-resources         [ OK ]
Executing S97create_platinum_forms.pl          [ OK ]
.


.


.

<command output>
```

Step 3.   When the initialization is complete, the Firepower login prompt appears. Enter the default username (**admin**) and password (**Admin123**) to log in to the CLI (see Example 4-7).

Example 4-7   *Logging In to the CLI of the FMC After the Initialization Is Complete*

```
Cisco Firepower Management Center 4000 v6.1.0 (build 330)
Sep 28 23:20:53 firepower SF-IMS[5124]: [5124] init script:system [INFO] pmmon
  Starting the Process Manager...
Sep 28 23:20:53 firepower SF-IMS[5125]: [5125] pm:pm [INFO] Using model number 66F
sfpacket: module license 'Proprietary' taints kernel.
Disabling lock debugging due to kernel taint
Sourcefire Bridging Packet Driver - version 6.0.0
Copyright (c) 2004-2010 Sourcefire, Inc.

Cisco Firepower Management Center 4000 v6.1.0 (build 330)
Firepower login:admin
Password:Admin123

Copyright 2004-2016, Cisco and/or its affiliates. All rights reserved.
Cisco is a registered trademark of Cisco Systems, Inc.
All other trademarks are property of their respective owners.

Cisco Fire Linux OS v6.1.0 (build 37)
Cisco Firepower Management Center 4000 v6.1.0 (build 330)

admin@FMC4000:~$
```

The command prompt at the end of Example 4-7 confirms that the installation is complete. The next step is to verify the network connectivity on the management interface and begin the registration process.

Verification and Troubleshooting Tools

This section describes the commands and tools you can run in the FMC to investigate any issues with the FMC.

Identifying the FMC on a Rack

If your rack is full of various hardware that is not labeled on the outside, it might be challenging to identify the FMC. However, when necessary, you can turn on an LED on your desired FMC, which will allow you locate the FMC on your rack on demand. Follow these steps to enable or disable the locator LED on the FMC:

Step 1.   Log in to the CIMC of your FMC through Secure Shell (SSH). Example 4-8 shows a successful login attempt from a Linux host to the CIMC of the FMC.

Example 4-8   *Logging In to the CIMC CLI*

```
localhost:~@ ssh admin@10.1.1.10
admin@10.1.1.10's password:
CIMC#
```

> **Tip**   If you are unable to remember the IP address or the password, you can change it from the CIMC configuration utility (by pressing F8 during the POST operation).

Step 2.   When you are in the CIMC shell, enter the chassis command mode:

```
CIMC# scope chassis
CIMC /chassis#
```

Step 3.   Run the **set locator-led** command to enable or disable the LED:

```
CIMC /chassis# set locator-led {on | off}
CIMC /chassis *#
```

Step 4.   Apply the new settings:

```
CIMC /chassis *# commit
CIMC /chassis #
```

Example 4-9 shows the whole process of managing the locator LED on the FMC.

Example 4-9   *Commands to Enable and Disable a Locator LED*

```
! Run the following commands to enable the locator LED
.
.
CIMC# scope chassis
CIMC /chassis# set locator-led on
CIMC /chassis *# commit
.
.
! Run the following commands to disable the locator LED
.
.
CIMC# scope chassis
CIMC /chassis# set locator-led off
CIMC /chassis *# commit
```

Determining the Hardware and Software Details of the FMC

After a successful login, the FMC displays a banner where you can find the software version and hardware model information.

Example 4-10 shows a successful login to the FMC.

Example 4-10 *Logging In to the FMC CLI*

```
login as: admin
Password:

Copyright 2004-2016, Cisco and/or its affiliates. All rights reserved.
Cisco is a registered trademark of Cisco Systems, Inc.
All other trademarks are property of their respective owners.

Cisco Fire Linux OS v6.1.0 (build 37)
Cisco Firepower Management Center 4000 v6.1.0 (build 330)

admin@FMC4000:~$
```

However, you can also run the **sfcli** command on demand to get all types of software versions and hardware model information as output. Example 4-11 confirms the hardware model as well as the software, rule update, and VDB versions of the FMC.

Example 4-11 *Output of the sfcli.pl show version Command*

```
admin@FMC4000:~$ sfcli.pl show version
Password:
-----------[ FMC4000 ]-------------
Model                 : Cisco Firepower Management Center 4000 (66) Version 6.1.0
  (Build 330)
UUID                  : 5bac032c-8bf5-11e6-a7c8-99be23cbc50d
Rules update version  : 2016-10-05-001-vrt
VDB version           : 270
--------------------------------------------------

admin@FMC4000:~$
```

Determining the RAID Battery Status

To determine the status of the RAID battery in the FMC, use the **MegaCLI** command with the necessary parameters. Example 4-12 shows confirmation that the battery status is good, and no replacement is necessary.

Example 4-12 *The RAID Battery Status Displayed in the* **MegaCLI** *Command Output*

```
admin@FMC4000:~$ sudo MegaCLI -AdpBbuCmd -aAll | grep -i battery
BatteryType: CVPM02
  Battery Pack Missing                 : No
  Battery Replacement required         : No
  Battery backup charge time : 0 hours
Battery FRU: N/A


admin@FMC4000:~$
```

Determining the Status of a Power Supply Unit (PSU)

Before you deploy the FMC in your production network, it is a best practice to check the status of the PSUs and make sure they are operational. Look at the rear panel of your FMC. What is the color of the power supply fault LED? If the color is amber, is it blinking or solid?

Table 4-4 explains the meaning of the power supply fault LED that is located at the rear of an FMC (FMC 2000 or FMC 4000 chassis).

Table 4-4 *Power Supply Fault LED States*

LED State	Condition
Off	Operational
Blinking amber	Operational with warning
Solid amber	Critical condition

Checking Logs on the CLI

You can check the LED status when you have physical access to the FMC, but how do you check the LED status if an FMC is in a remote location? Well, you could ask someone at that location to check the LED, or you could send someone there, which might take several hours or as long as several days, depending on the location.

Apart from checking the LED status, you can also investigate an issue with a PSU from the CLI or the GUI (assuming that the FMC is turned on and receives power from at least one of the PSUs). Example 4-13 shows that Power Supply 1 (PS1) has lost power, and Power Supply 2 is working.

Example 4-13 *Checking the Status of FMC PSUs*

```
admin@FMC4000:~$ cat /var/sf/run/power.status


PS1: 0x08: Power Supply input lost
PS2: 0x01: Presence detected


admin@FMC4000:~$
```

You can also confirm a failure event by using the IPMI tool. Example 4-14 demonstrates redundancy as soon as one PSU loses power. The FMC in this example receives power from the second PSU.

Example 4-14 *Events Generated When a PSU Loses Power*

```
admin@FMC4000:~$ sudo ipmitool sel list | grep -i power

2cf | 10/12/2016 | 18:42:33 | Power Supply #0x26 | Power Supply AC lost | Asserted
2d0 | 10/12/2016 | 18:42:33 | Power Supply #0x3a | Redundancy Degraded | Asserted
2da | 10/12/2016 | 18:43:58 | Power Supply #0x3a | Non-Redundant: Sufficient from
 Redundant | Asserted

admin@FMC4000:~$
```

Example 4-15 shows many different components (such as voltage, temperature, and so on) related to FMC power supplies, their values, and their current statuses.

Example 4-15 *Statuses of Various Components of FMC PSUs*

```
admin@FMC4000:~$ sudo ipmitool sdr | egrep -i "power|ps"
MAIN_POWER_PRS  | 0x00          | ok
POWER_ON_FAIL   | 0x00          | ok
PSU1_STATUS     | 0x00          | ok
PSU2_STATUS     | 0x00          | ok
PSU1_PWRGD      | 0x00          | ok
PSU1_AC_OK      | 0x00          | ok
PSU2_PWRGD      | 0x00          | ok
PSU2_AC_OK      | 0x00          | ok
LED_PSU_STATUS  | 0x00          | ok
PS_RDNDNT_MODE  | 0x00          | ok
POWER_USAGE     | 128 Watts     | ok
PSU1_VOUT       | 0 Volts       | ok
PSU1_IOUT       | 0 Amps        | ok
PSU1_POUT       | 0 Watts       | ok
PSU2_VOUT       | 12 Volts      | ok
PSU2_IOUT       | 9 Amps        | ok
PSU2_POUT       | 112 Watts     | ok
PSU1_PIN        | 0 Watts       | ok
PSU2_PIN        | 128 Watts     | ok
PSU1_TEMP       | 30 degrees C  | ok
PSU2_TEMP       | 32 degrees C  | ok
admin@FMC4000:~$
```

Enabling Alerts on the GUI

When a PSU fails, the FMC can display a health alert for it if the Power Supply health module is enabled in the current Health Policy. Figure 4-24 shows the health module setting for monitoring power supplies. To find this configuration page, go to **System > Health > Policy** and edit the active health policy.

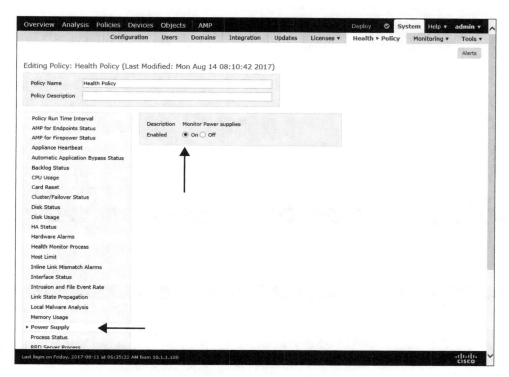

Figure 4-24 *Health Module to Monitor Power Supply Units*

When an alert appears, click on the health status icon. A red exclamation point indicates a critical alert, and a yellow triangle indicates a warning.

Figure 4-25 shows a critical health status icon when an FMC detects a PSU failure. After you click on the icon, a small window appears on top of the regular GUI. Select the Health tab to find the cause for an alert.

Figure 4-26 shows an alternative way to find descriptions for any health alerts—by navigating to the Health Monitor page at **System > Health > Monitor**.

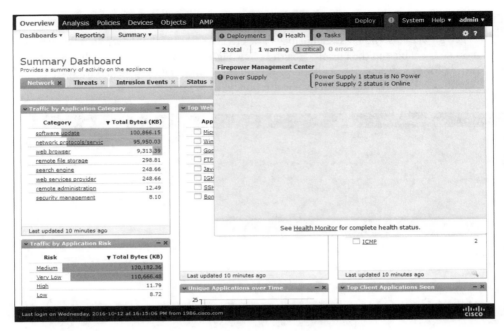

Figure 4-25   *Health Alert in the Top-Right Corner of the GUI*

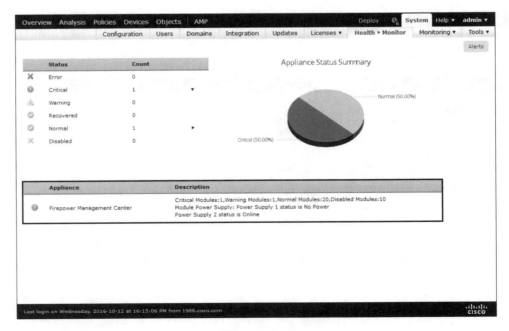

Figure 4-26   *Health Monitor Page of the FMC*

Performing a Complete Power Cycle

If both PSUs are connected but generate health alerts, performing a complete power cycle might resolve the issue. To perform a complete power cycle, follow these steps:

Step 1.   Gracefully shut down the FMC.

Step 2.   Unplug all the power cords from the device.

Caution   Pulling a power cord without a graceful shutdown can corrupt the database and file system of the FMC. You may have to reimage the whole system to recover from any database issues.

Step 3.   Wait five minutes.

Caution   The waiting period is necessary to discharge any internal electrical charges.

Step 4.   Reconnect the power cords to the FMC.

Step 5.   Turn on the FMC.

PSU Checklist

You have learned various techniques to investigate issues with PSUs. The following is a list of the items that need to be verified:

- Determine whether the power supply fault LED is amber.

- Ensure that the cords are properly connected to a power outlet.

- Verify whether a power cord is faulty.

- Confirm whether the power outlet is working.

- Check to see whether the fan on the faulty power supply unit is running.

- Try a complete power cycle to see whether it fixes the issue.

Verifying the Fans

The chassis of the FMC has a fan status LED. You can determine the fan status by looking into the front panel of the chassis. Table 4-5 explains the states of the fan status LED located at the front panel of an FMC (FMC 2000 or FMC 4000 chassis).

Table 4-5 *Fan Status LED States*

LED State	Condition
Green	Operating properly
Solid amber	One of the fan modules has failed
Blinking amber	More than one fan modules have failed

You can also confirm the status of a fan from the CLI. There are two ways to determine the status of the fans: by reading a log file and by running a command. Example 4-16 shows the information that is logged into the fans.status file.

Example 4-16 *Output of a Log File That Shows the Status of Various Fans on the FMC*

```
admin@FMC2000:~$ cat /var/sf/run/fans.status
$fan_status = {
        FAN11_name => 'FAN1_TACH1',
        FAN11_alertlevel => 'Green',
        FAN11_unit => 'RPM',
        FAN11_value => '3200',
        FAN12_name => 'FAN1_TACH2',
        FAN12_alertlevel => 'Green',
        FAN12_unit => 'RPM',
        FAN12_value => '3200',
        FAN21_name => 'FAN2_TACH1',
        FAN21_alertlevel => 'Green',
        FAN21_unit => 'RPM',
        FAN21_value => '3200',
        FAN22_name => 'FAN2_TACH2',
        FAN22_alertlevel => 'Green',
        FAN22_unit => 'RPM',
        FAN22_value => '3200',
        FAN31_name => 'FAN3_TACH1',
        FAN31_alertlevel => 'Green',
        FAN31_unit => 'RPM',
        FAN31_value => '3200',
        FAN32_name => 'FAN3_TACH2',
        FAN32_alertlevel => 'Green',
        FAN32_unit => 'RPM',
        FAN32_value => '3200',
        FAN41_name => 'FAN4_TACH1',
        FAN41_alertlevel => 'Green',
        FAN41_unit => 'RPM',
        FAN41_value => '3200',
```

```
        FAN42_name => 'FAN4_TACH2',
        FAN42_alertlevel => 'Green',
        FAN42_unit => 'RPM',
        FAN42_value => '3200',
        FAN51_name => 'FAN5_TACH1',
        FAN51_alertlevel => 'Green',
        FAN51_unit => 'RPM',
        FAN51_value => '3200',
        FAN52_name => 'FAN5_TACH2',
        FAN52_alertlevel => 'Green',
        FAN52_unit => 'RPM',
        FAN52_value => '3200',
};
admin@FMC2000:~$
```

If the output is too long, you can use the **grep** command, which is a regular expression tool that allows you to view concise output with desired keywords.

Example 4-17 shows the alert levels (green or amber) of the fans in the FMC. This is a concise view of the fans.status log file.

Example 4-17   *Determining the Fan Status LED from the CLI*

```
admin@FMC2000:~$ grep -i alert /var/sf/run/fans.status
        FAN11_alertlevel => 'Green',
        FAN12_alertlevel => 'Green',
        FAN21_alertlevel => 'Green',
        FAN22_alertlevel => 'Green',
        FAN31_alertlevel => 'Green',
        FAN32_alertlevel => 'Green',
        FAN41_alertlevel => 'Green',
        FAN42_alertlevel => 'Green',
        FAN51_alertlevel => 'Green',
        FAN52_alertlevel => 'Green',
admin@FMC2000:~$
```

You can also see the current status of the fans by running the **ipmitool** command with specific parameters. Example 4-18 shows the alert levels (green or amber) of the fans in the FMC. This is a concise view of the fans.status log file.

Example 4-18 *The RPM and Status of Each Fan in an FMC*

```
admin@FMC2000:~$ sudo ipmitool sdr list | grep -i fan | grep -i tach
FAN1_TACH1      | 7490 RPM       | ok
FAN1_TACH2      | 7062 RPM       | ok
FAN2_TACH1      | 7704 RPM       | ok
FAN2_TACH2      | 7276 RPM       | ok
FAN3_TACH1      | 7704 RPM       | ok
FAN3_TACH2      | 7276 RPM       | ok
FAN4_TACH1      | 7704 RPM       | ok
FAN4_TACH2      | 7062 RPM       | ok
FAN5_TACH1      | 7704 RPM       | ok
FAN5_TACH2      | 7062 RPM       | ok
admin@FMC2000:~$
```

Summary

This chapter discusses and compares various hardware platforms for the FMC. It illustrates the complete reimaging (also known as system restore) process and describes best practices for reimaging. This chapter also shows many different commands and tools that can help you determine whether you have any issues with FMC hardware.

Quiz

1. Which step is unique when reimaging the FMC from an older 5.x version to 6.1 directly?

   a. FMC supports reimaging from 5.x to 6.1 with zero downtime.

   b. You need to go through the System_Restore reimage process twice.

   c. Reimaging an FMC from 5.x to 6.1 is not supported.

   d. There is no need to reimage; just download the single Version 6.1 upgrade file and install it directly.

2. Which command shows the status of the RAID battery on the FMC?

   a. **sudo megacli -AdpBbuCmd -aAll | grep -i battery**

   b. **megacli -AdpBbuCmd -aAll | egrep -i battery**

   c. **MegaCLI -AdpBbuCmd -aAll | grep battery**

   d. **sudo MegaCLI -AdpBbuCmd -aAll | grep -i battery**

3. Which command would you run to determine the status of fans?

   a. **cat /var/log/run/fans.log | grep -i status**

   b. **cat /var/sf/run/fans | grep status**

   c. **cat /var/log/run/fans.status**

   d. **cat /var/sf/run/fans.status**

4. What does a blinking amber fan status LED mean?
   a. The fans are operational but the temperature is high.
   b. The fans are operational but one of the fan modules has failed.
   c. Two or more fan modules have failed.
   d. The fans are not working at all.

5. Which command confirms whether an FMC is running on a redundant power supply unit?
   a. **sudo ipmitool sdr | egrep -i "power|ps"**
   b. **sudo ipmitool sel list | grep -i power**
   c. **cat /var/sf/run/power.status**
   d. **cat /var/sf/run/power.log.status**

6. What does a blinking amber PSU LED mean?
   a. Overheated
   b. Critical condition
   c. Operational but has warning
   d. No problem as long as it is not solid amber

7. Which command shows the Firepower software version and hardware platform detail?
   a. **show version**
   b. **sfcli version**
   c. **show sfr version**
   d. **sfcli.pl show version**

Chapter 5

Firepower System Virtual on VMware

In the previous chapters, you have learned how to install the Firepower System software on Cisco hardware. If you choose not to purchase any additional hardware, you can still deploy the Firepower System in your existing virtual infrastructure. You can choose to virtualize both or one of the Firepower appliances—either the Firepower Management Center (FMC) or Firepower Threat Defense (FTD). This chapter discusses the implementation of FMC Virtual and FTD Virtual in VMware—one of the most popular virtual environments.

FMC and FTD Virtual Essentials

An FMC virtual appliance can manage any FTD physical appliance. Similarly, an FTD virtual appliance is fully interoperable with an FMC virtual appliance as well as FMC physical hardware. Before deploying a Firepower virtual appliance, let's take a moment to look at the key deployment options.

Supported Virtual Environments

Beginning with Version 6.1, the Firepower software supports a wide variety of virtual environments, such as VMware, Kernel-based Virtual Machine (KVM), and Amazon Web Services (AWS). This chapter uses VMware to demonstrate the deployment of a Firepower virtual appliance.

Table 5-1 provides a list of virtual environments that are compatible with Firepower Version 6.1.

Table 5-1   *Virtual Environments for Firepower Version 6.1*

Virtual Environment	Supported Platform
VMware	ESXi 5.5, 6.0
Amazon Web Services (AWS)	Virtual Private Cloud (VPC), Elastic Compute Cloud (EC2)
KVM	Tested on Ubuntu 14.04 LTS

Note   The Firepower software Version 6.1 does not support Microsoft virtualization platforms. The support of Azure begins from the Firepower software Version 6.2 or greater.

To manage a virtual appliance on a VMware ESXi server, you can use vCloud Director, vCenter, or vSphere Client. vSphere Client has two different variations—web and desktop—both of which are supported by the Firepower virtual appliances.

To host a Firepower virtual appliance, you can use VMware ESXi 5.5 and 6.0, but the following solutions are unsupported:

- VMware Workstation
- VMware Server
- VMware Player
- VMware Fusion

ESXi Versus VI

The tarball (.tar.gz file) of a Firepower virtual appliance includes templates for ESXi or the virtual infrastructure (VI). The key difference between them is the initial setup process, which includes configuring the network, setting up a password for the admin account, and so on.

In a VI template deployment, you configure the initial system settings by using a deployment wizard, before a Firepower virtual software is deployed. In an ESXi template, however, you configure the initial settings from the VMware console after an appliance is deployed.

The examples in this chapter use the ESXi OVF template to deploy a Firepower virtual appliance on VMware.

VMware Installation Package in a Tarball

The VMware installation package for Firepower virtual appliance comes in a .tar.gz file format, which includes three different types of files:

- **Open Virtual Format (.ovf) file:** An XML file that stores references to many elements of a Firepower System installation package

- **Virtual Machine Disk (.vmdk) file:** A compressed virtual disk that stores the Firepower System software

- **Manifest (.mf) file:** A clear-text file that stores the SHA1 digests of any OVF and VMDK files in a package

Figure 5-1 shows the files that are packaged in a tarball for a Firepower virtual appliance Version 6.1.

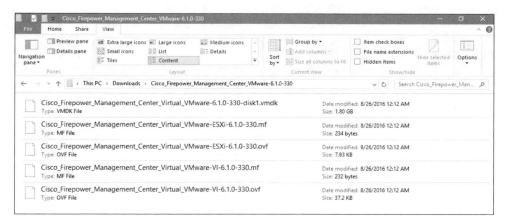

Figure 5-1   *Files in a Tarball for an FMC Virtual Appliance*

Disk Provisioning Options

During the deployment of a Firepower virtual appliance, you can choose one of the following options for provisioning your virtual disk:

- **Thick Provision Lazy Zeroed:** Space for a virtual disk is allocated during its creation but zeroed out later.

- **Thick Provision Eager Zeroed:** The space allocation and zeroing out of the data are performed at the time of virtual disk creation. Therefore, this method might take more time.

- **Thin Provision:** Disk space is allocated on an on-demand basis. The size of a virtual disk grows whenever there is a need, up to the maximum allocated limit.

Figure 5-2 shows these three options for provisioning a virtual disk on an ESXi host using the vSphere Client software. The examples in this book use the Thick Provision Lazy Zeroed option.

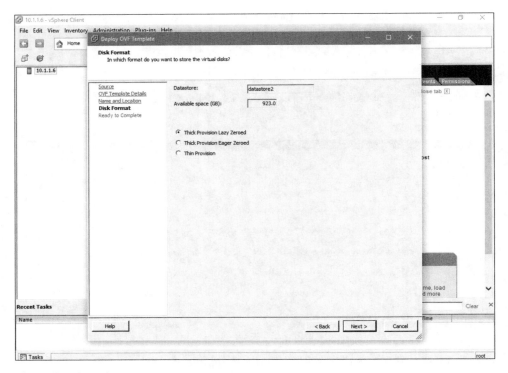

Figure 5-2   *Virtual Disk Provisioning Options*

Best Practices for Firepower Virtual Appliance Deployment

If you plan to deploy FMC Virtual and FTD Virtual Version 6.1, the FMC must be running Version 6.1 or greater. This chapter describes the process of reimaging the FMC to Version 6.1.

Pre-deployment Best Practices

Consider the following best practices before you deploy a Firepower virtual appliance:

- Depending on the hardware resources of a server, the process of deploying a new Firepower virtual appliance may take about an hour. You should plan for additional time to fulfill any prerequisites and post-deployment setup.

- Using an ISO file to build a Firepower appliance in a virtual environment is not supported. If your virtual network is based on VMware, use the Open Virtualization Format (OVF) file, which is compressed into a .tar.gz file. If your infrastructure is KVM-based, use the QEMU Copy On Write (.qcow2) file. Figure 5-3 shows a.tar.gz file and a .qcow2 file that are packaged for VMware and KVM, respectively. You can download them from the Cisco Software Download page.

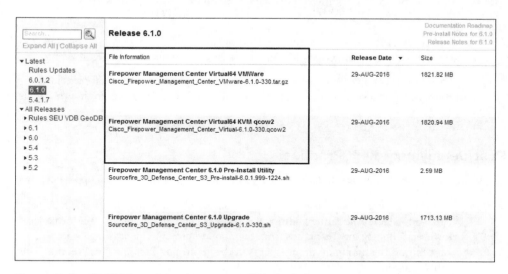

Figure 5-3 *FMC Virtual Appliance Installation Packages at cisco.com*

■ After you download an appropriate file for a Firepower virtual appliance from cisco.com, always verify the MD5 or SHA512 checksum of the files you have downloaded to confirm that the file is not corrupt and has not been modified during download. Figure 5-4 shows how the MD5 and SHA512 checksum values for the FTD Virtual installation package are displayed at cisco.com when you hover your mouse over a filename.

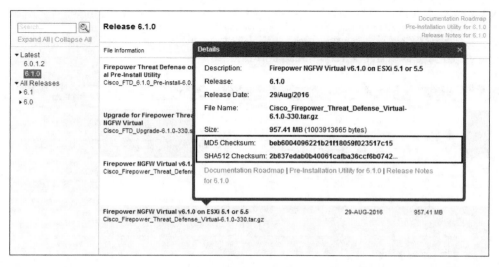

Figure 5-4 *Checksum Values of the FTD Installation Package Displayed in a Popup Box*

> **Tip**   Inside a tarball, you will find a manifest file (*.mf) that stores the individual SHA1 checksum values of the *.vmdk and *.ovf files in a tarball.

- Read the release notes to determine any known issues, any special requirements, and any instructions before you begin reimaging or performing a system restoration.

- Never power off a virtual appliance when the deployment or initialization is in progress. Upon a successful initialization, you will find a Firepower login prompt at the VMware console.

Post-deployment Best Practices

Consider the following best practices after you deploy a Firepower virtual appliance:

- If your ESXi server has unused resources, you can allocate them to your Firepower virtual appliance. Allocating additional resources can enhance system performance. However, reducing any resources from the minimum requirement is unsupported. You can find the minimum requirements in the "Fulfilling Prerequisites" section, later in this chapter.

- You can replace the E1000 network adapters with the VMXNET3 adapters for higher throughput.

> **Tip**   The steps to upgrade a default E1000 adapter with a VMXNET3 adapter are described in the "Verification and Troubleshooting Tools" section, later in this chapter.

- As a part of the disaster recovery plan, you should periodically make a backup of the existing events and configurations. Do not use any VMware-provided built-in features to make a backup of a Firepower virtual appliance. Instead, use the FMC's Backup/Restore tool. Figure 5-5 shows the FMC Backup Management page. It is located at **System > Tools > Backup/Restore**.

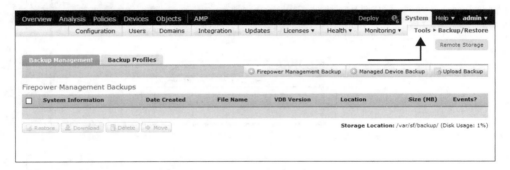

Figure 5-5   *The FMC's Backup Management Page*

Table 5-2 shows some of the backup tools provided by VMware. The Firepower virtual appliances do not support these tools.

Table 5-2   *VMware Backup and Migration Tools (Not Supported by Firepower)*

Feature	VMware Purpose
vMotion	Migration of a running virtual machine from one physical server to another, without any downtime
Cloning	Duplication of a virtual machine with the same configurations and applications
Snapshot	Saving of any particular state of a virtual machine

- You can also use the Import/Export tool in the FMC to copy a policy. During an import, the versions of a restored system must match with the FMC from which any policies were originally exported. Therefore, when you export, you must remember the software and Rule Update version information of the original FMC. Figure 5-6 shows the Import/Export page, which is located at **System > Tools > Import/Export.**

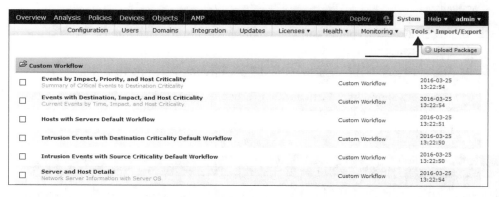

Figure 5-6   *The FMC Import/Export Page*

Installing and Configuring a Firepower Virtual Appliance

Deployment of a Firepower virtual appliance in VMware is not a one-click process. After you download a tarball for Firepower software from cisco.com and extract it onto your desktop, you need to complete the following steps:

Step 1.   Build an ESXi host that is compatible with Firepower.

Step 2.   Build a virtual Layer 2 network on the ESXi host.

Step 3.   Deploy the OVF file for the desired Firepower appliance.

Step 4.   Verify the resource allocation and network mapping.

Step 5.   Power on the Firepower appliance and initialize it.

Figure 5-7 shows the key steps in deploying a Firepower virtual appliance on a VMware ESXi host.

Figure 5-7   *Major Steps in Deploying a Firepower Virtual Appliance*

Fulfilling Prerequisites

You must fulfill the following requirements before you install a Firepower virtual appliance:

■ To deploy any Firepower software, your server must have a 64-bit CPU that supports the virtualization technology.

■ You must enable the virtualization functionality from the BIOS setup utility.

Figure 5-8 shows Intel Virtualization Technology enabled in the BIOS setup utility. Depending on the hardware vendor of an ESXi server, a setup utility may look different from this.

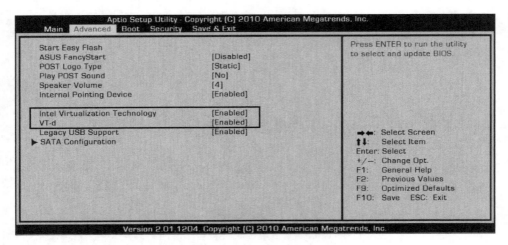

Figure 5-8   *Enabling the Virtualization Technology in the BIOS*

■ After you build an ESXi host, connect to the host by using vSphere Client. You can use either a web client or a desktop client.

Figure 5-9 shows the default home page of an ESXi host. To view this page, enter the IP address of your ESXi server into a browser. This page provides you with a link to download the vSphere Client software.

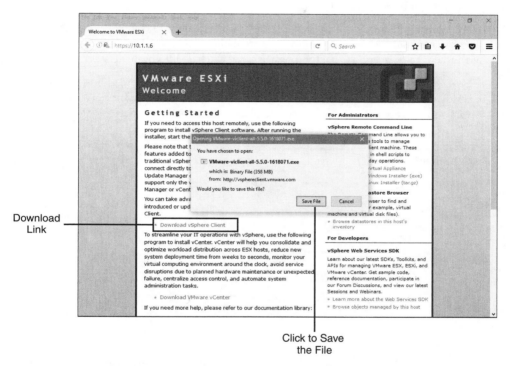

Figure 5-9 *Download Link for vSphere Client on an ESXi Home Page*

■ Whether your ESXi host runs Version 5.5 or Version 6.0, ensure that your Firepower virtual appliance is allocated the minimum amount of resources. Do not reduce the settings from the minimum requirements. Table 5-3 shows the minimum requirements for a Firepower virtual appliance.

Table 5-3 *Minimum Resource Allocation for a Firepower Virtual Appliance*

Resource Type	FMC	FTD
CPU	Four	Four
Memory	8 GB	8 GB
Disk space	250 GB	48.25 GB
Network interface	One	Four

> **Tip**   Read the "Verification and Troubleshooting Tools" section, later in this chapter, to learn how to add an additional resource.

Creating a Virtual Network

Let's say that you have just built an ESXi host. Now you want to deploy both of the Firepower virtual appliances—an FMC virtual appliance and an FTD virtual appliance. You need to create a Layer 2 virtual topology using vSwitch and VMware network adapter.

Figure 5-10 shows a topology created inside a virtual network. An ESXi host, FMC, and FTD are connected to a management network, and data from inside the network can traverse to the Internet. All the servers are placed in a DMZ network.

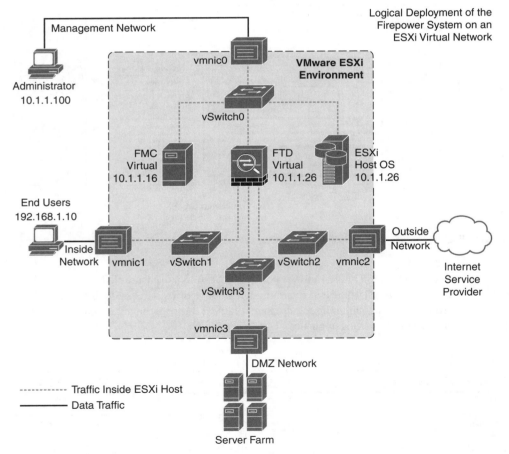

Figure 5-10   *A Virtual Network Topology on a VMware ESXi Host*

The number of steps to create a virtual topology could be different, depending on the number of required interfaces on a particular appliance you want to deploy. For example, by default, FMC Virtual requires only one interface for management communication, whereas FTD Virtual requires four interfaces—one interface for management communication and three interfaces for traffic inspection.

In the next few pages, you will learn how to create the virtual network shown in Figure 5-10 on a VMware ESXi host, using vSphere Client software.

Creating a Network for FMC Virtual

By default, a virtual switch is created on a new ESXi installation. To view a virtual switch, go to **Configuration > Networking** in vSphere Client.

Figure 5-11 shows a default virtual switch vSwitch0 that is created by the ESXi host. A physical adapter vmnic0 is connected with two default virtual ports: Management Network and VM Network.

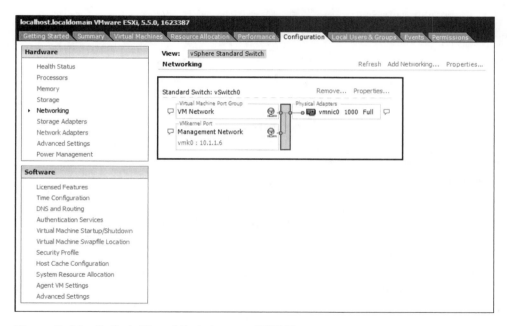

Figure 5-11   *Default Virtual Switch on an ESXi Host*

The Management Network port is automatically mapped with the management interface of the ESXi host. The VM Network port is available for use. You can use it as the management interface for your FMC virtual appliance. To make it clear and meaningful, you could optionally rename the default labels by following these steps:

Step 1.   Click the **Properties** option next to Standard Switch: vSwitch0. The vSwitch0 Properties window appears. Figure 5-12 shows two virtual ports created by the ESXi host during installation.

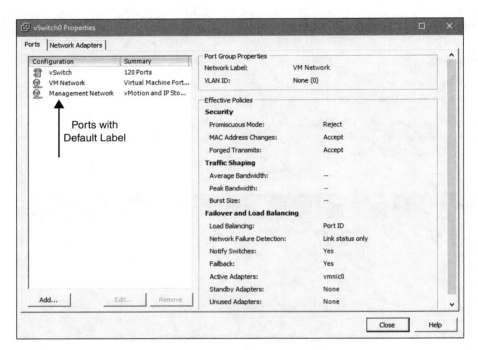

Figure 5-12   *The Ports Tab in the vSwitch0 Properties Window*

Step 2.   Select the **VM Network** port and click the **Edit** button. The VM Network Properties windows appears, as shown in Figure 5-13. This is where you can edit the default port VM Network.

Step 3.   Change Network Label from VM Network to **FMC Management** and click **OK**.

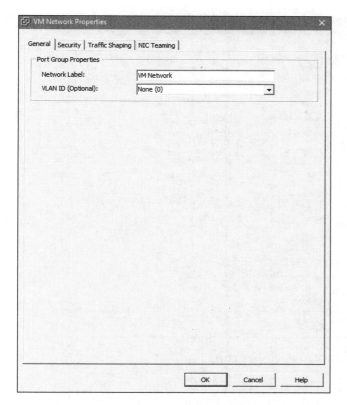

Figure 5-13   *The VM Network Properties Window*

Step 4.   Optionally, select the **Management Network** port, click the **Edit** button, and then change Network Label from Management Network to **VMware Management** and click **OK**.

Figure 5-14 shows the vSwitch0 Properties window with both of the ports renamed. From the new labels, it is now easy to see the purpose of each port.

Step 5.   Click **Close** to return to the Networking view, where you can find the newly labeled virtual ports connected to the same physical adapter.

If you plan to deploy FTD Virtual, read the next section. Otherwise, proceed to the section "Deploying an OVF Template."

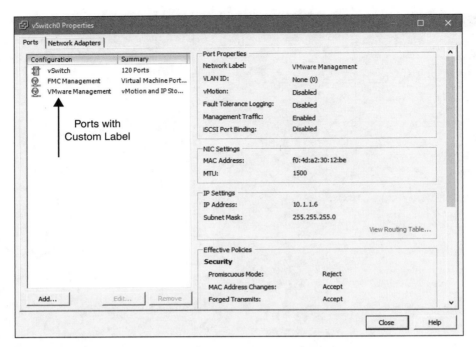

Figure 5-14   *The New Labels of the Two Virtual Ports*

Creating a Network for FTD Virtual

Earlier in this chapter, in the section "Fulfilling Prerequisites," you learned that an FTD virtual appliance requires at least four interfaces—one interface for management traffic and three interfaces for data traffic. Now you can follow these steps to add a network adapter for a virtual appliance:

Note   FTD Virtual can support up to 10 interfaces in total.

Step 1.   Go to the **Configuration > Networking** page in vSphere Client.

Step 2.   Select the **Add Networking** option, as shown in Figure 5-15. (In this window, you can also see the new labels of the default virtual ports that you renamed in the previous section. Both of them are connected to the vmnic0 physical adapter.) The Add Network Wizard window appears.

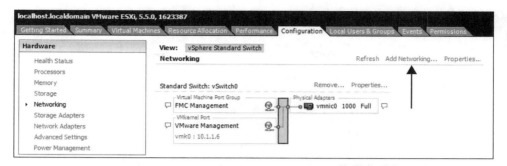

Figure 5-15   *The Default Virtual Switch vSwitch0 After the Label Change*

Step 3.   Select **Virtual Machine** as the connection type, as shown in Figure 5-16.

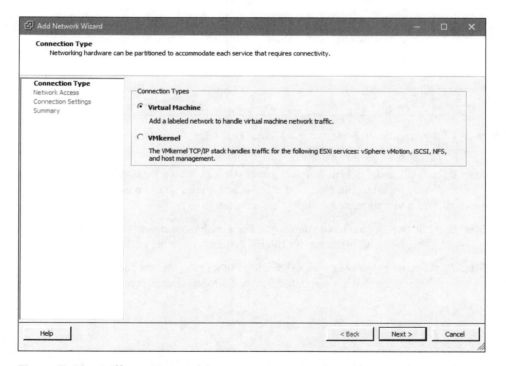

Figure 5-16   *Different Types of Connection Types in the Add Network Wizard*

Step 4.   Select an existing virtual switch (vSwitch) or create a new one that can map a physical adapter with a virtual port. You can configure each vSwitch to represent a segregated virtual network. Figure 5-17 shows that vmnic0 is mapped with vSwitch0, which connects the FTD Virtual management port.

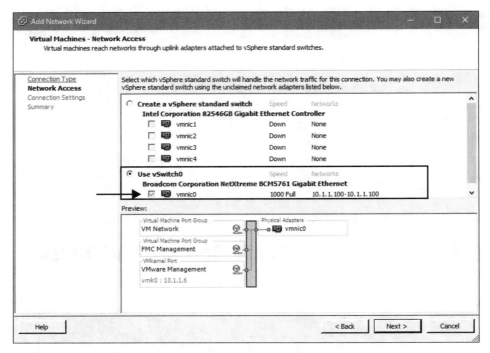

Figure 5-17   *Virtual Switch Mapping a Virtual Port with a Physical Adapter*

Step 5.   Replace the default Network Label setting with a meaningful name
(see Figure 5-18). Note that this window allows you to preview the mapping
of a virtual port with a physical adapter.

Step 6.   Click **Next** to view a summary. Click **Finish** to complete the configuration of
the vSwitch port group for the FTD Management network.

Step 7.   Repeat Steps 1–6 at least three more times to create the remaining three
vSwitches that are mandatory on an FTD virtual appliance.

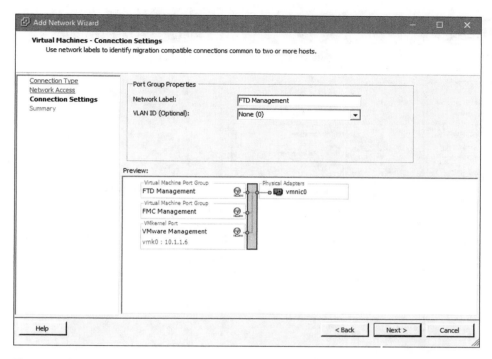

Figure 5-18 *Connection Settings and Port Group Properties for the Network Adapters*

Table 5-4 shows the mapping between the virtual ports and physical adapters that is used in the configuration example of this chapter.

Table 5-4 *Mapping Between the Virtual Ports and Physical Adapters*

Virtual Port	Physical Adapter	Purpose
FTD Management	vmnic0	For management traffic
Inside Network	vmnic1	For internal network
Outside Network	vmnic2	Toward the outside world
DMZ Network	vmnic3	Network for the server farm

Figure 5-19 shows the final view of the networking configuration page after you create four virtual ports and map them with four individual physical adapters. Each vSwitch can be configured separately by using the Properties option.

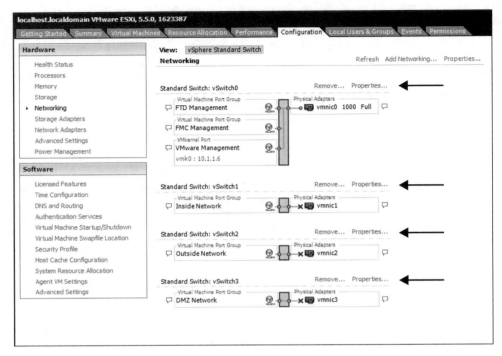

Figure 5-19   *Four Virtual Ports Mapped with Four Separate Physical Adapters*

Using Promiscuous Mode

Promiscuous mode allows a vSwitch to see any frames that traverse it. It allows an interface to see any packet in a network segment—even the packets that are not aimed for that interface. By default, this mode is disabled on a vSwitch. You must enable this mode on all the virtual ports of an FTD virtual appliance.

The following steps describe how to enable promiscuous mode on the management interface of an FTD virtual appliance. You can also use these steps to enable promiscuous mode on any data interfaces:

Step 1.   Select the **Properties** option next to vSwitch0. The vSwitch0 Properties window appears, as shown in Figure 5-20. (In this window, you can select any virtual port to find the Promiscuous Mode status, which is Reject, by default.)

Step 2.   Select the port on which you want to enable promiscuous mode and click **Edit**. The Properties window appears.

Step 3.   Select the **Security** tab. All the options, including the Promiscuous Mode option, are unchecked by default.

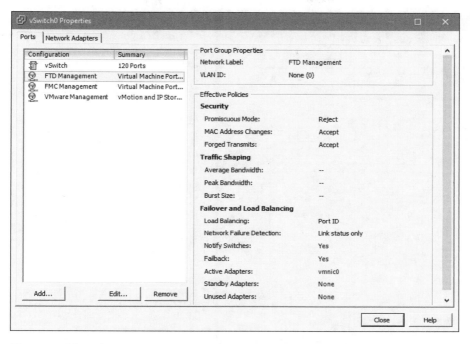

Figure 5-20 *The Properties Option That Allows You Edit a vSwitch*

Step 4.   Check all the boxes and select **Accept** from each dropdown, as shown in Figure 5-21.

Step 5.   When you are done, click **OK** to return to the vSwitch Properties window. Click the **Close** button to complete the configuration.

Step 6.   Repeat Steps 1–5 for all the interfaces on an FTD virtual appliance.

Caution   Enabling all the above options on all the FTD interfaces is a requirement. Failure to enable any single option on a single FTD interface can lead to an unexpected technical issue.

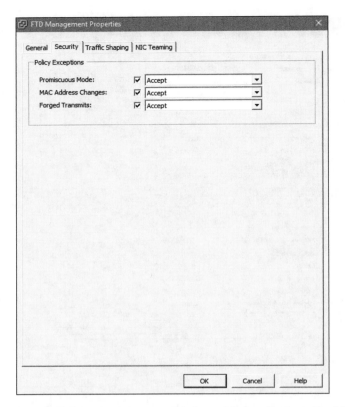

Figure 5-21   *Promiscuous Mode and Other Options Enabled*

Deploying an OVF Template

After building a Layer 2 topology in VMware, the next step is to deploy an OVF template file in an ESXi host. Use the following steps to deploy an OVF file:

Step 1.   In vSphere Client, from the File menu, select the **Deploy OVF Template** option (see Figure 5-22). The Deploy OVF Template window appears.

Step 2.   Click **Browse** and choose an appropriate OVF file for your virtual appliance. (Figure 5-23 shows the Cisco_Firepower_Threat_Defense_Virtual-ESXi-6.1.0-330.ovf file selected for deployment.) Click **Next** to continue.

> **Note**   If you want to deploy FMC Version 6.1 on an ESXi host, select the Cisco_Firepower_Management_Center_Virtual_VMware-ESXi-6.1.0-330.ovf file. Similarly, to deploy FTD Version 6.1, select the Cisco_Firepower_Threat_Defense_Virtual-ESXi-6.1.0-330.ovf file.

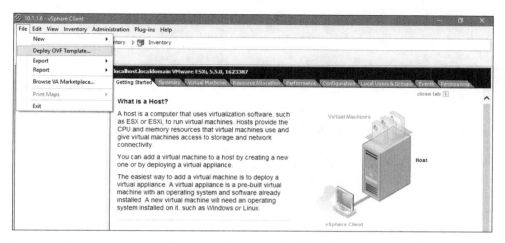

Figure 5-22 *Navigating to the Deploy OVF Template Option in vSphere Client*

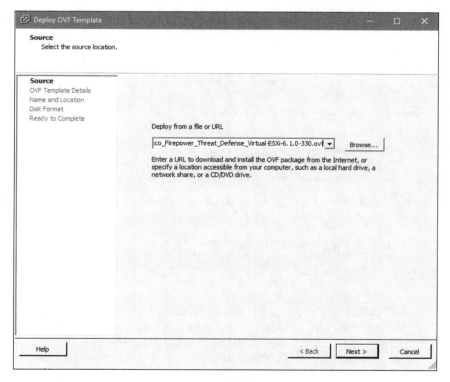

Figure 5-23 *Selection of an OVF File in the Deploy OVF Template*

Step 3. Verify that all the information in the OVF Template Details window is correct (see Figure 5-24). If everything looks good, click **Next** to continue.

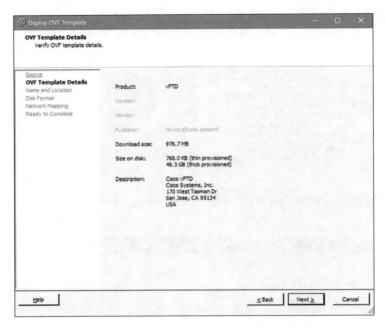

Figure 5-24 *Detail Description of an OVF Template*

Step 4. Specify a unique name for your virtual appliance. Figure 5-25 shows the custom name FTD for the virtual appliance. Keep in mind that this name must be unique within the inventory. Click **Next**.

Step 5. Select a disk format type for the virtual disk, such as the Thick Provisioned Lazy Zeroed (as shown in Figure 5-26), and click **Next**.

Tip Refer to the section "Disk Provisioning Options," earlier in this chapter, to learn about different types of disk formats.

Step 6. In the Network Mapping window, shown in Figure 5-27, map the destination networks (virtual ports) with the source networks (interfaces on a virtual appliance). Use the dropdown to find an appropriate interface. Figure 5-27 shows the selection of the FTD Management virtual port for the management interface of an FTD virtual appliance.

Note The number of networks you need to map depends on the type of virtual appliance. Remember that an FMC virtual appliance must have at least one interface, and an FTD virtual appliance must have at least four interfaces.

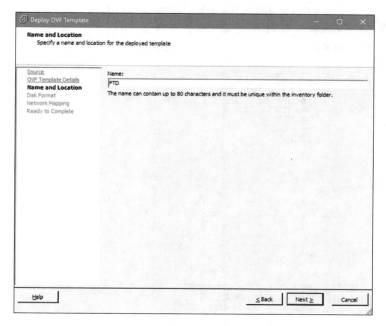

Figure 5-25 *Custom Name for a Deployed Template*

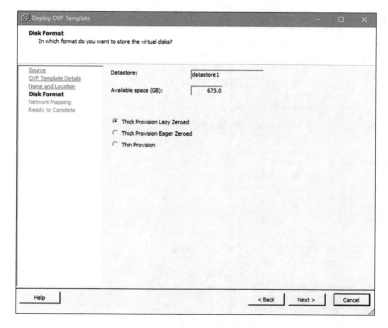

Figure 5-26 *Disk Format Options for a Virtual Appliance*

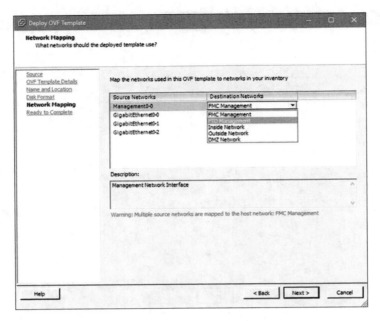

Figure 5-27   *Selecting a Virtual Port*

Figure 5-28 shows all the interfaces on an FTD virtual appliance after they are mapped with separate virtual ports.

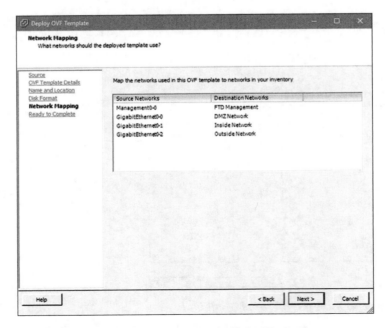

Figure 5-28   *Complete Mapping of All the Networks*

Step 7.   When you finish mapping the network, click **Next**. A summary of all the settings is displayed, as shown in Figure 5-29. If everything looks good, click **Finish** to complete the configuration.

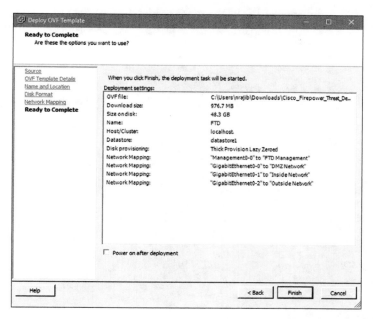

Figure 5-29   *Final Prompt to Confirm the Settings of an FTD Virtual Deployment*

Figure 5-30 shows an example of the pre-deployment settings of an FMC virtual appliance. A screenshot of the Ready to Complete window is provided here, so that you can compare Figure 5-30 (FMC Virtual deployment) with Figure 5-29 (FTD Virtual deployment). You can confirm that FMC allocates more spaces on disk and requires only one interface for management connection.

The deployment begins. The time it takes to complete a deployment depends on various factors, such as the type of Firepower virtual appliance you are deploying, the amount of resources available in the ESXi host, and the connection speed between the ESXi server and the endpoint where the OVF file is stored. Once complete, a confirmation message appears in a Deployment Completed Successfully window, as shown in Figure 5-31.

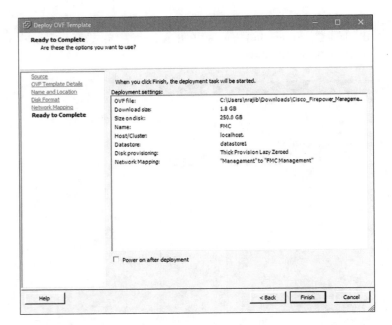

Figure 5-30   *Example of Settings for an FMC Virtual Deployment*

Figure 5-31   *Completion of a Successful FTD Deployment*

Initializing an Appliance

Use the following process to begin the initialization of any Firepower virtual appliances (either FMC or FTD):

Step 1.   Select the desired virtual appliance from the inventory, as shown in Figure 5-32.

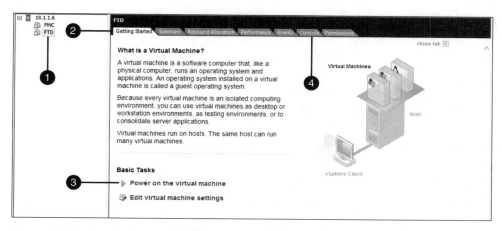

Figure 5-32 *Beginning an Initialization Process and Watching the Status on the Console Tab*

Step 2.   Go to the Getting Started tab.

Step 3.   Click the **Power On the Virtual Machine** option.

Step 4.   When the initialization begins, view the status in the Console tab.

Initializing an FMC Virtual Appliance

On an FMC virtual appliance, the initialization process ends automatically after 40 to 50 minutes. You can view the status on the Console tab. At the end of the process, a login prompt appears.

Example 5-1 shows the completion of the Firepower software initialization on VMware. As you can see, you can enter the CLI by using the default credentials—username admin and password Admin123.

Example 5-1 *Login Prompt for an FMC Virtual Appliance After Initialization Completion*

```
Cisco Firepower Management Center for VMWare v6.1.0 (build 330)
Oct 18 13:20:23 firepower SF-IMS[616]: [616] init script:system [INFO] pmmon
  Starting the Process Manager...
Oct 18 13:20:23 firepower SF-IMS[617]: [617] pm:pm [INFO] Using model number
  66ESad7: WRITE SAME failed. Manually zeroing.


Cisco Firepower Management Center for VMWare v6.1.0 (build 330)
Firepower login:admin
Password:Admin123
```

```
Copyright 2004-2016, Cisco and/or its affiliates. All rights reserved.
Cisco is a registered trademark of Cisco Systems, Inc.
All other trademarks are property of their respective owners.

Cisco Fire Linux OS v6.1.0 (build 37)
Cisco Firepower Management Center for VMWare v6.1.0 (build 330)

admin@firepower:~$
```

Initializing an FTD Virtual Appliance

On an FTD virtual appliance, the initialization process ends in approximately 20 minutes. At the end of the process, a login prompt appears. You can enter the CLI by using the default credentials—username admin and password Admin123.

Example 5-2 shows the initialization process for an FTD virtual appliance on VMware. The process prompts you to accept the end user license agreement (EULA) and configure the network before a login prompt appears.

Example 5-2 *Accepting the EULA and Configuring the Network to Get to the CLI Prompt of an FTD Virtual*

```
Cisco Firepower Threat Defense for VMWare v6.1.0 (build 330)
Firepower login:admin
Password:Admin123
You must accept the EULA to continue.
Press <ENTER> to display the EULA:
.

.

Output Omitted

.

.

Please enter 'YES' or press <ENTER> to AGREE to the EULA:

System initialization in progress. Please stand by.
You must change the password for 'admin' to continue.
Enter new password:
Confirm new password:
You must configure the network to continue.
You must configure at least one of IPv4 or IPv6.
Do you want to configure IPv4? (y/n) [y]:
Do you want to configure IPv6? (y/n) [n]:
Configure IPv4 via DHCP or manually? (dhcp/manual) [manual]:
Enter an IPv4 address for the management interface [192.168.45.45]: 10.1.1.21
Enter an IPv4 netmask for the management interface [255.255.255.0]:
Enter the IPv4 default gateway for the management interface [192.168.45.1]: 10.1.1.1
Enter a fully qualified hostname for this system [firepower]:
```

```
Enter a comma-separated list of DNS servers or 'none' []: none
Enter a comma-separated list of search domains or 'none' []: none
If your networking information has changed, you will need to reconnect.
For HTTP Proxy configuration, run 'configure network http-proxy'
Configure firewall mode? (routed/transparent) [routed]:
Configuring firewall mode ...
Update policy deployment information
    - add device configuration
    - add network discovery
    - add system policy


You can register the sensor to a Firepower Management Center and use the
Firepower Management Center to manage it. Note that registering the sensor
to a Firepower Management Center disables on-sensor Firepower Services
management capabilities.


When registering the sensor to a Firepower Management Center, a unique
alphanumeric registration key is always required.  In most cases, to register
a sensor to a Firepower Management Center, you must provide the hostname or
the IP address along with the registration key.
'configure manager add [hostname | ip address ] [registration key ]'


However, if the sensor and the Firepower Management Center are separated by a
NAT device, you must enter a unique NAT ID, along with the unique registration
key.
'configure manager add DONTRESOLVE [registration key ] [ NAT ID ]'


Later, using the web interface on the Firepower Management Center, you must
use the same registration key and, if necessary, the same NAT ID when you add
this sensor to the Firepower Management Center.
>
```

The > prompt at the end of Example 5-2 confirms that the installation is totally complete.

The next step is to verify the network connectivity on the management interface and then begin the registration process. (Chapter 6, "The Firepower Management Network," explains the management connection, and Chapter 7, "Firepower Licensing and Registration," describes the registration process.)

Verification and Troubleshooting Tools

In this section, you will learn how to investigate some common issues with Firepower virtual appliances. If you experience any issues with the ESXi host operating system, you should find a troubleshooting guide at the VMware website and read it.

Determining the Status of Allocated Resources

The amount of resources allocated to a Firepower virtual appliance is very critical for its system performance. You can verify resource allocation in two different places in vSphere Center:

■ **Summary page:** The Summary page of a virtual appliance provides an overview of the deployed OVF template and its allocated resources. Figure 5-33 shows the allocated CPU, memory, storage, and so on for an FMC virtual appliance.

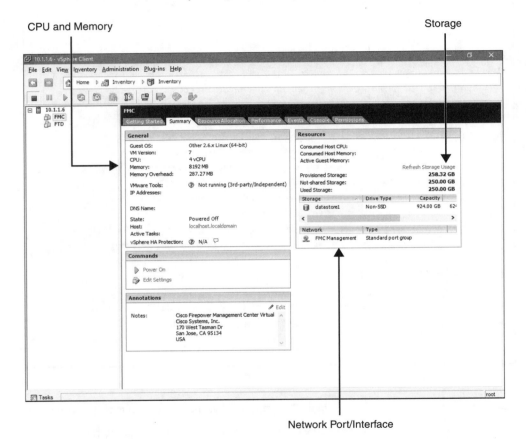

Figure 5-33   *Summary of Resource Allocations*

■ **Virtual machine settings editor:** This editor allows you to view, add, or remove resources allocated to a virtual machine. There are two ways to navigate to the virtual machine settings editor (see Figure 5-34):

■ **Option 1:** Right-click the name of a virtual appliance from the inventory list and select the **Edit Settings** option. The Virtual Machine Properties window appears.

■ **Option 2:** Go to the Getting Started page and click on the **Edit Virtual Machine Settings** option under Basic Tasks. The Virtual Machine Properties window appears.

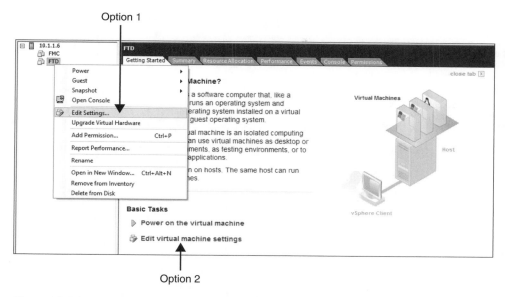

Figure 5-34   *Navigating to the Virtual Machine Settings Editor*

Determining the Status of a Network Adapter

If the management interface or data interface on a Firepower virtual appliance does not show up or stays always down, you need to verify the network adapter configuration of that virtual appliance. To verify an adapter using vSphere Client, follow these steps:

Step 1.   From the inventory list, select the virtual appliance that does not display an interface properly.

Step 2.   Open the Virtual Machine Properties window for a virtual machine, using one of the two options described in the previous section.

Step 3.   From the Hardware list, select the network adapter that is not functioning properly, as shown in Figure 5-35.

Step 4.   Under Device Status on the right side of the window, make sure both options—Connected and Connect at Power On—are checked. Figure 5-35 shows the status of the FTD management interface. It is currently connected, and it is configured to be connected when the FTD virtual appliance is powered on.

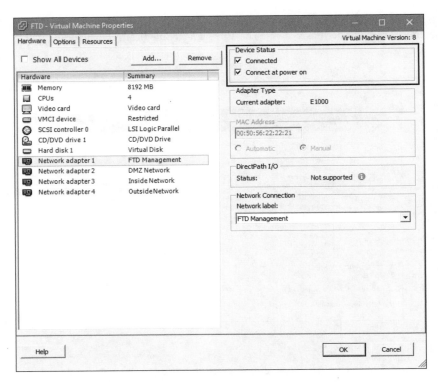

Figure 5-35   *The Connected and Connect at Power On Options of a Network Adapter*

Tip   If you are still experiencing an issue with a network adapter, did you complete
all the steps when you enabled promiscuous mode? Go back to the windows shown in
Figure 5-20 and Figure 5-21 and verify whether your vSwitch properties match the settings
shown in those images.

Upgrading a Network Adapter

When you deploy a virtual appliance, VMware uses the E1000 network adapter by
default. You can also choose a VMXNET3 adapter for your Firepower virtual appliance.
The difference between an E1000 adapter and a VMXNET3 adapter is in throughput. The
throughput of a VMXNET3 adapter is 10 Gbps, whereas an E1000 adapter supports up
to 1 Gbps.

On any given virtual appliance, all the adapters have to be the same type. In other words,
if you want to upgrade the type of an adapter, you must upgrade it for all the interfaces
on any single virtual interface. It is, however, not a requirement to have the same type

of network adapters on all the virtual appliances in any network. For example, if the management interface of an FMC virtual appliance is an E1000 adapter, it should be able to communicate with an FTD virtual appliance that has VMXNET3 type network adapters.

To upgrade a network adapter from the default type E1000 to VMXNET3, follow these steps:

Step 1.   Gracefully shut down the virtual appliance on which the new adapter will be added by running the **shutdown** command on the VMware console:

```
admin@FMCv:~$ sudo shutdown -h now
```

Caution   Do not power off a virtual appliance manually. Doing so could corrupt the Firepower System database. Instead, issue the **shutdown** command from the VMware console.

Step 2.   Edit the virtual machine settings and open the Virtual Machine Properties window. Figure 5-36 shows all the hardware resources that are allocated to an FTD virtual appliance in the FTD – Virtual Machine Properties window.

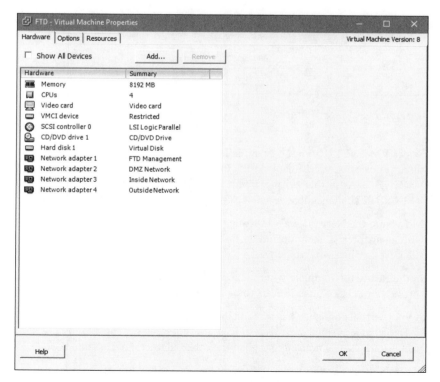

Figure 5-36   *The FTD – Virtual Machine Properties Window*

Step 3.   Click the **Remove** button and delete the network adapter that you want to upgrade from E1000 to VMXNET3.

Step 4.   Add a new VMXNET3 interface by clicking the **Add** button in the Virtual Machine Properties window. Then, in the Add Hardware window that appears (see Figure 5-37), select **Ethernet Adapter** from the device list.

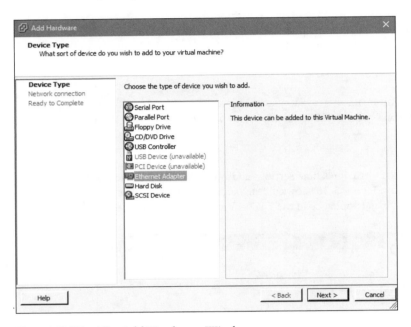

Figure 5-37   *The Add Hardware Window*

Step 5.   Select **VMXNET3** from the Adapter Type drop-down. Figure 5-38 shows three types of network adapters: E1000, VMXNET2 (Enhanced), and VMXNET3. As of this writing, Firepower software does not support the VMXNET2 (Enhanced) adapter.

Step 6.   Make sure the Network Label setting (that is, the association of a network with an adapter) is accurate and ensure that Connect at Power On is checked. Click **Next** when you are done.

Step 7.   In the Ready to Complete window, shown in Figure 5-39, check all the adapter settings and click **Finish** if everything looks good.

Step 8.   If your virtual appliance has more than one network adapter (for example, an FTD virtual appliance must have at least four interfaces), repeat Steps 1–7 as many times as needed to upgrade all the other adapters to the same type.

Figure 5-40 shows the Virtual Machine Properties window after the management interface is replaced with a VMXNET3 adapter.

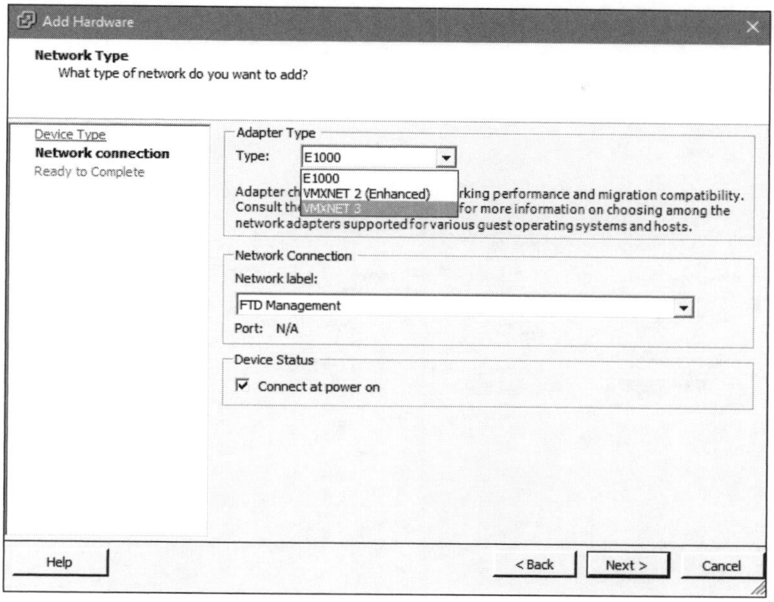

Figure 5-38 *Available Adapter Types in VMware ESXi*

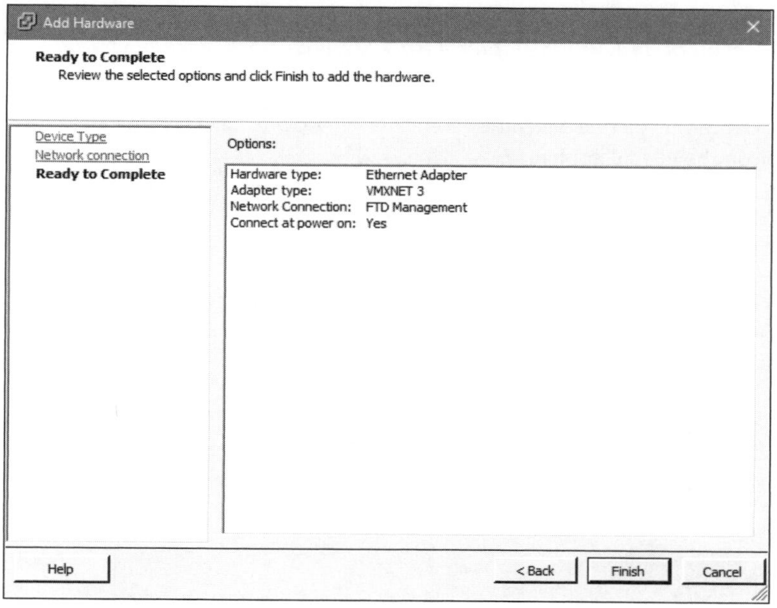

Figure 5-39 *An Overview of the Ethernet Adapter Options*

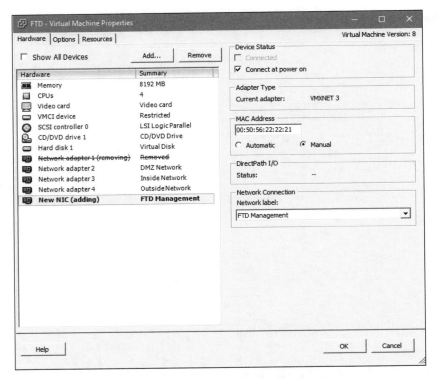

Figure 5-40   *Replacement of an E1000 Adapter with VMXNET3*

Step 9.   Click **OK** in the Virtual Machine Properties window to save the changes and power on the virtual appliance.

Summary

This chapter describes various aspects of Firepower virtual appliances. You have learned how to deploy a virtual appliance, how to tune the resources for optimal performance, and how to investigate issues with a new deployment.

Quiz

1. Which file can be deployed directly into an ESXi host?

   a. tar.gz

   b. VMDK

   c. OVF

   d. MF

2. Which of the following network adapters provides the maximum throughput?
   a. E1000
   b. VMXNET2 (Enhanced)
   c. VMXNET3
   d. VMXNET-X

3. Which of the following options should not contribute to any connectivity issues between two Firepower virtual appliances?
   a. The network adapter is configured as connected.
   b. The Connected at Power On option is checked.
   c. Promiscuous mode is enabled.
   d. The network adapter types of two appliances are different.

4. Which of the following resources should not be adjusted on the FMC?
   a. Network adapter
   b. Storage
   c. Memory
   d. CPU

5. Which of the following statements is false?
   a. An OVF file for VI completes the initial setup before deployment.
   b. You cannot adjust the resource allocations on an FTD virtual appliance to improve its performance.
   c. An FTD virtual appliance needs at least four interfaces.
   d. A large deployment can be scaled by cloning an FTD virtual appliance by using VMware.

Chapter 6

The Firepower Management Network

After you install the Firepower software, you might wonder how to manage a Firepower Threat Defense (FTD) system. For a smaller network, you can use the browser-based on-box application—the Firepower Device Manager (FDM)—which can manage one FTD device with limited functionalities. However, for a medium- to large-scale network, you must use the Firepower Management Center (FMC). Regardless of how you manage FTD, it is important that you properly design and configure the management network to secure the control traffic.

Firepower System Management Network Essentials

Before you begin the registration process, it is important to ensure that the FMC and FTD can communicate with each other and that they are deployed in appropriate locations in the network. In this section, you will learn about the anatomy of the Firepower management interface and various design scenarios for the Firepower management network.

The FTD Management Interface

The Firepower System uses the management interface to send and receive the control traffic. The implementation of a management interface differs, depending on the hardware platform. This section describes how a management interface works on FTD with two different platforms: Adaptive Security Appliance (ASA) hardware, and Firepower Security Appliance hardware.

- **On an Adaptive Security Appliance (ASA):** On Cisco ASA 5500-X Series hardware, the management interface is located at the rear panel of the ASA hardware, next to the console port (see Figure 6-1).

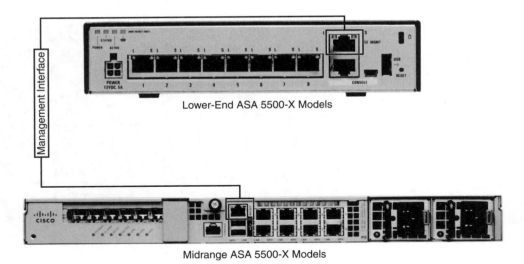

Figure 6-1   *Location of the Management Interface on ASA Hardware*

A physical management interface on an ASA comprises two logical interfaces: a logical management interface and a logical diagnostic interface.

FTD uses the logical management interface to complete the registration process with the FMC and to establish a secure tunnel with the FMC. The tunnel, thereafter, is used to set up the FTD, apply policies to the FTD, and transfer events from FTD to the FMC. During the FTD installation process, when you provide an IP address for the FTD management interface, it is actually assigned to the logical management interface.

Figure 6-2 illustrates the relationships between different logical interfaces with different software codes and how they are displayed on the CLI.

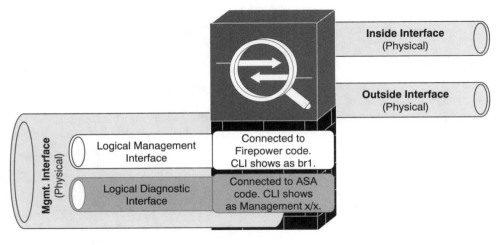

Figure 6-2   *ASA Logical Interfaces*

The diagnostic interface, on the other hand, is an optional logical interface. Cisco recommends that you not configure the diagnostic interface with an IP address if there is no router between the management network and the inside network. This also simplifies your network design and reduces configuration overhead.

Note Each of the FTD data interfaces is required to be on a different network. When a diagnostic interface is configured with an IP address, FTD considers it to be a data interface. Therefore, the diagnostic interface (which must be on the same subnet as the logical management interface, br1) and the inside interface must be on two different subnets. To transfer traffic between two different subnetworks, a router is necessary.

- **On a Firepower Security Appliance:** Each Firepower security appliance has one fixed management interface on the front panel of the chassis. Using this interface, you can administer the Firepower eXtensible Operating System (FXOS). An FTD logical device, however, does not use this interface to communicate with the FMC. For the management communication between FTD and the FMC, you can select any of the remaining Ethernet ports and configure them (with the **mgmt.** type) by using the Firepower Chassis Manager. (The configuration steps are described later in this chapter, in the section "Configuring a Management Network on a Firepower Security Appliance.")

Figure 6-3 shows the location of the management interface on the Firepower security appliances.

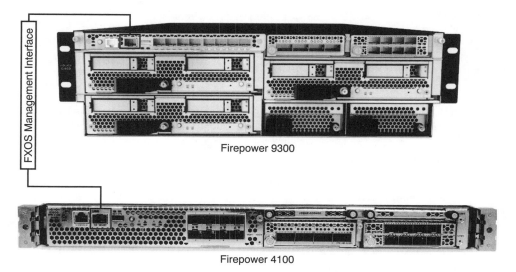

Firepower 9300

Firepower 4100

Figure 6-3 *Location of the Management Interface on Firepower Security Appliances*

Designing a Firepower Management Network

As long as the management interfaces can communicate with each other, the FMC can manage FTD from any location—either a local area network (LAN) or a wide area network (WAN). Depending on the placement and configuration of the management interfaces, a Firepower management network can be designed various ways.

Figure 6-4 categorizes the possible scenarios for deploying FTD with the FMC:

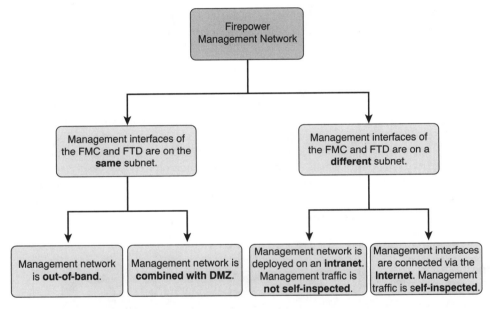

Figure 6-4 *Options for Firepower Management Network Design*

- **Management interfaces are on the same subnet:** You can configure the management interfaces of the FMC and FTD on the same subnetwork and connect them through a Layer 2 switch. The Layer 2 switch for a management network could be completely out-of-band or placed in a network where other servers are currently deployed.

  Figure 6-5 shows a deployment in which the management interfaces of the FMC and FTD are configured out-of-band.

- **Management interfaces are on different subnets:** The FMC and FTD can be deployed in two different subnets or branch offices of your company, or even in two different countries. In such a case, you need a router to route the management traffic between Firepower systems.

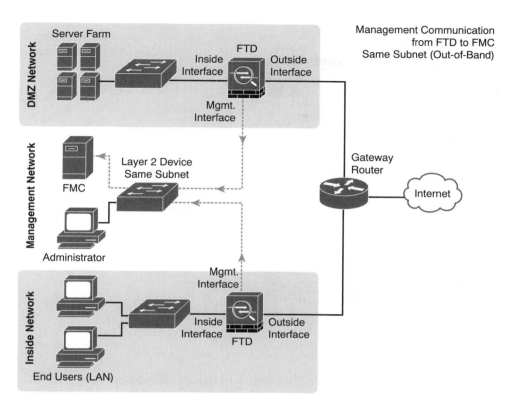

Figure 6-5 *Out-of-Band Firepower Management Network*

Figure 6-6 shows a design where the management interface of the FMC is connected to two FTD systems that are located at two different networks—one FTD system is in the same DMZ network as the FMC, and the other FTD system is in a separate inside network.

If you do not assign an IP address to the logical diagnostic interface, you can configure the logical management interface and inside interface within the same Layer 2 network and use the inside interface as the gateway for the logical management interface. This allows the FTD to communicate with the FMC over the Internet. However, if you configure the logical diagnostic interface with an IP address anyway (which is not recommended), you end up adding a router between your management network and inside network.

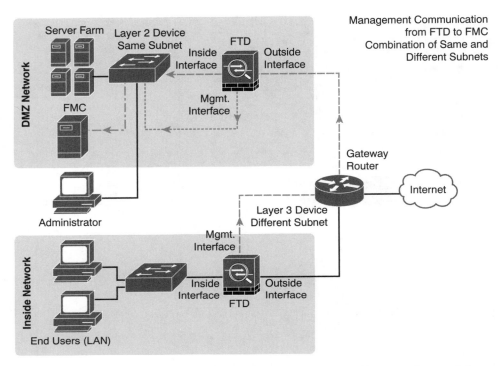

Figure 6-6   *FMC Connected with FTDs Simultaneously at Different and Same Subnets*

Caution   Be mindful when you consider sending Firepower management traffic through the FTD inside interface. If the inside interface flaps, FTD and the FMC can experience intermittent communication failures. If the inside interface goes down, FTD loses its connection to the FMC completely. In this circumstance, a console connection to FTD is critical for investigating the connectivity issue. If console access is not provisioned, you cannot troubleshoot further until physical access to the FTD is possible.

Note   When a Firepower appliance uses a private IP address for its management interface and needs to communicate with another Firepower appliance over the Internet, the private IP address has to be translated to a publicly routable IP address. It is usually performed by a router or firewall using Network Address Translation (NAT). When an intermediate device translates the management IP address of a Firepower appliance, the FMC and FTD must use a unique NAT ID during the registration process.

Figure 6-7 shows FTD systems positioned in various locations in a company and connected through the Internet.

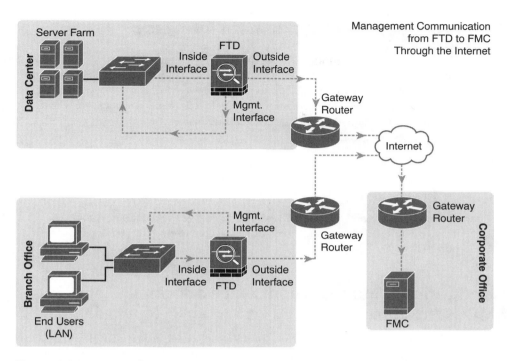

Figure 6-7 *FMC and FTD Communicating over the Internet*

Until an FTD system is registered with the FMC, the web interface does not let you configure the inside and outside interfaces. Hence, you are unable to select the inside interface as a gateway for the management interface until the inside interface is configured and
enabled. To address this challenge, follow these steps:

Step 1.   Register FTD with the FMC without sending the management traffic through
an inside interface. At this point, you can connect the management interfaces
of FTD and the FMC directly through a Layer 2 or Layer 3 device. (Refer to
Figure 6-5.)

Step 2.   After the registration is complete, configure the inside and outside interfaces.

Step 3.   When the inside and outside networks are able to communicate with each
other, gracefully delete the existing registration between the FMC and FTD.

Step 4.   Connect the management interface to the inside network.

Step 5.   Reregister the FTD with the FMC. This time, the management traffic should
go through the inside network to the FMC in the outside network.

Best Practices for Management Interface Configuration

You can configure a management interface when the Firepower System prompts you to set up the network automatically at the end of the software installation. If you misconfigure at that time or later want to modify the initially configured settings, you can also do that. When you design and configure a Firepower management network, there are a couple best practices you should consider:

- You should segregate the management traffic from the data traffic. Keeping the management network out-of-band secures the control-plane traffic in the event that the data network is attacked.

- Although the Firepower System allows you to change the default port for management communication, Cisco strongly recommends that you use the default port TCP 8305.

Configuring a Management Network on FMC Hardware

A brand-new FMC, out of the box, uses 192.168.45.45 as its management IP address. To connect to the FMC through the web interface for the first time, your computer must be able to reach the FMC management network 192.168.45.0/24. Once your computer is able to communicate with the FMC management interface, enter **https://192.168.45.45** in your browser to access the GUI.

Note   When you reimage a previously configured FMC, the FMC prompts you to confirm whether you want to keep the prior network settings during the reimaging process. Chapter 4, "Firepower Management Center (FMC) Hardware," describes the reimaging process in detail.

Configuration Options

You have several options for configuring or modifying the management IP address of the FMC. You can change the IP address during your first login to the FMC web interface or, later, you can use the GUI or CLI to modify the management IP address. These options are detailed in the following sections.

Using the GUI During the First Login

After reimaging, when you log in to the web interface of the FMC for the first time, the initialization page appears. In this page, you can change the default password, network settings, and so on. You can skip the licensing configuration on this page, as you will learn more about licensing in Chapter 7, "Firepower Licensing and Registration."

Note   The default username and password for the FMC are admin and Admin123, respectively.

Figure 6-8 shows the initial landing page of the FMC. This page appears when you enter the management IP address on a browser for the first time.

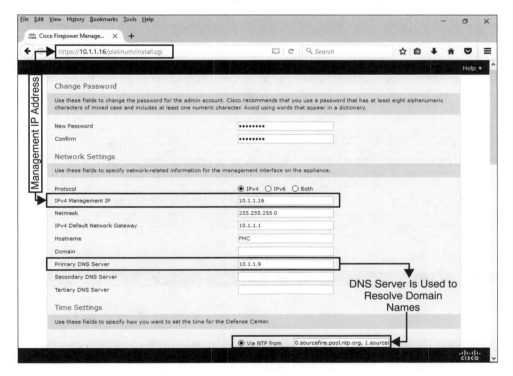

Figure 6-8   *System Initialization Page for the FMC*

After updating the default settings, you need to accept the end user license agreement (EULA) and click the **Apply** button.

Caution   As soon as you apply a new management IP address, any SSH or HTTPS session to the FMC is disconnected. You have to reconnect to the FMC by using the updated IP address.

Figure 6-9 shows the check box that you must select to accept the EULA and complete the system initialization.

You can skip adding
any licenses for now.

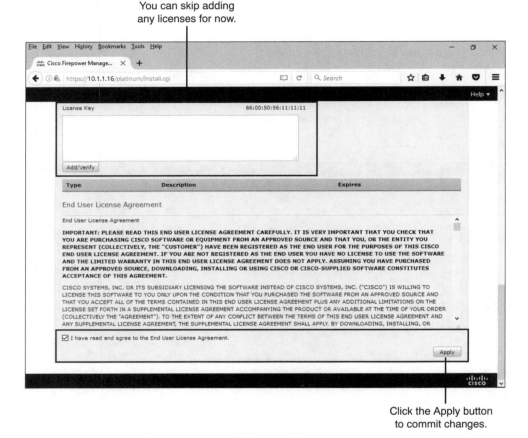

Click the Apply button
to commit changes.

Figure 6-9   *Accepting the FMC End User License Agreement (EULA)*

Using the GUI On Demand

Instead of using the GUI during the first login, you can change the management
IP address of the FMC whenever you need to. To change the existing network settings
of the FMC via the GUI, follow these steps:

Caution   If the FMC is currently managing any FTDs, deregister them from the FMC
before you change the management IP address. After you apply the new IP address,
reregister them with FMC. Doing this helps you avoid any potential registration or
communication issues.

Step 1.   Log in to the web interface of the FMC.

Step 2.   Go to **System** > **Configuration**.

Step 3. Select the **Management Interfaces** option in the left panel, as shown in Figure 6-10.

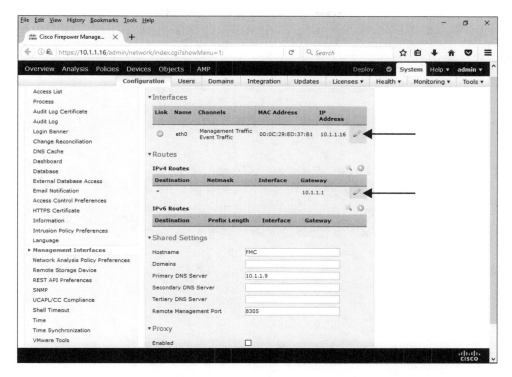

Figure 6-10 *Configurable Items for the Management Interface of an FMC*

Step 4. In the Configuration page, use the pencil icon to modify the IP addresses. In the Interfaces section, you can enter an IP address for the management interface. Similarly, in the Routes section, you can provide the gateway IP address.

Step 5. When all the necessary network settings are entered, click the **Save** button at the bottom of the page to save your changes. You are done, and now you should be able to access the FMC by using the new IP address.

Using the Command-Line Interface

To change the network settings on the FMC via the CLI, access the CLI by using Secure Shell (SSH) or the console terminal and run the **configure-network** command.

Example 6-1 shows the network configuration of a management interface on the FMC. It manually assigns 10.1.1.16/24 for the interface address and 10.1.1.1 for the gateway.

Example 6-1   *Configuring Network Settings from the FMC CLI*

```
admin@firepower:~$ sudo configure-network

We trust you have received the usual lecture from the local System
Administrator. It usually boils down to these three things:

    #1) Respect the privacy of others.
    #2) Think before you type.
    #3) With great power comes great responsibility.

Password:

Do you wish to configure IPv4? (y or n) y

Management IP address? [192.168.45.45] 10.1.1.16
Management netmask? [255.255.255.0]
Management default gateway? 10.1.1.1

Management IP address?        10.1.1.16
Management netmask?           255.255.255.0
Management default gateway?   10.1.1.1

Are these settings correct? (y or n) y
Do you wish to configure IPv6? (y or n) n

Updated network configuration.
Updated comms. channel configuration.

Please go to https://10.1.1.16/ or https://[]/ to finish installation.
admin@firepower:~$
```

Verification and Troubleshooting Tools

Before the registration process, if you experience any connectivity issues between the management interfaces of the FMC and FTD, you can run a couple of command-line tools to verify the network connectivity between your Firepower systems.

First, run the ping test from the CLI of the FMC to the management interface of your FTD device.

Example 6-2 shows a successful ping test from the FMC to 10.1.1.2—the IP address of the management interface. The **ping** command on the FMC requires root privilege, so you need to run **sudo** with the **ping** command.

Example 6-2 *Successful Ping Test Between the FMC and FTD*

```
admin@FMC:~$ sudo ping 10.1.1.2
Password:
PING 10.1.1.2 (10.1.1.2) 56(84) bytes of data.
64 bytes from 10.1.1.2: icmp_req=1 ttl=64 time=0.615 ms
64 bytes from 10.1.1.2: icmp_req=2 ttl=64 time=0.419 ms
64 bytes from 10.1.1.2: icmp_req=3 ttl=64 time=0.536 ms
64 bytes from 10.1.1.2: icmp_req=4 ttl=64 time=0.613 ms
^C
--- 10.1.1.2 ping statistics ---
4 packets transmitted, 4 received, 0% packet loss, time 2999ms
rtt min/avg/max/mdev = 0.419/0.545/0.615/0.084 ms
admin@FMC:~$
```

If the ping test from the FMC to FTD is unsuccessful, check whether the FMC can ping the gateway. Example 6-3 confirms the IP address of the gateway, 10.1.1.1, for eth0—the management interface of the FMC.

Example 6-3 *Verifying the Routing Table*

```
admin@FMC:~$ route -n
Kernel IP routing table
Destination     Gateway         Genmask         Flags Metric Ref    Use Iface
0.0.0.0         10.1.1.1        0.0.0.0         UG    0      0        0 eth0
10.1.1.0        0.0.0.0         255.255.255.0   U     0      0        0 eth0
admin@FMC:~$
```

If the FMC can successfully ping the gateway but fails to ping FTD, there must be a routing issue between the FMC and FTD. You can run the **traceroute** tool on the Firepower System to investigate this issue further, or you can check the configuration on any intermediate routers. The syntax to run the **traceroute** command on an FMC is as follows:

```
admin@FMC:~$ sudo traceroute IP_Address_of_FTD
```

If the connectivity between the FMC and the gateway fails, there is no reason for the FMC to connect to FTD successfully. You should see if the interface is up and connected with a cable. Also, you should make sure the IP address and subnet mask are configured properly. Run the **ifconfig** command to verify the settings and status.

Example 6-4 shows the assignment of IP address 10.1.1.16 and subnet mask 255.255.255.0. The status of the management interface, eth0, is up. This output also confirms whether the packets are dropped or have errors.

Example 6-4   *Verifying Interface Status and IP Address Assignment*

```
admin@FMC:~$ ifconfig
eth0      Link encap:Ethernet  HWaddr 00:0C:29:ED:37:B1
          inet addr:10.1.1.16  Bcast:10.1.1.255  Mask:255.255.255.0
          inet6 addr: fe80::20c:29ff:feed:37b1/64 Scope:Link
          UP BROADCAST RUNNING MULTICAST  MTU:1500  Metric:1
          RX packets:2190 errors:0 dropped:0 overruns:0 frame:0
          TX packets:197 errors:0 dropped:0 overruns:0 carrier:0
          collisions:0 txqueuelen:1000
          RX bytes:150210 (146.6 Kb)  TX bytes:25196 (24.6 Kb)

lo        Link encap:Local Loopback
          inet addr:127.0.0.1  Mask:255.255.255.0
          inet6 addr: ::1/128 Scope:Host
          UP LOOPBACK RUNNING  MTU:65536  Metric:1
          RX packets:9789370 errors:0 dropped:0 overruns:0 frame:0
          TX packets:9789370 errors:0 dropped:0 overruns:0 carrier:0
          collisions:0 txqueuelen:0
          RX bytes:2482195842 (2367.2 Mb)  TX bytes:2482195842 (2367.2 Mb)

admin@FMC:~$
```

Configuring a Management Network on ASA Hardware

FTD does not offer a GUI when you want to manage it from the FMC. Therefore, to configure or reconfigure the management interface for FTD, you need to access the CLI.

Configuration

Once you access the CLI, you can run the **configure network** command to configure all kinds of basic network settings, such as DHCP, manual, IPv4, IPv6, and so on.

To obtain an IP address from the DHCP server, run the following command:

```
> configure network ipv4 dhcp
```

To assign an IP address manually, use the following syntax:

```
> configure network ipv4 manual IP_Address Subnet_Mask Gateway_Address
```

> **Note**   The **configure network ipv4** command changes the IP address of the logical management interface, br1. It does not assign or make any changes on the logical diagnostic interface.

Example 6-5 shows the command to configure a static IP address 10.1.1.2/24 and a gateway IP address 10.1.1.1 for the FTD management interface br1.

Example 6-5   *Configuring an IPv4 Address on the FTD Management Interface*

```
> configure network ipv4 manual 10.1.1.2 255.255.255.0 10.1.1.1
Setting IPv4 network configuration.
Network settings changed.

>
```

Verification and Troubleshooting Tools

Like the FMC, FTD provides various tools to test network settings and connectivity; however, the command syntax is different for FTD. The following examples show some useful FTD commands.

Example 6-6 shows the network settings and the status of the logical management interface br1. The output proves the assignment of port 8305 for transferring management traffic and events. The IP address and MAC address of the logical management interface (br1) are 10.1.1.2 and A4:6C:2A:E4:6B:BE, respectively.

Example 6-6   *Verifying the Status of the Logical Management Interface br1*

```
> show network
===============[ System Information ]===============
Hostname                : firepower
Management port         : 8305
IPv4 Default route
  Gateway               : 10.1.1.1


======================[ br1 ]======================
State                   : Enabled
Channels                : Management & Events
Mode                    : Non-Autonegotiation
MDI/MDIX                : Auto/MDIX
MTU                     : 1500
MAC Address             : A4:6C:2A:E4:6B:BE
---------------------[ IPv4 ]---------------------
Configuration           : Manual
Address                 : 10.1.1.2
Netmask                 : 255.255.255.0
Broadcast               : 10.1.1.255
---------------------[ IPv6 ]---------------------
```

```
Configuration         : Disabled

===============[ Proxy Information ]===============
State                 : Disabled
Authentication        : Disabled

>
```

Did you notice that the command output shown in Example 6-6 does not show the status of the logical diagnostic interface, Management x/x? To determine the status of the diagnostic interface and any other interfaces, run the **show interface ip brief** command at the FTD CLI.

Example 6-7 shows an overview of all the interfaces. The output confirms that there is no IP address assigned to the logical diagnostic interface Management1/1.

Example 6-7 *A Brief Overview of the FTD Interfaces*

```
> show interface ip brief
Interface           IP-Address    OK? Method Status                 Protocol
Virtual0            127.1.0.1     YES unset  up                     up
GigabitEthernet1/1  unassigned    YES unset  administratively down  down
GigabitEthernet1/2  unassigned    YES unset  administratively down  down
GigabitEthernet1/3  unassigned    YES unset  administratively down  down
GigabitEthernet1/4  unassigned    YES unset  administratively down  down
GigabitEthernet1/5  unassigned    YES unset  administratively down  down
GigabitEthernet1/6  unassigned    YES unset  administratively down  down
GigabitEthernet1/7  unassigned    YES unset  administratively down  down
GigabitEthernet1/8  unassigned    YES unset  administratively down  down
Internal-Control1/1 127.0.1.1     YES unset  up                     up
Internal-Data1/1    unassigned    YES unset  up                     up
Internal-Data1/2    unassigned    YES unset  down                   down
Internal-Data1/3    unassigned    YES unset  up                     up
Internal-Data1/4    169.254.1.1   YES unset  up                     up
Management1/1       unassigned    YES unset  up                     up
>
```

Tip The diagnostic interface Management1/1 is an optional logical interface. Cisco recommends that you not configure the diagnostic interface with an IP address if there is no router between the management network and the inside network. This also simplifies your network design and reduces configuration overhead and any potential mistakes.

In your output, if you do not see 1/1 with the management interface name, it is okay. The numbering scheme of a management interface depends on the hardware platform you are running. Table 6-1 shows the management interface numbering for different hardware platforms.

Table 6-1 *Management Interface Numbering*

Hardware Platform	Interface Numbering
ASA 5506, 5508, 5516	Management1/1
ASA 5512, 5515, 5525, 5545, 5555	Management0/0
Firepower 4100, 9300	Management0

Example 6-8 shows that FTD is running a successful ping test to its manager, using the IP address of the FMC management interface, 10.1.1.16.

Example 6-8 *Running a Ping Test Appropriately*

```
> ping system 10.1.1.16
PING 10.1.1.16 (10.1.1.16) 56(84) bytes of data.
64 bytes from 10.1.1.16: icmp_seq=1 ttl=64 time=0.593 ms
64 bytes from 10.1.1.16: icmp_seq=2 ttl=64 time=0.654 ms
64 bytes from 10.1.1.16: icmp_seq=3 ttl=64 time=0.663 ms
64 bytes from 10.1.1.16: icmp_seq=4 ttl=64 time=0.699 ms
^C
--- 10.1.1.16 ping statistics ---
4 packets transmitted, 4 received, 0% packet loss, time 2999ms
rtt min/avg/max/mdev = 0.593/0.652/0.699/0.042 ms
>
```

Example 6-9 shows that FTD fails to ping the management IP address of the FMC when the ping request is sent from the diagnostic CLI instead of the default CLI. This happens because the diagnostic interface has no IP address. (Use the command as shown in Example 6-8 when you want to run a proper ping test from FTD.)

Example 6-9 *Ping Test Showing No Success Although the Connection Is Established*

```
> system support diagnostic-cli
Attaching to ASA console ... Press 'Ctrl+a then d' to detach.
Type help or '?' for a list of available commands.

firepower> enable
Password:
firepower# ping 10.1.1.16
```

```
Type escape sequence to abort.
Sending 5, 100-byte ICMP Echos to 10.1.1.16, timeout is 2 seconds:
No route to host 10.1.1.16

Success rate is 0 percent (0/1)
firepower#
```

Configuring a Management Network on a Firepower Security Appliance

To manage FTD, you have to configure one of the interfaces from the network modules for management communication. This section describes the steps to configure and verify the status of a management interface for both FXOS and FTD on a Firepower security appliance.

Configuring the FXOS Management Interface

The embedded management interface that is located on the front panel of a Firepower security appliance is used to manage FXOS. You can configure that interface by using the FXOS CLI.

To configure the network settings for a management interface that provides administrative access to the FXOS software, run the **set out-of-band** command at the CLI. After any changes, you must apply the configuration in order for it to take effect.

Example 6-10 shows how to assign an IP address and gateway to the FXOS management interface.

Example 6-10   *Setting Up an IP Address and Gateway for the FXOS Management Interface*

```
Firepower-9300# scope fabric-interconnect a
Firepower-9300 /fabric-interconnect # set out-of-band ip 10.1.1.28 netmask
  255.255.255.0 gw 10.1.1.1
Warning: When committed, this change may disconnect the current CLI session
Firepower-9300 /fabric-interconnect* #

! The above command does not take an effect until you run the following command and
  commit the changes.

Firepower-9300 /fabric-interconnect* # commit-buffer
Firepower-9300 /fabric-interconnect #

! If you misconfigured or do not want to apply a recent change, you could discard it
  from the buffer as well. To discard, run the following command.

Firepower-9300 /fabric-interconnect* # discard-buffer
Firepower-9300 /fabric-interconnect #
```

Verification of the FXOS Management Interface Configuration

The command syntax on FXOS is different from the syntax on an ASA or FTD software. In FXOS, when you run a particular command, you must enter an appropriate module or scope. The following are some testing tools that are run on the FMC or ASA hardware earlier in this chapter. Now you can see these tests performed once again, but this time with different command syntax that works only on FXOS.

Example 6-11 shows the command to connect to the local-mgmt module and how to run a ping test from there.

Example 6-11   *Successful Ping Test from FXOS to the FMC Management Interface*

```
Firepower-9300# connect local-mgmt
Firepower-9300(local-mgmt)# ping 10.1.1.1
PING 10.1.1.1 (10.1.1.1) from 10.1.1.28 eth0: 56(84) bytes of data.
64 bytes from 10.1.1.1: icmp_seq=1 ttl=255 time=0.298 ms
64 bytes from 10.1.1.1: icmp_seq=2 ttl=255 time=0.412 ms
64 bytes from 10.1.1.1: icmp_seq=3 ttl=255 time=0.392 ms
64 bytes from 10.1.1.1: icmp_seq=4 ttl=255 time=0.390 ms
^C
--- 10.1.1.1 ping statistics ---
4 packets transmitted, 4 received, 0% packet loss, time 3007ms
rtt min/avg/max/mdev = 0.298/0.373/0.412/0.044 ms
Firepower-9300(local-mgmt)#
```

Example 6-12 shows the command to verify the network settings and the status of the FXOS management interface.

Example 6-12   *Status of a Management Interface*

```
Firepower-9300# connect local-mgmt
Firepower-9300(local-mgmt)# show mgmt-port
eth0      Link encap:Ethernet   HWaddr B0:AA:77:2F:84:71
          inet addr:10.1.1.28  Bcast:10.122.144.255  Mask:255.255.255.0
          inet6 addr: fe80::b2aa:77ff:fe2f:8471/64 Scope:Link
          UP BROADCAST RUNNING MULTICAST   MTU:1500  Metric:1
          RX packets:4980815 errors:0 dropped:0 overruns:0 frame:0
          TX packets:2680187 errors:0 dropped:0 overruns:0 carrier:0
          collisions:0 txqueuelen:1000
          RX bytes:1124575588 (1.0 GiB)  TX bytes:1921268851 (1.7 GiB)
Firepower-9300(local-mgmt)#
```

Example 6-13 shows the command to determine the IP address of the gateway for the FXOS management interface.

Example 6-13   *Default Gateway for the FXOS Management Interface*

```
Firepower-9300# show fabric-interconnect


Fabric Interconnect:
ID  OOB IP Addr    OOB Gateway   OOB Netmask    OOB IPv6 Address OOB IPv6 Gateway
    Prefix Operability
--  -----------    -----------   -----------    ---------------- ----------------
    ------ -----------
A   10.1.1.28      10.1.1.1      255.255.255.0 ::                ::                 64
    Operable
Firepower-9300#
```

Configuring the FTD Management Interface

You cannot select the embedded management interface as the FTD management interface. This section describes how to set up a management interface for an FTD logical device.

To configure a new physical interface for management communication or to change the administrative state (enable/disable) of a management interface, follow these steps:

Step 1.   Go to the Interfaces page of the Firepower Chassis Manager. By default, you should be at the All Interfaces tab.

Step 2.   Click the pencil icon (at the right-hand side) for the interface you want to modify. The Edit Interface window appears.

Step 3.   Using the Type dropdown, select the type of traffic that you want the interface to carry. For example, if you want to select an interface for management communication between an FTD and FMC, select **mgmt** from the dropdown. Figure 6-11 shows that the Ethernet1/1 interface is enabled and configured for the mgmt (management) type of traffic.

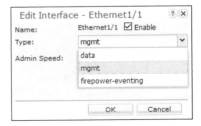

Figure 6-11   *The Configurable Options for an Interface*

Step 4.   Select the **Enable** check box if you want to enable this interface immediately with the updated settings.

Step 5. Click the **OK** button to save the changes. The Interfaces page returns, and it now reflects the changes you have made.

Figure 6-12 shows the status of each of the two types of management interfaces—one for FXOS and the other for FTD—after they are configured, administratively enabled, and physically connected.

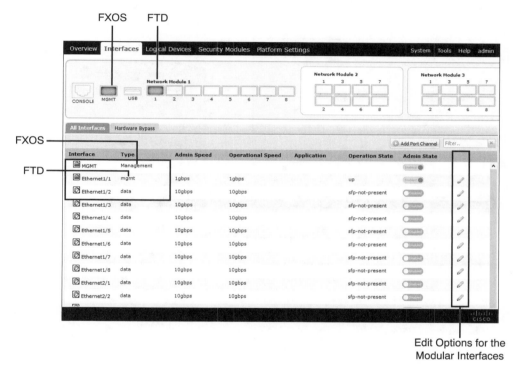

Figure 6-12 *Visual Changes in the GUI for Both Types of Management Interfaces*

If you want to modify the management IP address of an already configured FTD or intend to use a different physical management interface for an FTD, follow these steps:

Step 1. On the Firepower Chassis Manager, go to the Logical Devices page. The FTD logical device, if configured, should appear.

Step 2. Click the pencil icon (at the right-hand side) for the FTD logical device you want to modify. An FTD Provisioning page appears.

Step 3. Click the **Click to Configure** rectangular box. A configuration window appears. Figure 6-13 shows the FTD configuration window. In it, you can modify the settings of an FTD management interface.

Step 4. When you are done with any modification, click **OK**, and then click the **Save** button to apply the changes.

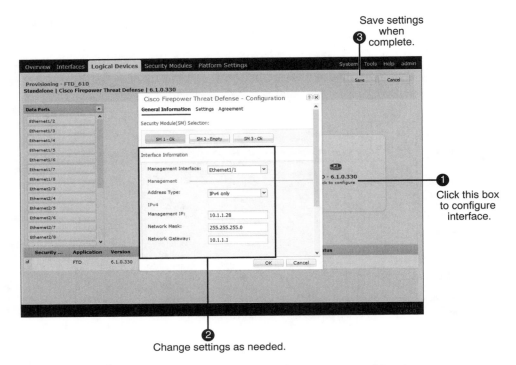

Figure 6-13 *Changing the Network Settings of an FTD Logical Device*

Caution   After you change the FTD management IP address and commit changes using the Firepower Chassis Manager, the FTD logical device reinitializes and resets all bootstrap settings.

Verification of the FTD Management Interface Configuration

Example 6-14 shows the interfaces for an FTD logical device. By running the **show configuration** command within the scope of **ssa**, you can verify whether the selected physical interfaces are properly mapped with a logical device.

Example 6-14 *Mapping Physical Interfaces with an FTD Logical Device*

```
Firepower-9300# scope ssa
Firepower-9300 /ssa # show configuration
 scope ssa
     enter logical-device FTD_61 ftd 1 standalone
          enter external-port-link Ethernet11_ftd Ethernet1/1 ftd
               set decorator ""
               set description ""
```

```
                    set port-name Ethernet1/1
            exit
            enter external-port-link Ethernet23_ftd Ethernet2/3 ftd
                set decorator ""
                set description ""
                set port-name Ethernet2/3
            exit
            enter external-port-link Ethernet24_ftd Ethernet2/4 ftd
                set decorator ""
                set description ""
                set port-name Ethernet2/4
            exit
            enter mgmt-bootstrap ftd
                enter ipv4 1 firepower
                    set gateway 10.1.1.1
                    set ip 10.1.1.28 mask 255.255.255.0
                exit
            exit
            set description ""
            set res-profile-name ""
        exit
.
.
.
<Output Omitted>

Firepower-9300 /ssa #
```

Example 6-15 shows the administrative and operational status of each of the interfaces
on a Firepower security appliance (except the member interfaces of a port channel). The
output shows that the FTD management interface (Ethernet1/1) and both data interfaces
(Ethernet2/3 and Ethernet2/4) are enabled and up.

Example 6-15 *Status of Each Fixed and Modular Interface from the FXOS CLI*

```
Firepower-9300# scope eth-uplink
Firepower-9300 /eth-uplink # scope fabric a
Firepower-9300 /eth-uplink/fabric # show interface

Interface:
    Port Name       Port Type           Admin State Oper State       State Reason
    --------------- ------------------- ----------- ---------------- ------------
    Ethernet1/1     Mgmt                Enabled     Up
    Ethernet1/2     Data                Disabled    Sfp Not Present  Unknown
```

```
Ethernet1/3      Data            Disabled      Sfp Not Present   Unknown
Ethernet1/4      Data            Disabled      Sfp Not Present   Unknown
Ethernet1/5      Data            Disabled      Sfp Not Present   Unknown
Ethernet1/6      Data            Disabled      Sfp Not Present   Unknown
Ethernet1/7      Data            Disabled      Sfp Not Present   Unknown
Ethernet1/8      Data            Disabled      Sfp Not Present   Unknown
Ethernet2/3      Data            Enabled       Up
Ethernet2/4      Data            Enabled       Up
Ethernet2/5      Data            Disabled      Sfp Not Present   Unknown
Ethernet2/6      Data            Disabled      Sfp Not Present   Unknown
Ethernet2/7      Data            Disabled      Sfp Not Present   Unknown
Ethernet2/8      Data            Disabled      Sfp Not Present   Unknown
Ethernet3/1      Data            Disabled      Sfp Not Present   Unknown
Ethernet3/2      Data            Disabled      Sfp Not Present   Unknown
Ethernet3/3      Data            Disabled      Sfp Not Present   Unknown
Ethernet3/4      Data            Disabled      Sfp Not Present   Unknown
Ethernet3/5      Data            Disabled      Sfp Not Present   Unknown
Ethernet3/6      Data            Disabled      Sfp Not Present   Unknown
Ethernet3/7      Data            Disabled      Sfp Not Present   Unknown
Ethernet3/8      Data            Disabled      Sfp Not Present   Unknown
Firepower-9300 /eth-uplink/fabric #
```

Example 6-16 shows how to connect to the FTD logical device from the FXOS CLI and then verify the network settings on the FTD logical device.

Example 6-16 *Verifying Network Settings That Are Specific to the FTD Application*

```
Firepower-9300# connect module 1 console
Telnet escape character is '~'.
Trying 127.5.1.1...
Connected to 127.5.1.1.
Escape character is '~'.
CISCO Serial Over LAN:
Close Network Connection to Exit


Firepower-module1> connect ftd
Connecting to ftd console... enter exit to return to bootCLI


> show network
===============[ System Information ]===============
Hostname                 : Firepower-module1
Management port          : 8305
```

```
IPv4 Default route
  Gateway                  : 10.1.1.1


=================[ management0 ]==================
State                      : Enabled
Channels                   : Management & Events
Mode                       : Non-Autonegotiation
MDI/MDIX                   : Auto/MDIX
MTU                        : 9210
MAC Address                : B0:AA:77:2F:84:5D
--------------------[ IPv4 ]---------------------
Configuration              : Manual
Address                    : 10.1.1.28
Netmask                    : 255.255.255.0
Broadcast                  : 10.1.1.255
--------------------[ IPv6 ]---------------------
Configuration              : Disabled


===============[ Proxy Information ]===============
State                      : Disabled
Authentication             : Disabled
>
```

Summary

In this chapter, you have learned the best practices for designing and configuring a management network for the Firepower System. This chapter discusses the tools you can use to verify any communication issues between the management interfaces of the FMC and FTD. Before you begin the registration process, which is described in Chapter 7, you must ensure that the FMC and FTD are successfully connected through your network.

Quiz

1. To run a ping test from FTD to the FMC, which command syntax would be correct?
   a. **ping** *IP_Address*
   b. **sudo ping** *IP_Address*
   c. **ping system** *IP_Address*
   d. **ping host** *IP_Address*

2. Which port does the Firepower System use for management communication by default?

    a. 22

    b. 443

    c. 8080

    d. 8305

3. During FTD software initialization, you have to configure a network. Which interface on an ASA device is assigned with an IP address from that initial configuration?

    a. GigabitEthernet0/0

    b. Management0/0

    c. Management1/1

    d. br1

4. Per Cisco recommendation, one of the interfaces on an ASA device should have no IP address configured. Which interface is this?

    a. Management0/0

    b. Management1/1

    c. br1

    d. Both a and b

5. To investigate a communication issue between the FMC and FTD, which of the following tools could be used?

    a. **ifconfig**

    b. **ping**

    c. **traceroute**

    d. All of the above

6. Which of the following statements is false?

    a. Segregation of management traffic improves security policy.

    b. The default Firepower management port should not be changed.

    c. The logical management interface is labeled Management0/0 on an ASA platform.

    d. FTD does not offer any web interface when it is configured for remote management.

Chapter 7

Firepower Licensing and Registration

At this point, you have the Firepower software running and the management interface configured. You are ready to begin the next steps: installing the licenses, enabling the Firepower features, and registering FTD with the FMC. The registration process takes place through an encrypted tunnel that is established between the management interfaces of the FMC and FTD. You cannot, however, register FTD with the FMC unless the FMC is licensed. This chapter shows you all the necessary steps for an initial deployment.

Licensing Essentials

The FMC accepts two types of licenses: Classic License and Smart License. To manage FTD, you must use a Smart License. A Classic License is used for earlier implementations of the Sourcefire technology, such as FirePOWER Services on ASA and legacy Sourcefire products. Because this book focuses on FTD, this section covers the Smart Licensing architecture.

The Smart Licensing Architecture

The Smart Licensing architecture offers two major benefits over the Classic License. It enables you to administer all your Firepower licenses from a single place and oversee their usage in real time. It also allows you to enable the full functionalities of the FMC and FTD without installing any licenses for the first 90 days of an initial deployment. This grace period allows you to complete any logistic or business processes related to your new Firepower deployment.

In the Smart Licensing architecture, the Firepower manager uses a process—Smart Agent—to communicate and register with the Cisco License Authority. After a successful registration, the License Authority issues an ID certificate. The Smart Agent process uses this certificate to communicate with the Cisco License Authority from time to time and track the status of entitlements.

Cisco offers two options to connect a Firepower manager to the Cisco License Authority. Depending on the security and connectivity policies of your organization, you can either choose to connect to the Cisco License Authority directly over the Internet or via a satellite server.

Cisco Smart Software Manager (CSSM)

After purchase, your Firepower Smart Licenses are assigned to an account that is created exclusively for your organization. You can manage any Smart Licenses your company owns by using the Cisco Smart Software Manager (CSSM)—a web-based application at cisco.com.

If you have administrative access to your account, the CSSM allows you to create additional virtual accounts within your company's master account. Doing this helps you organize Firepower licenses based on departments or locations. When necessary, you can also transfer licenses and devices between the virtual accounts.

Tip   To get access to the CSSM, contact the Cisco channel partner, sales representative, or Global Licensing Operations (GLO) team.

Figure 7-1 shows that the Smart Agent process of an FMC connects to the Cisco License Authority through the Internet, and an administrator can manage the licenses through the Internet by connecting to the CSSM application.

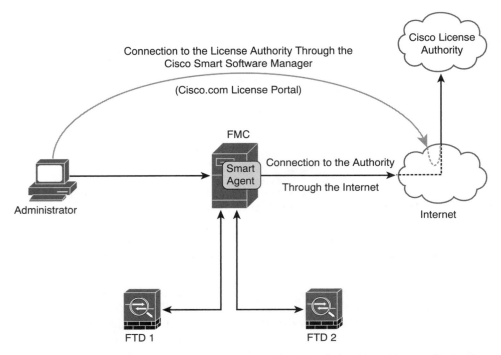

Figure 7-1   *Network Connectivity Between an FMC and the Cisco License Authority*

CSSM Satellite

Because the Cisco License Authority is hosted at cisco.com, you need Internet connectivity from the FMC to obtain a Smart License. For security or other reasons, if you cannot connect the management interface of the FMC to the Internet, you can use the CSSM satellite—a virtual version of the CSSM deployed from an OVA image. In a CSSM satellite deployment, the FMC is connected to a CSSM satellite server, and the CSSM satellite server is registered to the Cisco License Authority through the Internet.

> **Note** The CSSM application or a satellite server is designed to integrate a wide range of Cisco products. Describing the configuration of the CSSM satellite is beyond the scope of this book. Cisco publishes various documents on Smart Licensing, which you can download free from cisco.com. Please read them to learn more.

Figure 7-2 illustrates the connection of an FMC with the Cisco License Authority through the CSSM satellite server and Internet.

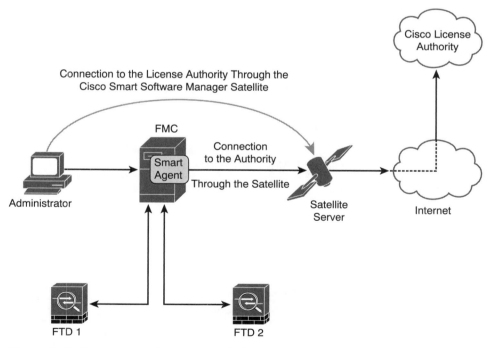

Figure 7-2 *Connection of an FMC with the Cisco License Authority via CSSM Satellite*

Firepower Licenses

The Cisco Firepower technology, an evolution from the Sourcefire technology, offers various features to protect your network from malicious activities. Firepower, by default, comes with a base license. A base license, however, does not enable all the security features. To enable all the functionalities, separate feature licenses are necessary.

Tip If you turn on the Evaluation Mode on the Firepower System, it enables all the security features on the FMC. You can apply these features on FTD for a 90-day period. Before the evaluation period expires, you must purchase a valid license and register the FMC with the Cisco License Authority for continuous operation.

Table 7-1 describes the functionalities of each Firepower license. Keep in mind that a Threat license is a prerequisite for a Malware license or a URL Filtering license.

Table 7-1 *Capabilities of the Firepower Licenses*

License	It Allows You to...
Base	Update the Firepower system
	Control applications and users
	Perform switching, routing, and NAT
Threat	Detect and prevent intrusion attempts
	Blacklist traffic based on intelligence
	Block transfer of certain types of files
Malware	Protect the network from malware, enable AMP for the network, and enable AMP Threat Grid features
URL Filtering	Filter URLs based on reputation and category

Table 7-2 describes the license subscription codes—T, TM, TMC, AMP, and URL—that you might notice during a purchase order. The Malware and URL Filtering licenses are available in two formats: as an add-on or in a bundle with a Threat license.

Table 7-2 *Firepower License Subscription Purchase Options*

License	Expiration	Which License to Purchase
Base	Permanent	No separate purchase; included automatically during a device purchase.
Threat	Term-based	T: Threat license only.

License	Expiration	Which License to Purchase
Malware	Term-based	**TM:** Threat and Malware licenses in a bundle. **AMP:** Malware license only; purchased if a Threat license is already available.
URL Filtering	Term-based	**TMC:** Threat, Malware, and URL Filtering licenses in a bundle. **URL:** URL Filtering license only; purchased if a Threat license is already available.

Best Practices for Licensing and Registration

When you register the FMC with FTD, there are a few things to consider:

- If you are in the middle of procuring a Firepower Smart License, you can avoid any delay by turning on the Evaluation Mode on the FMC. It enables all the security features on the FMC for 90 days and allows you to register FTD with the FMC immediately.

- If there is an intermediate device that translates the management IP addresses of your Firepower systems, use a unique NAT ID during the registration process.

- Before you begin the registration process, make sure the network settings on Firepower appliances are correct. FMC and FTD should be able to communicate with each other using IP addresses. If you choose to perform a registration using host names or domain names, verify the name resolution before you attempt to register. You can run a simple **ping** test between the FMC and FTD by using their fully qualified domain names (FQDNs). If the **ping** test fails due to name resolution failure, check to ensure that the Firepower appliances are configured with an appropriate DNS server and also make sure the DNS server is responding to the queries.

Licensing a Firepower System

Enabling a feature on Firepower is not a straightforward process. First, you need to purchase the necessary subscriptions. Then, you need to obtain the Smart Licenses by registering the FMC with the Smart Licensing Server. Finally, you have to enable a feature by applying the licenses to FTD from the web interface of the FMC.

Figure 7-3 summarizes the steps to obtain and apply a Smart License on the Firepower System.

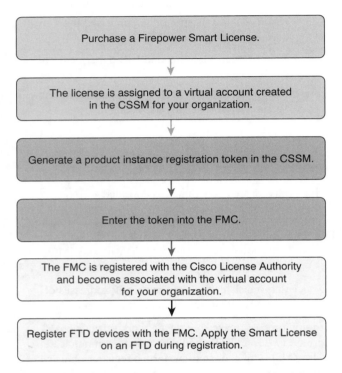

Figure 7-3   *Workflow to Purchase, Generate, and Apply a Smart License*

Licensing Configuration

You cannot register FTD with the FMC until you register the FMC with a Smart Licensing Server or enable the evaluation mode.

Figure 7-4 shows a notification in the Add Device window. This message appears when you attempt to register an FTD without registering the FMC with a Smart Licensing Server or without enabling Evaluation Mode.

If you are in the middle of procuring a Firepower Smart License, you can avoid any delay by turning on the Evaluation Mode on the FMC. It enables all the security features on the FMC for 90 days and allows you to register FTD with the FMC immediately. The following section describes how to enable Evaluation Mode on the FMC.

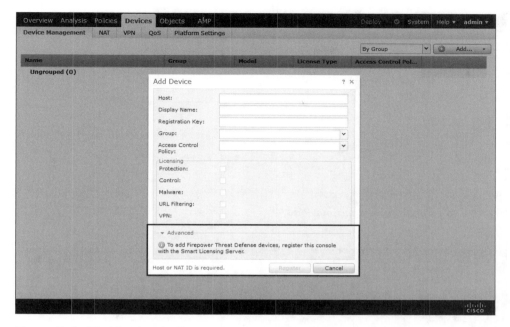

Figure 7-4   *Notification for Registering an FMC with the Smart Licensing Server*

Evaluation Mode

To enable Evaluation Mode, follow these steps:

Step 1.   Go to the **System > Licenses > Smart Licenses** page. Figure 7-5 shows the Evaluation Mode button that appears on the Smart Licenses page.

> **Note**   The Evaluation Mode button does not appear after the 90-day period expires; however, you can retrieve the button by reimaging the FMC.

Step 2.   Click the **Evaluation Mode** button. A confirmation message appears, reminding you that Evaluation Mode is a one-time option and available for a 90-day period (see Figure 7-6).

Step 3.   Click **Yes** to begin the 90-day period.

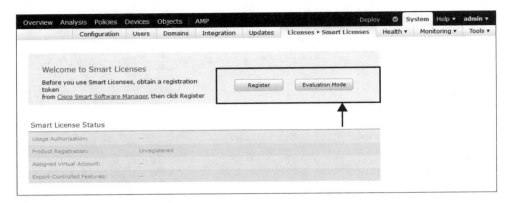

Figure 7-5   *Enabling Evaluation Mode*

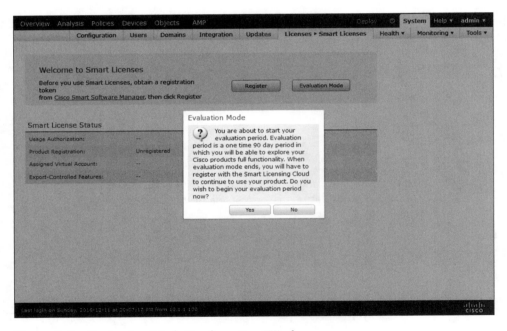

Figure 7-6   *Evaluation Mode Confirmation Window*

Registering with the CSSM

To register the FMC with the CSSM, follow these steps:

Step 1.   Log in to the cisco.com support portal and navigate to the CSSM.

Step 2. Access the virtual account created for your organization and click **New Token** to generate a new token (see Figure 7-7). A long string is randomly generated, and you can copy it by selecting the **Actions** option.

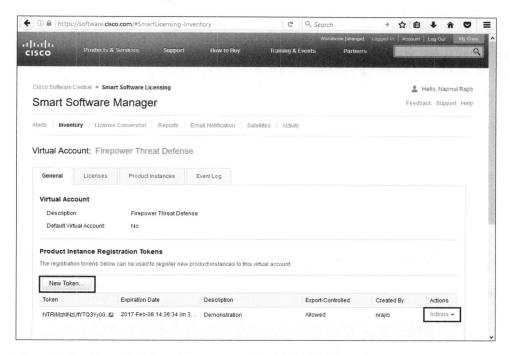

Figure 7-7   *View of a Virtual Account on the CSSM Web Portal*

Step 3. Copy the token from the CSSM and paste it in the Smart Licensing Product Registration form on the FMC (see Figure 7-8). To access the form, click the **Register** button on the Smart Licenses page.

Step 4. Click the **Apply Changes** button to begin the registration process with the Cisco License Authority. A confirmation message appears when registration is successful. Figure 7-9 confirms that the FMC is successfully registered with the Cisco License Authority. The Smart License Status shows healthy states (green checkmarks) and the name of the virtual account of your organization.

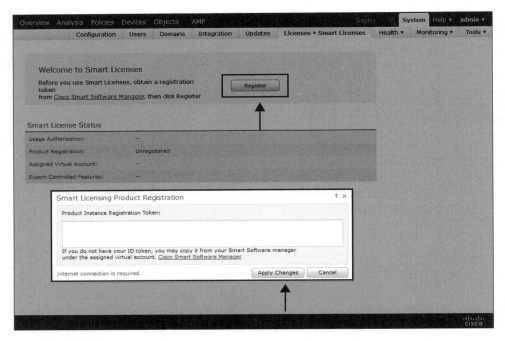

Figure 7-8 *Smart Licensing Product Registration Form*

Note You can apply your desired license on an FTD device during the registration process. Later, you can click the **Edit License** button on the Smart Licenses page to manage the associations of licenses with any managed devices.

Figure 7-9   *Confirmation of Registering the FMC with the Smart License Authority*

Verifying a Smart License Issue

If the FMC is unable to communicate with the Smart Licensing Server, make sure the FMC is configured to connect directly to the CSSM. You can confirm the setting from the **System > Integration > Smart Software Satellite** page.

Figure 7-10 shows two options to connect the FMC. By default, Connect Directly to Cisco Smart Software Manager is selected.

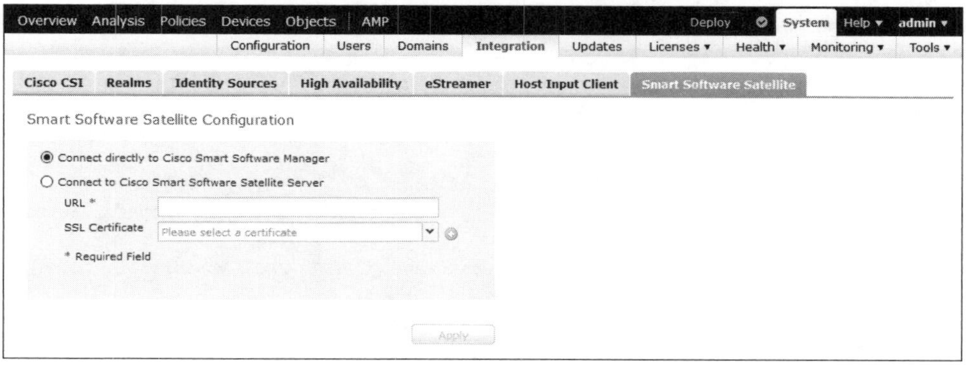

Figure 7-10   *Options to Connect an FMC with Different Types of License Servers*

The web interface of an FMC displays notifications when it successfully registers, or fails to register, with a License Server. To investigate any communication error, you can debug any related processes from the FMC CLI. Example 7-1 shows that the FMC can successfully connect and register with the Cisco License Authority.

Example 7-1   *Syslog Messages That Confirm a Successful Connection Between the FMC and a License Server*

```
admin@FMC:~$ sudo tail -f /var/log/sam.log
Password:


[timestamp] PID : 12133 Process : ActionQueueScrape.pl [SAM-DBG-LOG]:
  registerIdToken start: token(NGJmZThZjItZjVkNZC00TcyLWI5MTAAtNGRhMzExZDM5MzVmLTE0O
  DY1NjMZz%0AOD1MMDN8RmZweWJ5eG9Z0c…)
[timestamp] PID : 12133 Process : ActionQueueScrape.pl [SAM-DBG-LOG]: [socket conn]
  compose msg header: type[7], len[147], seq[1]
[timestamp] PID : 12133 Process : ActionQueueScrape.pl [SAM-DBG-LOG]: [socket conn]
  establishConnection start
[timestamp] PID : 12133 Process : ActionQueueScrape.pl [SAM-DBG-LOG]: [socket conn]
  Connected to server
[timestamp] PID : 12133 Process : ActionQueueScrape.pl [SAM-DBG-LOG]: [socket conn]
  '/var/sf/run/smart_agent.sock' Exiting the loop
[timestamp] PID : 12133 Process : ActionQueueScrape.pl [SAM-DBG-LOG]: [socket conn]
  Connection successful!
[timestamp] PID : 12133 Process : ActionQueueScrape.pl [SAM-DBG-LOG]: [socket conn]
  initSequence: 3
[timestamp] PID : 12133 Process : ActionQueueScrape.pl [SAM-DBG-LOG]: [socket conn]
  establishConnection done
[timestamp] PID : 12133 Process : ActionQueueScrape.pl [SAM-DBG-LOG]: [socket conn]
  sendMsg: successfully sent the msg!
[timestamp] PID : 12133 Process : ActionQueueScrape.pl [SAM-DBG-LOG]: [socket conn]
  recvMsg get: type[1007], len[141], seq[0], msg[error:0 authorization:AUTHORIZED,
  1483970615 registration:REGISTERED,1483970610 virtual_acct:Firepower Threat
  Defense export_control:1]
```

Example 7-2 demonstrates a scenario where the FMC can connect to the Smart Licensing Server successfully but fails to register with the server due to a token being invalid.

Example 7-2   *Debugging a Registration Failure Between the FMC and a License Server*

```
[timestamp] PID : 463 Process : mojo_server.pl [SAM-DBG-LOG]: [socket conn] Closing
  Connection
[timestamp] PID : 13540 Process : ActionQueueScrape.pl [SAM-DBG-LOG]:
  registerIdToken start: token(NGJmZThhZjItZjVkZCooyTcyLWI5MTAtNGRhMzExZDM5MzVmLTE0O
  DY1NjMz%0AODk1MDN8RmZweWJ5eG9ZY)
[timestamp] PID : 13540 Process : ActionQueueScrape.pl [SAM-DBG-LOG]: [socket conn]
  compose msg header: type[7], len[147], seq[1]
[timestamp] PID : 13540 Process : ActionQueueScrape.pl [SAM-DBG-LOG]: [socket conn]
  establishConnection start
[timestamp] PID : 13540 Process : ActionQueueScrape.pl [SAM-DBG-LOG]: [socket conn]
  Connected to server
```

```
[timestamp] PID : 13540 Process : ActionQueueScrape.pl [SAM-DBG-LOG]: [socket conn]
 '/var/sf/run/smart_agent.sock' Exiting the loop
[timestamp] PID : 13540 Process : ActionQueueScrape.pl [SAM-DBG-LOG]: [socket conn]
 Connection successful!
[timestamp] PID : 13540 Process : ActionQueueScrape.pl [SAM-DBG-LOG]: [socket conn]
 initSequence: 9
[timestamp] PID : 13540 Process : ActionQueueScrape.pl [SAM-DBG-LOG]: [socket conn]
 establishConnection done
[timestamp] PID : 13540 Process : ActionQueueScrape.pl [SAM-DBG-LOG]: [socket conn]
 sendMsg: successfully sent the msg!
[timestamp] PID : 13540 Process : ActionQueueScrape.pl [SAM-DBG-LOG]: [socket conn]
 recvMsg get: type[1003], len [203], seq[0], msg[Response error: {"token":
 ["The token 'NGJmZThhZjItZjVkZCooyTcyLWI5MTAtNGRhMzExZDM5MzVmLTE0ODY1NjMz%0AODk-
 1MDN8RmZweWJ5eG9ZY is not valid."]}]
[timestamp] PID : 13540 Process : ActionQueueScrape.pl [SAM-DBG-LOG]: [socket conn]
 Closing Connection
[timestamp] PID : 13540 Process : ActionQueueScrape.pl [SAM-DBG-LOG]:
 registerIdToken return: $VAR1 = {
        'error' => 17
      };
```

Registering a Firepower System

Registration of a Firepower System is a two-step process. You must begin the registration process from FTD. At first, you enter the FMC information in FTD, and then you provide the FTD information on the FMC.

Registration Configuration

To register FTD with the FMC, you need to have access to the FTD CLI and also to the web interface of the FMC. This section describes the entire process of completing a registration.

Setting Up FTD

After you install FTD software successfully, you should be able to connect to the FTD CLI through Secure Shell (SSH) or a console terminal. When you can successfully access the FTD software, you see the default CLI prompt, >.

Example 7-3 confirms that a fresh installation of FTD has no connection with a management appliance.

Example 7-3   *Output of the* **show managers** *Command*

```
> show managers
No managers configured.
>
```

To add the FMC to FTD, run the **configure manager add** command along with the management IP address of the FMC. You also have to provide a one-time registration key that is used only during the registration process. A unique NAT ID is necessary only if there is an intermediate networking device that translates the IP addresses of the Firepower System. The command syntax is as follows:

```
> configure manager add IP_Address_of_FMC Registration_Key NAT_ID
```

Example 7-4 demonstrates a successful addition of the FMC with management IP address 10.1.1.16. The configuration uses *RegKey* as the one-time temporary registration key and *NatId* as a NAT ID. The use of a NAT ID is optional when the management IP addresses are not translated by any intermediate devices.

Example 7-4   *Adding the FMC to FTD*

```
> configure manager add 10.1.1.16 RegKey NatId
Manager successfully configured.
Please make note of reg_key as this will be required while adding Device in FMC.
>
```

The configuration on your FTD is complete. The next step is to add FTD on the FMC. Before you go to the next step, you can optionally check the current status of the registration. Example 7-5 shows the pending registration status after you add the FMC to FTD. The registration status changes to completed after you perform the next step successfully.

Example 7-5   *Pending Status After Adding the FMC to FTD*

```
> show managers
Host                     : 10.1.1.16
Registration Key         : ****
Registration             : pending
RPC Status               :
>
```

Setting Up the FMC

The second step of the registration process is to enter the details of FTD on the web interface of the FMC. When you add FTD, you must use the same registration key (and the same NAT ID, if used) that you configured on the FTD previously. Here are the steps you have to follow:

Step 1.   Log in to the web interface of the FMC and go to **Devices > Device Management > Add Device** (see Figure 7-11). The Add Device window appears. You must add the FMC on FTD before you attempt to add the FTD details on this window.

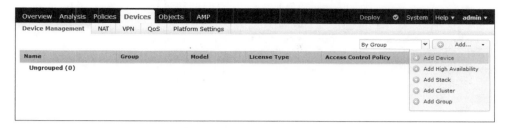

Figure 7-11 *Navigating to the Add Device Window*

Step 2. In the Host field, enter the IP address of the FTD management interface.

Step 3. In the Display Name field, provide a name that will be displayed on the FMC web interface to indicate this FTD.

Step 4. In the Registration Key field, enter **RegKey**—the same key you used when you added the FMC on FTD earlier.

Step 5. Use the Access Control Policy dropdown to select an access control policy that you want to initially apply to FTD. If this is a new deployment, the FMC may not have any preconfigured access control policy. You can, however, create a policy on the fly by choosing the **Create New Policy** option from the Access Control Policy dropdown. The New Policy window appears (see Figure 7-12).

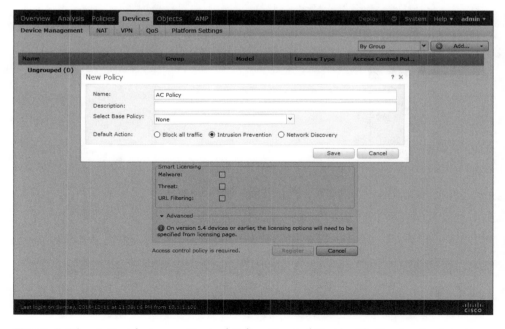

Figure 7-12 *A Simple Access Control Policy Created On the Fly During Registration*

Caution   The registration process can fail if you select an access control policy that was created for a different device model or configured with a component that is unsupported in FTD. Therefore, if you are not sure about the configuration of an old access control policy, you should create a new policy on the fly and select it to ensure that the registration will not fail due to an incompatible access control policy.

Figure 7-12 shows the creation of a new access control policy called *AC Policy*. This figure shows a very basic configuration that is good for a successful registration. You can edit and enhance this policy later. For now, click **Save**.

Step 6.   In the Smart Licensing section of the Add Device dialog, select the features that you want to apply, such as Malware, Threat, and URL Filtering.

Step 7.   In the Advanced section of the Add Device dialog, provide a unique NAT ID if there is an intermediate device that translates the management IP addresses of your Firepower systems. This is an optional step if there is no NAT device between the FMC and FTD. Figure 7-13 shows that the Add Device window is populated with the details of the FTD. Note that the same registration key (RegKey) and NAT ID (NatId) are used on the FMC and FTD.

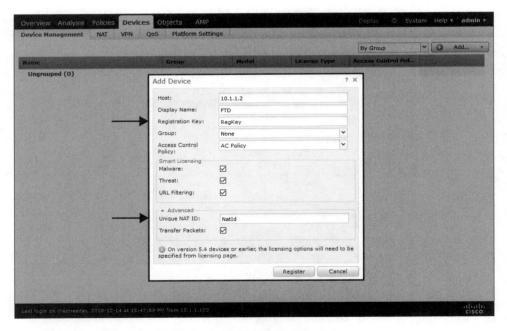

Figure 7-13   *Filling the Fields in the Add Device Window*

Step 8. Ensure that the Transfer Packets option is selected to allow FTD to send the associated packets to the FMC when any security events are generated.

Step 9. Click the **Register** button. The registration process begins, through an encrypted tunnel. Figure 7-14 demonstrates the in-progress registration process on the web interface.

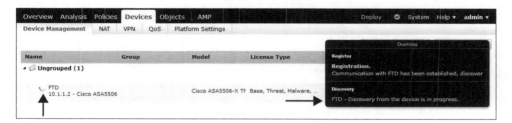

Figure 7-14 *Registration Process in Progress (Spinning Icon)*

Figure 7-15 shows the confirmation you get after a successful registration. The FTD device model, software version, and applied feature licenses are displayed after a successful registration.

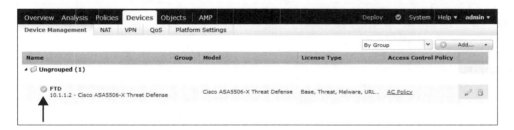

Figure 7-15 *Registration Process Complete (Spinning Icon Turns to Solid Icon)*

Verifying the Registration and Connection

If the registration process between FTD and the FMC is unsuccessful, the FMC displays an error message for it. In addition, you can run various commands to verify the communication status between FTD and the FMC.

Figure 7-16 shows an error message that can appear when a registration attempt fails due to a communication issue, an incompatible software version, or a mismatched registration key.

Example 7-6 shows two different registration statuses—pending and completed—that appear in the FTD CLI. The pending status appears after you add the FMC in the FTD CLI. The registration status changes to completed after you add FTD on the FMC web interface.

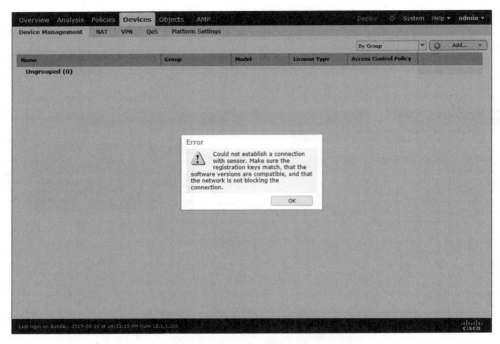

Figure 7-16 *Error Message on the GUI due to a Registration Failure*

Example 7-6 *Displaying the Registration Status from the FTD CLI*

```
! Registration status: After you complete the first step (Add an FMC on FTD CLI)


> show managers
Host                      : 10.1.1.16
Registration Key          : ****
Registration              : pending
RPC Status                :
>


! Registration status: After you complete the second and final step (Add an FTD on
  FMC GUI)


> show managers
Type                      : Manager
Host                      : 10.1.1.16
Registration              : Completed
>
```

As soon as you enter the FMC information in FTD, the FTD TCP port 8305 starts listening for incoming connections; it expects packets from the FMC. Similarly, as soon as you enter the FTD information on the FMC, the FMC begins listening on TCP port 8305.

Example 7-7 shows the transition of TCP port 8305 on FTD and the FMC during the registration process.

Example 7-7   *Verifying the Management Port Status*

```
! First, on the CLI of an FTD, when you enter the FMC detail, it opens the TCP port
  8305 on FTD.

admin@FTD:~$ sudo netstat -antp | grep -i 8305
tcp        0      0 10.1.1.2:8305           0.0.0.0:*             LISTEN
  933/sftunnel
admin@FTD:~$


! Then, on the GUI of an FMC, when you enter the FTD detail, the FMC begins
  listening on TCP port 8305. FMC responses the FTD's registration request from a
  random port 49707.

admin@FMC:~$ sudo netstat -antp | grep -i 8305
tcp        0      0 10.1.1.16:8305          0.0.0.0:*             LISTEN
  10095/sftunnel
tcp        0      0 10.1.1.16:49707         10.1.1.2:8305         ESTABLISHED
  10095/sftunnel
root@FMC:~#


! Upon a successful registration, the connections appear fully established on the
  FMC.

admin@FMC:~$ sudo netstat -antp | grep -i 8305
tcp        0      0 10.1.1.16:49707         10.1.1.2:8305         ESTABLISHED
  10095/sftunnel
tcp        0      0 10.1.1.16:8305          10.1.1.2:54998        ESTABLISHED
  10095/sftunnel
admin@FMC:~$
```

If the port status does not change from the listening state to the established state, the FMC may not have received any registration requests from FTD, or FTD may have not received any acknowledgements from the FMC. Let's take a look at what happens at the packet level during the registration process.

Caution   The following two examples use the built-in packet capture tools in FTD and the FMC to display the transactions of packets. Capturing packets in a product system can impact system performance. Therefore, if necessary, you should run this tool only during a maintenance window or in a lab environment.

Example 7-8 shows the exchange of packets right after you begin the registration process, which is after adding the FMC in the FTD CLI. Because at this stage you have not yet entered the details of FTD on the FMC, the FMC (IP address 10.1.1.6) keeps sending the RESET packets in response to the SYN packets from the FTD (IP address 10.1.1.2).

Example 7-8   *Packet Transaction After Adding an FMC on the FTD CLI*

```
! Capturing Packets on the FTD Management Interface

> capture-traffic

Please choose domain to capture traffic from:
  0 - br1

Selection? 0

Please specify tcpdump options desired.
(or enter '?' for a list of supported options)
Options: host 10.1.1.16

HS_PACKET_BUFFER_SIZE is set to 4.
tcpdump: verbose output suppressed, use -v or -vv for full protocol decode
listening on br1, link-type EN10MB (Ethernet), capture size 96 bytes

[timestamp] IP FTD.46373 > 10.1.1.16.8305: Flags [S], seq 1709676008, win 14600,
  options [mss 1460,sackOK,TS val 87180 ecr 0,nop,wscale 7], length 0
[timestamp] IP 10.1.1.16.8305 > FTD.46373: Flags [R.], seq 0, ack 1709676009, win 0,
  length 0
[timestamp] IP FTD.58441 > 10.1.1.16.8305: Flags [S], seq 3021847438, win 14600,
  options [mss 1460,sackOK,TS val 87380 ecr 0,nop,wscale 7], length 0
[timestamp] IP 10.1.1.16.8305 > FTD.58441: Flags [R.], seq 0, ack 3021847439, win 0,
  length 0
[timestamp] IP FTD.46814 > 10.1.1.16.8305: Flags [S], seq 1334198689, win 14600,
  options [mss 1460,sackOK,TS val 88317 ecr 0,nop,wscale 7], length 0
[timestamp] IP 10.1.1.16.8305 > FTD.46814: Flags [R.], seq 0, ack 1334198690, win 0,
  length 0
[timestamp] IP FTD.45854 > 10.1.1.16.8305: Flags [S], seq 1274367969, win 14600,
  options [mss 1460,sackOK,TS val 88517 ecr 0,nop,wscale 7], length 0
[timestamp] IP 10.1.1.16.8305 > FTD.45854: Flags [R.], seq 0, ack 1274367970, win 0,
  length 0
```

```
.
.
<Output Omitted>




! Capturing Packets on the FMC Management Interface

admin@FMC:~$ sudo tcpdump -i eth0 host 10.1.1.2
Password:

HS_PACKET_BUFFER_SIZE is set to 4.
tcpdump: verbose output suppressed, use -v or -vv for full protocol decode
listening on eth0, link-type EN10MB (Ethernet), capture size 96 bytes


[timestamp] IP 10.1.1.2.46373 > FMC.8305: Flags [S], seq 1709676008, win 14600,
  options [mss 1460,sackOK,TS val 87180 ecr 0,nop,wscale 7], length 0
[timestamp] IP FMC.8305 > 10.1.1.2.46373: Flags [R.], seq 0, ack 1709676009, win 0,
  length 0
[timestamp] IP 10.1.1.2.58441 > FMC.8305: Flags [S], seq 3021847438, win 14600,
  options [mss 1460,sackOK,TS val 87380 ecr 0,nop,wscale 7], length 0
[timestamp] IP FMC.8305 > 10.1.1.2.58441: Flags [R.], seq 0, ack 3021847439, win 0,
  length 0
[timestamp] IP 10.1.1.2.46814 > FMC.8305: Flags [S], seq 1334198689, win 14600,
  options [mss 1460,sackOK,TS val 88317 ecr 0,nop,wscale 7], length 0
[timestamp] IP FMC.8305 > 10.1.1.2.46814: Flags [R.], seq 0, ack 1334198690, win 0,
  length 0
[timestamp] IP 10.1.1.2.45854 > FMC.8305: Flags [S], seq 1274367969, win 14600,
  options [mss 1460,sackOK,TS val 88517 ecr 0,nop,wscale 7], length 0
[timestamp] IP FMC.8305 > 10.1.1.2.45854: Flags [R.], seq 0, ack 1274367970, win 0,
  length 0
.
.
<Output Omitted>
```

Example 7-9 shows the next phase of the registration process. As soon as you enter the FTD details on the web interface of the FMC, the FMC stops sending RESET packets.

Example 7-9 *Packet Transaction After Adding the FTD on the FMC GUI*

```
! On the FMC Interface


.
<Output Omitted>
.
```

```
[timestamp] IP FMC.51509 > 10.1.1.2.8305: Flags [S], seq 1804119299, win 14600,
  options [mss 1460,sackOK,TS val 258976 ecr 0,nop,wscale 7], length 0
[timestamp] IP 10.1.1.2.8305 > FMC.51509: Flags [S.], seq 4103916511, ack
  1804119300, win 14480, options [mss 1460,sackOK,TS val 93418 ecr 258976,nop,
  wscale 7], length 0
[timestamp] IP FMC.51509 > 10.1.1.2.8305: Flags [.], ack 1, win 115, options
  [nop,nop,TS val 258976 ecr 93418], length 0
[timestamp] IP FMC.51509 > 10.1.1.2.8305: Flags [P.], ack 1, win 115, options
  [nop,nop,TS val 258985 ecr 93418], length 247
[timestamp] IP 10.1.1.2.8305 > FMC.51509: Flags [.], ack 248, win 122, options
  [nop,nop,TS val 93422 ecr 258985], length 0
[timestamp] IP 10.1.1.2.8305 > FMC.51509: Flags [.], ack 248, win 122, options
  [nop,nop,TS val 93423 ecr 258985], length 1448
[timestamp] IP 10.1.1.2.8305 > FMC.51509: Flags [P.], ack 248, win 122, options
  [nop,nop,TS val 93423 ecr 258985], length 774
 .
<Output Omitted>
 .

! Press the Control+C keys to exit and stop capturing.




! On the FTD Interface


 .
<Output Omitted>
 .

[timestamp] IP 10.1.1.16.51509 > FTD.8305: Flags [S], seq 1804119299, win 14600,
  options [mss 1460,sackOK,TS val 258976 ecr 0,nop,wscale 7], length 0
[timestamp] IP FTD.8305 > 10.1.1.16.51509: Flags [S.], seq 4103916511, ack
  1804119300, win 14480, options [mss 1460,sackOK,TS val 93418 ecr 258976,nop,
  wscale 7], length 0
[timestamp] IP 10.1.1.16.51509 > FTD.8305: Flags [.], ack 1, win 115, options
  [nop,nop,TS val 258976 ecr 93418], length 0
[timestamp] IP 10.1.1.16.51509 > FTD.8305: Flags [P.], ack 1, win 115, options
  [nop,nop,TS val 258985 ecr 93418], length 247
[timestamp] IP FTD.8305 > 10.1.1.16.51509: Flags [.], ack 248, win 122, options
  [nop,nop,TS val 93422 ecr 258985], length 0
[timestamp] IP FTD.8305 > 10.1.1.16.51509: Flags [.], ack 248, win 122, options
  [nop,nop,TS val 93423 ecr 258985], length 1448
[timestamp] IP FTD.8305 > 10.1.1.16.51509: Flags [P.], ack 248, win 122, options
  [nop,nop,TS val 93423 ecr 258985], length 774
 .
<Output Omitted>
 .

! Press the Control+C keys to exit and stop capturing.
```

If you do not notice any activity on the management interfaces, check whether the TCP port 8305 is bidirectionally allowed on any intermediate network devices between the FMC and FTD. You can test this by connecting to the TCP port 8305 of FTD from the FMC directly.

Example 7-10 shows a successful telnet connection from the FMC to FTD port 8305. It confirms that FTD port 8305 (IP address 10.1.1.2) is allowed by any intermediate router or firewall.

Example 7-10   *Successful Telnet Connection from the FMC to FTD Port 8305*

```
admin@FMC:~$ telnet 10.1.1.2 8305
Trying 10.1.1.2...
Connected to 10.1.1.2.
Escape character is '^]'.
^]              ! Press the Ctrl and ] keys together
telnet> quit
Connection closed.
admin@fmc:~$
```

Analyzing the Encrypted SFTunnel

The FMC and FTD complete their registration process through the SFTunnel—an encrypted communication channel between the management interfaces of the FMC and FTD. Using TCP port 8305, FTD and the FMC establish this channel to complete any administrative tasks between them, such as registering FTD with the FMC, exchanging keepalive heartbeats, receiving new security policies and configurations from the FMC, sending security events to the FMC, synchronizing time with the FMC, and so on.

The **netstat** or **tcpdump** command that you ran earlier confirms the establishment of a tunnel between the FMC and FTD. However, it does not display what happens inside an encrypted tunnel at the application level. The Firepower System provides a command-line tool, **sftunnel-status**, that shows the status of each of the services running through an encrypted secure tunnel.

Example 7-11 shows output of the **sftunnel-status** command on FTD. From the output, you can conclude that the logical management interface of FTD (name br1, IP address 10.1.1.2) is connected to the management interface of the FMC (name eth0, IP address 10.1.1.16). Two channels, A and B, are connected for control packets and event traffic, respectively. The tunnel is encrypted using the AES256-GCM-SHA384 cipher.

Example 7-11   *Output of the* **sftunnel-status** *Command in FTD*

```
> sftunnel-status

SFTUNNEL Start Time: Sun Dec 11 23:51:56 2016

        Both IPv4 and IPv6 connectivity is supported
        Broadcast count = 2
        Reserved SSL connections: 0
        Management Interfaces: 1
        br1 (control events) 10.1.1.2,


**********************

**RUN STATUS****10.1.1.16*************
        Cipher used = AES256-GCM-SHA384 (strength:256 bits)
        ChannelA Connected: Yes, Interface br1
        Cipher used = AES256-GCM-SHA384 (strength:256 bits)
        ChannelB Connected: Yes, Interface br1
        Registration: Completed.
        IPv4 Connection to peer '10.1.1.16' Start Time: Mon Dec 12 00:13:44 2016


PEER INFO:
        sw_version 6.1.0
        sw_build 330
        Management Interfaces: 1
        eth0 (control events) 10.1.1.16,
        Peer channel Channel-A is valid  type (CONTROL), using 'br1', connected
to '10.1.1.16' via '10.1.1.2'
        Peer channel Channel-B is valid  type (EVENT), using 'br1', connected to
 '10.1.1.16' via '10.1.1.2'

        TOTAL TRANSMITTED MESSAGES <24> for Health Events service
        RECEIVED MESSAGES <12> for Health Events service
        SEND MESSAGES <12> for Health Events service
        HALT REQUEST SEND COUNTER <0> for Health Events service
        STORED MESSAGES for Health service (service 0/peer 0)
        STATE <Process messages> for Health Events service
        REQUESTED FOR REMOTE <Process messages> for Health Events service
        REQUESTED FROM REMOTE <Process messages> for Health Events service


        TOTAL TRANSMITTED MESSAGES <3> for Identity service
        RECEIVED MESSAGES <2> for Identity service
```

```
         SEND MESSAGES <1> for Identity service
         HALT REQUEST SEND COUNTER <0> for Identity service
         STORED MESSAGES for Identity service (service 0/peer 0)
         STATE <Process messages> for Identity service
         REQUESTED FOR REMOTE <Process messages> for Identity service
         REQUESTED FROM REMOTE <Process messages> for Identity service


         TOTAL TRANSMITTED MESSAGES <76> for RPC service
         RECEIVED MESSAGES <38> for RPC service
         SEND MESSAGES <38> for RPC service
         HALT REQUEST SEND COUNTER <0> for RPC service
         STORED MESSAGES for RPC service (service 0/peer 0)
         STATE <Process messages> for RPC service
         REQUESTED FOR REMOTE <Process messages> for RPC service
         REQUESTED FROM REMOTE <Process messages> for RPC service


         TOTAL TRANSMITTED MESSAGES <41> for IP(NTP) service
         RECEIVED MESSAGES <27> for IP(NTP) service
         SEND MESSAGES <14> for IP(NTP) service
         HALT REQUEST SEND COUNTER <0> for IP(NTP) service
         STORED MESSAGES for IP(NTP) service (service 0/peer 0)
         STATE <Process messages> for IP(NTP) service
         REQUESTED FOR REMOTE <Process messages> for IP(NTP) service
         REQUESTED FROM REMOTE <Process messages> for IP(NTP) service


         TOTAL TRANSMITTED MESSAGES <5> for IDS Events service
         RECEIVED MESSAGES <0> for service IDS Events service
         SEND MESSAGES <5> for IDS Events service
         HALT REQUEST SEND COUNTER <0> for IDS Events service
         STORED MESSAGES for IDS Events service (service 0/peer 0)
         STATE <Process messages> for IDS Events service
         REQUESTED FOR REMOTE <Process messages> for IDS Events service
         REQUESTED FROM REMOTE <Process messages> for IDS Events service
.
.
<Output omitted for brevity>
.
.
         Heartbeat Send Time:     Mon Dec 12 00:28:17 2016
         Heartbeat Received Time: Mon Dec 12 00:29:35 2016
```

```
************************
**RPC STATUS****10.1.1.16*************
  'ip' => '10.1.1.16',
  'uuid' => '7d3aa42c-95c7-11e6-a825-2c6c588f5f38',
  'ipv6' => 'IPv6 is not configured for management',
  'name' => '10.1.1.16',
  'active' => '1',
  'uuid_gw' => '',
  'last_changed' => 'Wed Oct 19 17:56:43 2016'

Check routes:


>
```

You can view similar statistics on an FMC by running the **sftunnel_status.pl** tool. By comparing the data on both devices, FMC and FTD, you can determine any potential issues with the SFTunnel. This is the command syntax on the FMC:

```
admin@FMC:~$ sudo sftunnel_status.pl <Management_IP_Address_of_the_FTD>
```

Example 7-12 shows output of the **sftunnel_status.pl** tool in the FMC. It confirms that the FMC (IP address 10.1.1.16) is registered with FTD (IP address 10.1.1.2) and is communicating actively.

Example 7-12   *Output of the* sftunnel_status.pl *Tool in the FMC*

```
admin@FMC:~$ sudo sftunnel_status.pl 10.1.1.2
Password:


Check peer 10.1.1.2 at /usr/local/sf/bin/sftunnel_status.pl line 19
SFTUNNEL Start Time: Mon Dec 12 01:17:21 2016


        Key File  = /etc/sf/keys/sftunnel-key.pem
        Cert File = /etc/sf/keys/sftunnel-cert.pem
        CA Cert   = /etc/sf/ca_root/cacert.pem
        FIPS,STIG,CC = 0,0,0
        Both IPv4 and IPv6 connectivity is supported
        Broadcast count = 1
        Reserved SSL connections: 0
        Management Interfaces: 1
        eth0 (control events) 10.1.1.16,


************************
```

```
**RUN STATUS****10.1.1.2*************
        Cipher used = AES256-GCM-SHA384 (strength:256 bits)
        ChannelA Connected: Yes, Interface eth0
        Cipher used = AES256-GCM-SHA384 (strength:256 bits)
        ChannelB Connected: Yes, Interface eth0
        Registration: Completed.
        IPv4 Connection to peer '10.1.1.2' Start Time: Mon Dec 12 02:58:54 2016

PEER INFO:
        sw_version 6.1.0
        sw_build 330
        Management Interfaces: 1
        br1 (control events) 10.1.1.2,
        Peer channel Channel-A is valid  type (CONTROL), using 'eth0', connected to
   '10.1.1.2' via '10.1.1.16'
        Peer channel Channel-B is valid  type (EVENT), using 'eth0', connected to
   '10.1.1.2' via '10.1.1.16'

        TOTAL TRANSMITTED MESSAGES <20> for Health Events service
        RECEIVED MESSAGES <10> for Health Events service
        SEND MESSAGES <10> for Health Events service
        HALT REQUEST SEND COUNTER <0> for Health Events service
        STORED MESSAGES for Health service (service 0/peer 0)
        STATE <Process messages> for Health Events service
        REQUESTED FOR REMOTE <Process messages> for Health Events service
        REQUESTED FROM REMOTE <Process messages> for Health Events service

        TOTAL TRANSMITTED MESSAGES <3> for Identity service
        RECEIVED MESSAGES <1> for Identity service
        SEND MESSAGES <2> for Identity service
        HALT REQUEST SEND COUNTER <0> for Identity service
        STORED MESSAGES for Identity service (service 0/peer 0)
        STATE <Process messages> for Identity service
        REQUESTED FOR REMOTE <Process messages> for Identity service
        REQUESTED FROM REMOTE <Process messages> for Identity service
   .
   .
<Output omitted>
```

After comparing the SFTunnel statistics on the FMC and FTD, if you notice any anomaly, you can use the **manage_procs.pl** tool in FTD to restart the channels between the FMC and FTD.

> **Caution** If you run the **manage_procs.pl** tool on the FMC, and the FMC is currently managing many FTD devices, it restarts the communication channel between the FMC and all the FTD devices at the same time. If you need to restart the channel between the FMC and one particular FTD device only, you should run the **manage_procs.pl** tool on the Expert Mode of the desired FTD.

Example 7-13 shows the operation of the **manage_procs.pl** tool on the Expert Mode of FTD. Select option 3 to restart the communication channel.

Example 7-13 *Menu of the* **manage_procs.pl** *Tool*

```
> expert
admin@FTD:~$ sudo manage_procs.pl
Password:
****************  Configuration Utility  *************

  1   Reconfigure Correlator
  2   Reconfigure and flush Correlator
  3   Restart Comm. channel
  4   Update routes
  5   Reset all routes
  6   Validate Network
  0   Exit


**************************************************************
Enter choice: 3

****************  Configuration Utility  *************

  1   Reconfigure Correlator
  2   Reconfigure and flush Correlator
  3   Restart Comm. channel
  4   Update routes
  5   Reset all routes
  6   Validate Network
  0   Exit


**************************************************************
Enter choice: 0
Thank you
admin@FTD:~$
```

While the channel restarts, the system generates debug logs for stopping and starting various services. These logs provide detailed insight about the Firepower System's communication at the application level and allow you to determine any complex communication issues.

Example 7-14 shows the debugging of a restart process from the FMC CLI. As soon as you begin the process in FTD, the FMC fails to connect to FTD. After the connection to FTD (IP address 10.1.1.2) is closed, the FMC (IP address 10.1.1.16) automatically begins the connection reestablishment process with the FTD.

Example 7-14 *Debugging Logs Generated During Communication Channel Restart*

```
admin@FMC:~$ sudo tail -f /var/log/messages | grep 10.1.1.2
Password:


! The following message appears on an FMC as soon as you begin the process on the
  FTD. It confirms that the FMC is unable to connect to the FTD.


[timestamp] sftunneld:sf_connections [INFO] Unable to receive message from peer
  10.1.1.2:Closed

[timestamp] sftunneld:sf_channel [INFO] >> ChannelState dropChannel peer 10.1.1.2 /
  channelA / CONTROL [ msgSock & ssl_context ] <<

[timestamp] sftunneld:sf_connections [INFO] Exiting channel (recv). Peer 10.1.1.2
  closed connection on interface eth0.

[timestamp] sftunneld:sf_connections [INFO] Failed to send in control channel for
  peer 10.1.1.2 (eth0)

[timestamp] sftunneld:sf_channel [INFO] >> ChannelState dropChannel peer 10.1.1.2 /
  channelA / DROPPED [ msgSock & ssl_context ] <<

[timestamp] sftunneld:sf_channel [INFO] >> ChannelState freeChannel peer 10.1.1.2 /
  channelA / DROPPED [ msgSock & ssl_context ] <<

[timestamp] sftunneld:sf_connections [INFO] Need to send SW version and Published
  Services to 10.1.1.2

[timestamp] sftunneld:sf_channel [INFO] >> ChannelState do_dataio_for_heartbeat peer
  10.1.1.2 / channelB / EVENT [ msgSock2 & ssl_context2 ] <<

[timestamp] sftunneld:control_services [INFO] Successfully Send Interfaces info to
  peer 10.1.1.2 over eth0

[timestamp] sftunneld:sf_connections [INFO] Unable to receive message from peer
  10.1.1.2:Closed

[timestamp] sftunneld:sf_channel [INFO] >> ChannelState dropChannel peer 10.1.1.2 /
  channelB / EVENT [ msgSock2 & ssl_context2 ] <<

[timestamp] sftunneld:sf_connections [INFO] Exiting channel (recv). Peer 10.1.1.2
  closed connection on interface eth0.

[timestamp] sftunneld:sf_connections [INFO] Failed to send in control channel for
  peer 10.1.1.2 (eth0)

[timestamp] sftunneld:sf_channel [INFO] >> ChannelState dropChannel peer 10.1.1.2 /
  channelB / DROPPED [ msgSock2 & ssl_context2 ] <<

[timestamp] sftunneld:sf_channel [INFO] >> ChannelState freeChannel peer 10.1.1.2 /
  channelB / DROPPED [ msgSock2 & ssl_context2 ] <<
```

```
[timestamp] sftunneld:sf_connections [INFO] ChannelState Peer 10.1.1.2 TOP OF THE
    LOOP CHANNEL COUNT 0
[timestamp] sftunneld:sf_connections [INFO] <<<<<<<<<<<<<<<<<<<<<<< ShutDownPeer
    10.1.1.2 >>>>>>>>>>>>>>>>>>>>>>>>
[timestamp] sfmgr:sfmanager [INFO] Exiting child-sftunnel for peer '10.1.1.2'.
    (relocated unix socket?)
[timestamp] sfmgr:sfmanager [INFO] Exiting child thread for peer 10.1.1.2
[timestamp] sfmgr:sfmanager [INFO] WRITE_THREAD:Terminated sftunnel write thread for
    peer 10.1.1.2
[timestamp] sftunneld:stream_file [INFO] Stream CTX destroyed for 10.1.1.2
[timestamp] sftunneld:sf_channel [INFO] >> ChannelState ShutDownPeer peer 10.1.1.2 /
    channelA / DROPPED [ msgSock & ssl context ] <<
[timestamp] sftunneld:sf_channel [INFO] >> ChannelState ShutDownPeer peer 10.1.1.2 /
    channelB / NONE [ msgSock & ssl_context ] <<
[timestamp] sftunneld:sf_connections [INFO] Peer 10.1.1.2 needs re-connect
[timestamp] sfmbservice:sfmb_service [INFO] Bad read/Connection closed to host
    10.1.1.2
[timestamp] sfmbservice:sfmb_service [INFO] Connection closed to host 10.1.1.2
[timestamp] sfmbservice:sfmb_service [INFO] (4)Exiting child for peer 10.1.1.2.
[timestamp] sfmbservice:sfmb_service [INFO] (2)Exiting child for peer 10.1.1.2


! Shortly after the FMC closes connection with the FTD, it automatically starts
    accepting connections from the FTD, and reestablishes connections with the FTD.


[timestamp] sftunneld:tunnsockets [INFO] Accepted IPv4 connection from
    10.1.1.2:34088/tcp
[timestamp] sftunneld:sf_ssl [INFO] Processing connection from 10.1.1.2:34088/tcp
    (socket 10)
[timestamp] sftunneld:sf_ssl [INFO] Accepted SSL connection from: 10.1.1.2:34088/tcp
[timestamp] sftunneld:sf_peers [INFO] Peer 10.1.1.2 needs the first connection
[timestamp] sftunneld:sf_ssl [INFO] Verify accepted: Need a new connection for peer
    10.1.1.2 (1)
[timestamp] sftunneld:sf_ssl [INFO] Peer 10.1.1.2 supports multiple ports
[timestamp] sftunneld:sf_ssl [INFO] Peer 10.1.1.2 supports separate events
    connection
[timestamp] sftunneld:sf_ssl [INFO] Peer 10.1.1.2 registration is complete remotely
[timestamp] sftunneld:sf_peers [INFO] Peer 10.1.1.2 needs the first connection
[timestamp] sftunneld:sf_ssl [INFO] Accept: Will start a child thread for peer
    '10.1.1.2'
[timestamp] sftunneld:sf_ssl [INFO] Accept: Start child thread for peer '10.1.1.2'
[timestamp] sftunneld:sf_channel [INFO] >>>>>>> initChannels peer: 10.1.1.2 <<<<<<
[timestamp] sftunneld:stream_file [INFO] Stream CTX initialized for 10.1.1.2
[timestamp] sftunneld:sf_connections [INFO] Peer 10.1.1.2 main thread started
[timestamp] sftunneld:control_services [INFO] Successfully Send Interfaces info to
    peer 10.1.1.2 over eth0
```

```
[timestamp] sftunneld:sf_heartbeat [INFO] Saved SW VERSION from peer 10.1.1.2
  (6.1.0)


[timestamp] sftunneld:sf_connections [INFO] Need to send SW version and Published
  Services to 10.1.1.2
[timestamp] sftunneld:sf_channel [INFO] >> ChannelState do_dataio_for_heartbeat peer
  10.1.1.2 / channelA / CONTROL [ msgSock & ssl_context ] <<
[timestamp] sftunneld:control_services [INFO] Interface br1 from 10.1.1.2 supports
  'control events'
[timestamp] sftunneld:control_services [INFO] Interface br1 from 10.1.1.2 supports
  events
[timestamp] sftunneld:control_services [INFO] Interface br1 (10.1.1.2) from 10.1.1.2
  is up
[timestamp] sftunneld:control_services [INFO] Peer 10.1.1.2 Notified that it is NOT
  configured for dedicated events interface
[timestamp] sftunneld:sf_connections [INFO] Need to send SW version and Published
  Services to 10.1.1.2
[timestamp] sftunneld:sf_channel [INFO] >> ChannelState do_dataio_for_heartbeat peer
  10.1.1.2 / channelA / CONTROL [ msgSock & ssl_context ] <<
[timestamp] sftunneld:sf_heartbeat [INFO] Saved SW VERSION from peer 10.1.1.2
  (6.1.0)
[timestamp] sfmgr:sfmanager [INFO] Established connection to sftunnel for peer
  10.1.1.2 (fd 8)
.

.

<Output omitted for brevity>
.

.

[timestamp] sftunneld:sf_heartbeat [INFO] Identity Service is published for peer
  10.1.1.2
[timestamp] sftunneld:sf_peers [INFO] Using a 20 entry queue for 10.1.1.2 - 7770
[timestamp] sfmbservice:sfmb_service [INFO] Start getting MB messages for 10.1.1.2
[timestamp] sfmbservice:sfmb_service [INFO] Established connection to peer 10.1.1.2
[timestamp] sftunneld:sf_heartbeat [INFO] Message Broker Service is published for
  peer 10.1.1.2
```

Summary

This chapter describes licensing and registration—two important initial tasks in Firepower deployment. In this chapter, you have learned the capabilities of different Firepower licenses and the steps to register the FMC with a Smart Licensing Server. This chapter also discusses the registration process and the tools you can use to investigate communication issues.

Quiz

1. Which tool is used in FTD to view the statistics of events inside the encrypted tunnel between FTD and the FMC?

   a. > **sftunnel**

   b. > **sftunnel-status**

   c. > **sftunnel_status**

   d. > **sftunnel status**

2. Which command confirms whether FTD is registered with the FMC?

   a. > **show fmc**

   b. > **show console**

   c. > **show managers**

   d. > **show registration**

3. Which statement about registration is incorrect?

   a. Always begin the registration process from FTD.

   b. NAT ID is necessary only when there is an intermediate NAT device between the FMC and FTD.

   c. Before registering FTD, the FMC must be connected to a license server.

   d. FTD and FMC use port 8305 for registration and management communication purposes.

4. Which command shows the logs between the FMC and a Smart Licensing Server?

   a. **sudo tail -f /var/log/messages**

   b. **sudo tail -f /var/log/messages.log**

   c. **sudo tail -f /var/log/cssm.log**

   d. **sudo tail -f /var/log/sam.log**

5. Which tool allows you to restart the communication channel between the FMC and FTD?

   a. **sftunnel_status.pl**

   b. **sftunnel_restart.pl**

   c. **manage_procs.pl**

   d. **manage_channel.pl**

6. Which statement is correct about the Smart Licensing architecture?

   a. Evaluation Mode allows you to test certain features but not all of them.

   b. FTD connects to the Smart Licensing Server to obtain licenses.

   c. The Cisco satellite server is an on-premises virtual machine.

   d. To register the FMC with the Smart Licensing Server, run the command **configure manager add** <*IP_Address_of_the_CSSM*>

Chapter 8

Firepower Deployment in Routed Mode

You can deploy a Firepower Threat Defense (FTD) device as a default gateway for your network so that the hosts can communicate with the FTD device in order to connect to any different subnet or the Internet. You can also deploy an FTD device transparently, so that it becomes invisible to the hosts in your network. In short, you can deploy an FTD device in two ways—Routed Mode and Transparent Mode. This chapter describes the processes involved in deploying an FTD device in routed mode. Chapter 9, "Firepower Deployment in Transparent Mode," covers Transparent Mode.

Routed Mode Essentials

In Routed Mode, FTD performs like a Layer 3 hop. Each interface on an FTD device connects to a different subnet. If configured to do so, an FTD device can act as a default gateway for any particular subnet and can route traffic between different subnets.

Figure 8-1 shows how a host interacts with an FTD device as its next Layer 3 hop. In Routed Mode, each FTD interface connects to a unique subnet.

Figure 8-2 shows the default gateways on each segment when an FTD device is deployed in a typical real-world network. The end users on a LAN use the FTD physical interface as their gateway. An FTD device can also use its inside interface as the default gateway for its management communication.

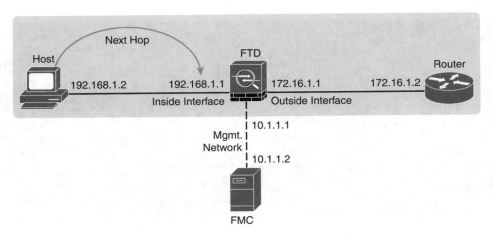

Figure 8-1 *Communication of a Host with an FTD Device in Routed Mode*

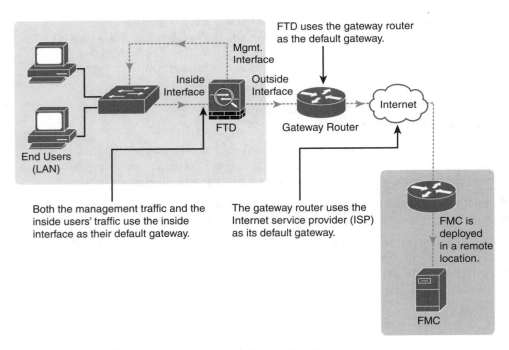

Figure 8-2 *Deploying an FTD Device in Routed Mode*

Best Practices for Routed Mode Configuration

If you want to deploy FTD in Routed Mode, consider the following suggestions:

- Cisco recommends that you not configure the diagnostic interface with an IP address. This simplifies the network design and reduces configuration overhead. When a diagnostic interface is configured with an IP address, FTD considers it a data interface. Each data interface on an FTD device is required to be on a different network. Therefore, the diagnostic interface (which must be on the same subnet as the logical management interface, br1) and the inside interface must be on two different subnets. To transfer traffic between two different subnetworks, a router is required.

- Changing the firewall mode wipes out any existing FTD configurations. Therefore, before you change the firewall mode from Transparent to Routed or vice versa, take note of your FTD configuration settings for future reference, in case you want to revert the FTD to the initial state. To view the current FTD configuration, run the **show running-config** command in the CLI.

If you just want to change the firewall mode on an FTD device, performing a backup of your security policy configuration is not necessary because the next-generation security policies are defined and stored on the FMC. After you configure the policies, FMC allows you to deploy the same policies to one or more FTD devices.

Configuring Routed Mode

Do you remember the last part of the FTD installation and initialization process? During the initialization, FTD prompts to confirm the firewall mode, and you can select between Routed Mode and Transparent Mode (see Example 8-1).

Example 8-1 *Configuring the Firewall Mode During the Initialization*

```
<Output Omitted>
.
.
.
Manage the device locally? (yes/no) [yes]: no
Configure firewall mode? (routed/transparent) [routed]:
Configuring firewall mode ...
Update policy deployment information
    - add device configuration
    - add network discovery
    - add system policy
.
.
.
<Output Omitted>
```

If you selected Routed Mode during the system initialization, you can skip the next two sections and read the section "Configuring the Routed Interfaces." If you selected Transparent Mode, read on.

Fulfilling Prerequisites

If you selected Transparent Mode during the system initialization and now you want to reconfigure FTD to Routed Mode, you must unregister FTD from the FMC. You cannot change the firewall mode when a manager is configured. To verify whether FTD is currently registered with the FMC, run the **show managers** command at the FTD CLI.

Example 8-2 shows that FTD is currently registered with the FMC with IP address 10.1.1.16.

Example 8-2   *Verifying the Registration Status—FTD Is Currently Registered*

```
> show managers
Type                    : Manager
Host                    : 10.1.1.16
Registration            : Completed
>
```

If you find that FTD is currently registered with the FMC, you can unregister it from the FMC web interface. To delete registration, go to the **Devices > Device Management** page and click the delete icon next to FTD (see Figure 8-3).

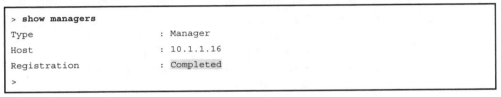

Figure 8-3   *Deleting a Firepower Registration*

Example 8-3 shows confirmation that FTD is currently not registered with the FMC.

Example 8-3   *Verifying the Registration Status—FTD Is Not Registered*

```
> show managers
No managers configured.
>
```

Configuring the Firewall Mode

If FTD is currently not registered with the FMC, you can change the firewall deployment mode. To configure an FTD with Routed Mode, log in to the FTD CLI and run the **configure firewall routed** command (see Example 8-4).

Example 8-4 *Configuring the Routed Mode*

```
> configure firewall routed

This will destroy the current interface configurations, are you sure that you want
  to proceed? [y/N] y
The firewall mode was changed successfully.
```

After configuring FTD with the desired mode, you can determine the status from the CLI. Example 8-5 shows confirmation that FTD is configured to Routed Mode.

Example 8-5 *Verifying the Firewall Deployment Mode*

```
> show firewall
Firewall mode: Router
>
```

Alternatively, upon a successful registration, the web interface of the FMC also displays the current firewall deployment mode. You can view it at the **Devices > Device Management** page. Figure 8-4 indicates that FTD is configured in Routed Mode.

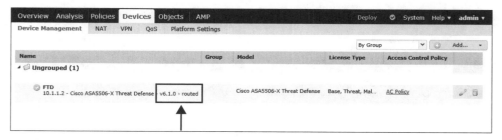

Figure 8-4 *Checking the Current FTD Deployment Mode*

Configuring the Routed Interface

In FTD, you can configure a data interface with a static IP address. FTD can also work as a DHCP client and obtain an IP address from a DHCP server. Furthermore, you can enable DHCP service on FTD to enable it to assign an IP address dynamically to its host.

Configuring an Interface with a Static IP Address

To configure a routed interface with a static IP address, follow these steps:

Step 1.   Navigate to the **Devices > Device Management** page. A list of the managed devices appears.

Step 2. Click the pencil icon that is next to the FTD device you want to configure. The device editor page appears, showing all the physical interfaces of an FTD device on the Interfaces tab (see Figure 8-5).

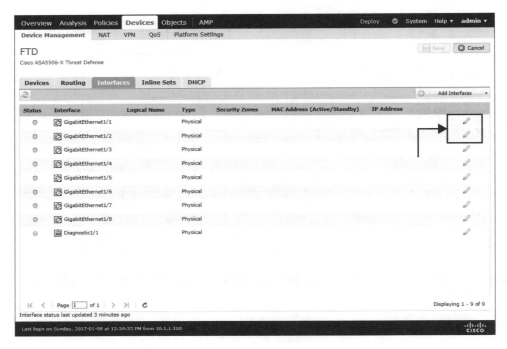

Figure 8-5 *The Interfaces Tab of the Device Editor Page*

Step 3. On the Interfaces tab, click the pencil icons next to GigabitEthernet1/1 and GigabitEthernet1/2 to configure these interfaces for the inside and outside networks. Use the settings shown in Table 8-1 to configure these two interfaces.

Table 8-1 *Configuration Settings for GigabitEthernet1/1 and GigabitEthernet1/2*

	GigabitEthernet1/1	GigabitEthernet1/2
Interface name	INSIDE_INTERFACE	OUTSIDE_INTERFACE
Security zone (optional)	INSIDE_ZONE	OUTSIDE_ZONE
IP address	192.168.1.1/24	172.16.1.1/24

Note To enable an interface, giving it a name is a requirement. However, configuring a security zone is an optional step.

Figure 8-6 shows these interfaces, which are each connected to two different subnets.

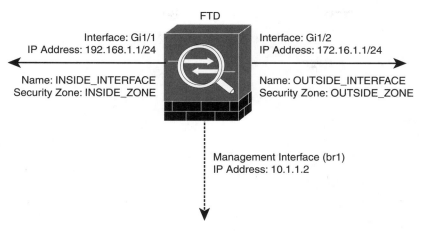

Figure 8-6 *Overview of FTD Interface Configurations*

Figure 8-7 shows the configurations on the GigabitEthernet1/1 interface that can act as the default gateway for the inside network.

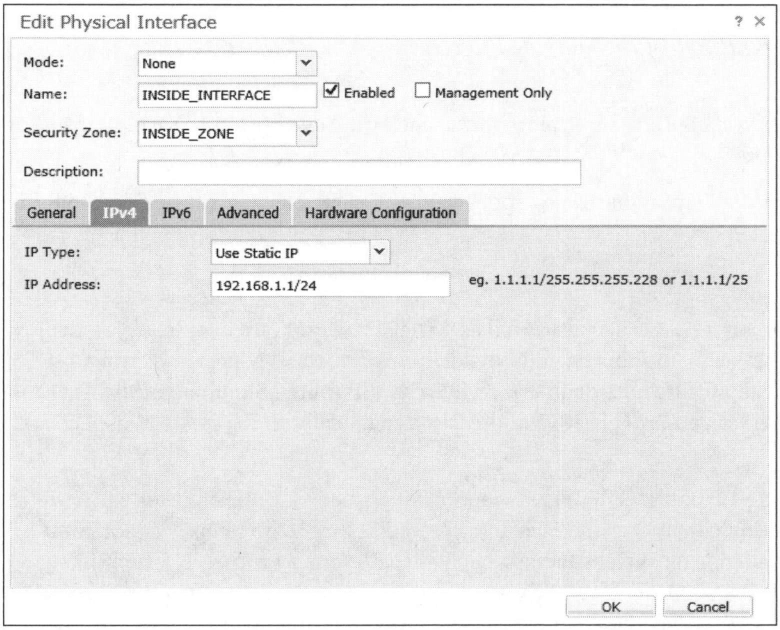

Figure 8-7 *Configurations of the Inside Interface GigabitEthernet1/1*

Figure 8-8 shows the configurations on the GigabitEthernet1/2 interface that is connected to the outside network.

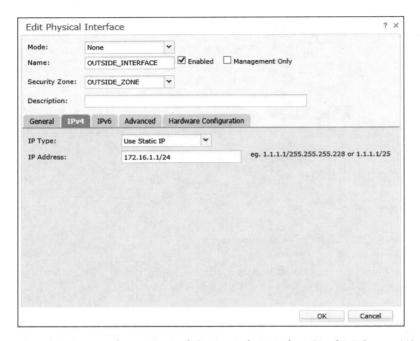

Figure 8-8   *Configurations of the Outside Interface GigabitEthernet1/2*

Step 4.   After you configure both interfaces, click the **Save** button to save the configurations.

Step 5.   Click the **Deploy** button to apply the configurations to FTD (see Figure 8-9).

DHCP Services

FTD can function as a DHCP server as well as a DHCP client. For example, if you deploy an FTD device between your inside and outside networks, the device can obtain an IP address dynamically for its outside interface from an ISP router. Simultaneously, FTD can act as a DHCP server and provide IPv4 addresses dynamically to the hosts it inspects.

Note   Configuring FTD as a DHCP server is an optional choice; it does not influence the deep packet inspection capability. The DHCP implementation on the Firepower software has limitations. It depends on various factors, such as the Internet Protocol version (IPv4 versus IPv6), FTD firewall mode (Routed versus Transparent), and the type of services (DHCP server versus DHCP relay). Read the official Cisco Firepower publications to find any version-specific limitations and enhancements.

Figure 8-9   *Saving the Configuration and Clicking the Deploy Button to Apply Changes*

Figure 8-10 illustrates two scenarios: The inside network obtains an IP address from the DHCP service running on FTD, while the outside interface of the FTD device gets an IP address from a service provider.

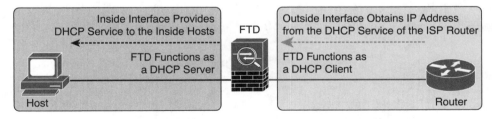

Figure 8-10   *FTD as a DHCP Server as well as a DHCP Client*

FTD as a DHCP Server

The following steps describe how to enable the DHCP service on an FTD device and allow the inside interface to provide IPv4 addresses to its connected host computers:

Step 1.   Go to the **Devices** > **Device Management** page and click the pencil icon to edit the FTD configuration.

Step 2.   Assign the static IP address 192.168.1.1 on GigabitEthernet1/1—the inside interface of FTD—as shown in Figure 8-11. Your end users (DHCP clients) will be using this IP address as their default gateway.

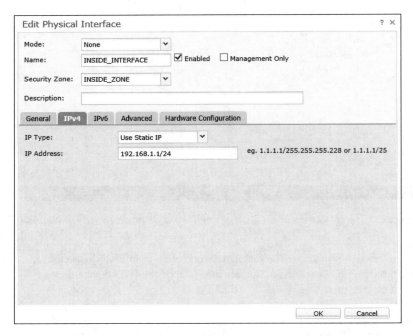

Figure 8-11   *Static IP Address Configuration on the Inside Interface*

Step 3.   In the device editor page, go to the DHCP tab. By default, the DHCP Server page appears.

Step 4.   Click the **Add** button in the Server tab (located in the bottom part of the DHCP Server page). The Add Server window appears.

Step 5.   In the Add Server window, select the inside interface from the dropdown list as it will be offering IP addresses to the inside network.

Step 6.   Create an address pool for the DHCP server. Remember that the addresses in the pool must be within the same subnet as the connected interface. For example, if you assign 192.168.1.1/24 to the inside interface, the DHCP address pool should be between 192.168.1.2 and 192.168.1.254.

Figure 8-12 shows that a DHCP server is enabled on the FTD inside interface with the address pool 192.168.1.2 to 192.168.1.10.

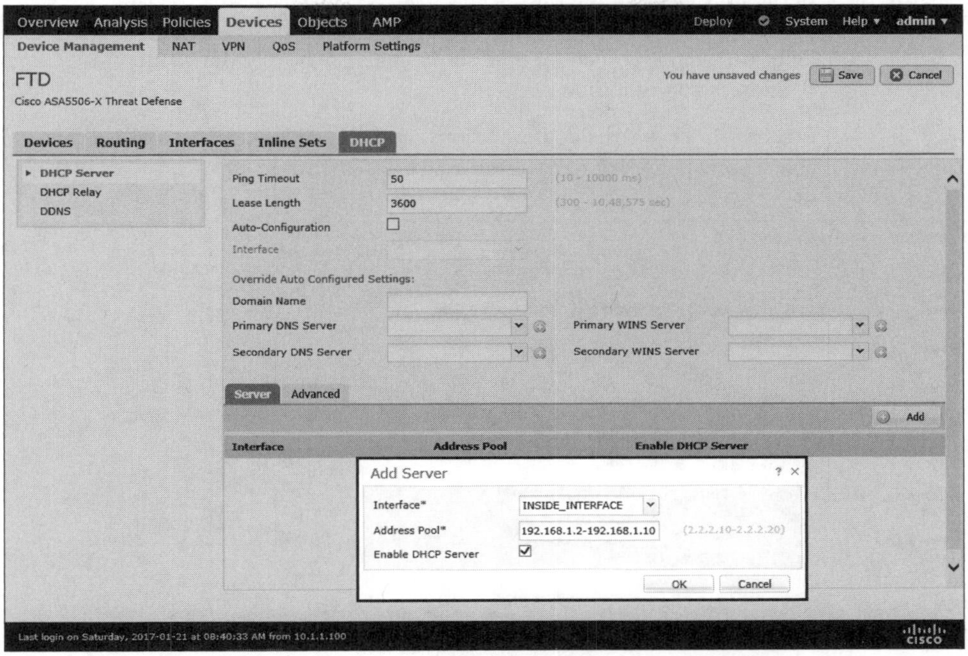

Figure 8-12 *DHCP Server FTD Configuration*

Step 7. Select the **Enable DHCP Server** check box to enable the service and click **OK**. You are returned to the device editor page.

Step 8. Optionally, through the DHCP service, transfer any DNS-related information to your DHCP clients. The DHCP Server page allows you to enter domain name and DNS addresses manually. Alternatively, you can select the **Auto-Configuration** check box to let FTD obtain any DNS information automatically from a DHCP client connected to a predefined interface.

Step 9. Click the **Save** button to save the configuration, and then click the **Deploy** button to apply the changes.

FTD as a DHCP Client

If you connect the outside interface of FTD with an Internet service provider (ISP), FTD can accept any dynamic IP address assigned by an ISP. To accept a DHCP offer from an external server, perform the following tasks in FTD:

Step 1. Go to the **Devices > Device Management** page and click the pencil icon next to the FTD device that you want to configure.

Step 2.   Edit the interface that is connected to an external DHCP server—in this example, the outside interface GigabitEthernet1/2.

Step 3.   In the Edit Physical Interface window, select the check box to enable the interface. Specify a name and a security zone for this interface. (Skip this step if you configured these items previously during the static IP address configuration.)

Figure 8-13 shows the configurations on the outside interface that will be able to obtain an IP address from a DHCP server.

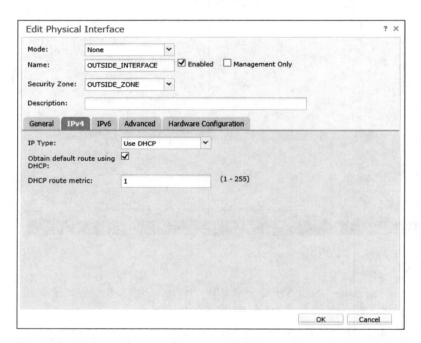

Figure 8-13   *Interface Configuration to Obtain an IP Address as a DHCP Client*

Step 4.   On the IPv4 tab, choose **Use DHCP** from the dropdown list and select the **Obtain Default Route Using DHCP** check box.

Step 5.   Click **OK** to exit the Edit Physical Interface window.

Step 6.   Click the **Save** button to save the configuration, and then click the **Deploy** button to apply the changes.

The outside interface now should see an offer from an external DHCP server.

Verification and Troubleshooting Tools

Once the ingress and egress interfaces are successfully configured and enabled, you should be able to ping from the inside network to the outside network and vice versa. While you run ICMP traffic, you can view the transaction of packets going through FTD by using the **debug** command.

Example 8-6 shows ICMP requests and replies exchanged between two computers located in inside and outside networks.

Example 8-6   *Debugging ICMP Traffic in FTD*

```
> debug icmp trace
debug icmp trace enabled at level 1
>
ICMP echo request from INSIDE_INTERFACE:192.168.1.2 to OUTSIDE_INTERFACE:172.16.1.100
  ID=4101 seq=1 len=56
ICMP echo reply from OUTSIDE_INTERFACE:172.16.1.100 to INSIDE_INTERFACE:192.168.1.2
  ID=4101 seq=1 len=56
ICMP echo request from INSIDE_INTERFACE:192.168.1.2 to OUTSIDE_INTERFACE:172.16.1.100
  ID=4101 seq=2 len=56
ICMP echo reply from OUTSIDE_INTERFACE:172.16.1.100 to INSIDE_INTERFACE:192.168.1.2
  ID=4101 seq=2 len=56
.

.
<Output Omitted>


> undebug all
>
```

If the ping test fails, you need to determine the status of the interfaces. You can run a couple commands in FTD to verify the configurations you applied from the FMC to the FTD. As shown in the following sections, command outputs are slightly different depending on the configuration method (static versus dynamic).

Verifying the Interface Configuration

The following commands are useful for verifying the interface configuration and status:

- **show ip**
- **show interface ip brief**
- **show interface** *interface_ID*
- **show running-config interface**

Example 8-7 shows output of the **show ip** command. You can view the mapping between the interface, logical name, and IP address in this output. You cannot, however, view the current status in the output.

Example 8-7   *Output of the* **show ip** *Command*

```
> show ip
System IP Addresses:
Interface               Name                IP address      Subnet mask       Method
GigabitEthernet1/1      INSIDE_INTERFACE    192.168.1.1     255.255.255.0     manual
GigabitEthernet1/2      OUTSIDE_INTERFACE   172.16.1.1      255.255.255.0     manual
Current IP Addresses:
Interface               Name                IP address      Subnet mask       Method
GigabitEthernet1/1      INSIDE_INTERFACE    192.168.1.1     255.255.255.0     manual
GigabitEthernet1/2      OUTSIDE_INTERFACE   172.16.1.1      255.255.255.0     manual
>
```

Example 8-8 confirms that both the GigabitEthernet1/1 and GigabitEthernet1/2 interfaces are up and configured manually (using static IP addresses). The **show interface ip brief** command provides an overview, including the current status, of each of the interfaces.

Example 8-8   *Overview of the Interface Status*

```
> show interface ip brief
Interface               IP-Address      OK? Method Status                  Protocol
Virtual0                127.1.0.1       YES unset  up                      up
GigabitEthernet1/1      192.168.1.1     YES manual up                      up
GigabitEthernet1/2      172.16.1.1      YES manual up                      up
GigabitEthernet1/3      unassigned      YES unset  administratively down   down
GigabitEthernet1/4      unassigned      YES unset  administratively down   down
GigabitEthernet1/5      unassigned      YES unset  administratively down   down
GigabitEthernet1/6      unassigned      YES unset  administratively down   down
GigabitEthernet1/7      unassigned      YES unset  administratively down   down
GigabitEthernet1/8      unassigned      YES unset  administratively down   down
Internal-Control1/1     127.0.1.1       YES unset  up                      up
Internal-Data1/1        unassigned      YES unset  up                      up
Internal-Data1/2        unassigned      YES unset  down                    down
Internal-Data1/3        unassigned      YES unset  up                      up
Internal-Data1/4        169.254.1.1     YES unset  up                      up
Management1/1           unassigned      YES unset  up                      up
>
```

Example 8-9 shows detailed statistics of the GigabitEthernet1/1 interface. By using the
show interface *interface_ID* command, you can determine any errors and drops that
may have occurred on an interface.

Example 8-9 *Detailed Statistics of Packets in the Interface Level*

```
> show interface GigabitEthernet 1/1
Interface GigabitEthernet1/1 "INSIDE_INTERFACE", is up, line protocol is up
  Hardware is Accelerator rev01, BW 1000 Mbps, DLY 10 usec
        Auto-Duplex(Full-duplex), Auto-Speed(1000 Mbps)
        Input flow control is unsupported, output flow control is off
        MAC address a46c.2ae4.6bc0, MTU 1500
        IP address 192.168.1.1, subnet mask 255.255.255.0
        3541 packets input, 379530 bytes, 0 no buffer
        Received 54 broadcasts, 0 runts, 0 giants
        0 input errors, 0 CRC, 0 frame, 0 overrun, 0 ignored, 0 abort
        0 pause input, 0 resume input
        0 L2 decode drops
        2875 packets output, 292832 bytes, 0 underruns
        0 pause output, 0 resume output
        0 output errors, 0 collisions, 0 interface resets
        0 late collisions, 0 deferred
        0 input reset drops, 0 output reset drops
        input queue (blocks free curr/low): hardware (938/895)
        output queue (blocks free curr/low): hardware (1023/1022)
  Traffic Statistics for "INSIDE_INTERFACE":
        3534 packets input, 315149 bytes
        2875 packets output, 240884 bytes
        658 packets dropped
      1 minute input rate 2 pkts/sec,  168 bytes/sec
      1 minute output rate 2 pkts/sec,  168 bytes/sec
      1 minute drop rate, 0 pkts/sec
      5 minute input rate 2 pkts/sec,  168 bytes/sec
      5 minute output rate 2 pkts/sec,  168 bytes/sec
      5 minute drop rate, 0 pkts/sec
>
```

Example 8-10 displays the interface configurations from the CLI. You can find all the settings you configured on the FMC and applied to FTD. The system, however, adds some
commands automatically when you apply the final configurations.

Example 8-10   *Running Configurations of GigabitEthernet1/1 and GigabitEthernet1/2*

```
> show running-config interface
!
interface GigabitEthernet1/1
 nameif INSIDE_INTERFACE
 cts manual
  propagate sgt preserve-untag
  policy static sgt disabled trusted
 security-level 0
 ip address 192.168.1.1 255.255.255.0
!
interface GigabitEthernet1/2
 nameif OUTSIDE_INTERFACE
 cts manual
  propagate sgt preserve-untag
  policy static sgt disabled trusted
 security-level 0
 ip address 172.16.1.1 255.255.255.0
!
.
.
<Output Omitted for Brevity>
>
```

Verifying DHCP Settings

If an FTD device does not offer an IP address to its DHCP clients, or if the FTD device cannot obtain an IP address from any external DHCP server, you can verify the configurations and debug any DHCP packets to and from the DHCP server. Let's take a look.

Example 8-11 confirms that GigabitEthernet1/2, connected to the outside network, can obtain the IP address 172.16.1.104 from a DHCP server.

Example 8-11   *Status of an Outside Interface—Configured with a Dynamic IP Address*

```
> show interface ip brief
Interface           IP-Address      OK? Method Status                Protocol
Virtual0            127.1.0.1       YES unset  up                    up
GigabitEthernet1/1  192.168.1.1     YES manual up                    up
GigabitEthernet1/2  172.16.1.104    YES DHCP   up                    up
GigabitEthernet1/3  unassigned      YES unset  administratively down down
GigabitEthernet1/4  unassigned      YES unset  administratively down down
GigabitEthernet1/5  unassigned      YES unset  administratively down down
```

```
GigabitEthernet1/6          unassigned      YES unset  administratively down down
GigabitEthernet1/7          unassigned      YES unset  administratively down down
GigabitEthernet1/8          unassigned      YES unset  administratively down down
Internal-Control1/1         127.0.1.1       YES unset  up                   up
Internal-Data1/1            unassigned      YES unset  up                   up
Internal-Data1/2            unassigned      YES unset  down                 down
Internal-Data1/3            unassigned      YES unset  up                   up
Internal-Data1/4            169.254.1.1     YES unset  up                   up
Management1/1               unassigned      YES unset  up                   up
>
```

Example 8-12 shows the differences between the configurations of two interfaces: The inside interface GigabitEthernet1/1 is configured with the static IP address 192.168.1.1/24, whereas the outside interface GigabitEthernet1/2 is configured to obtain an address from a DHCP server.

Example 8-12   *The Difference Between Static and DHCP Configurations in the CLI*

```
> show running-config interface
!
interface GigabitEthernet1/1
 nameif INSIDE_INTERFACE
 cts manual
  propagate sgt preserve-untag
  policy static sgt disabled trusted
 security-level 0
 ip address 192.168.1.1 255.255.255.0
!
interface GigabitEthernet1/2
 nameif OUTSIDE_INTERFACE
 cts manual
  propagate sgt preserve-untag
  policy static sgt disabled trusted
 security-level 0
 ip address dhcp setroute
!
.
.
.
<Output Omitted for Brevity>
>
```

Example 8-13 proves that FTD has dynamically assigned the IP address 192.168.1.2 to a host with MAC address C4:2C:03:3C:98:A8. This IP address is the first address from the DHCP address pool 192.168.1.2 to 192.168.1.10.

Example 8-13 *Verifying the IP Address Assignment from a DHCP Address Pool*

```
> show dhcpd binding

IP address         Client Identifier        Lease expiration       Type
    192.168.1.2        c42c.033c.98a8                 3580 seconds   Automatic
>
```

If you do not see any DHCP binding, you can debug the DHCP packets on the FTD device.

Example 8-14 demonstrates the process of a DHCP server assigning an IP address. In the debug output, you can analyze the four major stages of the DHCP protocol—Discovery, Offer, Request, and Acknowledgement (DORA).

Example 8-14 *Exchanging DHCP Packets Between FTD and a DHCP Server*

```
> debug dhcpd packet
debug dhcpd packet enabled at level 1
>


DHCPD/RA:  Server msg received, fip=ANY, fport=0 on INSIDE_INTERFACE interface
DHCPD: DHCPDISCOVER received from client c42c.033c.98a8 on interface INSIDE_INTERFACE.
DHCPD: send ping pkt to 192.168.1.2
DHCPD: ping got no response for ip: 192.168.1.2
DHCPD: Add binding 192.168.1.2 to radix tree
DHCPD/RA: Binding successfully added to hash table
DHCPD: Sending DHCPOFFER to client c42c.033c.98a8 (192.168.1.2).

DHCPD: Total # of raw options copied to outgoing DHCP message is 0.
DHCPD/RA: creating ARP entry (192.168.1.2, c42c.033c.98a8).
DHCPD: unicasting BOOTREPLY to client c42c.033c.98a8(192.168.1.2).
DHCPD/RA:  Server msg received, fip=ANY, fport=0 on INSIDE_INTERFACE interface
DHCPD: DHCPREQUEST received from client c42c.033c.98a8.
DHCPD: Extracting client address from the message
DHCPD: State = DHCPS_REBOOTING
DHCPD: State = DHCPS_REQUESTING
DHCPD: Client c42c.033c.98a8 specified it's address 192.168.1.2
DHCPD: Client is on the correct network
DHCPD: Client accepted our offer
DHCPD: Client and server agree on address 192.168.1.2
DHCPD: Renewing client c42c.033c.98a8 lease
DHCPD: Client lease can be renewed
DHCPD: Sending DHCPACK to client c42c.033c.98a8 (192.168.1.2).
```

```
DHCPD: Total # of raw options copied to outgoing DHCP message is 0.
DHCPD/RA: creating ARP entry (192.168.1.2, c42c.033c.98a8).
DHCPD: unicasting BOOTREPLY to client c42c.033c.98a8(192.168.1.2).

>
```

Summary

In this chapter, you have learned about the widely deployed firewall mode Routed Mode. This chapter describes the steps involved in configuring routed interfaces with static IP addresses as well as dynamic IP addresses. In addition, this chapter discusses various command-line tools you can use to determine any potential interface-related issues.

Quiz

1. Which of the following commands is used to debug and analyze ping requests?
   a. **debug icmp**
   b. **debug ip icmp**
   c. **debug icmp trace**
   d. **debug icmp reply**

2. Which of the following commands is used to configure FTD from Transparent Mode to Routed Mode?
   a. **configure routed**
   b. **configure firewall routed**
   c. **configure firepower routed**
   d. **configure transparent disable**

3. Which of the following statements is true?
   a. FTD in Transparent Mode cannot be configured by the FMC.
   b. You can change the firewall deployment mode by using the FMC.
   c. You cannot change the firewall mode until you unregister FTD from the FMC.
   d. When you change the firewall mode, FTD saves the running configurations.

4. Which of the following commands allows you to determine any interface-related issues?
   a. **show interface ip brief**
   b. **show interface** *interface_ID*
   c. **show running-config interface**
   d. All of the above

Chapter 9

Firepower Deployment in Transparent Mode

FTD Transparent Mode allows you to control your network traffic like a firewall, while the FTD device stays invisible to the hosts in your network. This chapter discusses the configuration of FTD Transparent Mode.

Transparent Mode Essentials

In Transparent Mode, FTD bridges the inside and outside interfaces into a single Layer 2 network and remains transparent to the hosts. When FTD is in Transparent Mode, the FMC does not allow you to assign an IPv4 address to a directly connected interface. As a result, the hosts are unable to communicate with any connected interfaces. Unlike with Routed Mode, you cannot configure the connected interfaces as the default gateway for the hosts.

You can, however, assign an IP address to the Bridge Virtual Interface (BVI) that comes with each bridge group. A bridge group represents a unique Layer 2 network. You can create multiple bridge groups on a single FTD device, but the hosts within different bridge groups cannot communicate with each other without a router. Within a bridge group, both the BVI and the hosts must have IP addresses from the same subnet. FTD uses the IP address of the BVI when it communicates with its hosts.

Figure 9-1 shows how a host finds a router, not an FTD device, as its next hop when you configure FTD in Transparent Mode.

Figure 9-2 shows an example of a real-world deployment of FTD in Transparent Mode. The management interfaces of the FMC and FTD are connected to the end users through the 192.168.1.0/24 subnet. The default gateway for the 192.168.1.0/24 subnet is the gateway router IP address 192.168.1.30/24.

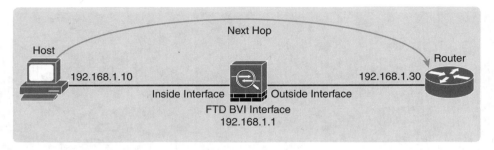

Figure 9-1 *Host Communicating with Its Next Hop When FTD Is Transparent*

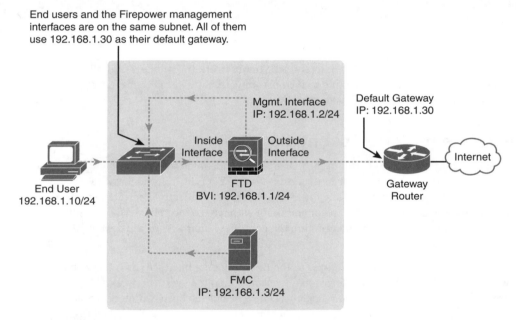

Figure 9-2 *Real-World Deployment Example of FTD in Transparent Mode*

Best Practices for Transparent Mode

Consider the following when you plan to deploy FTD in Transparent Mode:

■ Changing the firewall mode wipes out any existing FTD configurations. Therefore, before you change the firewall mode from Routed to Transparent or vice versa, take note of your FTD configuration settings for future reference, in case you want to revert the FTD to the initial state. To view the current FTD configuration, run the **show running-config** command in the CLI.

If you just want to change the firewall mode on an FTD device, performing a backup of your security policy configuration is not necessary because the next-generation security policies are defined and stored on the FMC. Once configured, FMC can deploy the same policies to one or more FTD devices.

- Do not use the BVI IP address as the default gateway for the connected hosts. Instead, use any connected router as the default gateway for the hosts in the bridged network.

- Do not forget to add access rules to allow any necessary network management traffic. By default, FTD in Transparent Mode blocks the DHCP traffic, multicast traffic, and dynamic routing protocol traffic (such as RIP, OSPF, EIGRP, BGP, and so on). If you select Access Control: Block All Traffic as the default action, make sure you have added access rules explicitly to allow any essential traffic. If you are not sure, you can use Intrusion Prevention: Balanced Security and Connectivity as the default action; it allows any unmatched traffic, as long as there are no malicious activities found.

- If your ultimate goal is to perform transparent inspection, you can choose the Inline IPS mode instead of the Transparent firewall mode. While both modes allow you to deploy FTD as a bump in the wire, Inline Mode has less configuration overhead than Transparent Mode. In addition, a dedicated IP address for each BVI is not necessary. To learn more, read Chapter 11, "Blocking Traffic Using Inline Interface Mode."

Configuring Transparent Mode

During system initialization, FTD provides you an option to choose between Routed Mode and Transparent Mode (see Example 9-1). To set up FTD with Transparent Mode, just type **transparent** when the system prompts and press Enter.

Example 9-1 *Configuring Transparent Firewall Mode During Initialization*

```
<Output Omitted>
.
.
Manage the device locally? (yes/no) [yes]: no
Configure firewall mode? (routed/transparent) [routed]: transparent
Configuring firewall mode ...
.
.
<Output Omitted>
```

If you selected Transparent Mode during the system initialization, you can skip the next two sections and read the section "Deploying Transparent Mode in a Layer 2 Network." If you selected Routed Mode, read on.

Fulfilling Prerequisites

You cannot change the firewall mode if FTD is currently registered with the FMC. If you initially configured FTD to Routed Mode and now you want to reconfigure it to Transparent Mode, you must unregister FTD from the FMC. To verify the registration status, run the **show managers** command at the FTD CLI.

Example 9-2 shows that FTD is currently registered with the FMC with IP address 10.1.1.16.

Example 9-2   *Verifying the Registration Status—FTD Is Currently Registered*

```
> show managers
Type                    : Manager
Host                    : 10.1.1.16
Registration            : Completed
>
```

If you find that FTD is currently registered with the FMC, unregister it by using the FMC web interface. To delete the registration, go to the **Devices > Device Management** page and click the delete icon next to the appropriate FTD device (see Figure 9-3).

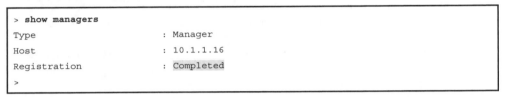

Figure 9-3   *Deleting a Firepower Registration*

Example 9-3 shows confirmation that FTD is currently not registered with the FMC.

Example 9-3   *Verifying the Registration Status—FTD Is Not Registered*

```
> show managers
No managers configured.
>
```

Changing the Firewall Mode

If an FTD device is currently not associated with a manager, you can change the firewall deployment mode. To configure an FTD device with Transparent Mode, log in to the FTD CLI and run the **configure firewall transparent** command (see Example 9-4).

Example 9-4 *Configuring Transparent Mode*

```
> configure firewall transparent

This will destroy the current interface configurations, are you sure that you want
  to proceed? [y/N] y
The firewall mode was changed successfully.
```

After configuring FTD with the desired mode, you can determine the status from the
CLI, as shown in Example 9-5.

Example 9-5 *Verifying Firewall Deployment Mode*

```
> show firewall
Firewall mode: Transparent
>
```

Alternatively, upon a successful registration, the web interface of the FMC also displays
the current firewall deployment mode. You can view it on the **Devices > Device
management** page (see Figure 9-4).

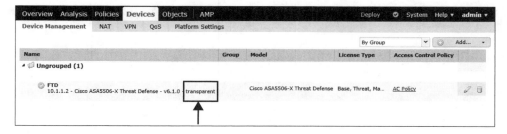

Figure 9-4 *Checking the Current FTD Deployment Mode*

Deploying Transparent Mode in a Layer 2 Network

An FTD device in Transparent Mode can control traffic as a firewall and inspect traffic
as an intrusion prevention system while it stays transparent in the network, like a Layer 2
switch. A transparent FTD supports the following deployment scenarios:

- You can deploy it in a single Layer 2 network, where all the hosts reside in the
  same subnet and can communicate without a dynamic routing protocol. This type
  of deployment works when you configure the physical and virtual interfaces in a
  bridge group.

- You can also deploy an FTD device between the Layer 3 networks, where hosts
  from different subnets communicate using a routing protocol. By default, when you

configure an FTD device in Transparent Mode, it blocks any underlying dynamic routing protocol traffic. Therefore, to allow this traffic, you need to add access rules explicitly.

Configuring the Physical and Virtual Interfaces

To configure the interfaces when an FTD device is in Transparent Mode, follow these steps:

Step 1.   Navigate to the **Devices > Device Management** page. A list of the managed devices appears.

Step 2.   Click the pencil icon that is next to the FTD device you want to configure. The device editor page appears, showing all the physical interfaces of an FTD device on the Interfaces tab (see Figure 9-5).

Figure 9-5   *The Interfaces Tab of the Device Editor Page*

Step 3.   On the Interfaces tab, click the pencil icons next to GigabitEthernet1/1 and GigabitEthernet1/2 to configure these interfaces for the inside and outside networks. Use the settings shown in Table 9-1 to configure these two interfaces.

Table 9-1 *Configuration Settings for GigabitEthernet1/1 and GigabitEthernet1/2*

	GigabitEthernet1/1	GigabitEthernet1/2
Interface name	INSIDE_INTERFACE	OUTSIDE_INTERFACE
Security zone (optional)	INSIDE_ZONE	OUTSIDE_ZONE
IP address	In Transparent Mode, an IP address is not required on a data interface. Instead, assign an address to the BVI.	

Note To enable an interface, giving it a name is a requirement; however, configuring a security zone is an optional step.

Figure 9-6 shows the configurations on the GigabitEthernet1/1 interface. Note that there is no option to configure an IPv4 address.

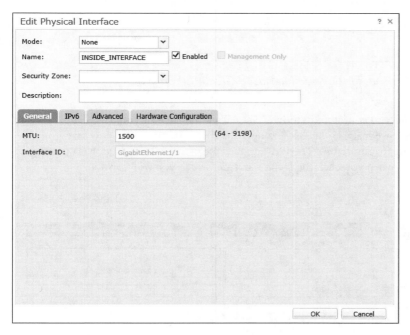

Figure 9-6 *Configuring the Inside Interface—GigabitEthernet1/1*

Figure 9-7 shows the configurations on the GigabitEthernet1/2 interface that is connected to the outside network.

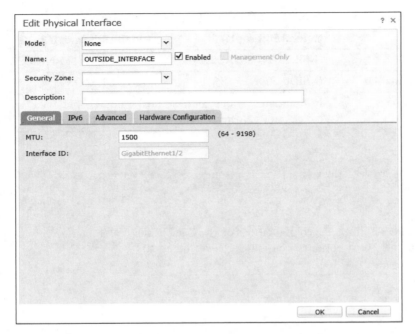

Figure 9-7 *Configuring the Outside Interface—GigabitEthernet1/2*

Step 4. After you configure both interfaces, click the **Save** button to save the changes you have made so far (see Figure 9-8). The configuration is now saved on the FMC for future use. The FMC applies the configuration to an FTD device only when you click the Deploy button, which you will do soon.

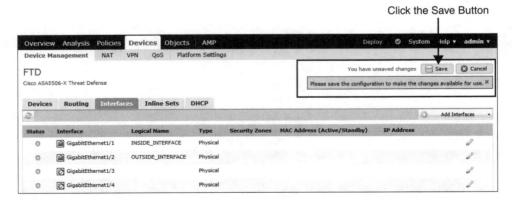

Figure 9-8 *Saving a Configuration*

Step 5.   To configure a BVI, on the right side of the Interfaces tab, click the **Add Interfaces** button. A list of different types of interfaces appears.

Step 6.   Select **Bridge Group Interface** from the list of interfaces (see Figure 9-9). The Add Bridge Group Interface window appears.

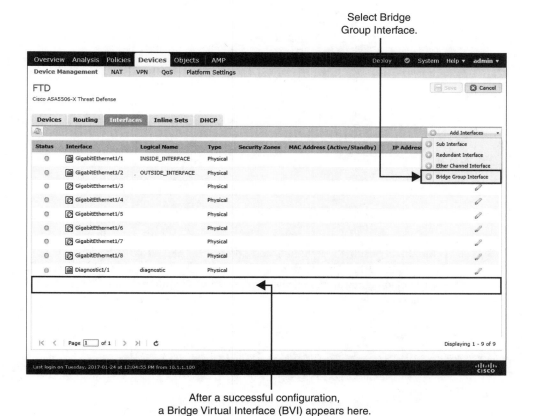

Figure 9-9 *Navigating to the Bridge Group Interface Configuration*

Step 7.   On the Interfaces tab of the Add Bridge Group Interface window, provide a bridge group ID between 1 and 250 and select the interfaces that are part of the bridged network—in this case GigabitEthernet1/1 and GigabitEthernet1/2, as shown in Figure 9-10.

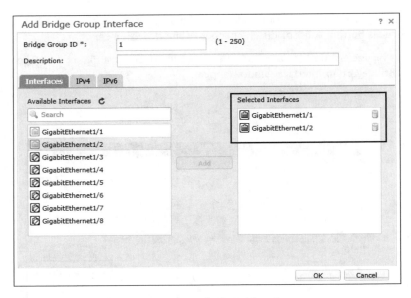

Figure 9-10   *Selecting Interfaces for a Bridge Group*

Step 8.   On the IPv4 subtab, configure the address 192.168.1.1 for the BVI (see Figure 9-11). The IP address must be on the same subnet as the hosts and default gateway router, and in this case it is within the same /24 subnet as its hosts.

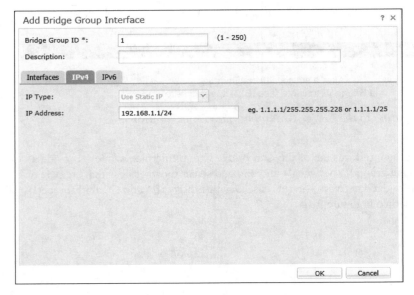

Figure 9-11   *Configuring an IP Address for the BVI*

Step 9.   Click **OK** to exit the Add Bridge Group Interface window. Figure 9-12
confirms the setup of a bridge group BVI1.

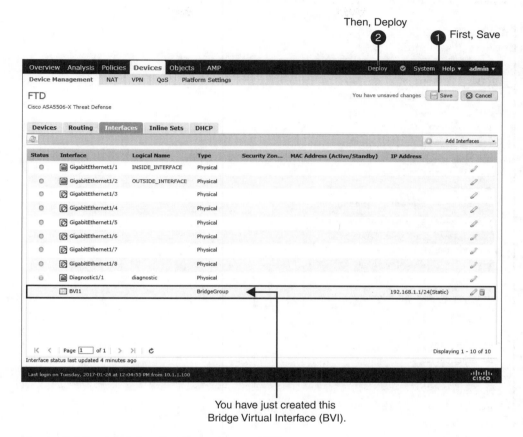

Figure 9-12   *Applying Configurations to FTD*

Step 10.   Click the **Save** button to save the changes, and then click the **Deploy** button
to apply the changes to the FTD device.

Verifying the Interface Status

After deploying an FTD device by using the FMC web interface, you can verify any
configuration settings from the FTD CLI.

Example 9-6 shows the interface configuration of FTD in Transparent Mode. Both of the
member interfaces are in bridge group 1 and have no IP addresses. Only BVI1 has an IP
address (192.168.1.1/24).

Example 9-6 *Interface Configurations on an FTD in Transparent Mode*

```
> show running-config interface
!
interface GigabitEthernet1/1
 nameif INSIDE_INTERFACE
 cts manual
  propagate sgt preserve-untag
  policy static sgt disabled trusted
 bridge-group 1
 security-level 0
!
interface GigabitEthernet1/2
 nameif OUTSIDE_INTERFACE
 cts manual
  propagate sgt preserve-untag
  policy static sgt disabled trusted
 bridge-group 1
 security-level 0
.
.
<Output Omitted for Brevity>
.
.
interface Management1/1
 management-only
 nameif diagnostic
 cts manual
  propagate sgt preserve-untag
  policy static sgt disabled trusted
 security-level 0
!
interface BVI1
 ip address 192.168.1.1 255.255.255.0
>
```

Example 9-7 highlights the status of the interfaces on a Transparent Mode FTD device. Although you do not configure IP addresses for the member interfaces of a bridge group, they use the same IP address as the BVI when you communicate with any connected hosts.

Example 9-7 *Interface Status of FTD in Transparent Mode*

```
> show interface ip brief
Interface               IP-Address      OK? Method Status                 Protocol
Virtual0                127.1.0.1       YES unset  up                     up
GigabitEthernet1/1      192.168.1.1     YES unset  up                     up
GigabitEthernet1/2      192.168.1.1     YES unset  up                     up
GigabitEthernet1/3      unassigned      YES unset  administratively down  down
GigabitEthernet1/4      unassigned      YES unset  administratively down  down
GigabitEthernet1/5      unassigned      YES unset  administratively down  down
GigabitEthernet1/6      unassigned      YES unset  administratively down  down
GigabitEthernet1/7      unassigned      YES unset  administratively down  down
GigabitEthernet1/8      unassigned      YES unset  administratively down  down
Internal-Control1/1     127.0.1.1       YES unset  up                     up
Internal-Data1/1        unassigned      YES unset  up                     up
Internal-Data1/2        unassigned      YES unset  down                   down
Internal-Data1/3        unassigned      YES unset  up                     up
Internal-Data1/4        169.254.1.1     YES unset  up                     up
Management1/1           unassigned      YES unset  up                     up
BVI1                    192.168.1.1     YES manual up                     up
>
```

Example 9-8 shows the status of the logical management interface br1, which is not
displayed in the previous example. FTD uses the IP address of br1 to communicate with
the FMC.

Example 9-8 *Status of the Logical Management Interface br1*

```
> show network
===============[ System Information ]===============
Hostname                : firepower
Management port         : 8305
IPv4 Default route
  Gateway               : 10.1.1.1


=====================[ br1 ]=====================
State                   : Enabled
Channels                : Management & Events
Mode                    : Non-Autonegotiation
MDI/MDIX                : Auto/MDIX
MTU                     : 1500
MAC Address             : A4:6C:2A:E4:6B:BE
---------------------[ IPv4 ]---------------------
Configuration           : Manual
Address                 : 10.1.1.2
```

```
Netmask                : 255.255.255.0
Broadcast              : 10.1.1.255
--------------------[ IPv6 ]--------------------
Configuration          : Disabled


==============[ Proxy Information ]===============
State                  : Disabled
Authentication         : Disabled

>
```

Verifying Basic Connectivity and Operations

After configuring an FTD device to Transparent Mode, you might want to verify whether the transparent FTD is working. Is it invisible in the network? You can prove this by using Address Resolution Protocol (ARP). When a host computer communicates through an FTD device, the host cannot see the FTD device. Instead, it can see the devices deployed on the other side of the FTD device.

Before testing the functionality, let's determine the MAC and IP addresses of all the participating interfaces. Figure 9-13 details the Layer 1, Layer 2, and Layer 3 addresses of the network devices in the OSPF area 1 network. Instead of seeing the FTD inside interface, the inside router sees the outside router as its next hop.

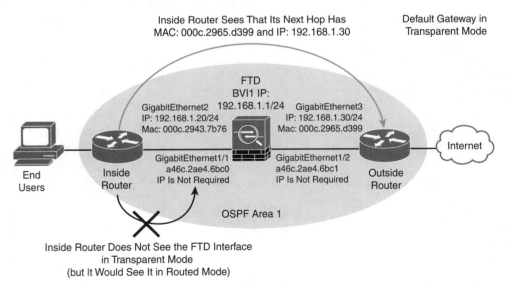

Figure 9-13 *Traffic Flow Between an Inside Router and a Default Gateway*

Example 9-9 shows the commands that allow you to find the MAC and IP addresses of an interface on an FTD device and a router.

Example 9-9 *Determining the MAC and IP Addresses*

```
! On FTD:


> show interface GigabitEthernet1/1 | include address
        MAC address a46c.2ae4.6bc0, MTU 1500
        IP address 192.168.1.1, subnet mask 255.255.255.0

> show interface GigabitEthernet1/2 | include address
        MAC address a46c.2ae4.6bc1, MTU 1500
        IP address 192.168.1.1, subnet mask 255.255.255.0



! On Router:


Inside-Router# show interfaces GigabitEthernet2 | include address
  Hardware is CSR vNIC, address is 000c.2943.7b76 (bia 000c.2943.7b76)
  Internet address is 192.168.1.20/24

Outside-Router## show interfaces GigabitEthernet3 | include address
  Hardware is CSR vNIC, address is 000c.2965.d399 (bia 000c.2965.d399)
  Internet address is 192.168.1.30/24
```

If you configured the interfaces according to the instructions in the previous section, you should be able to successfully ping from the inside router to the outside router.

Example 9-10 shows a successful ping test from the inside router to the outside router through the FTD. The dropping of the first packet is an expected behavior. It happens because the ARP table is empty at the beginning.

Example 9-10 *Sending a Successful Ping Request from Inside to Outside*

```
Inside-Router# ping 192.168.1.30
Type escape sequence to abort.
Sending 5, 100-byte ICMP Echos to 192.168.1.30, timeout is 2 seconds:
.!!!!
Success rate is 80 percent (4/5), round-trip min/avg/max = 5/5/6 ms
Inside-Router#
```

The ping test by the inside router (shown in Example 9-10) does not prove whether the ping replies come from the outside router or from the BVI of the FTD. You can determine this by enabling debugging on FTD for ICMP traffic, like this:

```
> debug icmp trace
debug icmp trace enabled at level 1

>
```

Once again, you can send the ping requests to the IP address of the outside router 192.168.1.30 from the inside router. The requests go through the FTD device as in the previous example. However, this time, the FTD device shows a log for the through traffic. There are two lines for each ping request—one for sending a request and one for receiving a reply:

```
ICMP echo request from INSIDE_INTERFACE:192.168.1.20 to OUTSIDE_
INTERFACE:192.168.1.30 ID=8 seq=1 len=72
ICMP echo reply from OUTSIDE_INTERFACE:192.168.1.30 to INSIDE_
INTERFACE:192.168.1.20 ID=8 seq=1 len=72
```

Now check the ARP table on the inside router to view the mapping of IP addresses with the inside interface. Compare the entries in the table with the MAC addresses that you found in the command output shown in Example 9-9.

Example 9-11 displays the mapping of the MAC addresses with the IP addresses. Besides the MAC address of its own interface (000c.2943.7b76), the ARP table of the inside router shows the MAC address of its next hop—the outside router (000c.2965.d399), not the FTD (a46c.2ae4.6bc0), which is transparent in the network.

Example 9-11 *Inside Router ARP Table—After Pinging from the Inside Router to the Outside Router*

```
Inside-Router# show arp
Protocol  Address       Age (min)  Hardware Addr   Type   Interface
Internet  192.168.1.20       -     000c.2943.7b76  ARPA   GigabitEthernet2
Internet  192.168.1.30       2     000c.2965.d399  ARPA   GigabitEthernet2
Inside-Router#
```

If you send a ping request from the FTD device, FTD uses its BVI IP address to send that request. In that case, the ARP table on the router shows the MAC address of the FTD interface that communicates with the router.

Example 9-12 demonstrates that when you ping from FTD to the inside router, it uses the BVI address 192.168.1.1 as its IP address. Remember that in Transparent Mode, you do not configure any IPv4 address on the FTD physical interface.

Example 9-12   *BVI IP Address Used When Traffic Originates from the FTD Itself*

```
> debug icmp trace
debug icmp trace enabled at level 1


> ping 192.168.1.20
ICMP echo request from 192.168.1.1 to 192.168.1.20 ID=52779 seq=30330 len=72
ICMP echo reply from 192.168.1.20 to 192.168.1.1 ID=52779 seq=30330 len=72
.
<Output Omitted for Brevity>
.

! To disable the debug of ICMP traffic:
> no debug icmp trace
debug icmp trace disabled.
>


! Alternatively, to disable all of the running debug processes:
> undebug all
>
```

Example 9-13 shows a new entry in the ARP table after you send the ping requests to the inside router from the FTD device. It now displays the MAC address of the GigabitEthernet1/1 interface (a46c.2ae4.6bc0) in FTD.

Example 9-13   *Inside Router ARP Table—After Pinging from FTD to the Inside Router*

```
Inside-Router# show arp
Protocol   Address         Age (min)   Hardware Addr   Type   Interface
Internet   192.168.1.1             1   a46c.2ae4.6bc0  ARPA   GigabitEthernet2
Internet   192.168.1.20            -   000c.2943.7b76  ARPA   GigabitEthernet2
Internet   192.168.1.30            5   000c.2965.d399  ARPA   GigabitEthernet2
Inside-Router#
```

Deploying an FTD Device Between Layer 3 Networks

After configuring the physical and virtual interfaces, you can communicate with any hosts, through an FTD device, within the same subnet. However, if you want to communicate with hosts that are in different subnets, a routing protocol is necessary.

When you configure a dynamic routing protocol across the network, FTD blocks the underlying routing traffic until you allow it in an access control policy. You can choose one of following options:

■ Select a nonblocking policy as the default action.

■ Add a custom access rule to allow desired traffic.

Figure 9-14 shows an FTD device deployed between an inside router and an outside router. Both routers use loopback interfaces to simulate a host and the Internet. The loopback and routing interfaces are on different subnets, and all of them are included in OSPF area 1.

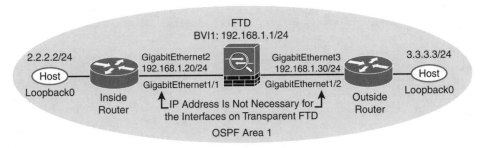

Figure 9-14 *Transparent FTD Deployment in an OSPF Network*

Selecting the Default Action

The default action in an access control policy determines how an FTD device handles traffic when there is no matching access rule. To define the default action, you can either go to the **Policies > Access Control** page to create a new policy or you can edit an existing policy. Figure 9-15 shows the options to create a new access control policy and to modify an existing one.

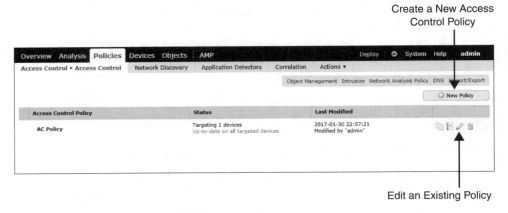

Figure 9-15 *Options to Create a New Access Control Policy and to Modify an Existing One*

When you are on the policy editor page, select the desired policy from the Default Action dropdown. You can select one of the system-provided policies that does not block traffic or a policy that you have created (if any). If you are not sure about selecting a policy, you can select the **Intrusion Prevention: Balanced Security and Connectivity** policy, which allows any unmatched traffic to go through an FTD device after being inspected for malicious activities.

Figure 9-16 shows a list of system-provided policies that you can select for default action. Once you select a policy, save the changes and deploy it on your FTD.

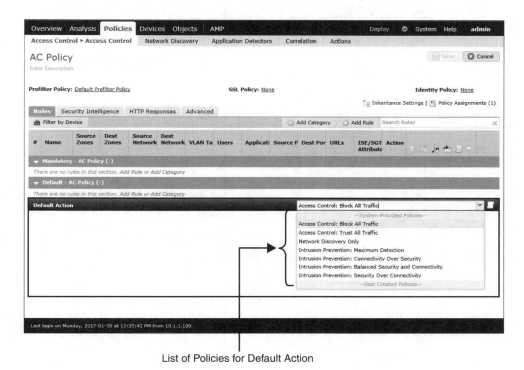

List of Policies for Default Action

Figure 9-16 *System-Provided Policies That Are Available for Default Action*

Adding an Access Rule

If you select the Access Control: Block All Traffic policy as the default action, traffic is blocked when it does not match with any custom access rules. Only the traffic that exclusively matches a rule is allowed through the FTD device.

If you create an access rule to allow a particular routing protocol, such as OSPF, and select the **Access Control: Block All Traffic** policy as the default action, the FTD device allows only OSPF management traffic. Any other data traffic, however, is dropped due to the default blocking action. In this scenario, two routers can build an OSPF neighbor relationship through an FTD device, but you are unable to ping the inside router from the outside router and vice versa. Similarly, you cannot use Secure Shell (SSH) to access a router from the other router even though the neighbor relation is established. To allow any additional traffic, you need to add the related protocols in the access rule and select the **Allow** action.

In the following configuration example, you will see how to create two access rules—one for the routing traffic (OSPF) and one for the data traffic (SSH).

To create an access rule for OSPF traffic, follow these steps:

Step 1. Go to the **Policies > Access Control** page. Click the **New Policy** button to create a new policy, or click on the pencil icon to edit an existing policy. The policy editor page appears.

Step 2. To create a new access rule, on the policy editor page, click the **Add Rule** button (see Figure 9-17). The Add Rule window appears.

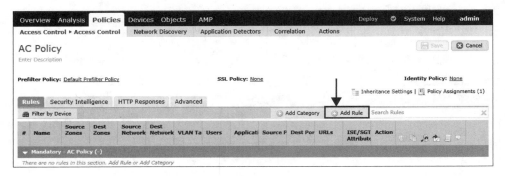

Figure 9-17 *Navigating to the Add Rule Button*

Step 3. Give a name to this particular access rule, select the **Enabled** check box, and set the action to **Allow**. Figure 9-18 shows how to enable a new access rule called Routing Access with the rule action set to Allow.

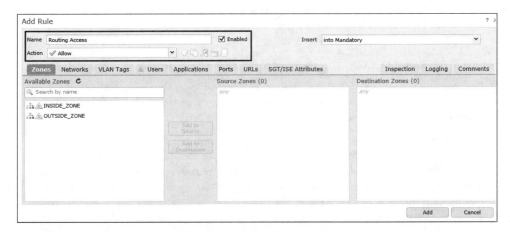

Figure 9-18 *The Add Rule Window, Where You Define a Rule for Access Control*

Warning   Routers exchange keepalives to determine the states of the neighbors. If an FTD device deployed between two routers inspects a very high volume of traffic, it may delay the traverse of keepalive packets even if you add an access rule to allow them. As a result, a router may take a longer time to call its neighbor down, which makes any reachability issues worse.

Tip   The Firepower System offers two unique rule actions—Trust and Fastpath—that can expedite the traverse of management traffic. In an access rule, you can set the action to Trust to let the OSPF traffic go through the FTD device without any further inspection. However, the more optimal method for bypassing an inspection is to add a prefilter rule for the OSPF protocol and set the action for it to Fastpath. To learn about the details of both options, see Chapter 14, "Bypassing Inspection and Trusting Traffic."

Step 4.   Go to the Ports tab and navigate to the Protocol dropdown that is under the Selected Destination Ports field.

Step 5.   Select the OSPF/OSPFIGP protocol and click the **Add** button next to the protocol dropdown. The selected protocol should be listed under the Selected Destination Ports box. Figure 9-19 shows the sequence for adding an access rule called Routing Access to allow the OSPF protocol.

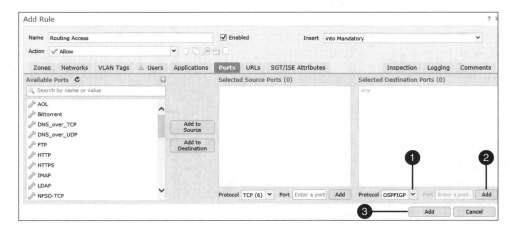

Figure 9-19   *Allowing OSPF in an Access Rule*

Step 6.   Click the **Add** button to return to the policy editor page, where you can see the rule you just created.

Creating an Access Rule for SSH

You can create a rule to allow data traffic through the SSH protocol. The following steps show how to allow destination port 22—the default port for SSH:

Step 1. Click the **Add Rule** button once again. In the Add Rule window, provide a name for the rule, select the **Enabled** check box, and set the **Allow** action.

Step 2. In the Available Ports section, select **SSH** and click the **Add to Destination** button. The SSH protocol appears under the Selected Destination Ports box. Figure 9-20 shows the steps to create an access rule named Shell Access to allow the SSH traffic via port 22.

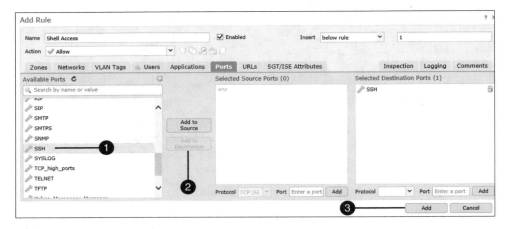

Figure 9-20   *Allowing the Default SSH Port 22 in an Access Rule*

Note   Step 2 allows SSH traffic that is destined for port 22, which is also the default port for the SSH protocol. If you want to allow any SSH application traffic, regardless of its destination port, you need to create a rule by using the Applications tab. To learn more about the Firepower application control, read Chapter 19, "Discovering Network Applications and Controlling Application Traffic."

Step 3. Click the **Add** button to return to the policy editor page and select the **Access Control: Block All Traffic** policy as the Default Action. Figure 9-21 shows that two rules—Routing Access and Shell Access—are added. As the default action, Access Control: Block All Traffic is added.

Step 4. Add more access rules as necessary. For now, in this configuration example, just create the above two access rules, save the policy, and deploy the new configuration on the FTD. Figure 9-22 shows that the new access control policy is being deployed. It may take several minutes to complete the deployment.

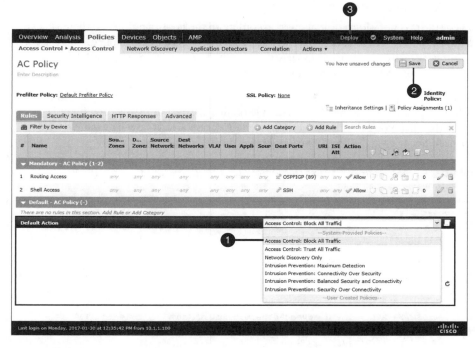

Figure 9-21 *Selecting a Default Action*

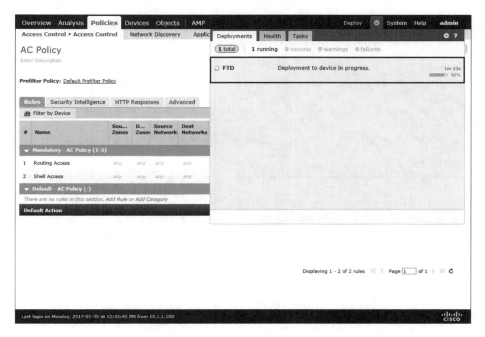

Figure 9-22 *Status of a New Policy Deployment*

Verifying Access Control Lists

When traffic is not blocked or allowed according to the configurations on the FMC, you can use the FTD CLI to verify whether the desired access rules are applied. You can run the **show access-list** command to view the custom access rules you created, as well as any implicit or system-generated rules that are applied to the FTD.

Example 9-14 shows the system-generated access rules when an access control policy with no custom rule is applied. The last rule on line 10, **permit ip any any**, is applied implicitly when you select a nonblocking default action. The following example uses the Balanced Security and Connectivity policy as the default action.

Example 9-14   *No Custom Rule with the Balanced Security and Connectivity Default Policy*

```
> show access-list
access-list cached ACL log flows: total 0, denied 0 (deny-flow-max 4096)
            alert-interval 300
access-list CSM_FW_ACL_; 6 elements; name hash: 0x4a69e3f3
access-list CSM_FW_ACL_ line 1 remark rule-id 9998: PREFILTER POLICY: Default Tunnel
  and Priority Policy
access-list CSM_FW_ACL_ line 2 remark rule-id 9998: RULE: DEFAULT TUNNEL ACTION RULE
access-list CSM_FW_ACL_ line 3 advanced permit ipinip any any rule-id 9998
  (hitcnt=0) 0xf5b597d6
access-list CSM_FW_ACL_ line 4 advanced permit 41 any any rule-id 9998 (hitcnt=0)
  0x06095aba
access-list CSM_FW_ACL_ line 5 advanced permit gre any any rule-id 9998 (hitcnt=0)
  0x52c7a066
access-list CSM_FW_ACL_ line 6 advanced permit udp any eq 3544 any range 1025 65535
  rule-id 9998 (hitcnt=0) 0x46d7839e
access-list CSM_FW_ACL_ line 7 advanced permit udp any range 1025 65535 any eq 3544
  rule-id 9998 (hitcnt=0) 0xaf1d5aa5
access-list CSM_FW_ACL_ line 8 remark rule-id 268434432: ACCESS POLICY: AC Policy -
  Default/1
access-list CSM_FW_ACL_ line 9 remark rule-id 268434432: L4 RULE: DEFAULT ACTION
  RULE
access-list CSM_FW_ACL_ line 10 advanced permit ip any any rule-id 268434432
  (hitcnt=3281) 0xa1d3780e
>
```

Example 9-15 shows two custom access rules on lines 10 and 13, along with other system-generated rules, that are created on the FMC and applied to FTD. These rules allow FTD to permit OSPF and SSH traffic. The last rule on line 16, **deny ip any any**, is applied implicitly when you select Access Control: Block All Traffic as the default action.

Example 9-15 *Two Custom Rules with Block All Traffic as the Default Policy*

```
> show access-list
access-list cached ACL log flows: total 0, denied 0 (deny-flow-max 4096)
            alert-interval 300
access-list CSM_FW_ACL_; 8 elements; name hash: 0x4a69e3f3
access-list CSM_FW_ACL_ line 1 remark rule-id 9998: PREFILTER POLICY: Default Tunnel
  and Priority Policy
access-list CSM_FW_ACL_ line 2 remark rule-id 9998: RULE: DEFAULT TUNNEL ACTION RULE
access-list CSM_FW_ACL_ line 3 advanced permit ipinip any any rule-id 9998
  (hitcnt=0) 0xf5b597d6
access-list CSM_FW_ACL_ line 4 advanced permit 41 any any rule-id 9998 (hitcnt=0)
  0x06095aba
access-list CSM_FW_ACL_ line 5 advanced permit gre any any rule-id 9998 (hitcnt=0)
  0x52c7a066
access-list CSM_FW_ACL_ line 6 advanced permit udp any eq 3544 any range 1025 65535
  rule-id 9998 (hitcnt=0) 0x46d7839e
access-list CSM_FW_ACL_ line 7 advanced permit udp any range 1025 65535 any eq 3544
  rule-id 9998 (hitcnt=0) 0xaf1d5aa5
access-list CSM_FW_ACL_ line 8 remark rule-id 268437504: ACCESS POLICY: AC Policy -
  Mandatory/1
access-list CSM_FW_ACL_ line 9 remark rule-id 268437504: L7 RULE: Routing Access
access-list CSM_FW_ACL_ line 10 advanced permit ospf any any rule-id 268437504
  (hitcnt=4) 0x385cc1f6
access-list CSM_FW_ACL_ line 11 remark rule-id 268437505: ACCESS POLICY: AC Policy -
  Mandatory/2
access-list CSM_FW_ACL_ line 12 remark rule-id 268437505: L7 RULE: Shell Access
access-list CSM_FW_ACL_ line 13 advanced permit tcp any any object-group SSH rule-id
  268437505 (hitcnt=8) 0x030eea01
  access-list CSM_FW_ACL_ line 13 advanced permit tcp any any eq ssh rule-id
    268437505 (hitcnt=8) 0xf8ca4a86
access-list CSM_FW_ACL_ line 14 remark rule-id 268434432: ACCESS POLICY: AC Policy -
  Default/1
access-list CSM_FW_ACL_ line 15 remark rule-id 268434432: L4 RULE: DEFAULT ACTION
  RULE
access-list CSM_FW_ACL_ line 16 advanced deny ip any any rule-id 268434432 event-log
  flow-start (hitcnt=826) 0x97aa021a
>
```

If you set the default action to block all traffic and do not permit the OSPF traffic through an access list, the neighbor relationship breaks. When a neighbor goes down, FTD triggers an alert on the CLI similar to the following:

```
Jan 31 04:00:51.434: %OSPF-5-ADJCHG: Process 1, Nbr 3.3.3.3 on GigabitEthernet2
from FULL to DOWN, Neighbor Down: Dead timer expired
```

Summary

This chapter discusses the Transparent firewall mode and how to configure the physical and virtual interfaces. Furthermore, you have learned about various command-line tools that enable you to investigate any potential configuration issues.

Quiz

1. Which of the following statements is true about deployment?

   a. You can replace a Layer 2 switch with a transparent FTD device; there is no difference between them.

   b. Switching between Transparent Mode and Routed Mode requires a restart.

   c. You can use the FMC to configure an FTD device from Routed Mode to Transparent Mode.

   d. Changing the firewall deployment mode erases any existing configuration.

2. Which of the following statements is true about an IP address?

   a. You should use the IP address of a BVI as the default gateway for the hosts in a bridged network.

   b. The IP address of a BVI should be on a different subnet than any hosts in the bridge group.

   c. The BVI's IP address is used as the source IP address for packets that originate from an FTD device.

   d. You can configure an IPv4 address on any physical interface.

3. Which of the following statements is true when you select the Access Control: Block All Traffic policy as the default action?

   a. It overrides any "allow" access rules deployed on an FTD device.

   b. It blocks the traffic when the intrusion prevention system of an FTD device finds no malicious activities.

   c. This policy is equivalent to the **deny tcp any any** access rule.

   d. It blocks any traffic that does not match an existing access rule.

4. Which of the following commands displays the access rule entries?

   a. **show access-control**

   b. **show access-control-rule**

   c. **show access-list**

   d. **show access-list-config**

Chapter 10

Capturing Traffic for Advanced Analysis

After deploying an FTD device, if your network exhibits any connectivity issues, one of the first steps is to verify the configurations. If, however, you cannot find any configuration errors, you might want to capture live traffic and analyze it. This chapter discusses the processes of capturing traffic using the built-in FTD tools.

Traffic Capture Essentials

As you have learned, Cisco introduces a unified image on the FTD software. It converges the features of a traditional Cisco ASA firewall and next-generation Firepower services, including various advanced security technologies, such as security intelligence, network discovery, application control, file control, and a Snort-based intrusion prevention system.

When FTD blocks the traverse of a packet from ingress to egress interface, this is actually performed by either the Firewall engine, or the Firepower engine. Therefore, if two hosts experience any connectivity issues while sending traffic through an FTD device, it is essential to analyze packets from both engines to determine the root cause of the problem. For example, to investigate any registration or communications issues between FTD and the FMC, capturing traffic from the Firepower management interfaces is one of the key troubleshooting steps.

Figure 10-1 provides a high-level overview of the flow of traffic through an FTD device. The Firewall Engine receives a packet from the ingress interface and redirects to the Firepower engine.

You can utilize any third-party packet sniffer to capture traffic from the Firepower interfaces. However, both Firepower systems—FMC and FTD—offer a native packet-capturing tool within the operating system.

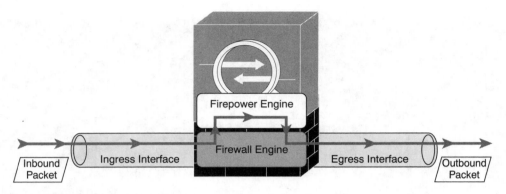

Figure 10-1   *Flow of Traffic Between Ingress and Egress Interfaces of FTD*

Best Practices for Capturing Traffic

Before you consider capturing traffic, make sure you understand the following:

■ The primary objective of a Firepower system is not to capture live traffic all the time. Besides controlling and inspecting traffic, a Firepower system supports capture of live traffic only for troubleshooting purposes. If you need to capture traffic for a long period, you should find a dedicated system designed for this purpose.

■ Capturing live traffic on a production system can degrade system performance. If necessary, you should capture traffic during a maintenance window.

■ Instead of displaying the packets on the console, redirect them into a file, copy the file from the Firepower system to your computer, and open it by using any packet analyzer. If you decide not to store the packet in a file anyway, you should limit the number of packets that you capture.

Configuring Firepower System for Traffic Analysis

The process of capturing traffic varies depending on where you want to probe. In the following sections, you will learn how to capture packets from the following hardware and software components:

■ The Firepower engine

■ The Firewall Engine

■ The FMC

Figure 10-2 shows the lab topology that is used in this chapter to capture traffic with various options.

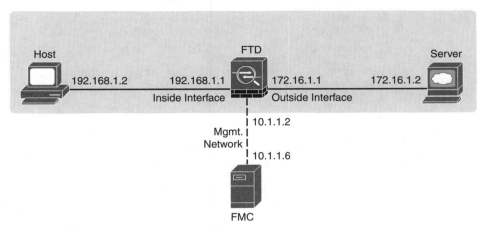

Figure 10-2 *Topology for the Packet Capture Lab*

Capturing Traffic from a Firepower Engine

To capture traffic from a Firepower engine, use the following steps:

Step 1.   Log in to the FTD CLI.

Step 2.   Run the **capture-traffic** command on the shell.

Step 3.   When the system prompts you to choose a domain, select the **Router** domain to capture traffic from the data interfaces. (The br1 domain captures traffic from the management interface.) Enter your selection to continue.

Example 10-1 shows the selection of a domain during traffic capturing. The option 1 - Router is selected, which enables the capture from the data interfaces.

Example 10-1 *Running the* **capture-traffic** *Command for the Data Interfaces*

```
> capture-traffic

Please choose domain to capture traffic from:
  0 - br1
  1 - Router

Selection? 1

Please specify tcpdump options desired.
(or enter '?' for a list of supported options)
Options:
```

Step 4.   When FTD prompts you to specify the **tcpdump** options, use the tables shown in the following section to determine the options you need. If you do not provide any options, you capture traffic without any filter by default.

Step 5.   After you add options, press Enter to begin the capture. To terminate a capture at any time, press Ctrl+C.

tcpdump Options

tcpdump offers a wide variety of options you can use to manage captured packets. It also supports Berkeley Packet Filter (BPF), which allows you to control and enhance the display of packet data.

Table 10-1 provides a list of some useful options that you can use during packet capture. Some of these options allow you to collect additional information from each packet, such as **-e**, **-n**, **-v**, and **-X**. The other options, such as **-c**, **-s**, and **-w**, enable you to manage the capturing process.

Table 10-1   *Useful* **tcpdump** *Options*

Option	Description
-c	Stops after a certain number of packets are captured.
-e	Displays the Ethernet header in the capture.
-n	Does not resolve the host name and port name.
-s	Defines the size (snaplength) of the captured packets.
-v	Shows extra packet data. **-vv** shows even more data.
-w	Saves the captured packets in a file instead of displaying them on the console.
-X	Shows packet contents in hex and ASCII.

Table 10-2 lists some of the useful BPF syntax that you can apply to filter traffic that you capture.

Table 10-2   *BPF Syntax to Filter Live Traffic During a Traffic Capture*

Options	Usage
host, net	Filters traffic to and from a single host or the entire network, respectively.
port, portrange	Filters traffic to and from a single or range of ports, respectively.
src, dst	Selects a direction for traffic flow—source or destination. Used in conjunction with the **host** and **port** options.
and, or, not	Combines or isolates traffic with a precise condition.
vlan	Captures traffic related to a particular VLAN. To capture VLAN tagged traffic, you must enter the **vlan** option followed by the desired vlan_id.

Tip   Whenever you capture traffic, you should view the actual IP address and port number (using the -n option) in the packet. You should also either save the capture (-w option) into a file or limit the number of packets you want to capture (-c option).

Example 10-2 shows the traffic capture using various **tcpdump** options. The packets in this example are captured by running the **capture-traffic** command separately. Remember that you can press Ctrl+C to exit a capture process.

Example 10-2   *Capturing Traffic Using* **tcpdump** *Options*

```
! To capture the 5 HTTP transactions between a web server and a host with IP address
  192.168.1.2:


Options: -n -c 5 host 192.168.1.2 and port 80


03:42:23.479970 IP 192.168.1.2.44694 > 172.16.1.2.80: Flags [S], seq 2622260089, win
  29200, options [mss 1380,sackOK,TS val 2174057 ecr 0,nop,wscale 7], length 0
03:42:23.479970 IP 172.16.1.2.80 > 192.168.1.2.44694: Flags [S.], seq 2877405527,
  ack 2622260090, win 28960, options [mss 1380,sackOK,TS val 1270689 ecr
  2174057,nop,wscale 7], length 0
03:42:23.479970 IP 192.168.1.2.44694 > 172.16.1.2.80: Flags [.], ack 1, win 229,
  options [nop,nop,TS val 2174058 ecr 1270689], length 0
03:42:23.479970 IP 192.168.1.2.44694 > 172.16.1.2.80: Flags [P.], ack 1, win 229,
  options [nop,nop,TS val 2174058 ecr 1270689], length 436
03:42:23.479970 IP 172.16.1.2.80 > 192.168.1.2.44694: Flags [.], ack 437, win 235,
  options [nop,nop,TS val 1270689 ecr 2174058], length 0
>


! To capture the client side traffic—originated by a host, destined to a web server:


Options: -n -c 5 src 192.168.1.2 and dst port 80


03:47:07.529956 IP 192.168.1.2.44698 > 172.16.1.2.80: Flags [S], seq 3873637979, win
  29200, options [mss 1380,sackOK,TS val 2245066 ecr 0,nop,wscale 7], length 0
03:47:07.529956 IP 192.168.1.2.44698 > 172.16.1.2.80: Flags [.], ack 3924903157, win
  229, options [nop,nop,TS val 2245066 ecr 1341696], length 0
03:47:07.529956 IP 192.168.1.2.44698 > 172.16.1.2.80: Flags [P.], ack 1, win 229,
  options [nop,nop,TS val 2245066 ecr 1341696], length 436
03:47:07.529956 IP 192.168.1.2.44698 > 172.16.1.2.80: Flags [.], ack 1369, win 251,
  options [nop,nop,TS val 2245067 ecr 1341697], length 0
03:47:07.529956 IP 192.168.1.2.44698 > 172.16.1.2.80: Flags [.], ack 2737, win 274,
  options [nop,nop,TS val 2245067 ecr 1341697], length 0
>


! To capture the server side traffic—originated by a web server, destined to host
  192.168.1.2:


Options: -n -c 5 dst 192.168.1.2 and src port 80
```

```
03:49:11.779943 IP 172.16.1.2.80 > 192.168.1.2.44702: Flags [S.], seq 212338482,
   ack 2358717416, win 28960, options [mss 1380,sackOK,TS val 1372759 ecr
   2276129,nop,wscale 7], length 0
03:49:11.789952 IP 172.16.1.2.80 > 192.168.1.2.44702: Flags [.], ack 437, win 235,
   options [nop,nop,TS val 1372759 ecr 2276129], length 0
03:49:11.789952 IP 172.16.1.2.80 > 192.168.1.2.44702: Flags [.], ack 437, win 235,
   options [nop,nop,TS val 1372759 ecr 2276129], length 1368
03:49:11.789952 IP 172.16.1.2.80 > 192.168.1.2.44702: Flags [.], ack 437, win 235,
   options [nop,nop,TS val 1372759 ecr 2276129], length 1368
03:49:11.789952 IP 172.16.1.2.80 > 192.168.1.2.44702: Flags [P.], ack 437, win 235,
   options [nop,nop,TS val 1372759 ecr 2276129], length 789
>
```

Example 10-3 shows the options to print additional data while you capture traffic.

Example 10-3   *Displaying Additional Packet Data by Using the* **tcpdump** *Tool*

```
! First, look at the following capture with default packet data:

Options: -n -c 5 host 192.168.1.2

04:36:10.329969 IP 192.168.1.2.58718 > 172.16.1.2.80: Flags [S], seq 193723078, win
   29200, options [mss 1380,sackOK,TS val 392486 ecr 0,nop,wscale 7], length 0
04:36:10.329969 IP 172.16.1.2.80 > 192.168.1.2.58718: Flags [S.], seq 2078424703,
   ack 193723079, win 28960, options [mss 1380,sackOK,TS val 2077347 ecr
   392486,nop,wscale 7], length 0
04:36:10.329969 IP 192.168.1.2.58718 > 172.16.1.2.80: Flags [.], ack 1, win 229,
   options [nop,nop,TS val 392486 ecr 2077347], length 0
04:36:10.329969 IP 192.168.1.2.58718 > 172.16.1.2.80: Flags [P.], ack 1, win 229,
   options [nop,nop,TS val 392486 ecr 2077347], length 436
04:36:10.329969 IP 172.16.1.2.80 > 192.168.1.2.58718: Flags [.], ack 437, win 235,
   options [nop,nop,TS val 2077347 ecr 392486], length 0
>


! The -vv option prints additional data including the checksum of a packet.

Options: -n -c 5 -vv host 192.168.1.2

04:36:44.729957 IP (tos 0x0, ttl 64, id 27818, offset 0, flags [DF], proto TCP (6),
   length 60)
    192.168.1.2.58720 > 172.16.1.2.80: Flags [S], cksum 0x730b (correct), seq
      2112778772, win 29200, options [mss 1380,sackOK,TS val 401086 ecr 0,nop,
      wscale 7], length 0
04:36:44.729957 IP (tos 0x0, ttl 64, id 0, offset 0, flags [DF], proto TCP (6),
   length 60)
```

```
    172.16.1.2.80 > 192.168.1.2.58720: Flags [S.], cksum 0x0515 (correct), seq
      2199066473, ack 2112778773, win 28960, options [mss 1380,sackOK,TS val 2085945
      ecr 401086,nop,wscale 7], length 0
04:36:44.729957 IP (tos 0x0, ttl 64, id 27819, offset 0, flags [DF], proto TCP (6),
    length 52)
    192.168.1.2.58720 > 172.16.1.2.80: Flags [.], cksum 0xa3cc (correct), seq 1,
      ack 1, win 229, options [nop,nop,TS val 401086 ecr 2085945], length 0
04:36:44.729957 IP (tos 0x0, ttl 64, id 27820, offset 0, flags [DF], proto TCP (6),
    length 488)
    192.168.1.2.58720 > 172.16.1.2.80: Flags [P.], cksum 0xf6e9 (correct), seq
      1:437, ack 1, win 229, options [nop,nop,TS val 401086 ecr 2085945], length 436
04:36:44.729957 IP (tos 0x0, ttl 64, id 65408, offset 0, flags [DF], proto TCP (6),
    length 52)
    172.16.1.2.80 > 192.168.1.2.58720: Flags [.], cksum 0xa212 (correct), seq 1,
      ack 437, win 235, options [nop,nop,TS val 2085945 ecr 401086], length 0
>
```

! The -e option displays the layer 2 header in the capture.

Options: **-n -c 5 -e host 192.168.1.2**

```
04:37:21.909941 c4:2c:03:3c:98:a8 > a4:6c:2a:e4:6b:c0, ethertype IPv4 (0x0800),
    length 74: 192.168.1.2.58722 > 172.16.1.2.80: Flags [S], seq 1691712365, win
    29200, options [mss 1380,sackOK,TS val 410383 ecr 0,nop,wscale 7], length 0
04:37:21.919935 00:23:24:72:1d:3c > a4:6c:2a:e4:6b:c1, ethertype IPv4 (0x0800),
    length 74: 172.16.1.2.80 > 192.168.1.2.58722: Flags [S.], seq 3252338695,
    ack 1691712366, win 28960, options [mss 1380,sackOK,TS val 2095242 ecr
    410383,nop,wscale 7], length 0
04:37:21.919935 c4:2c:03:3c:98:a8 > a4:6c:2a:e4:6b:c0, ethertype IPv4 (0x0800),
    length 66: 192.168.1.2.58722 > 172.16.1.2.80: Flags [.], ack 1, win 229, options
    [nop,nop,TS val 410383 ecr 2095242], length 0
04:37:21.919935 c4:2c:03:3c:98:a8 > a4:6c:2a:e4:6b:c0, ethertype IPv4 (0x0800),
    length 502: 192.168.1.2.58722 > 172.16.1.2.80: Flags [P.], ack 1, win 229, options
    [nop,nop,TS val 410383 ecr 2095242], length 436
04:37:21.919935 00:23:24:72:1d:3c > a4:6c:2a:e4:6b:c1, ethertype IPv4 (0x0800),
    length 66: 172.16.1.2.80 > 192.168.1.2.58722: Flags [.], ack 437, win 235, options
    [nop,nop,TS val 2095242 ecr 410383], length 0
>
```

! The -X option prints the hex and ASCII values of each packet. For example, the
  fourth packet in the following example shows the GET request to a HTTP server.

Options: **-n -c 5 -X host 192.168.1.2**

```
04:40:50.069988 IP 192.168.1.2.58724 > 172.16.1.2.80: Flags [S], seq 3090457163, win
    29200, options [mss 1380,sackOK,TS val 462423 ecr 0,nop,wscale 7], length 0
```

```
        0x0000:  4500 003c ac1c 4000 4006 1fe3 c0a8 0102   E..<..@.@.......
        0x0010:  ac10 0102 e564 0050 b834 a24b 0000 0000   .....d.P.4.K....
        0x0020:  a002 7210 18f0 0000 0204 0564 0402 080a   ..r........d....
        0x0030:  0007 0e57 0000 0000 0103 0307            ...W.......
04:40:50.069988 IP 172.16.1.2.80 > 192.168.1.2.58724: Flags [S.], seq 1195208673,
    ack 3090457164, win 28960, options [mss 1380,sackOK,TS val 2147276 ecr
    462423,nop,wscale 7], length 0
        0x0000:  4500 003c 0000 4000 4006 cbff ac10 0102   E..<..@.@.......
        0x0010:  c0a8 0102 0050 e564 473d 6fe1 b834 a24c   .....P.dG=o..4.L
        0x0020:  a012 7120 9ec3 0000 0204 0564 0402 080a   ..q........d....
        0x0030:  0020 c3cc 0007 0e57 0103 0307            .......W....
04:40:50.069988 IP 192.168.1.2.58724 > 172.16.1.2.80: Flags [.], ack 1, win 229,
    options [nop,nop,TS val 462423 ecr 2147276], length 0
        0x0000:  4500 0034 ac1d 4000 4006 1fea c0a8 0102   E..4..@.@.......
        0x0010:  ac10 0102 e564 0050 b834 a24c 473d 6fe2   .....d.P.4.LG=o.
        0x0020:  8010 00e5 3d7b 0000 0101 080a 0007 0e57   ....={.........W
        0x0030:  0020 c3cc                                 ....
04:40:50.069988 IP 192.168.1.2.58724 > 172.16.1.2.80: Flags [P.], ack 1, win 229,
    options [nop,nop,TS val 462423 ecr 2147276], length 436
        0x0000:  4500 01e8 ac1e 4000 4006 1e35 c0a8 0102   E.....@.@..5....
        0x0010:  ac10 0102 e564 0050 b834 a24c 473d 6fe2   .....d.P.4.LG=o.
        0x0020:  8018 00e5 9098 0000 0101 080a 0007 0e57   ...............W
        0x0030:  0020 c3cc 4745 5420 2f20 4854 5450 2f31   ....GET./.HTTP/1
        0x0040:  2e31 0d0a 486f 7374 3a20 3137 322e 3136   .1..Host:.172.16
        0x0050:  2e31 2e32 0d0a 5573 6572 2d41 6765 6e74   .1.2..User-Agent
        0x0060:  3a20 4d6f 7a69 6c6c 612f 352e 3020 2858   :.Mozilla/5.0.(X
        0x0070:  3131 3b20 5562 756e 7475 3b20 4c69 6e75   11;.Ubuntu;.Linu
        0x0080:  7820 7838 365f 3634 3b20 7276 3a34 382e   x.x86_64;.rv:48.
        0x0090:  3029 2047 6563 6b6f 2f32 3031 3030 3130   0).Gecko/2010010
        0x00a0:  3120 4669 7265 666f 782f 3438 2e30 0d0a   1.Firefox/48.0..
        0x00b0:  4163 6365 7074 3a20 7465 7874 2f68 746d   Accept:.text/htm
        0x00c0:  6c2c 6170 706c 6963 6174 696f 6e2f 7868   l,application/xh
        0x00d0:  746d 6c2b 786d 6c2c 6170 706c 6963 6174   tml+xml,applicat
        0x00e0:  696f 6e2f 786d 6c3b 713d 302e 392c 2a2f   ion/xml;q=0.9,*/
        0x00f0:  2a3b 713d 302e 380d 0a41 6363 6570 742d   *;q=0.8..Accept-
        0x0100:  4c61 6e67 7561 6765 3a20 656e 2d55 532c   Language:.en-US,
        0x0110:  656e 3b71 3d30 2e35 0d0a 4163 6365 7074   en;q=0.5..Accept
        0x0120:  2d45 6e63 6f64 696e 673a 2067 7a69 702c   -Encoding:.gzip,
        0x0130:  2064 6566 6c61 7465 0d0a 436f 6e6e 6563   .deflate..Connec
        0x0140:  7469 6f6e 3a20 6b65 6570 2d61 6c69 7665   tion:.keep-alive
        0x0150:  0d0a 5570 6772 6164 652d 496e 7365 6375   ..Upgrade-Insecu
        0x0160:  7265 2d52 6571 7565 7374 733a 2031 0d0a   re-Requests:.1..
        0x0170:  4966 2d4d 6f64 6966 6965 642d 5369 6e63   If-Modified-Sinc
        0x0180:  653a 2054 7565 2c20 3134 2046 6562 2032   e:.Tue,.14.Feb.2
        0x0190:  3031 3720 3136 3a32 343a 3339 2047 4d54   017.16:24:39.GMT
```

```
        0x01a0:   0d0a 4966 2d4e 6f6e 652d 4d61 7463 683a   ..If-None-Match:
        0x01b0:   2022 3263 3339 2d35 3438 3830 3030 3333   ."2c39-548800033
        0x01c0:   3730 6463 2d67 7a69 7022 0d0a 4361 6368   70dc-gzip"..Cach
        0x01d0:   652d 436f 6e74 726f 6c3a 206d 6178 2d61   e-Control:.max-a
        0x01e0:   6765 3d30 0d0a 0d0a                        ge=0....
04:40:50.069988 IP 172.16.1.2.80 > 192.168.1.2.58724: Flags [.], ack 437, win 235,
    options [nop,nop,TS val 2147276 ecr 462423], length 0
        0x0000:   4500 0034 1e39 4000 4006 adce ac10 0102   E..4.9@.@.......
        0x0010:   c0a8 0102 0050 e564 473d 6fe2 b834 a400   .....P.dG=o..4..
        0x0020:   8010 00eb 3bc1 0000 0101 080a 0020 c3cc   ....;..........
        0x0030:   0007 0e57                                  ...W
>
```

Downloading a .pcap File Generated by Firepower Engine

In addition to using the live view on a console, you can also redirect a capture into
a .pcap file. Later, you can retrieve the file by using packet analyzer software for further
analysis.

Example 10-4 shows the options to capture traffic to and from host 192.168.1.2. While
the packets are being captured, the system stores them in the traffic.pcap file.

Example 10-4   *Options to Save Packets into a .pcap File*

```
Options: -w traffic.pcap -s 1518 host 192.168.1.2
^C
Caught interrupt signal
Exiting.


>

! The following command confirms that the pcap file is created and stored on the
  disk.


> file list
Feb 15 05:03                886 /traffic.pcap
>
```

Once the traffic is captured and a .pcap file is created, you can download the file by
using either the GUI or the CLI.

Using the FMC GUI to Download a File

FTD does not have its own GUI. You can, however, use the FMC GUI to download a file,
as shown in the following steps.

Step 1.   Log in to the FMC GUI and navigate to the **System > Health > Monitor** page. The Appliance Status Summary chart appears.

Step 2.   Find the FTD device where you captured traffic. If you do not see your appliance, expand the arrow icon next to the health status. Figure 10-3 shows this icon next to the Normal status. You can expand this arrow icon to see all the appliances that have normal health status.

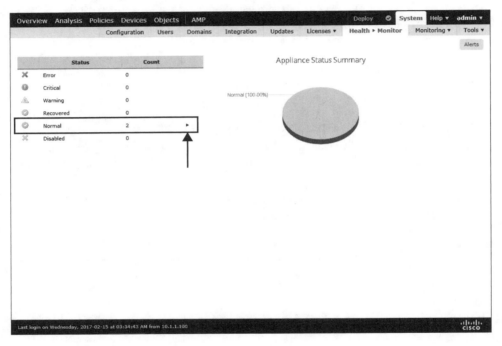

Figure 10-3   *Appliance Status Summary*

Step 3.   When you find the FTD device on this page, click on the appliance name, and the Health Monitor page for the FTD appears.

Step 4.   Click the **Advanced Troubleshooting** button (see Figure 10-4). The File Download page appears.

Step 5.   On the File Download page, in the field where you can enter the name of a .pcap file, enter the filename with .pcap file extension (for example, traffic. pcap, as shown in Figure 10-5).

Step 6.   Click the **Download** button to begin the file download.

Figure 10-4 *Advanced Troubleshooting Button*

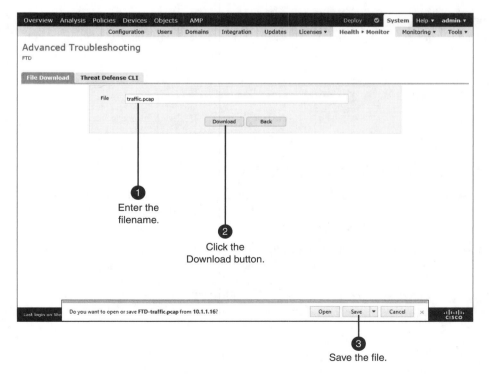

Figure 10-5 *The File Download Page Appears in the Advanced Troubleshooting Page*

Using the CLI to Copy a File to an External Computer

You can use the CLI to copy a file to an external system if the system runs the SSH daemon. To transfer files, FTD uses the Secure Copy (SCP) protocol, which is based on the Secure Shell (SSH) protocol. To copy a file, use the following command syntax:

```
file secure-copy IP_Address Username Path Filename
```

Example 10-5 show the traffic.pcap file being copied from FTD to an external computer.

Example 10-5 *Copying a File Securely from FTD to a Computer*

```
> file secure-copy 10.1.1.10 admin /var/tmp traffic.pcap
The authenticity of host '10.1.1.10 (10.1.1.10)' can't be established.
ECDSA key fingerprint is 71:cf:b1:17:86:78:bf:10:41:7d:60:75:87:c3:6b:f4.
Are you sure you want to continue connecting (yes/no)? yes
Password:
copy successful.

>
```

> **Note** You can also run the **file copy** command to transfer files over FTP.

When the .pcap file is transferred to the desired location, you can delete the original .pcap file in FTD to maintain free disk space. Use the **file delete** command from the CLI, as shown here, to delete a .pcap file:

```
> file delete traffic.pcap
Really remove file traffic.pcap?
Please enter 'YES' or 'NO': YES
>
```

Capturing Traffic from the Firewall Engine

In the previous section, you learned how to capture traffic from a Firepower engine. However, you cannot run the same command on a Firewall Engine. Follow these steps to capture traffic from the Firewall Engine:

Step 1.   Determine the name of the interface from which you want to capture traffic. Example 10-6 shows one of the ways to identify the name of an FTD interface. In this example, you will run the capture on the GigabitEthernet1/1 interface that is named INSIDE_INTERFACE.

Example 10-6 *Using the* **nameif** *Command to See the Interfaces with Names*

```
> show nameif
Interface              Name                    Security
GigabitEthernet1/1     INSIDE_INTERFACE        0
GigabitEthernet1/2     OUTSIDE_INTERFACE       0
Management1/1          diagnostic              0
>
```

Step 2.   Run the **capture** command along with the interface name, using the following syntax:

```
capture capture_name interface int_name match protocol_name source_
detail destination_detail
```

The following command captures ICMP traffic from a single host, 192.168.1.2, to any destinations. This particular capture process, labeled *icmp_traffic*, captures traffic only from INSIDE_INTERFACE.

```
> capture icmp_traffic interface INSIDE_INTERFACE match icmp host
192.168.1.2 any
```

Figure 10-6 clarifies the difference between the **capture** and **capture-traffic** commands. To capture traffic from the Firewall Engine, you use the **capture** command. The **capture-traffic** command captures the traffic from the Firepower engine.

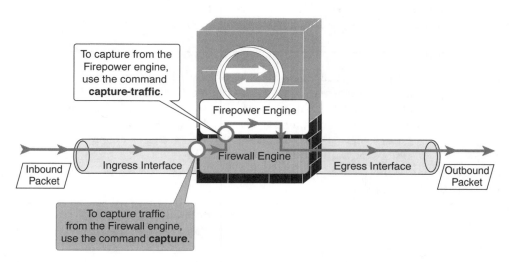

Figure 10-6   *The Difference Between the* **capture** *and* **capture-traffic** *Tools*

Step 3.   After you enter the **capture** command, run some ping tests through FTD. When the test traffic goes through, you can view it by running the **show capture** command in FTD.

Example 10-7 confirms that the condition in the *icmp_traffic* capture process is matching and capturing traffic. You can view the captured traffic on an on-demand basis.

Example 10-7   *Viewing Captured Traffic*

```
! Run the following command to view the condition within a capture process.

> show capture
capture icmp_traffic type raw-data interface INSIDE_INTERFACE [Capturing - 1140
  bytes]
  match icmp host 192.168.1.2 any
>
! Run the following command to view the captured traffic for a particular matching
  condition.

> show capture icmp_traffic

6 packets captured

   1: 05:47:38.406457        192.168.1.2 > 172.16.1.2: icmp: echo request
   2: 05:47:38.407205        172.16.1.2 > 192.168.1.2: icmp: echo reply
   3: 05:47:39.407617        192.168.1.2 > 172.16.1.2: icmp: echo request
   4: 05:47:39.408258        172.16.1.2 > 192.168.1.2: icmp: echo reply
   5: 05:47:40.408731        192.168.1.2 > 172.16.1.2: icmp: echo request
   6: 05:47:40.409478        172.16.1.2 > 192.168.1.2: icmp: echo reply
6 packets shown
>
```

Step 4.   The *icmp_traffic* capture process keeps growing as it matches more ICMP traffic. You can remove any previous captures and start capturing similar traffic by using the **clear** command. When you want to stop capturing completely, use the **no capture** command, as shown in Example 10-8. As you can see, this command clears the packets from an existing capture process and also stops the traffic capture.

Example 10-8   *Deleting a Capture*

```
! Run the following command to remove the previous captures.

> clear capture /all
>



! The following command confirms that all of the previously captured packets are
  cleared.
```

```
> show capture icmp_traffic

0 packet captured
0 packet shown
>



! To stop capturing any traffic that might match the icmp_traffic capturing condi-
  tion, run the following command:


> no capture icmp_traffic interface INSIDE_INTERFACE
>



! To confirm that a capture instance no longer runs on an interface, run the com-
  mand below. Note that an interface name is no longer associated the icmp_traffic
  capture.


> show capture
capture icmp_traffic type raw-data [Capturing - 1140 bytes]
  match icmp host 192.168.1.2 any
>



! To delete the icmp_traffic capture instance, run the following command:


> no capture icmp_traffic
>


! Now, if you try again, it ends with an error as the capture itself is deleted.


> show capture icmp_traffic
ERROR: Capture <icmp_traffic> does not exist
>
```

Downloading a .pcap File Generated by Firewall Engine

You can download a capture from a Firewall Engine to your desktop, save it as a .pcap
file, and retrieve it by using a packet analyzer for further analysis. Instead of looking at
simple ICMP traffic, let's examine how to capture TCP traffic and download the capture
to your desktop. Later in this section, you can view the full TCP handshakes of an HTTP
session. For now, follow these steps:

Step 1.   Create a capture for INSIDE_INTERFACE that will match any HTTP traffic
(TCP port 80):

```
> capture http_traffic interface INSIDE_INTERFACE match tcp any any eq 80
```

Step 2.   Go to a website in your browser. If the host computer is unable to access the website, check whether the host can communicate with INSIDE_INTERFACE.

Step 3.   After you access a website successfully, check the status of the capture in FTD. Example 10-9 confirms that the FTD is currently capturing HTTP traffic on INSIDE_INTERFACE.

Example 10-9   *Matching the HTTP Traffic*

```
> show capture
capture http_traffic type raw-data interface INSIDE_INTERFACE [Capturing - 5777
  bytes]
  match tcp any any eq www
>
```

Example 10-10 shows that an FTD device captures 15 packets by using the *http_traffic* matching condition. The capture demonstrates a complete TCP handshake process. Note the SYN, SYN-ACK, and ACK at the beginning of the session.

Example 10-10   *Capturing HTTP Traffic Through an FTD*

```
> show capture http_traffic

15 packets captured

   1: 09:19:38.442726        192.168.1.2.58808 > 172.16.1.2.80: S 1558097726:
      1558097726(0) win 29200 <mss 1460,sackOK,timestamp 4644956 0,nop,wscale 7>
   2: 09:19:38.444007        172.16.1.2.80 > 192.168.1.2.58808: S 1776867665:
      1776867665(0) ack 1558097727 win 28960 <mss 1380,sackOK,timestamp 6329332
      4644956,nop,wscale 7>
   3: 09:19:38.444129        192.168.1.2.58808 > 172.16.1.2.80: . ack 1776867666 win
      229 <nop,nop,timestamp 4644956 6329332>
   4: 09:19:38.444267        192.168.1.2.58808 > 172.16.1.2.80: P 1558097727:
      1558098163(436) ack 1776867666 win 229 <nop,nop,timestamp 4644956 6329332>
   5: 09:19:38.444999        172.16.1.2.80 > 192.168.1.2.58808: . ack 1558098163 win
      235 <nop,nop,timestamp 6329332 4644956>
   6: 09:19:38.446601        172.16.1.2.80 > 192.168.1.2.58808: . 1776867666:
      1776869034(1368) ack 1558098163 win 235 <nop,nop,timestamp 6329332 4644956>
   7: 09:19:38.446616        172.16.1.2.80 > 192.168.1.2.58808: . 1776869034:
      1776870402(1368) ack 1558098163 win 235 <nop,nop,timestamp 6329332 4644956>
   8: 09:19:38.446662        172.16.1.2.80 > 192.168.1.2.58808: P 1776870402:
      1776871191(789) ack 1558098163 win 235 <nop,nop,timestamp 6329332 4644956>
   9: 09:19:38.446800        192.168.1.2.58808 > 172.16.1.2.80: . ack 1776871191 win
      284 <nop,nop,timestamp 4644957 6329332>
  10: 09:19:38.488011        192.168.1.2.58808 > 172.16.1.2.80: P 1558098163:
      1558098553(390) ack 1776871191 win 284 <nop,nop,timestamp 4644967 6329332>
```

```
11: 09:19:38.489354        172.16.1.2.80 > 192.168.1.2.58808: P 1776871191:
    1776871371(180) ack 1558098553 win 243 <nop,nop,timestamp 6329343 4644967>
12: 09:19:38.489476        192.168.1.2.58808 > 172.16.1.2.80: . ack 1776871371 win
    305 <nop,nop,timestamp 4644968 6329343>
13: 09:19:43.397013        172.16.1.2.80 > 192.168.1.2.58808: F 1776871371:
    1776871371(0) ack 1558098553 win 243 <nop,nop,timestamp 6330570 4644968>
14: 09:19:43.397486        192.168.1.2.58808 > 172.16.1.2.80: F 1558098553:
    1558098553(0) ack 1776871372 win 305 <nop,nop,timestamp 4646195 6330570>
15: 09:19:43.397821        172.16.1.2.80 > 192.168.1.2.58808: . ack 1558098554 win
    243 <nop,nop,timestamp 6330570 4646195>
15 packets shown
>
```

Step 4. Download the packets shown in Example 10-10 by using a web browser. Use the following URL syntax in your browser to access FTD:

```
https://<IP_Address_of_FTD>/capture/<capture_name>/pcap/<capture_name>.
pcap
```

For example, if the IP address of the inside interface is 192.168.1.1, and the name of the capture is http_traffic, enter the following URL in your browser:

```
https://192.168.1.1/capture/http_traffic/pcap/http_traffic.pcap
```

If the browser is unable to connect to FTD, run the following command to check whether the HTTP service is running:

```
> show running-config http
>
```

If this command shows no output, the HTTP service is disabled. You need to enable it to access FTD through a bowser and download a capture in .pcap file format.

Enabling HTTP Service in FTD

Before you enable HTTP service in FTD, you can optionally turn on debugging. When you do, you get a confirmation when the HTTP server starts, which helps you determine the status of the service:

```
> debug http 255
debug http enabled at level 255.
>
```

By deploying a new platform setting policy from the FMC, you can enable the HTTP service on an FTD device. Here are the steps:

Step 1. Go to the **Devices > Platform Settings** page, click the **New Policy** button, and select the **Threat Defense Settings** option. Figure 10-7 confirms that there is no current Platform Settings policy available.

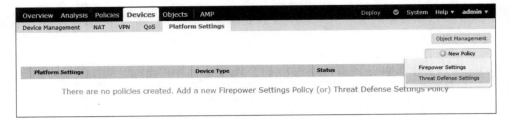

Figure 10-7   *Platform Settings Page Showing the Threat Defense Settings Option*

Step 2.   When the New Policy window appears, name the policy **FTD Platform Settings**, select an FTD device where you want to apply this new policy, and save the settings (see Figure 10-8).

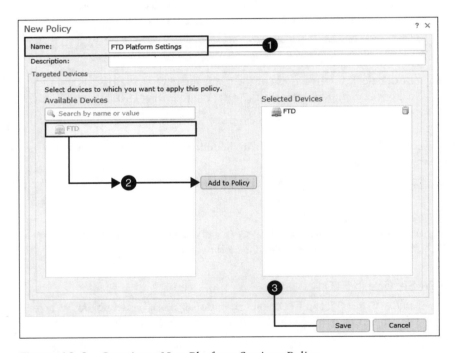

Figure 10-8   *Creating a New Platform Settings Policy*

Step 3.   In the FTD Platform Settings policy editor page, select **HTTP** from the left panel, and then select the check box for **Enable HTTP Server**. Figure 10-9 shows the HTTP service being enabled through port 443.

Step 4.   Click the **Add** button. The Add HTTP Configuration window appears.

Figure 10-9 *Enabling the HTTP Service*

Step 5.   Select the zones (INSIDE_ZONE) and IP addresses (192.168.0.0/16) that are allowed to access the HTTP service on FTD, as shown in Figure 10-10.

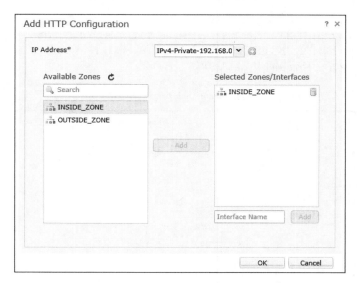

Figure 10-10 *Add HTTP Configuration Page*

Step 6. Click **OK** to return to the policy editor page. You should now see the zone and IP address you just selected.

Step 7. Click the **Save** button to save the changes, and then click the **Deploy** button to commit the changes to the FTD device (see Figure 10-11).

Figure 10-11 *Deploying the Platform Settings with the HTTP Service*

You can now use the CLI to verify the deployment status. When the HTTP service starts in FTD, it generates a debug message (if you enabled **debug http** already) and changes the running configurations.

Example 10-11 confirms that the HTTP server has been enabled. Per this configuration, users who are connected to INSIDE_INTERFACE are able to access FTD by using a browser if the requests originate from the 192.168.0.0/16 network.

Example 10-11 *Verifying HTTP Server Configuration in FTD*

```
! As soon as the HTTP service starts, FTD generates the following debug message:

http_enable: Enabling HTTP server
HTTP server starting.

! To verify the current HTTP server configuration:

> show running-config http
http server enable
http 192.168.0.0 255.255.0.0 INSIDE_INTERFACE
>
```

After the deployment is verified, run the **undebug all** command to disable debugging. Now, in a browser, enter the IP address of the inside interface as a URL with the following syntax:

```
https://<IP_Address_of_FTD>/capture/<capture_name>/pcap/<capture_name>.pcap
```

For example, if the IP address of the FTD inside interface is 192.168.1.1/24, and the name of the capture is http_traffic, then enter the following URL in your browser:

```
https://192.168.1.1/capture/http_traffic/pcap/http_traffic.pcap
```

A browser, upon successful connection to the FTD, should prompt you to save the traffic.pcap file. After you save the file on your computer, you can use a third-party packet analyzer to view the packets.

Figure 10-12 shows the same HTTP traffic that you viewed earlier in this section. Previously, you viewed this traffic on the FTD console. Now, you are viewing the traffic using the third-party packet analyzer Wireshark.

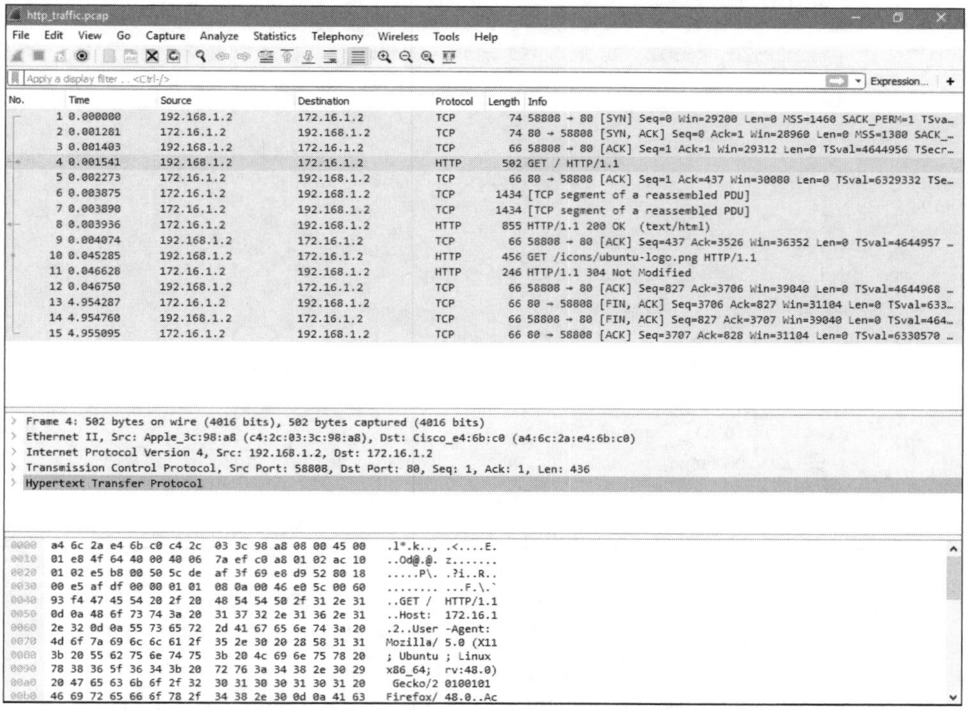

Figure 10-12 *HTTP Traffic Capture in the Wireshark Packet Analyzer*

When you finish working with a packet capture, delete the rule to prevent the FTD device from capturing any further traffic. This ensures that the system will not be wasting any resources by capturing unwanted traffic in the future.

```
> no capture http_traffic
```

Capturing Traffic from the FMC

To investigate any complicated communication issue between the FMC and FTD, analysis of the management traffic is one of the key troubleshooting tools. You cannot run exactly the same commands to capture traffic on the FMC and FTD. This section describes a different process for capturing traffic from the management interface of the FMC.

First, you need to determine the name of the FMC management interface. Example 10-12 indicates two interfaces on the FMC. The first one, eth0 with 10.1.1.16, is the management interface. The second one, lo with 127.0.0.1, is a loopback interface.

Example 10-12   *Output of the* ifconfig *Command*

```
admin@FMC:~$ ifconfig
eth0      Link encap:Ethernet  HWaddr 00:0     C:29:ED:37:B1
          inet addr:10.1.1.16  Bcast:10.1.1.255  Mask:255.255.255.0
          inet6 addr: fe80::20c:29ff:feed:37b1/64 Scope:Link
          UP BROADCAST RUNNING MULTICAST  MTU:1500  Metric:1
          RX packets:99519 errors:0 dropped:0 overruns:0 frame:0
          TX packets:591461 errors:0 dropped:0 overruns:0 carrier:0
          collisions:0 txqueuelen:1000
          RX bytes:21356354 (20.3 Mb)  TX bytes:145518227 (138.7 Mb)

lo        Link encap:Local Loopback
          inet addr:127.0.0.1  Mask:255.255.255.0
          inet6 addr: ::1/128 Scope:Host
          UP LOOPBACK RUNNING  MTU:65536  Metric:1
          RX packets:79815237 errors:0 dropped:0 overruns:0 frame:0
          TX packets:79815237 errors:0 dropped:0 overruns:0 carrier:0
          collisions:0 txqueuelen:0
          RX bytes:32518661679 (31012.2 Mb)  TX bytes:32518661679 (31012.2 Mb)

admin@FMC:~$
```

Then you need to run the **tcpdump** command on the management interface to capture traffic. You can apply BPF syntax and filtering options similar to the ones you used on a Firepower engine earlier in this chapter.

Example 10-13 shows a capture of ICMP traffic between FTD and the FMC. The **host** option, in this example, limits the capture of traffic only from a particular host, 10.1.1.2, which is an FTD device. The **-i eth0** option allows the **tcpdump** tool to listen to only the eth0 management interface.

Example 10-13   *Capturing Traffic on the eth0 Interface of the FMC*

```
admin@FMC:~$ sudo tcpdump -i eth0 host 10.1.1.2
Password:
HS_PACKET_BUFFER_SIZE is set to 4.
tcpdump: verbose output suppressed, use -v or -vv for full protocol decode
listening on eth0, link-type EN10MB (Ethernet), capture size 96 bytes

11:11:52.121238 IP 10.1.1.2 > FMC: ICMP echo request, id 16625, seq 1, length 64
11:11:52.121293 IP FMC > 10.1.1.2: ICMP echo reply, id 16625, seq 1, length 64
11:11:53.121786 IP 10.1.1.2 > FMC: ICMP echo request, id 16625, seq 2, length 64
11:11:53.121856 IP FMC > 10.1.1.2: ICMP echo reply, id 16625, seq 2, length 64
^C
4 packets captured
4 packets received by filter
0 packets dropped by kernel
admin@FMC:~$
```

Downloading a .pcap File Generated by FMC

To analyze a capture using a third-party packet analyzer, you need to save the packets in .pcap file format and then transfer the file to your computer.

Example 10-14 shows 10 packets captured into the traffic.pcap file. When you redirect packets into a .pcap file, it is no longer displayed in a console and thus reduces resource utilization.

Example 10-14   *Saving the Packet Capture into a .pcap File*

```
admin@FMC:~$ sudo tcpdump -i eth0 host 10.1.1.2 -w /var/common/fmc_traffic.pcap
HS_PACKET_BUFFER_SIZE is set to 4.
tcpdump: listening on eth0, link-type EN10MB (Ethernet), capture size 96 bytes
^C
10 packets captured
10 packets received by filter
0 packets dropped by kernel
admin@FMC:~$
```

Note   To store any user-generated file, use the /var/common directory on the FMC. If you save a file on this directory, the FMC allows you to download it directly using the GUI.

You can use either the GUI or CLI to download a packet capture. If you want to use the GUI to download a .pcap file, the file should be located in the /var/common directory of the FMC.

To download a file from the FMC by using its GUI, use the following steps:

Step 1.   Go to the **Health > Monitor** page and find the FMC in the appliance health status list.

Step 2.   Click on the FMC name. A detail view of the FMC health status appears.

Step 3.   Click the **Advanced Troubleshooting** button (see Figure 10-13). The File Download tab appears.

Figure 10-13   *Health Module Status and Details of Alerts on the FMC*

Step 4.   Enter the name of the .pcap file (including the file extension) in the File field.

Step 5.   Click the **Download** button. (Figure 10-14 shows the sequence to download the fmc_traffic.pcap file by using the Advanced Troubleshooting page.) The browser prompts you to save the file on your computer.

Alternatively, you can use the CLI to copy a file to an external system if the system runs SSH daemon. To transfer files, the FMC uses the Secure Copy (SCP) protocol, which is based on the Secure Shell (SSH) protocol.

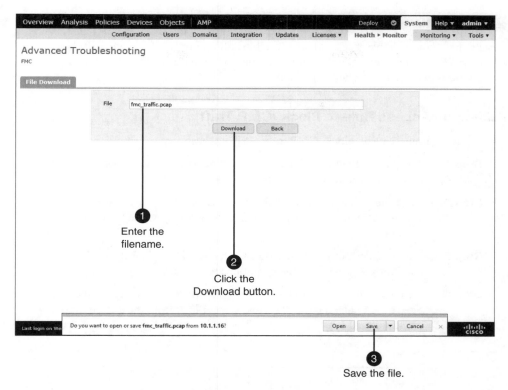

Figure 10-14   *Downloading a User-Generated File by Using the GUI*

Example 10-15 shows the command to copy a file from the FMC to an external computer by using SCP.

Example 10-15   *Transferring a .pcap File from the FMC to an External Computer*

```
admin@FMC:~$ scp /var/common/fmc_traffic.pcap admin@10.1.1.10:/home/user
The authenticity of host '10.1.1.10 (10.1.1.10)' can't be established.
ECDSA key fingerprint is SHA256:HBe6vA5zp014kDANRmJuAUxwW5Q5z/9Hy9B4nF+TVWA.
Are you sure you want to continue connecting (yes/no)? yes
Warning: Permanently added '10.1.1.10' (ECDSA) to the list of known hosts.
admin@10.1.1.10's password:
fmc_traffic.pcap                                                100%  886
  0.9KB/s   00:00
admin@FMC:~$
```

Once the .pcap file is transferred to the desired location, you can delete the original .pcap file on the FMC to maintain free disk space.

Verification and Troubleshooting Tools

By deploying a simple access rule that can block ICMP traffic, you can verify how a Firewall Engine receives traffic from a physical interface and then redirects it to a Firepower engine for further inspection.

Adding an Access Rule to Block ICMP Traffic

To create a rule that can block ICMP traffic, follow these steps:

Step 1.   Navigate to **Policy > Access Control > Access Control**. A list of available access control policies appears.

Step 2.   Click the pencil icon next to the policy called AC Policy that you created in Chapter 9, "Firepower Deployment in Transparent Mode." The policy editor page opens.

Step 3.   On the Rules tab, click the **Add Rule** button. The Add Rule window appears, and in it you can define the conditions for a rule.

Step 4.   Assign a name for the rule that suits its purpose (for example, **Ping Access**). Select the **Enabled** check box, and select **Block** from the Action dropdown (see Figure 10-15).

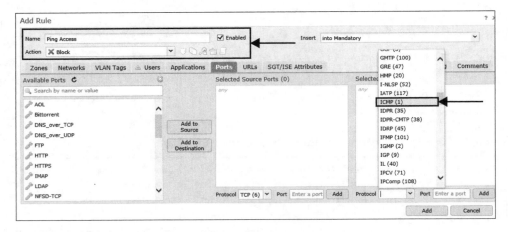

Figure 10-15   *Creating an Access Rule with the Block Action*

Step 5.   On the Ports tab, select the **ICMP (1)** protocol as the destination port.

Step 6.   In the Logging tab, select the **Log at Beginning of Connection** check box. Send the connection events to the Event Viewer to view them in the FMC GUI.

Figure 10-16 shows the options to enable logging. This optional step generates events and displays them in the FMC when the Ping Access access rule blocks any ICMP traffic.

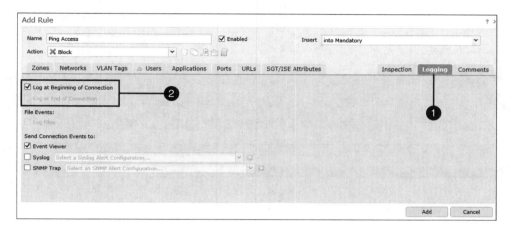

Figure 10-16   *Enabling Logging for an Access Rule*

Step 7.   Click the **Add** button to create the Ping Access rule. You return to the policy editor page.

Step 8.   Click the **Save** button to save the changes, and then click the **Deploy** button to apply the new access control policy on the FTD device.

Figure 10-17 shows the final view of the access control policy editor page. Because Default Action is set to Balanced Security and Connectivity, any nonmalicious traffic except the ICMP traffic is permitted by this access control policy.

Analyzing the Traffic Flow by Using a Block Rule

Right after you click the Deploy button, you can start sending ICMP requests from an inside host to the outside network. At the beginning, both the ASA and Firepower engines can see the ICMP echo requests and echo replies. As soon as the new ICMP rule is activated on the FTD device, the Firewall Engine begins to see the echo requests only, and no echo replies are received.

Example 10-16 shows what happens after a new access control policy with an ICMP block rule is deployed. The Firewall Engine stops seeing any ICMP replies because the requests cannot even reach the outside network.

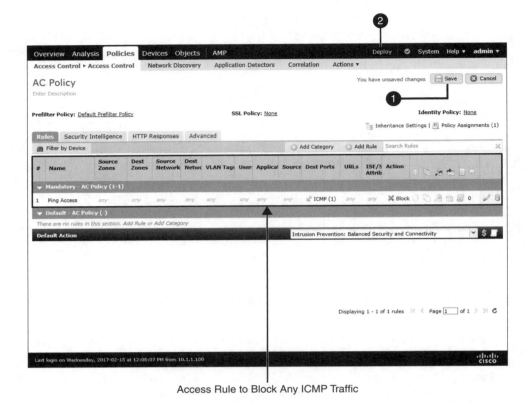

Access Rule to Block Any ICMP Traffic

Figure 10-17 *Access Control Policy to Block Only ICMP Traffic and Permit Other Traffic*

Example 10-16 *Capturing Traffic on a Firewall Engine During the Deployment of an ICMP Block Rule*

```
> capture icmp_traffic interface INSIDE_INTERFACE match icmp any any

> show capture icmp_traffic

20 packets captured

  1: 16:39:55.255159      172.16.1.2 > 192.168.1.2: icmp: echo reply
  2: 16:39:56.255769      192.168.1.2 > 172.16.1.2: icmp: echo request
  3: 16:39:56.256548      172.16.1.2 > 192.168.1.2: icmp: echo reply
  4: 16:39:57.257127      192.168.1.2 > 172.16.1.2: icmp: echo request
  5: 16:39:57.257753      172.16.1.2 > 192.168.1.2: icmp: echo reply
  6: 16:39:58.258333      192.168.1.2 > 172.16.1.2: icmp: echo request
  7: 16:39:58.259019      172.16.1.2 > 192.168.1.2: icmp: echo reply
```

```
 8:  16:39:59.259630        192.168.1.2 > 172.16.1.2: icmp: echo request
 9:  16:39:59.260286        172.16.1.2 > 192.168.1.2: icmp: echo reply
10:  16:40:00.260835        192.168.1.2 > 172.16.1.2: icmp: echo request
11:  16:40:00.262315        172.16.1.2 > 192.168.1.2: icmp: echo reply
12:  16:40:01.262971        192.168.1.2 > 172.16.1.2: icmp: echo request
13:  16:40:02.273759        192.168.1.2 > 172.16.1.2: icmp: echo request
14:  16:40:03.279663        192.168.1.2 > 172.16.1.2: icmp: echo request
15:  16:40:04.287735        192.168.1.2 > 172.16.1.2: icmp: echo request
16:  16:40:05.295776        192.168.1.2 > 172.16.1.2: icmp: echo request
17:  16:40:06.303664        192.168.1.2 > 172.16.1.2: icmp: echo request
18:  16:40:07.311919        192.168.1.2 > 172.16.1.2: icmp: echo request
19:  16:40:08.320006        192.168.1.2 > 172.16.1.2: icmp: echo request
20:  16:40:09.328031        192.168.1.2 > 172.16.1.2: icmp: echo request
20 packets shown
>
```

Example 10-17 confirms that as soon as the new ICMP block rule is activated, the
Firepower engine stops seeing any ICMP traffic.

Example 10-17   *Capturing Traffic on a Firepower Engine During the Deployment of
an ICMP Block Rule*

```
> capture-traffic

Please choose domain to capture traffic from:
  0 - br1
  1 - Router

Selection? 1

Please specify tcpdump options desired.
(or enter '?' for a list of supported options)
Options: icmp
16:39:57.249971 IP 192.168.1.2 > 172.16.1.2: ICMP echo request, id 12845, seq 148,
  length 64
16:39:57.249971 IP 172.16.1.2 > 192.168.1.2: ICMP echo reply, id 12845, seq 148,
  length 64
16:39:58.249971 IP 192.168.1.2 > 172.16.1.2: ICMP echo request, id 12845, seq 149,
  length 64
16:39:58.249971 IP 172.16.1.2 > 192.168.1.2: ICMP echo reply, id 12845, seq 149,
  length 64
16:39:59.249971 IP 192.168.1.2 > 172.16.1.2: ICMP echo request, id 12845, seq 150,
  length 64
```

```
16:39:59.259965 IP 172.16.1.2 > 192.168.1.2: ICMP echo reply, id 12845, seq 150,
  length 64
16:40:00.259965 IP 192.168.1.2 > 172.16.1.2: ICMP echo request, id 12845, seq 151,
  length 64
16:40:00.259965 IP 172.16.1.2 > 192.168.1.2: ICMP echo reply, id 12845, seq 151,
  length 64
.
.
^C
Caught interrupt signal
Exiting.

>
```

You see this behavior because of the Ping Access rule you deployed earlier. You can confirm this by navigating to the **Analysis > Connection Events** page, where you should find an event generated by the Ping Access rule. Figure 10-18 shows a connection event that is generated when the Firewall Engine blocks the ICMP traffic by using the Ping Access rule.

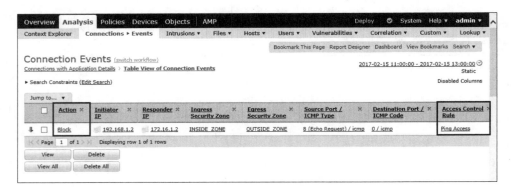

Figure 10-18   *An Event with the Block Action—Triggered by the Ping Access Rule*

Figure 10-19 shows the behavior of the traffic flow before and after an ICMP block rule is deployed. The Firepower engine does not see Packet 12 in the capture because this packet matches an access rule condition, and the ASA firewall engine blocks it.

Packet Processing by an Interface

If you do not see any desired packets in the capture, make sure the filtering condition in the **capture** or **capture-traffic** command is correct. If the condition looks correct, and there are no underlying networking issues, it is important that you check the statistics of the FTD interface and determine whether any packets are dropped by the interface.

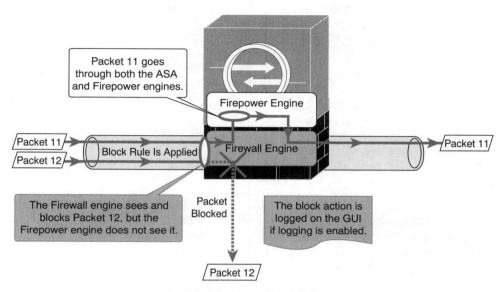

Figure 10-19 *Traffic Flow Before and After a Block Rule Is Activated*

Example 10-18 shows confirmation that the FTD ingress interface is not dropping traffic due to the filling of the FIFO queue (no buffer) or the memory (overrun).

Example 10-18 *Verifying Packet Drops from the Interface Statistics*

```
> show interface GigabitEthernet 1/1
Interface GigabitEthernet1/1 "INSIDE_INTERFACE", is down, line protocol is down
  Hardware is Accelerator rev01, BW 1000 Mbps, DLY 10 usec
        Auto-Duplex, Auto-Speed
        Input flow control is unsupported, output flow control is off
        MAC address a46c.2ae4.6bc0, MTU 1500
        IP address 192.168.1.1, subnet mask 255.255.255.0
        5200 packets input, 531929 bytes, 0 no buffer
        Received 68 broadcasts, 0 runts, 0 giants
        0 input errors, 0 CRC, 0 frame, 0 overrun, 0 ignored, 0 abort
        0 pause input, 0 resume input
        0 L2 decode drops
        2922 packets output, 2340459 bytes, 0 underruns
        0 pause output, 0 resume output
        0 output errors, 0 collisions, 0 interface resets
        0 late collisions, 0 deferred
        0 input reset drops, 0 output reset drops
        input queue (blocks free curr/low): hardware (985/891)
        output queue (blocks free curr/low): hardware (1023/997)
```

```
Traffic Statistics for "INSIDE_INTERFACE":
      5153 packets input, 432852 bytes
      2922 packets output, 2285241 bytes
      3023 packets dropped
   1 minute input rate 0 pkts/sec,  0 bytes/sec
   1 minute output rate 0 pkts/sec,  0 bytes/sec
   1 minute drop rate, 0 pkts/sec
   5 minute input rate 0 pkts/sec,  33 bytes/sec
   5 minute output rate 0 pkts/sec,  1 bytes/sec
   5 minute drop rate, 0 pkts/sec
>
```

While traffic is being received, if an FTD device is not fast enough in pulling the packets from its ingress interface, the interface that uses the FIFO queuing algorithm becomes full. Therefore, any further incoming packets get dropped. When this occurs, you can find the number of these dropped packets in the overrun counter.

Similarly, when an FTD device has to process more traffic than a particular model is designed to handle, FTD can run out of memory, and any incoming packets are dropped as a consequence. The no buffer counter in the interface statistics provides the number of dropped packets.

Figure 10-20 illustrates the processing of incoming packets by an FTD device. In this example, Packet 16 is dropped due to lack of space in the FIFO queue, and Packet 10 is dropped due to lack of memory or buffer.

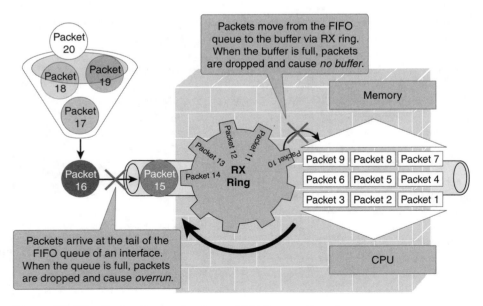

Figure 10-20 *Packet Processing by an FTD Ingress Interface*

Summary

This chapter describes the processes of capturing live traffic on an FTD device using the system-provided capturing tool. To demonstrate the benefit of the tool, this chapter shows various **tcpdump** options and BPF syntax to filter and manage packet capture.

Quiz

1. In terms of system performance, which of the following statements about capturing traffic is true?

   a. When capturing traffic, always display the packets on the console to avoid system overload.

   b. Capturing traffic on a production system has no impact on system performance.

   c. Redirecting traffic into a file can increase the utilization of resources.

   d. None of the above.

2. Which of the following filters captures HTTP client traffic only from the client host 192.168.1.2?

   a. **src 192.168.1.2 and src port 80**

   b. **host 192.168.1.2 or src port 80**

   c. **src 192.168.1.2 and dst port 80**

   d. **host 192.168.1.2 or dst port 80**

3. Which option would prevent **tcpdump** from oversubscribing an FTD for a long time?

   a. **-c 10**

   b. **-e**

   c. **-vv**

   d. **-X**

4. To copy a .pcap file from the FMC to your local computer using the GUI, which of the following conditions must be fulfilled?

   a. You must enable the HTTP service through the Platform Settings policy.

   b. The FMC must be registered with an FTD device.

   c. The .pcap file must be stored in the /var/common directory.

   d. All of the above

Chapter 11

Blocking Traffic Using Inline Interface Mode

An FTD device in Inline interface mode can block unintended traffic while it remains invisible to the network hosts. However, in Chapter 9, "Firepower Deployment in Transparent Mode," you learned about Transparent Mode, which can also block traffic and keeps itself transparent in the network. So, why would someone choose Inline Mode? This chapter explores the advantages of Inline Mode and demonstrates its action and configuration.

Inline Mode Essentials

FTD supports a wide variety of block actions, such as simple blocking, blocking with reset, interactive blocking, and interactive blocking with reset. However, a block action cannot drop any suspicious packet if the interfaces are not set up properly.

Figure 11-1 shows a list of the actions that you can apply to an access rule. Note the different types of block actions FTD supports.

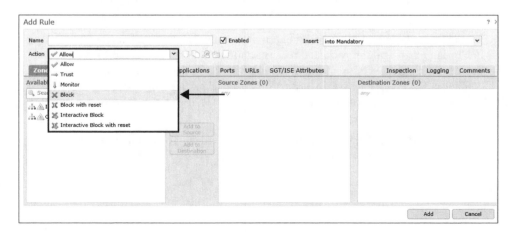

Figure 11-1 *Available Actions, Including Blocking Actions*

FTD enables you to choose any interface mode, regardless of the underlying deployment mode—Routed or Transparent. However, ultimately, the capability of an interface mode defines whether FTD is able to block any suspicious traffic it sees.

Table 11-1 lists various FTD modes and describes their abilities to block traffic. The deployment mode in this table defines how FTD functions as a firewall. The interface mode defines how FTD acts on the traffic in case of any suspicious activities.

Table 11-1   *Ability to Block Traffic in Various Modes*

Deployment Mode	Interface Mode	Able to Block Traffic?
Routed		Yes
Transparent		Yes
	Inline	Yes
	Inline-tap	No
	Passive	No
	Passive (ERSPAN)	No

Inline Mode Versus Passive Mode

An intrusion detection and prevention system detects suspicious activities and prevents network attacks. You can deploy an FTD device either as an intrusion detection system (IDS) or to function as an intrusion prevention system (IPS). To prevent any potential intrusion attempt in real time, you must deploy an FTD device in Inline Mode. In Inline Mode, the ingress and egress interfaces are bundled into an interface pair. Each pair must be associated with an inline set, which is a logical group of one or more interface pairs.

Figure 11-2 illustrates how two interfaces (GigabitEthernet1/1 with GigabitEthernet1/2 and GigabitEthernet1/3 with GigabitEthernet1/4) can build the inline pairs. Note that both of the inline pairs are included in Inline Set 1 in this illustration.

An FTD device in Passive Mode, on the contrary, can only detect intrusion attempts. A switch or tap mirrors all the packets it receives and sends a copy of each packet to the FTD device using port mirroring. Because the original traffic does not go through an FTD device, FTD is unable to take any action on a packet. In other words, an FTD device in Passive Mode cannot block any intrusion attempt; it can only detect an attempt based on the traffic it sees.

Figure 11-3 provides an example of a typical FTD deployment. The topology shows two FTD devices deployed in two different modes—Inline (IPS) and Passive (IDS).

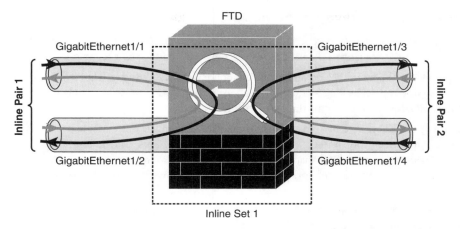

Figure 11-2 *Understanding an Inline Interface, Interface Pair, and Inline Set*

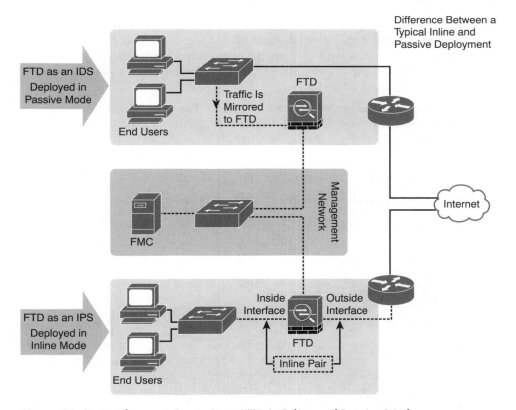

Figure 11-3 *Deployment Scenarios—FTD in Inline and Passive Modes*

Inline Mode Versus Transparent Mode

Both Inline Mode and Transparent Mode work like *bumps in the wire*, which means they are invisible to the connected devices. However, they are two different techniques.

In Inline Mode, the interfaces on an interface pair are network agnostic. They can send and receive any traffic, as long as the policies permit. In addition, you do not need to configure IP addresses on any of the member interfaces of an inline-pair.

In contrast, an FTD device in Transparent Mode places the inside and outside networks into a virtual bridge group and creates a Layer 2 bridging network. Traffic originates from an FTD device using a Bridged Virtual Interface (BVI) as its source interface. The BVI, inside network, and outside network must all be configured with the IP addresses from a single subnet.

You can enable Network Address Translation (NAT) in the Transparent Mode; however, FTD does not support NAT in the Inline Mode.

Tracing a Packet Drop

After receiving a packet from the ingress interface, FTD processes the packets and takes an action based on the deployed access rules and intrusion rules. In Chapter 10, "Capturing Traffic for Advanced Analysis," you learned how to capture live traffic from an interface. In this chapter, you are going to leverage the capturing tool to trace a drop of a packet through an FTD device.

Figure 11-4 illustrates the potential reasons for a packet drop by an FTD device. After FTD filters traffic using its traditional firewall rules, the Firepower/Snort engine inspects traffic.

To record additional tracing data during a capture, you need to use the **trace** parameter with the **capture** command. For example, to capture any HTTP traffic received on an inside interface, you used the following command in Chapter 10:

```
> capture http_traffic interface INSIDE_INTERFACE match tcp any any eq 80
```

Now, to capture tracing data for each packet, you can add the **trace** parameter, as shown here:

```
> capture http_traffic trace interface INSIDE_INTERFACE match tcp any any eq 80
```

To view the additional tracing data for a specific packet, add the number of that packet with the **trace** keyword, as shown here:

```
> show capture http_traffic packet-number 1 trace
```

Moreover, FTD provides a tool called **packet-tracer**, which can generate simulated packets using the information of five tuples: source IP address, destination IP address, source port number, destination port number, and protocol. By considering the deployed rule conditions, this tool simulates traffic flow from the ingress interface to the egress interface, as if a client and server were communicating using a network protocol through the FTD. Here is an example:

```
> packet-tracer input INSIDE_INTERFACE tcp 192.168.1.2 10000 192.168.1.200 80
```

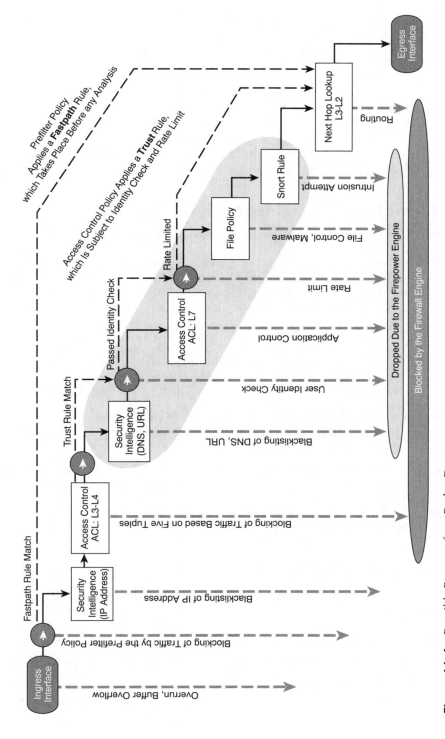

Figure 11-4   *Possible Reasons for a Packet Drop*

This command generates a virtual packet flow from the INSIDE_INTERFACE with the following header information:

```
Source IP Address: 192.168.1.2
Destination IP Address: 192.168.1.200
Source Port: 10000
Destination Port: 80
Protocol: TCP
```

Later in this chapter you will use both **capture trace** and **packet-trace** tools to determine where a packet gets dropped. For now, just keep this concept in mind.

Best Practices for Inline Mode Configuration

When you create an inline set, consider the following during configurations:

- If your network uses asynchronous routing, and the inbound and outbound traffic go through two different interface pairs, you should include both interface pairs in the same interface set. Doing so ensures that FTD does not see just half of the traffic; it can see the flows from both directions and recognize them when they are part of a single connection.

- If the interfaces of an inline pair are connected to switches that run Spanning Tree Protocol (STP), you should enable PortFast on the associated switch ports. It allows those switch ports to transition to the forwarding state immediately and reduces hardware bypass time.

- You should enable the FailSafe feature on the inline interface set. In case of a software failure, this feature allows FTD to continue its traffic flow through the device by bypassing the detection.

- You should allow the inline set to propagate its link state. This reduces the routing convergence time when one of the interfaces in an inline set goes down.

The configuration examples in this chapter discuss the steps to enable FailSafe and the Propagate Link State feature on an inline set.

Configuring Inline Mode

In this section, you are going to configure and verify three important elements of an inline interface:

- You will create a simple inline set and verify traffic flow.

- You will enable the fault tolerance features on an inline set to avoid downtime in case of a failure.

- You will learn how to block a particular service or port through an inline interface.

Figure 11-5 provides an overview of the lab topology that is used in this chapter. The configuration examples and the command outputs in this chapter are based on this topology.

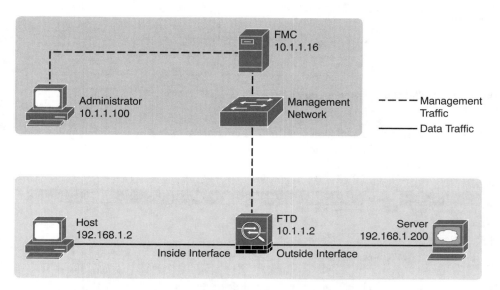

Figure 11-5 *Lab Topology Used in the Configuration Examples in This Chapter*

Fulfilling Prerequisites

If you previously configured an FTD device as a firewall in routed mode, you need to remove any platform settings, the IP address, and DHCP server configurations from the FTD data interfaces, as they are not necessary in Inline Mode.

Creating an Inline Set

An inline set is a logical group of one or more interface pairs. Before you add an inline set, you must create an inline interface pair and associate the pair with the inline set you want to add.

To create an inline set, follow these steps:

Step 1.   Navigate to the **Devices** > **Device Management** page. A list of all the devices that are registered with FMC appears.

Step 2.   Click the pencil icon next to the FTD device (see Figure 11-6).

Step 3.   Select the **Interfaces** tab. A list of the available interfaces appears, and you can set up or modify interface settings by using this page.

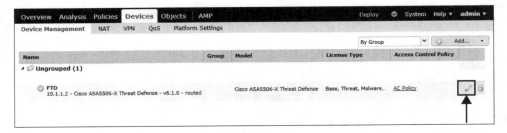

Figure 11-6   *The Device Management Page of the FMC*

Step 4.   Select the pencil icon next to each interface that will be part of an inline pair—in this case, the GigabitEthernet1/1 and GigabitEthernet1/2 interfaces (see Figure 11-7).

Figure 11-7   *Available Interfaces on an FTD Device*

Step 5.   In the Edit Physical Interface window, the default value of the Mode drop-down is None. Keep it unchanged, as this represents Inline Mode. Then assign a name to the interface and click the **Enabled** check box to enable it. An IP address is not necessary.

Figure 11-8 shows the settings on the GigabitEthernet1/1 interface. This example uses the names INSIDE_INTERFACE and OUTSIDE_INTERFACE for the GigabitEthernet1/1 and GigabitEthernet1/2 interfaces, respectively.

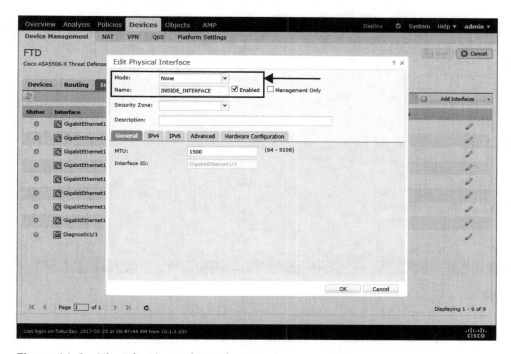

Figure 11-8   *The Edit Physical Interface Window*

Step 6.   Click **OK** to return to the Interfaces tab and repeat Steps 4 and 5 for the other interface of the pair.

Step 7.   After both interfaces are named and enabled, click the **Save** button to save the changes.

Figure 11-9 shows an overview of each interface configuration. Note that the IP address or security zone is not configured. Only the logical interface is necessary for an inline interface.

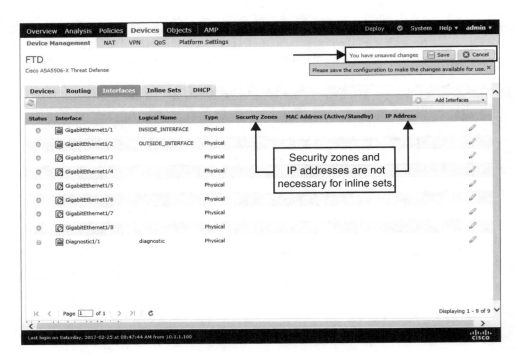

Figure 11-9 *Overview of the Interface Configuration*

Now, begin the second part of the configuration—adding the interface pair to an inline set—by following these steps:

Step 1.   On the **Devices > Device Management** page, go to the Inline Sets tab and click the **Add Inline Set** button. The Add Inline Set window appears.

Step 2.   In the Add Inline Set window, give a name to the inline set, select an interface pair, and add it to the inline set (see Figure 11-10).

Note   Do not configure any additional settings at this moment. You will come back here when you learn the fault tolerance configuration later in this chapter.

Step 3.   Click **OK** to return to the Inline Sets tab.

Step 4.   Click **Save** to save the configuration, and click **Deploy** to deploy it to FTD (see Figure 11-11).

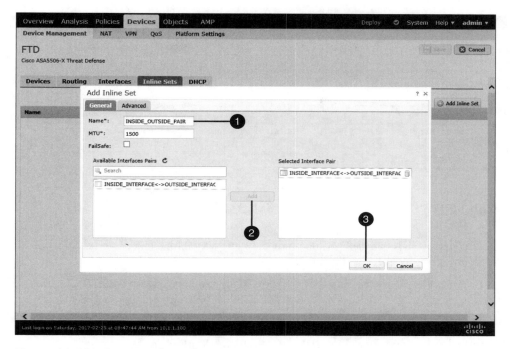

Figure 11-10 *Settings of an Inline Set*

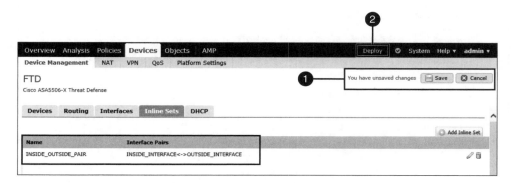

Figure 11-11 *Deploying an Inline Set Configuration*

Verifying the Configuration

Upon a successful deployment, you should be able to ping from your inside host 192.168.1.2 to the outside server 192.168.1.200.

Figure 11-12 shows the table view of a connection event. The event confirms that host 192.168.1.2 is able to send ICMP echo requests to 192.168.1.200.

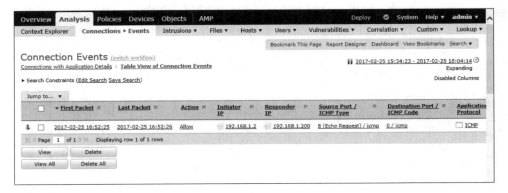

Figure 11-12 *Connection Event for the ICMP Traffic*

If a ping test fails but the FMC does not show any reason for a failure, you can troubleshoot by checking the interface status.

Example 11-1 shows the output of the **show inline-set** command on the FTD CLI. This command provides various components of an inline set configuration, such as member interfaces of an inline pair, the status of each interface, and advanced settings.

Example 11-1 *Status of the INSIDE_OUTSIDE_PAIR Inline Set*

```
> show inline-set

Inline-set INSIDE_OUTSIDE_PAIR
  Mtu is 1500 bytes
  Failsafe mode is off
  Failsecure mode is off
  Tap mode is off
  Propagate-link-state option is off
  hardware-bypass mode is disabled
  Interface-Pair[1]:
    Interface: GigabitEthernet1/1 "INSIDE_INTERFACE"
      Current-Status: UP
    Interface: GigabitEthernet1/2 "OUTSIDE_INTERFACE"
      Current-Status: UP
    Bridge Group ID: 500
>
```

Example 11-2 shows the overall status of the available interfaces on an FTD device. It confirms that the GigabitEthernet1/1 and GigabitEthernet1/2 interfaces are up and configured with no IP address. However, it does not confirm if they are part of an inline pair.

Example 11-2 *Summary of the FTD Interface Status*

```
> show interface ip brief
Interface                 IP-Address      OK? Method Status               Protocol
Virtual0                  127.1.0.1       YES unset  up                   up
GigabitEthernet1/1        unassigned      YES unset  up                   up
GigabitEthernet1/2        unassigned      YES unset  up                   up
GigabitEthernet1/3        unassigned      YES unset  administratively down down
GigabitEthernet1/4        unassigned      YES unset  administratively down down
GigabitEthernet1/5        unassigned      YES unset  administratively down down
GigabitEthernet1/6        unassigned      YES unset  administratively down down
GigabitEthernet1/7        unassigned      YES unset  administratively down down
GigabitEthernet1/8        unassigned      YES unset  administratively down down
Internal-Control1/1       127.0.1.1       YES unset  up                   up
Internal-Data1/1          unassigned      YES unset  up                   up
Internal-Data1/2          unassigned      YES unset  down                 down
Internal-Data1/3          unassigned      YES unset  up                   up
Internal-Data1/4          169.254.1.1     YES unset  up                   up
Management1/1             unassigned      YES unset  up                   up
>
```

Example 11-3 confirms that the GigabitEthernet1/1 interface is in Inline Mode, and it is included in an inline pair called INSIDE_OUTSIDE_PAIR. It also provides detailed statistics about the traffic.

Example 11-3 *Detailed Statistic About the GigabitEthernet1/1 Interface*

```
> show interface GigabitEthernet1/1
Interface GigabitEthernet1/1 "INSIDE_INTERFACE", is up, line protocol is up
  Hardware is Accelerator rev01, BW 1000 Mbps, DLY 10 usec
        Auto-Duplex(Full-duplex), Auto-Speed(1000 Mbps)
        Input flow control is unsupported, output flow control is off
        MAC address a46c.2ae4.6bc0, MTU 1500
        IPS Interface-Mode: inline, Inline-Set: INSIDE_OUTSIDE_PAIR
        IP address unassigned
        2382 packets input, 258694 bytes, 0 no buffer
        Received 142 broadcasts, 0 runts, 0 giants
        0 input errors, 0 CRC, 0 frame, 0 overrun, 0 ignored, 0 abort
        0 pause input, 0 resume input
        0 L2 decode drops
        2079 packets output, 234133 bytes, 0 underruns
        0 pause output, 0 resume output
        0 output errors, 0 collisions, 0 interface resets
        0 late collisions, 0 deferred
        0 input reset drops, 2 output reset drops
```

```
        input queue (blocks free curr/low): hardware (946/894)
        output queue (blocks free curr/low): hardware (1023/1020)
 Traffic Statistics for "INSIDE_INTERFACE":
        592 packets input, 53381 bytes
        530 packets output, 63776 bytes
        11 packets dropped
    1 minute input rate 1 pkts/sec,   85 bytes/sec
    1 minute output rate 1 pkts/sec,   88 bytes/sec
    1 minute drop rate, 0 pkts/sec
    5 minute input rate 1 pkts/sec,   79 bytes/sec
    5 minute output rate 0 pkts/sec,  103 bytes/sec
    5 minute drop rate, 0 pkts/sec
>
```

Verifying Packet Flow by Using packet-tracer

If the interface status and configuration seem correct but the hosts in the inside and outside networks are still unable to communicate, you can use a simulated packet to determine the flow of a packet through an FTD device. The **packet-tracer** command can generate a virtual packet based on the parameters you enter with it. In the next example, you will simulate the flow of an ICMP packet using the following syntax:

packet-tracer input *source_interface protocol_name source_address ICMP_type ICMP_code destination_address*

Note   The **packet-tracer** command syntax is different for a TCP packet. You will learn how to use it near the end of this chapter, when the blocking of a TCP service/port is simulated.

In an ICMP header, the **type** and **code** fields contain the control messages. There are many different types of ICMP control messages available. In the following exercise, however, you are going to use two types of messages—echo request and echo reply.

Figure 11-13 shows the format of an ICMP packet. The 8-bit type and 8-bit code fields carry the ICMP control messages.

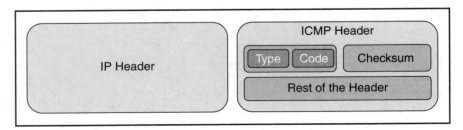

Figure 11-13   *Type and Code Fields on an ICMP Header*

Table 11-2 shows the values of the type and code fields. Using these values, you can generate a particular ICMP control message.

Table 11-2   *Values for the Echo Request and Echo Reply Messages*

Control Message	Type	Code
Echo request	8	0
Echo reply	0	0

Example 11-4 demonstrates the simulation of ICMP traffic, sent from the inside interface. The host 192.168.1.2 from the inside network sends an ICMP echo request to an outside system, 192.168.1.200. The ingress and egress interfaces of this simulated packet are determined by the inline set configuration of the FTD device.

Example 11-4   *Simulating an ICMP Echo Request*

```
> packet-tracer input INSIDE_INTERFACE icmp 192.168.1.2 8 0 192.168.1.200

Phase: 1
Type: ACCESS-LIST
Subtype:
Result: ALLOW
Config:
Implicit Rule
Additional Information:
MAC Access list


Phase: 2
Type: NGIPS-MODE
Subtype: ngips-mode
Result: ALLOW
Config:
Additional Information:
The flow ingressed an interface configured for NGIPS mode and NGIPS services will be
  applied


Phase: 3
Type: ACCESS-LIST
Subtype: log
Result: ALLOW
Config:
access-group CSM_FW_ACL_ global
access-list CSM_FW_ACL_ advanced permit ip any any rule-id 268434432
access-list CSM_FW_ACL_ remark rule-id 268434432: ACCESS POLICY: AC Policy - Default/1
```

```
access-list CSM_FW_ACL_ remark rule-id 268434432: L4 RULE: DEFAULT ACTION RULE
Additional Information:
 This packet will be sent to snort for additional processing where a verdict will be
   reached


Phase: 4
Type: NGIPS-EGRESS-INTERFACE-LOOKUP
Subtype: Resolve Egress Interface
Result: ALLOW
Config:
Additional Information:
Ingress interface INSIDE_INTERFACE is in NGIPS inline mode.
Egress interface OUTSIDE_INTERFACE is determined by inline-set configuration


Phase: 5
Type: FLOW-CREATION
Subtype:
Result: ALLOW
Config:
Additional Information:
New flow created with id 269, packet dispatched to next module


Result:
input-interface: INSIDE_INTERFACE
input-status: up
input-line-status: up
Action: allow


>
```

Example 11-5 concludes that an ICMP echo reply packet, originated by the host
192.168.1.200, should be able to reach its destination, 192.168.1.2.

Example 11-5 *Simulating an ICMP Echo Reply*

```
> packet-tracer input OUTSIDE_INTERFACE icmp 192.168.1.200 0 0 192.168.1.2


Phase: 1
Type: ACCESS-LIST
Subtype:
Result: ALLOW
Config:
Implicit Rule
Additional Information:
MAC Access list
```

```
Phase: 2
Type: NGIPS-MODE
Subtype: ngips-mode
Result: ALLOW
Config:
Additional Information:
The flow ingressed an interface configured for NGIPS mode and NGIPS services will be
  applied

Phase: 3
Type: ACCESS-LIST
Subtype: log
Result: ALLOW
Config:
access-group CSM_FW_ACL_ global
access-list CSM_FW_ACL_ advanced permit ip any any rule-id 268434432
access-list CSM_FW_ACL_ remark rule-id 268434432: ACCESS POLICY: AC Policy - Default/1
access-list CSM_FW_ACL_ remark rule-id 268434432: L4 RULE: DEFAULT ACTION RULE
Additional Information:
 This packet will be sent to snort for additional processing where a verdict will be
  reached

Phase: 4
Type: NGIPS-EGRESS-INTERFACE-LOOKUP
Subtype: Resolve Egress Interface
Result: ALLOW
Config:
Additional Information:
Ingress interface OUTSIDE_INTERFACE is in NGIPS inline mode.
Egress interface INSIDE_INTERFACE is determined by inline-set configuration

Phase: 5
Type: FLOW-CREATION
Subtype:
Result: ALLOW
Config:
Additional Information:
New flow created with id 271, packet dispatched to next module

Result:
input-interface: OUTSIDE_INTERFACE
input-status: up
input-line-status: up
Action: allow
>
```

Verifying Packet Flow by Using Real Packet Capture

In the previous section, you used virtually generated packets to simulate the flow of packets. In this section, you are going to use real ping requests to determine the flow of a packet through an FTD. Follow these steps:

Step 1.   Enter two capture rules with tracing capability, as shown in Example 11-6. They begin capturing ICMP traffic. To trace packets from both directions, you need to capture traffic from both of the interfaces of an inline pair.

Example 11-6 demonstrates the use of the **trace** keyword with the **capture** command. The example uses the **capture** command twice, to capture traffic from the ingress and egress interfaces separately. The **Capturing - 0 bytes** message on the **show capture** command confirms that the process is running but has not seen any packets yet.

Example 11-6   *Creating and Verifying Matching Conditions for Packet Captures*

```
> capture inside_icmp trace interface INSIDE_INTERFACE match icmp any any

> capture outside_icmp trace interface OUTSIDE_INTERFACE match icmp any any

> show capture

capture inside_icmp type raw-data trace interface INSIDE_INTERFACE [Capturing - 0
  bytes]
  match icmp any any
capture outside_icmp type raw-data trace interface OUTSIDE_INTERFACE [Capturing - 0
  bytes]
  match icmp any any
>
```

Step 2.   Send a few ping requests from your inside host to the outside system. After sending and receiving two to four ICMP packets, stop the ping request. You should now be able to see the capture between the inside and outside systems. Example 11-7 shows the captures of ICMP traffic from both directions on both interfaces.

Example 11-7   *Captures of the ICMP Traffic*

```
> show capture inside_icmp

4 packets captured

  1: 21:52:25.988428        192.168.1.2 > 192.168.1.200: icmp: echo request
  2: 21:52:25.989405        192.168.1.200 > 192.168.1.2: icmp: echo reply
  3: 21:52:26.989862        192.168.1.2 > 192.168.1.200: icmp: echo request
  4: 21:52:26.990412        192.168.1.200 > 192.168.1.2: icmp: echo reply
```

```
4 packets shown

>


> show capture outside_icmp

4 packets captured

    1: 21:52:25.989038          192.168.1.2 > 192.168.1.200: icmp: echo request
    2: 21:52:25.989252          192.168.1.200 > 192.168.1.2: icmp: echo reply
    3: 21:52:26.990106          192.168.1.2 > 192.168.1.200: icmp: echo request
    4: 21:52:26.990305          192.168.1.200 > 192.168.1.2: icmp: echo reply
4 packets shown

>
```

Step 3. From Example 11-7, select a packet you want to trace, using its associated number on the left. In this lab scenario, the host 192.168.1.2 sends the echo request packet from the inside interface. That's why you use the inside_icmp capture to view the tracing data. Similarly, when you want to trace the echo reply packet from the host 192.168.1.200, you need to use the outside_icmp capture.

Example 11-8 shows the flow of packet number 1 from Example 11-7. You must use the **trace** keyword to view the tracing data.

Example 11-8 *Tracing an Echo-Request Packet Originated by the Host 192.168.1.2*

```
> show capture inside_icmp packet-number 1 trace

4 packets captured

    1: 21:52:25.988428          192.168.1.2 > 192.168.1.200: icmp: echo request
Phase: 1
Type: CAPTURE
Subtype:
Result: ALLOW
Config:
Additional Information:
MAC Access list


Phase: 2
Type: ACCESS-LIST
Subtype:
```

```
Result: ALLOW
Config:
Implicit Rule
Additional Information:
MAC Access list


Phase: 3
Type: NGIPS-MODE
Subtype: ngips-mode
Result: ALLOW
Config:
Additional Information:
The flow ingressed an interface configured for NGIPS mode and NGIPS services will be
   applied


Phase: 4
Type: ACCESS-LIST
Subtype: log
Result: ALLOW
Config:
access-group CSM_FW_ACL_ global
access-list CSM_FW_ACL_ advanced permit ip any any rule-id 268434432
access-list CSM_FW_ACL_ remark rule-id 268434432: ACCESS POLICY: AC Policy - Default/1
access-list CSM_FW_ACL_ remark rule-id 268434432: L4 RULE: DEFAULT ACTION RULE
Additional Information:
 This packet will be sent to snort for additional processing where a verdict will be
   reached


Phase: 5
Type: NGIPS-EGRESS-INTERFACE-LOOKUP
Subtype: Resolve Egress Interface
Result: ALLOW
Config:
Additional Information:
Ingress interface INSIDE_INTERFACE is in NGIPS inline mode.
Egress interface OUTSIDE_INTERFACE is determined by inline-set configuration


Phase: 6
Type: FLOW-CREATION
Subtype:
Result: ALLOW
```

```
Config:
Additional Information:
New flow created with id 279, packet dispatched to next module

Phase: 7
Type: EXTERNAL-INSPECT
Subtype:
Result: ALLOW
Config:
Additional Information:
Application: 'SNORT Inspect'

Phase: 8
Type: SNORT
Subtype:
Result: ALLOW
Config:
Additional Information:
Snort Verdict: (pass-packet) allow this packet

Phase: 9
Type: CAPTURE
Subtype:
Result: ALLOW
Config:
Additional Information:
MAC Access list

Result:
input-interface: OUTSIDE_INTERFACE
input-status: up
input-line-status: up
Action: allow


1 packet shown
>
```

Example 11-9 shows two different outputs for tracing the same packet. Only the second command shows the desired detail because the outside interface receives the echo reply packet.

Example 11-9   *Tracing an Echo Reply Packet Originated by the Host 192.168.1.200*

```
> show capture inside_icmp packet-number 2 trace

4 packets captured

   2: 21:52:25.989405        192.168.1.200 > 192.168.1.2: icmp: echo reply
1 packet shown
>


> show capture outside_icmp packet-number 2 trace

4 packets captured

   2: 21:52:25.989252        192.168.1.200 > 192.168.1.2: icmp: echo reply
Phase: 1
Type: CAPTURE
Subtype:
Result: ALLOW
Config:
Additional Information:
MAC Access list

Phase: 2
Type: ACCESS-LIST
Subtype:
Result: ALLOW
Config:
Implicit Rule
Additional Information:
MAC Access list

Phase: 3
Type: FLOW-LOOKUP
Subtype:
Result: ALLOW
Config:
Additional Information:
Found flow with id 279, using existing flow

Phase: 4
Type: EXTERNAL-INSPECT
Subtype:
```

```
Result: ALLOW
Config:
Additional Information:
Application: 'SNORT Inspect'

Phase: 5
Type: SNORT
Subtype:
Result: ALLOW
Config:
Additional Information:
Snort Verdict: (pass-packet) allow this packet

Phase: 6
Type: CAPTURE
Subtype:
Result: ALLOW
Config:
Additional Information:
MAC Access list

Result:
input-interface: INSIDE_INTERFACE
input-status: up
input-line-status: up
Action: allow


1 packet shown
>
```

Tip To learn how to inactivate a capture on an interface or how to delete a capture process permanently, see Chapter 10.

Enabling Fault Tolerance Features

In Inline Mode, traffic goes through an FTD device. FTD can interrupt the traffic flow in case of any software or hardware failure. To avoid any network outage, the Firepower system offers various fault tolerance features, such as FailSafe and Link State Propagation, as described in the following sections.

Configuring Fault Tolerance Features

This section assumes that you have already configured your FTD device in basic Inline Mode by following the steps described in the previous section. Now, you are going to edit that configuration to enable two fault tolerance features:

- **FailSafe:** In the event of any software failure, if FTD stops processing traffic, and the buffer becomes full, FTD drops traffic. The FailSafe feature watches the use of the buffer. When the buffer is full, FailSafe allows the traffic to go through FTD without any inspection. Hence, users do not experience any permanent network outage.

- **Propagate Link State:** If one of the links of an inline pair goes down, the second link can stay up and able to receive traffic. However, FTD cannot transfer traffic through an interface that has no link. The Propagate Link State feature automatically brings the remaining interface down if one of the interfaces in an inline pair goes down. This feature improves routing convergence time by not sending traffic through a failed link.

Follow these steps to enable FailSafe and Propagate Link State:

Step 1.   Navigate to the **Devices** > **Device Management** page. Click the pencil icon next to the FTD device where you created the inline set.

Step 2.   In the device editor page, go to the Inline Sets tab. Click the pencil icon next to the inline set that you want to modify. The Add Inline Set window appears.

Step 3.   Go to the General tab and select the **FailSafe** check box (see Figure 11-14).

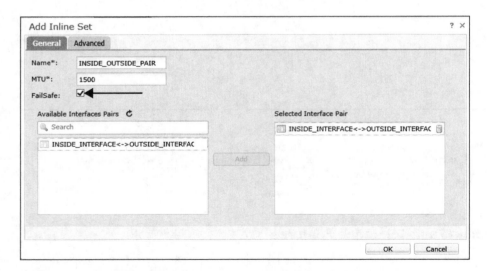

Figure 11-14   *The FailSafe Feature on the General Tab*

Step 4.   Go to the Advanced tab and select the **Propagate Link State** check box (see Figure 11-15).

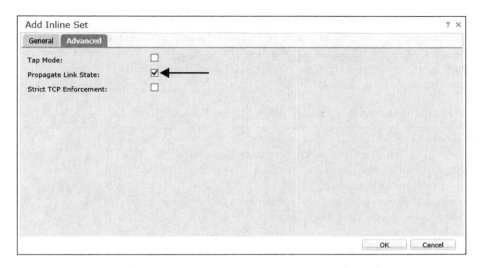

Figure 11-15 *The Propagate Link State Feature on the Advanced Tab*

Step 5.   Click the **OK** button to return to the device editor page.

Step 6.   Click **Save** to save the changes, and click **Deploy** to deploy the settings to FTD.

Verifying Fault Tolerance Features

After you reconfigure an inline set with the FailSafe and Propagate Link State features, you can run the **show inline-set** command to verify the changes. Example 11-10 confirms that the FailSafe and Propagate Link State features are enabled successfully.

Example 11-10 *Viewing the Inline Set Configuration from the CLI*

```
> show inline-set

Inline-set INLINE_OUTSIDE_PAIR
  Mtu is 1500 bytes
  Failsafe mode is on/activated
  Failsecure mode is off
  Tap mode is off
  Propagate-link-state option is on
  hardware-bypass mode is disabled
  Interface-Pair[1]:
    Interface: GigabitEthernet1/1 "INSIDE_INTERFACE"
      Current-Status: Down(Propagate-Link-State-Activated)
    Interface: GigabitEthernet1/2 "OUTSIDE_INTERFACE"
      Current-Status: Down(Down-By-Propagate-Link-State)
    Bridge Group ID: 500
>
```

To verify that the Propagate Link State feature works as expected, you can unplug the cable from one of the interfaces and run the **show interface** command to determine the status. Example 11-11 shows the output of the **show interface** command. After unplugging the cable from the GigabitEthernet1/1 interface, the second interface, GigabitEthernet1/2, has also gone down.

Example 11-11   *Viewing the Status of the Propagate Link State Feature*

```
> show interface GigabitEthernet1/1
Interface GigabitEthernet1/1 "INSIDE_INTERFACE", is down, line protocol is down
  Hardware is Accelerator rev01, BW 1000 Mbps, DLY 10 usec
        Auto-Duplex, Auto-Speed
        Input flow control is unsupported, output flow control is off
        MAC address a46c.2ae4.6bc0, MTU 1500
        IPS Interface-Mode: inline, Inline-Set: INSIDE_OUTSIDE_PAIR
        Propagate-Link-State-Activated
        IP address unassigned
        14779 packets input, 1512926 bytes, 0 no buffer
        Received 147 broadcasts, 0 runts, 0 giants
  .
  .
  .
<Output Omitted for Brevity>



> show interface GigabitEthernet1/2
Interface GigabitEthernet1/2 "OUTSIDE_INTERFACE", is administratively down, line
  protocol is down
  Hardware is Accelerator rev01, BW 1000 Mbps, DLY 10 usec
        Auto-Duplex, Auto-Speed
        Input flow control is unsupported, output flow control is off
        MAC address a46c.2ae4.6bc1, MTU 1500
        IPS Interface-Mode: inline, Inline-Set: INSIDE_OUTSIDE_PAIR
        Down-By-Propagate-Link-State
        IP address unassigned
        15397 packets input, 1558479 bytes, 0 no buffer
        Received 930 broadcasts, 0 runts, 0 giants
  .
  .
  .
<Output Omitted for Brevity>
```

Blocking a Specific Port

Now that you have configured the inline interface pair, you will try to block a particular port or service using an FTD device. In the previous section, you used ICMP to determine the traffic flow. In this section, you will configure an FTD device to block the cleartext Telnet traffic—a TCP protocol that uses port 23.

Configuring Blocking a Specific Port

The following steps describe how to add an access rule that can block any packets destined for port 23:

Step 1.   Navigate to the **Policies > Access Control > Access Control** page.

Step 2.   Click the pencil icon next to an access control policy that you want to deploy to an FTD device.

Step 3.   When the policy editor page appears, click the **Add Rule** button to create a new rule. The Add Rule window appears. Figure 11-16 shows the addition of an access rule that blocks traffic destined for port 23 (the Telnet service port).

Figure 11-16   *Access Rule to Block the Telnet Port*

Step 4.   Give the access rule a name, enable the rule, and select the **Block** action.

Step 5.   In the Ports tab, find the Telnet service in the Available Ports list and add the Telnet port to the destination.

Step 6.   Go to the Logging tab and select **Log at Beginning of Connection**.
This optional step allows you to view an event when a Telnet connection is blocked. Figure 11-17 shows logging being enabled for the Shell Access access rule. When this access rule blocks a Telnet connection, the web interface displays a Block event for it.

Step 7.   Click the **Add** button to return to the policy editor page.

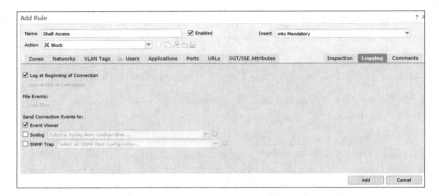

Figure 11-17   *Enabling Logging for an Access Rule*

Step 8.   To define a default action, select **Balanced Security and Connectivity** from the dropdown. This allows any nonmalicious traffic other than the Telnet traffic to go through.

Figure 11-18 shows the policy editor page after you add the rule to block Telnet traffic.

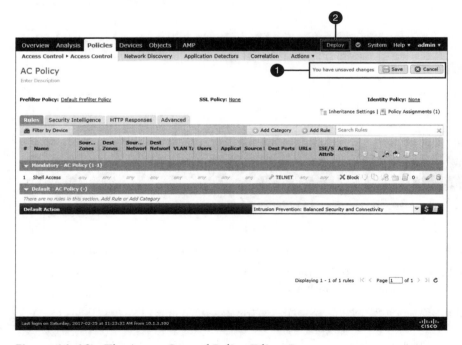

Figure 11-18   *The Access Control Policy Editor Page*

Step 9.   Click **Save** to save the configuration, and click **Deploy** to deploy the Access Control Policy to FTD.

Verifying Blocking of a Specific Port

After a successful deployment of the updated access control policy, you can go to your inside host 192.168.1.2 to access the outside system 192.168.1.200 using Telnet. Your attempt to connect through the Telnet port should not work because FTD is now blocking any traffic destined for port 23. For a blocked connection, the FMC should also log a connection event.

Figure 11-19 illustrates two types of connection events—block and allow. The Telnet traffic is blocked by the Shell Access rule, while any other traffic (such as ping requests) is allowed by the Default Action rule.

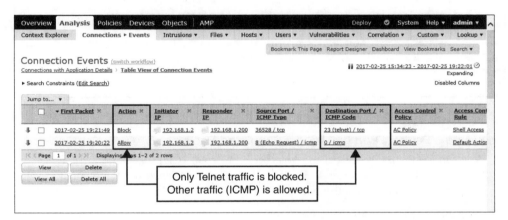

Figure 11-19 *Events Logged for a Blocked Telnet Connection*

Example 11-12 displays the Shell Access rule that you created to block Telnet traffic. In the line following this rule, you can find the default action to permit any other traffic. The hitcnt value increases as more Telnet traffic is blocked by FTD.

Example 11-12 *Viewing the Access Control Rules from the CLI*

```
> show access-list
access-list cached ACL log flows: total 0, denied 0 (deny-flow-max 4096)
          alert-interval 300
access-list CSM_FW_ACL_; 7 elements; name hash: 0x4a69e3f3
access-list CSM_FW_ACL_ line 1 remark rule-id 9998: PREFILTER POLICY: Default Tunnel
  and Priority Policy
access-list CSM_FW_ACL_ line 2 remark rule-id 9998: RULE: DEFAULT TUNNEL ACTION RULE
access-list CSM_FW_ACL_ line 3 advanced permit ipinip any any rule-id 9998 (hitcnt=0)
  0xf5b597d6
access-list CSM_FW_ACL_ line 4 advanced permit 41 any any rule-id 9998 (hitcnt=0)
  0x06095aba
access-list CSM_FW_ACL_ line 5 advanced permit gre any any rule-id 9998 (hitcnt=0)
  0x52c7a066
```

```
access-list CSM_FW_ACL_ line 6 advanced permit udp any eq 3544 any range 1025 65535
  rule-id 9998 (hitcnt=0) 0x46d7839e
access-list CSM_FW_ACL_ line 7 advanced permit udp any range 1025 65535 any eq 3544
  rule-id 9998 (hitcnt=0) 0xaf1d5aa5
access-list CSM_FW_ACL_ line 8 remark rule-id 268440576: ACCESS POLICY: AC Policy -
  Mandatory/1
access-list CSM_FW_ACL_ line 9 remark rule-id 268440576: L4 RULE: Shell Access
access-list CSM_FW_ACL_ line 10 advanced deny tcp any any object-group TELNET
  rule-id 268440576 event-log flow-start (hitcnt=2) 0xae7f8544
  access-list CSM_FW_ACL_ line 10 advanced deny tcp any any eq telnet rule-id
    268440576 event-log flow-start (hitcnt=2) 0x2bcbaf06
access-list CSM_FW_ACL_ line 11 remark rule-id 268434432: ACCESS POLICY: AC Policy -
  Default/1
access-list CSM_FW_ACL_ line 12 remark rule-id 268434432: L4 RULE: DEFAULT ACTION RULE
access-list CSM_FW_ACL_ line 13 advanced permit ip any any rule-id 268434432
  (hitcnt=134) 0xa1d3780e
>
```

Analyzing a Packet Drop by Using a Simulated Packet

You can use the **packet-tracer** tool to generate a virtual TCP packet and simulate the flow of the packet through an FTD device. It allows you to analyze any potential packet drop due to the access control policy.

Example 11-13 simulates the requests for Telnet traffic access from both networks— inside and outside—in two **packet-tracer** outputs. Both requests are blocked by the Shell Access rule that you created earlier. This example uses port 23 as the destination port and assumes port number 10000 as a randomly generated source port.

Example 11-13 *Simulating a TCP Packet Drop*

```
! Packet originates from the inside network, Telnet server is located at the outside
  network


> packet-tracer input INSIDE_INTERFACE tcp 192.168.1.2 10000 192.168.1.200 23

Phase: 1
Type: NGIPS-MODE
Subtype: ngips-mode
Result: ALLOW
Config:
Additional Information:
The flow ingressed an interface configured for NGIPS mode and NGIPS services will be
  applied
```

```
Phase: 2
Type: ACCESS-LIST
Subtype: log
Result: DROP
Config:
access-group CSM_FW_ACL_ global
access-list CSM_FW_ACL_ advanced deny tcp any any object-group TELNET rule-id
  268440576 event-log flow-start
access-list CSM_FW_ACL_ remark rule-id 268440576: ACCESS POLICY: AC Policy -
  Mandatory/1
access-list CSM_FW_ACL_ remark rule-id 268440576: L4 RULE: Shell Access
object-group service TELNET tcp
 port-object eq telnet
Additional Information:

Result:
input-interface: INSIDE_INTERFACE
input-status: up
input-line-status: up
Action: drop
Drop-reason: (acl-drop) Flow is denied by configured rule

>



! Packet originates from the outside network, Telnet server is located at the inside
  network

> packet-tracer input OUTSIDE_INTERFACE tcp 192.168.1.200 10000 192.168.1.2 23

Phase: 1
Type: NGIPS-MODE
Subtype: ngips-mode
Result: ALLOW
Config:
Additional Information:
The flow ingressed an interface configured for NGIPS mode and NGIPS services will be
  applied

Phase: 2
Type: ACCESS-LIST
Subtype: log
Result: DROP
Config:
```

```
access-group CSM_FW_ACL_ global
access-list CSM_FW_ACL_ advanced deny tcp any any object-group TELNET rule-id
  268440576 event-log flow-start
access-list CSM_FW_ACL_ remark rule-id 268440576: ACCESS POLICY: AC Policy -
  Mandatory/1
access-list CSM_FW_ACL_ remark rule-id 268440576: L4 RULE: Shell Access
object-group service TELNET tcp
 port-object eq telnet
Additional Information:


Result:
input-interface: OUTSIDE_INTERFACE
input-status: up
input-line-status: up
Action: drop
Drop-reason: (acl-drop) Flow is denied by configured rule

>
```

Analyzing a Packet Drop by Using a Real Packet

If your network experiences any connectivity issue, and you do not see any configuration errors, you can capture the live traffic with the tracing feature enabled. This allows you to analyze a real packet—how it goes through an FTD device and how it is blocked by an access rule when it matches a condition. The following steps describe the process:

Step 1.   Create a rule that can capture any traffic destined for port 23. You must apply the rule on the interface that sees the incoming requests.

Example 11-14 shows a command that is able to capture any traffic with destination port 23. You must use the **trace** keyword to capture additional tracing data. After you enter the command, you can view the status of a capture by using the **show capture** command.

Example 11-14   *Capturing Telnet Traffic with Tracing Data*

```
> capture inside_telnet trace interface INSIDE_INTERFACE match tcp any any eq 23
>
> show capture
capture inside_telnet type raw-data trace interface INSIDE_INTERFACE [Capturing - 0
  bytes]
  match tcp any any eq telnet
>
```

Step 2.   Try to access the Telnet server. Although it fails due to the Shell Access rule, your failure attempt generates Telnet traffic that you will analyze next.

Example 11-15 displays four packets with destination port 23. They are captured using the command provided in Example 11-14.

Example 11-15   *FTD Capturing Four Telnet Packets*

```
> show capture inside_telnet

4 packets captured

   1: 01:24:06.440422       192.168.1.2.36534 > 192.168.1.200.23: S 2986077586:
      2986077586(0) win 29200 <mss 1460,sackOK,timestamp 3482899 0,nop,wscale 7>
   2: 01:24:07.437965       192.168.1.2.36534 > 192.168.1.200.23: S 2986077586:
      2986077586(0) win 29200 <mss 1460,sackOK,timestamp 3483149 0,nop,wscale 7>
   3: 01:24:09.442009       192.168.1.2.36534 > 192.168.1.200.23: S 2986077586:
      2986077586(0) win 29200 <mss 1460,sackOK,timestamp 3483650 0,nop,wscale 7>
   4: 01:24:13.450217       192.168.1.2.36534 > 192.168.1.200.23: S 2986077586:
      2986077586(0) win 29200 <mss 1460,sackOK,timestamp 3484652 0,nop,wscale 7>
4 packets shown

>
```

Step 3.   Select a packet by using its number and view the packet by using the **show capture** command. Add the **trace** parameter with the command in order to view additional tracing data. Example 11-16 shows the dropping of a TCP packet through an FTD device. The tracing data confirms that the packet was dropped due to an access rule.

Example 11-16   *Viewing a Captured Packet with Tracing Data*

```
> show capture inside_telnet packet-number 2 trace

4 packets captured

   2: 01:24:07.437965       192.168.1.2.36534 > 192.168.1.200.23: S 2986077586:
      2986077586(0) win 29200 <mss 1460,sackOK,timestamp 3483149 0,nop,wscale 7>
Phase: 1
Type: CAPTURE
Subtype:
Result: ALLOW
Config:
Additional Information:
MAC Access list
Phase: 2
Type: ACCESS-LIST
Subtype:
Result: ALLOW
Config:
```

```
Implicit Rule
Additional Information:
MAC Access list

Phase: 3
Type: NGIPS-MODE
Subtype: ngips-mode
Result: ALLOW
Config:
Additional Information:
The flow ingressed an interface configured for NGIPS mode and NGIPS services will be
  applied

Phase: 4
Type: ACCESS-LIST
Subtype: log
Result: DROP
Config:
access-group CSM_FW_ACL_ global
access-list CSM_FW_ACL_ advanced deny tcp any any object-group TELNET rule-id
  268440576 event-log flow-start
access-list CSM_FW_ACL_ remark rule-id 268440576: ACCESS POLICY: AC Policy -
  Mandatory/1
access-list CSM_FW_ACL_ remark rule-id 268440576: L4 RULE: Shell Access
object-group service TELNET tcp
 port-object eq telnet
Additional Information:

Result:
input-interface: INSIDE_INTERFACE
input-status: up
input-line-status: up
Action: drop
Drop-reason: (acl-drop) Flow is denied by configured rule


1 packet shown
>
```

Summary

In this chapter, you have learned how to configure an FTD device in Inline Mode, how to enable fault tolerance features on an inline set, and how to trace a packet in order to analyze the root cause of a drop. This chapter also describes various command-line tools that you can use to verify the status of an interface, an inline pair, and an inline set.

Quiz

1. Which of the following statements is true?

   a. The configuration steps for Inline Mode and Transparent Mode are the same.

   b. An inline pair uses a loopback IP address for communication.

   c. The FailSafe feature is enabled on an inline set by default.

   d. The Propagate Link State feature is not enabled by default on an inline set.

2. Which of the following statements is true?

   a. You should include both interface pairs in the same inline set to ensure the recognition of asynchronous traffic.

   b. The FailSafe feature allows an FTD device to continue its traffic flow through the device by bypassing the detection.

   c. Propagate Link State reduces the routing convergence time when one of the interfaces in an inline set goes down.

   d. All of the above.

3. Which command provides an overview of the various components of an inline interface set?

   a. **show interface ip brief**

   b. **show inline-set**

   c. **show interface detail**

   d. **show interface inline detail**

4. To determine whether a packet is dropped by an access rule, which of the following options is provided by FTD?

   a. Capture traffic in .pcap file format and open the file in an external packet analyzer.

   b. Use the **packet-tracer** tool to trace a live packet directly.

   c. Capture the traffic and use the trace functionality, and view the packets by using the **capture** command.

   d. None of the above.

Chapter 12

Inspecting Traffic Without Blocking It

An FTD device can block packets when you deploy it in Inline Mode. However, there are some scenarios where you may not want to block a packet right away but instead want to watch the traffic pattern, determine the effectiveness of your access rules or intrusion rules on live traffic, and then tune the overall access control policy accordingly. Sometimes, you want to analyze any suspicious activities on your honeypot and detect any potential attacks. Occasionally, the business continuity policy of your organization may demand passive detection rather than inline protection. In this chapter, you will learn how to deploy FTD to inspect traffic and detect any suspicious activities without dropping the traffic in real time.

Traffic Inspection Essentials

When you consider deploying FTD for detection-only purposes, you mainly have two choices—Passive Mode and Inline Tap Mode. The following sections emphasize the differences between various interface modes and monitoring technologies.

Passive Monitoring Technology

To understand the architecture of a passive deployment, you must be familiar with the underlying technologies, including the following:

- **Promiscuous Mode:** On an FTD device, when you configure an interface in passive mode, you set the interface into Promiscuous Mode. Promiscuous Mode allows an interface to see any packet in a network segment—even packets that are not aimed at that interface. This capability empowers an FTD device to monitor the network activities without being an active part of a network.

Figure 12-1 introduces Promiscuous Mode and SPAN port, which are technologies used in a passive FTD deployment.

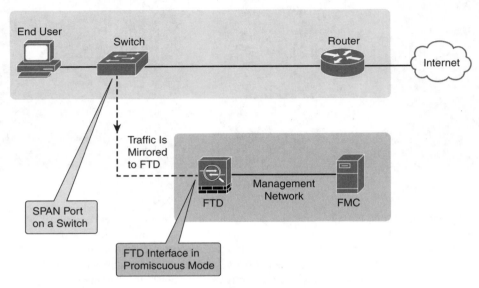

Figure 12-1   *Basic Architecture of a Passive Deployment*

- **SPAN port:** Some switch models can replicate traffic from multiple switch ports and send the copies to a specific switch port. An FTD device can monitor a network without being an active part of the network flow; this feature is called *port mirroring*. A switch port enabled with the port mirroring feature is known as the switch port analyzer (SPAN) port.

  A SPAN port can receive mirrored traffic from the same Layer 2 switch. However, if you want to send the replicated traffic to multiple switches, you can use the Encapsulated Remote Switched Port Analyzer (ERSPAN) technology. ERSPAN transports mirrored traffic over a Layer 3 network by encapsulating it using the Generic Routing Encapsulation (GRE) tunneling protocol.

  FTD supports inspection of both SPAN and ERSPAN traffic. However, the configuration examples in this chapter use only SPAN port.

  Figure 12-2 illustrates the differences between two types of passive deployments—using SPAN and ERSPAN ports.

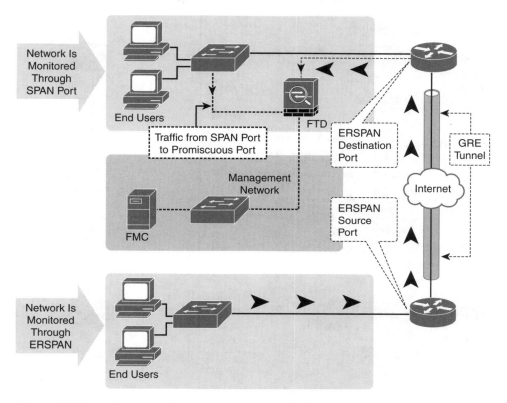

Figure 12-2   *Difference Between a SPAN Port and an ERSPAN Port*

- **TAP:** A TAP is a network device that copies and transfers traffic to another system. Unlike a SPAN port on a switch, which is configured at the software level, a network TAP is dedicated hardware that is designed to replicate and transfer traffic. For an additional cost, a TAP offers numerous advantages over a SPAN port. One of the most important benefits is that a TAP is able to capture and copy all the traffic (including any errors) from a highly utilized network and transfer it to a monitoring device, such as FTD, without any packet drop.

  A SPAN port, in contrast, drops packets if the utilization of a SPAN link exceeds its capacity. In a highly utilized network, if a SPAN port fails to transfer all the traffic from all the switch ports, an FTD device loses the complete visibility of a network and may miss detecting any suspicious activities.

Figure 12-3 shows two types of cabling that an FTD device supports. Both deployments are operational in detection-only mode.

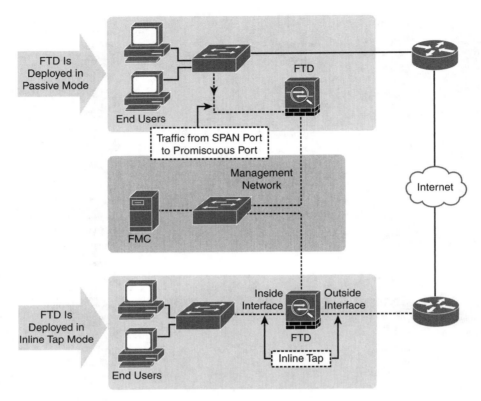

Figure 12-3   *Cabling of Interfaces in Passive Mode and Inline Tap Mode*

Inline Versus Inline Tap Versus Passive

In Chapter 11, "Blocking Traffic Using Inline Interface Mode," you learned about the operation of an FTD device in Inline Mode, which can block traffic based on the access control and intrusion rules you enable.

In contrast, if you apply a rule to block packets with certain conditions, an FTD device does not actually block the original traffic when you configure it in Inline Tap Mode or Passive Mode. It only generates an event and lets the packet go through the FTD.

Figure 12-4 provides a flowchart of various security components of the Firepower software that can block a packet. However, the Passive Mode and Inline Tap Mode deployments do not block any traffic; they only generate an event when a packet matches a rule.

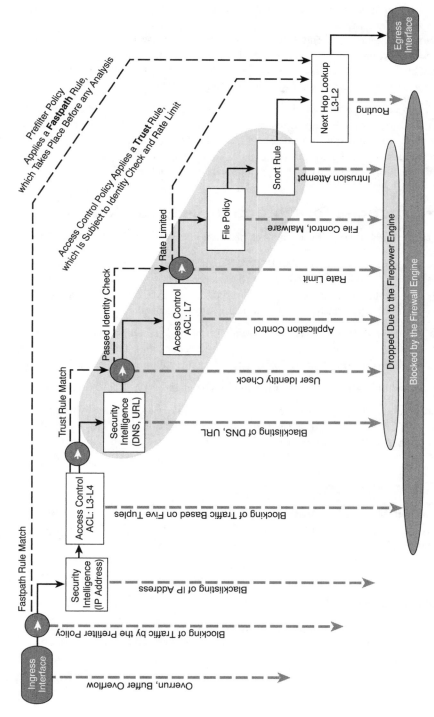

Figure 12-4 *Overview of the FTD Components That Can Trigger a Block Action*

From a user standpoint, a block or drop action on both modes—Passive and Inline Tap—has the same effect. For example, if a packet matches an access rule with a Block action, it triggers a connection event displaying the Block action, while the original packet goes through. Likewise, if a packet matches an intrusion rule with the Drop and Generate Event rule state, FTD displays the matching packets with the Would Have Dropped action and lets the traffic go through the FTD.

Although the outcomes are the same, the big advantage of Inline Tap Mode over Passive Mode is the ease of transition to the inline mode, when necessary. The physical cabling of Inline Mode and Inline Tap Mode is exactly same. If your FTD is currently deployed in Inline Tap mode, and you decide to switch to Inline Mode to block traffic in real time, you can do it simply by changing a setting in the GUI.

Best Practices for Detection-Only Deployment

Consider the following best practices before you deploy an FTD in Passive Mode:

- If your plan is to deploy an FTD device in Detection-Only Mode, so that you could observe any network activities and tune the security policies accordingly, you may choose Inline Tap Mode over the traditional Passive Mode. This allows you to switch to Inline Mode faster, without touching any physical cables.

- If your ultimate plan is to deploy an FTD device in Detection-Only Mode permanently, you can choose Passive Mode over Inline Tap Mode to eliminate any chance of traffic interruption due to an accidental outage of the FTD device.

- If the utilization of a network is medium to high, use a TAP instead of a SPAN port.

- Although an FTD device in Passive Mode cannot block traffic, you should still select an FTD model based on the throughput specification to ensure that the FTD device inspects all the traffic without dropping it.

Fulfilling Prerequisites

If you previously configured an FTD device as a firewall in Routed Mode, you need to remove any platform settings, IP addresses, and DHCP server configurations from the FTD data interfaces, as they are not necessary in Inline, Inline Tap, and Passive Modes.

Inline Tap Mode

Inline Tap Mode comes as an add-on feature to an inline set configuration. To enable Inline Tap Mode, at first, you have to perform all the steps to add an inline set in Inline Mode.

Configuring Inline Tap Mode

The following steps are necessary to create an inline set with Inline Tap Mode and to verify the operation:

- Part 1: Configuration

  Step 1. Build an inline pair.

  Step 2. Associate an inline pair with the inline set.

  Step 3. Turn on the fault tolerance features.

  Step 4. Enable Inline Tap Mode.

  Step 5. Save the changes, and deploy the new settings.

- Part 2: Verification

  Step 1. Add an access rule with Block action.

  Step 2. Save the changes, and deploy the new settings.

  Step 3. Run traffic that matches the access rule.

Note Except for Step 4 in Part 1—enabling Inline Tap Mode—all of the above steps are described and configured in Chapter 11. If you skipped that chapter, please read it now. This section discusses only the additional step—enabling Inline Tap Mode.

If your FTD is currently running in Inline Mode, follow these steps to enable Inline Tap Mode:

Step 1. Log in to the FMC GUI.

Step 2. Navigate to the **Devices > Device Management** page. A list of managed devices appears.

Step 3. Click the pencil icon next to the FTD device where you want to enable Inline Tap Mode. The device editor page appears.

Step 4. Select the **Inline Sets** tab. If you configured an inline set earlier, it appears here (see Figure 12-5).

Step 5. Click the pencil icon next to the inline set to modify the existing settings. The Edit Inline Set window appears.

Step 6. Select the **Advanced** tab.

Step 7. Enable the **Tap Mode** check box (see Figure 12-6).

Step 8. Click **OK** to return to the Inline Sets tab.

Step 9. Click **Save** to save the settings, and click **Deploy** to deploy them.

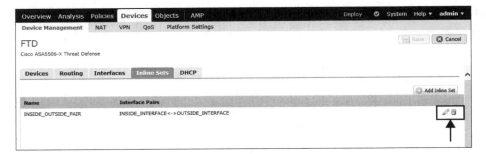

Figure 12-5   *Option to Modify an Existing Inline Pair Configuration*

Figure 12-6   *Advanced Settings for an Inline Set Configuration*

Verifying an Inline Tap Mode Configuration

Upon a successful deployment, you should be able to communicate from your inside host 192.168.1.2 to the outside server 192.168.1.200. The examples in this chapter use a TCP service, Telnet, to test connectivity and generate a Block event for it.

> **Note**   This section assumes that the FTD device is running the same access control policy that you created in Chapter 11, which blocks any traffic destined for port 23 (Telnet). If you revoked that policy or skipped Chapter 11, please read it now to learn how to block Telnet traffic in Inline Mode.

After you deploy an access control policy to block traffic with destination port 23, try to Telnet into the outside system 192.168.1.200 from the inside host 192.168.1.2. You should be able to access the system successfully. You should also be able to view an event for the corresponding connections.

FTD generates only one event—for its Block action—when it is in Inline Mode because it logs an event at the beginning of a connection and is unable to see the rest of the connection. However, when an FTD device is in Detection-Only Mode, it generates multiple events—for Block and Allow actions—because it can see the entire connection without interrupting the flow.

Figure 12-7 shows two Block events that are generated in Inline Tap Mode and Inline Mode at the beginning of a Telnet connection.

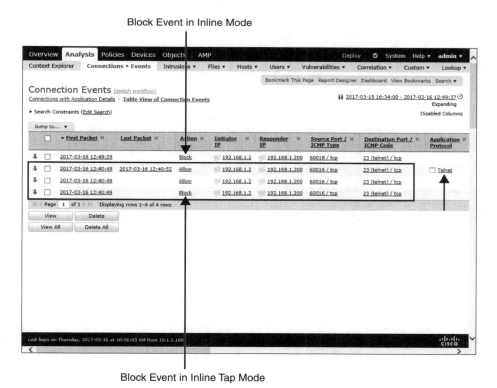

Figure 12-7   *Connection Events for a Block Action in Inline Tap Mode and Inline Mode*

If a communication attempt fails and the FMC does not indicate an error for it, you can begin troubleshooting by using the FTD CLI.

Example 12-1 confirms that the interface set is in Inline Tap Mode. The command output displays various components of an inline set configuration, such as member interfaces of an inline pair, their statuses, and advanced settings.

Example 12-1 *Tap Mode Enabled on the INSIDE_OUTSIDE_PAIR Inline Set*

```
> show inline-set

Inline-set INSIDE_OUTSIDE_PAIR
  Mtu is 1500 bytes
  Failsafe mode is on/activated
  Failsecure mode is off
  Tap mode is on
  Propagate-link-state option is on
  hardware-bypass mode is disabled
  Interface-Pair[1]:
    Interface: GigabitEthernet1/1 "INSIDE_INTERFACE"
      Current-Status: UP
    Interface: GigabitEthernet1/2 "OUTSIDE_INTERFACE"
      Current-Status: UP
    Bridge Group ID: 0
>
```

Example 12-2 demonstrates that the GigabitEthernet1/1 and GigabitEthernet1/2
interfaces are in Inline Tap Mode. Both of them are part of an inline pair called INSIDE_
OUTSIDE_PAIR. The command output also provides detailed statistics about the packets.

Example 12-2 *Status of Each Interface of an Inline Pair*

```
> show interface GigabitEthernet 1/1
Interface GigabitEthernet1/1 "INSIDE_INTERFACE", is up, line protocol is up
  Hardware is Accelerator rev01, BW 1000 Mbps, DLY 10 usec
        Auto-Duplex(Full-duplex), Auto-Speed(1000 Mbps)
        Input flow control is unsupported, output flow control is off
        MAC address a46c.2ae4.6bc0, MTU 1500
        IPS Interface-Mode: inline-tap, Inline-Set: INSIDE_OUTSIDE_PAIR
        IP address unassigned
        9241 packets input, 945431 bytes, 0 no buffer
        Received 89 broadcasts, 0 runts, 0 giants
  .
  .

> show interface GigabitEthernet 1/2
Interface GigabitEthernet1/2 "OUTSIDE_INTERFACE", is up, line protocol is up
  Hardware is Accelerator rev01, BW 1000 Mbps, DLY 10 usec
        Auto-Duplex(Full-duplex), Auto-Speed(1000 Mbps)
        Input flow control is unsupported, output flow control is off
        MAC address a46c.2ae4.6bc1, MTU 1500
```

```
IPS Interface-Mode: inline-tap, Inline-Set: INSIDE_OUTSIDE_PAIR
IP address unassigned
9065 packets input, 924609 bytes, 0 no buffer
Received 30 broadcasts, 0 runts, 0 giants
```

Passive Interface Mode

A passive interface is simpler to configure than an inline set. You can use just one interface to receive traffic from a mirror port. An egress interface is not necessary, as an FTD does not forward traffic in Passive Mode.

Configuring Passive Interface Mode

An FTD device supports both SPAN and ERSPAN ports, but the ports require additional configuration on a switch or router. However, you can install a plug-and-play TAP that can mirror traffic without any additional software configuration.

The following section details the steps to connect an FTD passive interface with a SPAN port on a switch—one of the most common port mirroring options.

Configuring Passive Interface Mode on an FTD Device

To configure a passive interface on an FTD device, follow these steps:

Step 1. Log in to the FMC GUI.

Step 2. Navigate to the **Devices** > **Device Management** page. A list of managed devices appears.

Step 3. Click the pencil icon next to the device name where you want to enable the passive interface mode. The device editor page appears.

Step 4. On the Interfaces tab, select an interface that will function in Promiscuous Mode. The interface connects to a SPAN port on a switch. The Edit Physical Interface window appears. Figure 12-8 shows the configuration of GigabitEthernet1/1 interface as a passive interface.

Step 5. From the Mode dropdown, select **Passive**.

Step 6. Give the interface a name and select the **Enabled** check box.

Step 7. Click **OK** to return to the device editor page.

Step 8. Click **Save** to save the configuration, and click **Deploy** to deploy it.

Figure 12-9 shows an overview of the FTD interfaces. Note that you do not need to copy an IP address and security zone for a passive interface.

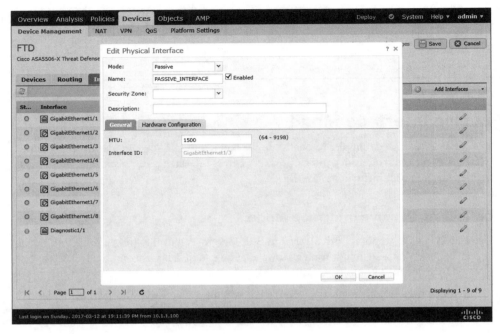

Figure 12-8   *The Edit Physical Interface Window*

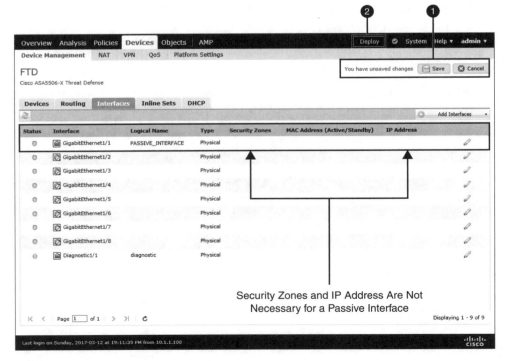

Figure 12-9   *Overview of FTD Interface Configurations*

Configuring a SPAN Port on a Switch

If you are using a Cisco switch to transmit mirrored traffic to an FTD device, you have to define the source ports (the ports from which the traffic is copied) and a destination port (the port that sends duplicated traffic to an FTD device).

Example 12-3 shows the setup of a SPAN port on a Cisco switch. According to the following configuration, this switch receives traffic on the GigabitEthernet0/1 and GigabitEthernet0/2 interfaces, duplicates them, and retransmits the duplicated traffic through the GigabitEthernet0/8 interface.

Example 12-3 *Essential Commands to Configure a SPAN Port*

```
Switch(config)# monitor session 1 source interface gigabitEthernet 0/1
Switch(config)# monitor session 1 source interface gigabitEthernet 0/2

Switch(config)# monitor session 1 destination interface g0/8
```

Verifying a Passive Interface Mode Configuration

After you deploy configuration, initiate a Telnet connection from inside to outside systems. You will notice that, although the access control policy is configured to block Telnet traffic, FTD does not block any traffic in Passive Mode; it just generates events.

Figure 12-10 shows three Block actions that are generated in three different interface modes during three Telnet connection attempts.

If a passive interface on an FTD device does not see traffic, you need to check both devices—FTD and switch. The following examples demonstrate some commands that you run during investigation.

Example 12-4 offers two useful commands that you can run on an FTD device. First, enter the **show nameif** command to determine the active interfaces. Then you can run the **show interface** command with the interface to identify the interface status, mode, traffic statistics, and so on

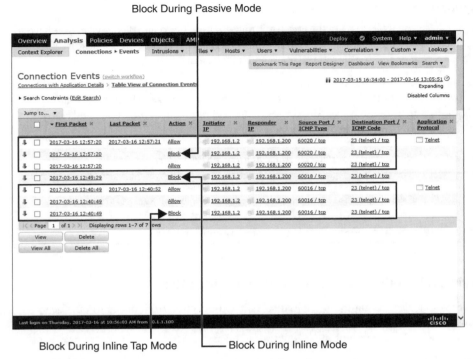

Figure 12-10   *Block Actions of a Telnet Connection in Different Interface Modes*

Example 12-4   *Verifying a Passive Interface*

```
> show nameif
Interface                 Name                    Security
GigabitEthernet1/1        PASSIVE_INTERFACE          0
Management1/1             diagnostic                 0
>



> show interface GigabitEthernet 1/1
Interface GigabitEthernet1/1 "PASSIVE_INTERFACE", is up, line protocol is up
  Hardware is Accelerator rev01, BW 1000 Mbps, DLY 10 usec
        Auto-Duplex(Full-duplex), Auto-Speed(1000 Mbps)
        Input flow control is unsupported, output flow control is off
        MAC address a46c.2ae4.6bc0, MTU 1500
        IPS Interface-Mode: passive
        IP address unassigned
        289 packets input, 30173 bytes, 0 no buffer
```

```
        Received 7 broadcasts, 0 runts, 0 giants
        0 input errors, 0 CRC, 0 frame, 0 overrun, 0 ignored, 0 abort
        0 pause input, 0 resume input
        0 L2 decode drops
        161 packets output, 17774 bytes, 0 underruns
        0 pause output, 0 resume output
        0 output errors, 0 collisions, 0 interface resets
        0 late collisions, 0 deferred
        0 input reset drops, 24 output reset drops
        input queue (blocks free curr/low): hardware (991/894)
        output queue (blocks free curr/low): hardware (1023/1018)
Traffic Statistics for "PASSIVE_INTERFACE":
        104 packets input, 6520 bytes
        0 packets output, 0 bytes
        104 packets dropped
    1 minute input rate 0 pkts/sec,  0 bytes/sec
    1 minute output rate 0 pkts/sec,  0 bytes/sec
    1 minute drop rate, 0 pkts/sec
    5 minute input rate 0 pkts/sec,  0 bytes/sec
    5 minute output rate 0 pkts/sec,  0 bytes/sec
    5 minute drop rate, 0 pkts/sec
>
```

Example 12-5 provides two useful commands that can confirm the SPAN port status on a switch.

Example 12-5 *Configuring and Verifying a SPAN Port*

```
Switch# show running-config | include monitor
monitor session 1 source interface Gi0/1 - 2
monitor session 1 destination interface Gi0/8
Switch#


Switch# show monitor session 1
Session 1
---------
Type                   : Local Session
Source Ports           :
    Both               : Gi0/1-2
Destination Ports      : Gi0/8
    Encapsulation      : Native
          Ingress      : Disabled

Switch#
```

Analyzing Traffic Inspection Operation

If a host experiences any connectivity issues despite the FTD device being deployed in Detection-Only Mode, you can determine the root cause of an issue by analyzing the tracing information of a packet, as described in the following sections.

Analyzing a Connection Event with a Block Action

The following sections show how to analyze the packets that trigger connection events. There are two ways to analyze them: by capturing live traffic with the trace functionality and by running the **packet-tracer** tool.

Analyzing Live Traffic

Follow these steps to capture live Telnet traffic and analyze the flow of packets in Inline Tap Mode:

Step 1. Enter a capture rule with the **trace** keyword. Example 12-6 shows the use of the **trace** keyword with the **capture** command. It probes the inside interface and matches any packets with destination port 23. The *Capturing - 0 Bytes* message on the **show capture** command confirms that the process is running but has not seen a packet yet.

Example 12-6 *Capturing Telnet Traffic with Tracing Information*

```
> capture telnet_inside trace interface INSIDE_INTERFACE match tcp any any eq 23
>

> show capture
capture telnet_inside type raw-data trace interface INSIDE_INTERFACE [Capturing - 0
  bytes]
  match tcp any any eq telnet
>
```

Step 2. Initiate a Telnet request from the inside host to the outside server. Although you enabled an access rule to block Telnet traffic, the traffic is able to go through because the interface is in Inline Tap Mode.

Example 12-7 shows the capture of 13 packets with destination port 23 (Telnet). The output displays only three packets for brevity. Each packet has a sequence number on its left.

Example 12-7 *Capturing Telnet Traffic*

```
> show capture telnet_inside


13 packets captured


  1: 01:56:01.756735        192.168.1.2.59358 > 192.168.1.200.23: S 1923550801:
     1923550801(0) win 29200 <mss 1460,sackOK,timestamp 2340482 0,nop,wscale 7>
  2: 01:56:01.757101        192.168.1.2.59358 > 192.168.1.200.23: . ack 2745314499
     win 229 <nop,nop,timestamp 2340483 1541951>
  3: 01:56:01.757239        192.168.1.2.59358 > 192.168.1.200.23: P 1923550802:
     1923550829(27) ack 2745314499 win 229 <nop,nop,timestamp 2340483 1541951>
.
.
<Output_Omitted_for_Brevity>
```

Step 3. From the **show capture** output shown in Example 12-6, select a packet you
want to trace by using its associated number on the left. Example 12-8 shows
the tracing data for a Telnet packet. Note the final action of the flow: *Access-
list would have dropped, but packet forwarded due to inline-tap.*

Example 12-8 *Detail Tracing Data of a Telnet Packet*

```
> show capture telnet_inside packet-number 1 trace


13 packets captured


  1: 01:56:01.756735        192.168.1.2.59358 > 192.168.1.200.23: S 1923550801:
     1923550801(0) win 29200 <mss 1460,sackOK,timestamp 2340482 0,nop,wscale 7>
Phase: 1
Type: CAPTURE
Subtype:
Result: ALLOW
Config:
Additional Information:
MAC Access list


Phase: 2
Type: ACCESS-LIST
Subtype:
Result: ALLOW
Config:
Implicit Rule
Additional Information:
MAC Access list
```

```
Phase: 3
Type: NGIPS-MODE
Subtype: ngips-mode
Result: ALLOW
Config:
Additional Information:
The flow ingressed an interface configured for NGIPS mode and NGIPS services will be
  applied

Phase: 4
Type: ACCESS-LIST
Subtype: log
Result: WOULD HAVE DROPPED
Config:
access-group CSM_FW_ACL_ global
access-list CSM_FW_ACL_ advanced deny tcp any any object-group TELNET rule-id
  268441600 event-log flow-start
access-list CSM_FW_ACL_ remark rule-id 268441600: ACCESS POLICY: AC Policy -
  Mandatory/1
access-list CSM_FW_ACL_ remark rule-id 268441600: L4 RULE: Shell Access
object-group service TELNET tcp
 port-object eq telnet
Additional Information:

Result:
input-interface: INSIDE_INTERFACE
input-status: up
input-line-status: up
Action: Access-list would have dropped, but packet forwarded due to inline-tap

1 packet shown
>
```

Analyzing a Simulated Packet

You can also use the **packet-tracer** tool to simulate the flow of a Telnet packet through the FTD. The tool uses the active access control policy to simulate the packet flow.

Example 12-9 simulates a Telnet packet that would have dropped, but FTD forwards it due to the Inline Tap Mode setting.

Example 12-9 *Simulating Telnet Traffic Through Inline Tap Mode*

```
> packet-tracer input INSIDE_INTERFACE tcp 192.168.1.2 10000 192.168.1.200 23


Phase: 1
Type: ACCESS-LIST
Subtype:
Result: ALLOW
Config:
Implicit Rule
Additional Information:
MAC Access list


Phase: 2
Type: NGIPS-MODE
Subtype: ngips-mode
Result: ALLOW
Config:
Additional Information:
The flow ingressed an interface configured for NGIPS mode and NGIPS services will be
  applied


Phase: 3
Type: ACCESS-LIST
Subtype: log
Result: WOULD HAVE DROPPED
Config:
access-group CSM_FW_ACL_ global
access-list CSM_FW_ACL_ advanced deny tcp any any object-group TELNET rule-id
  268441600 event-log flow-start
access-list CSM_FW_ACL_ remark rule-id 268441600: ACCESS POLICY: AC Policy -
  Mandatory/1
access-list CSM_FW_ACL_ remark rule-id 268441600: L4 RULE: Shell Access
object-group service TELNET tcp
 port-object eq telnet
Additional Information:


Result:
input-interface: INSIDE_INTERFACE
input-status: up
input-line-status: up
Action: Access-list would have dropped, but packet forwarded due to inline-tap


>
```

Analyzing an Intrusion Event with an Inline Result

So far, you have seen how to analyze the connection events when an FTD device is deployed in Passive Mode or Inline Tap Mode. For an access rule with a Block action, the FMC shows a connection event with a Block action, while FTD allows the traffic to go through without an interruption. However, when a packet matches against an intrusion rule with Drop and Generate Events state, the FMC shows a reason for logging the connection as well.

> **Note**   Because this chapter is about inspecting traffic without blocking it, this section takes an opportunity to demonstrate the behavior of an FTD device when you deploy an intrusion policy in Detection-Only Mode. It will help you understand and compare different actions in different interface modes. However, to learn about the configuration and troubleshooting of an intrusion policy, read Chapter 21, "Preventing Cyber Attacks by Blocking Intrusion Attempts."

To understand various actions on connections and the reasons for their logging, this section shows how to deploy and analyze an FTD device in various interface modes with different intrusion policy settings. You will notice different behaviors on FTD when host 192.168.1.2 attempts to connect to a Telnet server 192.168.1.200 in different deployment scenarios.

Table 12-1 highlights the deployment scenarios (1, 2, and 6) when the FTD device would have dropped a packet. A gray down arrow in the Inline Result column confirms it (refer to Figure 12-12, which appears after the table). However, an FTD device blocks a connection when it meets all three conditions together—Interface Mode is inline, the intrusion rule state is set to Drop and Generate Events, and the intrusion policy is configured with the Drop When Inline option enabled. In this case (Scenario 5), the down arrow turns black.

Table 12-1   *Inline Result Behavior in Various Deployment Scenarios*

Scenario	Interface Mode	Intrusion Rule State	Drop When Inline Option	Connection Event (Action, Reason)	Intrusion Event (Inline Result)
1	Inline Tap	Drop and Generate	Enabled	Allow, Intrusion Block	Down arrow (Gray)
2	Inline Tap	Drop and Generate	Disabled	Allow, Intrusion Block	Down arrow (Gray)
3	Inline Tap	Generate	Enabled	Allow, Intrusion Monitor	Blank
4	Inline Tap	Generate	Disabled	Allow, Intrusion Monitor	Blank
5	Inline	Drop and Generate	Enabled	**Block**, Intrusion Block	Down arrow (**Black**)

Scenario	Interface Mode	Intrusion Rule State	Drop When Inline Option	Connection Event (Action, Reason)	Intrusion Event (Inline Result)
6	Inline	Drop and Generate	Disabled	Allow, Intrusion Block	Down arrow (Gray)
7	Inline	Generate	Enabled	Allow, Intrusion Monitor	Blank
8	Inline	Generate	Disabled	Allow, Intrusion Monitor	Blank

Figure 12-11 shows different types of connection events in different deployment scenarios. Although the reasons for logging show Intrusion Block, FTD "allows" all these connections (in Scenarios 1, 2, and 6) due to its interface modes and intrusion policies.

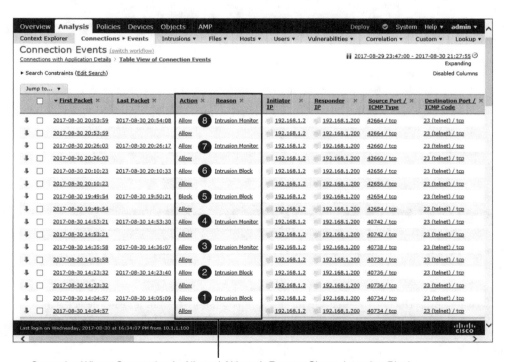

Scenarios Where Connection Is Allowed Although Reason Shows Intrusion Block:
- Scenario 1 and 2: Interface Is In Inline Tap Mode
- Scenario 6: Inline Mode with Drop When Inline Option Is Disabled

Figure 12-11 *Connection Event—Action Versus Reason*

Figure 12-12 shows three types of inline results—blank, gray arrow, and black arrow. Inline results appear blank when FTD does not drop the original packet but generates an event only. The gray down arrow (Scenarios 1, 2 and 6) indicates that the packet would have dropped, and the black arrow (Scenario 5) denotes a drop of the original packet. Modes that can trigger "Would Have Dropped" events are Passive Mode, Inline Tap Mode, and Inline Mode with the "Drop When Inline" option disabled. All the events in this example (and in the previous example) are created using the same client host, the same server host, and the same application protocol.

Figure 12-12 *Intrusion Event—Inline Result Appears as Blank, Gray Arrow, and Black Arrow*

Example 12-10 confirms that the intrusion policy (Snort rule) of an FTD device would have dropped a Telnet packet, but FTD forwards it due to the Inline Tap Mode setting.

Example 12-10 *Analyzing Telnet Traffic Through Inline Tap Mode*

```
> show capture telnet_inside packet-number 1 trace

36 packets captured

  1: 19:39:24.086177        192.168.1.2.40744 > 192.168.1.200.23: S 2884265905:
    2884265905(0) win 29200 <mss 1460,sackOK,timestamp 6199376 0,nop,wscale 7>
```

```
Phase: 1
Type: CAPTURE
Subtype:
Result: ALLOW
Config:
Additional Information:
MAC Access list

Phase: 2
Type: ACCESS-LIST
Subtype:
Result: ALLOW
Config:
Implicit Rule
Additional Information:
MAC Access list

Phase: 3
Type: NGIPS-MODE
Subtype: ngips-mode
Result: ALLOW
Config:
Additional Information:
The flow ingressed an interface configured for NGIPS mode and NGIPS services will be
  applied

Phase: 4
Type: ACCESS-LIST
Subtype: log
Result: ALLOW
Config:
access-group CSM_FW_ACL_ global
access-list CSM_FW_ACL_ advanced permit ip any any rule-id 268434432
access-list CSM_FW_ACL_ remark rule-id 268434432: ACCESS POLICY: AC Policy -
  Default/1
access-list CSM_FW_ACL_ remark rule-id 268434432: L4 RULE: DEFAULT ACTION RULE
Additional Information:
 This packet will be sent to snort for additional processing where a verdict will be
  reached

Phase: 5
Type: NGIPS-EGRESS-INTERFACE-LOOKUP
Subtype: Resolve Egress Interface
Result: ALLOW
Config:
```

```
Additional Information:
Ingress interface INSIDE_INTERFACE is in NGIPS inline mode.
Egress interface OUTSIDE_INTERFACE is determined by inline-set configuration

Phase: 6
Type: FLOW-CREATION
Subtype:
Result: ALLOW
Config:
Additional Information:
New flow created with id 257, packet dispatched to next module

Phase: 7
Type: EXTERNAL-INSPECT
Subtype:
Result: ALLOW
Config:
Additional Information:
Application: 'SNORT Inspect'

Phase: 8
Type: SNORT
Subtype:
Result: DROP
Config:
Additional Information:
Snort Verdict: (block-packet) drop this packet

Result:
input-interface: INSIDE_INTERFACE
input-status: up
input-line-status: up
Action: Access-list would have dropped, but packet forwarded due to inline-tap


1 packet shown
>
```

Summary

This chapter explains the configuration and operation of various detection-only modes
of an FTD device, such as Passive Mode, Inline Tap Mode, and Inline Mode with drop
when the inline option is disabled. It also shows various command-line tools you can use
to determine the status of interfaces and traffic.

Quiz

1. Which of the following interface modes does not block a packet?

   a. Transparent Mode

   b. Routed Mode

   c. Inline Tap Mode

   d. All of the above

2. Which of the following actions ensures the analysis of maximum traffic when it goes through an FTD device?

   a. Using a SPAN port on a switch

   b. Deploying a TAP to replicate traffic

   c. Configuring Inline Tap Mode instead of Passive Mode

   d. Any FTD model can handle all of the traffic and ensures 100% detection.

3. Which of the following statements is true?

   a. Passive Mode can work with just one interface, whereas an inline set requires at least two interfaces.

   b. An inline interface does not require that port mirroring features—such as TAP or SPAN port—be available.

   c. Transition between Detection-Only Mode and Prevention Mode is faster and easier in Inline Tap Mode.

   d. All of the above.

4. Which of the following commands shows whether an interface is set to Inline Tap Mode?

   a. **show inline-tap**

   b. **show inline-set**

   c. **show interface ip brief**

   d. **show interface inline-tap**

Chapter 13

Handling Encapsulated Traffic

FTD can analyze encapsulated traffic. It can take an action based on the outermost and innermost headers of an encapsulated packet. As of this writing, FTD supports the Generic Routing Encapsulation (GRE), IP-in-IP, IPv6-in-IP, and Teredo encapsulation protocols. This chapter demonstrates how an FTD device handles an encapsulated packet over a tunnel.

Encapsulation and Prefilter Policy Essentials

An encapsulation protocol, also known as a tunneling protocol, is used to mask the original IP header of a packet and encapsulate the packet with a completely different IP header. Routers can leverage this protocol to transport certain types of traffic that may not be allowed via the underlying network. Some of that traffic includes (but is not limited to) multicast traffic, nonroutable IP traffic, and non-IP traffic. Through encapsulation technology, a user is able to access a network or service that may be denied in the original network.

This chapter uses the GRE encapsulation protocol in its configuration examples. In GRE, one tunnel endpoint encapsulates data packets with an additional header and forwards them to another tunnel endpoint for decapsulation. A router acts as a GRE tunnel endpoint.

Figure 13-1 shows how a GRE header and an IP header (outer) encapsulate a TCP header and its original IP header (inner).

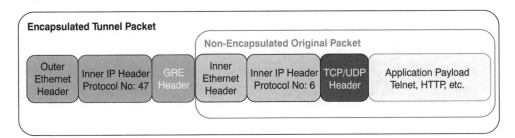

Figure 13-1 *GRE Encapsulated Packet*

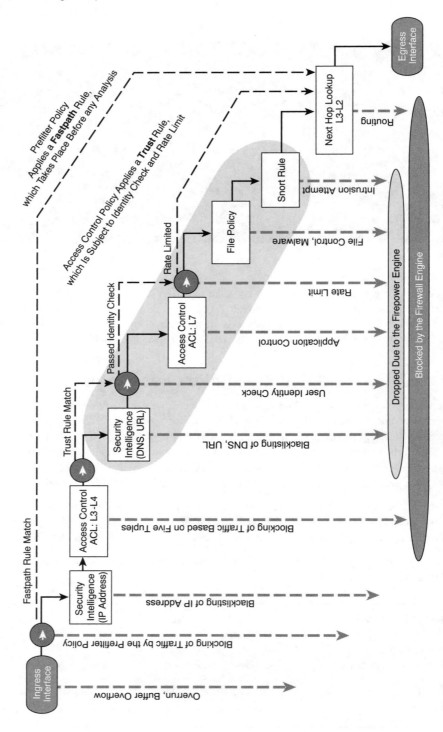

Figure 13-2 *Position of a Prefilter Policy in the Workflow*

You can deploy a prefilter policy in FTD to analyze the encapsulated packets based on their outermost headers. When a packet matches with a rule on a prefilter policy, FTD takes an appropriate action before the packet hits any other security policies.

Figure 13-2 illustrates how a prefilter policy can act as a gatekeeper to the rest of the security policies.

FTD, by default, enables a default prefilter policy. You can change the settings of the default policy. However, you cannot delete this system-provided policy, nor can you add a new rule to this policy. The only configurable option is the default action against the traffic. There are two choices for the default action—*Analyze All Tunnel Traffic* and *Block All Tunnel Traffic*. These default actions are illustrated later in the "Prefilter Policy Settings" section of this chapter (see Figure 13-5).

A custom prefilter policy allows you to add a tunnel rule, which can offer granular control over the tunnel traffic. By using a custom tunnel rule, you can bypass the encapsulated pass-through traffic from any further inspection.

This chapter uses both the default policy and a custom policy to demonstrate the flow of an encapsulated packet in various conditions.

Best Practices for Adding a Prefilter Rule

You can deploy a prefilter policy on an FTD device to define how the FTD should handle any encapsulated traffic. When a prefilter rule matches encapsulated traffic, the remaining non-encapsulated traffic is automatically forwarded to the next level of inspection. You do not need to create a separate prefilter rule to allow the non-encapsulated traffic.

Fulfilling Prerequisites

This chapter assumes that you have prior experience with GRE protocol implementation. In addition, to prepare a lab to implement the examples in this chapter, you need to complete the following tasks:

■ Deploy an FTD device between two routers and configure a simple GRE tunnel between them. FTD must be able to see all the traffic between the routers.

■ Build two pairs of subnetworks, where one subnet pair transfers traffic over an encapsulated tunnel, and the other pair uses a regular non-encapsulated network. You can use either physical hosts or loopback interfaces to represent the endpoints.

Figure 13-3 shows two subnets in each location—a branch office and a data center. Network 2 in the branch office and Network 200 in the data center are connected over a GRE tunnel. The remaining subnets (Network 1 and Network 100) use the non-encapsulated route.

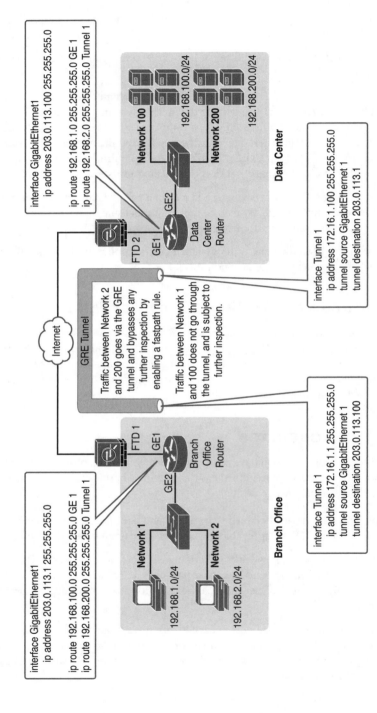

Figure 13-3 *Lab Topology and Router Configuration Used in This Chapter*

Table 13-1 provides a summary of the addressing scheme used in this chapter. The lab exercises in this chapter demonstrate that when Network 2 and Network 200 communicate, the traffic uses the GRE tunnel and is subject to the action in a prefilter policy. The packet flow between Network 1 and Network 100 always remains the same, regardless of any action you define for tunnel traffic.

Table 13-1   *Overview of the IP Addresses Used in This Lab*

Network	Location	Subnet	Packet Header
Network 1	Branch	192.168.1.0/24	Not encapsulated
Network 2	Branch	192.168.2.0/24	Encapsulated
Network 100	Data center	192.168.100.0/24	Not encapsulated
Network 200	Data center	192.168.200.0/24	Encapsulated

- To demonstrate a TCP connection between the subnetworks, this chapter uses Telnet service. The method to initiate a Telnet connection varies, depending on the Telnet client or operating system you use. This book assumes that you know how to establish a Telnet connection.

Transferring and Capturing Traffic on the Firewall Engine

To examine the flows of both encapsulated and non-encapsulated packets through an FTD device, enable two independent capture processes—one for GRE encapsulated packets and the other one for non-encapsulated Telnet packets:

```
> capture gre_traffic trace interface INSIDE_INTERFACE match gre any any
> capture telnet_traffic trace interface INSIDE_INTERFACE match tcp any any eq 23
>
```

Make sure the capture is running but not capturing any data until you manually send traffic. Example 13-1 shows confirmation that the capture process is running. The "0 bytes" output indicates that the FTD device has not received any packets.

Example 13-1   *The Capture Process Is Running but FTD Has Not Received Any Packets to Capture*

```
> show capture
capture gre_traffic type raw-data trace interface INSIDE_INTERFACE [Capturing - 0
  bytes]
  match gre any any
capture telnet_traffic type raw-data trace interface INSIDE_INTERFACE [Capturing - 0
  bytes]
  match tcp any any eq telnet
>
```

To transfer and capture traffic on the firewall engine, follow these steps:

Step 1.   Connect to host 192.168.100.1/24 from host 192.168.1.1/24, using the Telnet application. It should generate non-encapsulated Telnet packets. You can verify this by viewing the capture process, as shown in Example 13-2, which demonstrates that the Telnet connection between 192.168.1.1/24 and 192.168.100.1/24 triggers the *telnet_traffic* access rule and generates 3572 bytes of traffic.

Example 13-2   *Capture is Running—FTD has Captured Telnet Packets*

```
> show capture
capture gre_traffic type raw-data trace interface INSIDE_INTERFACE [Capturing - 0
  bytes]
  match gre any any
capture telnet_traffic type raw-data trace interface INSIDE_INTERFACE
  [Capturing - 3572 bytes]
  match tcp any any eq telnet
>
```

Note   The method to initiate a Telnet connection varies, depending on the Telnet client you use. You can use any tool or an operating system to establish a Telnet connection.

Step 2.   Connect to host 192.168.200.1/24 from host 192.168.2.1/24 by using the Telnet application. This should generate GRE encapsulated packets. Although you have used the Telnet application, the packets have TCP headers inside and the GRE headers outside. You can verify this by viewing the GRE traffic statistics in the capture process. Example 13-3 shows that the Telnet connection between 192.168.2.1/24 and 192.168.200.1/24 triggers the *gre_traffic* access rule instead of the *telnet_traffic* access rule. It proves that the Telnet connection between these two subnets uses the GRE tunnel.

Example 13-3   *FTD Capturing GRE Packets After Sending Traffic over the Tunnel*

```
> show capture
capture gre_traffic type raw-data trace interface INSIDE_INTERFACE [Capturing - 4748
  bytes]
  match gre any any
capture telnet_traffic type raw-data trace interface INSIDE_INTERFACE
  [Capturing - 3572 bytes]
  match tcp any any eq telnet
>
```

> **Note**   Hosts in this lab use two different paths to transfer encapsulated and non-encapsulated traffic. The "Fulfilling Prerequisites" section of this chapter describes the router configurations in Figure 13-3.

To clear the previously captured packets from memory and to begin the capture again, run the **clear capture** command:

```
> clear capture /all
```

Scenario 1: Analyzing Encapsulated Traffic

This first scenario shows how to enable the analysis of encapsulated traffic. Here is a summary of the steps you need to perform:

Step 1.   Configure prefilter and access control policies on the FMC and deploy them in FTD.

Step 2.   Transfer traffic through the encapsulated tunnel and the non-encapsulated path.

Step 3.   Capture packets with tracing data for further analysis.

Configuring Policies to Analyze Encapsulated Traffic

To analyze encapsulated traffic, Firepower uses the settings from both a prefilter policy and an access control policy. A prefilter policy allows you to select an encapsulation protocol and an action on encapsulated traffic. An access control policy invokes a prefilter policy and deploys it on an FTD device. By default, a new access control policy invokes the settings from the system-provided default prefilter policy.

> **Tip**   If your goal is to simply *analyze* or *block* all tunnel traffic, select a default action in the default prefilter policy to keep the configuration simple. However, if you need separate tunnel rules for different types of encapsulated traffic, create a custom prefilter policy. A default prefilter policy does not allow you to add custom rules.

Prefilter Policy Settings

To verify the settings of the default prefilter policy, go to the **Policies > Access Control > Prefilter** page. Use the pencil icon to edit the default prefilter policy. Figure 13-4 shows the Prefilter Policy page. By default, FTD provides the default prefilter policy, and uses it in an access control policy.

To analyze encapsulated traffic, select the **Analyze All Tunnel Traffic** option. This allows an FTD device to forward an encapsulated packet to the next level of inspection.

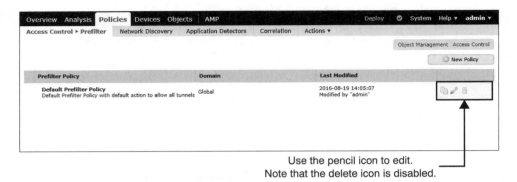

Use the pencil icon to edit.
Note that the delete icon is disabled.

Figure 13-4   *The Prefilter Policy Page Shows the System-Provided Default Policy*

Figure 13-5 shows the configurable options in the default prefilter policy. You cannot add rules to the default prefilter policy; you can only select a default action from the dropdown.

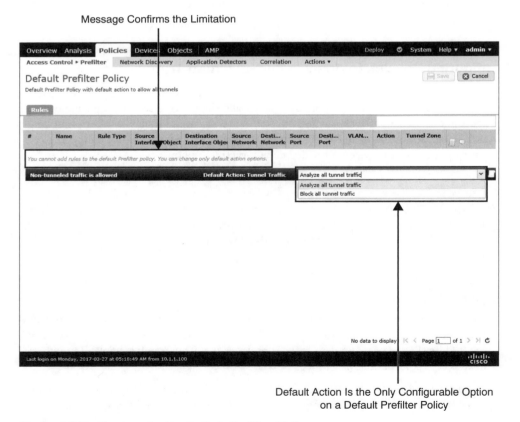

Default Action Is the Only Configurable Option
on a Default Prefilter Policy

Figure 13-5   *Settings for the Default Prefilter Policy*

Access Control Policy Settings

By default, FTD does not generate a connection event when an access control policy has no access rule. You can change this behavior by enabling logging for the default action of an access control policy. Receiving connection events for a default action indicates that traffic is going through the access control policy. Therefore, this chapter does not use a custom access rule.

Figure 13-6 shows the selection of Intrusion Prevention: Balanced Security and Connectivity as the default action. Select the logging icon located next to the Default Action dropdown. The Logging window appears.

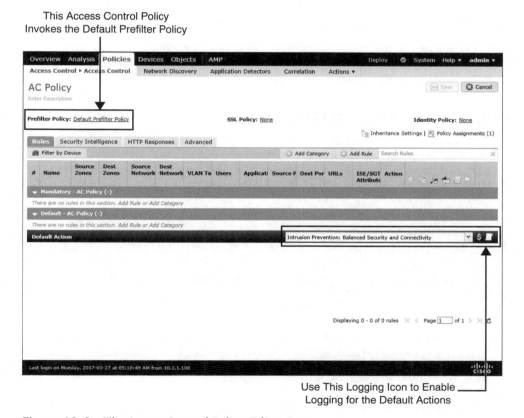

Figure 13-6   *The Access Control Policy Editor Page*

Figure 13-7 shows the Logging window. You can enable logging either at the beginning or at the end of a connection, but not for both because doing so could affect the system performance.

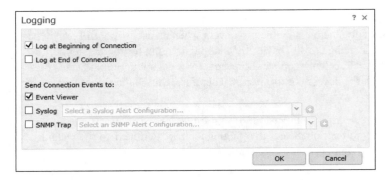

Figure 13-7 *Enabling Logging for the Default Action*

After you make any changes to the prefilter or access control policies, you must save the settings and redeploy the access control policy to activate the new changes.

Verifying the Configuration and Connection

After you have configured the policies to generate connection events for both types of traffic—encapsulated and non-encapsulated—to verify their operation, you need to capture traffic from the ASA firewall engine. If a capture is already running, you can remove the previously captured packets by running the **clear capture** command:

```
> clear capture /all
```

Note The steps for capturing Telnet and GRE traffic are described earlier in this chapter, in the section "Transferring and Capturing Traffic on the Firewall Engine." To learn more about the packet capture option, read Chapter 10, "Capturing Traffic for Advanced Analysis."

Once you enable the captures, use Telnet to connect to Network 100 from Network 1. Similarly, connect to Network 200 from Network 2. Both connection attempts should be successful. You can view the associated connection events in the FMC.

Figure 13-8 shows two connection events for two separate Telnet connections— originated from Network 1 and Network 2. Because FTD can analyze the inner header of an encapsulated packet, the FMC shows the original IP address—not the address on the outermost header—in a connection event.

If you do not see the events as shown in Figure 13-8, make sure you have enabled logging for the default action. You can verify the logging settings by running the **show access-control-config** command (see Example 13-4). If you did not enable logging, read the section "Configuring Policies to Analyze Encapsulated Traffic," earlier in this chapter.

Although the packets between Network 2 and 200 are
encapsulated, the FTD can inspect the innermost IP header.

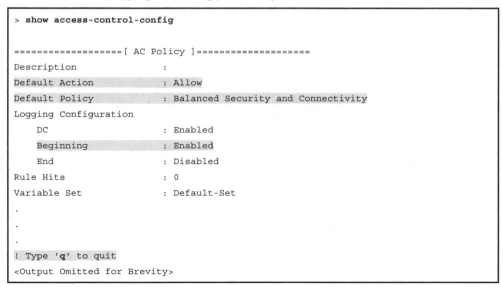

The default action under the Tunnel/Prefilter Rule column confirms that a
prefilter policy allowed this traffic for further inspection.

Figure 13-8   *Connection Events Due to Encapsulated and Non-encapsulated Traffic*

Example 13-4 shows confirmation that the default action of the access control policy is
configured to generate a log at the beginning of a connection.

Example 13-4   *Verifying the Setting for the Default Action*

```
> show access-control-config


==================[ AC Policy ]==================
Description              :
Default Action           : Allow
Default Policy           : Balanced Security and Connectivity
Logging Configuration
   DC                    : Enabled
   Beginning             : Enabled
   End                   : Disabled
Rule Hits                : 0
Variable Set             : Default-Set
.
.
.
! Type 'q' to quit
<Output Omitted for Brevity>
```

If you do not see an expected connection event, you can turn on the **firewall-engine-debug** tool to determine if (and why) a packet goes through the engines. As an access rule inspects a packet, the tool displays the internal ID for an active rule and its associated action in real time.

Example 13-5 shows debug messages for both encapsulated and non-encapsulated Telnet connections. If FTD generates debug messages during both connection attempts, it confirms that the Firepower inspection engines are able to see and inspect traffic inside and outside a tunnel.

Example 13-5 *Debugging the Firewall Engine*

```
> system support firewall-engine-debug

Please specify an IP protocol: tcp
Please specify a client IP address:
Please specify a client port:
Please specify a server IP address:
Please specify a server port:
Monitoring firewall engine debug messages

! The following messages appear when you connect to 192.162.100.1/24 from the host
  192.168.1.1/24 over the non-encapsulated path. It triggers the default action
  (rule id: 268434432) on the Access Control policy:

.
192.168.1.1-43286 > 192.168.100.1-23 6 AS 5 I 1 New session
192.168.1.1-43286 > 192.168.100.1-23 6 AS 5 I 1 using HW or preset rule order 2,
  id 268434432 action Allow and prefilter rule 0
192.168.1.1-43286 > 192.168.100.1-23 6 AS 5 I 1 allow action
192.168.1.1-43286 > 192.168.100.1-23 6 AS 5 I 1 Deleting session

.
.
! The following output appears when you connect to 192.162.200.1/24 from the host
  192.168.2.1/24 over the GRE tunnel. It triggers the prefilter rule id 9988:

.
192.168.2.1-23208 > 192.168.200.1-23 6 AS 5 I 0 New session
192.168.2.1-23208 > 192.168.200.1-23 6 AS 5 I 0 using prefilter rule 9998 with
  tunnel zone -1
192.168.2.1-23208 > 192.168.200.1-23 6 AS 5 I 0 Starting with minimum 0, id 0 and
  SrcZone first with zones -1 -> -1, geo 0(0) -> 0, vlan 0, sgt tag: untagged,
  svc 0, payload 0, client 0, misc 0, user 9999997, url , xff
192.168.2.1-23208 > 192.168.200.1-23 6 AS 5 I 0 match rule order 2, id 268434432
  action Allow
192.168.2.1-23208 > 192.168.200.1-23 6 AS 5 I 0 allow action

.
.
<Output Omitted for Brevity>
```

If you want to know exactly which rule will trigger a message on the **firewall-engine-debug** output, first take note of the rule ID from the debug output, and then find it in the list of active access rules. Example 13-6 shows the list of active access rules on an FTD device. You can find any tunnel, prefilter, and access rules with their associated internal rule IDs in this list.

Example 13-6 *Verifying Prefilter Policy Configuration by Using the CLI*

```
> show access-list
access-list cached ACL log flows: total 0, denied 0 (deny-flow-max 4096)
          alert-interval 300
access-list CSM_FW_ACL_; 6 elements; name hash: 0x4a69e3f3
access-list CSM_FW_ACL_ line 1 remark rule-id 9998: PREFILTER POLICY: Default Tunnel
  and Priority Policy
access-list CSM_FW_ACL_ line 2 remark rule-id 9998: RULE: DEFAULT TUNNEL ACTION RULE
access-list CSM_FW_ACL_ line 3 advanced permit ipinip any any rule-id 9998
  (hitcnt=0) 0xf5b597d6
access-list CSM_FW_ACL_ line 4 advanced permit 41 any any rule-id 9998 (hitcnt=0)
  0x06095aba
access-list CSM_FW_ACL_ line 5 advanced permit gre any any rule-id 9998 (hitcnt=3)
  0x52c7a066
access-list CSM_FW_ACL_ line 6 advanced permit udp any eq 3544 any range 1025 65535
  rule-id 9998 (hitcnt=0) 0x46d7839e
access-list CSM_FW_ACL_ line 7 advanced permit udp any range 1025 65535 any eq 3544
  rule-id 9998 (hitcnt=0) 0xaf1d5aa5
access-list CSM_FW_ACL_ line 8 remark rule-id 268434432: ACCESS POLICY: AC Policy -
  Default/1
access-list CSM_FW_ACL_ line 9 remark rule-id 268434432: L4 RULE: DEFAULT ACTION RULE
access-list CSM_FW_ACL_ line 10 advanced permit ip any any rule-id 268434432
  (hitcnt=2) 0xa1d3780e
>
```

Analyzing Packet Flows

Now that you have captured Telnet and GRE packets, you can retrieve any particular captured packets directly on the CLI of the FTD device. Remember that in order to view the detailed tracing data of a packet, you must add the **trace** keyword with the **capture** command. To learn more, read the section "Transferring and Capturing Traffic on the Firewall Engine," earlier in this chapter.

Example 13-7 shows the output of the **show capture** command, which enables you to view the three-way handshake (SYN, SYN-ACK, and ACK) of a TCP connection. Each packet is assigned a number (on the left side of each row) that you can use for further analysis.

Example 13-7 *Retrieving Non-encapsulated Telnet Packets*

```
> show capture telnet_traffic

49 packets captured

  1: 12:57:33.942105        192.168.1.1.46774 > 192.168.100.1.23: S 636710801:
     636710801(0) win 4128 <mss 536>
  2: 12:57:33.945706        192.168.100.1.23 > 192.168.1.1.46774: S 1516450804:
     1516450804(0) ack 636710802 win 4128 <mss 536>
  3: 12:57:33.947140        192.168.1.1.46774 > 192.168.100.1.23: . ack 1516450805
     win 4128
  4: 12:57:33.947186        192.168.1.1.46774 > 192.168.100.1.23: P 636710802:
     636710814(12) ack 1516450805 win 4128
.
.
.
<Output Omitted for Brevity>
```

Example 13-8 shows the detailed flow of a captured packet. This example uses packet
number 1, which is a SYN packet from 192.168.1.1 to 192.168.100.1.

Example 13-8 *Analyzing a Non-encapsulated Telnet Packet*

```
> show capture telnet_traffic packet-number 1 trace

49 packets captured

  1: 12:57:33.942105        192.168.1.1.46774 > 192.168.100.1.23: S 636710801:
     636710801(0) win 4128 <mss 536>
Phase: 1
Type: CAPTURE
Subtype:
Result: ALLOW
Config:
Additional Information:
MAC Access list

Phase: 2
Type: ACCESS-LIST
Subtype:
Result: ALLOW
Config:
Implicit Rule
Additional Information:
MAC Access list
```

```
Phase: 3
Type: NGIPS-MODE
Subtype: ngips-mode
Result: ALLOW
Config:
Additional Information:
The flow ingressed an interface configured for NGIPS mode and NGIPS services will be
   applied

Phase: 4
Type: ACCESS-LIST
Subtype: log
Result: ALLOW
Config:
access-group CSM_FW_ACL_ global
access-list CSM_FW_ACL_ advanced permit ip any any rule-id 268434432
access-list CSM_FW_ACL_ remark rule-id 268434432: ACCESS POLICY: AC Policy -
   Default/1
access-list CSM_FW_ACL_ remark rule-id 268434432: L4 RULE: DEFAULT ACTION RULE
Additional Information:
 This packet will be sent to snort for additional processing where a verdict will be
 reached

Phase: 5
Type: NGIPS-EGRESS-INTERFACE-LOOKUP
Subtype: Resolve Egress Interface
Result: ALLOW
Config:
Additional Information:
Ingress interface INSIDE_INTERFACE is in NGIPS inline mode.
Egress interface OUTSIDE_INTERFACE is determined by inline-set configuration

Phase: 6
Type: FLOW-CREATION
Subtype:
Result: ALLOW
Config:
Additional Information:
New flow created with id 102, packet dispatched to next module

Phase: 7
Type: EXTERNAL-INSPECT
Subtype:
Result: ALLOW
Config:
```

```
Additional Information:
Application: 'SNORT Inspect'


Phase: 8
Type: SNORT
Subtype:
Result: ALLOW
Config:
Additional Information:
Snort Verdict: (pass-packet) allow this packet


Result:
input-interface: INSIDE_INTERFACE
input-status: up
input-line-status: up
Action: allow



1 packet shown
>
```

Example 13-9 shows the packets encapsulated with GRE headers (IP number 47). The external IP address 203.0.113.1 represents the internal host 192.168.1.1. Each packet has a reference number (on the left side of each row) that you can use later, during flow analysis.

Example 13-9 *Retrieving the Encapsulated GRE Packets*

```
> show capture gre_traffic

49 packets captured

  1: 12:59:01.441536        203.0.113.1 > 203.0.113.100:   ip-proto-47, length 48
  2: 12:59:01.444190        203.0.113.100 > 203.0.113.1:   ip-proto-47, length 48
  3: 12:59:01.446525        203.0.113.1 > 203.0.113.100:   ip-proto-47, length 44
  4: 12:59:01.446571        203.0.113.1 > 203.0.113.100:   ip-proto-47, length 56
  5: 12:59:01.446601        203.0.113.1 > 203.0.113.100:   ip-proto-47, length 44
  6: 12:59:01.449378        203.0.113.100 > 203.0.113.1:   ip-proto-47, length 44
  7: 12:59:01.450156        203.0.113.100 > 203.0.113.1:   ip-proto-47, length 56
  8: 12:59:01.450217        203.0.113.100 > 203.0.113.1:   ip-proto-47, length 84
.
.
<Output Omitted for Brevity>
```

Example 13-10 shows tracing data for a GRE-encapsulated packet. Because this is tunnel traffic, the default prefilter policy forwards it to the inspection engine for further analysis.

Example 13-10 *Analyzing a GRE-Encapsulated Packet*

```
> show capture gre_traffic packet-number 1 trace

49 packets captured

   1: 12:59:01.441536       203.0.113.1 > 203.0.113.100:  ip-proto-47, length 48
Phase: 1
Type: CAPTURE
Subtype:
Result: ALLOW
Config:
Additional Information:
MAC Access list


Phase: 2
Type: ACCESS-LIST
Subtype:
Result: ALLOW
Config:
Implicit Rule
Additional Information:
MAC Access list


Phase: 3
Type: NGIPS-MODE
Subtype: ngips-mode
Result: ALLOW
Config:
Additional Information:
The flow ingressed an interface configured for NGIPS mode and NGIPS services will be
   applied


Phase: 4
Type: ACCESS-LIST
Subtype: log
Result: ALLOW
Config:
access-group CSM_FW_ACL_ global
access-list CSM_FW_ACL_ advanced permit gre any any rule-id 9998
access-list CSM_FW_ACL_ remark rule-id 9998: PREFILTER POLICY: Default Tunnel and
   Priority Policy
access-list CSM_FW_ACL_ remark rule-id 9998: RULE: DEFAULT TUNNEL ACTION RULE
```

```
Additional Information:
This packet will be sent to snort for additional processing where a verdict will be
  reached


Phase: 5
Type: NGIPS-EGRESS-INTERFACE-LOOKUP
Subtype: Resolve Egress Interface
Result: ALLOW
Config:
Additional Information:
Ingress interface INSIDE_INTERFACE is in NGIPS inline mode.
Egress interface OUTSIDE_INTERFACE is determined by inline-set configuration


Phase: 6
Type: FLOW-CREATION
Subtype:
Result: ALLOW
Config:
Additional Information:
New flow created with id 103, packet dispatched to next module


Phase: 7
Type: EXTERNAL-INSPECT
Subtype:
Result: ALLOW
Config:
Additional Information:
Application: 'SNORT Inspect'


Phase: 8
Type: SNORT
Subtype:
Result: ALLOW
Config:
Additional Information:
Snort Verdict: (pass-packet) allow this packet


Result:
input-interface: INSIDE_INTERFACE
input-status: up
input-line-status: up
Action: allow



1 packet shown
>
```

Scenario 2: Blocking Encapsulated Traffic

In this second scenario, FTD blocks tunnel traffic due to a configuration on the default prefilter policy. The physical topology or the router configurations remains unchanged.

Configuring Policies to Block Encapsulated Traffic

To block all tunnel traffic, you can use the FTD default prefilter policy. However, if you want to block tunnel traffic from a particular source and destination, you need to add a prefilter rule for it. This exercise uses the default prefilter policy because the goal is to analyze the flow of a blocked packet over the tunnel:

Step 1.   Go to **Policies > Access Control > Prefilter**.

Step 2.   Click the pencil icon to edit the default prefilter policy.

Step 3.   In the policy editor page, from the Default Action dropdown select **Block All Tunnel Traffic** (see Figure 13-9).

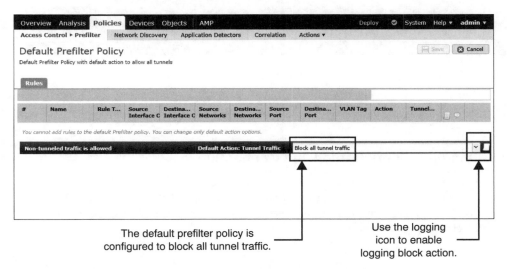

Figure 13-9   *Setting the Prefilter Policy to Block All Tunnel Traffic*

Step 4.   Optionally, use the logging icon, next to the dropdown, to enable logging when the default prefilter policy blocks any tunnel traffic (see Figure 13-10).

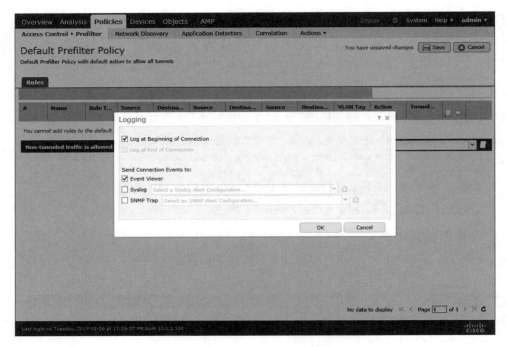

Figure 13-10   *Logging for the Block Action on the Default Prefilter Policy*

Step 5.   Click **Save** to save the policy, and click **Deploy** to deploy it to the FTD device.

Verifying the Configuration and Connection

After you have reconfigured the prefilter policy to block all tunnel traffic, to verify its operation, enable two independent captures for Telnet and GRE traffic. If the FTD device has been running **capture**, you can remove any previously captured packets by running the **clear capture** command:

```
> clear capture /all
```

> **Note**   The steps for capturing Telnet and GRE traffic are described in the section "Transferring and Capturing Traffic on the Firewall Engine," earlier in this chapter. If you want to learn more about packet capture option, read Chapter 10.

In addition, run the **firewall-engine-debug** tool at the FTD CLI. It allows you to analyze any activities in real time as the traffic comes.

When you enable both the **capture** and the **firewall-engine-debug** tools, you can generate live traffic through the FTD device by attempting to establish Telnet connections to Network 100 and Network 200 from Network 1 and Network 2, respectively. In this scenario,

Network 1 and Network 100 should be able to establish a Telnet connection, but Network 2 should fail to connect to Network 200 due to the Block action on the prefilter policy.

Example 13-11 does not show any tunnel traffic in the **firewall-engine-debug** output. Because the traffic is blocked before it hits an inspection engine, the **firewall-engine-debug** tool cannot see and log the Block action.

Example 13-11   *Debugging Connections When a Prefilter Policy Blocks All Tunnel Traffic*

```
! The non-encapsulated traffic from 192.168.1.1 to 192.168.100.1 is allowed by a
  rule (id 268434432).


> system support firewall-engine-debug


Please specify an IP protocol: tcp
Please specify a client IP address:
Please specify a client port:
Please specify a server IP address:
Please specify a server port:

Monitoring firewall engine debug messages

! An action on the traffic from 192.168.1.1 to 192.168.100.1 is logged below:

192.168.1.1-36257 > 192.168.100.1-23 6 AS 5 I 0 New session
192.168.1.1-36257 > 192.168.100.1-23 6 AS 5 I 0 using HW or preset rule order 2, id
  268434432 action Allow and prefilter rule 0
192.168.1.1-36257 > 192.168.100.1-23 6 AS 5 I 0 allow action
192.168.1.1-36257 > 192.168.100.1-23 6 AS 5 I 0 Deleting session

! Traffic from 192.168.2.1 to 192.168.200.1 does not appear here; because they are
  encapsulated and therefore, blocked by the Prefilter policy.

^C
Caught interrupt signal
Exiting.

>
```

The **firewall-engine-debug** output shows rule ID 268434432 with the Allow action, but it does not display the condition that triggers this particular rule. To learn about a rule condition, you can view the list of all active access rules and find the associated rule ID for a specific rule.

Example 13-12 elaborates the default actions of both the prefilter and access control policies. The tunnel traffic is denied by rule 9998, and any other traffic is permitted by rule 268434432 and forwarded for Firepower deep packet inspection.

Example 13-12 *List of Access Rules by the Prefilter and Access Control Default Actions*

```
> show access-list
access-list cached ACL log flows: total 0, denied 0 (deny-flow-max 4096)
          alert-interval 300
access-list CSM_FW_ACL_; 6 elements; name hash: 0x4a69e3f3
access-list CSM_FW_ACL_ line 1 remark rule-id 9998: PREFILTER POLICY: Default Tunnel
  and Priority Policy
access-list CSM_FW_ACL_ line 2 remark rule-id 9998: RULE: DEFAULT TUNNEL ACTION RULE
access-list CSM_FW_ACL_ line 3 advanced deny ipinip any any rule-id 9998 event-log
  flow-start (hitcnt=0) 0x128a09cb
access-list CSM_FW_ACL_ line 4 advanced deny 41 any any rule-id 9998 event-log
  flow-start (hitcnt=0) 0x6e21b1ba
access-list CSM_FW_ACL_ line 5 advanced deny gre any any rule-id 9998 event-log
  flow-start (hitcnt=4) 0xe9c037af
access-list CSM_FW_ACL_ line 6 advanced deny udp any eq 3544 any range 1025 65535
  rule-id 9998 event-log flow-start (hitcnt=0) 0x77ac07e0
access-list CSM_FW_ACL_ line 7 advanced deny udp any range 1025 65535 any eq 3544
  rule-id 9998 event-log flow-start (hitcnt=0) 0x3054708b
access-list CSM_FW_ACL_ line 8 remark rule-id 268434432: ACCESS POLICY: AC Policy -
  Default/1
access-list CSM_FW_ACL_ line 9 remark rule-id 268434432: L4 RULE: DEFAULT ACTION RULE
access-list CSM_FW_ACL_ line 10 advanced permit ip any any rule-id 268434432
  (hitcnt=12) 0xa1d3780e
>
```

For the successful and unsuccessful Telnet attempts, the FMC should display connection events. You can find them in the **Analysis > Connections > Events** page.

Table 13-2 summarizes the actions in a lab network when FTD is configured to block all tunnel traffic.

Table 13-2 *Expected Behavior in Lab Scenario 2 When the Tunnel Traffic Is Blocked*

Network	Policy Action	Event Log
Non-encapsulated traffic between Network 1 and Network 100	The prefilter policy does not interrupt traffic because the traffic is non-encapsulated. It is allowed by the default action of the access control policy.	An Allow event is logged by the default action of the access control policy.
Encapsulated traffic between Network 2 and Network 200	The prefilter policy blocks all of the tunnel traffic, per configuration, before it hits any inspection engines.	A Blocked event is logged by the default action of the prefilter policy.

Figure 13-11 shows that the default action of the default prefilter policy blocks a GRE connection. Because the packet is blocked and not analyzed afterward, FTD does not reveal the innermost IP header. As a result, the connection event shows the IP addresses of the router interfaces.

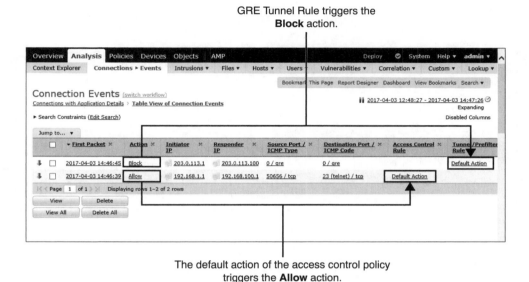

Figure 13-11 shows that the default action of the default prefilter policy blocks a GRE

Figure 13-11   *Connection Events Showing the Blocking of a GRE Connection*

If you do not see an event that you expect to see, make sure you enabled logging for the default actions on both the prefilter and access control policies. In addition, you must check to make sure the latest access control policy where you saved the recent changes is active. You can verify it by checking the status of the access control policy, at **Policies > Access Control > Access Control**.

Analyzing Packet Flows

The packet flows between 192.168.1.1/24 and 192.168.100.1/24 are identical in Scenario 1 and Scenario 2—regardless of the default action you choose for tunnel traffic—because these hosts transfer traffic over a non-encapsulated path. However, in Scenario 2, FTD blocks traffic between the hosts 192.168.2.1/24 and 192.168.200.1/24 because they attempt to route their traffic over the tunnel.

Example 13-13 displays the Telnet traffic over a tunnel. First, it shows the encapsulation of a packet with a GRE header (IP number 47). Then it analyzes the blocking of a GRE packet due to the default tunnel action rule 9998.

Example 13-13   *Analyzing the GRE-Encapsulated Traffic When It Is Blocked by FTD*

```
> show capture gre_traffic

4 packets captured

   1: 18:46:45.801670        203.0.113.1 > 203.0.113.100:  ip-proto-47, length 48
   2: 18:46:47.802708        203.0.113.1 > 203.0.113.100:  ip-proto-47, length 48
   3: 18:46:51.802952        203.0.113.1 > 203.0.113.100:  ip-proto-47, length 48
   4: 18:46:59.803165        203.0.113.1 > 203.0.113.100:  ip-proto-47, length 48
4 packets shown
>


> show capture gre_traffic packet-number 1 trace

4 packets captured

   1: 18:46:45.801670        203.0.113.1 > 203.0.113.100:  ip-proto-47, length 48
Phase: 1
Type: CAPTURE
Subtype:
Result: ALLOW
Config:
Additional Information:
MAC Access list


Phase: 2
Type: ACCESS-LIST
Subtype:
Result: ALLOW
Config:
Implicit Rule
Additional Information:
MAC Access list


Phase: 3
Type: NGIPS-MODE
Subtype: ngips-mode
Result: ALLOW
Config:
Additional Information:
The flow ingressed an interface configured for NGIPS mode and NGIPS services will be
  applied
```

```
Phase: 4
Type: ACCESS-LIST
Subtype: log
Result: DROP
Config:
access-group CSM_FW_ACL_ global
access-list CSM_FW_ACL_ advanced deny gre any any rule-id 9998 event-log flow-start
access-list CSM_FW_ACL_ remark rule-id 9998: PREFILTER POLICY: Default Tunnel and
  Priority Policy
access-list CSM_FW_ACL_ remark rule-id 9998: RULE: DEFAULT TUNNEL ACTION RULE
Additional Information:


Result:
input-interface: INSIDE_INTERFACE
input-status: up
input-line-status: up
Action: drop
Drop-reason: (acl-drop) Flow is denied by configured rule


1 packet shown
>
```

Scenario 3: Bypassing Inspection

In this third scenario, FTD bypasses only the tunnel traffic, while any other
non-encapsulated traffic can still go through the FTD device, as in Scenarios 1 and 2.
The physical topology or the router configurations remain untouched.

Configuring Policies to Bypass Inspection

The default prefilter policy can allow or block the tunnel traffic, but it does not offer an
option to bypass inspection. To bypass, you need to create a custom prefilter policy and
invoke it in an access control policy that you want to deploy.

Custom Prefilter Policy

Use the following steps to create a custom prefilter policy:

Step 1.   Navigate to **Policies > Access Control > Prefilter**.

Step 2.   In the Prefilter Policy page that appears, click the **New Policy** button to create
a new prefilter policy. Figure 13-12 shows the name of a new policy—Custom
Tunnel and Prefilter Policy. In the background, you can see the New Policy
button as well.

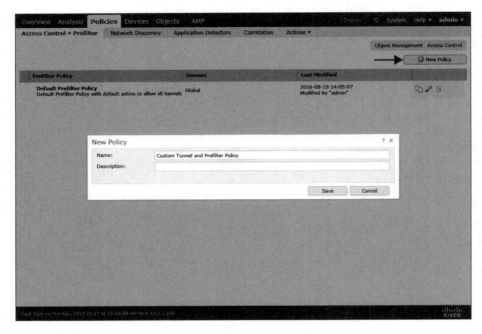

Figure 13-12   *The New Policy Window*

Step 3.   When the New Policy window appears, name the policy and click the **Save** button for the policy. The policy editor page appears.

Step 4.   On the policy editor page, click the **Add Tunnel Rule** button. The Add Tunnel Rule configuration window appears. Figure 13-13 shows the prefilter policy editor page. A user-created policy offers two additional options—Add Tunnel Rule and Add Prefilter Rule.

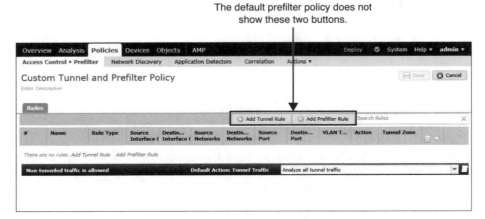

Figure 13-13   *Buttons to Add Custom Tunnel and Prefilter Rules*

Step 5. Assign a name to your custom tunnel rule and select **Fastpath** from the Action dropdown.

Step 6. Make sure the rule is enabled, and select the radio button **Match Tunnels from Source and Destination**.

Step 7. Click the **Encapsulation & Ports** tab and enable GRE in the list of encapsulation protocols. Optionally, you can go to the Tunnel Endpoints tab and select the source and destination tunnel endpoints. These tunnel endpoints are the IP addresses of both sides of the tunnels. You can configure them the same way you would configure a network address within an access rule or a prefilter rule.

Figure 13-14 shows the configuration of a tunnel rule named GRE Tunnel Rule. The rule matches GRE tunnel traffic from source and destination, and it uses Fastpath with them for any further inspection.

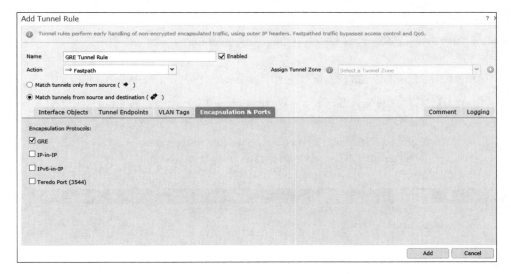

Figure 13-14 *A Fastpath Rule to Bypass Only GRE Traffic*

Step 8. Optionally, go to the Logging tab and enable logging at the beginning of a connection (see Figure 13-15). This allows an FTD device to generate a log when this particular rule triggers.

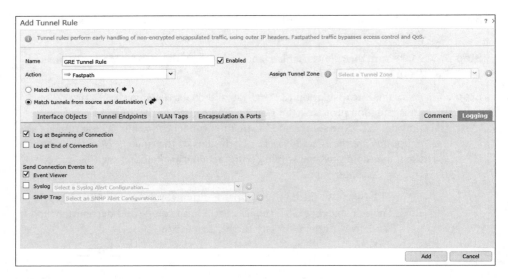

Figure 13-15 *Enabling Logging for a Custom Tunnel Rule*

Step 9.   Click the **Add** button. The GUI returns to the policy editor page.

Step 10.   Click the **Save** button to save the policy. To activate the new custom prefilter policy, you must invoke it in the current access control policy.

Figure 13-16 shows a basic but complete configuration of a tunnel rule. It enables any GRE packets to bypass further inspection.

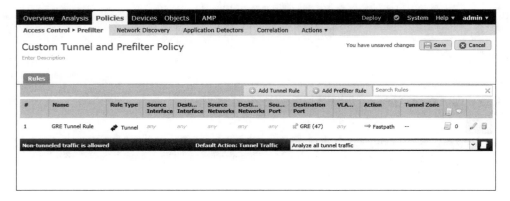

Figure 13-16 *Adding a Tunnel Rule*

Access Control Policy Settings

FTD, by default, invokes the default prefilter policy. You can select a particular policy using the access control policy editor page. Here are the steps to follow:

Step 1.   Go to **Policies > Access Control**. A list of available access control policies appears.

Step 2.   Select the pencil icon to edit the desired policy. The access control policy editor page appears.

Step 3.   In the top-left corner, click the **Default Prefilter Policy** link.

Step 4.   In the Prefilter Policy popup window that appears, select your desired policy from the dropdown. Figure 13-17 shows the access control policy configurations for Scenario 3. First, you must select a custom prefilter policy that has the Fastpath rule. Then you need to enable logging for default action. Finally, you can save and deploy the policy.

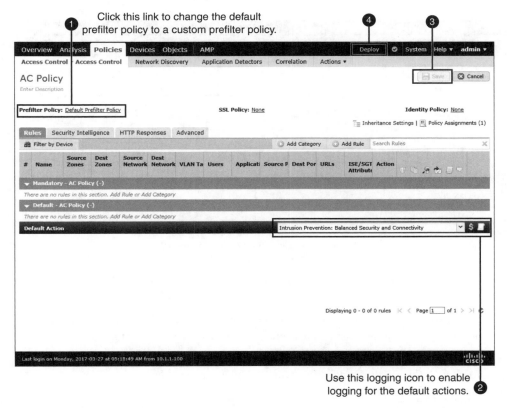

Figure 13-17   *Configuration Items on an Access Control Policy for Scenario 3*

Step 5.   Optionally, enable logging for the default action. This allows you to determine whether a packet hits the default action of an access control policy or bypasses the inspection before it hits the default action.

Step 6.   Finally, click **Save** to save the changes, and click **Deploy** to deploy the revised access control policy to your FTD device. It should activate the revised prefilter policy as well.

Now, connect to Network 200 from Network 2 via Telnet. Because these networks are connected over the GRE tunnel, FTD allows the traffic between them to bypass any additional inspection. You can verify this by viewing the associated connection events on the **Analysis > Connection > Events** page.

Figure 13-18 shows a Fastpath event that is triggered by the GRE tunnel rule. In this case, because FTD does not analyze the inside of the encapsulated traffic, the connection event shows the outermost headers (IP addresses of the router interfaces) instead of the innermost headers.

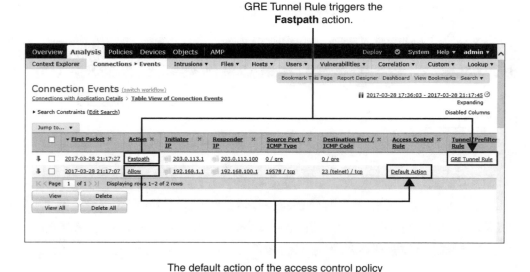

Figure 13-18   *Connection Event Triggered by the Fastpath Action*

If FTD still does not bypass the tunnel traffic and acts based on the previous prefilter policy, try clearing the existing connections on the FTD. This forces the hosts to establish new connections by using the new policy.

To clear all the existing connections, run the following command:

```
> clear conn all
```

To clear connections from a certain host, run the following command:

```
> clear conn address IP_Address_of_a_Host
```

Verifying the Configuration and Connection

You have just enabled a custom prefilter policy to bypass all tunnel traffic. To verify its operation, enable two independent captures for the Telnet and GRE protocols. If FTD has been running **capture**, you can remove any previously captured packets by running the **clear capture** command:

```
> clear capture /all
```

> **Note** The steps for capturing Telnet and GRE traffic are described in the section "Transferring and Capturing Traffic on the Firewall Engine," earlier in this chapter. If you want to learn more about packet capture option, read Chapter 10.

In addition, run the **firewall-engine-debug** tool on the CLI of your FTD device to analyze any activities in real time as the traffic comes.

Once you enable both the **capture** and the **firewall-engine-debug** tools, you can generate live traffic through the FTD device by trying to establish Telnet connections between Network 1 and Network 100 and between Network 2 and Network 200. In Scenario 3, both connection attempts are successful; however, the debug engine does not see traffic from Network 2 and Network 200 because it is encapsulated and bypasses further inspection.

Example 13-14 shows the debugging of a connection between Network 1 and Network 100. Although the Telnet connection was successful, the output does not show any related debug message because a Fastpath rule in the custom prefilter policy allows the encapsulated traffic to bypass any further inspection.

Example 13-14 *Firewall Engine Debug Output—When the Tunnel Traffic Bypasses FTD*

```
> system support firewall-engine-debug

Please specify an IP protocol: tcp
Please specify a client IP address:
Please specify a client port:
Please specify a server IP address:
Please specify a server port:


Monitoring firewall engine debug messages

! Traffic from 192.168.1.1 to 192.168.100.1 is non-encapsulated, therefore it is
  inspected by a rule (id 268434432).


192.168.1.1-40591 > 192.168.100.1-23 6 AS 5 I 1 New session
192.168.1.1-40591 > 192.168.100.1-23 6 AS 5 I 1 using HW or preset rule order 3,
  id 268434432 action Allow and prefilter rule 0
```

```
192.168.1.1-40591 > 192.168.100.1-23 6 AS 5 I 1 allow action
192.168.1.1-40591 > 192.168.100.1-23 6 AS 5 I 1 Deleting session


! Traffic from 192.168.2.1 to 192.168.200.1 are transferred over a GRE tunnel.
  Therefore, they are bypassed from any further inspection, and do not appear here
  in the firewall-engine-debug output.


^C
Caught interrupt signal
Exiting.

>
```

Example 13-15 confirms the deployment of the Fastpath rule named GRE Tunnel Rule.
An FTD device trusts the traffic when the rule uses the Fastpath action.

Example 13-15 *A Fastpath Rule Shows a Trust Action in the CLI Access List*

```
> show access-list
access-list cached ACL log flows: total 0, denied 0 (deny-flow-max 4096)
            alert-interval 300
access-list CSM_FW_ACL_; 7 elements; name hash: 0x4a69e3f3
access-list CSM_FW_ACL_ line 1 remark rule-id 268438530: PREFILTER POLICY: Custom
  Tunnel and Prefilter Policy
access-list CSM_FW_ACL_ line 2 remark rule-id 268438530: RULE: GRE Tunnel Rule
access-list CSM_FW_ACL_ line 3 advanced trust gre any any rule-id 268438530
  event-log both (hitcnt=3) 0xbc125eb0
access-list CSM_FW_ACL_ line 4 remark rule-id 268438529: PREFILTER POLICY: Custom
  Tunnel and Prefilter Policy
access-list CSM_FW_ACL_ line 5 remark rule-id 268438529: RULE: DEFAULT TUNNEL ACTION
  RULE
access-list CSM_FW_ACL_ line 6 advanced permit ipinip any any rule-id 268438529
  (hitcnt=0) 0xf5b597d6
access-list CSM_FW_ACL_ line 7 advanced permit 41 any any rule-id 268438529
  (hitcnt=0) 0x06095aba
access-list CSM_FW_ACL_ line 8 advanced permit gre any any rule-id 268438529
  (hitcnt=0) 0x52c7a066
access-list CSM_FW_ACL_ line 9 advanced permit udp any eq 3544 any range 1025 65535
  rule-id 268438529 (hitcnt=0) 0x46d7839e
access-list CSM_FW_ACL_ line 10 advanced permit udp any range 1025 65535 any eq 3544
  rule-id 268438529 (hitcnt=0) 0xaf1d5aa5
access-list CSM_FW_ACL_ line 11 remark rule-id 268434432: ACCESS POLICY: AC Policy -
  Default/1
access-list CSM_FW_ACL_ line 12 remark rule-id 268434432: L4 RULE: DEFAULT ACTION
  RULE
access-list CSM_FW_ACL_ line 13 advanced permit ip any any rule-id 268434432
  (hitcnt=16) 0xa1d3780e

>
```

Analyzing Packet Flows

The packet flows between 192.168.1.1/24 and 192.168.100.1/24 are the same in all three scenarios in this chapter—regardless of any action you apply on the tunnel traffic—because these hosts transfer traffic over a non-encapsulated path. However, in Scenario 3, FTD allows the traffic between the hosts 192.168.2.1/24 and 192.168.200.1/24 to bypass inspection, because these hosts transfer traffic over the GRE encapsulated tunnel.

Example 13-16 shows the capture of encapsulated packets with GRE headers (IP number 47). Due to the Fastpath rule **trust gre any any**, FTD bypasses them without any further inspection.

Example 13-16   *Analyzing the Bypassing of a GRE-Encapsulated Packet*

```
> show capture gre_traffic

49 packets captured

   1: 01:17:27.046475      203.0.113.1 > 203.0.113.100:  ip-proto-47, length 48
   2: 01:17:27.048871      203.0.113.100 > 203.0.113.1:  ip-proto-47, length 48
   3: 01:17:27.050397      203.0.113.1 > 203.0.113.100:  ip-proto-47, length 44
.
.
.
<Output Omitted for Brevity>

> show capture gre_traffic packet-number 1 trace

49 packets captured

   1: 01:17:27.046475      203.0.113.1 > 203.0.113.100:  ip-proto-47, length 48
Phase: 1
Type: CAPTURE
Subtype:
Result: ALLOW
Config:
Additional Information:
MAC Access list

Phase: 2
Type: ACCESS-LIST
Subtype:
Result: ALLOW
Config:
Implicit Rule
Additional Information:
MAC Access list
```

```
Phase: 3
Type: NGIPS-MODE
Subtype: ngips-mode
Result: ALLOW
Config:
Additional Information:
The flow ingressed an interface configured for NGIPS mode and NGIPS services will be
  applied

Phase: 4
Type: ACCESS-LIST
Subtype: log
Result: ALLOW
Config:
access-group CSM_FW_ACL_ global
access-list CSM_FW_ACL_ advanced trust gre any any rule-id 268438530 event-log both
access-list CSM_FW_ACL_ remark rule-id 268438530: PREFILTER POLICY: Custom Tunnel
  and Prefilter Policy
access-list CSM_FW_ACL_ remark rule-id 268438530: RULE: GRE Tunnel Rule
Additional Information:

Phase: 5
Type: NGIPS-EGRESS-INTERFACE-LOOKUP
Subtype: Resolve Egress Interface
Result: ALLOW
Config:
Additional Information:
Ingress interface INSIDE_INTERFACE is in NGIPS inline mode.
Egress interface OUTSIDE_INTERFACE is determined by inline-set configuration

Phase: 6
Type: FLOW-CREATION
Subtype:
Result: ALLOW
Config:
Additional Information:
New flow created with id 131, packet dispatched to next module

Result:
input-interface: INSIDE_INTERFACE
input-status: up
input-line-status: up
Action: allow


1 packet shown
>
```

Summary

In this chapter, you have learned how to analyze and block traffic that is encapsulated with the GRE protocol, and how to bypass inspection when the traffic is transferred over a tunnel. This chapter also presents various tools you can use to analyze the actions of the prefilter and access control policies.

Quiz

1. Which of the following statements is true?
   a. To analyze any tunnel traffic, you must create and apply a prefilter policy.
   b. An access control policy overrides the rules in a prefilter policy.
   c. The Fastpath action in a prefilter policy bypasses the rules in an access control policy; however, traffic is still subject to intrusion policy inspection.
   d. None of the above.

2. Which of the following tunnel protocols is supported by FTD?
   a. GRE
   b. IP-in-IP
   c. IPv6-in-IP
   d. All of the above

3. Which of the following commands confirms whether logging is enabled for the default action in an access control policy?
   a. **show logging**
   b. **show access-list**
   c. **show default-action**
   d. **show access-control-config**

4. The **firewall-engine-debug** tool shows debug-level messages for which of the following components?
   a. A tunnel rule
   b. A prefilter rule
   c. An access rule
   d All of the above

Chapter 14

Bypassing Inspection and Trusting Traffic

If you do not want FTD to inspect certain traffic, because, for example, it is completely trusted, you can configure FTD to bypass inspection for that particular traffic while it continues deep packet inspection for the rest of the network. Doing so offloads the FTD hardware resources, reduces overall processing delay, and improves network performance. This chapter describes the options for bypassing Firepower inspection of any particular traffic.

Bypassing Inspection and Trusting Traffic Essentials

A Firepower system offers the following tools to bypass deep packet inspection:

- **Fastpath rule:** Enabled through a prefilter policy

- **Trust rule:** Activated over an access control policy

While their goals are identical—to bypass deep packet inspection—the architecture and implementation of each tool is different, as described in the following sections.

The Fastpath Rule

A prefilter policy allows you to bypass traffic before a packet even reaches the ASA and Firepower engines. This functionality is known as Fastpath. A rule enabled with the Fastpath action is also known as a *fastpath rule*. You can apply the Fastpath action on the following rule types, which filter packets based on the outermost header data, and therefore do not offer deep packet inspection:

- **Tunnel rule:** A tunnel rule, as the name suggests, filters tunnel traffic that is encapsulated by an additional IP header. As of this writing, a tunnel rule supports GRE, IP-in-IP, IPv6-in-IP, and Teredo encapsulation protocols, as discussed in Chapter 13, "Handling Encapsulated Traffic."

- **Prefilter rule:** A prefilter rule is able to filter traffic based on basic networking criteria. As of this writing, it supports a rule condition based on an IP address, a port number, a VLAN tag, and an interface.

Rules in a prefilter policy support three types of actions—Fastpath, Analyze, and Block. Whereas the Fastpath action bypasses traffic from further inspection, the Analyze action forwards the traffic to the next level of inspection, and the Block action drops a packet without any additional security check.

Figure 14-1 shows the position of a fastpath rule in an FTD workflow. When a packet matches a fastpath rule, it bypasses the Firepower deep packet inspection completely.

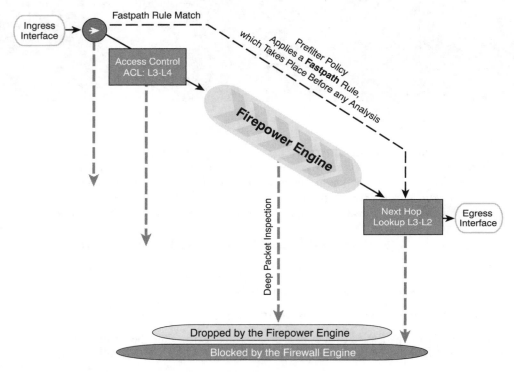

Figure 14-1   *Workflow of the Fastpath Action in a Prefilter Policy*

The Trust Rule

An access rule is known as a *trust rule* when you assign the Trust action to it. A trust rule can bypass traffic without performing any deep packet inspection and network discovery. To ensure the entitlements, the trusted traffic, however, checks for identity and quality of service (QoS) requirements.

Besides the simple filtering conditions that are available in a prefilter rule, an access rule offers additional granular filters. For example, you can match and trust traffic based on network conditions, applications, URLs, users, and so on. Unlike a prefilter rule, an access rule uses the innermost header of a packet to filter traffic.

Figure 14-2 shows the position of a trust rule and a fastpath rule in an FTD workflow. When a packet matches a trust rule or a fastpath rule, it bypasses various inspection components.

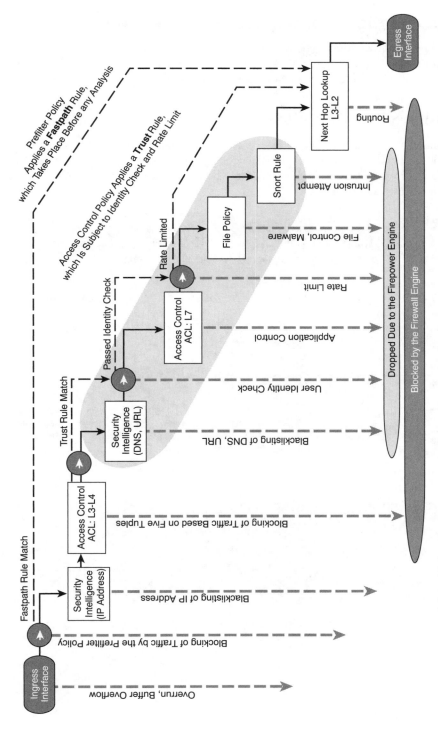

Figure 14-2 *Workflow of the Trust Action in an Access Control Policy*

Best Practices for Bypassing Inspection

To bypass inspection, if you want to filter traffic based on simple conditions, such as network address, port number, VLAN tags, and interface objects, you should use a prefilter rule instead of an access rule with Trust action.

Fulfilling Prerequisites

This chapter assumes that an FTD device is deployed between a client and a server. The client can access the server by using Secure Shell (SSH) and Telnet services. The configuration examples in this chapter use both of these services to verify the action of the fastpath and trust rules.

Note The method to initiate a Telnet or SSH connection varies, depending on the client software or operating system you use. This book does not recommend any particular client, and therefore it does not display any Telnet or SSH client commands.

Figure 14-3 shows a simple topology that is used in this chapter to demonstrate bypassing inspection.

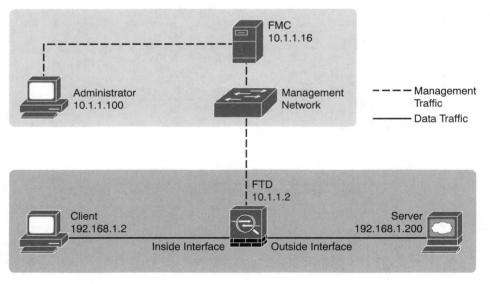

Figure 14-3 *Topology Used in the Configuration Examples of This Chapter*

Implementing Fastpath Through a Prefilter Policy

The default prefilter policy that comes with an FTD device out of the box provides limited configurable options. However, you can create your own prefilter policy, which supports a custom prefilter rule based on basic filtering conditions, such as network address, port numbers, VLAN tags, and interface objects.

A custom prefilter rule supports three types of actions: Analyze, Block, and Fastpath. As an example, the following sections demonstrate how to create a custom prefilter policy, add a custom prefilter rule to it, and fastpath any traffic over port 22—the default port for the SSH protocol.

Configuring Traffic Bypassing

The configurations for bypassing traffic can be divided into two parts:

- Configuring a prefilter policy
- Invoking the prefilter policy into an access control policy

Configuring a Prefilter Policy

To configure a custom prefilter rule for traffic over port 22, follow these steps:

Step 1.   Navigate to **Policies > Access Control > Prefilter**. The Prefilter Policy page appears.

Step 2.   Click the **New Policy** button to create a new prefilter policy. If you created a custom tunnel and prefilter policy in Chapter 13, you can reuse that policy for this exercise. Just use the pencil icon to edit the policy and delete any tunnel rule you created earlier.

Figure 14-4 shows the list of available policies in the Prefilter Policy page. The top one, custom tunnel and prefilter policy, is from Chapter 13. The bottom one, default prefilter policy, comes with FTD by default. You can also create a brand-new prefilter policy by clicking the **New Policy** button.

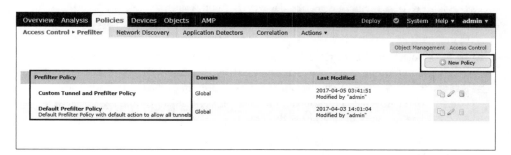

Figure 14-4   *The Prefilter Policy Page Shows Available Policies and the New Policy Button*

Step 3.   In the prefilter policy editor page, click the **Add Prefilter Rule** button (see Figure 14-5). A configuration window appears.

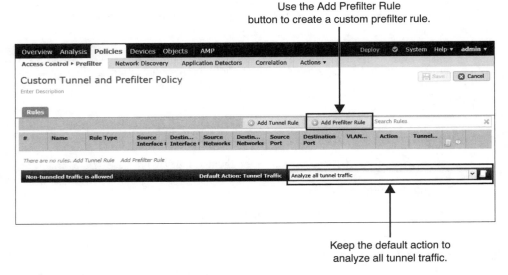

Figure 14-5 shows: Use the Add Prefilter Rule button to create a custom prefilter rule.

Keep the default action to analyze all tunnel traffic.

Figure 14-5   *The Prefilter Policy Editor Page*

Step 4.   Give a name to the rule and set the Action dropdown to **Fastpath**.

Step 5.   Click the **Port** tab and select **SSH** from the Available Ports list.

Step 6.   Click the **Add to Destination** button to select port 22 as the destination port. Figure 14-6 shows the creation of a custom prefilter rule, named Shell Prefilter. The rule uses Fastpath action, and selects the default port for the SSH protocol (port 22) as the destination port.

Note   You could save the rule right here, and it would enable any traffic that is transferred over port 22 to bypass further inspection. However, if you want to enable traffic originated from only a particular subnet to bypass inspection, proceed with the next steps.

Step 7.   Select the **Networks** tab. By default, FTD has preconfigured objects for some common networks, such as private IP addresses, multicast addresses, and so on. If they match with your network-addressing scheme, you can select them here. Alternatively, you can create a network object on the fly. Otherwise, you can just add an IP address directly as a source or destination.

Figure 14-7 illustrates the options available for defining the source and destination for a prefilter rule.

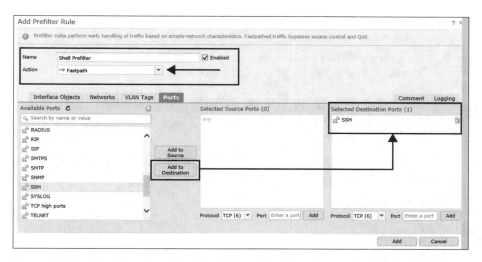

Figure 14-6   *Configuring a Prefilter Rule with Name, Action, and Destination Port*

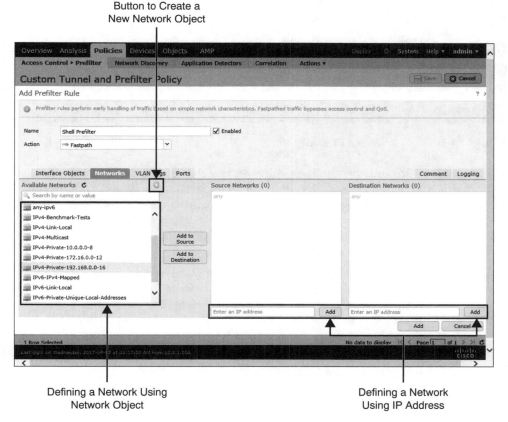

Figure 14-7   *The Network Tab's Options for Adding Networks*

Step 8.   Click on the green plus icon. The New Network Objects popup window appears.

Step 9.   As shown in Figure 14-8, create a custom network object, Corporate-Network, for the 192.168.1.0/24 subnet and click **Save**.

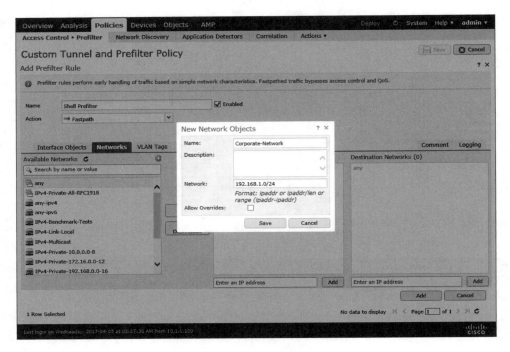

Figure 14-8   *A New Network Object*

Step 10.   Once you have saved a new network object, it is available for selection. You may need to click the refresh icon for it to show up in the list. Click the **Add to Source** button to select your custom network object as the source network. This enables the FTD device to match traffic coming from your desired subnet. Figure 14-9 shows a custom network object, Corporate-Network, selected as the source network.

Step 11.   Optionally, enable logging for every time a fastpath rule triggers. This helps you to determine whether a policy is operational. To do this, go to the Logging tab and select either **Log at Beginning of Connection** or **Log at End of Connection**. (However, do not select both as doing so can affect the system performance.)

Step 12.   Click the **Add** button to complete the rule configuration, and you return to the policy editor page. Click the **Save** button to save the changes.

Caution   Do not select the Deploy button at this stage because you have to make sure this new prefilter policy is invoked by the required access control policy. The next section, "Invoking a Prefilter Policy in an Access Control Policy," describes how to do that. For now, just click the Save button to store the changes.

Figure 14-10 shows a complete view of the Shell Prefilter rule. It also illustrates the buttons that you should and should not click at this stage.

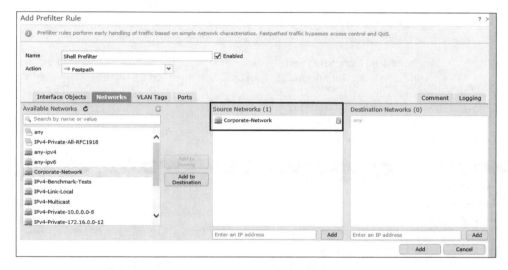

Figure 14-9   *Configuring a Rule to Match 192.168.1.0/24 as the Source Network*

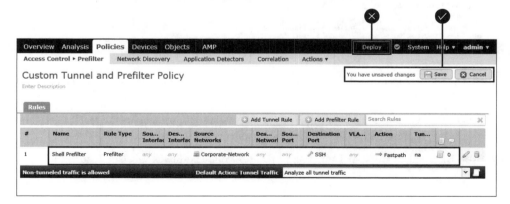

Figure 14-10   *View of a Prefilter Rule That Can Bypass SSH Traffic from 192.168.1.0/24*

Invoking a Prefilter Policy in an Access Control Policy

To invoke a custom prefilter policy in your desired access control policy, follow these steps:

Step 1.   Navigate to **Policies** > **Access Control** > **Access Control**. The Access Control Policy page appears.

Step 2.   To edit the policy that you want to deploy on your FTD device, use the pencil icon next to the name of a policy to open the access control policy editor page.

Step 3.   Look at the top-left side of the policy editor page. You should be able to find a link to the currently selected prefilter policy. Click this link. By default, an access control policy uses the default prefilter policy.

Figure 14-11 confirms that this access control policy invokes the prefilter rules from the default prefilter policy. Click the name of the prefilter policy to make a change.

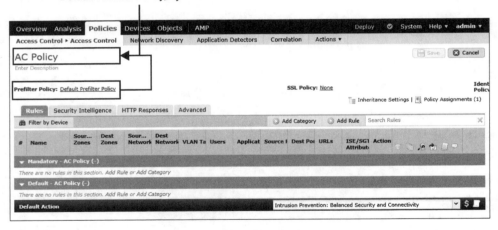

Figure 14-11   *By Default, An Access Control Policy Uses the Default Prefilter Policy*

Step 4.   After you click the link, the Prefilter Policy popup window appears. It presents the available prefilter policies in a dropdown.

Step 5.   Select **Custom Tunnel and Prefilter Policy** and click **OK** (see Figure 14-12).

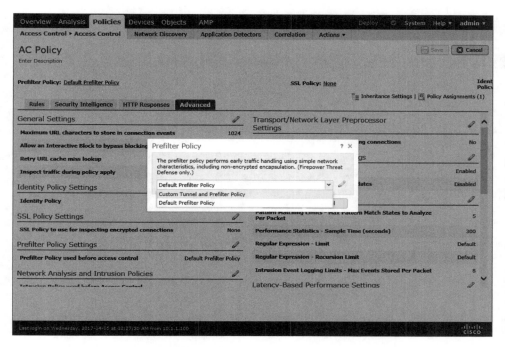

Figure 14-12   *Prefilter Policy Dropdown*

You could save and deploy the access control policy at this stage. However, to determine whether an access control policy inspects a connection, you can enable the logging for the default action. This helps in understanding the life cycle of a packet and troubleshooting any potential issues. Here are the steps:

Step 1.   Go to the Rules tab of the access control policy editor page.

Step 2.   Select the logging icon that is next to the Default Action dropdown (see Figure 14-13).

Step 3.   Select either **Log at Beginning of Connection** or **Log at End of Connection**. (However, do not select both as doing so can affect the system performance.)

Step 4.   Click the **OK** button to return to the policy editor page.

Step 5.   Click **Save** to save the changes, and then click **Deploy** to deploy the changes to your FTD device.

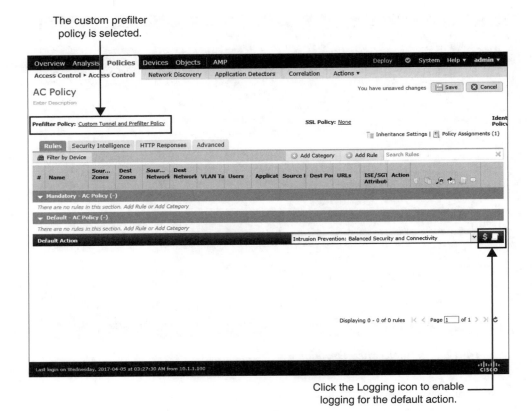

Figure 14-13 *Logging Icon for the Default Action*

Verifying the Prefilter Rule Configuration

By using the CLI, you can verify whether a prefilter rule is active on an FTD device. Example 14-1 shows the list of access rules that are active on an FTD device. The custom prefilter rule shell prefilter is positioned on top of any other access rules because a prefilter policy acts on traffic before any security policies.

Example 14-1 *Position of a Prefilter Rule on the Active Ruleset*

```
> show access-list
access-list cached ACL log flows: total 0, denied 0 (deny-flow-max 4096)
            alert-interval 300
access-list CSM_FW_ACL_; 7 elements; name hash: 0x4a69e3f3
access-list CSM_FW_ACL_ line 1 remark rule-id 268440577: PREFILTER POLICY: Custom
   Tunnel and Prefilter Policy
access-list CSM_FW_ACL_ line 2 remark rule-id 268440577: RULE: Shell Prefilter
access-list CSM_FW_ACL_ line 3 advanced trust tcp object Corporate-Network any
   object-group SSH rule-id 268440577 event-log both (hitcnt=0) 0xe9257885
```

```
access-list CSM_FW_ACL_ line 3 advanced trust tcp 192.168.1.0 255.255.255.0 any eq
ssh rule-id 268440577 event-log both (hitcnt=0) 0xad5d48f9

access-list CSM_FW_ACL_ line 4 remark rule-id 268438529: PREFILTER POLICY: Custom
Tunnel and Prefilter Policy

access-list CSM_FW_ACL_ line 5 remark rule-id 268438529: RULE: DEFAULT TUNNEL ACTION
RULE

access-list CSM_FW_ACL_ line 6 advanced permit ipinip any any rule-id 268438529
(hitcnt=0) 0xf5b597d6

access-list CSM_FW_ACL_ line 7 advanced permit 41 any any rule-id 268438529
(hitcnt=0) 0x06095aba

access-list CSM_FW_ACL_ line 8 advanced permit gre any any rule-id 268438529
(hitcnt=0) 0x52c7a066

access-list CSM_FW_ACL_ line 9 advanced permit udp any eq 3544 any range 1025 65535
rule-id 268438529 (hitcnt=0) 0x46d7839e

access-list CSM_FW_ACL_ line 10 advanced permit udp any range 1025 65535 any eq 3544
rule-id 268438529 (hitcnt=0) 0xaf1d5aa5

access-list CSM_FW_ACL_ line 11 remark rule-id 268434432: ACCESS POLICY: AC Policy -
Default/1

access-list CSM_FW_ACL_ line 12 remark rule-id 268434432: L4 RULE: DEFAULT ACTION
RULE

access-list CSM_FW_ACL_ line 13 advanced permit ip any any rule-id 268434432
(hitcnt=34) 0xa1d3780e

>
```

Enabling Tools for Advanced Analysis

Before you run live SSH traffic, you need to enable a few debugging tools so you can
better understand the action of a rule and the flow of a packet. Follow these steps:

Step 1.   Capture the SSH traffic from the ASA firewall engine:

```
> capture ssh_traffic trace interface INSIDE_INTERFACE match tcp any
any eq 22
```

You can run the **show capture** command to confirm that the capture process
is running. 0 bytes in the output indicates that the FTD has not received
any packets:

```
> show capture
capture ssh_traffic type raw-data trace interface INSIDE_INTERFACE
  [Capturing - 0 bytes]
  match tcp any any eq ssh
  >
```

To clear any previously captured packets from the memory and to restart the
capture from the next matched packets, run the **clear capture** command.

```
> clear capture /all
```

Step 2.   Begin the capture of TCP traffic from the Firepower Snort engine. This
helps you determine whether the Snort engine sees any bypassed traffic.
Example 14-2 shows the command to capture TCP traffic from an inline pair.

Example 14-2   *Capturing Traffic from the Firepower Snort Engine*

```
> capture-traffic

Please choose domain to capture traffic from:
  0 - br1
  1 - INSIDE_OUTSIDE_PAIR inline set

Selection? 1

Please specify tcpdump options desired.
(or enter '?' for a list of supported options)
Options: -n tcp
```

Because the current CLI terminal has entered the Packet Capture Mode, you need to access the FTD from a different terminal. You can connect through SSH or a console connection. On the second terminal connection to the FTD, perform the following steps.

Step 3.   Reset the counters for Snort statistics, which helps you determine the exact number of events for your test traffic:

```
> clear snort statistics
```

Step 4.   Enable debugging for the firewall engine, which allows you to determine the actions applied to any traffic. Example 14-3 shows the command that generates debugging data when FTD inspects TCP traffic.

Example 14-3   *Collecting Debugging Data from the Firewall Engine*

```
> system support firewall-engine-debug

Please specify an IP protocol: tcp
Please specify a client IP address:
Please specify a client port:
Please specify a server IP address:
Please specify a server port:
Monitoring firewall engine debug messages
```

Analyzing the Fastpath Action

It's a good idea to verify the action of the custom prefilter policy. Since the prefilter policy has a rule to bypass SSH traffic, you need to generate SSH traffic between the client (192.168.1.2) and server (192.168.1.200) to verify the Fastpath action. Follow these steps:

Step 1.   Connect to the server (192.168.1.200) from the host (192.168.1.2), using an SSH client. The FTD should fastpath the SSH traffic.

Step 2.   Go to the **Analysis > Connection > Events** page; you should be able view a connection event for the Fastpath action. Figure 14-14 shows a connection event triggered by the shell prefilter—a custom prefilter rule.

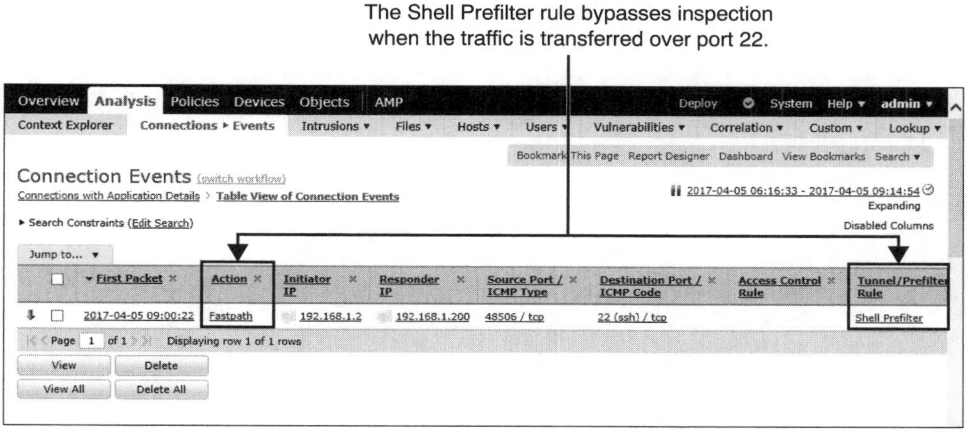

The Shell Prefilter rule bypasses inspection
when the traffic is transferred over port 22.

Figure 14-14   *Connection Event for the Fastpath Action*

Step 3.   Go to the CLI terminal where **firewall-engine-debug** is running. Check the status of the tool. You should see some logs (see Example 14-4).

Example 14-4   *Bypassed Connection Generates Event Logs and Increases Counters*

```
! The firewall-engine-debug tool receives events from hardware in real time.

> system support firewall-engine-debug

Please specify an IP protocol: tcp
Please specify a client IP address:
Please specify a client port:
Please specify a server IP address:
Please specify a server port:
Monitoring firewall engine debug messages

192.168.1.2-48506 > 192.168.1.200-22 6 AS 5 I 0 Got start of flow event from
  hardware with flags 84000001
192.168.1.2-48506 > 192.168.1.200-22 6 AS 5 I 0 Got end of flow event from hardware
  with flags 84000001
^C
Caught interrupt signal
Exiting.

>
```

```
! The Snort statistics keeps a record of these events under the Miscellaneous
  Counters section.


> show snort statistics

Packet Counters:
  Passed Packets                                                    0
  Blocked Packets                                                   0
  Injected Packets                                                  0

Flow Counters:
  Fast-Forwarded Flows                                              0
  Blacklisted Flows                                                 0
  Flows bypassed (Snort Down)                                       0
  Flows bypassed (Snort Busy)                                       0

Miscellaneous Counters:
  Start-of-Flow events                                              1
  End-of-Flow events                                                1
  Denied flow events                                                0
  Frames forwarded to Snort before drop                             0
  Inject packets dropped                                            0
>
```

Step 4.   Go to the terminal where the **capture-traffic** command is running, and analyze the captured packets. Example 14-5 demonstrates that the Firepower
Snort engine does not see any SSH traffic. However, the ASA Firewall engine
can see and capture that traffic.

Example 14-5 *Firewall and Firepower Engines Showing Different Behavior
During Capture*

```
> capture-traffic

Please choose domain to capture traffic from:
  0 - br1
  1 - INSIDE_OUTSIDE_PAIR inline set

Selection? 1

Please specify tcpdump options desired.
(or enter '?' for a list of supported options)
Options: -n tcp
```

```
! If the Firepower Snort engine would see traffic, it would appear here.
! Press the Control+C keys to exit from the capture-traffic tool.


^C
Caught interrupt signal
Exiting.



! Check the status of the capture on the ASA Firewall engine.


> show capture ssh_traffic


61 packets captured


    1: 13:00:22.730156        192.168.1.2.48506 > 192.168.1.200.22: S 1199563799:
        1199563799(0) win 29200 <mss 1460,sackOK,timestamp 4732110 0,nop,wscale 7>
    2: 13:00:22.730492        192.168.1.200.22 > 192.168.1.2.48506: S 2739603340:
        2739603340(0) ack 1199563800 win 28960 <mss 1460,sackOK,timestamp 1446067
        4732110,nop,wscale 7>
    3: 13:00:22.730659        192.168.1.2.48506 > 192.168.1.200.22: . ack 2739603341
        win 229 <nop,nop,timestamp 4732110 1446067>
    4: 13:00:22.730949        192.168.1.2.48506 > 192.168.1.200.22: P 1199563800:
        1199563841(41) ack 2739603341 win 229 <nop,nop,timestamp 4732110 1446067>
    5: 13:00:22.731132        192.168.1.200.22 > 192.168.1.2.48506: . ack 1199563841
        win 227 <nop,nop,timestamp 1446067 4732110>
.
.
! You can see all of the SSH packets generated by your connection. The above output
shows only the first TCP three way handshake, as an example. The remaining outputs
are omitted for brevity.
```

Example 14-6 analyzes the flow of a packet that bypasses the FTD inspection due to the
Fastpath action on the shell prefilter rule. Note the absence of the Snort inspection phase
in this trace data.

Example 14-6 *Analyzing a Packet Flow That Follows the Fastpath Action*

```
> show capture ssh_traffic packet-number 1 trace


61 packets captured


    1: 13:00:22.730156        192.168.1.2.48506 > 192.168.1.200.22: S 1199563799:
        1199563799(0) win 29200 <mss 1460,sackOK,timestamp 4732110 0,nop,wscale 7>
Phase: 1
Type: CAPTURE
Subtype:
```

```
Result: ALLOW
Config:
Additional Information:
MAC Access list


Phase: 2
Type: ACCESS-LIST
Subtype:
Result: ALLOW
Config:
Implicit Rule
Additional Information:
MAC Access list


Phase: 3
Type: NGIPS-MODE
Subtype: ngips-mode
Result: ALLOW
Config:
Additional Information:
The flow ingressed an interface configured for NGIPS mode and NGIPS services will be
  applied


Phase: 4
Type: ACCESS-LIST
Subtype: log
Result: ALLOW
Config:
access-group CSM_FW_ACL_ global
access-list CSM_FW_ACL_ advanced trust tcp object Corporate-Network any object-group
  SSH rule-id 268440577 event-log both
access-list CSM_FW_ACL_ remark rule-id 268440577: PREFILTER POLICY: Custom Tunnel
  and Prefilter Policy
access-list CSM_FW_ACL_ remark rule-id 268440577: RULE: Shell Prefilter
object-group service SSH tcp
 port-object eq ssh
Additional Information:


Phase: 5
Type: NGIPS-EGRESS-INTERFACE-LOOKUP
Subtype: Resolve Egress Interface
Result: ALLOW
Config:
Additional Information:
Ingress interface INSIDE_INTERFACE is in NGIPS inline mode.
Egress interface OUTSIDE_INTERFACE is determined by inline-set configuration
```

```
Phase: 6
Type: FLOW-CREATION
Subtype:
Result: ALLOW
Config:
Additional Information:
New flow created with id 81, packet dispatched to next module

Result:
input-interface: INSIDE_INTERFACE
input-status: up
input-line-status: up
Action: allow

1 packet shown
>
```

Establishing Trust Through an Access Policy

A trust rule can bypass traffic without performing any deep packet inspection and network discovery. It supports granular filters based on Security Intelligence data, application fingerprints, URL filtering, user identities, and so on. In the following sections, you will learn how to trust Telnet traffic as an example of trusting a TCP protocol.

> **Warning**   This chapter uses Telnet service to demonstrate the flow of a TCP packet. However, you should not trust any connection unless you have a complete understanding of the particular traffic and its source and destination.

Configuring Trust with an Access Policy

This section describes how to trust the default port of the Telnet protocol, port 23. Follow these steps:

Step 1.   Navigate to **Policies > Access Control > Access Control**. The access control policy page appears.

Step 2.   To edit the policy that you want to deploy on your FTD device, use the pencil icon next to the name of a policy to open the access control policy editor page.

Step 3.   Click the **Add Rule** button to create a new access rule (see Figure 14-15). The Add Rule window appears.

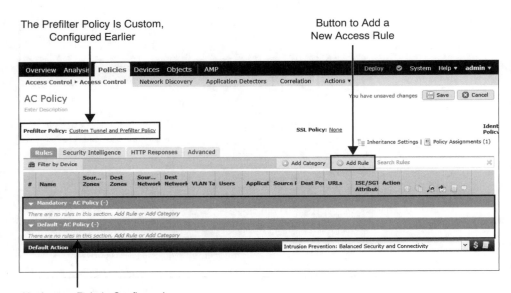

Figure 14-15 *Access Control Policy Editor Showing the Status and the Add Rule Button*

Step 4. Give a name to the access rule and select the **Trust** action.

Step 5. To define the condition of the access rule, go to the Networks tab and select **Corporate-Network** as the source network. Figure 14-16 shows the configuration of the Telnet access rule, which trusts any Telnet traffic coming from 192.168.1.0/24, the internal corporate network.

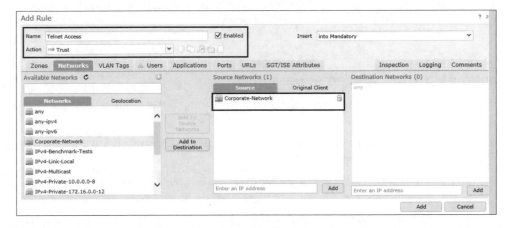

Figure 14-16 *Access Rule to Trust Telnet Traffic—Configuration of the Source Network*

Step 6. On the Ports tab, select **Telnet** as the destination ports (see Figure 14-17).

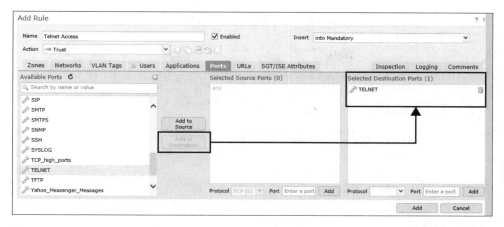

Figure 14-17 *Access Rule to Trust Telnet Traffic—Configuration of the Destination Port*

Step 7. Optionally, go to the Logging tab to enable logging so that you can determine when FTD trusts a connection. Select either **Log at Beginning of Connection** or **Log at End of Connection**. (However, do not select both as doing so can affect the system performance.)

Step 8. Click the **Add** button to complete the trust rule configuration. You are returned to the policy editor page.

Step 9. Click the **Save** button to save the changes, and then click the **Deploy** button to activate the rule.

Verifying the Trust Rule Configuration

Using the CLI, you can verify whether a trust rule is active on an FTD device. Example 14-7 shows the list of access rules that are active on an FTD device. The trust rule Telnet access is placed below the prefilter rule shell prefilter.

Example 14-7 *Position of a Trust Rule on the Active Ruleset*

```
> show access-list
access-list cached ACL log flows: total 0, denied 0 (deny-flow-max 4096)
          alert-interval 300
access-list CSM_FW_ACL_; 8 elements; name hash: 0x4a69e3f3
access-list CSM_FW_ACL_ line 1 remark rule-id 268440577: PREFILTER POLICY: Custom
  Tunnel and Prefilter Policy
access-list CSM_FW_ACL_ line 2 remark rule-id 268440577: RULE: Shell Prefilter
access-list CSM_FW_ACL_ line 3 advanced trust tcp object Corporate-Network any
  object-group SSH rule-id 268440577 event-log both (hitcnt=4) 0xe9257885
  access-list CSM_FW_ACL_ line 3 advanced trust tcp 192.168.1.0 255.255.255.0 any eq
    ssh rule-id 268440577 event-log both (hitcnt=4) 0xad5d48f9
```

```
access-list CSM_FW_ACL_ line 4 remark rule-id 268438529: PREFILTER POLICY: Custom
  Tunnel and Prefilter Policy
access-list CSM_FW_ACL_ line 5 remark rule-id 268438529: RULE: DEFAULT TUNNEL ACTION
  RULE
access-list CSM_FW_ACL_ line 6 advanced permit ipinip any any rule-id 268438529
  (hitcnt=0) 0xf5b597d6
access-list CSM_FW_ACL_ line 7 advanced permit 41 any any rule-id 268438529
  (hitcnt=0) 0x06095aba
access-list CSM_FW_ACL_ line 8 advanced permit gre any any rule-id 268438529
  (hitcnt=0) 0x52c7a066
access-list CSM_FW_ACL_ line 9 advanced permit udp any eq 3544 any range 1025 65535
  rule-id 268438529 (hitcnt=0) 0x46d7839e
access-list CSM_FW_ACL_ line 10 advanced permit udp any range 1025 65535 any eq 3544
  rule-id 268438529 (hitcnt=0) 0xaf1d5aa5
access-list CSM_FW_ACL_ line 11 remark rule-id 268440580: ACCESS POLICY: AC Policy -
  Mandatory/1
access-list CSM_FW_ACL_ line 12 remark rule-id 268440580: L7 RULE: Telnet Access
access-list CSM_FW_ACL_ line 13 advanced permit tcp object Corporate-Network any
  object-group TELNET rule-id 268440580 (hitcnt=3) 0x388a3b9d
access-list CSM_FW_ACL_ line 13 advanced permit tcp 192.168.1.0 255.255.255.0 any eq
  telnet rule-id 268440580 (hitcnt=3) 0x4a6c1f4c
access-list CSM_FW_ACL_ line 14 remark rule-id 268434432: ACCESS POLICY: AC Policy -
  Default/1
access-list CSM_FW_ACL_ line 15 remark rule-id 268434432: L4 RULE: DEFAULT ACTION
  RULE
access-list CSM_FW_ACL_ line 16 advanced permit ip any any rule-id 268434432
  (hitcnt=144) 0xa1d3780e
>
```

Enabling Tools for Advanced Analysis

Before you generate live Telnet traffic, you need to enable a few debugging tools,
which will help you understand the action of a rule and the flow of a packet. Follow these
steps:

Step 1.   Capture the Telnet traffic from the ASA firewall engine:

```
> capture telnet_traffic trace interface INSIDE_INTERFACE match tcp any
any eq 23
```

You can run the **show capture** command to confirm that the capture process
is running. 0 bytes in the output indicates that the FTD device has not
received any packets:

```
> show capture
capture telnet_traffic type raw-data trace interface INSIDE_INTERFACE
  [Capturing - 0 bytes]
  match tcp any any eq telnet
>
```

If the FTD device is running a capture for SSH traffic that you enabled earlier, you can remove it by using the **no** keyword with the **capture** command, as it not necessary for this example:

```
> no capture ssh_traffic
```

To clear any previously captured packets from memory and to restart the capture from the next matched packets, run the **clear capture** command.

```
> clear capture /all
```

Step 2.   Begin the capture of TCP traffic from the Firepower Snort engine. This helps you to determine whether the Snort engine sees any bypassed traffic. Example 14-8 shows the command to capture TCP traffic from an inline pair.

Example 14-8   *Capturing Traffic from the Firepower Snort Engine*

```
> capture-traffic

Please choose domain to capture traffic from:
  0 - br1
  1 - INSIDE_OUTSIDE_PAIR inline set

Selection? 1

Please specify tcpdump options desired.
(or enter '?' for a list of supported options)
Options: -n tcp
```

Because the current CLI terminal has entered the Packet Capture Mode, you need to access the FTD from a new separate terminal. You can connect through an SSH client or a console terminal. On the second terminal connection to the FTD, perform the following steps.

Step 3.   Reset the counters for Snort statistics, which helps you determine the exact number of events for your test traffic:

```
> clear snort statistics
```

Step 4.   Enable debugging for the firewall engine. This helps you determine the actions applied to any traffic. Example 14-9 shows the command that generates debugging data when FTD inspects TCP traffic.

Example 14-9 *Collecting Debugging Data from the Firewall Engine*

```
> system support firewall-engine-debug

Please specify an IP protocol: tcp
Please specify a client IP address:
Please specify a client port:
Please specify a server IP address:
Please specify a server port:
Monitoring firewall engine debug messages
```

In the next section, you will generate traffic to analyze the action of a trust rule. Both tools that you have just enabled on two different terminals—**capture-traffic** and **firewall-engine-debug**—will display data in real time when the traffic will go through the FTD.

Analyzing the Trust Action

It's a good idea to verify the action of the trust rule you created. Because the access control policy has a rule to bypass Telnet traffic, you need to generate Telnet traffic between the client (192.168.1.2) and server (192.168.1.200) to verify the trust action.

Step 1.   Connect to the server (192.168.1.200) from the host (192.168.1.2), using a Telnet client. The FTD device should trust the Telnet traffic.

Step 2.   Go to the **Analysis > Connection > Events** page; you should be able view a connection event for the Trust action. Figure 14-18 shows a new connection event triggered by the Telnet access rule—an access rule with a Trust action.

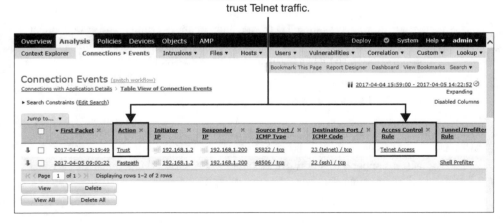

Figure 14-18 *Connection Event for the Trust Action*

Step 3.   Go to the CLI terminal where **firewall-engine-debug** is running (you enabled it in the previous section, "Enabling Tools for Advanced Analysis"). Check the status of the tool. You should see some logs. Example 14-10 shows analysis of the debugging data from an FTD when an access rule applies the Trust action on the Telnet traffic.

Example 14-10   *Trusted Connection Generating Event Logs*

```
! The firewall-engine-debug tool shows that the "Telnet Access" rule applies Trust
  action.

> system support firewall-engine-debug

Please specify an IP protocol: tcp
Please specify a client IP address:
Please specify a client port:
Please specify a server IP address:
Please specify a server port:

Monitoring firewall engine debug messages

192.168.1.2-55822 > 192.168.1.200-23 6 AS 5 I 1 New session
192.168.1.2-55822 > 192.168.1.200-23 6 AS 5 I 1 using HW or preset rule order 3,
  'Telnet Access', action Trust and prefilter rule 0
192.168.1.2-55822 > 192.168.1.200-23 6 AS 5 I 1 Deleting session

^C
Caught interrupt signal
Exiting.

>
```

Step 4.   Go to the terminal where the **capture-traffic** command is running (you enabled it in the previous section, "Enabling Tools for Advanced Analysis"), and analyze the captured packets. Example 14-11 shows that the Firepower Snort engine starts trusting the Telnet traffic after the initial TCP three-way handshake is complete. Therefore, the traffic does not appear in the **capture-traffic** output. However, the ASA firewall engine can see and capture all the traffic.

Example 14-11 *Firewall and Firepower Engines Showing Different Actions During Capture*

```
! The Firepower Snort engine stops seeing traffic after the initial TCP three-way
  handshake.


> capture-traffic


Please choose domain to capture traffic from:
  0 - br1
  1 - INSIDE_OUTSIDE_PAIR inline set


Selection? 1


Please specify tcpdump options desired.
(or enter '?' for a list of supported options)
Options: -n tcp
17:19:49.089991 IP 192.168.1.2.55822 > 192.168.1.200.23: Flags [S], seq 1700253547,
  win 29200, options [mss 1460,sackOK,TS val 7177698 ecr 0,nop,wscale 7], length 0
17:19:49.089991 IP 192.168.1.200.23 > 192.168.1.2.55822: Flags [S.], seq 495495803,
  ack 1700253548, win 28960, options [mss 1460,sackOK,TS val 3421593 ecr 7177698,
  nop,wscale 7], length 0
17:19:49.109979 IP 192.168.1.2.55822 > 192.168.1.200.23: Flags [.], ack 1, win 229,
  options [nop,nop,TS val 7177701 ecr 3421593], length 0
17:19:49.109979 IP 192.168.1.2.55822 > 192.168.1.200.23: Flags [P.], ack 1, win 229,
  options [nop,nop,TS val 7177701 ecr 3421593], length 27

! Nothing appears after the above packets, because they are trusted.


^C
Caught interrupt signal
Exiting.


>



! However, the ASA Firewall engine sees all of the traffic generated by the telnet
  connection.


> show capture telnet_traffic


78 packets captured

  1: 17:19:49.096766        192.168.1.2.55822 > 192.168.1.200.23: S 1700253547:
     1700253547(0) win 29200 <mss 1460,sackOK,timestamp 7177698 0,nop,wscale 7>
  2: 17:19:49.109781        192.168.1.200.23 > 192.168.1.2.55822: S 495495803:
     495495803(0) ack 1700253548 win 28960 <mss 1460,sackOK,timestamp 3421593
     7177698,nop,wscale 7>
```

```
  3: 17:19:49.110086        192.168.1.2.55822 > 192.168.1.200.23: . ack 495495804
     win 229 <nop,nop,timestamp 7177701 3421593>
  4: 17:19:49.110391        192.168.1.2.55822 > 192.168.1.200.23: P 1700253548:
     1700253575(27) ack 495495804 win 229 <nop,nop,timestamp 7177701 3421593>
  5: 17:19:49.110651        192.168.1.200.23 > 192.168.1.2.55822: . ack 1700253575
     win 227 <nop,nop,timestamp 3421596 7177701>
  6: 17:19:49.116037        192.168.1.200.23 > 192.168.1.2.55822: P 495495804:
     495495816(12) ack 1700253575 win 227 <nop,nop,timestamp 3421597 7177701>
  7: 17:19:49.116159        192.168.1.2.55822 > 192.168.1.200.23: . ack 495495816
     win 229 <nop,nop,timestamp 7177703 3421597>
.
.
.
! Output is Omitted for Brevity
```

When a packet matches a prefilter rule with the Fastpath action, the packet does not go through the Snort inspection phase. You verified that earlier in this chapter by analyzing the trace data of a captured packet.

Now, this section demonstrates that the Firepower Snort engine processes the initial TCP handshake before it begins trusting the rest of a connection. Therefore, the initial packets appear in the **capture-traffic** output. You can verify the cause of this behavior by looking into the tracing data. You should see two different Snort verdicts: The first Telnet packet is allowed, and the subsequent flows are fast-forwarded.

Example 14-12 shows an analysis of the first packet of a trusted TCP connection. The Snort verdict is to allow this packet.

Example 14-12 *Analyzing the First Packet of a Trusted Telnet Connection*

```
> show capture telnet_traffic packet-number 1 trace

78 packets captured

  1: 17:19:49.096766        192.168.1.2.55822 > 192.168.1.200.23: S 1700253547:
     1700253547(0) win 29200 <mss 1460,sackOK,timestamp 7177698 0,nop,wscale 7>
Phase: 1
Type: CAPTURE
Subtype:
Result: ALLOW
Config:
Additional Information:
MAC Access list


Phase: 2
Type: ACCESS-LIST
Subtype:
```

```
Result: ALLOW
Config:
Implicit Rule
Additional Information:
MAC Access list

Phase: 3
Type: NGIPS-MODE
Subtype: ngips-mode
Result: ALLOW
Config:
Additional Information:
The flow ingressed an interface configured for NGIPS mode and NGIPS services will be
  applied

Phase: 4
Type: ACCESS-LIST
Subtype: log
Result: ALLOW
Config:
access-group CSM_FW_ACL_ global
access-list CSM_FW_ACL_ advanced permit tcp object Corporate-Network any
  object-group TELNET rule-id 268440580
access-list CSM_FW_ACL_ remark rule-id 268440580: ACCESS POLICY: AC Policy -
  Mandatory/1
access-list CSM_FW_ACL_ remark rule-id 268440580: L7 RULE: Telnet Access
object-group service TELNET tcp
 port-object eq telnet
Additional Information:
 This packet will be sent to snort for additional processing where a verdict will be
  reached

Phase: 5
Type: NGIPS-EGRESS-INTERFACE-LOOKUP
Subtype: Resolve Egress Interface
Result: ALLOW
Config:
Additional Information:
Ingress interface INSIDE_INTERFACE is in NGIPS inline mode.
Egress interface OUTSIDE_INTERFACE is determined by inline-set configuration

Phase: 6
Type: FLOW-CREATION
Subtype:
```

```
Result: ALLOW
Config:
Additional Information:
New flow created with id 282, packet dispatched to next module


Phase: 7
Type: EXTERNAL-INSPECT
Subtype:
Result: ALLOW
Config:
Additional Information:
Application: 'SNORT Inspect'


Phase: 8
Type: SNORT
Subtype:
Result: ALLOW
Config:
Additional Information:
Snort Verdict: (pass-packet) allow this packet


Result:
input-interface: INSIDE_INTERFACE
input-status: up
input-line-status: up
Action: allow


1 packet shown
>
```

Example 14-13 shows an analysis of the third and fourth packets of a trusted TCP connection. The Snort verdicts for both packets are to fast-forward them.

Example 14-13   *Analyzing the Subsequent Packets of a Trusted Telnet Connection*

```
! Packet Number 3:


> show capture telnet_traffic packet-number 3 trace


78 packets captured


   3: 17:19:49.110086      192.168.1.2.55822 > 192.168.1.200.23: . ack 495495804
      win 229 <nop,nop,timestamp 7177701 3421593>
```

```
Phase: 1
Type: CAPTURE
Subtype:
Result: ALLOW
Config:
Additional Information:
MAC Access list

Phase: 2
Type: ACCESS-LIST
Subtype:
Result: ALLOW
Config:
Implicit Rule
Additional Information:
MAC Access list

Phase: 3
Type: FLOW-LOOKUP
Subtype:
Result: ALLOW
Config:
Additional Information:
Found flow with id 282, using existing flow

Phase: 4
Type: EXTERNAL-INSPECT
Subtype:
Result: ALLOW
Config:
Additional Information:
Application: 'SNORT Inspect'

Phase: 5
Type: SNORT
Subtype:
Result: ALLOW
Config:
Additional Information:
Snort Verdict: (fast-forward) fast forward this flow

Result:
input-interface: INSIDE_INTERFACE
input-status: up
input-line-status: up
Action: allow
```

```
1 packet shown
>



! Packet Number 4:


> show capture telnet_traffic packet-number 4 trace


78 packets captured


   4: 17:19:49.110391       192.168.1.2.55822 > 192.168.1.200.23: P 1700253548:
     1700253575(27) ack 495495804 win 229 <nop,nop,timestamp 7177701 3421593>
Phase: 1
Type: CAPTURE
Subtype:
Result: ALLOW
Config:
Additional Information:
MAC Access list
.
.
! Output is Omitted for Brevity
.
.
Phase: 5
Type: SNORT
Subtype:
Result: ALLOW
Config:
Additional Information:
Snort Verdict: (fast-forward) fast forward this flow

Result:
input-interface: INSIDE_INTERFACE
input-status: up
input-line-status: up
Action: allow

1 packet shown
>
```

Example 14-14 shows statistics of the passed packet and fast-forwarded flows. In this example, an FTD device passes two Telnet packets before it fast-forwards (trusts) the rest of the flows of a connection.

Example 14-14 *Counters for a Trusted Telnet Connection*

```
! The Snort statistics keep a record of these events using two types of counters.

> show snort statistics

Packet Counters:
  Passed Packets                                                    2
  Blocked Packets                                                   0
  Injected Packets                                                  0

Flow Counters:
  Fast-Forwarded Flows                                              1
  Blacklisted Flows                                                 0
  Flows bypassed (Snort Down)                                       0
  Flows bypassed (Snort Busy)                                       0

Miscellaneous Counters:
  Start-of-Flow events                                              0
  End-of-Flow events                                                0
  Denied flow events                                                0
  Frames forwarded to Snort before drop                            0
  Inject packets dropped                                            0

>
```

Using the Allow Action for Comparison

The Allow action passes a packet after it matches all the conditions in an access rule. Unlike the Trust action, the Allow action does not fast-forward any packets. All the packets in a connection are subject to inspection. To verify this behavior, deploy an access rule with the Allow action. As described here, you can redeploy the previously created Telnet access rule by changing the action type from Trust to Allow.

Figure 14-19 shows an access rule with the Allow action. The rule allows Telnet traffic when it originates from the corporate network 192.168.1.0/24.

After deploying the Telnet access rule, if you connect from host 192.168.1.2 to server 192.168.1.200, you should be able to access the server. This time, the FMC shows an Allow action for it.

Figure 14-20 shows a connection event with the Allow action. FTD generates this event if you enable logging for the Telnet access rule and the rule matches with a Telnet packet.

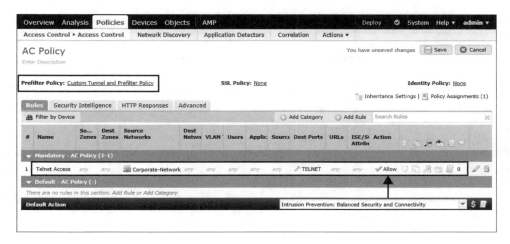

Figure 14-19 *An Access Rule with the Allow Action*

The Allow action makes the Telnet access rule permit
Telnet traffic upon all enabled inspections.

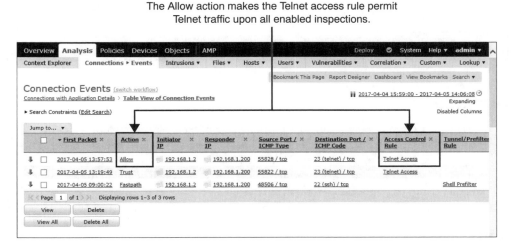

Figure 14-20 *A Connection Event for Allowing a Telnet Connection*

To verify the operation of the Allow action, you follow the same steps that you performed earlier in this chapter for Fastpath and Trust actions. However, you can just view the Snort statistics to determine whether the Allow action passed all the packets or fast-forwarded them.

Example 14-15 proves that the Allow action inspects and passes all the packets. It does not fast-forward any packets the way the Trust action does with traffic.

Example 14-15   *Statistics of Packets After an Allowed Connection*

```
> show snort statistics

Packet Counters:
  Passed Packets                                          78
  Blocked Packets                                          0
  Injected Packets                                         0

Flow Counters:
  Fast-Forwarded Flows                                     0
  Blacklisted Flows                                        0
  Flows bypassed (Snort Down)                              0
  Flows bypassed (Snort Busy)                              0

Miscellaneous Counters:
  Start-of-Flow events                                     0
  End-of-Flow events                                       0
  Denied flow events                                       0
  Frames forwarded to Snort before drop                    0
  Inject packets dropped                                   0
>
```

Summary

This chapter discusses the techniques for bypassing packet inspection. It provides the steps for configuring different methods. The chapter also shows how to analyze the flows of bypassed packets to demonstrate how an FTD device acts with different bypassing options. This chapter also shows various debugging tools, which help you to determine whether the bypass process is working as designed.

Quiz

1. Which of the following rules can bypass one or more types of security inspection?

   a. Prefilter rule

   b. Tunnel rule

   c. Access rule

   d. All of the above

2. Which of the following commands shows a statistic of the bypassed packets?

   a. **show trust statistics**

   b. **show snort statistics**

   c. **show bypass statistics**

   d. **show fastpath statistics**

3. You are running the **capture-traffic** command on FTD. When you initiate a connection between two hosts, you do not see any packet in the capture output, but the hosts can connect successfully. Which of the following scenarios may be related?

   a. Traffic between two hosts is inspected by the Snort engine, but events are suppressed.

   b. Traffic between two hosts is trusted by the access control policy.

   c. Traffic between two hosts is fastpathed by the prefilter policy.

   d. None of the above. If the traffic goes through an FTD device and the hosts are connected, FTD must see the traffic.

4. What is the difference between a prefilter rule and an access rule?

   a. A prefilter rule matches for traffic prior to an access rule.

   b. A prefilter rule analyzes traffic based on the outermost header of a packet, whereas an access rule analyzes the innermost header.

   c. A prefilter rule supports limited options to create a rule condition, whereas an access rule offers many granular options.

   d. All of the above

Chapter 15

Rate Limiting Traffic

You can use FTD to limit the rate of network traffic after an access control rule allows or trusts the traffic. An FTD device, however, does not regulate the rate of any particular traffic when a Prefilter policy applies the Fastpath action on them. Limiting the rate of traffic is a way to manage the bandwidth of a network and to ensure quality of service (QoS) for business-critical applications. This chapter discusses the steps in configuring a QoS policy on an FTD device and to verify its operations.

Rate Limiting Essentials

There are multiple ways to enable QoS in a network. FTD implements the traffic policing mechanism to limit the rate of traffic. With this method, FTD drops excessive traffic when the traffic rate reaches a predefined limit. As of this writing, FTD does not support traffic shaping, where excessive traffic is queued in a buffer—rather than being dropped—for later transmission.

Figure 15-1 illustrates the crests and troughs of the traffic pattern when an FTD device rate limits traffic using the policing method.

Figure 15-2 shows a typical graph illustrating traffic that is rate limited by the shaping mechanism.

At any given time, an FTD device can have only one active QoS policy. However, you can add multiple QoS rules within a QoS policy. Each QoS rule must be associated with a source interface and a destination interface, where both of them have to be routed interfaces. You can set separate upload and download speed limits for the traffic that match the conditions of a QoS rule. Furthermore, FTD allows you to define the QoS rule conditions based on advanced networking characteristics, such as network address, port number, application, URL, and user identity.

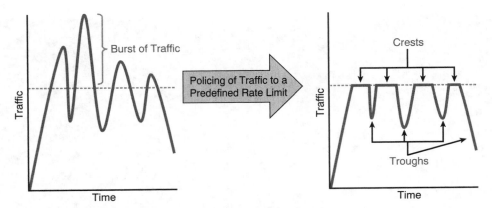

Figure 15-1   *Traffic Policing Method Dropping Excessive Traffic*

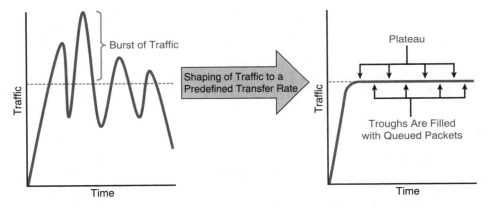

Figure 15-2   *Traffic Shaping Queues Excessive Traffic for Later Transmission*

The Firepower engine evaluates a QoS rule and classifies traffic. When a packet matches with a QoS rule, the Firepower engine sends the ID of the matching rule to the Firewall engine. The firewall engine limits the rate of individual flows based on the download and upload speed limits defined on a QoS rule. You must enable logging at the end of a connection to view QoS-related information.

Figure 15-3 shows a workflow of the QoS feature on the Firepower System. You use the FMC to configure and apply a QoS policy and view any QoS events. FTD ensures that the traffic conforms to the QoS rule.

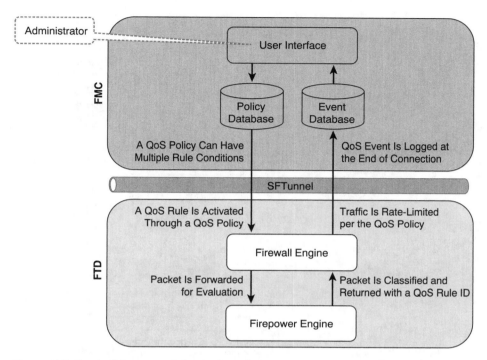

Figure 15-3 *Architecture of the QoS Implementation on an FTD Device*

Best Practices for QoS Rules

As of this writing, FTD supports up to 32 QoS rules within a single QoS policy. FTD allows you to add different rule conditions for different network segments that are connected to different FTD interfaces. However, you should enable a QoS rule as close to the source as possible to ensure that the traffic does not consume the network and system resources more than it should.

Figure 15-4 shows an example of a typical network where FTD enables different QoS rules through the same QoS policy. Traffic is originated from different source networks and rate limited by different QoS rules.

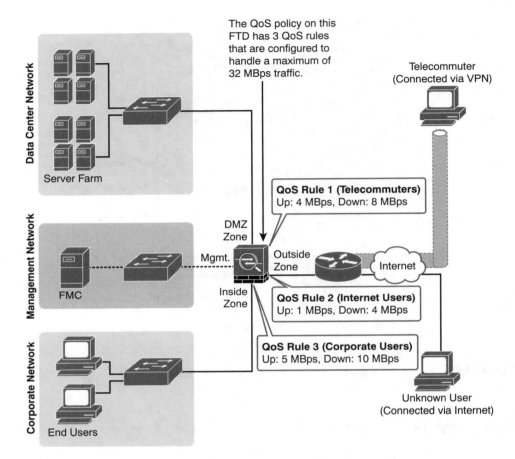

Figure 15-4 *Deploying Different QoS Rules on Different Network Segments*

Fulfilling Prerequisites

Each interface participating in a QoS policy must be in Routed Mode and associated with an interface object. You cannot apply a QoS policy to an interface that is in Inline Mode, Passive Mode, or Switched Mode. (Read Chapter 8, "Firepower Deployment in Routed Mode," to learn about Routed Mode.)

Figure 15-5 shows the configuration of the FTD interface. Both of the participating interfaces are in Routed Mode (assigned with IP addresses) and associated with security zones (interface objects).

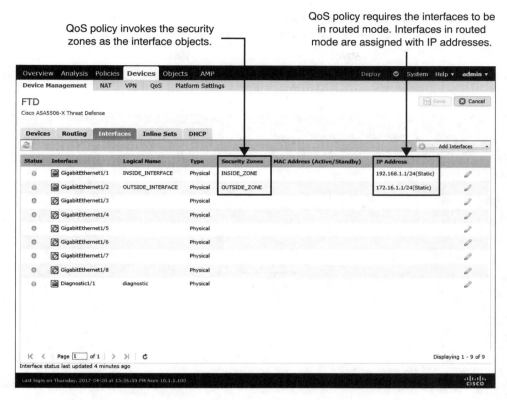

Figure 15-5 *Supported Interface Settings for a QoS Policy*

Configuring Rate Limiting

Follow these steps to create a QoS policy and add a rule within it:

Step 1.   Navigate to the **Devices > QoS** page. FTD does not provide a default policy, so click the **New Policy** button to create one (see Figure 15-6). The New Policy window appears.

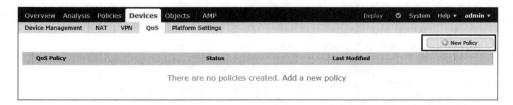

Figure 15-6 *Home Page for the QoS Policy*

Step 2.   Give a name to the new policy and add a target device to which you want to apply this policy. Click **Save** to save the changes. The QoS policy editor page appears.

Step 3.   As shown in Figure 15-7, select a device for the new QoS policy you want to create and click **Add to Policy**. Then click **Save**.

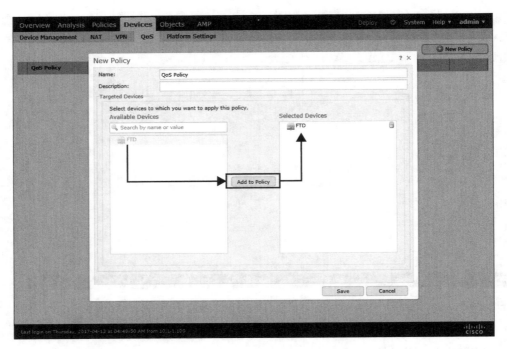

Figure 15-7   *Assigning a QoS Policy to FTD*

Step 4.   On the QoS policy editor page, notice that there is a link to the Policy Assignments option that you can use to associate a new managed device with this policy. Click the **Add Rule** button (see Figure 15-8). The Add Rule window appears, and in it you can define a rule condition.

Step 5.   Give a name to the new QoS rule. Using the Apply QoS On dropdown, define where you want to rate limit traffic. In addition, on the Interface Objects tab, add a source and destination interface to the rule condition.

Tip   You should rate limit traffic as close to the source as possible to ensure that the traffic rate does not go beyond an entitled limit throughout the network.

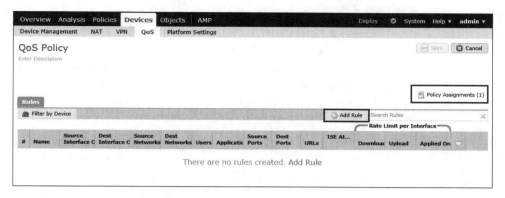

Figure 15-8   *The QoS Policy Editor Page*

Figure 15-9 shows a new QoS rule, named Rate Limiting Rule, that is applied on Interfaces in Source Interface Objects. This rule limits rates only when the traffic originates from Inside_Zone interface and is destined for Outside_Zone.

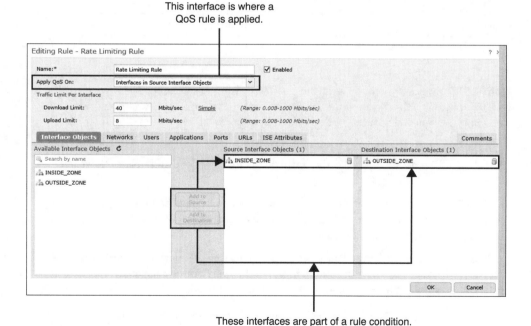

Figure 15-9   *Selecting an Interface Object in a Rule*

Step 6.   Enter a desired traffic limit for the interface. FTD allows you to enter upload and download limits separately. If you do not enter a value, FTD supports the maximum throughput for that physical interface.

Table 15-1 provides a conversion chart for commonly used traffic rates. When you enter a traffic limit, FTD considers the value as megabit per second (Mbps), not megabytes per second (MBps). The highlighted rows of this table are used in the configuration example in this chapter.

Table 15-1   *Megabits per Second to Megabytes per Second Conversion Table*

Megabits per Second	Megabytes per Second
1 Mbps	0.125 MBps
4 Mbps	0.5 MBps
8 Mbps	1 MBps
10 Mbps	1.25 MBps
16 Mbps	2 MBps
40 Mbps	5 MBps
80 Mbps	10 MBps
100 Mbps	12.5 MBps

Note   FTD supports the rate limit 0.008 to 1000 Mbps per interface. If you want to allocate *below* 0.008 Mbps to any hosts, it implies that those hosts are not important to you. You may just want to consider blocking them by using an access rule or a prefilter rule.

Figure 15-10 shows the traffic limits for download and upload flows, 40 Mbps and 8 Mbps, respectively.

Step 7.   Optionally, add a precise rate limiting condition based on any additional networking characteristics, such as network address, port number, application, URL, user identity, and so on.

Step 8.   Once you outline a rule condition, click the **OK** button to create the QoS rule. The browser returns to the QoS policy editor page. Click the **Save** button to preserve the QoS rules you have created.

Figure 15-11 shows the custom QoS rule you have just created.

Limits for Download
and Upload

Available Criteria That You
Can Use as a Rule Condition

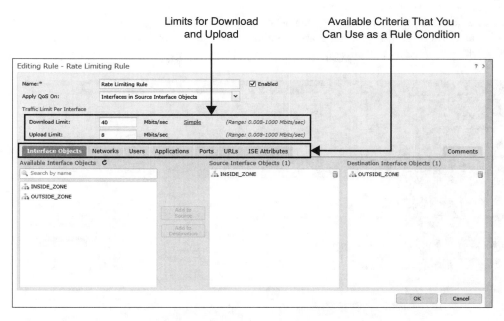

Figure 15-10   *Traffic Limit for a QoS Rule*

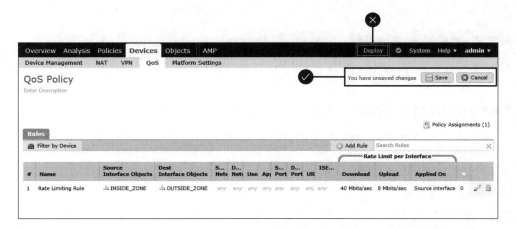

Figure 15-11   *The Overview of All of the QoS Rules on the QoS Policy Editor Page*

At this point, you can click the **Deploy** button to activate a QoS rule, but by default, FTD does not generate a log when a QoS rule triggers. A QoS policy does not offer an option for logging. If you want to view QoS-related statistics for any specific connection, you must identify the associated access rule that triggers the QoS rule and enable logging at the end of that connection. To accomplish that, you have to edit the access control policy and redeploy the revised policy.

Figure 15-12 shows the steps to enable logging. Because this exercise does not use any custom access rules, you can enable logging for the default action to generate QoS data when a connection hits the default action.

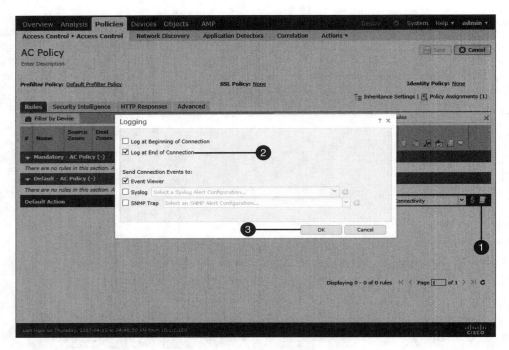

Figure 15-12   *Enabling Logging at the End of Connection in an Access Control Policy*

Verifying the Rate Limit of a File Transfer

After you successfully deploy a QoS policy, you can verify the deployment status from the FTD CLI. Example 15-1 shows confirmation of the QoS policy configurations and the interface where the policy is deployed.

Example 15-1   *Policy Map Showing the Active QoS Policy on an Interface*

```
! To view the rate-limiting settings:

> show running-config policy-map
!
policy-map type inspect dns preset_dns_map
 parameters
  message-length maximum client auto
  message-length maximum 512
  no tcp-inspection
```

```
policy-map type inspect ip-options UM_STATIC_IP_OPTIONS_MAP
 parameters
   eool action allow
   nop action allow
   router-alert action allow
policy-map global_policy
 class inspection_default
   inspect dns preset_dns_map
   inspect ftp
   inspect h323 h225
   inspect h323 ras
   inspect rsh
   inspect rtsp
   inspect sqlnet
   inspect skinny
   inspect sunrpc
   inspect xdmcp
   inspect sip
   inspect netbios
   inspect tftp
   inspect icmp
   inspect icmp error
   inspect dcerpc
   inspect ip-options UM_STATIC_IP_OPTIONS_MAP
 class class-default
   set connection advanced-options UM_STATIC_TCP_MAP
policy-map policy_map_INSIDE_INTERFACE
 match flow-rule qos 268442624
   police input 8000000 250000
   police output 40000000 1250000
!
>




! To determine where a policy is applied:

> show running-config service-policy
service-policy global_policy global
service-policy policy_map_INSIDE_INTERFACE interface INSIDE_INTERFACE
>
```

Now, you can verify the impact of the QoS policy you have deployed. First, download a file from the server to a client system. Then upload a file from the client PC to the server. You should notice two different traffic rates.

Figure 15-13 shows the topology of a simple deployment that you can use to verify the download and upload speeds through an FTD device.

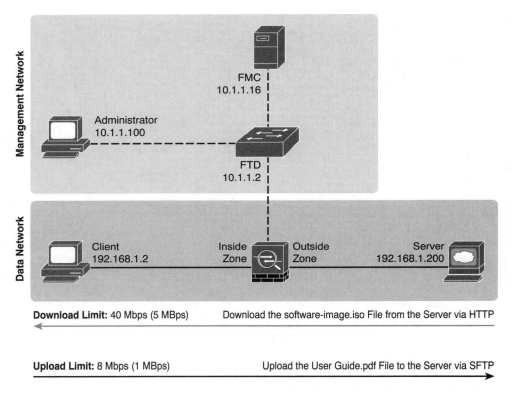

Download Limit: 40 Mbps (5 MBps)   Download the software-image.iso File from the Server via HTTP

Upload Limit: 8 Mbps (1 MBps)   Upload the User Guide.pdf File to the Server via SFTP

Figure 15-13   *A Simple Lab Topology to Test Rate Limiting of Traffic Through an FTD Device*

Figure 15-14 shows the download of a software image file. FTD enforces the download rate within 5 MBps.

Figure 15-15 shows the upload of a PDF file. FTD regulates the upload rate below 1 MBps.

Both of these transfers—download of the ISO and upload of the PDF—are initiated by a host that is located at the inside zone. Therefore, the traffic matches the QoS rule Rate Limiting Rule, and FTD regulates the traffic rate. However, if the connection is initiated by an outside system, it does not match the QoS rule condition. Hence, the QoS policy does not limit the traffic rate; the source and destination should be able to utilize the full capacity of the FTD interface bandwidth.

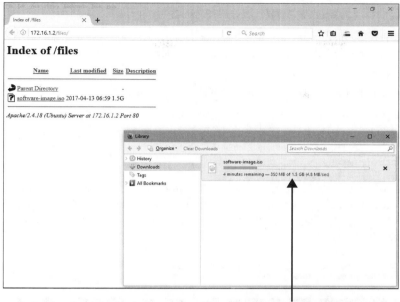

Download Speed Is Within 5 MBps (4.8 MBps)

Figure 15-14   *Compliance of the Download Rate with a QoS Policy*

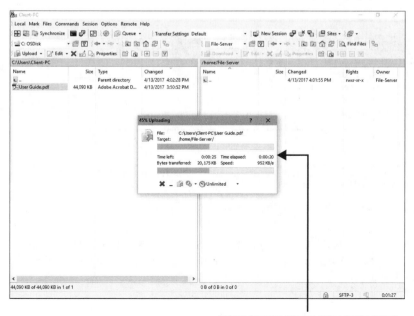

Upload Speed Is Within 1 MBps (0.952 MBps)

Figure 15-15   *Compliance of the Upload Rate with a QoS Policy*

Analyzing QoS Events and Statistics

If you have enabled logging for the connections that also match your QoS rule conditions, you can view the QoS-related statistics in the Connection Events page. Here are the steps to view them:

Step 1.   Navigate to the **Analysis > Connections > Events** page.

Step 2.   Select the **Connection Events** as the table view.

Step 3.   Expand the Search Constraints arrow on the left.

Step 4.   Select the necessary QoS-related data points.

Figure 15-16 shows two sets of connection events. The bottom two connections are originated by an inside client; they match the conditions in the Rate Limiting Rule, and rate is limited. However, the top two connections are not rate limited because they are initiated by an outside system.

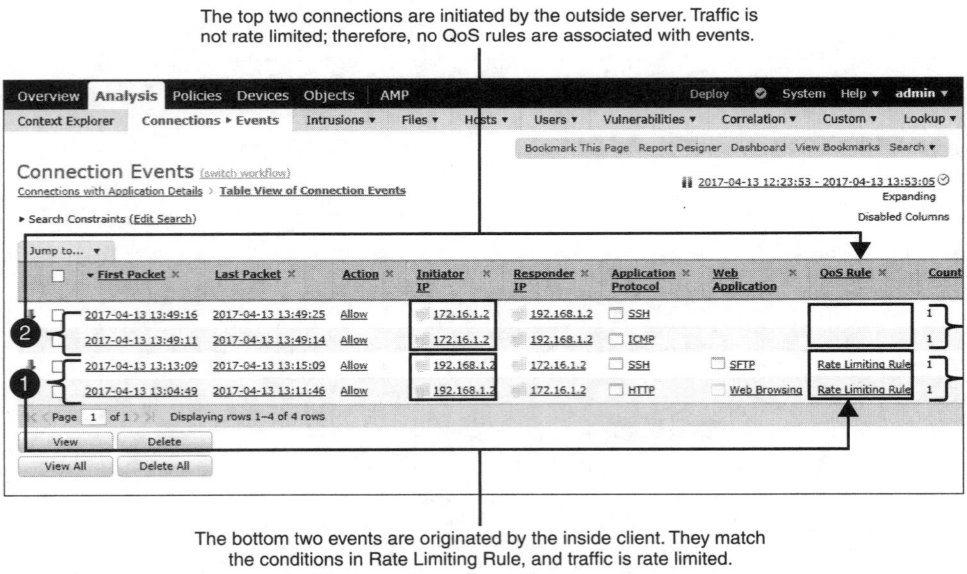

The top two connections are initiated by the outside server. Traffic is not rate limited; therefore, no QoS rules are associated with events.

The bottom two events are originated by the inside client. They match the conditions in Rate Limiting Rule, and traffic is rate limited.

Figure 15-16   *Connection Events Showing Associated QoS Rules*

Example 15-2 demonstrates the actions of a QoS policy on an FTD device. This example provides two commands that you can use to determine any drop due to a rate limiting rule during a file transfer.

Example 15-2 *Statistics of Dropped Packets Due to a QoS Policy (Rule ID: 268442624)*

```
! Record on the service policy statistics


> show service-policy police

Interface INSIDE_INTERFACE:
  Service-policy: policy_map_INSIDE_INTERFACE
    Flow-rule QoS id: 268442624
      Input police Interface INSIDE_INTERFACE:
        cir 8000000 bps, bc 250000 bytes
        conformed 334152 packets, 21168506 bytes; actions:  transmit
        exceeded 0 packets, 0 bytes; actions:  drop
        conformed 473456 bps, exceed 0 bps
      Output police Interface INSIDE_INTERFACE:
        cir 40000000 bps, bc 1250000 bytes
        conformed 1129736 packets, 1618239735 bytes; actions:  transmit
        exceeded 127629 packets, 182986654 bytes; actions:  drop
        conformed 36194128 bps, exceed 4092744 bps
>




! Statistics of the Accelerated Security Path (ASP) counts


> show asp drop

Frame drop:
  No route to host (no-route)                                         79
  TCP packet SEQ past window (tcp-seq-past-win)                        1
  Output QoS rate exceeded (rate-exceeded)                        127629
  Slowpath security checks failed (sp-security-failed)                 4
  FP L2 rule drop (l2_acl)                                            18

Last clearing: 00:51:31 UTC Apr 10 2017 by enable_1

Flow drop:

Last clearing: 00:51:31 UTC Apr 10 2017 by enable_1
>
```

Example 15-3 reveals the connections that are rate limited by a QoS rule. The flags associated with a connection confirm whether it is going through a Firepower deep packet inspection process.

Example 15-3   *Identifying the Status of a Rate Limited Connection*

```
! You can use a QoS Rule ID to view any associated active connections.


> show conn flow-rule qos 268442624
1 in use, 4 most used


TCP OUTSIDE_INTERFACE  172.16.1.2:80 INSIDE_INTERFACE  192.168.1.2:47072, idle
  0:00:00, bytes 1199375239, flags UIO N

>




! To determine the meaning of each flag, you can use the "detail" keyword. For exam-
  ple, the flag 'N' confirms that the Firepower Snort engine inspects the connection.


> show conn detail
1 in use, 4 most used
Flags: A - awaiting responder ACK to SYN, a - awaiting initiator ACK to SYN,
       b - TCP state-bypass or nailed,
       C - CTIQBE media, c - cluster centralized,
       D - DNS, d - dump, E - outside back connection, e - semi-distributed,
       F - initiator FIN, f - responder FIN,
       G - group, g - MGCP, H - H.323, h - H.225.0, I - initiator data,
       i - incomplete, J - GTP, j - GTP data, K - GTP t3-response
       k - Skinny media, M - SMTP data, m - SIP media, N - inspected by Snort, n - GUP
       O - responder data, P - inside back connection,
       q - SQL*Net data, R - initiator acknowledged FIN,
       R - UDP SUNRPC, r - responder acknowledged FIN,
       T - SIP, t - SIP transient, U - up,
       V - VPN orphan, v - M3UA W - WAAS,
       w - secondary domain backup,
       X - inspected by service module,
       x - per session, Y - director stub flow, y - backup stub flow,
       Z - Scansafe redirection, z - forwarding stub flow


TCP OUTSIDE_INTERFACE: 172.16.1.2/80 INSIDE_INTERFACE: 192.168.1.2/47072,
    flags UIO N, qos-rule-id 268442624, idle 0s, uptime 4m42s, timeout 1h0m, bytes
  1529246551


>
```

Example 15-4 shows the real-time debug messages generated by the firewall and Firepower engines, due to the match of a QoS rule (ID: 268442624).

Example 15-4   *Debugging the QoS Rule–Related Events in Real Time*

```
! Debug messages in the ASA Firewall Engine:


> system support firewall-engine-debug


Please specify an IP protocol: tcp
Please specify a client IP address:
Please specify a client port:
Please specify a server IP address:
Please specify a server port:


Monitoring firewall engine debug messages


192.168.1.2-47072 > 172.16.1.2-80 6 AS 1 I 0 New session
192.168.1.2-47072 > 172.16.1.2-80 6 AS 1 I 0 using HW or preset rule order 2, id
  268434432 action Allow and prefilter rule 0
192.168.1.2-47072 > 172.16.1.2-80 6 AS 1 I 0 allow action
192.168.1.2-47072 > 172.16.1.2-80 6 AS 1 I 0 Starting with minimum 0, id 0 and
  SrcZone first with zones 2 -> 1, geo 0(0) -> 0, vlan 0, sgt tag: untagged, svc 0,
  payload 0, client 0, misc 0, user 9999997, url , xff
192.168.1.2-47072 > 172.16.1.2-80 6 AS 1 I 0 match rule order 1, id 268442624 action
  Rate Limit
192.168.1.2-47072 > 172.16.1.2-80 6 AS 1 I 0 QoS policy match status (match found),
  match action (Rate Limit), QoS rule id (268442624)
192.168.1.2-47072 > 172.16.1.2-80 6 AS 1 I 0 Got end of flow event from hardware
  with flags 40000001


^C
Caught interrupt signal
Exiting.


>




! Debug messages in the Firepower Snort Engine:


> debug snort event
>
Flow from 192.168.1.2/47072 to 172.16.1.2/80 matched qos_rule_id 268442624 flag
  Regular flow
RL pkts  = 0, RL Bytes = 0, Rv RL pkts = 153693, Rv RL Byt = 220395762, Qos_on_Src 1


> undebug all
>
```

The statistics in these examples were captured when a client PC was downloading a large ISO file from the server using a web browser. You could perform similar analysis on uploaded traffic. Before you begin uploading a file from the client PC to the server, you can run the following commands to reset the counters.

```
> clear service-policy interface INSIDE_INTERFACE
> clear asp drop
```

Summary

In this chapter, you have learned the steps to configure QoS policy on an FTD device. This chapter also provides an overview to the common rate limiting mechanisms and how an FTD device implements QoS. Finally, this chapter provides the command-line tools you can use to verify the operation of QoS policies in FTD.

Quiz

1. Which of the following statements is correct?
   a. The Firepower engine not only evaluates but also enforces a QoS rule.
   b. Snort rate limits traffic as soon as it receives it.
   c. The ASA firewall engine enforces the actual rate limit.
   d. All of the above.

2. Which step is necessary to view any QoS-related events?
   a. In a QoS policy, enable logging at the beginning of a connection.
   b. In a QoS policy, enable logging at the end of a connection.
   c. In an access control policy, enable logging at the beginning of a connection.
   d. In an access control policy, enable logging at the end of a connection.

3. To limit the download rate to 50 MBps, which value should you enter in a QoS rule?
   a. 5
   b. 50
   c. 400
   d. 500

4. Which of the following commands confirms whether traffic is rate limited by FTD?
   a. **show service-policy police**
   b. **show conn detail**
   c. **show asp drop**
   d. All of the above

Chapter 16

Blacklisting Suspicious Addresses by Using Security Intelligence

To compromise a network, an attacker uses various techniques, such as spam, command-and-control (CNC) servers, phishing, and malware. The volume and sources of new threats are increasing every day. As a security engineer, you might find it challenging to keep the access control list of a firewall up to date with all the new suspicious addresses. To make this job easier, FTD offers a unique threat defense mechanism called Security Intelligence. This chapter describes the processes of configuring the Security Intelligence technology and verifying its operations.

Security Intelligence Essentials

Security Intelligence enables you to blacklist a suspicious address without any manual modification to the access control policy. It can block a packet before the packet goes through a deep packet inspection by the Firepower Snort engine. Therefore, it helps reduce the CPU utilization of an FTD device and hence improves performance.

Figure 16-1 shows that any traffic that is not prefiltered goes through the Security Intelligence inspection.

Several enhancements have been made to the Security Intelligence technology since the Firepower System introduced this feature. Besides blacklisting an IP address, which is one of the most common uses of Security Intelligence, FTD also supports the blacklisting of URLs and domain names. To demonstrate the operations of Security Intelligence, this chapter primarily focuses on the blacklisting of IP addresses.

So far, you have been using the diagram shown in Figure 16-1 to understand the flows and drops of packets through an FTD device. In this chapter, we zoom in on both firewall and Firepower engines, view the low-level components of both engines, and determine the flows of packets through them.

Figure 16-2 shows the low-level architecture of an FTD device. It shows that Security Intelligence is one of the earliest lines of defense in a Firepower engine.

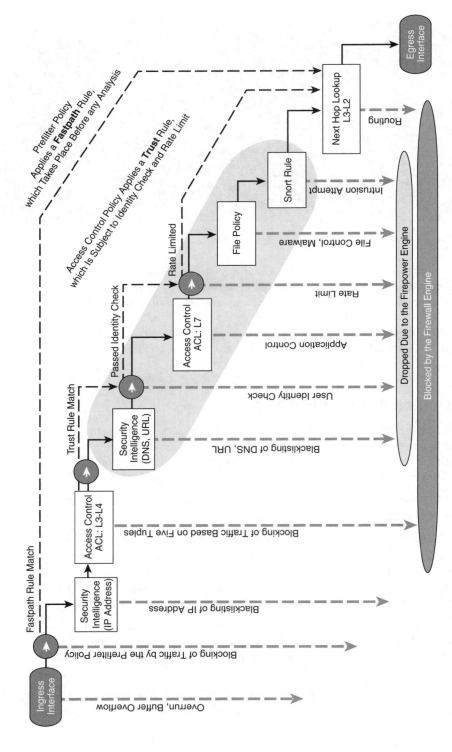

Figure 16-1 *Drops of Packets by an FTD—A High-Level Overview*

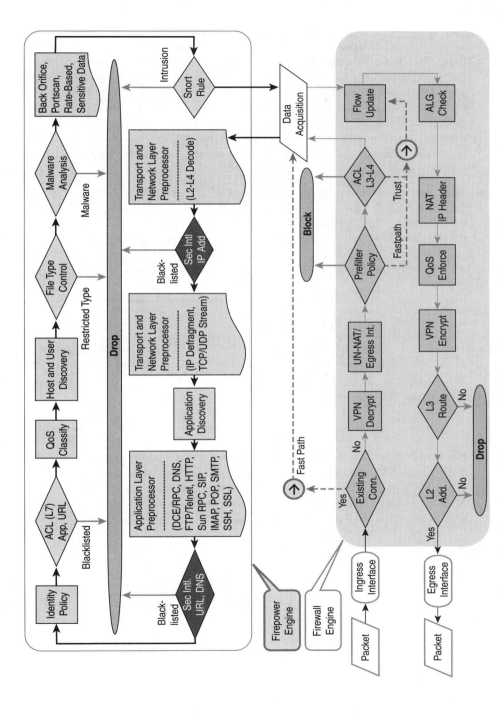

Figure 16-2 *Flows of Packets Through the Firewall and Firepower Engines*

Input Methods

To input a potential suspicious address, Security Intelligence supports three methods:

- **Feed:** Cisco has a dedicated threat intelligence and research team, known as Talos. The team analyzes the behavior of Internet traffic, performs in-depth analysis on any suspicious activities, categorizes the potential addresses based on their characteristics, and lists these addresses in a file called the Cisco Intelligence Feed. One of the processes running on the FMC, CloudAgent, periodically communicates with the Cisco cloud to download the latest feed. When the FMC downloads a feed, it sends the feed to its managed devices automatically; redeployment of the access control policy is not necessary.

- **List:** FMC also allows you to input custom addresses for blacklisting. You can list the addresses in a text file (.txt format) and upload the file manually to the FMC through a web browser. The file requires you to enter one address per line. Table 16-1 shows the key differences between the feed and list types of Security Intelligence input.

Table 16-1 *Security Intelligence Feed Versus Security Intelligence List*

	Feed	List
Provider	Created by the Cisco threat intelligence team	Created by you
Maintenance	Automatically updates the existing feed	You can manually update an old list on demand
File transfer	The update file is transferred via HTTPS or HTTP	You can upload an update file using a local web browser

- **Blacklist IP Now:** You can blacklist a suspicious address instantly—without adding a new access rule for it. In case of an immediate need, you can avoid the process of scheduling a maintenance window for policy modification and use the Blacklist IP Now option for an instant block. Any addresses that you blacklist using the Blacklist IP Now option become part of the global blacklist.

Figure 16-3 illustrates the key operational steps of the Security Intelligence feature on the FMC, FTD, and Cisco Cloud.

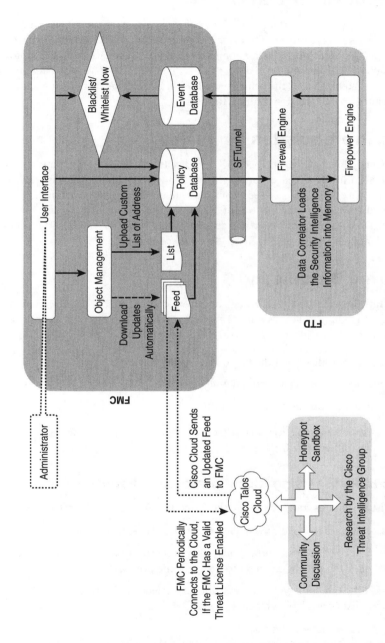

Figure 16-3 *Architecture of the Security Intelligence Technology*

Best Practices for Blacklisting

Security Intelligence is an effective tool for controlling suspicious traffic that a traditional firewall is unable to recognize. However, if your goal is to block or monitor traffic based on five tuples—source port, destination port, source IP, destination IP, and protocol— you should consider deploying an access rule with the *Block* or *Monitor* action. Do not use Security Intelligence as the primary method of monitoring or blocking all traffic because doing so can affect system performance.

Fulfilling Prerequisites

To use Security Intelligence, you need a Threat license. If that license expires after you enable the Security Intelligence feature, the FMC stops communicating with the cloud for the latest Cisco Intelligence feed. While you are in the process of purchasing a license, you can enable Evaluation Mode to configure an access rule with the Security Intelligence condition, and to deploy the associated access control policy to an FTD. To learn more about Evaluation Mode, read Chapter 7, "Firepower Licensing and Registration."

Configuring Blacklisting

Security Intelligence is enabled through an access control policy. However, you do not need to add an additional access rule. There are three ways to blacklist an address, as described in the following sections:

- Automatic blacklist using the Cisco Intelligence Feed
- Manual blacklist using a custom intelligence list
- Immediate blacklist using a connection event

Figure 16-4 shows a simple topology that is used in this chapter to demonstrate the configurations of Security Intelligence.

Automatic Blacklist Using Cisco Intelligence Feed

To blacklist suspicious traffic by using the Cisco Intelligence Feed, perform these steps:

Step 1.   Navigate to **Policies > Access Control > Access Control**.

Step 2.   Select an access control policy that you want to deploy to an FTD device and click the pencil icon next to it to edit the policy.

Step 3.   When the policy editor page appears, select the **Security Intelligence** tab. A list of available objects and zones appears.

Note   If you are configuring a newly installed system, the list of Security Intelligence objects might not be available for selection. To populate the Security Intelligence categories in the Available Objects field, you might need to update the Cisco Intelligence Feed from the cloud at least once. Without populating these objects, you cannot use them as rule conditions.

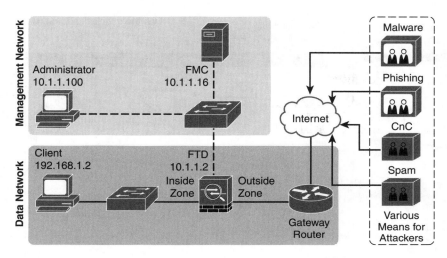

Figure 16-4   *Topology Used in the Configuration Examples of This Chapter*

Figure 16-5 shows the page to update the Security Intelligence feed and list. The list of intelligence categories may not be available for selection until you update the Cisco Intelligence Feed from the cloud.

Step 4.   On the Network subtab, select a category that you want to blacklist. You can also select a specific zone for inspection. By default, FTD inspects traffic from Any zone.

Note   This chapter shows how to enable the Security Intelligence feature based on network and IP addresses. If you want to enable this feature based on URL conditions, select the URL subtab. The remaining configuration steps are identical.

Step 5.   Click the **Add to Blacklist** button. The categories appear inside the Blacklist field. Figure 16-6 illustrates the detailed steps to add the Security Intelligence categories for blacklist.

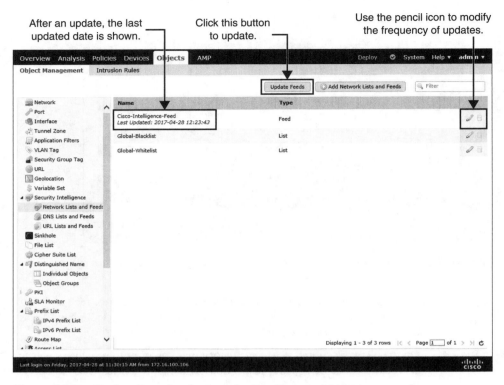

Figure 16-5   *Update Page for the Security Intelligence Objects*

Step 6.   Next to the Blacklist field, click the logging icon to verify whether Log Connections is checked for Security Intelligence events. Click **OK** to return to the Security Intelligence tab. Figure 16-7 shows the steps to verify logging for the connections that are subject to Security Intelligence blacklist.

Step 7.   When the configuration is complete, click **Save** to save the changes, and click **Deploy** to deploy the new access control policy to your FTD device.

Now if you attempt to access a malicious IP address that is included in the Cisco Intelligence Feed, FTD should block the connection.

Tip   The "Verification and Troubleshooting Tools" section of this chapter discusses how to reverse engineer the Cisco Intelligence Feed data to identify the addresses that are selected for blacklisting.

Figure 16-8 shows the action of Security Intelligence. After it is enabled, the host is blocked from accessing certain addresses. These addresses, as of this writing, are known for spreading malware and spam.

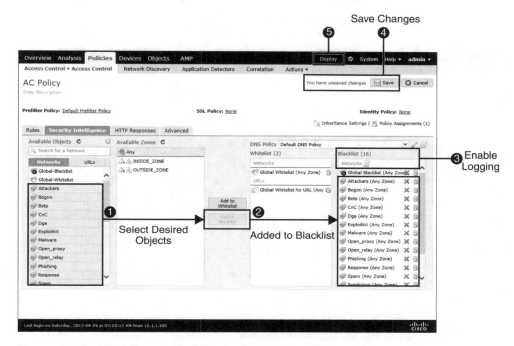

Figure 16-6 *Workflow to Blacklist the Security Intelligence Categories*

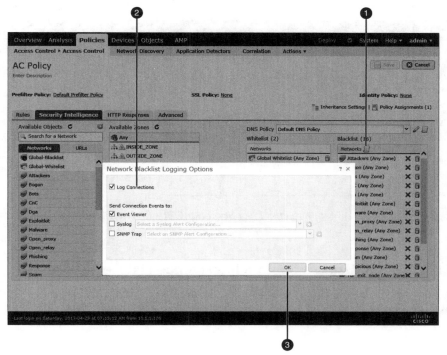

Figure 16-7 *Logging for the Security Intelligence Events*

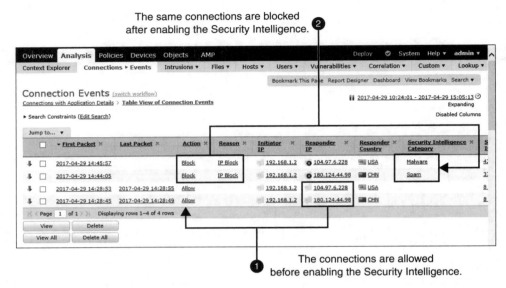

Figure 16-8   *Connection Events Page Shows the Security Intelligence Events*

Figure 16-9 shows an individual page that allows you to find any connections that are triggered due to Security Intelligence.

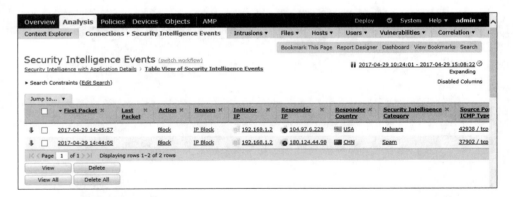

Figure 16-9   *Security Intelligence Events Page Showing Only Its Own Events*

Manual Blacklisting Using a Custom Intelligence List

As a security engineer, you always need to track the latest threats and vulnerabilities to make sure your network is protected from zero-day threats. Let's say, for example, that you have found a new security advisory in a security-related community forum or website. While Cisco is investigating the new information, you just want to blacklist the potential malicious address on your own without any delay. Using a text editor, you can create a file to list any potential IP addresses. Firepower System enables you to input this file to blacklist any custom list of IP addresses.

To blacklist a custom list of IP addresses, follow these steps:

Step 1.   Write or copy the potential malicious addresses into a text editor, and save the file in .txt format. When you create a list, enter one record per line. Optionally, if you want to insert a comment on an IP address for future reference, use the hash sign (#) at the beginning of a line.

Figure 16-10 shows the creation of a .txt file using notepad. The file contains a custom list of IP addresses. These addresses are listed for demonstration purpose only, and should not be considered as a definitive guideline. Perform your own research before you consider an address for blacklisting; otherwise, a legitimate site might get blocked.

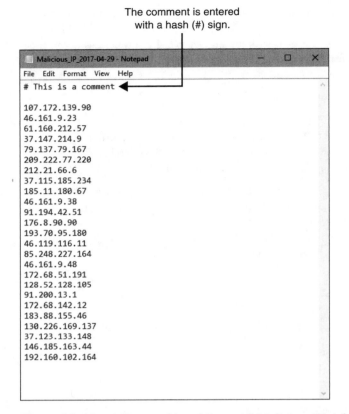

Figure 16-10   *A Custom List of Potential Malicious IP Addresses Saved in a .txt File*

Step 2.   In the FMC, navigate to **Object > Object Management**.

Step 3.   On the left panel, select an appropriate option under Security Intelligence. For example, if you want to add a custom list of IP addresses, select the **Network Lists and Feeds** option. Then click the **Add Network Lists and Feeds** button to upload your text file to the FMC. Figure 16-11 shows a configuration window for a Security Intelligence list. After you select **List** from the Type dropdown, you can browse your text file. Upon successful upload, the FMC can show the number of addresses you uploaded.

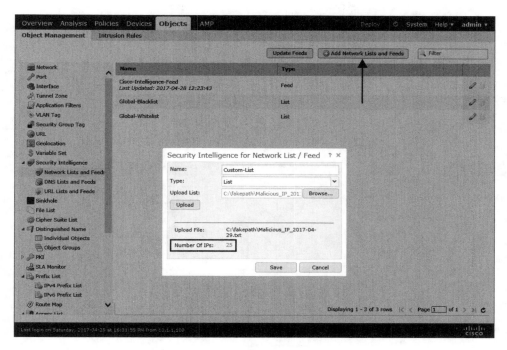

Figure 16-11 *Uploading a Security Intelligence List File*

Step 4.   Once the file is uploaded, navigate to **Policies > Access Control > Access Control** and edit the access control policy that you want to deploy to an FTD.

Step 5.   When the policy editor page appears, select the **Security Intelligence** tab. A list of available objects and zones appears.

Step 6.   On the Network subtab, select the custom object you want to blacklist. You can also select a specific zone for inspection. By default, FTD inspects traffic from Any zone.

Note   This chapter enables the Security Intelligence feature based on network and IP addresses. If you want to enable this feature based on URL conditions, select the URL subtab. The remaining configuration steps are identical.

Step 7.   Click the **Add to Blacklist** button, and the custom object appears in the Blacklist field.

Step 8.   Next to the Blacklist field, click the logging icon to verify whether Log Connections is checked for Security Intelligence events. Click **OK** to return to the Security Intelligence tab. Figure 16-12 illustrates the workflow of blacklisting a custom Security intelligence list.

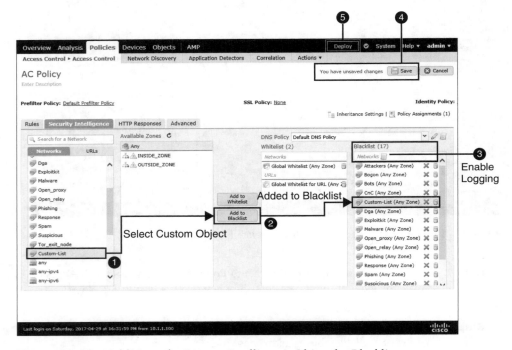

Figure 16-12   *Addition of a Custom Intelligence Object for Blacklist*

Step 9.   When the configuration is complete, click **Save** to save the changes and deploy the new access control policy to your FTD device. Now if you attempt to access one of the addresses that you included in the text file, FTD will block the connection.

Figure 16-13 shows the blocking of a connection due to a match with the Security Intelligence list.

The connection is blocked due to the
custom Security Intelligence list.

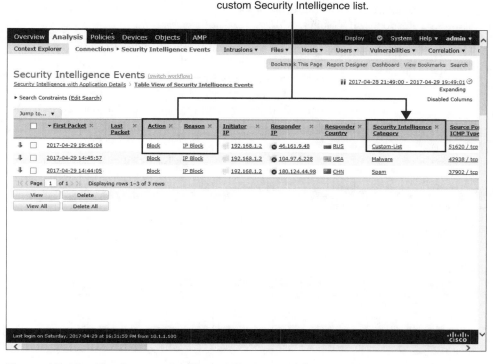

Figure 16-13 *The Security Intelligence Category Column Confirms the
Matching List Name*

Immediate Blacklisting Using a Connection Event

The Firepower System enables you to blacklist an address instantly by right-clicking
your mouse. This feature is useful when you notice a connection event for a suspicious
address but you cannot modify and reapply the access control policy without scheduling
a maintenance window.

Adding an Address to a Blacklist

Let's say, for example, that you have noticed an event from an address that you believe
could potentially be malicious activity. Here are the steps to blacklist the address
immediately:

Step 1.   Navigate to **Analysis > Connections > Events**.

Step 2. Right-click the address you want to blacklist. For example, if you want blacklist an unknown suspicious address, right-click an address under the Responder IP column.

Step 3. From the context menu that appears, select the **Blacklist IP Now** option. A confirmation window appears. Click the **Blacklist Now** button to confirm. Figure 16-14 shows the steps to blacklist an IP address using the context menu. No additional configuration is necessary after these steps. The configuration is complete. If you attempt to connect to that IP address, FTD will block it.

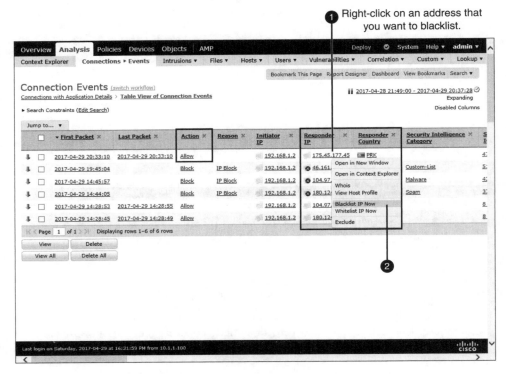

Figure 16-14 *Context Menu Displays the Blacklist IP Now Option*

Figure 16-15 shows the result of an immediate blacklist. Although Action and Reason look identical, Security Intelligence categorizes this event as a Global-Blacklist event.

The second connection is blocked
after selecting Blacklist IP Now.

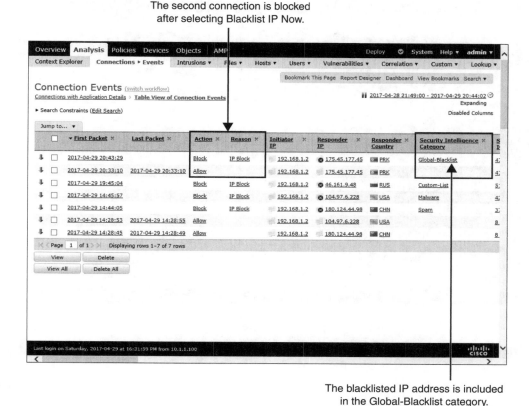

Figure 16-15 *The FMC Displays a Block Event due to the Blacklist IP Now Action*

The blacklisted IP address is included
in the Global-Blacklist category.

Deleting an Address from a Blacklist

Any addresses that you blacklist by using the Blacklist IP Now option are included in the Global-Blacklist category. If you want to remove the blacklisting attribute from an address and allow the address again, go to the Object Management page and edit Global-Blacklist to remove the address.

> **Warning**   If you delete the entire Global-Blacklist object by using the Security Intelligence configuration page, the access control policy does not enforce the Blacklist IP Now function.

Figure 16-16 shows the IP address that you blacklisted earlier by using the Blacklist IP Now option. To allow this IP address once again, click **Delete** and then click **Save** to save the changes.

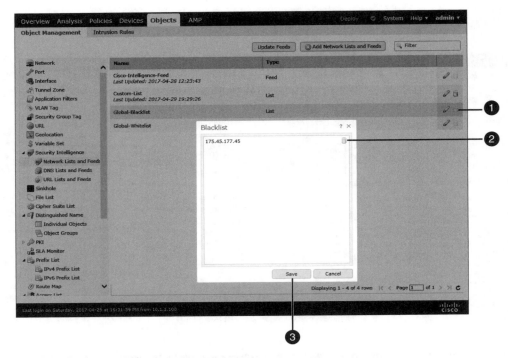

Figure 16-16 *Steps to Remove Blacklisting of an Address*

Monitoring a Blacklist

Occasionally, you might want to monitor the activities of certain hosts in a network instead of blocking them completely. Doing so allows you to analyze the characteristics of suspicious traffic and helps you build an appropriate defense. Follow these steps to enable monitoring functionality using Security Intelligence:

Note The following steps assume that you have already blacklisted certain traffic by using the instructions in the previous section. This time, you just want to change the action (monitor only instead of block) for certain traffic.

Step 1.   In the access control policy editor page, go to the Security Intelligence tab.

Step 2.   From the Blacklist field, right-click a category that you want to monitor.

Note FTD does not support the Monitor-only mode for the Global-Blacklist category.

Step 3. From the context menu that appears, select the **Monitor-only (do not block)** option. The icon changes from a red × to a green down arrow.

Figure 16-17 shows the steps to enable Monitor-only mode for a certain Security Intelligence category while leaving all other categories in Block mode.

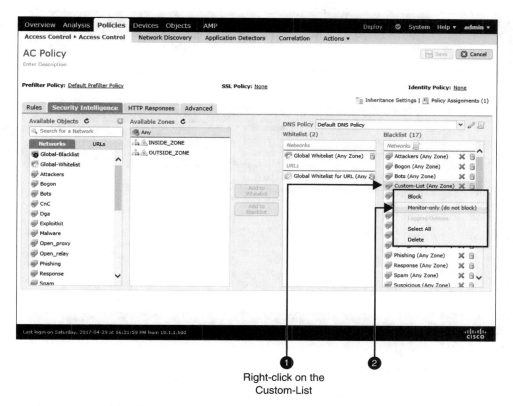

Right-click on the
Custom-List

Figure 16-17 *Configuration of Monitor-only Mode*

Step 4. When the configuration is complete, click **Save** to save the changes and redeploy the access control policy.

This configuration changes the action from Block to Monitor-only for any addresses in the custom list. To test the operation of Monitor-only mode, access one of the addresses from the custom list, and FTD allows that connection and generates a monitor event.

Figure 16-18 shows the difference between the Block and Monitor-only actions. The first connection attempt from host 192.168.1.2 to 46.161.9.48 was blocked; however, the second attempt was allowed, and the connection was monitored.

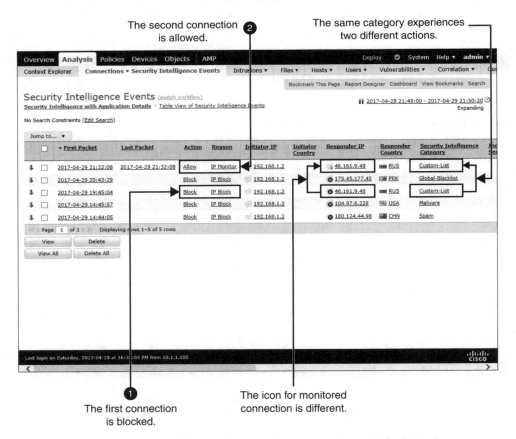

Figure 16-18   *Security Intelligence Events in Monitor-only and Block Modes*

Bypassing a Blacklist

If you find an address blacklisted by the Cisco Intelligence Feed, but it has been essential for your regular business, you can report it to Cisco. If you want to access the address anyway while Cisco reinvestigates, you can whitelist that particular address. Whitelisting bypasses the Security Intelligence check, but traffic is still subject to any subsequent inspection. If other components of an FTD device find any anomaly, they can still block the connection, although Security Intelligence whitelists it initially.

Adding an Address to a Whitelist

The process of whitelisting an address is identical to the process of blacklisting an address. You can add a whitelist in the access control policy as a Security Intelligence object. Alternatively, you can right-click an address and select the **Whitelist IP Now** option from the context menu (see Figure 16-19).

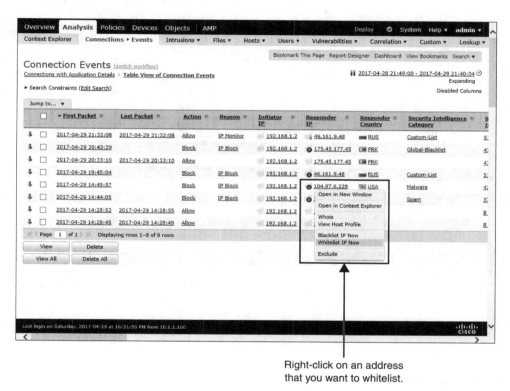

Right-click on an address
that you want to whitelist.

Figure 16-19   *Whitelisting an Address Without Modifying an Access Control Policy*

Figure 16-20 shows an example of a successful whitelisted connection. After overriding a blacklisted address with a whitelist action, a connection looks like a regular allowed event.

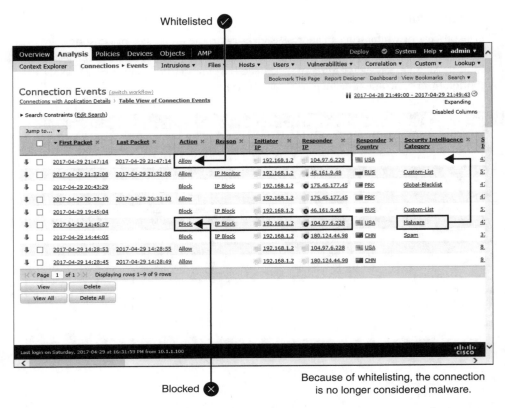

Figure 16-20   *A Whitelist Action Bypassing the Security Intelligence Check*

Deleting an Address from a Whitelist

When you whitelist an address by using the Whitelist IP Now option, the address is included in the Global-Whitelist object. If you want to stop whitelisting an address, you need to delete the address from the Global-Whitelist object.

> **Warning**   If you delete the entire Global-Whitelist object by using the Security Intelligence configuration page, the access control policy stops enforcing the Whitelist IP Now function.

Figure 16-21 shows the steps to delete an address from the Global-Whitelist object.

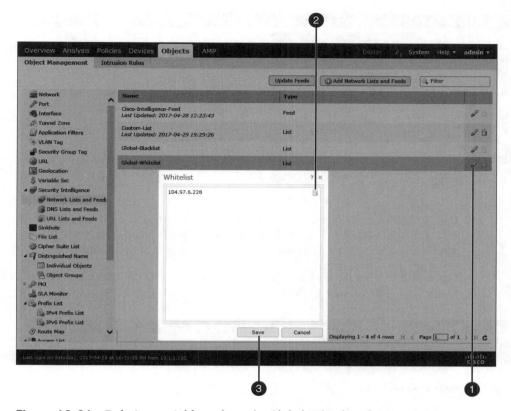

Figure 16-21   *Deleting an Address from the Global-Whitelist object*

Verification and Troubleshooting Tools

Before you begin investigating an issue with Security Intelligence, you should check the
following:

■ Check whether Security Intelligence's health module is enabled on the health policy.
This module allows the FMC to generate alerts if the system fails to download the
Security Intelligence data, and it loads the data into memory.

Figure 16-22 shows the option to enable the health module for Security Intelligence.
To find this page, go to **System > Health > Policy**, edit a health policy, and select
Security Intelligence from the left panel. You must redeploy a health policy if you
change any settings.

Figure 16-22   *Security Intelligence Health Module*

- Check whether the FMC has a valid Threat license and whether the license is applied on the desired FTD device. If the Threat license is disabled or expired, the FMC stops obtaining the latest Cisco Intelligence Feed from the Cisco cloud.

  Figure 16-23 shows the device management page where you can enable and disable a Threat license for a managed device.

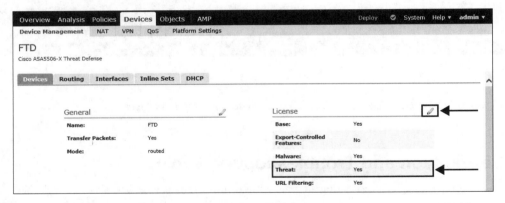

Figure 16-23   *Device Management Page with Options for License Administration*

Verifying the Download of the Latest Files

By using the CLI, you can verify whether the FMC has downloaded the Cisco Intelligence Feed from the Cisco cloud. Similarly, by accessing the FTD CLI, you can verify whether an FTD device has received the latest Security Intelligence files from the FMC.

Example 16-1 shows the Security Intelligence files on the FMC before and after a Cisco Intelligence Feed is downloaded.

Example 16-1 *Security Intelligence (for IP Address) Files on the FMC*

```
! Right after a fresh installation, an FMC does not contain any blacklist files by
  default:

admin@FMC:~$ ls -halp /var/sf/iprep_download/
total 20K
drwxr-xr-x  5 www   www   4.0K Apr 28 01:22 ./
drwxr-xr-x 64 root  root  4.0K Apr 28 02:20 ../
-rw-r--r--  1 www   www      0 Apr 28 01:22 IPRVersion.dat
drwxr-xr-x  2 www   www   4.0K Apr 28 01:22 health/
drwxr-xr-x  2 www   www   4.0K Apr 28 01:22 peers/
drwxr-xr-x  2 www   www   4.0K Apr 28 01:22 tmp/
admin@FMC:~$


! After updating the Cisco Intelligence Feed from the cloud, FMC shows the blacklist
  files:

admin@FMC~$ ls -halp /var/sf/iprep_download/
total 7.3M
drwxr-xr-x  5 www   www   4.0K Apr 28 16:39 ./
drwxr-xr-x 64 root  root  4.0K Apr 28 02:20 ../
-rw-r--r--  1 root  root  225K Apr 28 16:23 032ba433-c295-11e4-a919-d4ae5275a468
-rw-r--r--  1 root  root    37 Apr 28 16:23 1b117672-7453-478c-be31-b72e89ca1acb
-rw-r--r--  1 root  root   43K Apr 28 16:23 23f2a124-8278-4c03-8c9d-d28fe08b5e98
-rw-r--r--  1 root  root  5.3K Apr 28 16:23 2CCDA18E-DDFF-4F5C-AF9A-F009852183F4
-rw-r--r--  1 root  root  9.4K Apr 28 16:23 2b15cb6f-a3fc-4e0e-a342-ccc5e5803263
-rw-r--r--  1 root  root    52 Apr 28 16:23 30f9e69c-d64c-479c-821d-0e4edab8217a
-rw-r--r--  1 root  root  682K Apr 28 16:23 3e2af68e-5fc8-4b1c-b5bc-b4e7cab598ba
-rw-r--r--  1 root  root    48 Apr 28 16:23 5a0b6d6b-e2c3-436f-b4a1-48248b330a26
-rw-r--r--  1 root  root    32 Apr 28 16:23 5f8148f1-e5e4-427a-aa3b-ee1c2745c350
-rw-r--r--  1 root  root   47K Apr 28 16:23 60f4e2ab-d96c-44a0-bd38-830252b63f46
-rw-r--r--  1 root  root    31 Apr 28 16:23 6ba968f4-7a25-4793-a2c8-7cc77f1ff437
-rw-r--r--  1 root  root   165 Apr 28 16:23 A27C6AAE-8E52-4174-A81A-47C59FECC092
-rw-rw-r--  1 www   www     39 Apr 28 16:42 IPRVersion.dat
-rw-r--r--  1 root  root  6.2M Apr 28 16:22 Sourcefire_Intelligence_Feed
-rw-r--r--  1 root  root    30 Apr 28 16:23 b1df3aa8-2841-4c88-8e64-bfaacec7fedd
-rw-r--r--  1 root  root  1.7K Apr 28 16:23 d7d996a6-6b92-4a56-8f10-e8506e431ca5
drwxr-xr-x  2 www   www   4.0K Apr 28 01:22 health/
drwxr-xr-x  2 www   www   4.0K Apr 28 01:22 peers/
-rw-r--r--  1 root  root  4.6K Apr 28 16:22 rep_dd.yaml
drwxr-xr-x  2 www   www   4.0K Apr 28 16:32 tmp/
admin@FMC:~$
```

Example 16-2 shows the Security Intelligence blacklist (.blf) and whitelist (.wlf) files.
A new FTD installation comes with the global blacklist and whitelist files. The Cisco
Intelligence Feed files appear as soon as the FTD device receives an access control policy
from the FMC.

Example 16-2 *Security Intelligence (for IP Address) Files on an FTD Device*

```
! After a fresh installation, FTD shows only the empty blacklist (.blf) and
  whitelist (.wlf) files. At this point, FMC has not applied a Cisco Intelligence
  Feed yet:


> expert
admin@firepower:~$ ls -halp /var/sf/iprep_download/
total 40K
drwxr-xr-x  5 www  www  4.0K Apr 28 10:44 ./
drwxr-xr-x 66 root root 4.0K Dec 12 00:19 ../
-rw-rw-r--  1 www  www   118 Apr 28 10:17 .zones
-rw-rw-r--  1 www  www    17 Apr 28 10:44 IPRVersion.dat
-rw-r--r--  1 root root   40 Apr 28 10:17 c76556bc-6167-11e1-88e8-479de99bfdf1.blf
-rw-r--r--  1 root root   40 Apr 28 10:17 d8eea83e-6167-11e1-a154-589de99bfdf1.wlf
drwxr-xr-x  2 www  www  4.0K Sep 19  2016 health/
drwxr-xr-x  2 www  www  4.0K Sep 19  2016 peers/
drwxr-xr-x  2 www  www  4.0K Apr 28 10:44 tmp/
-rw-rw-r--  1 www  www   151 Apr 28 10:44 zone.info
admin@firepower:~$



! Upon a successful deployment of an Access Control policy, FTD received the
  necessary blacklist (.blf) and whitelist (.wlf) files from an FMC. Each of these
  files represent a Security Intelligence category.


admin@firepower:~$ ls -halp /var/sf/iprep_download/
total 1.1M
drwxr-xr-x  5 www  www  4.0K May  7 16:05 ./
drwxr-xr-x 66 root root 4.0K Dec 12 00:19 ../
-rw-rw-r--  1 www  www  1003 May  7 16:04 .zones
-rw-r--r--  1 root root 225K May  7 16:04 032ba433-c295-11e4-a919-d4ae5275a468.blf
-rw-r--r--  1 root root   37 May  7 16:04 1b117672-7453-478c-be31-b72e89ca1acb.blf
-rw-r--r--  1 root root  43K May  7 16:04 23f2a124-8278-4c03-8c9d-d28fe08b5e98.blf
-rw-r--r--  1 root root 9.4K May  7 16:04 2b15cb6f-a3fc-4e0e-a342-ccc5e5803263.blf
-rw-r--r--  1 root root 5.3K May  7 16:04 2ccda18e-ddff-4f5c-af9a-f009852183f4.blf
-rw-r--r--  1 root root   52 May  7 16:04 30f9e69c-d64c-479c-821d-0e4edab8217a.blf
-rw-r--r--  1 root root 682K May  7 16:04 3e2af68e-5fc8-4b1c-b5bc-b4e7cab598ba.blf
-rw-r--r--  1 root root   48 May  7 16:04 5a0b6d6b-e2c3-436f-b4a1-48248b330a26.blf
-rw-r--r--  1 root root   32 May  7 16:04 5f8148f1-e5e4-427a-aa3b-ee1c2745c350.blf
-rw-r--r--  1 root root  47K May  7 16:04 60f4e2ab-d96c-44a0-bd38-830252b63f46.blf
-rw-r--r--  1 root root   31 May  7 16:04 6ba968f4-7a25-4793-a2c8-7cc77f1ff437.blf
```

```
-rw-r--r--   1 root root   373 May   7 16:04 808e55a2-2d33-11e7-ab29-ad43fb3c690a.blf
-rw-r--r--   1 root root    17 May   7 16:04 IPRVersion.dat
-rw-r--r--   1 root root   165 May   7 16:04 a27c6aae-8e52-4174-a81a-47c59fecc092.blf
-rw-r--r--   1 root root    30 May   7 16:04 b1df3aa8-2841-4c88-8e64-bfaacec7fedd.blf
-rw-r--r--   1 root root    40 May   7 16:04 c76556bc-6167-11e1-88e8-479de99bfdf1.blf
-rw-r--r--   1 root root  1.7K May   7 16:04 d7d996a6-6b92-4a56-8f10-e8506e431ca5.blf
-rw-r--r--   1 root root    53 May   7 16:04 d8eea83e-6167-11e1-a154-589de99bfdf1.wlf
drwxr-xr-x   2 www  www   4.0K Sep  19  2016 health/
drwxr-xr-x   2 www  www   4.0K May   7 14:26 peers/
drwxr-xr-x   2 www  www   4.0K May   7 16:04 tmp/
-rw-rw-r--   1 www  www   1006 May   7 16:04 zone.info
admin@firepower:~$
```

Tip   If you have enabled Security Intelligence based on URL, you can find the list of blacklisted and whitelisted URLs in similar format. The files are located in the /var/sf/siurl_download directory.

Verifying the Loading of Addresses into Memory

Example 16-2 in the preceding section confirms that an FTD device has received the Security Intelligence category files from the FMC. However, it does not prove that all the blacklisted addresses are loaded successfully into the FTD memory. You can verify this by looking at the debugging messages at the FTD CLI while an access control policy is being deployed.

Example 16-3 shows the debugging messages in FTD when it loads the Security Intelligence configuration and entries into the device's memory. The following messages confirm that the Custom-List object has loaded all 25 of the addresses into its memory.

Example 16-3   *FTD Loads the Security Intelligence Data into Its Memory*

```
admin@firepower:~$ sudo tail -f /var/log/messages | grep -i reputation


May  7 16:05:40 ciscoasa SF-IMS[12223]:     Reputation Preprocessor: Size of shared
  memory segment SFIPReputation.rt.0.0.1 is 134217728
May  7 16:05:40 ciscoasa SF-IMS[12223]:     Reputation entries loaded: 1, invalid:
  0, re-defined: 0 (from file /ngfw/var/sf/iprep_download/d8eea83e-6167-11e1-a154-
  589de99bfdf1.wlf)
May  7 16:05:40 ciscoasa SF-IMS[12223]:     Reputation entries loaded: 0, invalid:
  0, re-defined: 0 (from file /ngfw/var/sf/iprep_download/c76556bc-6167-11e1-88e8-
  479de99bfdf1.blf)
May  7 16:05:40 ciscoasa SF-IMS[12223]:     Reputation entries loaded: 25, invalid:
  0, re-defined: 0 (from file /ngfw/var/sf/iprep_download/808e55a2-2d33-11e7-ab29-
  ad43fb3c690a.blf)
```

```
May  7 16:05:40 ciscoasa SF-IMS[12223]:    Reputation entries loaded: 3310,
   invalid: 0, re-defined: 7 (from file /ngfw/var/sf/iprep_download/60f4e2ab-d96c-
   44a0-bd38-830252b63f46.blf)
May  7 16:05:40 ciscoasa SF-IMS[12223]:    Reputation entries loaded: 0, invalid:
   0, re-defined: 0 (from file /ngfw/var/sf/iprep_download/6ba968f4-7a25-4793-a2c8-
   7cc77f1ff437.blf)
May  7 16:05:40 ciscoasa SF-IMS[12223]:    Reputation entries loaded: 3050,
   invalid: 0, re-defined: 1 (from file /ngfw/var/sf/iprep_download/23f2a124-8278-
   4c03-8c9d-d28fe08b5e98.blf)
May  7 16:05:40 ciscoasa SF-IMS[12223]:    Reputation entries loaded: 112, invalid:
   0, re-defined: 0 (from file /ngfw/var/sf/iprep_download/d7d996a6-6b92-4a56-8f10-
   e8506e431ca5.blf)
May  7 16:05:40 ciscoasa SF-IMS[12223]:    Reputation entries loaded: 1, invalid:
   0, re-defined: 0 (from file /ngfw/var/sf/iprep_download/5a0b6d6b-e2c3-436f-b4a1-
   48248b330a26.blf)
May  7 16:05:40 ciscoasa SF-IMS[12223]:    Reputation entries loaded: 0, invalid:
   0, re-defined: 0 (from file /ngfw/var/sf/iprep_download/5f8148f1-e5e4-427a-aa3b-
   ee1c2745c350.blf)
May  7 16:05:40 ciscoasa SF-IMS[12223]:    Reputation entries loaded: 676, invalid:
   0, re-defined: 3 (from file /ngfw/var/sf/iprep_download/2b15cb6f-a3fc-4e0e-a342-
   ccc5e5803263.blf)
May  7 16:05:40 ciscoasa SF-IMS[12223]:    Reputation entries loaded: 0, invalid:
   0, re-defined: 0 (from file /ngfw/var/sf/iprep_download/1b117672-7453-478c-be31-
   b72e89ca1acb.blf)
May  7 16:05:40 ciscoasa SF-IMS[12223]:    Reputation entries loaded: 1, invalid:
   0, re-defined: 0 (from file /ngfw/var/sf/iprep_download/30f9e69c-d64c-479c-821d-
   0e4edab8217a.blf)
May  7 16:05:40 ciscoasa SF-IMS[12223]:    Reputation entries loaded: 48044,
   invalid: 0, re-defined: 0 (from file /ngfw/var/sf/iprep_download/3e2af68e-5fc8-
   4b1c-b5bc-b4e7cab598ba.blf)
May  7 16:05:40 ciscoasa SF-IMS[12223]:    Reputation entries loaded: 15962,
   invalid: 0, re-defined: 112 (from file /ngfw/var/sf/iprep_download/032ba433-c295-
   11e4-a919-d4ae5275a468.blf)
May  7 16:05:40 ciscoasa SF-IMS[12223]:    Reputation entries loaded: 0, invalid:
   0, re-defined: 0 (from file /ngfw/var/sf/iprep_download/b1df3aa8-2841-4c88-8e64-
   bfaacec7fedd.blf)
May  7 16:05:40 ciscoasa SF-IMS[12223]:    Reputation entries loaded: 9, invalid:
   0, re-defined: 0 (from file /ngfw/var/sf/iprep_download/a27c6aae-8e52-4174-a81a-
   47c59fecc092.blf)
May  7 16:05:40 ciscoasa SF-IMS[12223]:    Reputation entries loaded: 377, invalid:
   0, re-defined: 0 (from file /ngfw/var/sf/iprep_download/2ccda18e-ddff-4f5c-af9a-
   f009852183f4.blf)
May  7 16:05:40 ciscoasa SF-IMS[12223]: Reputation Preprocessor shared memory
   summary:
May  7 16:05:40 ciscoasa SF-IMS[12223]:    Reputation total memory usage: 9442496
   bytes
May  7 16:05:40 ciscoasa SF-IMS[12223]:    Reputation total entries loaded: 71568,
   invalid: 0, re-defined: 123
   .
   .
   .

! <Output is Omitted for Brevity>
```

To determine whether the memory is loaded with the latest set of Security Intelligence data, you can verify the timestamp of the FTD shared memory file. The timestamp should record the UTC time of the latest access control policy applied:

```
admin@firepower:~$ ls -halp /dev/shm/ | grep -i reputation
-rw-rw-rw-  1 root root 128M May  7 16:05 SFIPReputation.rt.0.0.1
admin@firepower:~$
```

Finding a Specific Address in a List

Let's say you have just learned about malware and its potential source address. You want to confirm whether the address is included in the active Cisco Intelligence Feed or whether you should consider blacklisting it manually. You can verify this from the FTD CLI by following these steps:

Step 1.   Run the following command to search for a specific IP address within the list file:

```
admin@firepower:/var/sf/iprep_download$ egrep 209.222.77.220 *.blf
60f4e2ab-d96c-44a0-bd38-830252b63f46.blf:209.222.77.220
admin@firepower:/var/sf/iprep_download$
```

This command uses the IP address 209.222.77.220 as an example; replace it as appropriate.

Step 2.   The output from Step 1 shows the list file where the IP address is listed, but it does not display the category. To determine the category type, run the following command to view the first line of the file:

```
admin@firepower:/var/sf/iprep_download$ head -n1 60f4e2ab-d96c-44a0-
bd38-830252b63f46.blf
#Cisco intelligence feed: CnC
admin@firepower:/var/sf/iprep_download$
```

Verifying URL-Based Security Intelligence Rules

You can leverage the Security Intelligence technology to blacklist, monitor, and whitelist a suspicious website. The configuration of URL-based Security Intelligence is similar to the configuration of IP address–based Security Intelligence. The only difference is that instead of selecting the Network type intelligence object, you select the URL type intelligence object. This section assumes that you have already selected URL-based intelligence by following a procedure similar to the one you used for configuring IP-based Security Intelligence. Now, you want to verify whether your deployment is successful.

Figure 16-24 shows the Security Intelligence configuration page. To blacklist or whitelist malicious URLs, select the **URL** subtab (instead of the Network subtab, which you selected for IP-based intelligence).

Likewise, you can apply the same troubleshooting techniques to investigate issues with URL-based Security Intelligence. You can find the blacklist and whitelist files for URL-based Security Intelligence at /var/sf/siurl_download.

Example 16-4 shows the blacklist and whitelist files for URL-based Security Intelligence. Unlike with IP-based Security Intelligence, all the URL-based Security Intelligence files use .lf (list file) as their file extensions.

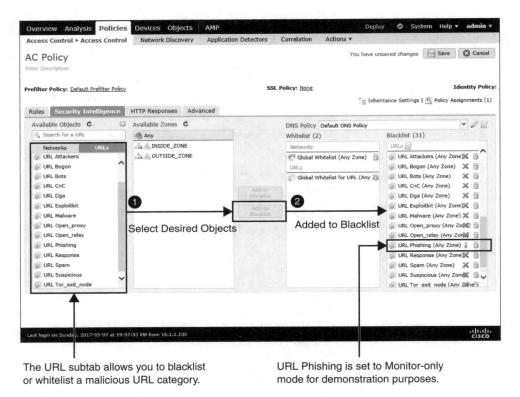

The URL subtab allows you to blacklist or whitelist a malicious URL category.

URL Phishing is set to Monitor-only mode for demonstration purposes.

Figure 16-24 *URL Subtab Showing the Categories of the Malicious Sites*

Example 16-4 *Blacklist and Whitelist Files for URL-Based Security Intelligence*

```
admin@firepower:~$ ls -halp /var/sf/siurl_download/
total 31M
drwxrwxr-x  5 www  detection 4.0K May  8 18:09 ./
drwxr-xr-x 66 root root      4.0K Dec 12 00:19 ../
-rw-rw-r--  1 www  www        930 May  8 18:08 .zones
-rw-r--r--  1 root root      422K May  8 18:08 032ba433-c295-11e4-a919-
  d4ae5275d599.lf
-rw-r--r--  1 root root        82 May  8 18:08 127dc4a2-1ea3-4423-a02d-
  1f02069828ac.lf
```

```
-rw-r--r--  1 root root        69 May  8 18:08 1b117672-7453-478c-be31-
   b72e89ca4bfc.lf
-rw-r--r--  1 root root       21M May  8 18:08 23f2a124-8278-4c03-8c9d-
   d28fe08b8fc9.lf
-rw-r--r--  1 root root        56 May  8 18:08 2b15cb6f-a3fc-4e0e-a342-
   ccc5e5806394.lf
-rw-r--r--  1 root root      147K May  8 18:08 2ccda18e-ddff-4f5c-af9a-
   f0098521b525.lf
-rw-r--r--  1 root root        53 May  8 18:08 30f9e69c-d64c-479c-821d-
   0e4edab852ab.lf
-rw-r--r--  1 root root      8.8K May  8 18:08 3e2af68e-5fc8-4b1c-b5bc-
   b4e7cab5c9eb.lf
-rw-r--r--  1 root root        65 May  8 18:08 5915d129-0d33-4e9c-969a-
   eab3cde32156.lf
-rw-r--r--  1 root root        52 May  8 18:08 5a0b6d6b-e2c3-436f-b4a1-
   48248b333b57.lf
-rw-r--r--  1 root root        48 May  8 18:08 5f8148f1-e5e4-427a-aa3b-
   ee1c2745f481.lf
-rw-r--r--  1 root root      187K May  8 18:08 60f4e2ab-d96c-44a0-bd38-
   830252b67077.lf
-rw-r--r--  1 root root        47 May  8 18:08 6ba968f4-7a25-4793-a2c8-
   7cc77f1f1256.lf
-rw-r--r--  1 root root        17 May  8 18:08 IPRVersion.dat
-rw-r--r--  1 root root       20K May  8 18:08 a27c6aae-8e52-4174-a81a-
   47c59fecf1c3.lf
-rw-r--r--  1 root root      2.2M May  8 18:08 b1df3aa8-2841-4c88-8e64-
   bfaacec71300.lf
-rw-r--r--  1 root root      2.6M May  8 18:08 d7d996a6-6b92-4a56-8f10-
   e8506e434dd6.lf
-rw-rw-r--  1 root root      5.1M May  8 18:09 dm_url0.acl
drwxr-xr-x  2 www  www       4.0K Sep 19  2016 health/
drwxr-xr-x  2 www  www       4.0K May  1 17:18 peers/
drwxr-xr-x  2 www  www       4.0K May  8 18:08 tmp/
-rw-rw-r--  1 www  www       1015 May  8 18:08 url.rules
admin@firepower:~$
```

Because both blacklist and whitelist files use the same .lf extension, you cannot distinguish the purpose of a file by looking at the extension. However, you can use the url.rules file to determine this.

Example 16-5 shows the purpose of each list file. The first file is a whitelist file, and the last file is set to Monitor-only mode. All other list files are configured to block traffic.

Example 16-5   *The url.rules File, Showing the Action or Purpose of Each List File*

```
admin@firepower:~$ cat /var/sf/siurl_download/url.rules
#security intelligence manifest file
si,5915d129-0d33-4e9c-969a-eab3cde32156.lf,1048597,white,any
si,127dc4a2-1ea3-4423-a02d-1f02069828ac.lf,1048613,block,any
```

```
si,5a0b6d6b-e2c3-436f-b4a1-48248b333b57.lf,1048599,block,any
si,5f8148f1-e5e4-427a-aa3b-ee1c2745f481.lf,1048600,block,any
si,6ba968f4-7a25-4793-a2c8-7cc77f1f1256.lf,1048601,block,any
si,30f9e69c-d64c-479c-821d-0e4edab852ab.lf,1048607,block,any
si,2b15cb6f-a3fc-4e0e-a342-ccc5e5806394.lf,1048612,block,any
si,1b117672-7453-478c-be31-b72e89ca4bfc.lf,1048606,block,any
si,3e2af68e-5fc8-4b1c-b5bc-b4e7cab5c9eb.lf,1048610,block,any
si,a27c6aae-8e52-4174-a81a-47c59fecf1c3.lf,1048604,block,any
si,2ccda18e-ddff-4f5c-af9a-f0098521b525.lf,1048611,block,any
si,60f4e2ab-d96c-44a0-bd38-830252b67077.lf,1048602,block,any
si,032ba433-c295-11e4-a919-d4ae5275d599.lf,1048609,block,any
si,b1df3aa8-2841-4c88-8e64-bfaacec71300.lf,1048603,block,any
si,23f2a124-8278-4c03-8c9d-d28fe08b8fc9.lf,1048605,block,any
si,d7d996a6-6b92-4a56-8f10-e8506e434dd6.lf,1048608,monitor,any
admin@firepower:~$
```

A list file uses a universally unique identifier (UUID) as its filename. It does not state the type of intelligence category it contains. To find that answer, you can view the first line of the list file. For example, the following example confirms that d7d996a6-6b92-4a56-8f10- e8506e434dd6.lf stores the URLs of the phishing websites.

```
admin@firepower:~$ head -n1 /var/sf/siurl_download/d7d996a6-6b92-4a56-8f10-
e8506e434dd6.lf
#Cisco DNS and URL intelligence feed: URL Phishing
admin@firepower:~$
```

Summary

In this chapter, you have learned how to detect a malicious address by using the Security Intelligence feature. When there is a match, you can ask an FTD device to block, monitor, or whitelist an address. This chapter also describes the back-end file systems for the Security Intelligence feature. You can apply this knowledge to troubleshooting issues with Security Intelligence.

Quiz

1. Security Intelligence is a first-level-defense mechanism implemented on which of the following?

   a. Firewall engine

   b. Firepower engine

   c. Firepower Management Center

   d. All of the above

2. Which of the following statements is true?

   a. FTD allows a whitelisted address to bypass any further inspection.

   b. FTD requires a direct connection to the Internet in order to obtain the Cisco Intelligence Feed.

   c. The Blacklist IP Now option allows you to block an address without redeploying an access control policy.

   d. Monitor-only mode of Security Intelligence works only when FTD is deployed in passive mode.

3. Which of the following commands displays the name of the Security Intelligence category from a blacklist file?

   a. **tail -f** *filename.blf*

   b. **tail** *filename.blf*

   c. **head** *filename.blf*

   d. **grep** *category_name filename.blf*

4. Which of the following commands displays an exact IP address and confirms that the address is included in the current blacklist file?

   a. **cat** *filename.blf*

   b. **head** *ip_address filename.blf*

   c. **grep** *ip_address *.blf*

   d. **tail** *ip_address filename.blf*

Chapter 17

Blocking a Domain Name System (DNS) Query

Attackers often send phishing emails with links to malware websites. A user in your network may be deceived by the hoax content and click on an obfuscated link by mistake. Firepower can intelligently prevent a user from accessing a malicious website by blocking its DNS query—one of the first things a client computer performs to access a website. This chapter describes the implementation of a DNS policy on an FTD system.

Firepower DNS Policy Essentials

Before diving into DNS policy configuration, let's take a look at how a host computer learns the IP address of a website through a DNS query and how a Firepower system can prevent a user from making a DNS query for a malicious domain.

Domain Name System (DNS)

When you want to call one of your friends, what do you usually do? You pick up your phone, go to the Contacts app, find your friend in the app, and select his or her name. You do not need to memorize or type the phone number. The phone originates a call for you, using the number stored in the Contacts app. If you do not find the number you need in your Contacts app, you ask someone who knows your friend for the phone number. This whole process is an analogy of how a DNS server works.

When you want to visit a website, you open a browser and enter the URL. However, before your browser learns the IP address of a website, the following tasks happen behind the scenes:

Step 1. The browser sends a query to the local DNS server in your network.

Step 2. If the local network has no internal DNS server or the DNS server has no information about the site you want to visit, a query is sent to the recursive

DNS server of your Internet service provider (ISP). If the recursive server has information about the IP address in its cache, your browser receives that information. No additional queries are performed.

Step 3. However, if the recursive server does not know the IP address, the recursive server sends the query to one of the 13 sets of root name servers located worldwide. A root server knows the DNS information about a top-level domain (TLD).

Step 4. The DNS server of a TLD sends information about the second-level domain and its authoritative name server. An authoritative name server knows all the addressing information for a particular domain.

Step 5. The authoritative name server responds to a query by returning the Address Record (A record) to your ISP. The ISP's recursive server stores the record on its cache for a specific amount of time and sends the IP address to your browser.

Figure 17-1 shows various levels of DNS queries for a domain. Depending on the records on the intermediate server cache, the number of queries can be higher or lower. The process can happen within less than a second.

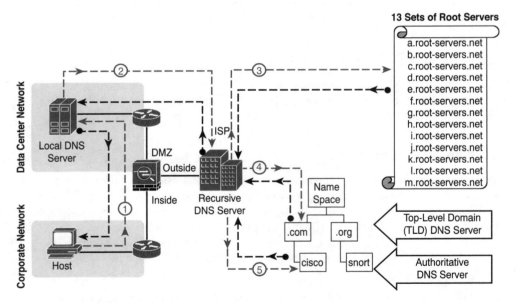

Figure 17-1 *DNS Queries Throughout a Network*

Blocking of a DNS Query Using a Firepower System

You can add an access rule to an access control policy to block DNS traffic; however, a traditional access rule is unable to identify a harmful domain based on the characteristics of its web contents.

Figure 17-2 shows an access rule that blocks DNS traffic solely based on DNS service ports. This static rule is unable to determine the risk level of a domain, and, therefore, it cannot block an unsafe domain dynamically.

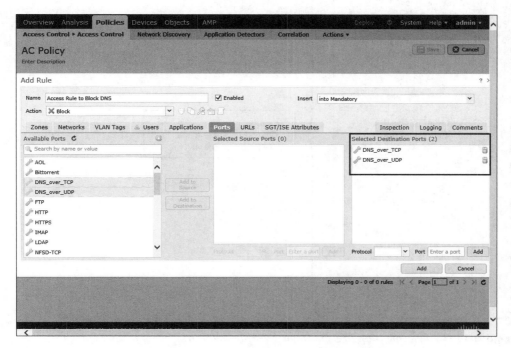

Figure 17-2 *Identifying and Blocking DNS Traffic Based on Service Ports*

The DNS-based Security Intelligence feature of Firepower allows you to identify a susceptible DNS query and blacklist the resolution of an unsafe domain name, while any queries to legitimate websites are allowed. It leads to a browser not being able to obtain the IP address of a website. FTD blocks the request for a website before a potential HTTP connection is even established. Consequently, FTD does not need to engage its resources for further HTTP inspection.

Figure 17-3 shows the workflow of a DNS query. It also shows where an FTD device functions.

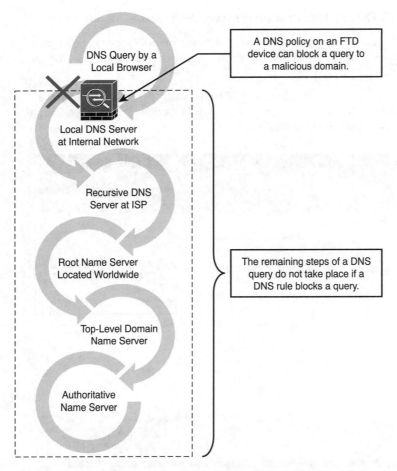

Figure 17-3 *Placement of an FTD Device Within the Workflow of a DNS Query*

DNS Rule Actions

Depending on your organization's security policy, you can add a DNS rule to a blacklist or to a whitelist, or you can monitor a DNS query.

Actions That Can Interrupt a DNS Query

Firepower offers various options for interrupting a DNS query (see Figure 17-4):

■ **Drop:** With this option, FTD simply drops the DNS query for a particular domain.

Warning   A user may still access a website if the client computer caches the DNS records and the existing records are not expired.

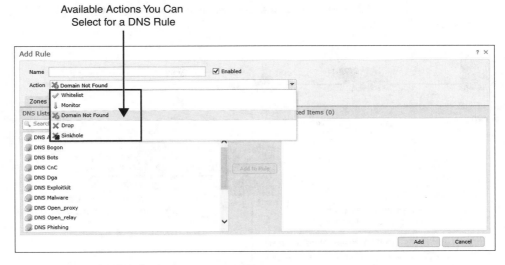

Figure 17-4 *DNS Rule Actions*

Figure 17-5 illustrates the drop action on an FTD device. The device simply drops the DNS query, and no response is provided to the client.

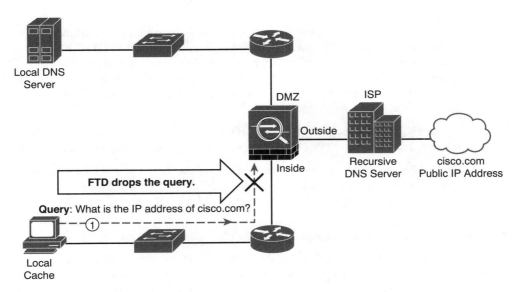

Figure 17-5 *DNS Drop Action*

- **Domain Not Found:** With this option, as a response to a DNS query, a user receives an NXDOMAIN (nonexistent domain name) message (see Figure 17-6). The NXDOMAIN message indicates that the requested domain name does not exist.

The browser cannot resolve the IP address for a domain. Consequently, the user fails to access the website.

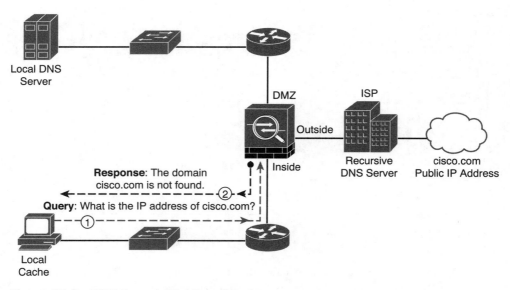

Figure 17-6   *DNS Domain Not Found Action*

- **Sinkhole:** With this option, FTD responds to a DNS query with a false IP address. A browser does not realize that an intermediate security device—FTD in this example—acts as a spoof DNS server, and it responds to its query with a false IP address. The IP address may or may not be assigned to an existing DNS server. Using Sinkhole functionality, you can redirect malicious traffic to an alternate location for further security analysis.

  Figure 17-7 shows a spoof DNS server. FTD uses the IP address of this spoof DNS server as a response to a DNS query only when the domain is categorized as harmful.

  Figure 17-8 shows the implementation of a sinkhole without a physical spoof server. You can assign any false IP address within a sinkhole object. Then FTD uses this false address to respond to any query to a harmful domain.

Actions That Allow a DNS Query

Let's say the Cisco Intelligence Feed blocks a query to your trusted domain. You have asked Cisco to reinvestigate the domain. While you are waiting on Cisco, you can use one of the following actions to allow a desired DNS query:

- **Whitelist:** This action allows the traffic to bypass an intelligence-based check; however, the traffic is still subject to other security inspections.

- **Monitor:** This action allows an FTD device to generate alerts when there is any match, but FTD does not interrupt traffic flow.

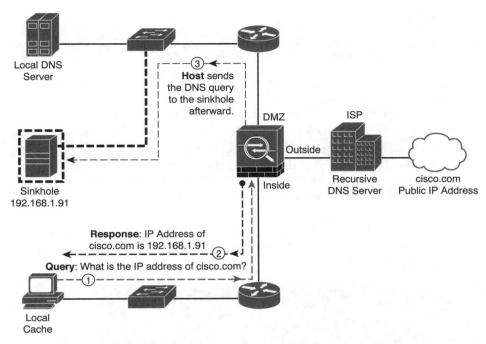

Figure 17-7   *DNS Sinkhole Action (Fake Address Represents a Spoof DNS Server)*

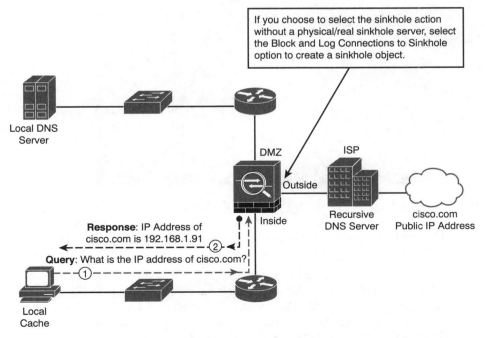

Figure 17-8   *DNS Sinkhole Action (Fake Address Does Not Represent any Server)*

Sources of Intelligence

To learn about the new suspicious domains, the Firepower System updates its intelligence database from the following sources:

■ **Feed:** Cisco has a dedicated threat intelligence and research team, known as Talos, that analyzes the behavior of Internet traffic, performs in-depth analysis on any suspicious activities, categorizes the potential domains based on their characteristics, and lists the domains in a file.

One of the processes running on the FMC, CloudAgent, periodically communicates with the Cisco cloud to download the latest feed. The frequency for updating the feed is configurable. Once the FMC downloads a feed, it sends the feed to its managed devices automatically. Redeployment of the access control policy is not necessary.

Figure 17-9 shows the configuration of the update frequency for the Cisco Intelligence Feed. To find this page, go to **Object > Object Management**. Under Security Intelligence, select **DNS Lists and Feeds** and edit Cisco-DNS-and-URL-Intelligence-Feed by using the pencil icon.

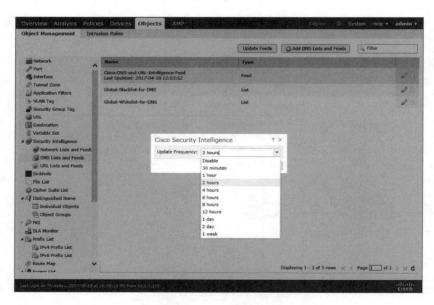

Figure 17-9   *Frequency of Cisco Intelligence Feed Update*

Table 17-1 shows the key differences between the feed and list types of Security Intelligence input.

■ **List:** FMC supports the blacklisting or whitelisting of custom lists of domains. You can list the domains in a text file (.txt format) and upload the file manually to the FMC. Upon a successful upload, a custom DNS object appears along with the system-provided DNS objects. The process to add a DNS rule is described later in this chapter, in the section "Configuring DNS Query Blocking."

Table 17-1 *Intelligence Feed Versus Intelligence List*

	Feed	List
Provider	The Cisco threat intelligence team creates and manages the feed. The FMC also supports the input of custom domains through an internal feed URL.	Created by you, based on your own research and selection.
Maintenance	The FMC can download the latest feed periodically.	You can manually update an old list on demand

Tip When you create your own list of domains for blacklisting, enter one domain name per line. You can add a comment for future reference. Use the hash sign (#) at the beginning of a line to enter a comment.

Figure 17-10 shows the DNS List/Feed configuration window. To find this window, go to Object Management and select the **DNS Lists and Feeds** option under Security Intelligence. Then click the **Add DNS Lists and Feeds** button. The DNS List/Feed configuration window then appears when you select List from the Type dropdown.

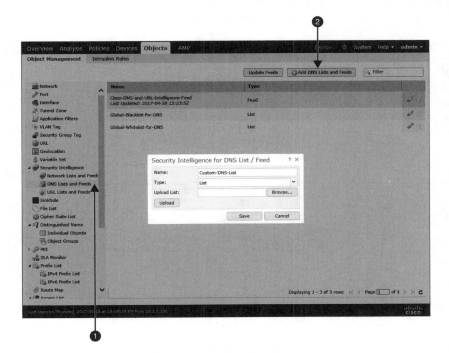

Figure 17-10 *Option to Upload a DNS List File*

Best Practices for Blocking DNS Query

Depending on the placement of an FTD device in a network, you may have to wait some time before you notice a new DNS policy take effect. For example, if your one and only FTD device is placed at the perimeter edge—between your company network and ISP network—your network hosts may continue resolving an undesired website until the local DNS cache expires. The hosts can notice the effect of a new DNS policy once the DNS cache of the client computer and local DNS server expires.

You can clear the cache of a DNS server manually. However, it may not be feasible to clear the cache of all of the network hosts manually in real time. To expedite the enforcement of a new Firepower DNS policy, you can consider the following best practices:

■ Enable IP address–based Security Intelligence as well.

■ Disable DNS caching on the local workstations. The system administrator of your organization can confirm this setting.

■ Position your FTD device between the local area network (LAN) and the DNS server so that any egress traffic from the LAN is subject to Firepower inspection. Placing an FTD device at the perimeter edge allows the hosts to resolve an address by using the cache of the internal DNS server.

Figure 17-11 shows different options for placement of an FTD device. In Network A, FTD allows queries to an internal DNS server and blocks the queries to an external DNS server. However, the FTD in Network B blocks queries to any DNS servers, local or external.

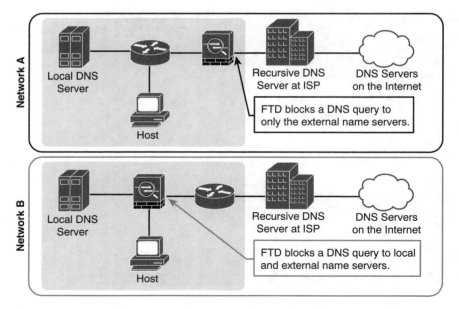

Figure 17-11 *Effectiveness of a DNS Rule in Different FTD Deployments*

Fulfilling Prerequisites

Before you configure a DNS policy, make sure the following prerequisites are fulfilled:

- If the DNS policy requires a Threat license and you are in the process of purchasing a license, you can enable Evaluation Mode to avoid any logistic and administrative delays. Evaluation Mode allows you to configure and deploy any features as if you have already installed a paid license.

- If you want to redirect a DNS query to a sinkhole, you must configure a sinkhole object (with a real or fake IP address) before you select the Sinkhole action for a DNS rule. You can create multiple sinkhole objects using different IP addresses and use them for different purposes (for example, one object for malware, one object for phishing, and so on).

Figure 17-12 shows the configuration of a sinkhole object. To find this configuration window, navigate to **Objects > Object Management > Sinkhole** and click the **Add Sinkhole** button.

Note If you want to set up the sinkhole functionality without a physical DNS server, select the Block and Log Connections to Sinkhole option shown in Figure 17-12.

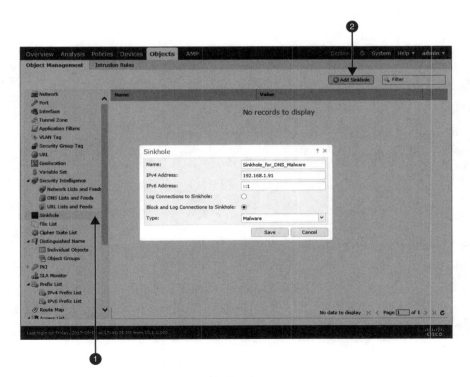

Figure 17-12 *Configuring a Sinkhole Object*

Configuring DNS Query Blocking

To block a DNS query using a Firepower System, you must perform the following two tasks on your FMC:

■ Create a new DNS policy or edit an existing one by adding the necessary DNS rule conditions.

■ Invoke the desired DNS policy within an access control policy and deploy the policies on an FTD device.

The following sections describe the process of enabling DNS policies successfully on an FTD device. Figure 17-13 shows the lab topology that is used in this chapter to configure DNS-based Security Intelligence (DNS policy).

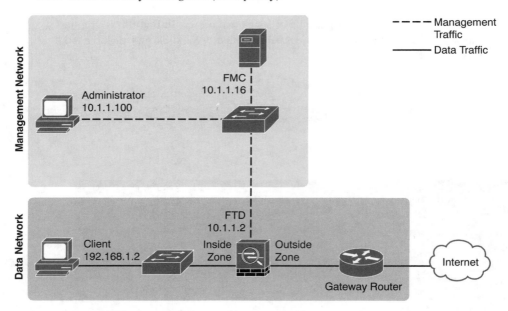

Figure 17-13   *Topology Used in the Configuration Examples of This Chapter*

Adding a New DNS Rule

To add a new DNS rule, follow these steps:

Step 1.   Navigate to **Policies > Access Control > DNS**. The system-provided Default DNS Policy appears. You can edit this default policy and add your custom DNS rules to it.

Alternatively, you can create a brand new DNS policy and customize it. To do that, click the **Add DNS Policy** button. The system prompts you to name your new DNS policy. After you save the name, the DNS policy editor page appears. The remaining steps in this example describe how to customize a new DNS policy.

Figure 17-14 shows a DNS policy editor page. Each DNS policy, by default, comes with two items—a global whitelist and global blacklist—that have higher precedence than a custom DNS rule.

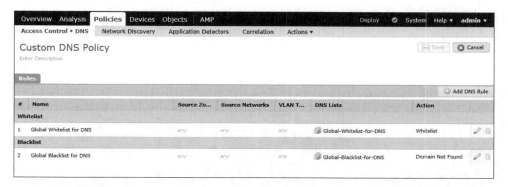

Figure 17-14 *DNS Policy Editor Page*

Step 2. When the DNS policy editor page appears, click the **Add DNS Rule** button. The Add Rule window appears.

Step 3. Give a name to your DNS rule and select a desired action from the Action dropdown. The section "DNS Query Blocking Essentials," earlier in this chapter, describes the functions of each action.

Step 4. Select the **Zones**, **Networks**, and **VLAN** tabs and define the source and destination traffic, as appropriate.

Step 5. Select the **DNS** tab, which shows the categories for unsafe DNS traffic. Add the desired categories to your rule.

Figure 17-15 shows the DNS rule editor window, which allows you to select a Security Intelligence category that you want to detect and to define an action for any matching traffic.

Step 6. When the rule configuration is complete, click the **OK** button to exit the DNS rule editor. Click the **Save** button to save the changes on your DNS policy.

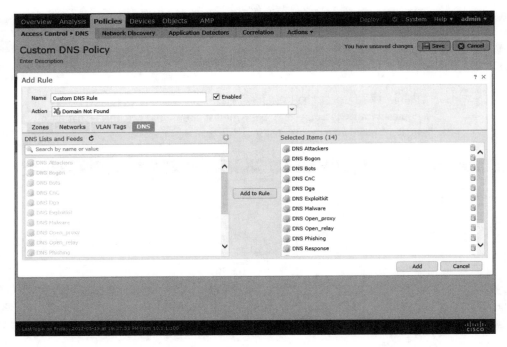

Figure 17-15 *DNS Rule Editor Window*

Invoking a DNS Policy

Once you have created a DNS policy, to deploy this policy on an FTD device, you need to invoke it manually within an access control policy. By default, an access control policy invokes the system-provided default DNS policy.

To activate a desired DNS policy, follow these steps:

Step 1.   Navigate to **Policies > Access Control > Access Control**. Edit the access control policy that will be applied on an FTD device.

Step 2.   In the access control policy editor page that appears, select the **Security Intelligence** tab.

Step 3.   In the Security Intelligence tab, from the DNS Policy dropdown select the desired DNS policy (see Figure 17-16).

Step 4.   Click **Save** to save the configuration and deploy the policy to your FTD device.

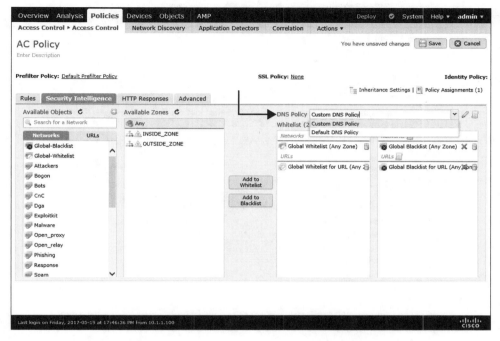

Figure 17-16 *Invoking DNS Policy in the Security Intelligence Tab*

Verification and Troubleshooting Tools

You can use the FTD CLI in Expert Mode to investigate an issue with DNS policy configuration and inspection.

Verifying the Configuration of a DNS Policy

FTD generates logs in the syslog messages file when the FMC deploys a DNS policy on it, and the FTD device loads the rules into its memory. You can review any historical logs to determine any prior failure or debug the logs in real time.

To review the old logs that are related to DNS policy, run the following command:

```
admin@firepower:~$ sudo grep -i dns /var/log/messages
```

To debug the deployment of a DNS policy in real time, run the following command:

```
admin@firepower:~$ sudo tail -f /var/log/messages | grep -i dns
```

Example 17-1 shows confirmation that the DNS policy is allocated with a shared memory of 5 MB, and the size of the DNS blacklisting database is 4.32 MB. There are 341440 rules on this DNS policy that are loaded from 13 blacklisting categories.

Example 17-1 *Debugging Logs Related to a DNS Policy*

```
admin@firepower:~$ sudo tail -f /var/log/messages | grep -i dns
Password:


May 21 20:56:35 ciscoasa SF-IMS[4397]: [4546] SFDataCorrelator:URLUserIP_
  CorrelatorThread [INFO] Writer swap dns database 2
May 21 20:56:35 ciscoasa SF-IMS[4397]: [4546] SFDataCorrelator:ShmemDB [INFO] DNS
  Blacklisting load database to segment 0 load mode 2
May 21 20:56:35 ciscoasa SF-IMS[4397]: [4546] SFDataCorrelator:ShmemDB [INFO]
  loading firewall rule ID file: /var/sf/sidns_download/dns.rules
May 21 20:56:35 ciscoasa SF-IMS[4397]: [4546] SFDataCorrelator:ShmemDB [INFO] number
  of SI category for DNS Blacklisting is 13
May 21 20:56:35 ciscoasa SF-IMS[4397]: [4546] SFDataCorrelator:ShmemDB [INFO]
  reading dns/url memcap file /ngfw/etc/sf/dns_url.memcap
May 21 20:56:35 ciscoasa SF-IMS[4397]: [4546] SFDataCorrelator:ShmemDB [INFO]
  Setting up shared memory memcap DNS Blacklisting 5242880
May 21 20:56:37 ciscoasa SF-IMS[4397]: [4546] SFDataCorrelator:ShmemDB [INFO]
  DNS BL database size: 4532600, number of entries: 341440
May 21 20:56:37 ciscoasa SF-IMS[4397]: [4546] SFDataCorrelator:DMShmMgmt [INFO]
  new database available, type:0, segment:0, path:/ngfw/var/sf/sidns_download/
  dm_dns0.acl
May 21 20:56:37 ciscoasa SF-IMS[4397]: [4546] SFDataCorrelator:ShmemDB [INFO]
  reading dns/url memcap file /ngfw/etc/sf/dns_url.memcap
May 21 20:56:45 ciscoasa SF-IMS[20862]: [20868] sfpreproc:DMShmMgmt [INFO]
  successfully removed unused database /ngfw/var/sf/sidns_download/dm_dns1.acl
.

.
.
<Output Omitted for Brevity>
```

Upon a successful deployment, the DNS Security Intelligence rules are stored in the /var/sf/sidns_download directory, in list file (.lf) format. The DNS policy configuration file, dns.rules, is also located in this directory. FTD creates all these files at the time when you deploy a DNS policy. Therefore, matching the timestamp, which uses the UTC time zone, is an important indicator of whether the latest policy is deployed.

Example 17-2 shows the list files that contain the blacklisted and whitelisted DNS addresses. These files are created at the same time the dns.rules file is created.

Example 17-2 *List Files (.lf) That Store the Blacklisted and Whitelisted DNS Addresses*

```
admin@firepower:~$ ls -halp /var/sf/sidns_download/
total 11M
drwxrwxr-x  5 www  detection 4.0K May 21 20:58 ./
drwxr-xr-x 66 root root      4.0K Dec 12 00:19 ../
-rw-r--r--  1 root root      400K May 21 20:56 032ba433-c295-11e4-a919-d4ae5275b77b.
  lf
-rw-r--r--  1 root root         0 May 21 20:56 17a11eb0-ff56-11e4-9081-764afb0f5dcb.
  lf
```

```
-rw-r--r--  1 root root            69 May 21 20:56 1b117672-7453-478c-be31-b72e89ca2dde.
  lf
-rw-r--r--  1 root root             0 May 21 20:56 1fca9c10-ff56-11e4-866e-ad4afb0f5dcb.
  lf
-rw-r--r--  1 root root          1.9M May 21 20:56 23f2a124-8278-4c03-8c9d-d28fe08b71ab.
  lf
-rw-r--r--  1 root root          145K May 21 20:56 2ccda18e-ddff-4f5c-af9a-f00985219707.
  lf
-rw-r--r--  1 root root            53 May 21 20:56 30f9e69c-d64c-479c-821d-0e4edab8348d.
  lf
-rw-r--r--  1 root root          8.8K May 21 20:56 3e2af68e-5fc8-4b1c-b5bc-b4e7cab5abcd.
  lf
-rw-r--r--  1 root root            52 May 21 20:56 5a0b6d6b-e2c3-436f-b4a1-48248b331d39.
  lf
-rw-r--r--  1 root root            48 May 21 20:56 5f8148f1-e5e4-427a-aa3b-ee1c2745d663.
  lf
-rw-r--r--  1 root root          187K May 21 20:56 60f4e2ab-d96c-44a0-bd38-830252b65259.
  lf
-rw-r--r--  1 root root            66 May 21 20:56 663da2e4-32f4-44d2-ad1f-8d6182720d32.
  lf
-rw-r--r--  1 root root            47 May 21 20:56 6ba968f4-7a25-4793-a2c8-7cc77f1f1074.
  lf
-rw-r--r--  1 root root            17 May 21 20:56 IPRVersion.dat
-rw-r--r--  1 root root           20K May 21 20:56 a27c6aae-8e52-4174-a81a-47c59fecd3a5.
  lf
-rw-r--r--  1 root root          2.2M May 21 20:56 b1df3aa8-2841-4c88-8e64-bfaacec7111f.
  lf
-rw-r--r--  1 root root          1.8M May 21 20:56 d7d996a6-6b92-4a56-8f10-e8506e432fb8.
  lf
-rw-r--r--  1 root root            66 May 21 20:56 ded9848d-3580-4ca1-9d3c-04113549f129.
  lf
-rw-rw-r--  1 root root          4.4M May 21 20:57 dm_dns1.acl
-rw-r--r--  1 root root          1.7K May 21 20:56 dns.rules
drwxr-xr-x  2 www  www          4.0K Sep 19  2016 health/
drwxr-xr-x  3 www  www          4.0K Apr 29 16:17 peers/
drwxr-xr-x  2 www  www          4.0K May 21 20:56 tmp/
admin@firepower:~$
```

After you configure a DNS policy using the GUI and deploy it on an FTD device, the FTD device writes the configurations into the dns.rules file. A dns.rules file saves the DNS rule conditions and associates the actions with the related blacklist and whitelist files. The file also records the time when the latest DNS policy is deployed.

Example 17-3 explains the contents of a dns.rules file. The example elaborates the sinkhole rule as an example. The sinkhole rule (rule ID 7) matches the domain names on the 23f2a124-8278-4c03-8c9d-d28fe08b71ab.lf list file (list ID 1048587). When there is a match, the rule responds to a DNS query with the sinkhole IP address 192.168.1.91.

Example 17-3   *DNS Policy Configurations—View from the CLI*

```
admin@firepower:~$ cat /var/sf/sidns_download/dns.rules
#### dns.rules
##########################################################################
#
# DNS Policy Name : Custom DNS Policy
#
# File Written    : Sun May 21 20:56:42 2017 (UTC)
#
##########################################################################
#
policy e5d989f8-3d01-11e7-8dc5-a7ffd42f66c2
revision e5d989f8-3d01-11e7-8dc5-a7ffd42f66c2

interface 1 e2b1d576-2cf5-11e7-8ea7-e184e4106fb3
interface 2 e295985c-2cf5-11e7-8ea7-e184e4106fb3

dnslist 1048594 663da2e4-32f4-44d2-ad1f-8d6182720d32.lf
dnslist 1048585 032ba433-c295-11e4-a919-d4ae5275b77b.lf
dnslist 1048599 ded9848d-3580-4ca1-9d3c-04113549f129.lf
dnslist 1048597 b1df3aa8-2841-4c88-8e64-bfaacec7111f.lf
dnslist 1048590 3e2af68e-5fc8-4b1c-b5bc-b4e7cab5abcd.lf
dnslist 1048587 23f2a124-8278-4c03-8c9d-d28fe08b71ab.lf
dnslist 1048598 d7d996a6-6b92-4a56-8f10-e8506e432fb8.lf
dnslist 1048595 6ba968f4-7a25-4793-a2c8-7cc77f1f1074.lf
dnslist 1048589 30f9e69c-d64c-479c-821d-0e4edab8348d.lf
dnslist 1048591 5a0b6d6b-e2c3-436f-b4a1-48248b331d39.lf
dnslist 1048592 5f8148f1-e5e4-427a-aa3b-ee1c2745d663.lf
dnslist 1048586 1b117672-7453-478c-be31-b72e89ca2dde.lf
dnslist 1048593 60f4e2ab-d96c-44a0-bd38-830252b65259.lf
sinkhole 1 7e550616-3e61-11e7-a338-d8a9a7208ff6 192.168.1.91 ::1

1 allow any   any any 1048594
3 nxdomain any   any any 1048599
5 nxdomain any   any any 1048591
5 nxdomain any   any any 1048592
5 nxdomain any   any any 1048595
5 nxdomain any   any any 1048593
6 block any   any any 1048597
6 block any   any any 1048586
6 block any   any any 1048589
7 sinkhole any   any any 1048587 (sinkhole: 1)
8 monitor any   any any 1048598
8 monitor any   any any 1048585
8 monitor any   any any 1048590
admin@firepower:~$
```

To determine the category of domains that are listed in an .lf file, view the first line of the file. For example, the following command confirms that the file 23f2a124-8278-4c03-8c9d-d28fe08b71ab.lf (DNS list ID 1048587) lists all the domains that are susceptible for malware:

```
admin@firepower:~$ head -n1 /var/sf/sidns_download/23f2a124-8278-4c03-8c9d-
d28fe08b71ab.lf
#Cisco DNS and URL intelligence feed: DNS Malware
admin@firepower:~$
```

Figure 17-17 shows some of the contents in a dns.rules file on the GUI—accessible from the DNS policy configuration editor. The example highlights the rule that enables the sinkhole action.

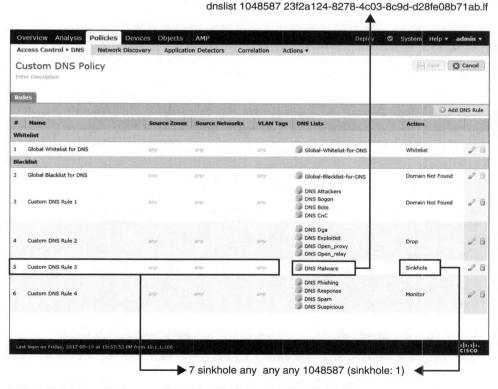

Figure 17-17   *DNS Policy Configurations—View from the GUI*

Verifying the Operation of a DNS Policy

To verify the operation of a DNS policy and inspection of a DNS query, you need to access a domain that is blocked by the current DNS policy. To help you better understand this, this chapter uses three different websites that can trigger the Security Intelligence events for three different categories.

> **Warning** If your computer is connected to the Internet, you should not attempt to access a malicious website until an FTD device is actively protecting your network.

The status of categorization or inclusion of a domain may vary in different versions of a feed. If you want to determine the inclusion of any particular domain in the current Cisco Intelligence Feed, search that particular domain within all the list files. The following command can perform that search:

```
admin@firepower:~$ grep [domain_name] /var/sf/sidns_download/*.lf
```

Example 17-4 shows the DNS intelligence category for the domains that you will be testing next.

Example 17-4 *Identifying the DNS Intelligence Category for Certain Domains*

```
admin@firepower:~$ egrep iolmau.com /var/sf/sidns_download/*.lf
/var/sf/sidns_download/23f2a124-8278-4c03-8c9d-d28fe08b71ab.lf:iolmau.com
admin@firepower:~$ head -n1 /var/sf/sidns_download/23f2a124-8278-4c03-8c9d-
    d28fe08b71ab.lf
#Cisco DNS and URL intelligence feed: DNS Malware
admin@firepower:~$


admin@firepower:~$ egrep mrreacher.net /var/sf/sidns_download/*.lf
/var/sf/sidns_download/60f4e2ab-d96c-44a0-bd38-830252b65259.lf:mrreacher.net
admin@firepower:~$ head -n1 /var/sf/sidns_download/60f4e2ab-d96c-44a0-bd38-
    830252b65259.lf
#Cisco DNS and URL intelligence feed: DNS CnC
admin@firepower:~$


admin@firepower:~$ egrep rent.sinstr.ru /var/sf/sidns_download/*.lf
/var/sf/sidns_download/d7d996a6-6b92-4a56-8f10-e8506e432fb8.lf:rent.sinstr.ru
admin@firepower:~$
admin@firepower:~$ head -n1 /var/sf/sidns_download/d7d996a6-6b92-4a56-8f10-
    e8506e432fb8.lf
#Cisco DNS and URL intelligence feed: DNS Phishing
admin@firepower:~$
```

Table 17-2 summarizes the domains that you will query from a client computer to test the DNS policy operation. As of writing this book, they are available in the current revision of the Cisco Intelligence Feed and added in the DNS rule.

Table 17-2 *Selection of Domains from Three Different Intelligence Categories (for Lab Test)*

Domain Name	DNS/Security Intelligence Category	DNS Rule Action
iolmau.com	Malware	Sinkhole
mrreacher.net	Command and control (CnC)	Domain not found
rent.sinstr.ru	Phishing	Monitor

Before you begin testing, enable the **firewall-engine-debug** command on the FTD CLI so that FTD device generates debug output while a client performs a DNS query. The following pages show you how to access the selected domains one by one from a client computer in your inside network.

Tip Depending on the placement of your FTD device, the DNS-based Security Intelligence may not begin to function if the existing cache of your DNS server is not cleared. Therefore, before you begin an investigation, wait until the existing cache expires or manually delete the cache entries from your DNS server. Read the "DNS Query Blocking Best Practices" section of this chapter for more information.

Example 17-5 shows the debugging messages that are generated by the **firewall-debug-engine** tool on the FTD device. Each time a domain name is queried by the host 192.168.1.2, FTD matches the domain with the names on the list files. When there is a match, FTD triggers the action configured on the matching DNS rule.

Example 17-5 *Debugging the DNS Queries Through an FTD Device*

```
> system support firewall-engine-debug

Please specify an IP protocol:
Please specify a client IP address: 192.168.1.2
Please specify a client port:
Please specify a server IP address:
Please specify a server port:

Monitoring firewall engine debug messages

192.168.1.2-37868 > 192.168.1.1-53 17 AS 4 I 1 DNS SI shared mem lookup returned 1
  for iolmau.com
192.168.1.2-37868 > 192.168.1.1-53 17 AS 4 I 1 Starting SrcZone first with intfs -1
  -> 0, vlan 0
192.168.1.2-37868 > 192.168.1.1-53 17 AS 4 I 1 match rule order 1, id 1 action Allow
192.168.1.2-37868 > 192.168.1.1-53 17 AS 4 I 1 match rule order 2, id 3 action DNS
  NXDomain
192.168.1.2-37868 > 192.168.1.1-53 17 AS 4 I 1 match rule order 3, id 5 action DNS
  NXDomain
192.168.1.2-37868 > 192.168.1.1-53 17 AS 4 I 1 match rule order 4, id 6 action Block
```

```
192.168.1.2-37868 > 192.168.1.1-53 17 AS 4 I 1 match rule order 5, id 7 action DNS
   Sinkhole
192.168.1.2-37868 > 192.168.1.1-53 17 AS 4 I 1 Got DNS list match. si list 1048587
192.168.1.2-37868 > 192.168.1.1-53 17 AS 4 I 1 match rule order 6, id 8 action Audit
192.168.1.2-37868 > 192.168.1.1-53 17 AS 4 I 1 Firing DNS action DNS Sinkhole
192.168.1.2-37868 > 192.168.1.1-53 17 AS 4 I 1 DNS SI: Matched rule order 5, Id 7,
   si list id 1048587, action 23, reason 2048, SI Categories 1048587,0



192.168.1.2-37868 > 192.168.1.1-53 17 AS 4 I 1 DNS SI shared mem lookup returned 1
   for mrreacher.net
192.168.1.2-37868 > 192.168.1.1-53 17 AS 4 I 1 Starting SrcZone first with intfs -1
   -> 0, vlan 0
192.168.1.2-37868 > 192.168.1.1-53 17 AS 4 I 1 match rule order 1, id 1 action Allow
192.168.1.2-37868 > 192.168.1.1-53 17 AS 4 I 1 match rule order 2, id 3 action DNS
   NXDomain
192.168.1.2-37868 > 192.168.1.1-53 17 AS 4 I 1 match rule order 3, id 5 action DNS
   NXDomain
192.168.1.2-37868 > 192.168.1.1-53 17 AS 4 I 1 Got DNS list match. si list 1048593
192.168.1.2-37868 > 192.168.1.1-53 17 AS 4 I 1 match rule order 4, id 6 action Block
192.168.1.2-37868 > 192.168.1.1-53 17 AS 4 I 1 match rule order 5, id 7 action DNS
   Sinkhole
192.168.1.2-37868 > 192.168.1.1-53 17 AS 4 I 1 match rule order 6, id 8 action Audit
192.168.1.2-37868 > 192.168.1.1-53 17 AS 4 I 1 Firing DNS action DNS NXDomain
192.168.1.2-37868 > 192.168.1.1-53 17 AS 4 I 1 DNS SI: Matched rule order 3, Id 5,
   si list id 1048593, action 22, reason 2048, SI Categories 1048593,0



192.168.1.2-37868 > 192.168.1.1-53 17 AS 4 I 1 DNS SI shared mem lookup returned 1
   for rent.sinstr.ru
192.168.1.2-37868 > 192.168.1.1-53 17 AS 4 I 1 Starting SrcZone first with intfs -1
   -> 0, vlan 0
192.168.1.2-37868 > 192.168.1.1-53 17 AS 4 I 1 match rule order 1, id 1 action Allow
192.168.1.2-37868 > 192.168.1.1-53 17 AS 4 I 1 match rule order 2, id 3 action DNS
   NXDomain
192.168.1.2-37868 > 192.168.1.1-53 17 AS 4 I 1 match rule order 3, id 5 action DNS
   NXDomain
192.168.1.2-37868 > 192.168.1.1-53 17 AS 4 I 1 match rule order 4, id 6 action Block
192.168.1.2-37868 > 192.168.1.1-53 17 AS 4 I 1 match rule order 5, id 7 action DNS
   Sinkhole
192.168.1.2-37868 > 192.168.1.1-53 17 AS 4 I 1 match rule order 6, id 8 action Audit
192.168.1.2-37868 > 192.168.1.1-53 17 AS 4 I 1 Got DNS list match. si list 1048598
192.168.1.2-37868 > 192.168.1.1-53 17 AS 4 I 1 Firing DNS action Audit
192.168.1.2-37868 > 192.168.1.1-53 17 AS 4 I 1 DNS SI: Matched rule order 6, Id 8,
   si list id 1048598, action 6, reason 4096, SI Categories 1048598,0
```

Now, for the three DNS queries in Example 17-5, the FMC should log events. You can view them on the **Analysis > Connections > Security Intelligence Events** page.

Figure 17-18 shows three types of DNS-based Security Intelligence actions. FTD triggered these events when a client attempted to access three different matching websites.

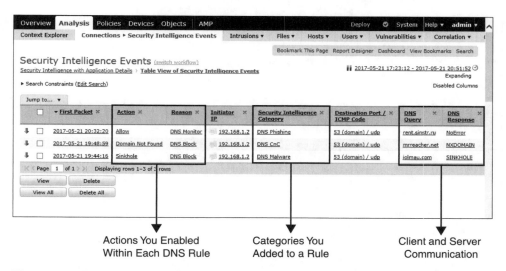

Actions You Enabled   Categories You   Client and Server
Within Each DNS Rule   Added to a Rule   Communication

Figure 17-18 *Security Intelligence Event Page Showing Events Triggered by DNS Rules*

You can also use the **nslookup** command-line tool to resolve a domain name to its IP address. The tools is available on both Windows and Linux operating systems. It allows you to view the IP address of a domain without accessing the web contents.

Example 17-6 shows the resolutions of the same domain names used in the previous examples from a network host. The client uses the **nslookup** command-line tool and receives three different types of results.

Example 17-6 *Resolving Domain Names by Using the* **nslookup** *Command*

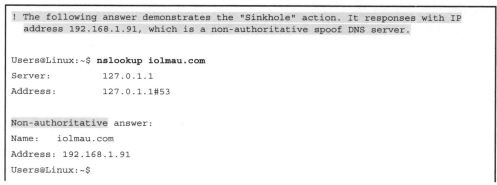

```
! The following answer demonstrates the "Sinkhole" action. It responses with IP
  address 192.168.1.91, which is a non-authoritative spoof DNS server.


Users@Linux:~$ nslookup iolmau.com
Server:          127.0.1.1
Address:         127.0.1.1#53


Non-authoritative answer:
Name:    iolmau.com
Address: 192.168.1.91
Users@Linux:~$
```

```
! The following answer reflects the "Domain Not Found" action. The DNS query fails
  with NXDOMAIN message, which means the domain appears to be non-existent.


Users@Linux:~$ nslookup mrreacher.net
Server:         127.0.1.1
Address:        127.0.1.1#53


** server can't find mrreacher.net: NXDOMAIN
Users@Linux:~$



! The following answer reflects the "Monitor" action. The DNS query is able to
  resolve the domain name. It shows the public IP address for the domain.


Users@Linux:~$ nslookup rent.sinstr.ru
Server:         127.0.1.1
Address:        127.0.1.1#53


Name:   rent.sinstr.ru
Address: 81.222.82.37
Users@Linux:~$
```

Summary

This chapter describes various techniques for administering DNS queries using a Firepower DNS policy. Besides using a traditional access control rule, an FTD device can incorporate Cisco Intelligence Feed and dynamically blacklist suspicious domains. In this chapter, you have learned various ways to configure and deploy a DNS policy. This chapter also demonstrates several command-line tools you can run to verify, analyze, and troubleshoot issues with DNS policy.

Quiz

1. Which of the following actions does not interrupt traffic flow immediately?
   a. Domain Not Found
   b. Whitelist
   c. Blacklist
   d. Monitor

2. Which of the following directories stores the files related to a DNS policy?
   a. /var/sf/sidns_intelligence
   b. /var/sf/sidns_download
   c. /var/log/sidns_policy
   d. /var/log/sidns_list

3. Which of the following statements is incorrect?

   a. Sinkhole configuration requires a unique type of sinkhole object.

   b. DNS policy requires a Threat license.

   c. FTD downloads the latest Cisco Intelligence Feed directly from the cloud.

   d. The FMC supports the blacklisting of custom domain lists.

4. Which of the following actions sends an address of a spoof DNS server?

   a. Domain Not Found

   b. Sinkhole

   c. Monitor

   d. Drop

Chapter 18

Filtering URLs Based on Category, Risk, and Reputation

New websites are coming out every day. A security analyst strives to determine the relevance of a new website for business operations and its risk level for security reasons. However, it is challenging to catch up with the exponentially growing number of new websites every day. In this chapter, you will learn how Firepower can empower you with automatic classification of millions of websites using the Web Reputation technology.

URL Filtering Essentials

The URL Filtering feature of a Firepower system is able to categorize millions of URLs and domains. You can enable this feature to prevent your network hosts from accessing a specific type of URL. This feature empowers you to enforce the IT security and legal policies of your organization dynamically—without continually making manual changes to the access rule conditions.

Reputation Index

You can download the Firepower URL database from the cloud by using the FMC GUI. As of this writing, the cloud has analyzed more than 600 million domains and more than 27 billion URLs and categorized them into more than 83 different classes. The analysis engine in the cloud can categorize more than 2500 URLs per second. The URL database maintains the Web Reputation Index (WRI), which is based on many different data points, such as age and history of the site, reputation and location of the hosting IP address, subject and context of the content, and so on.

Table 18-1 shows the WRI descriptions. WRI is calculated dynamically based on collective intelligence from various sources.

Table 18-1 *Web Reputation Index Used in a URL Database*

Reputation Level	Index	Description
1. High risk	01–20	Sites are at high risk. Known for exposure to malicious data.
2. Suspicious	21–40	Sites are suspicious. Threat level is higher than average.
3. Moderate risk	41–60	Benign sites but exposed to some unsafe characteristics.
4. Low risk	61–80	Benign sites but showed risks once or twice—though very rarely.
5. Trustworthy	81–100	Well-known sites with very strong security features.

Figure 18-1 shows the implementation of URL categories and reputations in the FMC web interface.

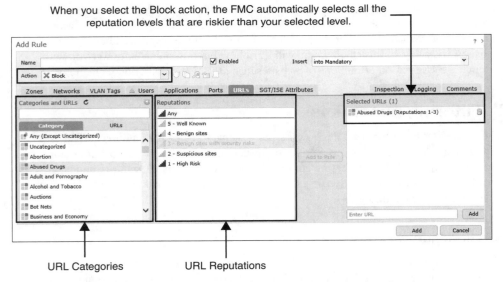

Figure 18-1 *URL Categories and Reputations in the Access Rule Editor*

Based on the type of action—Allow or Block—you select for an access rule, the FMC automatically adds extra URL reputation levels along with your original selection. For example, when you select the Allow action for a certain reputation level, the FMC allows all the URLs of that level as well as the URLs that are more benign than your selected level. Likewise, if you select the Block action for a particular reputation level, FMC blocks all the URLs of that level along with any URLs that are riskier than the level you selected.

Figure 18-2 shows different behaviors between the Allow and Block actions. Compare this image with Figure 18-1. Note that both show the same reputation level selected (3 - Benign sites with security risks), but the ultimate reputation selections are different due to the actions—Allow versus Block.

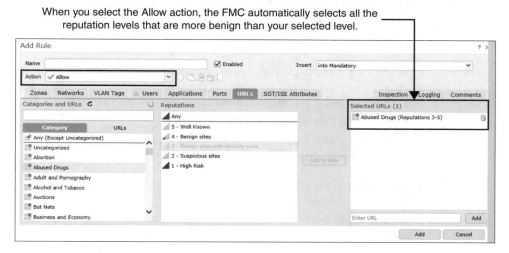

Figure 18-2 *FMC Selecting Extra URL Reputations—Depending on the Selected Action*

Operational Architecture

The Firepower system loads the URL dataset into its memory for a faster lookup. Depending on the size of available memory on a Firepower system, the cloud publishes two types of datasets in a URL database—20 million URLs and 1 million URLs. After the initial download of a database, the FMC receives updates from the cloud periodically, as long as the automatic update is enabled. The periodic updates are incremental and smaller. However, the total download time depends on the last URL database installed on the FMC and, of course, the download speed.

Table 18-2 shows that the number of URLs included in a database depends on the available memory on a Firepower system.

Table 18-2 *Available Memory Versus the Number of URLs in a Dataset*

Available Memory	Number of URLs in the Dataset
More than 3.4 GB	20 million URLs
Less than or equal to 3.4 GB	1 million URLs

During traffic inspection, an FTD device can resolve most of the URLs the first time it sees them. However, depending on other factors, an FTD device might have to go through multiple steps to resolve a URL by category and reputation. Here are some steps, for example:

Step 1.   The Firepower Snort engine on an FTD device performs an immediate lookup on the local URL dataset. FTD is able to determine the category in most cases. If the URL is unavailable in the FTD cache, FTD forwards the query to the FMC.

Step 2.   If the FMC can retrieve the URL category from its local database, it sends the query result to the FTD device so that FTD can act on traffic according to the access control policy. Figure 18-3 shows the steps to resolve an unknown new URL into its category and reputation.

Step 3.   If the FMC is unable to resolve the URL category from its local database, it checks the Cisco Collective Security Intelligence (CSI) configuration:

- If the query to the CSI is disabled, the FMC places the unknown URL into the Uncategorized group.

- If the query to the CSI is enabled, the FMC queries the cloud for the unknown URL.

Fulfilling Prerequisites

Before you begin configuring an access rule with URL Filtering conditions, fulfill the following requirements:

- A URL Filtering license is necessary to use the URL classification and reputation database of a Firepower system. Furthermore, as a prerequisite, the FMC requires you to enable a Threat license before you enable URL Filtering.

    Figure 18-4 shows the page where you can enable or disable any license for an FTD device. To find this page, navigate to **Devices > Device Management**. Edit the device where you want to enable URL Filtering license and then select the **Devices** tab.

    Without a URL Filtering license, you can create an access rule based on any URL conditions; however, you cannot deploy an access control policy with the URL conditions until you enable a URL Filtering license on your FTD device. Similarly, if the URL license expires after you deploy an access control policy, FTD stops matching any access rule with URL conditions, and the FMC stops updating the URL database.

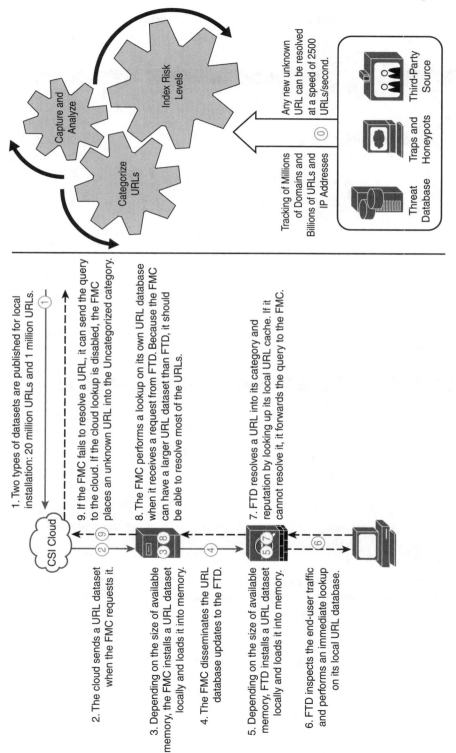

1. Two types of datasets are published for local installation: 20 million URLs and 1 million URLs.

2. The cloud sends a URL dataset when the FMC requests it.

3. Depending on the size of available memory, the FMC installs a URL dataset locally and loads it into memory.

4. The FMC disseminates the URL database updates to the FTD.

5. Depending on the size of available memory, FTD installs a URL dataset locally and loads it into memory.

6. FTD inspects the end-user traffic and performs an immediate lookup on its local URL database.

7. FTD resolves a URL into its category and reputation by looking up its local URL cache. If it cannot resolve it, it forwards the query to the FMC.

8. The FMC performs a lookup on its own URL database when it receives a request from FTD. Because the FMC can have a larger URL dataset than FTD, it should be able to resolve most of the URLs.

9. If the FMC fails to resolve a URL, it can send the query to the cloud. If the cloud lookup is disabled, the FMC places an unknown URL into the Uncategorized category.

Any new unknown URL can be resolved at a speed of 2500 URLs/second.

Tracking of Millions of Domains and Billions of URLs and IP Addresses

Figure 18-3 *Architecture of the Firepower System URL Lookup*

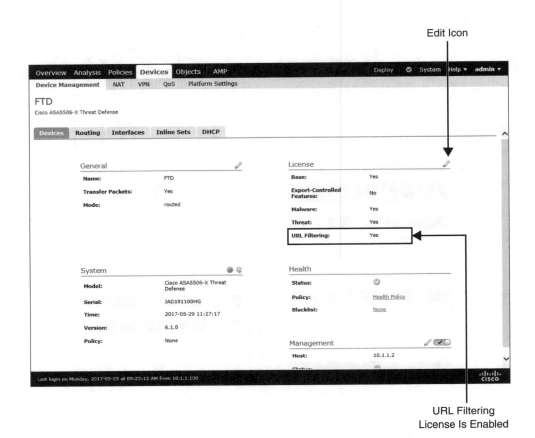

Figure 18-4 *Enabling the URL Filtering License on an FTD Device*

Tip   If you are in the process of purchasing a license, you can enable Evaluation Mode to avoid any administrative delays. Evaluation Mode allows you to configure and deploy any features as if you have already enabled a paid license.

■ Make sure the URL Filtering and Cisco CSI communication are enabled. The FMC should enable them automatically after you add a valid URL Filtering license. Figure 18-5 confirms that URL Filtering and automatic updating of the URL database have been enabled.

Both Options Are Enabled

Figure 18-5 *Enabling URL Filtering and Automatic Updating*

Best Practices for URL Filtering Configuration

Consider the following best practices when enabling the URL Filtering feature in Firepower:

- Check whether the URL Filtering Monitor health module is enabled in the current health policy. If this module is enabled, the FMC generates alerts if it fails to deploy a URL dataset to the managed devices or fails to download the latest URL database from the Cisco CSI.

  Figure 18-6 shows the option to enable the health module for URL Filtering. To find this page, go to **System > Health > Policy**, edit a health policy, and select **URL Filtering Monitor** from the left panel. You must redeploy a health policy after you change any settings.

- The FMC communicates with Cisco CSI every 30 minutes to determine if a new update for the URL Filtering database is available. Therefore, if the automatic update option is enabled, you should not create a separate scheduled task for URL database updates. However, a recurring scheduled task for URL database updates is useful if you want to manage the URL database update manually.

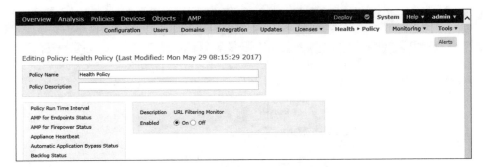

Figure 18-6   *Health Module for URL Filtering Monitor*

Figure 18-7 shows the options to create a scheduled task for URL database updates. In this configuration, the FMC updates the URL Filtering database daily at 5 a.m., as opposed to the system default of every 30 minutes.

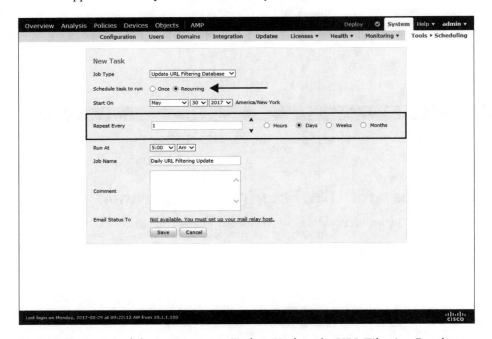

Figure 18-7   *Scheduling a Recurring Task to Update the URL Filtering Database*

■ To prevent access to any suspicious websites, you can consider blocking the DNS queries to those domains. If an FTD device can block a connection during DNS resolution, a URL lookup for that connection will no longer be necessary. Hence, it can improve system performance.

Figure 18-8 highlights the positions of the Firepower engine components. The URL-based Security Intelligence (DNS policy) can block a packet *before* it is categorized and blocked by a URL Filtering rule.

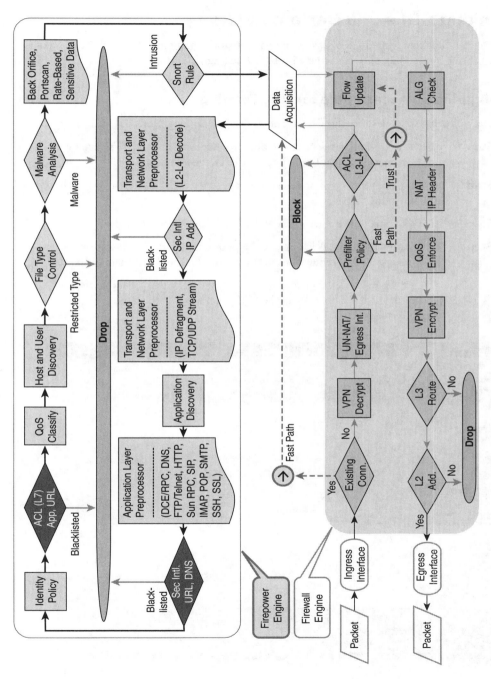

Figure 18-8 *Workflow of URL Filtering Within a Firepower Engine*

Blocking URLs of a Certain Category

You can block undesired URLs based on their categories and reputations. You can accomplish this by enabling an access rule with URL Filtering conditions.

Configuring an Access Rule for URL Filtering

The following steps describe how to add an access rule to block certain URL categories:

Step 1. Navigate to **Policies > Access Control > Access Control** and select an existing access control policy to edit or create a new one.

Step 2. On the access control policy editor page, click the **Add Rule** button. The Add Rule window appears.

Step 3. Give a name to the access rule and select an action for the rule.

Step 4. Click the **URLs** tab. A list of URL categories and reputations appear. Select the categories and reputations you want to block and add them to the rule.

Figure 18-9 shows the creation of an access rule with a URL Filtering condition. The rule blocks all the URLs that are related to the Job Search category.

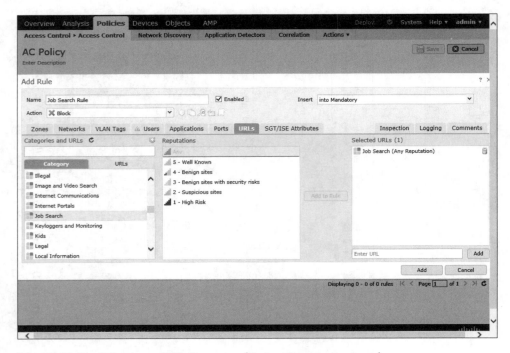

Figure 18-9 *Selecting a URL Category for Any Reputation Levels*

Step 5.   On the Logging tab, enable Log at Beginning of Connection. This step is optional, but it allows you to view events when FTD blocks a connection due to a URL Filtering condition.

Figure 18-10 shows how to enable logging at the beginning of a connection. Once this is enabled, FTD generates a connection event whenever it blocks a URL in the Job Search category.

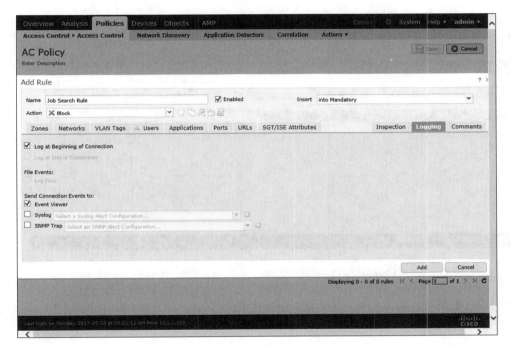

Figure 18-10   *Enabling Logging for an Access Rule with a URL Filtering Condition*

Step 6.   Click the **Add** button to create the access rule.

Step 7.   Click **Save** to save the changes on the access control policy. Finally, activate the policy by clicking the **Deploy** button.

Figure 18-11 shows the creation of a simple access rule called Job Search Rule. This rule blocks any URLs that are within the Job Search category.

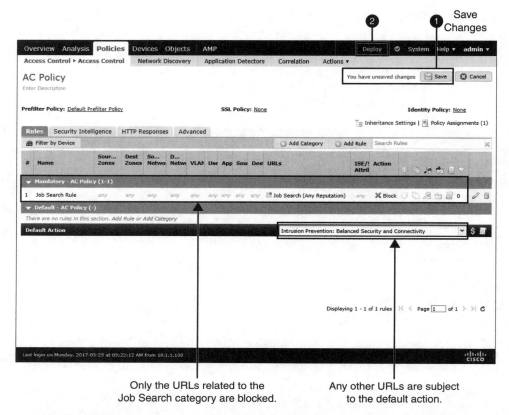

Figure 18-11 *Viewing a Simple URL Filtering Rule on the Access Control Policy Editor*

Verification and Troubleshooting Tools

To verify the actions of the access rule that you created in the previous section, select two URLs—one URL from the matching category, such as Job Search, and the other URL from any nonmatching category. If an access rule with a URL condition is operational, it only blocks the Job Search–related URLs, while the default action allows any other URL categories.

Attempt to visit the following websites and notice the result in each case:

- google.com (a general search engine)

- careerbuilder.com (a job search engine)

- dice.com (a job search engine)

Figure 18-12 shows the blocking of both job search engines, dice.com and careerbuilder.com. However, because of the default action, FTD does not block the general search engine google.com.

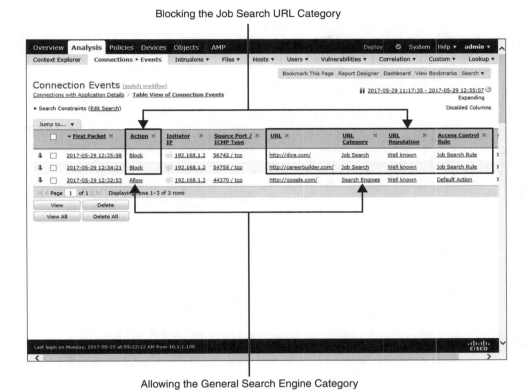

Figure 18-12 shows the blocking of both job search engines, dice.com and

Blocking the Job Search URL Category

Allowing the General Search Engine Category

Figure 18-12 *Access Rule with URL Filtering Conditions Blocking Desired Connections*

You can also debug the actions in an FTD device and analyze the **firewall-engine-debug** messages for troubleshooting purposes.

Example 18-1 shows the **firewall-engine-debug** messages when FTD allows you access to a general search engine, such as google.com. The debug message shows that FTD can perform a URL lookup successfully, but the URL itself does not match with a URL Filtering condition. The default action allows the URL.

Example 18-1   *Debug Messages by an Access Rule with a URL Condition (Action: Allow)*

```
> system support firewall-engine-debug

Please specify an IP protocol:
Please specify a client IP address: 192.168.1.2
Please specify a client port:
Please specify a server IP address:
Please specify a server port:
Monitoring firewall engine debug messages


192.168.1.2-44374 > XX.XX.XX.XX-80 6 AS 4 I 1 New session
192.168.1.2-44374 > XX.XX.XX.XX-80 6 AS 4 I 1 Starting with minimum 2, 'Job Search
  Rule', and SrcZone first with zones -1 -> -1, geo 0(0) -> 0, vlan 0, sgt tag:
  untagged, svc 0, payload 0, client 0, misc 0, user 9999997, url , xff
192.168.1.2-44374 > XX.XX.XX.XX-80 6 AS 4 I 1 pending rule order 2, 'Job Search
  Rule', URL
192.168.1.2-44374 > XX.XX.XX.XX-80 6 AS 4 I 1 Starting with minimum 2, 'Job Search
  Rule', and SrcZone first with zones -1 -> -1, geo 0(0) -> 0, vlan 0, sgt tag:
  untagged, svc 0, payload 0, client 0, misc 0, user 9999997, url , xff
192.168.1.2-44374 > XX.XX.XX.XX-80 6 AS 4 I 1 pending rule order 2, 'Job Search
  Rule', URL
192.168.1.2-44374 > XX.XX.XX.XX-80 6 AS 4 I 1 Starting with minimum 2, 'Job Search
  Rule', and SrcZone first with zones -1 -> -1, geo 0(0) -> 0, vlan 0, sgt tag:
  untagged, svc 0, payload 0, client 0, misc 0, user 9999997, url , xff
192.168.1.2-44374 > XX.XX.XX.XX-80 6 AS 4 I 1 pending rule order 2, 'Job Search
  Rule', URL
192.168.1.2-44374 > XX.XX.XX.XX-80 6 AS 4 I 1 URL SI:
  ShmDBLookupURL("http://google.com/") returned 0
192.168.1.2-44374 > XX.XX.XX.XX-80 6 AS 4 I 1 Starting with minimum 2, 'Job Search
  Rule', and SrcZone first with zones -1 -> -1, geo 0(0) -> 0, vlan 0, sgt tag:
  untagged, svc 676, payload 184, client 638, misc 0, user 9999997, url
  http://google.com/, xff
192.168.1.2-44374 > XX.XX.XX.XX-80 6 AS 4 I 1: DataMessaging_GetURLData: Returning
  URL_BCTYPE for google.com
192.168.1.2-44374 > XX.XX.XX.XX-80 6 AS 4 I 1 rule order 2, 'Job Search Rule', URL
  Lookup Success: http://google.com/ waited: 0ms
192.168.1.2-44374 > XX.XX.XX.XX-80 6 AS 4 I 1 no match rule order 2, 'Job Search
  Rule', url=(http://google.com/) c=50 r=81
192.168.1.2-44374 > XX.XX.XX.XX-80 6 AS 4 I 1 match rule order 3, id 268435458
  action Allow
192.168.1.2-44374 > XX.XX.XX.XX-80 6 AS 4 I 1 allow action
192.168.1.2-44374 > XX.XX.XX.XX-80 6 AS 4 I 1 Deleting session
```

Example 18-2 shows the **firewall-engine-debug** messages when FTD denies you access
to a job search engine, such as dice.com. The debug message confirms that FTD is able to
perform a URL lookup successfully, but the URL itself is blocked due to a matching
condition in the job search rule access rule.

Example 18-2   *Debug Messages by an Access Rule with a URL Condition (Action: Block)*

```
> system support firewall-engine-debug


Please specify an IP protocol:
Please specify a client IP address: 192.168.1.2
Please specify a client port:
Please specify a server IP address:
Please specify a server port:
Monitoring firewall engine debug messages


192.168.1.2-56742 > XX.XX.XX.XX-80 6 AS 4 I 0 New session

192.168.1.2-56742 > XX.XX.XX.XX-80 6 AS 4 I 0 Starting with minimum 2, 'Job Search
  Rule', and SrcZone first with zones -1 -> -1, geo 0(0) -> 0, vlan 0, sgt tag:
  untagged, svc 0, payload 0, client 0, misc 0, user 9999997, url , xff

192.168.1.2-56742 > XX.XX.XX.XX-80 6 AS 4 I 0 pending rule order 2, 'Job Search
  Rule', URL

192.168.1.2-56742 > XX.XX.XX.XX-80 6 AS 4 I 0 Starting with minimum 2, 'Job Search
  Rule', and SrcZone first with zones -1 -> -1, geo 0(0) -> 0, vlan 0, sgt tag:
  untagged, svc 0, payload 0, client 0, misc 0, user 9999997, url , xff

192.168.1.2-56742 > XX.XX.XX.XX-80 6 AS 4 I 0 pending rule order 2, 'Job Search
  Rule', URL

192.168.1.2-56742 > XX.XX.XX.XX-80 6 AS 4 I 0 Starting with minimum 2, 'Job Search
  Rule', and SrcZone first with zones -1 -> -1, geo 0(0) -> 0, vlan 0, sgt tag:
  untagged, svc 0, payload 0, client 0, misc 0, user 9999997, url , xff

192.168.1.2-56742 > XX.XX.XX.XX-80 6 AS 4 I 0 pending rule order 2, 'Job Search
  Rule', URL

192.168.1.2-56742 > XX.XX.XX.XX-80 6 AS 4 I 0 URL SI:
  ShmDBLookupURL("http://dice.com/") returned 0

192.168.1.2-56742 > XX.XX.XX.XX-80 6 AS 4 I 0 Starting with minimum 2, 'Job Search
  Rule', and SrcZone first with zones -1 -> -1, geo 0(0) -> 0, vlan 0, sgt tag:
  untagged, svc 676, payload 0, client 638, misc 0, user 9999997, url
  http://dice.com/, xff

192.168.1.2-56742 > XX.XX.XX.XX-80 6 AS 4 I 0: DataMessaging_GetURLData: Returning
  URL_BCTYPE for dice.com

192.168.1.2-56742 > XX.XX.XX.XX-80 6 AS 4 I 0 rule order 2, 'Job Search Rule', URL
  Lookup Success: http://dice.com/ waited: 0ms

192.168.1.2-56742 > XX.XX.XX.XX-80 6 AS 4 I 0 rule order 2, 'Job Search Rule', URL
  http://dice.com/ Matched Category: 26:96 waited: 0ms

192.168.1.2-56742 > XX.XX.XX.XX-80 6 AS 4 I 0 match rule order 2, 'Job Search Rule',
  action Block

192.168.1.2-56742 > XX.XX.XX.XX-80 6 AS 4 I 0 deny action

192.168.1.2-56742 > XX.XX.XX.XX-80 6 AS 4 I 0 Deleting session
```

Allowing a Specific URL

If you do not want FTD to block a particular URL along with the other URLs that are in
the same category, you can override the default reputation score of that URL. To accomplish this, you just need to add a separate access rule with the Allow action.

Configuring FTD to Allow a Specific URL

The following steps describe how to create an access rule to allow a certain URL:

Step 1.   Go to **Objects > Object Management** and create an object of type URL. Figure 18-13 shows the workflow to create a new URL object. In this example, the URL-Object-for-Dice.com custom object represents the dice.com site.

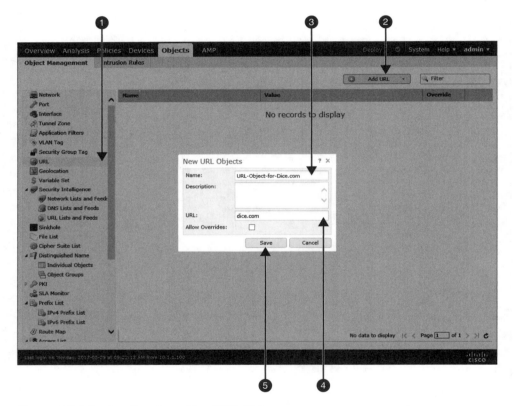

Figure 18-13   *Configuring a New URL Object*

Step 2.   Once a URL object is created, create a new access rule to allow this URL object. Figure 18-14 shows an access rule that allows the URL-Object-for-Dice.com object. Note that the job search whitelist rule is placed above the existing rule #1. The custom URL object is located under the URLs subtab.

Note   Because an FTD device analyzes rules top to bottom, a whitelist rule must be positioned above a block rule. You can define the position as you add the rule. Alternatively, after adding a rule, you can go to the access control policy editor page to drag a rule to a desired position.

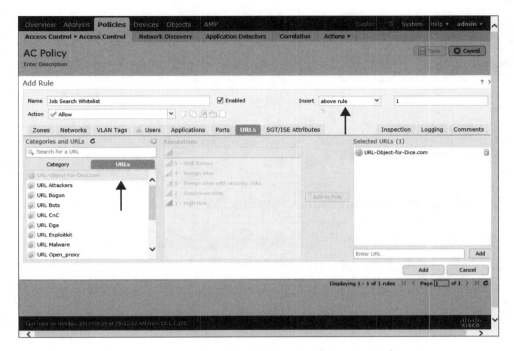

Figure 18-14 *Adding an Access Rule to Allow/Whitelist a Desired URL*

Step 3.   Optionally, go to the Logging tab and enable Log at Beginning of Connection. This optional step allows an FTD to generate events due to any matching URL Filtering condition.

Step 4.   Click the **Add** button to complete the creation of the access rule. The browser returns to the access control policy editor page.

Figure 18-15 shows all the access rules on a policy editor page. The rule that allows/whitelists your desired URL is positioned above the rule that blocks the entire Job Search category. This page allows you to drag a rule and place it in a different order.

Step 5.   Click **Save** to save the changes in the access control policy, and click **Deploy** to deploy the policy to your FTD device.

FTD analyzes rules top to bottom, and an
Allow rule must be above a Block rule for early analysis.

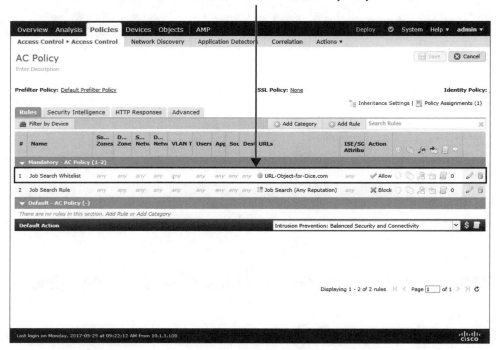

Figure 18-15 *Access Control Policy Editor Page Showing a Summary of the Access Rules*

Verification and Troubleshooting Tools

To verify the operation of the Allow action, perform the same test that you did in the previous section: Attempt to visit three search engines. This time, FTD should allow your access to dice.com, although this is a job search engine. However, FTD should continue blocking access to other job search engines, such as careerbuilder.com. Any URL categories except Job Search are allowed.

Attempt to visit the same three websites once again and notice the difference:

Figure 18-16 shows that dice.com is now allowed, while the careerbuilder.com site remains blocked. Because of the default action on the access control policy, FTD allows the general search engine google.com.

You can use the **firewall-engine-debug** tool to debug the whitelisting actions. The debugging messages are helpful for troubleshooting purposes.

This connection is allowed; only dice.com is allowed via a custom URL object.

The field is blank because the traffic was not evaluated by a rule that had to perform a URL category lookup.

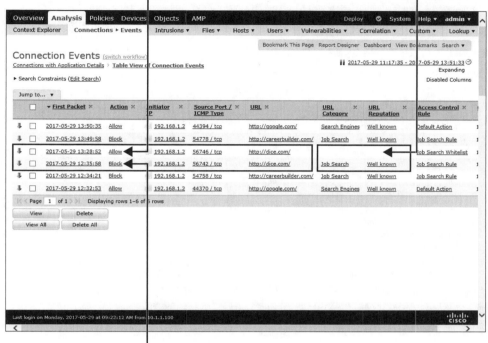

This connection is blocked because all the URLs in the Job Search category are blocked.

Figure 18-16   *Whitelisting a URL by Using the Allow Action*

Example 18-3 shows the **firewall-engine-debug** messages when FTD allows you to access the whitelisted URL dice.com.

Example 18-3   *Debugging Messages When Access to Dice.com Is Whitelisted/Allowed*

```
> system support firewall-engine-debug


Please specify an IP protocol:
Please specify a client IP address: 192.168.1.2
Please specify a client port:
Please specify a server IP address:
Please specify a server port:
Monitoring firewall engine debug messages
```

```
192.168.1.2-56746 > XX.XX.XX.XX-80 6 AS 4 I 0 New session
192.168.1.2-56746 > XX.XX.XX.XX-80 6 AS 4 I 0 Starting with minimum 2, 'Job Search
  Whitelist', and SrcZone first with zones -1 -> -1, geo 0(0) -> 0, vlan 0, sgt tag:
  untagged, svc 0, payload 0, client 0, misc 0, user 9999997, url , xff
192.168.1.2-56746 > XX.XX.XX.XX-80 6 AS 4 I 0 pending rule order 2, 'Job Search
  Whitelist', URL
192.168.1.2-56746 > XX.XX.XX.XX-80 6 AS 4 I 0 Starting with minimum 2, 'Job Search
  Whitelist', and SrcZone first with zones -1 -> -1, geo 0(0) -> 0, vlan 0, sgt tag:
  untagged, svc 0, payload 0, client 0, misc 0, user 9999997, url , xff
192.168.1.2-56746 > XX.XX.XX.XX-80 6 AS 4 I 0 pending rule order 2, 'Job Search
  Whitelist', URL
192.168.1.2-56746 > XX.XX.XX.XX-80 6 AS 4 I 0 Starting with minimum 2, 'Job Search
  Whitelist', and SrcZone first with zones -1 -> -1, geo 0(0) -> 0, vlan 0, sgt tag:
  untagged, svc 0, payload 0, client 0, misc 0, user 9999997, url , xff
192.168.1.2-56746 > XX.XX.XX.XX-80 6 AS 4 I 0 pending rule order 2, 'Job Search
  Whitelist', URL
192.168.1.2-56746 > XX.XX.XX.XX-80 6 AS 4 I 0 URL SI:
  ShmDBLookupURL("http://dice.com/") returned 0
192.168.1.2-56746 > XX.XX.XX.XX-80 6 AS 4 I 0 Starting with minimum 2, 'Job Search
  Whitelist', and SrcZone first with zones -1 -> -1, geo 0(0) -> 0, vlan 0, sgt tag:
  untagged, svc 676, payload 0, client 638, misc 0, user 9999997, url
  http://dice.com/, xff
192.168.1.2-56746 > XX.XX.XX.XX-80 6 AS 4 I 0 match rule order 2, 'Job Search
  Whitelist', action Allow
192.168.1.2-56746 > XX.XX.XX.XX-80 6 AS 4 I 0 allow action
192.168.1.2-56746 > XX.XX.XX.XX-80 6 AS 4 I 0 Deleting session
```

Example 18-4 shows the **firewall-engine-debug** messages when FTD denies you access to a job search engine, such as careerbuilder.com. The debugging messages confirm that FTD is able to perform a URL lookup successfully, but the URL itself is blocked due to a matching condition in the job search rule access rule.

Example 18-4   *Debugging Messages When Access to careerbuilder.com Is Blocked*

```
> system support firewall-engine-debug


Please specify an IP protocol:
Please specify a client IP address: 192.168.1.2
Please specify a client port:
Please specify a server IP address:
Please specify a server port:
Monitoring firewall engine debug messages
192.168.1.2-54772 > XX.XX.XX.XX-80 6 AS 4 I 1 New session
192.168.1.2-54772 > XX.XX.XX.XX-80 6 AS 4 I 1 Starting with minimum 2, 'Job Search
  Whitelist', and SrcZone first with zones -1 -> -1, geo 0(0) -> 0, vlan 0, sgt tag:
  untagged, svc 0, payload 0, client 0, misc 0, user 9999997, url , xff
```

```
192.168.1.2-54772 > XX.XX.XX.XX-80 6 AS 4 I 1 pending rule order 2, 'Job Search
    Whitelist', URL
192.168.1.2-54772 > XX.XX.XX.XX-80 6 AS 4 I 1 Starting with minimum 2, 'Job Search
    Whitelist', and SrcZone first with zones -1 -> -1, geo 0(0) -> 0, vlan 0, sgt tag:
    untagged, svc 0, payload 0, client 0, misc 0, user 9999997, url , xff
192.168.1.2-54772 > XX.XX.XX.XX-80 6 AS 4 I 1 pending rule order 2, 'Job Search
    Whitelist', URL
192.168.1.2-54772 > XX.XX.XX.XX-80 6 AS 4 I 1 Starting with minimum 2, 'Job Search
    Whitelist', and SrcZone first with zones -1 -> -1, geo 0(0) -> 0, vlan 0, sgt tag:
    untagged, svc 0, payload 0, client 0, misc 0, user 9999997, url , xff
192.168.1.2-54772 > XX.XX.XX.XX-80 6 AS 4 I 1 pending rule order 2, 'Job Search
    Whitelist', URL
192.168.1.2-54772 > XX.XX.XX.XX-80 6 AS 4 I 1 URL SI:
    ShmDBLookupURL("http://careerbuilder.com/") returned 0
192.168.1.2-54772 > XX.XX.XX.XX-80 6 AS 4 I 1 Starting with minimum 2, 'Job Search
    Whitelist', and SrcZone first with zones -1 -> -1, geo 0(0) -> 0, vlan 0, sgt tag:
    untagged, svc 676, payload 1491, client 638, misc 0, user 9999997, url
    http://careerbuilder.com/, xff
192.168.1.2-54772 > XX.XX.XX.XX-80 6 AS 4 I 1 no match rule order 2, 'Job Search
    Whitelist', url=(http://careerbuilder.com/) c=0 r=0
192.168.1.2-54772 > XX.XX.XX.XX-80 6 AS 4 I 1: DataMessaging_GetURLData: Returning
    URL_BCTYPE for careerbuilder.com
192.168.1.2-54772 > XX.XX.XX.XX-80 6 AS 4 I 1 rule order 3, 'Job Search Rule', URL
    Lookup Success: http://careerbuilder.com/ waited: 0ms
192.168.1.2-54772 > XX.XX.XX.XX-80 6 AS 4 I 1 rule order 3, 'Job Search Rule', URL
    http://careerbuilder.com/ Matched Category: 26:92 waited: 0ms
192.168.1.2-54772 > XX.XX.XX.XX-80 6 AS 4 I 1 match rule order 3, 'Job Search Rule',
    action Block
192.168.1.2-54772 > XX.XX.XX.XX-80 6 AS 4 I 1 deny action
192.168.1.2-54772 > XX.XX.XX.XX-80 6 AS 4 I 1 Deleting session
```

Querying the Cloud for Uncategorized URLs

In most cases, FTD resolves a URL into its category and reputation the first time it sees the web request. If FTD is unable to resolve a URL, it forwards the query to the FMC. The FMC performs a lookup on its own URL database. Because the FMC typically has a larger URL dataset than FTD, it should be able to resolve most of the URLs.

If you enter a new and uncommon URL, the FMC may be unable to resolve the category by looking up its local database. In such a case, it can send the query to the Cisco CSI cloud. If the cloud lookup times out, or if the query to the CSI is disabled due to privacy concerns, the FMC places the unknown URL into the Uncategorized group.

Warning When a host attempts to connect an uncategorized URL, FTD does not match a connection against an access rule that uses the URL Filtering condition.

Figure 18-17 illustrates the reason for receiving an uncategorized URL event. When the FMC is unable to query an unknown URL to the cloud, it marks that URL as Uncategorized.

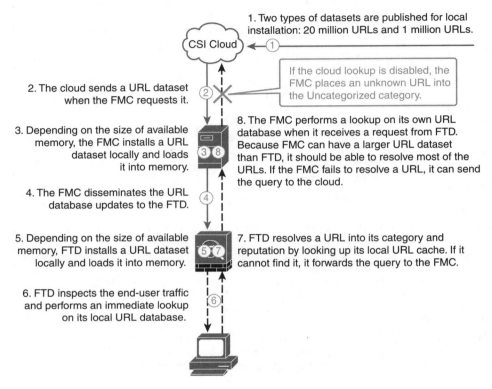

Figure 18-17   *Workflow of an Uncategorized URL Event*

Configuring FMC to Perform a Query

To allow the FMC to perform a cloud lookup for unknown URLs, follow these steps:

Step 1.   Go to **System > Integration > Cisco CSI**.

Step 2.   Enable the Query Cisco CSI for Unknown URLs option.

Step 3.   Save the changes.

Figure 18-18 shows the configuration page to enable cloud lookup for unknown URLs.

Figure 18-18   *Enabling Cloud Lookup for Unknown URLs*

While resolving a URL category, FTD does not let the uncategorized traffic pass until the URL lookup is complete or a lookup process times out, whichever comes first. If the volume of uncategorized traffic grows, FTD keeps holding the traffic in memory. FTD considers a URL uncategorized until an appropriate category is determined during a cloud lookup. FTD allows the initial flows, but for subsequent connections, it continues to look up that URL with the hope of resolving and caching it.

This behavior, however, can lead to performance degradation. To avoid this situation, you can let an FTD device pass traffic immediately whenever a URL appears uncached and the URL category cannot be determined locally. The following steps show how to disable a retry when a local cache fails the first lookup:

Step 1.   Go to **Policies > Access Control > Access Control** and edit the access control policy that is deployed on your FTD device.

Step 2.   In the access control policy editor page that appears, select the **Advanced** tab.

Step 3.   Select the pencil icon next to General Settings. The General Settings configuration window appears.

Step 4.   Disable the **Retry URL Cache Miss Lookup** option and click **OK** to return to the access control policy editor page.

Step 5.   Click **Save** to save the changes and click **Deploy** to redeploy the policy to your FTD device.

Figure 18-19 shows an advanced setting in an access control policy that allows an FTD device to pass uncategorized traffic immediately, without holding it for continuous cloud lookups.

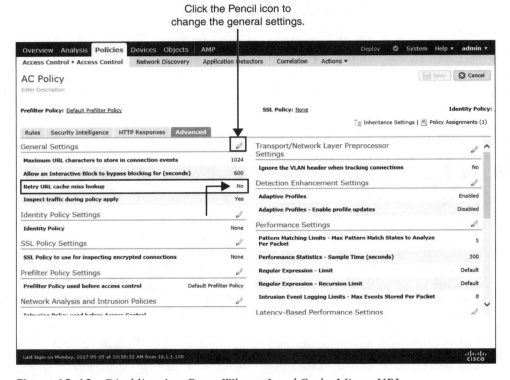

Figure 18-19   *Disabling Any Retry When a Local Cache Misses URLs*

Verification and Troubleshooting Tools

Find a URL that is new or unknown and try to access it. If the URL is found uncategorized, the default action of the access control policy should allow you access to that URL.

Figure 18-20 shows a connection event for accessing nazmulrajib.com. The URL category is marked as Uncategorized.

The URL category is Uncategorized.

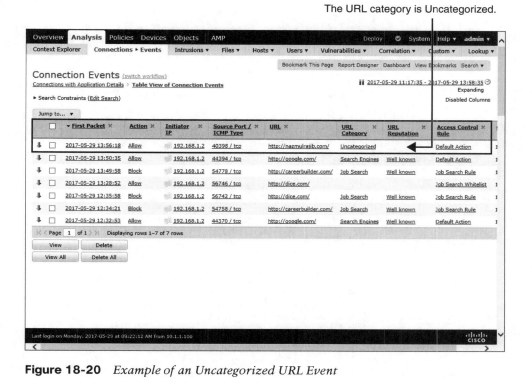

Figure 18-20   *Example of an Uncategorized URL Event*

Example 18-5 displays the debugging messages that result from connecting to the
unknown URL nazmulrajib.com. First, the FTD device performs a lookup on its local
shared memory (see the keyword **ShmDBLookupURL** in the example). Then it attempts
to query the cloud (see the keyword **useVendorService**). Because the cloud lookup is disabled in this example (see the keyword **feature not set**), the URL lookup eventually fails.

Example 18-5   *Debugging a Connection to an Uncategorized URL*

```
> system support firewall-engine-debug


Please specify an IP protocol:
Please specify a client IP address: 192.168.1.2
Please specify a client port:
Please specify a server IP address:
Please specify a server port:
Monitoring firewall engine debug messages
```

```
192.168.1.2-40398 > XX.XX.XX.XX-80 6 AS 4 I 0 New session
192.168.1.2-40398 > XX.XX.XX.XX-80 6 AS 4 I 0 Starting with minimum 2, 'Job Search
  Whitelist', and SrcZone first with zones -1 -> -1, geo 0(0) -> 0, vlan 0, sgt tag:
  untagged, svc 0, payload 0, client 0, misc 0, user 9999997, url , xff
192.168.1.2-40398 > XX.XX.XX.XX-80 6 AS 4 I 0 pending rule order 2, 'Job Search
  Whitelist', URL
192.168.1.2-40398 > XX.XX.XX.XX-80 6 AS 4 I 0 Starting with minimum 2, 'Job Search
  Whitelist', and SrcZone first with zones -1 -> -1, geo 0(0) -> 0, vlan 0, sgt tag:
  untagged, svc 0, payload 0, client 0, misc 0, user 9999997, url , xff
192.168.1.2-40398 > XX.XX.XX.XX-80 6 AS 4 I 0 pending rule order 2, 'Job Search
  Whitelist', URL
192.168.1.2-40398 > XX.XX.XX.XX-80 6 AS 4 I 0 Starting with minimum 2, 'Job Search
  Whitelist', and SrcZone first with zones -1 -> -1, geo 0(0) -> 0, vlan 0, sgt tag:
  untagged, svc 0, payload 0, client 0, misc 0, user 9999997, url , xff
192.168.1.2-40398 > XX.XX.XX.XX-80 6 AS 4 I 0 pending rule order 2, 'Job Search
  Whitelist', URL
192.168.1.2-40398 > XX.XX.XX.XX-80 6 AS 4 I 0 URL SI:
  ShmDBLookupURL("http://nazmulrajib.com/") returned 0
192.168.1.2-40398 > XX.XX.XX.XX-80 6 AS 4 I 0 Starting with minimum 2,
  'Job Search Whitelist', and SrcZone first with zones -1 -> -1, geo 0(0) -> 0,
  vlan 0, sgt tag: untagged, svc 676, payload 0, client 638, misc 0, user 9999997,
  url http://nazmulrajib.com/, xff
192.168.1.2-40398 > XX.XX.XX.XX-80 6 AS 4 I 0 no match rule order 2, 'Job Search
  Whitelist', url=(http://nazmulrajib.com/) c=0 r=0
192.168.1.2-40398 > XX.XX.XX.XX-80 6 AS 4 I 0: DataMessaging_GetURLData:
  useVendorService_feature not set, returning URL_FAILEDTYPE
192.168.1.2-40398 > XX.XX.XX.XX-80 6 AS 4 I 0 rule order 3, 'Job Search Rule',
  URL Lookup Failed: http://nazmulrajib.com/ waited: 0ms
192.168.1.2-40398 > XX.XX.XX.XX-80 6 AS 4 I 0 no match rule order 3, 'Job Search
  Rule', url=(http://nazmulrajib.com/) c=65534 r=0
192.168.1.2-40398 > XX.XX.XX.XX-80 6 AS 4 I 0 match rule order 4, id 268435458
  action Allow
192.168.1.2-40398 > XX.XX.XX.XX-80 6 AS 4 I 0 allow action
192.168.1.2-40398 > XX.XX.XX.XX-80 6 AS 4 I 0 Deleting session
```

If the Firepower System can't categorize a URL, there are a couple items you can check on both the FMC and FTD:

Step 1.   Verify whether the FMC is updated with the latest URL database.

Example 18-6 shows two types of URL database files on the FMC file system. The full_bcdb_rep_1m_5.174.bin file is smaller and applied to an FTD device for an immediate URL lookup. It is 22 MB in size and has approximately 1 million URLs. The larger database file, full_bcdb_rep_5.174.bin, is used by the FMC when FTD misses a URL lookup.

Example 18-6   *Two Types of URL Datasets Available on an FMC*

```
admin@FMC:~$ ls -halp /var/sf/cloud_download/
total 450M
drwxr-xr-x  3 www   www   4.0K Apr 28 23:18 ./
drwxr-xr-x 64 root  root  4.0K Apr 28 02:20 ../
-rw-r--r--  1 root  root    78 Apr 28 23:18 cloudagent_dlupdate_health
-rw-r--r--  1 root  root   22M Apr 28 16:24 full_bcdb_rep_1m_5.174.bin
-rw-r--r--  1 root  root  429M Apr 28 16:24 full_bcdb_rep_5.174.bin
-rw-r--r--  1 www   www   5.4K Aug 26  2016 sfrep_catg
-rw-r--r--  1 www   www    433 Aug 26  2016 sfrep_index
drwxr-xr-x  2 www   www   4.0K Apr 28 23:52 tmp/
admin@FMC:~$
```

If you do not see an up-to-date file, you should check whether the automatic update of the URL database is enabled. If it is enabled, verify whether the latest update attempt was successful. You can view the urldb_log file to determine the status of the URL database update. To view it, run the following command on the FMC:

```
admin@FMC:~$ cat /var/log/urldb_log
```

The urldb_log file can contain the following keywords:

- **Successfully downloaded:** This message confirms that the FMC was able to download the latest database update. Along with this message, you should also find the name of the update file, as in this example:

```
Successfully downloaded, applied and moved, full_bcdb_rep_5.174.bin,...
Success, called perl transaction,
```

- **Up to date:** This message confirms that there is no new update available on the cloud since the database on the FMC was updated last time.

- **Download failed:** This message indicates that an attempt to download a URL database file failed.

Step 2.   Determine whether the current URL dataset on the FTD device is derived from the latest URL database on the FMC. Example 18-7 confirms that the FTD device can obtain a smaller version of the latest URL dataset from the FMC.

Example 18-7   *FTD Downloading a Subset of the URL Database from the FMC*

```
admin@FTD:~$ ls -halp /var/sf/cloud_download/
total 22M
drwxr-xr-x  3 www   www  4.0K Apr 28 22:01 ./
drwxr-xr-x 66 root  root 4.0K Dec 12 00:19 ../
-rw-r--r--  1 root  root   78 Sep 19  2016 cloudagent_dlupdate_health
-rw-r--r--  1 root  root  22M Apr 28 22:01 full_bcdb_rep_5.174.bin
-rw-r--r--  1 www   www  5.4K Aug 26  2016 sfrep_catg
-rw-r--r--  1 www   www   433 Aug 26  2016 sfrep_index
drwxr-xr-x  2 www   www  4.0K Apr 28 22:01 tmp/
admin@FTD:~$
```

Step 3.   Check whether the shared memory of FTD loaded with the latest URL data-set. Example 18-8 shows the URL database files on the shared memory of an FTD device. The timestamp on the file indicates that the FTD is loaded with the latest URL dataset.

Example 18-8   *Loading the Latest URL Dataset on FTD Memory*

```
admin@FTD:~$ ls -halp /dev/shm/ | grep -i bcdb
-rwxrwxrwx  1 root root  23M Apr  28 23:17 Global.bcdb1
-rwxrwxrwx  1 root root 6.1M Apr  28 23:17 Global.bcdb1acc
-rwxrwxrwx  1 root root 256K Apr  28 23:17 Global.bcdb1cacheinx
admin@FTD:~$
```

Summary

This chapter describes techniques to filter traffic based on the category and reputation of a URL. It illustrates how Firepower performs a URL lookup and how an FTD device takes an action based on the query result. This chapter explains the connection to a URL through debugging messages, which is critical for troubleshooting.

Quiz

1. Which of the following licenses is necessary to block a URL based on its category and reputation?

   a. Threat
   b. URL
   c. Malware
   d. Both A and B

2. Which of the following statements is true about the URL lookup?

   a. FTD, by itself, can resolve any URLs on the Internet within a millisecond.

   b. Only the FMC can resolve any URLs on the Internet within a millisecond.

   c. Neither the FMC nor FTD can resolve all the URLs on the Internet.

   d. Both the FMC and FTD can resolve any URLs on the Internet independently.

3. Which of the following statements about URL database updates is true?

   a. New URLs are packaged in a binary file and downloadable from the Cisco website.

   b. A recurring scheduled task for URL database updates is required to update the URL database.

   c. The FMC communicates with CSI automatically every 30 minutes to check for a new update and downloads an update if available.

   d. All of the above.

4. Which of the following are true about uncategorized URLs?

   a. FTD can hold uncategorized traffic in the buffer if the URL lookup is pending.

   b. Connections associated with an uncategorized URL are not matched against an access rule if the rule uses a URL Filtering condition.

   c. Uncategorized URLs can be categorized if the FMC is able to communicate with CSI.

   d. All of the above.

Chapter 19

Discovering Network Applications and Controlling Application Traffic

The Firepower System can dynamically discover what applications are running in a network. It can also identify the host and user who are running a particular application. FTD can discover a network application with or without the help of any active scanner. FTD allows you to block certain traffic solely based on the type of an application a user might be running. This chapter describes how to configure network discovery policy to enable Application Visibility and Control (AVC) with Firepower.

Application Discovery Essentials

When you access a website, you interact with at least three types of applications: a browser on a client computer that originates the web communication, an underlying protocol that establishes the communication channel to the web, and the web contents for which you want to access a website. When an FTD device is configured and deployed properly, it is able to discover all three of these applications in a network. Moreover, it can categorize applications based on risk level, business relevance, content category, and so on.

Application Detectors

The Firepower System uses application detectors to identify the network applications running on a monitored network. The detection capability can vary, depending on the source of the detectors. There are mainly two sources for detectors:

■ **System-provided detectors:** The Firepower software, by default, comes with a set of application detectors. However, for a precise detection of the latest applications, you must update the Vulnerability Database (VDB).

The VDB contains the fingerprints of various applications, operating systems, and client software. It also keeps a record of the known vulnerabilities. When a Firepower system discovers an application, it can correlate the application with any known vulnerabilities to determine its impact within a network.

■ **User-created detectors:** You can create your own detectors based on patterns you notice on custom applications. The FMC provides full administrative control over your custom detectors, so that you can modify or disable them as necessary. Behind the scenes, it leverages OpenAppID—an open source application detection module.

> **Note**   When a host from a monitored network connects to a server in a nonmonitored network, the FMC infers the application protocol (on the nonmonitored network) by using the information on the client software (of the monitored network).

Table 19-1 shows the type of application detectors supported by Firepower. Except for the built-in internal detectors, you can activate or deactivate any types of detector, as necessary.

Table 19-1   *Types of Application Detector*

Type of Detector	Functions
Internal detector	Detects protocol, client, and web applications. Internal detectors are always on; they are built in within the software.
Client detector	Detects client traffic. It also helps to infer an application protocol on a nonmonitored network.
Web application detector	Detects traffic based on the contents in a payload of HTTP traffic.
Port-based application protocol detector	Detects traffic based on well-known ports.
Firepower-based application protocol detector	Detects traffic based on application fingerprints.
Custom application detector	Detects traffic based on user-defined patterns.

Figure 19-1 shows the application detector page on the FMC. To find this page, go to **Policies > Application Detectors**. You can search for any desired application to determine its coverage. For example, Figure 19-1 shows retrieval of 69 detectors that are related to Facebook. The total number of detectors can vary, depending on the VDB version running on the FMC.

Search for detectors that are
related to the Facebook application.

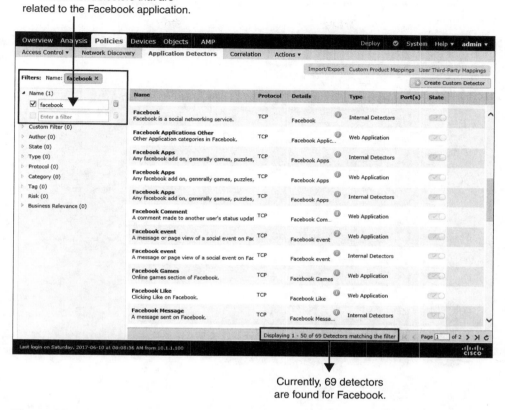

Currently, 69 detectors
are found for Facebook.

Figure 19-1   *The Application Detector Page on the FMC*

Operational Architecture

FTD can control an application when a monitored connection is established between
a client and server, and the application in a session is identified. To identify an
application, FTD has to analyze the first few packets in a session. Until the identification
is complete, FTD cannot apply an application rule. To ensure protection during the
analysis period, FTD inspects those early packets by using the default intrusion policy
of an active access control policy. Upon successful identification, FTD is able to act
on the rest of the session traffic based on the access rule created using an application
filtering condition. If a prefilter policy or an access control policy is configured to
block any particular traffic, FTD does not evaluate the traffic further against a network
discovery policy.

Figure 19-2 illustrates the operational workflow of the Firepower engine. It demonstrates that a connection is subject to Application Visibility and Control (AVC) only if it
passes the Security Intelligence inspection.

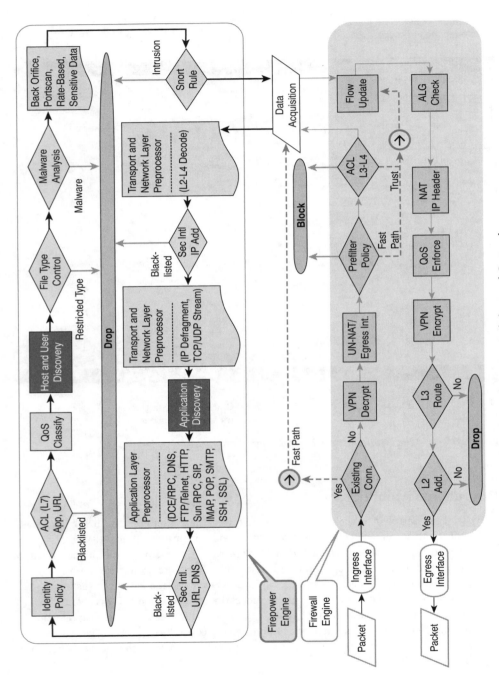

Figure 19-2 *Firepower Engine Workflow for Application Visibility and Control*

Best Practices for Network Discovery Configuration

FTD discovers a network passively; it does not directly affect the traffic flow. However, to ensure the performance of an FTD device, you should consider the following best practices when you enable network discovery:

> **Note**   Network discovery policy on a Firepower system consists of three functionalities: application discovery, host discovery, and user discovery. This chapter primarily focuses on discovery and control of network applications. You can also learn how to perform host discovery.

- Keep the VDB version up to date. Installing the latest version ensures the detection of the latest software with more precise version information.

- By default, the FMC comes with an application discovery rule, which uses 0.0.0.0/0 and ::/0 as the network address. This address enables a Firepower system to discover applications from any observed networks. Do not remove this default rule, as Snort leverages the application discovery data for intrusion detection and prevention by detecting the service metadata of a packet.

- When you add a custom rule for host and user discovery, include only the network addresses you own. Do not add the network address 0.0.0.0/0 and ::/0 to a host and user discovery rule, because doing so can deplete the host and user licenses quickly.

- Exclude the IP addresses of any NAT and load balancing devices from the list of monitored networks. These types of IP address can represent multiple computers running in a LAN, which leads an FTD device to generate excessive discovery events whenever there are activities in the LAN. Exclusion of NAT and load balancing IP addresses can improve the performance of FTD.

  Figure 19-3 shows the positions of two types of intermediate devices—a router and a load balancer—that can each represent multiple network hosts.

- You can also exclude any ports from monitoring if you are sure about the service a port might be running. Doing so reduces the number of discovery events for known ports and services.

- Avoid creating overlapping rules that include the same hosts multiple times to prevent performance degradation.

- Deploy the FTD device as close as possible to the hosts. The lower the hop count between an FTD device and a host, the faster the FTD device detects the host and with a higher confidence value.

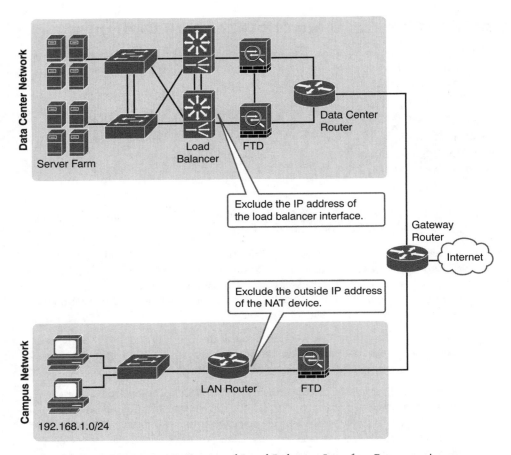

Figure 19-3   *NAT Device (Router) and Load Balancer Interface Representing Multiple Hosts*

Fulfilling Prerequisites

Before you begin configuring a network discovery rule, fulfill the following requirements:

■ The Firepower System uses the Adaptive Profiles option to perform application control. This option enhances detection capabilities of an FTD. The Adaptive Profile Updates option leverages the service metadata and helps an FTD determine whether a particular intrusion rule is pertinent to an application running on a particular host and whether the rule should be enabled.

By default, the Adaptive Profiles option is enabled (see Figure 19-4). You can verify the configuration status in the Advanced tab of an access control policy, under Detection Enhancement Settings.

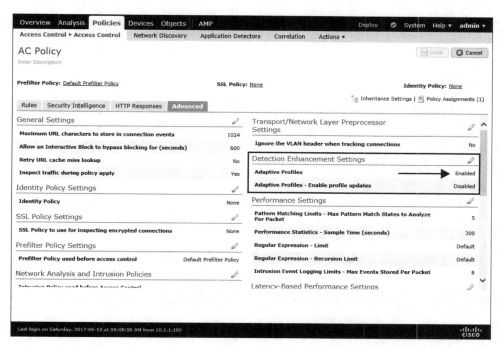

Figure 19-4 *Adaptive Profiles Setting for an Access Control Policy*

■ Create network objects for the network addresses that you want to add to a discovery rule. This helps you manage your configuration once you deploy a network discovery policy. To create an object, go to **Objects > Object Management** on the GUI. This page also enables you to modify the value of a custom object if necessary. However, you cannot modify a system-provided network object. To determine the type of an object, look at the rightmost column—a custom network object shows a pencil icon (see Figure 19-5), which you can select to modify the value of the object.

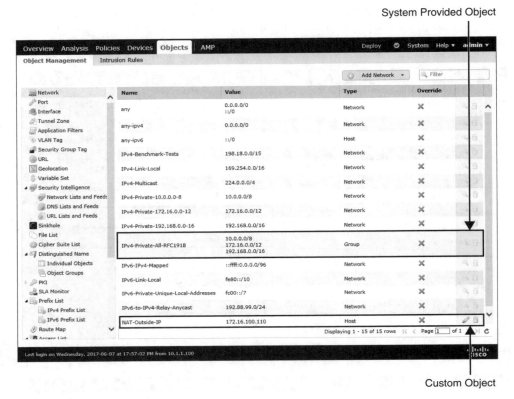

Figure 19-5   *Object Management Page*

Tip   The system also enables you to create an object on the fly directly from the rule editor window (see Figure 19-8, later in the chapter).

Discovering Applications

In the following sections, you will learn how to configure a network discovery policy to discover network applications as well as network hosts. To demonstrate the impact of an intermediate networking device representing multiple internal hosts, a router has been placed between the FTD device and the LAN switch in the topology.

Figure 19-6 shows the topology that is used in this chapter to demonstrate the configuration of a network discovery policy.

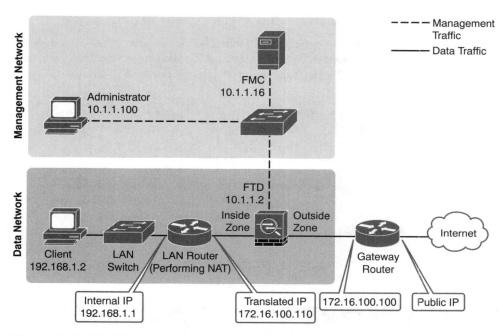

Figure 19-6 *Topology to Demonstrate the Operation of a Network Discovery Policy*

Configuring a Network Discovery Policy

To configure a network discovery policy, follow these steps:

Step 1.   In the FMC, navigate to **Policies > Network Discovery**. The default rule for application discovery appears (see Figure 19-7). It monitors traffic from any network to discover applications.

Figure 19-7 *Default Rule for a Network Discovery Policy*

Step 2.   Click the **Add Rule** button. The Add Rule window appears.

Step 3.   First, add a rule to exclude the IP address of any intermediate NAT and load balancing devices. To do that, select **Exclude** from the Action dropdown, and then select a network object that represents your desired IP address.

Tip   If you did not create a network object previously in the Fulfilling Prerequisites section, you can do it now on the fly using the green plus icon. Alternatively, you can add an IP address directly on the rule editor window.

Figure 19-8 shows a discovery rule that excludes a network object, NAT-Outside-IP. The object maps the IP address of the router's outside interface. The figure also highlights the available options to add an object or address on the fly.

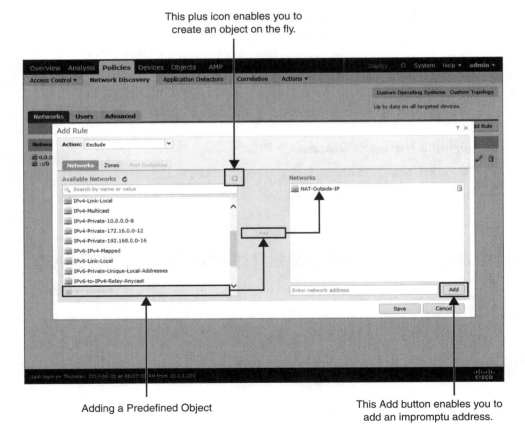

Adding a Predefined Object

This plus icon enables you to create an object on the fly.

This Add button enables you to add an impromptu address.

Figure 19-8   *Adding a Rule to Exclude a Network Object*

Step 4.   Click the **Save** button to return to the network discovery policy page.

Step 5.   Next, to include the network you want to monitor, click the **Add Rule** button again. The Add Rule window appears.

Step 6.   Select **Discover** from the Action dropdown, and then select a network object that represents your desired IP network.

Tip   If you want to monitor a private network, you can select one of the system-provided network objects.

Figure 19-9 shows a network discovery rule that can discover hosts and applications running on a network with private IP addresses (RFC 1918).

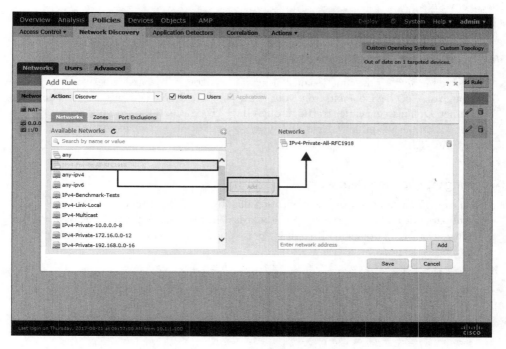

Figure 19-9   *Adding a Rule to Discover Hosts and Applications*

Step 7.   Click the **Save** button to return to the network discovery policy page, and then click the **Deploy** button to deploy the network discovery policy on your FTD device.

Figure 19-10 shows the two network discovery rules you have just created.

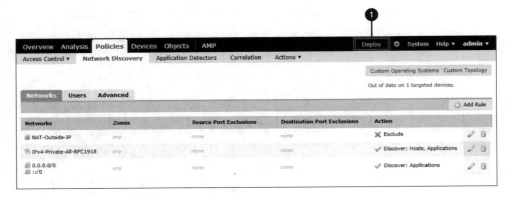

Figure 19-10   *A New Exclusion Rule, a Custom Discovery Rule, and the Default Discovery Rule*

Verification and Troubleshooting Tools

Now you can verify the functionality of network discovery by passing network traffic through an FTD device. First, from your client computers, go to various websites on the Internet. Doing so generates traffic through the FTD device. If the network discovery policy is properly configured and deployed, you will be able to view discovery events in the FMC GUI.

Analyzing Application Discovery

You can view a summary of the application data by using the Application Statistics dashboard, located at **Overview > Dashboards > Application Statistics**. The dashboard shows several data points in different widgets. You can add, remove, or modify any widgets, as desired.

Figure 19-11 shows six widgets in the Application Statistics dashboard. Each widget displays a unique statistic of the application running in a monitored network.

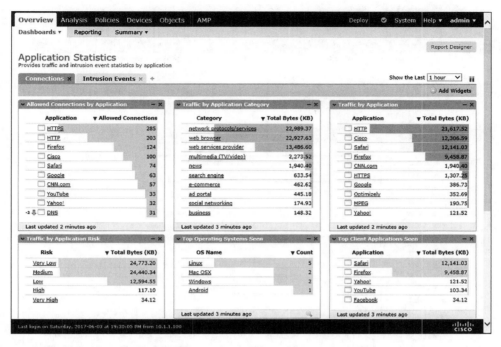

Figure 19-11   *Application Statistics Dashboard*

Figure 19-12 shows different types of discovery events. They are generated when a user connects an Apple Mac OS X to a network and opens a web browser, Safari. This figure also shows subsequent discoveries of various applications on the Mac.

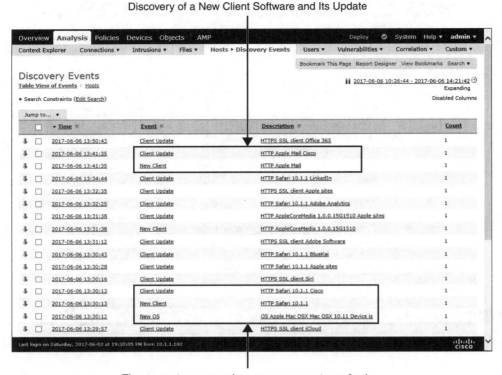

Figure 19-12   *Network Discovery Events*

Analyzing Host Discovery

You can view the operating systems running on a monitored network from the **Analysis > Hosts > Hosts** page. The Firepower System can identify most of the operating systems, along with their version detail. Click the Summary of the OS Versions to view the version information.

If some operating systems appear as *pending*, it is because FTD is currently analyzing the collected data or waiting on further packets to conclude. The *unknown* state indicates that the pattern of packets does not match an application detector. Updating the VDB to the latest version can reduce the number of unknown discovery events.

Figure 19-13 shows the name and version of operating systems running on a monitored network. It also shows examples of *unknown* and *pending* operating system.

Operating systems on some of the
hosts are not yet discovered.

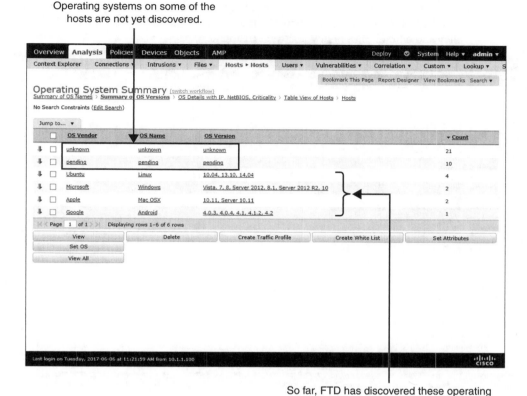

So far, FTD has discovered these operating
systems in a monitored network.

Figure 19-13   *Operating Systems on the Monitored Hosts*

Tip   Remember this best practice: The lower the hop count between an FTD device and
a host, the faster the FTD device detects the host and with a higher confidence value.
Moreover, additional intermediate devices between an FTD device and hosts can alter or
truncate important packet data. Therefore, you should deploy an FTD device as close as
possible to the monitored hosts.

Undiscovered New Hosts

If you find a new host undetected by your FTD device, you should check a couple items:

■ Check whether the FMC generates any health alerts for exceeding the host limits.
To receive an alert due to the oversubscription of host discovery, the health monitor
module for Host Limit must be enabled.

Figure 19-14 shows the option to enable a health module that can trigger an alert when the FMC exceeds its host limit. To find this page, go to **System > Health > Policy** and edit a health policy you want to apply.

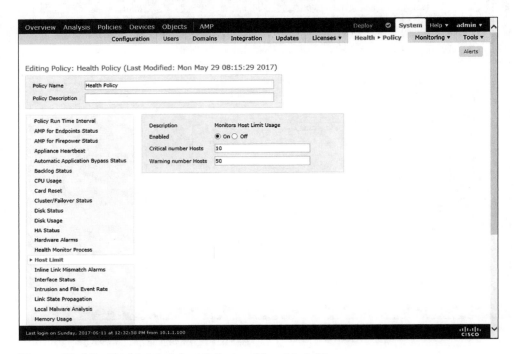

Figure 19-14   *Health Module to Monitor Host Limit Usage*

■ By analyzing the network map on the FMC, you can determine the number of unique hosts identified by a Firepower system and compare the number with the host limit for an FMC model. You can also recognize any hosts that might be representing multiple hosts, such as a router with NAT feature enabled or a load balancer. It helps you to select an IP address for exclusion.

Table 19-2 shows the maximum number of hosts the FMC can discover at any time.

Table 19-2   *FMC Limitation for Host Discovery*

FMC Model	Host Limit
FS 2000	150,000
FS 4000	600,000
Virtual	50,000

Note   As of this writing, Cisco supports additional FMC models, such as FS750, FS1500, and FS3500, which were designed prior to the Sourcefire acquisition. While this book uses the latest hardware models, you can still apply this knowledge on any legacy hardware models. For any specific information on the legacy hardware models, read the official user guide.

Figure 19-15 demonstrates that, although there are only 3 hosts in an internal network, FTD discovers more than 300 hosts in the external network within a few minutes. This discovery consumes additional resources and licenses from the Firepower System. To find this page, go to **Analysis > Hosts > Network Map**.

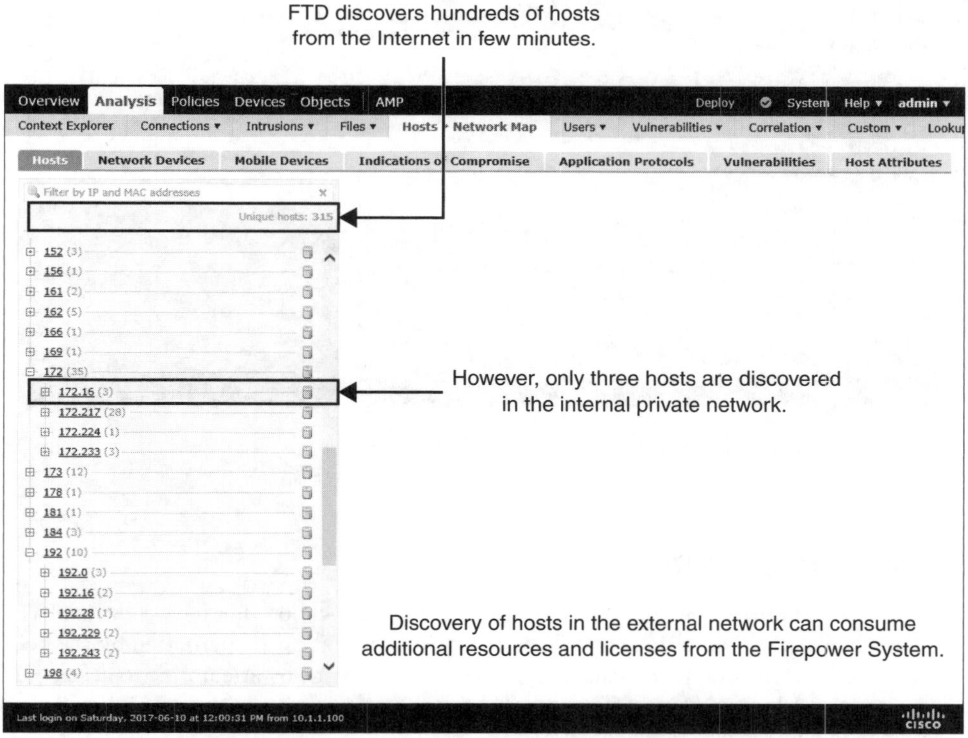

Figure 19-15   *A Network Map on the FMC Shows All of the Hosts an FTD Device Discovers*

■ Check how the network discovery policy is configured to handle a host when the FMC reaches the threshold for host limit. You can configure a policy to stop discovering any new hosts or to drop the earliest discoveries when the FMC reaches its limit.

Figure 19-16 shows the navigation to a dropdown where you can choose between dropping an old host and locking down any new entries.

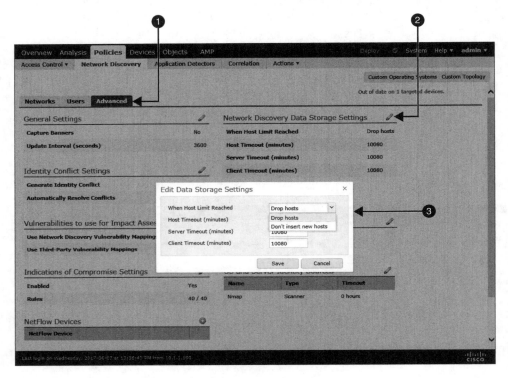

Figure 19-16   *Advanced Network Discovery Settings*

Blocking Applications

If an access control policy has no access rule with an application filtering condition, FTD allows any applications as long as connections to an application are permitted by the policy on the default action. You can verify this default behavior by attempting to access an application such as Facebook. However, if you want to restrict access to an application, you need to add an access rule for it.

Configuring Blocking of Applications

To block access to an application, you need to create an access rule by following these steps:

Step 1.   Navigate to **Policies > Access Control > Access Control**. A list of available access control policies appears.

Step 2. Use the pencil icon to edit the access control policy that you want to deploy on an FTD device. The access control policy editor page appears.

Step 3. Click the **Add Rule** button. The rule editor window appears.

Step 4. Give a name to the rule and select a desired action for the matched traffic.

Step 5. Select the **Applications** tab. A list of available application filters appears.

Figure 19-17 shows an access rule with an application filtering condition. FTD uses the rule to block a connection by sending reset packets whenever it detects an application in the Social Networking category.

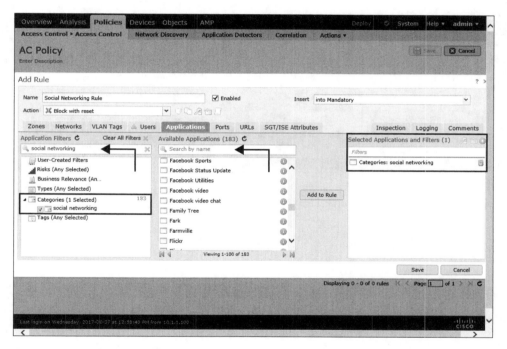

Figure 19-17 *Access Rule to Block Any Applications in the Social Networking Category*

Step 6. Use the search field in the Application Filter section to find a desired application category. You can select traffic based on categories, business relevance, risks, types, and so on. Alternatively, to find a specific application, you can just enter the application name in the search field in the Available Applications section.

Step 7. After you select the desired applications, add them to the rule.

Step 8. Go to the Logging tab to enable logging for any matching connections. This is an optional step, but it allows you to view an event when FTD blocks a connection.

Step 9. Click the **Save** button in the rule editor window to complete the creation of an access rule with an application filtering condition.

Figure 19-18 shows this new access rule, which blocks any applications that are related to the Social Networking category only. Any other applications are subject to the default action.

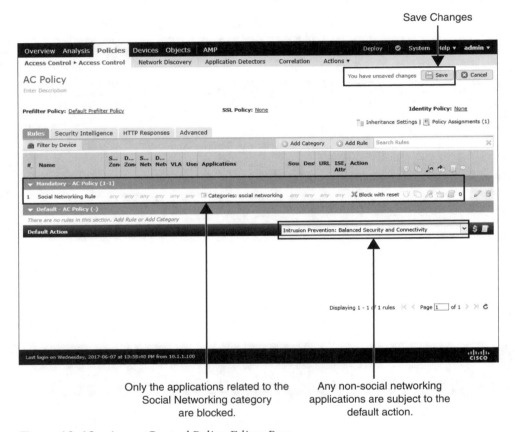

Only the applications related to the
Social Networking category
are blocked.

Any non-social networking
applications are subject to the
default action.

Figure 19-18 *Access Control Policy Editor Page*

Step 10. Finally, on the policy editor page, click **Save** to save the configurations, and click **Deploy** to deploy the policy on an FTD device.

Verification and Troubleshooting Tools

After deploying the policy that you created earlier in this chapter, in this section you'll try to access the Facebook application once again. This time the connection should be blocked.

Figure 19-19 shows two types of connections to the Facebook application. When a connection is allowed, it hits the default action. However, when the social networking rule finds a match, it inspects the connection and blocks with reset packets.

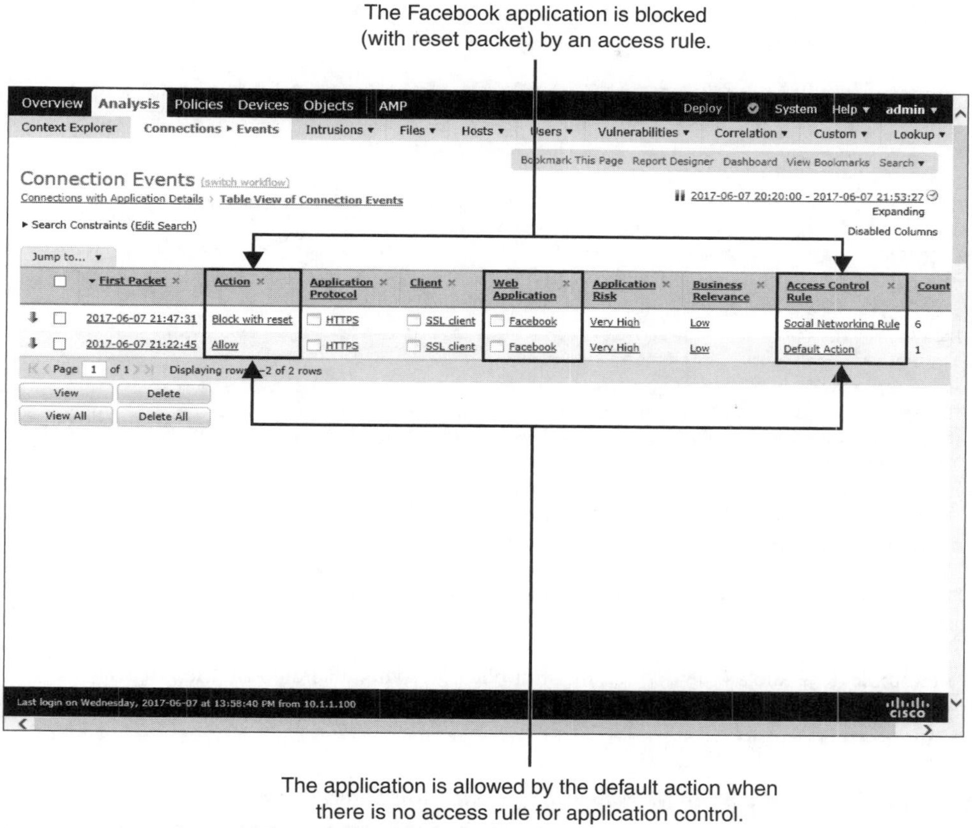

The Facebook application is blocked
(with reset packet) by an access rule.

The application is allowed by the default action when
there is no access rule for application control.

Figure 19-19   *Connection Events Displaying the Actions of Application Control*

Example 19-1 shows the debugging data generated by the firewall engine. It confirms that FTD is able to detect facebook.com and then applies the rule action to block with reset.

Example 19-1   *Debugging Messages Generated by the Firewall Engine*

```
> system support firewall-engine-debug

Please specify an IP protocol: tcp
Please specify a client IP address:
Please specify a client port:
Please specify a server IP address:
Please specify a server port:
Monitoring firewall engine debug messages
```

```
172.16.100.110-4677 > 31.13.65.36-443 6 AS 4 I 1 New session
172.16.100.110-4677 > 31.13.65.36-443 6 AS 4 I 1 Starting with minimum 2, 'Social
    Networking Rule', and SrcZone first with zones -1 -> -1, geo 0(0) -> 0, vlan 0,
    sgt tag: untagged, svc 0, payload 0, client 0, misc 0, user 9999997, url , xff
172.16.100.110-4677 > 31.13.65.36-443 6 AS 4 I 1 pending rule order 2,
    'Social Networking Rule', AppId
172.16.100.110-4677 > 31.13.65.36-443 6 AS 4 I 1 Starting with minimum 2, 'Social
    Networking Rule', and SrcZone first with zones -1 -> -1, geo 0(0) -> 0, vlan 0,
    sgt tag: untagged, svc 0, payload 0, client 0, misc 0, user 9999997, url , xff
172.16.100.110-4677 > 31.13.65.36-443 6 AS 4 I 1 pending rule order 2,
    'Social Networking Rule', AppId
172.16.100.110-4677 > 31.13.65.36-443 6 AS 4 I 1 Starting with minimum 2, 'Social
    Networking Rule', and SrcZone first with zones -1 -> -1, geo 0(0) -> 0, vlan 0,
    sgt tag: untagged, svc 0, payload 0, client 0, misc 0, user 9999997, url , xff
172.16.100.110-4677 > 31.13.65.36-443 6 AS 4 I 1 pending rule order 2,
    'Social Networking Rule', AppId
172.16.100.110-4677 > 31.13.65.36-443 6 AS 4 I 1 URL SI: ShmDBLookupURL
    ("www.facebook.com") returned 0
172.16.100.110-4677 > 31.13.65.36-443 6 AS 4 I 1 Starting with minimum 2, 'Social
    Networking Rule', and SrcZone first with zones -1 -> -1, geo 0(0) -> 0, vlan 0,
    sgt tag: untagged, svc 1122, payload 629, client 1296, misc 0, user 9999997, url
    www.facebook.com, xff
172.16.100.110-4677 > 31.13.65.36-443 6 AS 4 I 1 match rule order 2,
    'Social Networking Rule', action Reset
172.16.100.110-4677 > 31.13.65.36-443 6 AS 4 I 1 reset action
    172.16.100.110-4677 > 31.13.65.36-443 6 AS 4 I 1 Deleting session
```

Example 19-2 shows the debugging of application data generated by the Firepower engine. It displays the identification number (appID) of the application that is detected by the FTD device.

Example 19-2   *Debugging Messages for Application Identification*

```
> system support application-identification-debug

Please specify an IP protocol: tcp
Please specify a client IP address:
Please specify a client port:
Please specify a server IP address:
Please specify a server port:
Monitoring application identification debug messages
.
.
.
172.16.100.110-4677 -> 31.13.65.36-443 6 R AS 4 I 1 port service 0
172.16.100.110-4677 -> 31.13.65.36-443 6 AS 4 I 1 3rd party returned 847
172.16.100.110-4677 -> 31.13.65.36-443 6 AS 4 I 1 SSL is service 1122,
  portServiceAppId 1122
```

```
172.16.100.110-4677 -> 31.13.65.36-443 6 AS 4 I 1 ssl returned 10
172.16.100.110-4677 -> 31.13.65.36-443 6 AS 4 I 1 appId: 629
  (safe)search_support_type=NOT_A_SEARCH_ENGINE
^C
Caught interrupt signal
Exiting
```

Example 19-3 shows a query from the FMC database. It retrieves the mapping of the appID with an associated application name (appName). It confirms that the FTD device was able to identify the Facebook application correctly.

Example 19-3   *Mapping Application ID with an Application Name*

```
admin@FMC:~$ sudo OmniQuery.pl -db mdb -e "select appId,appName from appIdInfo where
  appId=629";
Password:
getting filenames from [/usr/local/sf/etc/db_updates/index]
getting filenames from [/usr/local/sf/etc/db_updates/base-6.1.0]


+-------+----------+
| appId | appName  |
+-------+----------+
| 629   | Facebook |
+-------+----------+


--------------------------
OmniQuery v2.1
(c) 2016 Cisco Systems, Inc.
.:|:.:|:.
--------------------------

mdb> exit
admin@FMC:~$
```

Summary

This chapter describes how the Firepower System can make you aware of the applications running on your network and empower you to control access to any unwanted applications. It also shows how to verify whether an FTD device can identify an application properly.

Quiz

1. Which of the following statements is true?

   a. A network discovery policy allows you to exclude network addresses but not any port numbers.

   b. You cannot determine the number of unique hosts identified by a Firepower system until it reaches the license limit.

   c. If a prefilter policy or an access control policy is configured to block any particular traffic, FTD does not evaluate the traffic further against a network discovery policy.

   d. All of the above.

2. Which of the following commands provides the ID for a discovered application?

   a. **system support app-id-debug**

   b. **system support firewall-debug**

   c. **system support firepower-engine-debug**

   d. **system support application-identification-debug**

3. Which of the following can affect the accuracy of network discovery?

   a. Snort rule database

   b. URL Filtering database

   c. Vulnerability Database

   d. Discovery event database

4. To improve the performance of network discovery, which of the following should you consider?

   a. Ensure that the network discovery policy is set to monitor the load balancer devices.

   b. Use the network address 0.0.0.0/0 and ::/0 in any discovery rules you create.

   c. Enable Firepower Recommendations in an intrusion policy.

   d. Keep the Vulnerability Database (VDB) version up to date.

Chapter 20

Controlling File Transfer and Blocking the Spread of Malware

As a security professional, you might not want your users to download and open random files from the Internet. While you allow your users to visit certain websites, you might want to block their attempts to download files from the sites they visit or to upload files to external websites. Unsafe downloads can spread viruses, malware, exploit kits, and other dangers on your network, and they can make the entire network vulnerable to various types of attacks. Likewise, to comply with the policy of your organization, you might not want your users to upload any particular types of files to the Internet from your corporate network.

The Firepower system enables you to block the download and upload of files based on file type (extension) and suspicious activity (malware).

File Policy Essentials

To govern the transfer of a file within a network, the Firepower System offers a standalone policy known as a *file policy*. A file policy allows you detect any file type, such as media files (.mp3, .mpeg), executable files (.exe, .rpm), and so on. In addition, an FTD device can analyze a file for potential malware when the file traverses a network. By design, FTD can detect and block files with a particular type before it performs lookups for malware.

Figure 20-1 shows an architectural diagram of the Firepower engine. The figure highlights both components of a file policy—file type control and malware analysis—which are described in the following sections.

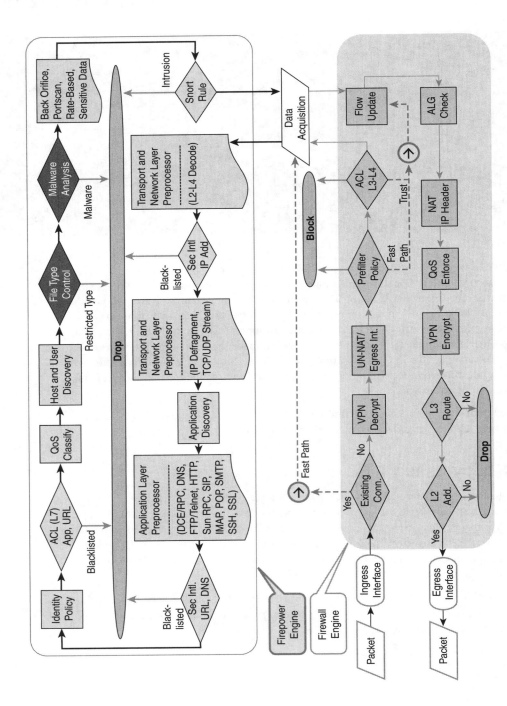

Figure 20-1 *Placement of the File Policy Components in the Firepower Architecture*

File Type Detection Technology

The Firepower System uses special metadata about a file, known as a magic number, to identify the file format. A magic number is a sequence of unique numbers that are encoded within files. When a file traverses a network, FTD can match the magic numbers from the stream of packets to determine the format of a file. For example, for a Microsoft executable (MSEXE) file, the magic number is 4D 5A. To find this number, Snort uses the following rule on FTD:

```
file type:MSEXE; id:21; category:Executables,Dynamic Analysis Capable,Local
Malware Analysis Capable; msg:"Windows/DOS executable file "; rev:1; content:
| 4D 5A|; offset:0;
```

Figure 20-2 demonstrates the magic number on a TCP packet. This packet is captured when a client downloads an executable file from a website. After completing the TCP three-way handshake, the server (172.16.100.100) sends this information to the client (192.168.1.200).

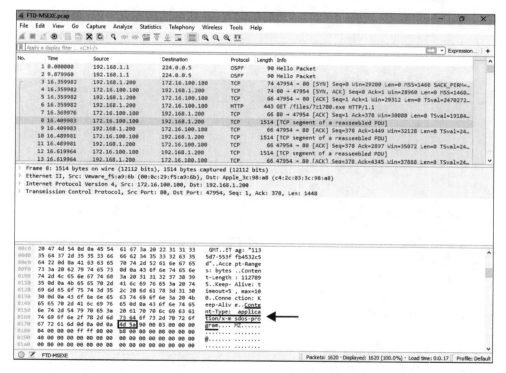

Figure 20-2 *Retrieval of the Magic Number from the Stream of Packets*

Malware Analysis Technology

To empower a network with the latest threat intelligence, Cisco has integrated the Advanced Malware Protection (AMP) technology with the Firepower System. AMP enables an FTD device to analyze a file for potential malware and viruses while the file traverses a network. To expedite the analysis process and to conserve resources, FTD can perform both types of malware analysis—local and dynamic. Let's take a look at the technologies behind them.

Figure 20-3 illustrates the purposes of any interactions between the Firepower System and the Cisco clouds.

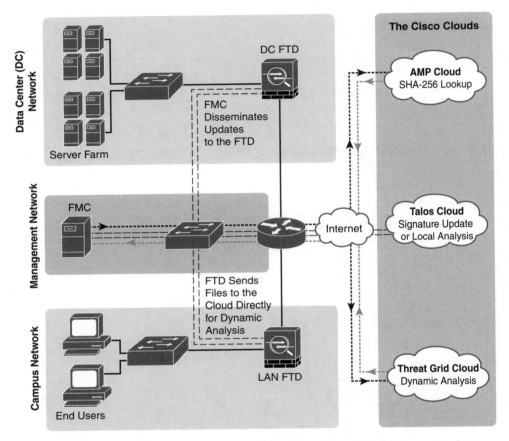

Figure 20-3   *Firepower Communications to the Cisco Clouds for Malware Analysis*

FTD calculates the SHA-256 hash value (Secure Hash Algorithm with 256 bits) of a file and uses the value to determine a disposition. The FMC performs a lookup on the cached disposition before it sends a new query to the AMP cloud. It provides a faster lookup result and improves overall performance. Depending on the action you select on a file policy, a Firepower system can perform additional advanced analysis in the following order:

■ **Spero analysis:** The Spero analysis engine examines the MSEXE files only. It analyzes the structure of an MSEXE file and submits the Spero signature to the cloud.

- **Local analysis:** FTD uses two types of rulesets for local analysis: high-fidelity rules and preclassification rules. The FMC downloads high-fidelity malware signatures from Talos and disseminates the rulesets to FTD. FTD matches the patterns and analyzes files for known malware. It also uses the file preclassification filters to optimize resource utilization.

- **Dynamic analysis:** The dynamic analysis feature submits a captured file to the threat grid sandbox for dynamic analysis. A sandbox environment can be available in the cloud or on premises. Upon analysis, the sandbox returns a threat score—a scoring system for considering a file as potential malware. A file policy allows you to adjust the threshold level of the dynamic analysis threat score. Thus, you can define when an FTD device should treat a file as potential malware.

  Dynamic analysis provides an option called capacity handling that allows a Firepower system to store a file temporarily if the system fails to submit the file to a sandbox environment. Some of the potential reasons for such a failure would be communication issues between Firepower and the sandbox (cloud or on premises), exceeding the limit for file submission, and so on.

Figure 20-4 shows an architectural workflow of the malware analysis techniques on a Firepower system.

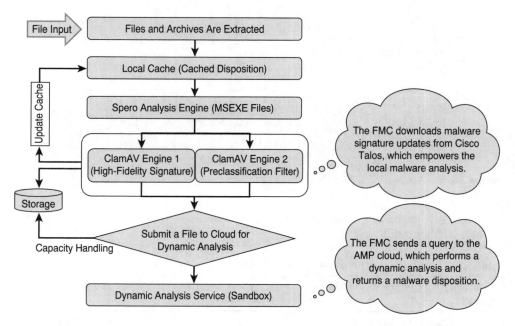

Figure 20-4 *Architecture of the Advanced Malware Protection (AMP) Technology*

Licensing Capability

With the installation of a Threat license, a Firepower system automatically enables the *file type control*. This means that if you are currently using the security intelligence and intrusion prevention features on an FTD device, you should be able to control the transfer of a particular file type without the need for any new license. However, to perform a malware analysis, Firepower requires an additional license, known as a Malware license.

Figure 20-5 shows the actions and features you can enable by using the Threat and Malware licenses.

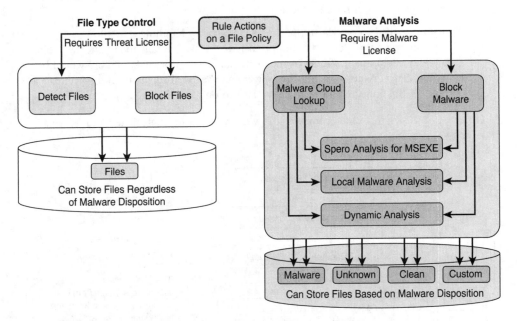

Figure 20-5   *Actions on a File Rule and Their Necessary Licenses*

Table 20-1 summarizes the differences between the capabilities of a Threat license and a Malware license.

Table 20-1   *Differences Between a Threat License and a Malware License*

When Only a Threat License Is Applied...	When a Malware License Is Also Applied...
FTD can block a file based on its file type.	FTD can block a file based on its malware dispositions.
FTD utilizes the file's magic numbers to determine the file type.	FTD matches malware signatures to perform local malware analysis.

When Only a Threat License Is Applied...	When a Malware License Is Also Applied...
FTD does not require a connection to the cloud for file type detection.	It needs to connect to the cloud for various purposes—for example, to update signature of the latest malware, to send a file to the cloud to perform dynamic file analysis, and to perform a SHA-256 lookup.
You can apply only two rule actions: Detect Files and Block Files.	You can apply any rule actions available, including Malware Cloud Lookup and Block Malware.

Best Practices for File Policy Deployment

You should consider the following best practices when you configure a file policy:

- When you want to block a file by using file policy, use the Reset Connection option. It allows an application session to close before the connection times out by itself.

- If you want to download a captured file to your desktop, make sure you take extra precautions on your desktop before you download. The file might be infected with malware that could be harmful to your desktop.

- Keep the file size limit low to improve performance. An access control policy allows you to limit the file size. It can impact the following activities:

  - Sending a file to the cloud for dynamic analysis

  - Storing a file locally

  - Calculating the SHA-256 hash value of a file

- In case of a communication failure between the Firepower System and the Cisco clouds, FTD can hold the transfer of a file for a short period of time when the file matches a rule with the Block Malware action. Although this holding period is configurable, Cisco recommends that you use the default value.

Figure 20-6 displays the advanced settings of an access control policy in which you can define the file holding period and file size limits.

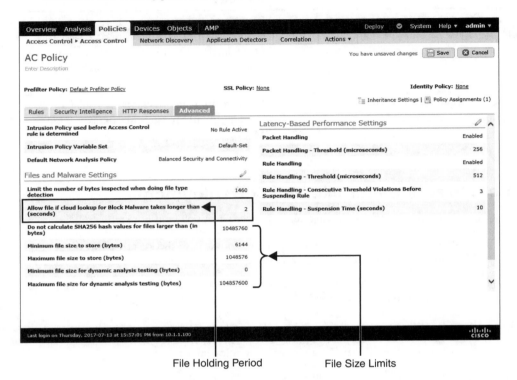

File Holding Period   **File Size Limits**

Figure 20-6 *Configuration of the File Holding Period and File Size Limits*

Fulfilling Prerequisites

The following items are necessary for a successful file policy deployment:

- Make sure to install an appropriate license. To control the transfer of a particular file type, only a Threat license is necessary. To perform malware analysis, an additional Malware license is required.

- A file policy uses the adaptive profile feature. Make sure the feature is enabled in the advanced settings of an access control policy (see Figure 20-7).

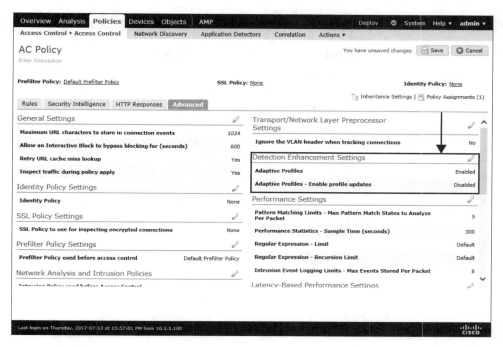

Figure 20-7   *Option to Enable Adaptive Profile Updates*

- Make sure the Enable Automatic Local Malware Detection Updates option is checked (see Figure 20-8). It allows the FMC to communicate with Talos cloud every 30 minutes. When a new ruleset is available, the FMC downloads it to enrich the local malware analysis engine.

- A file policy leverages the application detection functionality to determine whether an application is capable of carrying a file. Make sure a network discovery policy is deployed to discover applications. To learn about application detection and control, read Chapter 19, "Discovering Network Applications and Controlling Application Traffic."

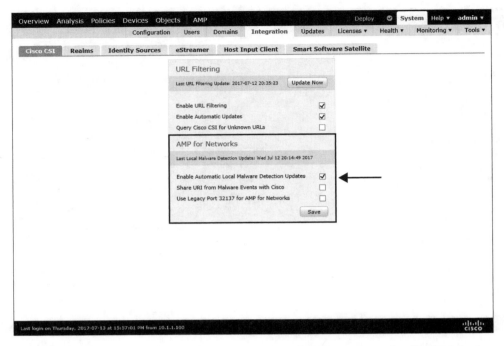

Figure 20-8   *Option to Enable the Automatic Local Malware Detection Updates*

Configuring a File Policy

Deployment of a file policy is a multistep process. First, you need to create a file policy
and add any necessary file rules to it. A file rule allows you to select the file type
category, application protocol, direction of transfer, and action. However, you cannot add
any source or destination details on a file rule. To assign network addresses, you need to
create an access rule within an access control policy and invoke the file policy within the
access rule.

Creating a File Policy

To create a file policy, follow these steps:

Step 1.   Navigate to **Policies > Access Control > Malware & File**. The Malware & File
Policy page appears.

Step 2.   Click the **New File Policy** button, and the New File Policy window appears
(see Figure 20-9).

Step 3.   Give a name to the policy and click the **Save** button. The file policy editor
appears.

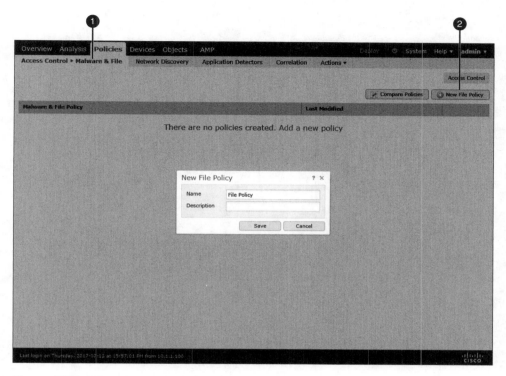

Figure 20-9   *Creating a New File Policy*

Step 4. Click the **Add Rule** button. The file rule editor appears.

Step 5. Select **Any** from the Application Protocol dropdown to detect files over multiple application protocols.

Step 6. Make a selection from the Direction of Transfer dropdown. Depending on the underlying application protocol for a file transfer, the direction can be limited. For example, the HTTP, FTP or NetBIOS-ssn (SMB) protocol allows any direction—upload or download. However, SMTP (upload only) and POP3/IMAP (download only) support unidirectional transfer.

Figure 20-10 explains the reasons for unidirectional transfer with the SMTP, POP3, and IMAP protocols. While SMTP is used for outbound transfers, POP3/IMAP is used to download incoming emails and any attachments.

Step 7. Select the file type categories you want to block, and click **Add** to add them to the rule. You can also search for a specific file type directly.

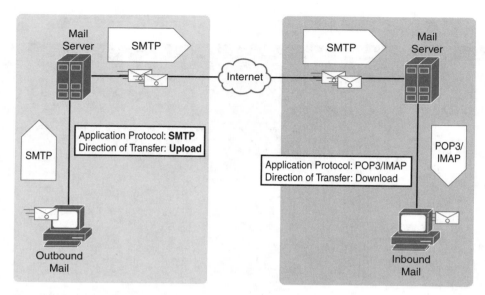

Figure 20-10 *Directions of Protocols Associated with Inbound and Outbound Emails*

> **Step 8.** Select an action from the Action dropdown. The following options are available:

Note A file policy does not evaluate a file rule based on its position; rather, it uses the order of actions. The order of actions is Block Files, Block Malware, Malware Cloud Lookup, and Detect Files. When performing an advanced analysis, FTD engages Spero analysis, local malware analysis, and dynamic analysis, successively—if you have enabled all of them in a particular file rule.

- **Detect Files:** This action detects a file transfer and logs it as a file event without interrupting the transfer.

- **Block Files:** This action blocks certain files—depending on the file formats selected on a file rule.

Tip If you want to block a file, select the **Reset Connection** option. It allows an application session to close before the connection times out by itself.

Figure 20-11 displays a file rule that blocks the transfer of any system, executable, encoded, and archive files without analyzing them for malware. According to the configuration, when a file matches this rule, FTD stores the file on local storage and sends reset packets to terminate any associated connection.

Click on the Add Rule button to open the file rule editor

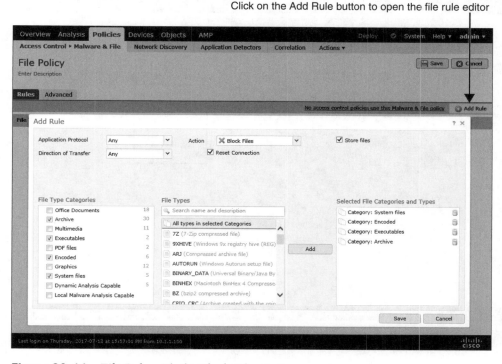

Figure 20-11 *File Rule with the Block Files Action*

Figure 20-12 shows the creation of two file rules. The first rule blocks system, encoded, executable, and archive files with reset packets and stores the blocked file in local storage. The second rule detects the graphic, PDF, multimedia, and Office document files but does not block or store them as they traverse the network.

■ **Malware Cloud Lookup:** This action enables an FTD device to perform malware analysis locally and remotely. FTD allows an uninterrupted file transfer regardless of the malware disposition.

■ **Block Malware:** This action performs the same tasks as the Malware Cloud Lookup action, with an addition of blocking the original file if the disposition is determined to be malware.

Note When you select the Malware Cloud Analysis or Block Malware action, the Firepower System offers various analysis methods. Read the previous section for more information on malware analysis methodologies.

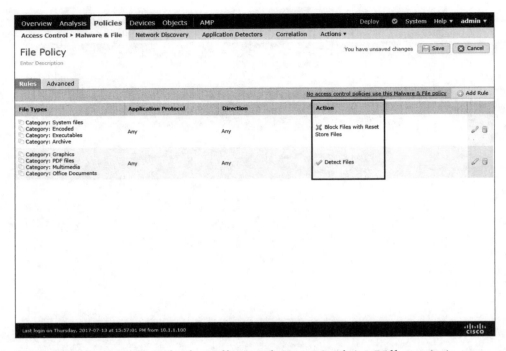

Figure 20-12 *Two File Rules for Different File Types Applying Different Actions*

Figure 20-13 shows another option for a file rule (which requires a Malware license). This rule enables an FTD device to block the transfer of a file and to store it locally if the file has one of three criteria: infected with malware, disposition is unknown, or matches a custom detection list. When blocking the file transfer, FTD sends reset packets to terminate any associated connection. This rule does not allow an FTD device to store a file if the file appears to be clean. It prevents storage from getting full of clean or benign files.

Step 9.   Optionally, on the Advanced tab, you can enable additional features for advanced analysis and inspection. Figure 20-14 shows the advanced settings of a file policy. For example, here you can adjust the threshold level of the dynamic analysis threat score, enable inspection for the archived contents, define the depth of inspection for a nested archive file, and so on.

Step 10.   Click the **Save** button on the policy editor to save the changes on the file policy.

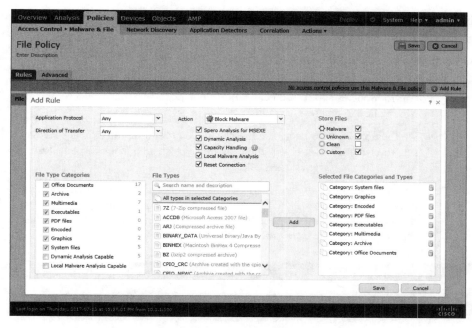

Figure 20-13 *File Rule with a Block Malware Action*

A lower threat score increases the number of
files that are going to be considered malware.

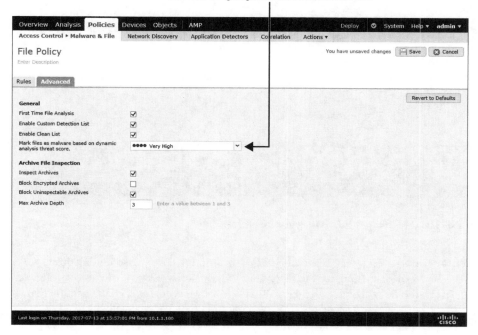

Figure 20-14 *Advanced Settings of a File Policy*

Applying a File Policy

To apply a file policy on an FTD device, you need to create an access rule within an access control policy and invoke the file policy in the access rule. Here are the detailed steps:

Step 1. Navigate to **Policies > Access Control > Access Control**. The available access control policies appear. You can modify one of the existing policies or click **New Policy** to create a new one.

Step 2. On the policy editor page, use the pencil icon to modify an existing access rule to invoke a file policy. If there are no rules created, click the **Add Rule** button to create a new access rule.

Step 3. On the rule editor window, go to the Inspection tab. You will notice drop-downs for Intrusion Policy, Variable Set, and File Policy. Figure 20-15 shows the dropdowns on the Inspection tab. The file policy you configured earlier should populate here, under the File Policy dropdown.

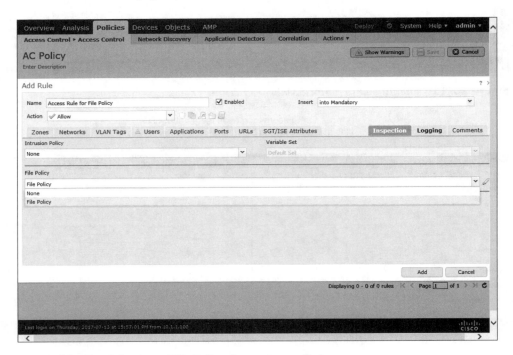

Figure 20-15 *Selecting a File Policy for an Access Rule*

Step 4. Choose a policy from the File Policy dropdown. Doing so automatically enables logging for the file event. You can verify it by viewing the settings on the Logging tab (see Figure 20-16). To view events for each connection that matches a particular access rule condition, you can manually enable Log at Beginning of Connection.

Manually Enabled

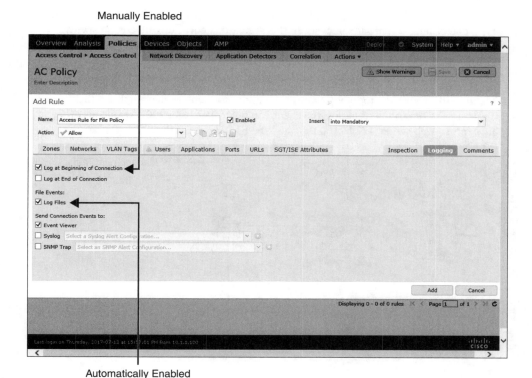

Automatically Enabled

Figure 20-16 *Options to Enable Logging for File Events and Connection Events*

Step 5. Click the **Add** button to save the changes. You are returned to the access control policy editor page. If you are editing an existing access rule, you can click the **Save** button instead.

Step 6. On the access control policy editor page, select a default action. You cannot select a file policy as the default action of an access control policy. You can only invoke a file policy within an individual access rule.

Step 7. Finally, click **Save** to save the changes, and click **Deploy** to deploy the configuration to the FTD device.

Verification and Troubleshooting Tools

A file policy can generate two types of events: file events and malware events. FTD generates a *file event* when it detects or blocks a certain type of file without a malware lookup. FTD generates a *malware event* when it performs an analysis for malware or blocks a file due to malware disposition.

The following sections of this chapter demonstrate the operation of both policies—file type detection and malware analysis. In this scenario, a client downloads files with two different formats—Microsoft executable (MSEXE) file format and Portable Document Format (PDF). As a security engineer, you need to verify whether a file policy is operational and whether the transfer of files complies with the active file policy.

Figure 20-17 shows the topology that is used in the configuration examples in this chapter. To demonstrate various scenarios, the client computer (192.168.1.200) downloads different files from a web server (172.16.100.100), and the FTD device in the LAN acts on them.

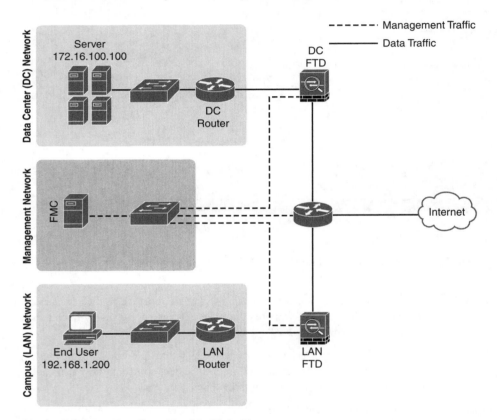

Figure 20-17   *Topology Used in This Chapter*

Analyzing File Events

Using a web browser on your client computer, you can attempt to download two files—7z1700.exe and userguide.pdf—from a web server. If the FTD device is running the following file policy, it should block the download of the 7z1700.exe file and allow and detect the download of userguide.pdf.

Figure 20-18 shows the currently enabled rules on a file policy. The first rule detects and blocks files in four categories, and the second rule only detects files in four different categories.

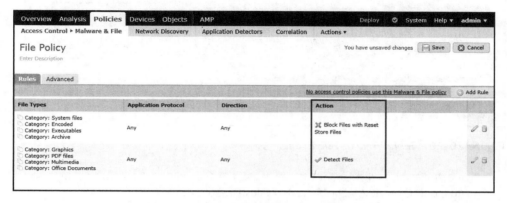

Figure 20-18 *Overview of the Active Rules Used in This Exercise*

Navigate to **Files > File Events** to view the file events. By default, the FMC shows the File Summary page. However, to find useful contextual information about file events, you should also check the Table View of File Events page.

Figure 20-19 confirms the blocking and detection of an MSEXE file and a PDF file. Because the Block Files action does not perform malware analysis, the Disposition column is blank.

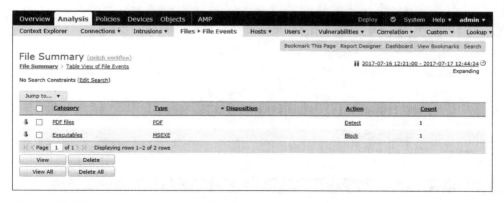

Figure 20-19 *Summary View of File Events*

Figure 20-20 shows detailed information about the detected and blocked files and their associated source and destination hosts. The SHA256 and Threat Score columns are blank because the FTD device does not perform any kind of malware analysis but detects file type only.

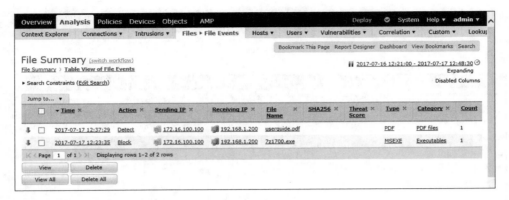

Figure 20-20   *Table View of File Events*

Figure 20-21 shows the data of file events visually in various widgets. To find this dashboard, go to **Overview > Dashboards > Files Dashboard**.

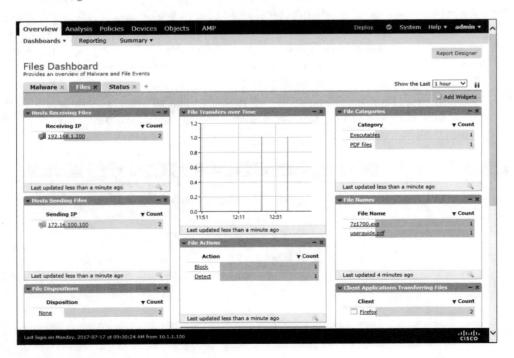

Figure 20-21   *Dashboard of File Events*

If you do not see a file event that you expected to see, you can use the CLI to debug the action of a file rule and verify the operation of a file policy. If you run the **system support firewall-engine-debug** command while you attempt to transfer a file, you see detailed logs associated with file inspection and analysis.

Example 20-1 shows the detailed debugging messages that appear when a client computer attempts to download the executable file 7z1700.exe and the FTD device blocks it due to the actions Block Files, Reset Connection, and Store Files.

Example 20-1   *Blocking a Microsoft Executable (MSEXE) File*

```
! First, run the debug command and specify necessary parameters.


> system support firewall-engine-debug


Please specify an IP protocol: tcp
Please specify a client IP address: 192.168.1.200
Please specify a client port:
Please specify a server IP address:
Please specify a server port:
Monitoring firewall engine debug messages


! Now, begin the transfer of an executable file.


192.168.1.200-47954 > 172.16.100.100-80 6 AS 4 I 0 New session
192.168.1.200-47954 > 172.16.100.100-80 6 AS 4 I 0 using HW or preset rule order 2,
  'Access Rule for File Policy', action Allow and prefilter rule 0
192.168.1.200-47954 > 172.16.100.100-80 6 AS 4 I 0 allow action
192.168.1.200-47954 > 172.16.100.100-80 6 AS 4 I 0 URL SI:
  ShmDBLookupURL("http://172.16.100.100/files/7z1700.exe") returned 0
192.168.1.200-47954 > 172.16.100.100-80 6 AS 4 I 0 File Policy verdict is Type,
  Malware, and Capture
192.168.1.200-47954 > 172.16.100.100-80 6 AS 4 I 0 File type verdict Unknown,
  fileAction Block, flags 0x00203500, and type action Reject for type 21 of
  instance 0


! At this stage, the file is being transferred through the FTD. The following
messages appear after the file is stored on the FTD. FTD blocks the file transfer
as soon as it detects the end-of-file marker on a packet.


192.168.1.200-47954 > 172.16.100.100-80 6 AS 4 I 0 File type storage finished within
  signature using verdict Reject
192.168.1.200-47954 > 172.16.100.100-80 6 AS 4 I 0 File signature reserved file data
  of partial file with flags 0x00203500 and status Exceeded Max Filesize
192.168.1.200-47954 > 172.16.100.100-80 6 AS 4 I 0 File signature verdict Reject and
  flags 0x00203500 for partial file of instance 0
192.168.1.200-47954 > 172.16.100.100-80 6 AS 4 I 0 File type event for file named
  7z1700.exe with disposition Type and action Block
192.168.1.200-47954 > 172.16.100.100-80 6 AS 4 I 0 Archive childs been processed No
192.168.1.200-47954 > 172.16.100.100-80 6 AS 4 I 0 Deleting session
^C
Caught interrupt signal
Exiting.

>
```

Example 20-2 shows the debugging messages that appears when a client computer downloads the file userguide.pdf. FTD generates a log, but it does not block the PDF file because the rule action is Detect Files.

Example 20-2   *Detecting a Portable Document Format (PDF) File*

```
> system support firewall-engine-debug

Please specify an IP protocol: tcp
Please specify a client IP address: 192.168.1.200
Please specify a client port:
Please specify a server IP address:
Please specify a server port:
Monitoring firewall engine debug messages



192.168.1.200-58374 > 172.16.100.100-80 6 AS 4 I 0 New session
192.168.1.200-58374 > 172.16.100.100-80 6 AS 4 I 0 Starting with minimum 0, id 0 and
  SrcZone first with zones -1 -> -1, geo 0(0) -> 0, vlan 0, sgt tag: untagged,
  svc 0, payload 0, client 0, misc 0, user 9999997, url , xff
192.168.1.200-58374 > 172.16.100.100-80 6 AS 4 I 0 match rule order 2, 'Access Rule
  for File Policy', action Allow
192.168.1.200-58374 > 172.16.100.100-80 6 AS 4 I 0 allow action
192.168.1.200-58374 > 172.16.100.100-80 6 AS 4 I 0 URL SI:
  ShmDBLookupURL("http://172.16.100.100/files/userguide.pdf") returned 0
192.168.1.200-58374 > 172.16.100.100-80 6 AS 4 I 0 Starting with minimum 0, id 0 and
  SrcZone first with zones -1 -> -1, geo 0(0) -> 0, vlan 0, sgt tag: untagged, svc
  676, payload 0, client 638, misc 0, user 9999997, url http://172.16.100.100/files/
  userguide.pdf, xff
192.168.1.200-58374 > 172.16.100.100-80 6 AS 4 I 0 match rule order 2, 'Access Rule
  for File Policy', action Allow
192.168.1.200-58374 > 172.16.100.100-80 6 AS 4 I 0 allow action
.
<Output omitted for brevity>
.
192.168.1.200-58374 > 172.16.100.100-80 6 AS 4 I 0 File policy verdict is Type,
  Malware, and Capture
192.168.1.200-58374 > 172.16.100.100-80 6 AS 4 I 0 File type verdict Log, fileAction
  Log, flags 0x00001100, and type action Log for type 285 of instance 0
192.168.1.200-58374 > 172.16.100.100-80 6 AS 4 I 0 File type event for file named
  userguide.pdf with disposition Type and action Log
.
<Output omitted for brevity>
^C
Caught interrupt signal
Exiting.
>
```

Analyzing Malware Events

In this section, when you attempt to download the same MSEXE file 7z1700.exe as before by using a web server, you will notice different behavior on the FTD device because it applies a different rule action—Block Malware instead of Block Files. You will analyze the following scenarios in this section:

- The FMC is unable to communicate with the cloud.

- The FMC performs a cloud lookup.

- FTD blocks malware.

Figure 20-22 shows a file rule that blocks the transfer of any malicious files. When FTD determines that a file is a malicious file, this rule allows an FTD device to store the file in local storage and send reset packets to terminate any associated connection. To conserve disk space, files with clean disposition are not stored.

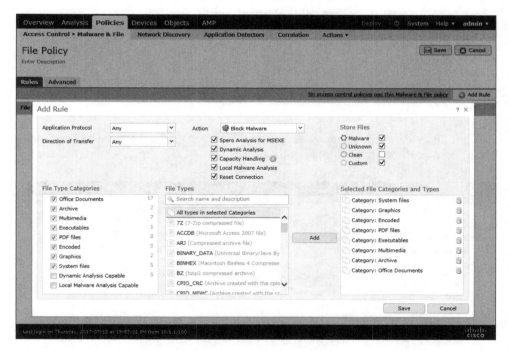

Figure 20-22 *Defining the Active Rule Used in This Exercise*

The FMC Is Unable to Communicate with the Cloud

After deploying a file policy with the Block Malware rule action, you can attempt to download the same MSEXE file 7z1700.exe as before but now using a web server.

Unlike in the previous section, where you used file type detection, you will find the FTD to calculate the SHA-256 checksum of the file. FTD later attempts to perform a cloud lookup for the hash value.

Figure 20-23 shows a file event (table view) for downloading the same 7z1700.exe file. Because the file policy enables malware analysis, FTD calculates the SHA-256 hash value. However, the cloud lookup process times out.

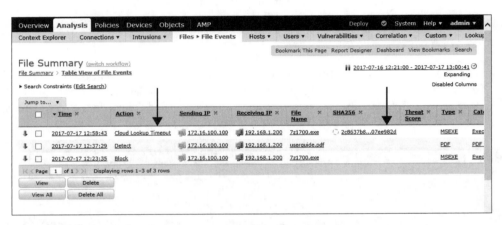

Figure 20-23 *Malware Analysis Verdict—Cloud Lookup Timeout*

Figure 20-24 shows the summary view of the file events. Due to the cloud lookup timeout, malware disposition is listed as Unavailable.

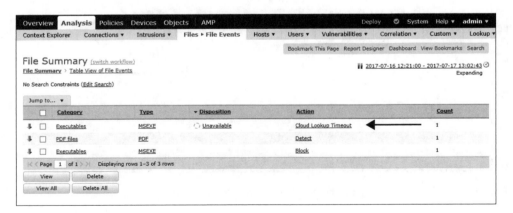

Figure 20-24 *Malware Disposition Is Unavailable Due to Cloud Lookup Timeout*

Example 20-3 demonstrates that the FTD device is able to calculate the SHA-256 checksum locally. However, when it sends the calculated hash value for a lookup, the query times out (due to a communication failure to the Cisco cloud). This leads the FMC to display the disposition as Unavailable.

Example 20-3   *The FMC Calculates SHA-256 Hash Value but Is Unable to Complete a Lookup*

```
> system support firewall-engine-debug


Please specify an IP protocol: tcp
Please specify a client IP address: 192.168.1.200
Please specify a client port:
Please specify a server IP address:
Please specify a server port:


Monitoring firewall engine debug messages


192.168.1.200-58466 > 172.16.100.100-80 6 AS 4 I 0 New session
192.168.1.200-58466 > 172.16.100.100-80 6 AS 4 I 0 using HW or preset rule order 2,
  'Access Rule for File Policy', action Allow and prefilter rule 0
192.168.1.200-58466 > 172.16.100.100-80 6 AS 4 I 0 allow action
192.168.1.200-58466 > 172.16.100.100-80 6 AS 4 I 0 URL SI: ShmDBLookupURL("h
  ttp://172.16.100.100/files/7z1700.exe") returned 0
192.168.1.200-58466 > 172.16.100.100-80 6 AS 4 I 0 File policy verdict is Type,
  Malware, and Capture
192.168.1.200-58466 > 172.16.100.100-80 6 AS 4 I 0 File type verdict Unknown,
  fileAction Malware Lookup, flags 0x01BDDA00, and type action Stop for type 21 of
  instance 0


! Next, FTD calculates the SHA-256 hash value of the file, which is
  2c8637b812f7a47802f4f91f8bfaccb978df9b62de558d038485ddb307ee982d.


192.168.1.200-58466 > 172.16.100.100-80 6 AS 4 I 0 File signature verdict Unknown
  and flags 0x01BDDA00 for partial file of instance 0
192.168.1.200-58466 > 172.16.100.100-80 6 AS 4 I 0 File signature cache query
  returned Cache Miss for 2c8637b812f7a47802f4f91f8bfaccb978df9b62de558d038485dd-
  b307ee982d with disposition Cache Miss, spero Cache Miss, severity 0, and transmit
  Not Sent
192.168.1.200-58466 > 172.16.100.100-80 6 AS 4 I 0 File signature reserved file data
  of 2c8637b812f7a47802f4f91f8bfaccb978df9b62de558d038485ddb307ee982d with flags
  0x01BDDA00 and status Exceeded Max Filesize
192.168.1.200-58466 > 172.16.100.100-80 6 AS 4 I 0 File signature verdict Pending
  and flags 0x01BDDA00 for 2c8637b812f7a47802f4f91f8bfaccb978df9b62de558d038485dd-
  b307ee982d of instance 0
192.168.1.200-58466 > 172.16.100.100-80 6 AS 4 I 0 File signature cache query
  returned Cache Miss for 2c8637b812f7a47802f4f91f8bfaccb978df9b62de558d038485dd-
  b307ee982d with disposition Cache Miss, spero Cache Miss, severity 0, and transmit
  Not Sent
192.168.1.200-58466 > 172.16.100.100-80 6 AS 4 I 0 File signature reserved file data
  of 2c8637b812f7a47802f4f91f8bfaccb978df9b62de558d038485ddb307ee982d with flags
  0x01BDDA00 and status Exceeded Max Filesize
```

```
192.168.1.200-58466 > 172.16.100.100-80 6 AS 4 I 0 File signature verdict Pending
    and flags 0x01BDDA00 for 2c8637b812f7a47802f4f91f8bfaccb978df9b62de558d038485dd-
    b307ee982d of instance 0
192.168.1.200-58466 > 172.16.100.100-80 6 AS 4 I 0 File malware event for
    2c8637b812f7a47802f4f91f8bfaccb978df9b62de558d038485ddb307ee982d named 7z1700.exe
    with disposition Cache Miss and action Timeout
192.168.1.200-58466 > 172.16.100.100-80 6 AS 4 I 0 Archive childs been processed No
192.168.1.200-58466 > 172.16.100.100-80 6 AS 4 I 0 Deleting session
^C
Caught interrupt signal
Exiting.
>
```

To find the root cause of a lookup failure, you can analyze the syslog messages on the FMC. To view the messages, you can use any convenient Linux commands, such as **less**, **cat**, or **tail**, as needed. Note that the timestamps of messages use coordinated universal time (UTC).

Tip   Cloud Lookup Timeout in the Action column indicates that the FMC is unable to connect to the cloud. When you see this, check whether the management interface of the FMC is connected to the Internet. If the Internet connectivity is operational, then make sure the FMC can resolve a DNS query.

Example 20-4 shows various states of the FMC cloud communication. The syslog messages are automatically generated by the Firepower software. To view them in real time, you can use the **tail** command with the **-f** parameter.

Example 20-4   *Analyzing Syslog Messages for FMC Communications to the Cloud*

```
admin@FMC:~$ sudo tail -f /var/log/messages
Password:
.
<Output is omitted for brevity>
.
! If FMC is connected to the internet, but fails to resolve a DNS query, the
    following error message appears in the Syslog.
.
[timestamp] FMC stunnel: LOG3[3953:140160119551744]: Error resolving 'cloud-sa.amp.
    sourcefire.com': Neither nodename nor servname known (EAI_NONAME)
.
! After you fix any communication issues, FMC should be able to connect to the
    cloud. The following Syslog messages confirm a successful connection.
.
```

```
[timestamp] FMC SF-IMS[25954]: [26657] SFDataCorrelator:FireAMPCloudLookup [INFO]
  cloud server is cloud-sa.amp.sourcefire.com
[timestamp] FMC SF-IMS[25954]: [26657] SFDataCorrelator:imcloudpool [INFO] connect
  to cloud using stunnel
.

! Once the FMC is connected to the cloud, it begins the registration process. The
  following messages confirm successful registrations to the Cisco Clouds.
.

[timestamp] FMC SF-IMS[25954]: [26657] SFDataCorrelator:FireAMPCloudLookup [INFO]
  Successfully registered with fireamp cloud
[timestamp] FMC SF-IMS[25954]: [25954] SFDataCorrelator:FileExtract [INFO]
  Successfully registered with sandbox cloud
.

! Upon successful registration, FMC is able to perform cloud lookup and obtains
  updates. The following messages confirm a successful check for malware database
  update.
.

[timestamp] FMC SF-IMS[25275]: [25275] CloudAgent:CloudAgent [INFO] ClamUpd, time to
  check for updates
.

[timestamp] FMC SF-IMS[25275]: [25298] CloudAgent:CloudAgent [INFO] Nothing to do,
  database is up to date
.
```

Figure 20-25 shows the DNS setting on an FMC management interface. To find this page, go to **System > Configuration** and select **Management Interfaces**. Make sure the FMC can communicate with the configured DNS server and resolve a domain name using this DNS server.

The FMC Performs a Cloud Lookup

If the FMC is able to resolve a DNS query, it should be able to connect and register with the Cisco clouds as well. Registration with clouds allows the FMC to perform cloud look-ups for malware disposition. As of this writing, Cisco uses cloud-sa.amp.sourcefire.com for Advanced Malware Protection (AMP) services.

This section assumes that you have fixed any connectivity or DNS issues you experienced in the last section. Here you will download the MSEXE file 7z1700.exe once again. You should notice a different type of event this time.

Figure 20-26 shows two different actions on file events for downloading the same file. Because the FMC can communicate with the Cisco clouds, FTD returns Malware Cloud Lookup instead of Cloud Lookup Timeout.

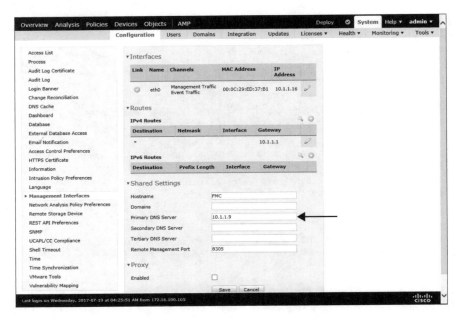

Figure 20-25   *DNS Settings on the FMC*

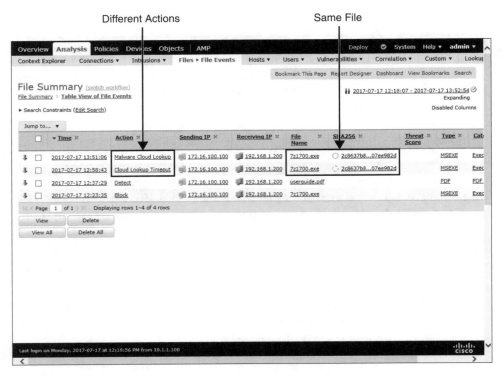

Figure 20-26   *Successful Malware Cloud Lookup*

You can go to the File Summary view to find the malware dispositions. The Cisco clouds can return one of the following dispositions for a query:

- **Malware:** If Cisco determines that a file is malware

- **Clean:** If Cisco finds no malicious pattern on a file

- **Unknown:** If Cisco has not assigned a disposition (malware or clean) to a file

Figure 20-27 compares two types of dispositions—unknown and unavailable—for the 7z1700.exe file. Unknown confirms a successful cloud communication with no cloud-assigned category, whereas Unavailable indicates an issue with cloud communication.

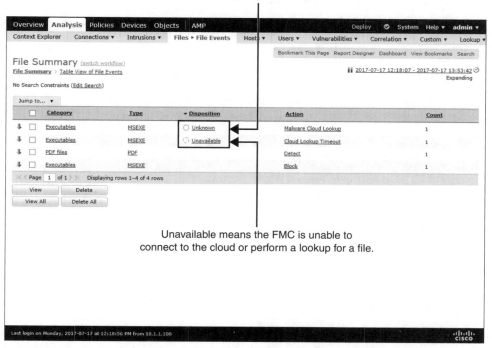

Figure 20-27   *Malware Disposition—Unknown Versus Unavailable*

Example 20-5 proves that the Firepower System checks its local cached disposition first before it sends the query to the Cisco clouds.

Example 20-5   *Firepower Queries Cached Disposition Before Performing a Cloud Lookup*

```
> system support firewall-engine-debug

Please specify an IP protocol: tcp
Please specify a client IP address: 192.168.1.200
Please specify a client port:
Please specify a server IP address:
Please specify a server port:


Monitoring firewall engine debug messages

! Now, begin the transfer of an executable file.


192.168.1.200-58552 > 172.16.100.100-80 6 AS 4 I 0 New session
192.168.1.200-58552 > 172.16.100.100-80 6 AS 4 I 0 using HW or preset rule order 2,
   'Access Rule for File Policy', action Allow and prefilter rule 0
192.168.1.200-58552 > 172.16.100.100-80 6 AS 4 I 0 allow action
192.168.1.200-58552 > 172.16.100.100-80 6 AS 4 I 0 URL SI:
   ShmDBLookupURL("http://172.16.100.100/files/7z1700.exe") returned 0
192.168.1.200-58552 > 172.16.100.100-80 6 AS 4 I 0 File policy verdict is Type,
   Malware, and Capture
192.168.1.200-58552 > 172.16.100.100-80 6 AS 4 I 0 File type verdict Unknown,
   fileAction Malware Lookup, flags 0x01BDDA00, and type action Stop for type 21 of
   instance 0


! First, Firepower System checks the cached disposition.


192.168.1.200-58552 > 172.16.100.100-80 6 AS 4 I 0 File signature verdict Unknown
   and flags 0x01BDDA00 for partial file of instance 0
192.168.1.200-58552 > 172.16.100.100-80 6 AS 4 I 0 File signature cache query returned
   Cache Miss for 2c8637b812f7a47802f4f91f8bfaccb978df9b62de558d038485ddb307ee982d with
   disposition Cache Miss, spero Cache Miss, severity 0, and transmit Not Sent
192.168.1.200-58552 > 172.16.100.100-80 6 AS 4 I 0 File signature reserved file data
   of 2c8637b812f7a47802f4f91f8bfaccb978df9b62de558d038485ddb307ee982d with flags
   0x01BDDA00 and status Exceeded Max Filesize
192.168.1.200-58552 > 172.16.100.100-80 6 AS 4 I 0 File signature verdict Pending
   and flags 0x01BDDA00 for 2c8637b812f7a47802f4f91f8bfaccb978df9b62de558d038485dd-
   b307ee982d of instance 0


! Here, Firepower System performs a query to the cloud for disposition.


192.168.1.200-58552 > 172.16.100.100-80 6 AS 4 I 0 File signature cache query returned
   Neutral for 2c8637b812f7a47802f4f91f8bfaccb978df9b62de558d038485ddb307ee982d with
   disposition Neutral, spero Cache Miss, severity 0, and transmit Not Sent
192.168.1.200-58552 > 172.16.100.100-80 6 AS 4 I 0 File signature reserved file data
   of 2c8637b812f7a47802f4f91f8bfaccb978df9b62de558d038485ddb307ee982d for spero with
   flags 0x01BDDA00 and status Exceeded Max Filesize
```

```
192.168.1.200-58552 > 172.16.100.100-80 6 AS 4 I 0 File signature reserved file data
   of 2c8637b812f7a47802f4f91f8bfaccb978df9b62de558d038485ddb307ee982d with flags
   0x01BDDA00 and status Exceeded Max Filesize
192.168.1.200-58552 > 172.16.100.100-80 6 AS 4 I 0 File signature reserved file data
   of 2c8637b812f7a47802f4f91f8bfaccb978df9b62de558d038485ddb307ee982d with flags
   0x01BDDA00 and status Exceeded Max Filesize
192.168.1.200-58552 > 172.16.100.100-80 6 AS 4 I 0 File signature verdict Log and
   flags 0x01BDDA00 for 2c8637b812f7a47802f4f91f8bfaccb978df9b62de558d038485dd-
   b307ee982d of instance 0
192.168.1.200-58552 > 172.16.100.100-80 6 AS 4 I 0 File malware event for
   2c8637b812f7a47802f4f91f8bfaccb978df9b62de558d038485ddb307ee982d named 7z1700.exe
   with disposition Neutral and action Malware Lookup
192.168.1.200-58552 > 172.16.100.100-80 6 AS 4 I 0 Archive childs been processed No
192.168.1.200-58552 > 172.16.100.100-80 6 AS 4 I 0 Deleting session
^C
Caught interrupt signal
Exiting.
>
```

FTD Blocks Malware

This section shows how to analyze Firepower actions on malware. To emulate a malicious file, this chapter leverages an anti-malware test file available in the European Institute for Computer Antivirus Research (EICAR) website. Cisco does not develop or maintain this test file; however, you can download the latest copy from eicar.org. Alternatively, you can create a test file by your own using a text editor. It consists of the following characters:

X5O!P%@AP[4\PZX54(P^)7CC)7}$EICAR-STANDARD-ANTIVIRUS-TEST-FILE!$H+H*

Figure 20-28 shows the creation of suspicious.exe, an anti-malware test file. The example uses notepad—a text editor for Microsoft Windows—to create the file. The file simply contains the test string. After you copy the string, save the file in the Windows executable (.exe) format.

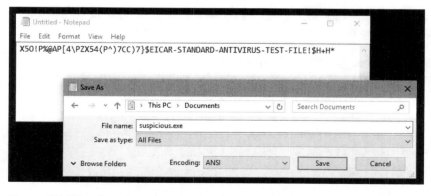

Figure 20-28 *Creation of an Anti-Malware Test File, suspicious.exe, Using a Text Editor*

To perform an experiment, at first, store the anti-malware test file (suspicious.exe) on a web server in your lab network. Then attempt to download the test file to a client computer by using a web browser. FTD should block the attempt.

Figure 20-29 demonstrates that FTD blocks a client's attempt to download the suspicious.exe file. The cloud lookup returns a very high threat score for this anti-malware test file, because the cloud detects the test string within the file and considers it malware.

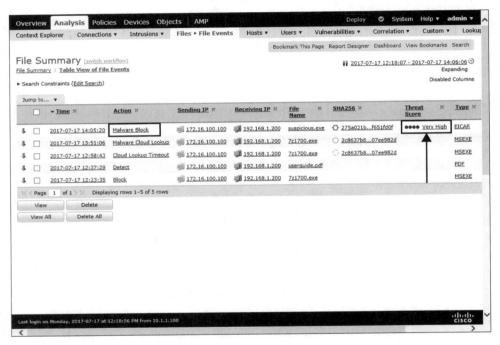

Figure 20-29   *FTD Blocking a File with a Malware Signature*

Example 20-6 details the operations of an FTD device when it analyzes a file, performs a cloud lookup, and blocks the file based on its malware disposition.

Example 20-6   *Blocking a File Due to Its Malware Disposition*

```
> system support firewall-engine-debug

Please specify an IP protocol: tcp
Please specify a client IP address: 192.168.1.200
Please specify a client port:
Please specify a server IP address:
Please specify a server port:

Monitoring firewall engine debug messages
```

```
! First, client attempts to download the suspicious.exe file using a web browser.


192.168.1.200-58566 > 172.16.100.100-80 6 AS 4 I 0 New session

192.168.1.200-58566 > 172.16.100.100-80 6 AS 4 I 0 using HW or preset rule order 2,
  'Access Rule for File Policy', action Allow and prefilter rule 0

192.168.1.200-58566 > 172.16.100.100-80 6 AS 4 I 0 allow action

192.168.1.200-58566 > 172.16.100.100-80 6 AS 4 I 0 URL SI: ShmDBLookupURL
  ("http://172.16.100.100/files/suspicious.exe") returned 0

192.168.1.200-58566 > 172.16.100.100-80 6 AS 4 I 0 File policy verdict is Type,
  Malware, and Capture

192.168.1.200-58566 > 172.16.100.100-80 6 AS 4 I 0 File type verdict Unknown,
  fileAction Malware Lookup, flags 0x0025DA00, and type action Stop for type 273 of
  instance 0


! Firepower System performs a lookup on cached disposition before sending a query to
  the cloud.


192.168.1.200-58566 > 172.16.100.100-80 6 AS 4 I 0 File signature cache
  query returned Cache Miss for 275a021bbfb6489e54d471899f7db9d1663f-
  c695ec2fe2a2c4538aabf651fd0f with disposition Cache Miss, spero Cache Miss,
  severity 0, and transmit Sent

192.168.1.200-58566 > 172.16.100.100-80 6 AS 4 I 0 File signature reserved file data
  of 275a021bbfb6489e54d471899f7db9d1663fc695ec2fe2a2c4538aabf651fd0f with flags
  0x0025DA00 and status Smaller than Min Filesize

192.168.1.200-58566 > 172.16.100.100-80 6 AS 4 I 0 File signature verdict
  Pending and flags 0x0025DA00 for 275a021bbfb6489e54d471899f7db9d1663f-
  c695ec2fe2a2c4538aabf651fd0f of instance 0

192.168.1.200-58566 > 172.16.100.100-80 6 AS 4 I 0 File signature cache
  query returned Cache Miss for 275a021bbfb6489e54d471899f7db9d1663f-
  c695ec2fe2a2c4538aabf651fd0f with disposition Cache Miss, spero Cache Miss,
  severity 0, and transmit Sent

192.168.1.200-58566 > 172.16.100.100-80 6 AS 4 I 0 File signature reserved file data
  of 275a021bbfb6489e54d471899f7db9d1663fc695ec2fe2a2c4538aabf651fd0f with flags
  0x0025DA00 and status Smaller than Min Filesize

192.168.1.200-58566 > 172.16.100.100-80 6 AS 4 I 0 File signature
  verdict Pending and flags 0x0025DA00 for 275a021bbfb6489e54d471899f7db9d1663f-
  c695ec2fe2a2c4538aabf651fd0f of instance 0


! At this stage, FMC receives a malware disposition from the cloud. FTD acts on the
  file based on the File Policy.


192.168.1.200-58566 > 172.16.100.100-80 6 AS 4 I 0 File signature cache
  query returned Malware for 275a021bbfb6489e54d471899f7db9d1663f-
  c695ec2fe2a2c4538aabf651fd0f with disposition Malware, spero Cache Miss, severity
  76, and transmit Sent

192.168.1.200-58566 > 172.16.100.100-80 6 AS 4 I 0 File signature reserved file data
  of 275a021bbfb6489e54d471899f7db9d1663fc695ec2fe2a2c4538aabf651fd0f with flags
  0x0025DA00 and status Smaller than Min Filesize

192.168.1.200-58566 > 172.16.100.100-80 6 AS 4 I 0 File signature verdict
  Reject and flags 0x0025DA00 for 275a021bbfb6489e54d471899f7db9d1663f-
  c695ec2fe2a2c4538aabf651fd0f of instance 0
```

```
192.168.1.200-58566 > 172.16.100.100-80 6 AS 4 I 0 File malware event for
  275a021bbfb6489e54d471899f7db9d1663fc695ec2fe2a2c4538aabf651fd0f named suspicious.
  exe with disposition Malware and action Block Malware
192.168.1.200-58566 > 172.16.100.100-80 6 AS 4 I 0 Archive childs been processed No
192.168.1.200-58566 > 172.16.100.100-80 6 AS 4 I 0 Deleting session
.
<Output Omitted for Brevity>
.
^C
Caught interrupt signal
Exiting.

>
```

Overriding a Malware Disposition

If you disagree with a file disposition—whether it is analyzed locally by the FTD device or dynamically by the cloud—the FMC allows you to override an outcome by using a file list. There are two types of file list:

- **Clean list:** If FTD blocks a file due to its malware disposition, you could manually allow the file by adding it to the clean list. This lets the file go through FTD moving forward.

- **Custom detection list:** If the local or dynamic analysis engine identifies a file as clean or unknown and, therefore, FTD allows the file to transfer, you could change this behavior by adding the file to the custom detection list. In the future, if a client attempts to transfer the same file, FTD will block it, regardless of the disposition by the local or dynamic analysis engine.

In short, the clean list allows you to *whitelist* a file, whereas you can *blacklist* a file by adding it to the custom detection list.

To deploy a new file list, the FTD device must be running a file policy with the following rule conditions:

- The rule matches the same file type as your selected file format for a file list. For example, if you want to add an executable file to the clean or custom detection list, the rule on a file policy needs to match the executable file types as well.

- The action of the rule is set to one of the malware analysis rules, such as malware cloud lookup or block malware.

Once these conditions are fulfilled, you can add a file to a file list in two ways: by using the right-click context menu or by using a file list object. The context menu allows you to add a file on the fly.

Figure 20-30 shows the addition of the 7z1700.exe file to the custom detection list through the context menu.

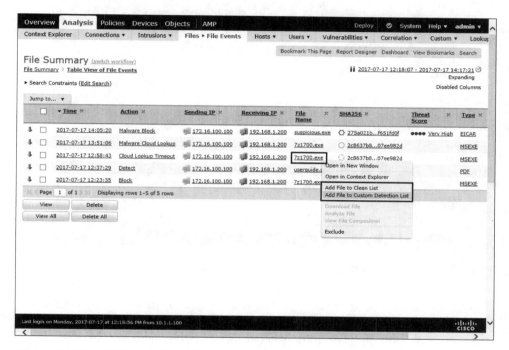

Figure 20-30   *Adding a File to the Custom Detection List by Using the Context Menu*

Figure 20-31 shows the navigation to the file list object configuration page. Besides adding the files and their SHA hash values, this page allows you to manage any previously added files.

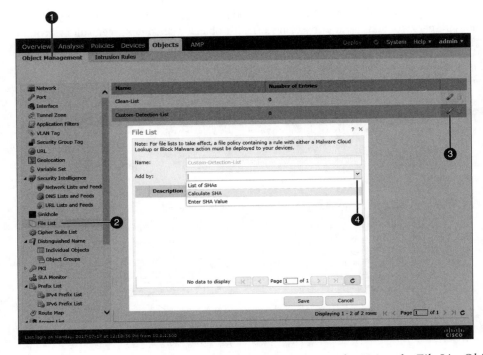

Figure 20-31   *Adding a File to the Custom Detection List by Using the File List Object*

Once you add your desired file to a file list, you can redeploy the file policy to FTD.
Then you can attempt to redownload the file you have just added. If you added the file to
the custom detection list, the client should no longer be able to download the file.

Figure 20-32 confirms the block of the latest download attempt due to custom detection.
This time, FTD blocks the same 7z1700.exe file that was allowed earlier due to unavailable
and unknown dispositions.

Example 20-7 displays the debugging messages for a Custom Detection Block event.
Here, FTD blacklists the 7z1700.exe file due to its addition to the custom detection list.

The File Is Blocked Due to Custom Detection

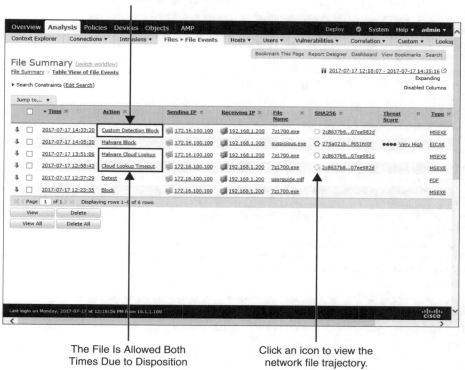

The File Is Allowed Both
Times Due to Disposition

Click an icon to view the
network file trajectory.

Figure 20-32 *File Event for the Custom Detection Block*

Example 20-7 *Adding a File to the Custom Detection List Blacklists the File*

```
> system support firewall-engine-debug

Please specify an IP protocol: tcp
Please specify a client IP address: 192.168.1.200
Please specify a client port:
Please specify a server IP address:
Please specify a server port:
Monitoring firewall engine debug messages

192.168.1.200-58588 > 172.16.100.100-80 6 AS 4 I 0 New session
192.168.1.200-58588 > 172.16.100.100-80 6 AS 4 I 0 using HW or preset rule order 2,
   'Access Rule for File Policy', action Allow and prefilter rule 0
```

```
192.168.1.200-58588 > 172.16.100.100-80 6 AS 4 I 0 allow action

192.168.1.200-58588 > 172.16.100.100-80 6 AS 4 I 0 URL SI:
   ShmDBLookupURL("http://172.16.100.100/files/7z1700.exe") returned 0

192.168.1.200-58588 > 172.16.100.100-80 6 AS 4 I 0 File policy verdict is Type,
   Malware, and Capture

192.168.1.200-58588 > 172.16.100.100-80 6 AS 4 I 0 File type verdict Unknown,
   fileAction Malware Lookup, flags 0x01BDDA00, and type action Stop for type 21 of
   instance 0

192.168.1.200-58588 > 172.16.100.100-80 6 AS 4 I 0 File signature verdict Unknown
   and flags 0x01BDDA00 for partial file of instance 0

192.168.1.200-58588 > 172.16.100.100-80 6 AS 4 I 0 File signature blacklist
   2c8637b812f7a47802f4f91f8bfaccb978df9b62de558d038485ddb307ee982d

192.168.1.200-58588 > 172.16.100.100-80 6 AS 4 I 0 File signature reserved file data
   of 2c8637b812f7a47802f4f91f8bfaccb978df9b62de558d038485ddb307ee982d with flags
   0x00A5DA00 and status Exceeded Max Filesize

192.168.1.200-58588 > 172.16.100.100-80 6 AS 4 I 0 File signature verdict Reject
   and flags 0x00A5DA00 for 2c8637b812f7a47802f4f91f8bfaccb978df9b62de558d038485dd-
   b307ee982d of instance 0

192.168.1.200-58588 > 172.16.100.100-80 6 AS 4 I 0 File malware event for
   2c8637b812f7a47802f4f91f8bfaccb978df9b62de558d038485ddb307ee982d named 7z1700.exe
   with disposition Custom and action Custom Block

192.168.1.200-58588 > 172.16.100.100-80 6 AS 4 I 0 Archive childs been processed No

192.168.1.200-58588 > 172.16.100.100-80 6 AS 4 I 0 Deleting session

^C

Caught interrupt signal

Exiting.

>
```

The FMC allows you to track and visualize the path of a file by using the network file trajectory feature. This feature can save you analysis time when you want to determine the spread of a suspicious file. You can look up a particular file by entering its SHA-256 hash value on the **Files > Network Trajectory** page. Alternatively, on the file event page, you can click a disposition icon in the SHA256 column to open the file trajectory page (as shown in the Figure 20-32).

Figure 20-33 shows the network file trajectory for the 7z1700.exe file. Throughout the exercises on this chapter, the file has gone through various disposition states that you can see on this page.

Figure 20-33 *Network File Trajectory Page*

Summary

Cisco integrates the Advanced Malware Protection (AMP) technology with the Firepower technology. This chapter explains how these technologies work together to help you detect and block the spread of infected files across your network. This chapter also shows the configurations and operations of a file policy on a Firepower system, and it demonstrates various logs and debugging messages that are useful for determining any issues with cloud lookup and file disposition.

Quiz

1. Which of the following does not require a Malware license?

   a. Sending a file to the cloud for dynamic analysis

   b. Enabling a local analysis engine

   c. Performing a cloud lookup without blocking a file

   d. Blocking a file transfer based on its file format

2. Which type of analysis requires a connection to the cloud?

    a. Spero
    b. Sandbox
    c. High-fidelity
    d. Prefilter

3. Which of the following is recommended?

    a. Use the Reset Connection option on a file rule.
    b. Avoid storing all the files that FTD detects.
    c. Limit the file size for analysis.
    d. All of the above.

4. Which of the following is not true?

    a. FTD can interrupt traffic in case of a cloud lookup failure.
    b. A file policy uses the adaptive profile feature.
    c. The FMC sends a query to the cloud to detect a file type.
    d. The FMC connects to the cloud to obtain new signatures for malware.

Chapter 21

Preventing Cyber Attacks by Blocking Intrusion Attempts

One of the most popular features of Firepower Threat Defense (FTD) is that it can function as an intrusion detection system (IDS) as well as an intrusion prevention system (IPS). FTD uses Snort, an open-source IDS/IPS, to perform deep packet inspection. Snort can detect intrusion attempts and prevent cyber attacks in real time. When an FTD device runs Snort along with many other next-generation security technologies (described in recent chapters), the device turns into a next-generation intrusion prevention system (NGIPS). In this chapter, you will learn how to configure and deploy an intrusion policy on an FTD device.

Figure 21-1 shows a packet analyzed against a Snort ruleset as the last phase of the Firepower engine inspection. However, any bypassed or trusted traffic is not subject to Snort rule inspection.

Firepower NGIPS Essentials

To deploy an FTD as an NGIPS, you need to work with three different policies in the FMC:

- **Network analysis policy:** This policy works in conjunction with preprocessor rules to normalize traffic.

- **Intrusion policy:** This policy employs the Snort rules to perform deep packet inspection.

- **Access control policy:** This policy invokes the network analysis policy and intrusion policy for matching and nonmatching traffic.

The following sections describe all the essential components that are part of an intrusion policy deployment.

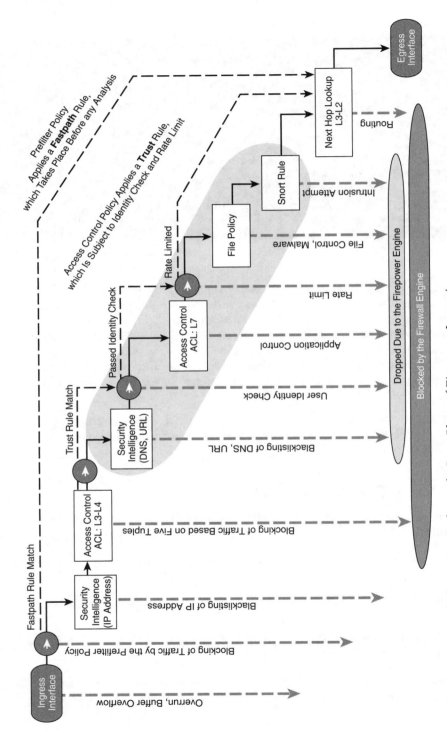

Figure 21-1 *Snort Rule Drops a Packet at the Later Phase of Firepower Inspection*

Network Analysis Policy and Preprocessor

Before performing deep packet inspection, Snort decodes a packet and streamlines its header and payload into a format that a Snort rule can analyze easily. The component that performs this normalization is called a *preprocessor*. Snort has various protocol-specific preprocessors. They can identify anomalies within the stream of packets, detect evasion techniques, and drop them when there is an inconsistency, such as an invalid checksum or unusual ports.

The implementation of preprocessors on open source Snort and FTD are not exactly the same. The Firepower engine normalizes traffic in various phases as a packet goes through additional advanced security checks.

Figure 21-2 shows the position of preprocessor in the open source Snort architecture. All the preprocessor plugins operate at the same level—after decoding a packet and before the Snort rule inspection.

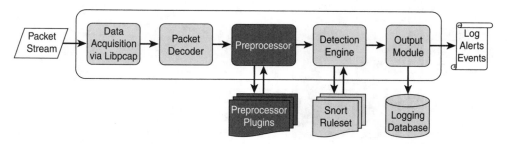

Figure 21-2 *Implementing Preprocessor Plugins on Open Source Snort*

Figure 21-3 illustrates the multiphase implementation of preprocessors on an FTD device. You can enable any of these preprocessors from one place: the network analysis policy.

A network analysis policy on a Firepower system allows you to enable a certain preprocessor and fine-tune any granular settings within. A preprocessor allows Snort to preprocess, decode, and normalize traffic for advance inspection. If you disable a preprocessor manually but Snort deems the preprocessor necessary, FTD can still engage that particular preprocessor in the backend to protect your network from a potential threat. However, a network analysis policy configuration does not indicate when FTD enables an essential preprocessor automatically. Visually, the preprocessor setting remains disabled on the FMC GUI.

Figure 21-4 shows the network analysis policy editor page, where you can enable and disable a desired preprocessor. Later in this chapter, you will learn how to create and deploy a network analysis policy from scratch.

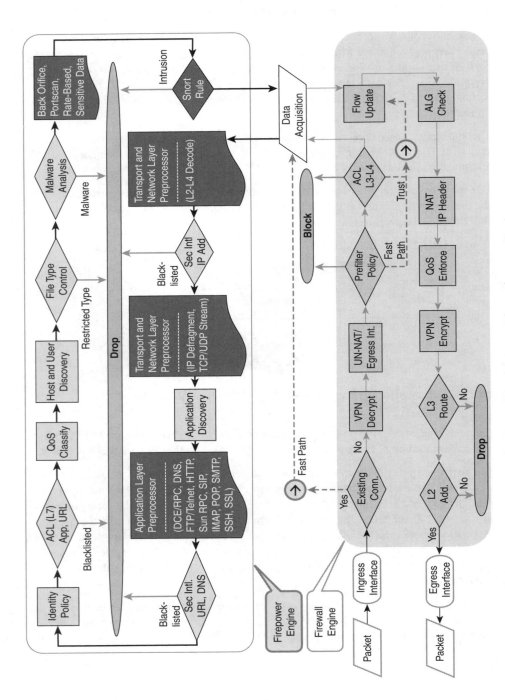

Figure 21-3   *Network Analysis Policy Acting in Multiple Phases Throughout an Engine*

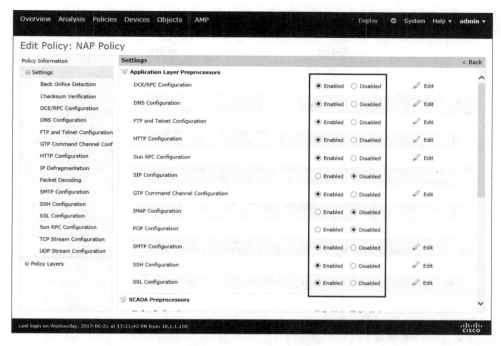

Figure 21-4 *Enabling and Disabling Preprocessor Settings in the Network Analysis Policy Editor*

The Application Layer Preprocessors section of a network analysis policy editor allows you to configure the advanced settings of various protocols traffic, such as DCE/RPC, DNS, FTP and Telnet, HTTP, Sun RPC, SIP, GTP Command Channel, IMAP, POP, SMTP, SSH, and SSL.

The Transport and Network Layer Preprocessors section of a network analysis policy editor offers granular configurable options for checksum verification, inline normalization, IP defragmentation, packet decoding, TCP stream configuration, UDP stream configuration, and so on.

The FMC also provides preprocessors for very specific environments and detection. For example, DNP3 and Modbus preprocessors have been developed for the Supervisory Control and Data Acquisition (SCADA) network environment. Similarly, three additional preprocessors are designed to detect very specific traffic patterns and threats, including Back Orifice, Portscan, and Rate-Based.

Intrusion Policy and Snort Rules

After decoding and normalizing a packet, FTD uses the intrusion ruleset to perform deep packet inspection. An intrusion rule is written based on Snort rule syntax and contains the signature of a specific vulnerability. The Firepower System supports Snort rules from various sources, including the following:

- **Standard text rules:** The Cisco Talos security intelligence and research group writes these rules in clear-text format. The Snort detection engine uses them to analyze packets.

- **Shared object (SO) rules:** Talos writes SO rules in the C programming language and compiles them for Snort use. The content of an SO rule is made irretrievable for various reasons, such as proprietary agreements between Cisco and third-party vendors.

- **Preprocessor rules:** The Snort development team creates these rules, which the Firepower engine uses to decode packets with various protocols.

- **Local rules:** The FMC enables you to create a custom Snort rule by using its GUI. You can also write your own rule in a text editor, save the file in .txt format, and upload it to the FMC. When you create your own Snort rule and import it into the FMC, the Firepower System labels it as a *local rule*. Similarly, if you obtain a Snort rule from a community-based Internet forum, the system considers it a local rule as well. The Firepower System supports text-based local rules only; it does not support the creation and compilation of your own SO rules.

Warning   Although the FMC enables you to import the community-provided rules or to write your own local rules, you should always consider enabling a Cisco-provided rule over a local rule. Cisco-provided rules are developed by Talos—a group of world-class researchers who are primarily responsible for writing and improving Snort rules. An ill-structured rule created by a new Snort user can affect the performance of an FTD device.

Snort uses a unique generator ID (GID) and Snort rule ID (SID) to identify a rule. Depending on who creates a rule, the numbering schemes of GIDs and SIDs are different. Table 21-1 provides the identification numbers that you can use to distinguish one type of Snort rule from another.

Table 21-1   *Types of Snort Rules and Their Identification Numbers*

Type of Rule	Identification Number
Standard text rule	GID is 1. SID is lower than 1,000,000.
Shared object rule	GID is 3.
Preprocessor rule	GID can be anything other than 1 or 3.
Local rule	SID is 1,000,000 or higher.

Once you create an intrusion policy, you can enter the intrusion policy editor page to find and enable a specific Snort rule or all of the rules within a category.

Figure 21-5 shows a search query for all the Snort rules with Telnet metadata. You can perform a similar search to find rules with many other criteria. For now, just take a look how the intrusion policy editor displays rules in a search query. Later in this chapter, you will learn how to create, edit, and deploy an intrusion policy from scratch.

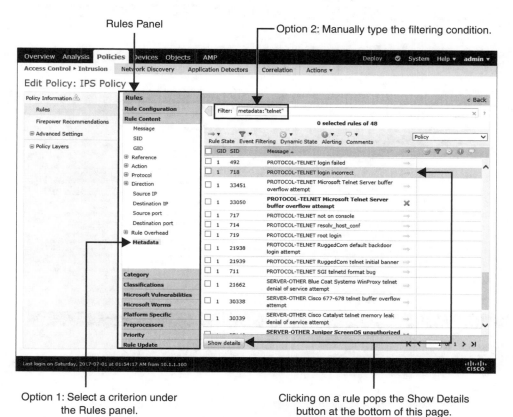

Figure 21-5 *Granular Options to Search for a Specific Snort Rule in the Intrusion Policy Editor*

Tip   If you want to search for rule 718 directly, enter **SID:718** in the filter—rather than just 718. If you want to perform a new search, you should clear the existing search result by clicking the X icon in the Filter bar.

Once you find a rule, you can select the rule and click the **Show Details** button to view detailed information about it.

Figure 21-6 shows the syntax of Snort rule 1:718. It also provides detailed rule documentation. Later in this chapter, you will learn how to create an intrusion policy from scratch and enable a desired rule within it.

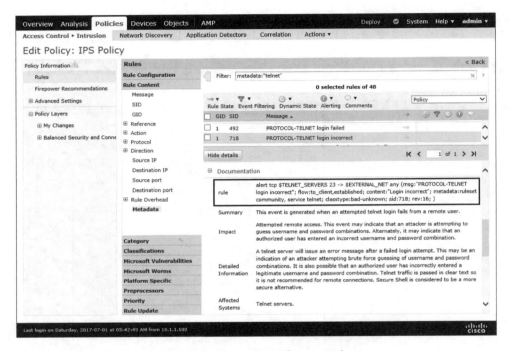

Figure 21-6 *Viewing Additional Information About a Rule*

Note   Throughout this chapter, Snort rule 1:718 is used as an example to demonstrate various configurations. You can replace SID:718 with any desired rule.

System-Provided Variables

Besides using a static IP address or port number, a Snort rule can use variables to represent the source and destination information. This empowers you to enable a rule in any network environment without modifying the original Snort rule.

Figure 21-7 illustrates Snort rule 1:718, which analyzes traffic from the $TELNET_ SERVERS variable to detect a potential brute-force attack. If you do not change the default value of the $TELNET_SERVERS variable, Snort analyzes packets from additional IP addresses—along with your real Telnet server—for the "Login incorrect" content with the payloads.

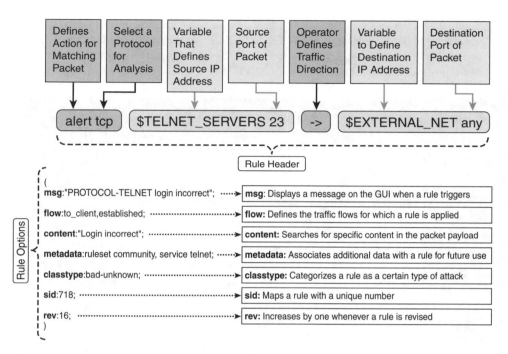

Figure 21-7 *Anatomy of Snort Rule 1:718 (GID:1, SID:718)*

You must define the $HOME_NET variable based on the network address used in your LAN. If the default value of a variable that represents a specific server is set to any or $HOME_NET, you must change it to a more specific value. It makes a Snort rule more effective and reduces the probability of false positive alerts. Thus, a proper variable setting can improve performance.

The purpose of a variable is explained by the variable's name. The names ending with $*_NET, $*_SERVERS and $*_PORTS define network addresses, IP addresses, and port numbers, respectively. Consider these examples:

■ **$HOME_NET, $EXTERNAL_NET:** Defines the internal network and external network addresses, respectively.

■ **$HTTP_SERVERS, $DNS_SERVERS:** Defines the IP addresses of the web servers and domain name servers, respectively.

■ **$FTP_PORTS, $HTTP_PORTS:** Defines the port numbers of the FTP servers and web servers, respectively.

Note In this chapter, the configuration examples use the Cisco-provided Snort rules. If you want to write your own local rules, you need to know the usage of Snort variables and rule options, which are beyond the scope of this chapter. To learn more about custom rule writing, read the documentation on open-source Snort at www.snort.org.

Figure 21-8 shows a list of variables in the default variable set. You must redefine both variables—$HOME_NET and $TELNET_SERVERS—to trigger SID:718 efficiently in the appropriate condition. The list in this figure has been shortened to accommodate both the $HOME_NET and $TELNET_SERVERS in one screenshot.

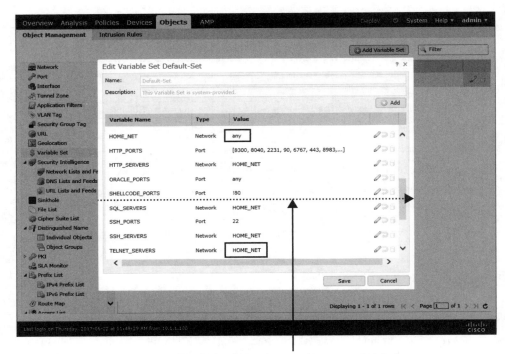

The list has been shortened to accommodate the
essential variables in one page.

Figure 21-8   *Redefining the Default Values of Variables with Specific Values*

System-Provided Policies

To help you expedite a deployment, Firepower software comes with several preconfig-ured network analysis policies and intrusion policies. You can use one of the following system-provided policies as the default security policy for your network or as a baseline for a custom security policy:

- **Balanced Security and Connectivity:** Cisco Talos recommends this policy for the best system performance without compromising the detection of the latest critical vulnerabilities.

- **Connectivity over Security:** This policy prioritizes connection speed while main-taining detection of a few critical vulnerabilities.

- **Security over Connectivity:** Security has higher priority than connection speed and reachability.

- **Maximum Detection:** Security has supreme priority over business continuity. Due to the deeper inspection of packets, end users may experience latency, and FTD may drop some legitimate traffic.

Figure 21-9 shows four system-provided policies that you can use as a base policy for a network analysis policy (NAP).

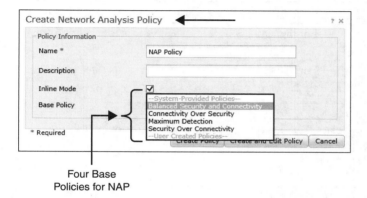

Figure 21-9   *System-Provided Base Policies for Network Analysis*

Figure 21-10 shows five system-provided policies in the dropdown that you can use as a base policy for an intrusion policy. The base policy No Rules Active allows you to create an empty intrusion policy with all the rules disabled. You can use it for two purposes: to create an intrusion policy from scratch or to investigate any technical issues with the Snort engine.

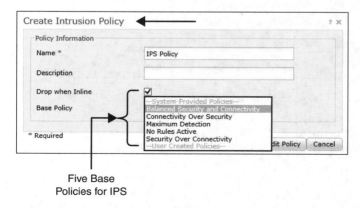

Figure 21-10   *System-Provided Base Policies for Intrusion Detection and Prevention*

The number of rules enabled by default in a system-provided policy varies. Cisco uses a Common Vulnerability Scoring System (CVSS) score that is associated with a vulnerability to determine whether a rule should be part of any system-provided policy.

Table 21-2 shows the criteria to determine the inclusion of an intrusion rule in a system-provided policy.

Table 21-2   *System-Provided Policies and Their Associations with CVSS Scores*

Intrusion Policy	CVSS Score	Age of Vulnerability
Connectivity over Security	10	Current year plus two prior years
Balanced Security and Connectivity	9 or higher	Current year plus two prior years
Security over Connectivity	8 or higher	Current year plus three prior years
Maximum Detection	7.5 or higher	All the years since 2005

Figure 21-11 shows the correlation among the system-provided intrusion policies, their detection coverages, and processing overheads. The higher the threat coverage, the higher the utilization of the FTD resources.

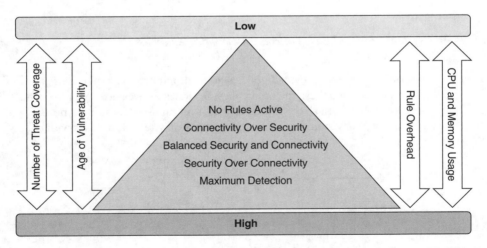

Figure 21-11   *System-Provided Policies, Coverages, and Processing Overheads*

Cisco releases rule updates periodically. The FMC can update the ruleset automatically from the cloud through a scheduled task. You can also manually download a rule update file and upload it to the FMC for installation. Each rule update comes with a unique ruleset. While the exact number of available rules on a specific rule update is unpredictable, the ratio of enabled rules among the system-provided policies is similar. For example, the Security over Connectivity policy enables the highest number of intrusion rules, whereas the Connectivity over Security policy enables the lowest number of rules. (However, the No Rules Active policy has no rules enabled.)

Figure 21-12 shows the Policy Information page in an intrusion policy editor. Here you can determine the number of enabled rules and the rule update version of a base policy.

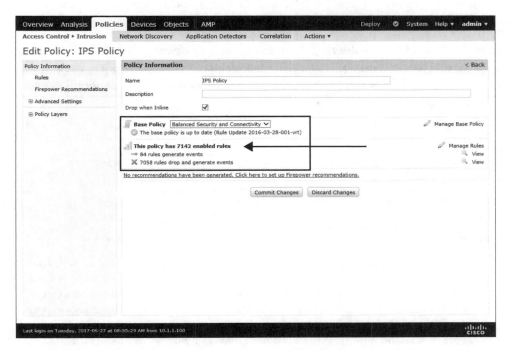

Figure 21-12   *Determining the Number of Enabled Rules on a Base Policy*

Table 21-3 shows the number of rules enabled by default by Rule Update 2016-03-28-001-vrt. Firepower Version 6.1 comes with rule update 2016-03-28-001-vrt preinstalled.

Table 21-3   *Enabled Rules in the Default Ruleset of Rule Update 2016-03-28-001-vrt*

Intrusion Policy	Total Number of Enabled Rules	Rules to Generate Events	Rules to Drop and Generate Events
No Rules Active	0	0	0
Connectivity over Security	459	9	450
Balanced Security and Connectivity	7142	84	7058
Security over Connectivity	10,069	235	9834
Maximum Detection	5533	39	5494

Table 21-4 shows the number of rules enabled by default by Rule Update 2017-06-15-001-vrt. You can compare the statistics shown here with the number of rules enabled on 2016-03-28-001-vrt, as shown in Table 21-3. These rule updates were released one year apart, but the ratio of the enabled rules is similar.

Table 21-4   *Enabled Rules in the Default Ruleset of Rule Update 2017-06-15-001-vrt*

Intrusion Policy	Total Number of Rules Enabled	Rules to Generate Events	Rules to Drop and Generate Events
No Rules Active	0	0	0
Connectivity over Security	474	9	465
Balanced Security and Connectivity	8779	71	8708
Security over Connectivity	12,716	245	12,471
Maximum Detection	6732	40	6692

As the name suggests, the Maximum Detection policy is meant to enable the maximum number of intrusion rules. However, the numbers in Tables 21-3 and 21-4 do not support this assumption. Actually, the Security over Connectivity policy enables the maximum number of rules. So, how does the Maximum Detection policy ensure the maximum threat detection? It actually performs a much deeper analysis of packets to detect any protocol anomalies.

Table 21-5 shows the number of preprocessors enabled on different system-provided network analysis policies. The Maximum Detection policy has the highest number of preprocessors enabled, by default.

Table 21-5   *Number of Preprocessors Enabled on Rule Update 2017-06-15-001-vrt*

Intrusion Policy	Number of Enabled Preprocessors
Connectivity over Security	15
Balanced Security and Connectivity	15
Security over Connectivity	17
Maximum Detection	18

Figure 21-13 illustrates the default configuration settings of the HTTP preprocessor on the Maximum Detection policy. As you can see, much deeper inspections are enabled.

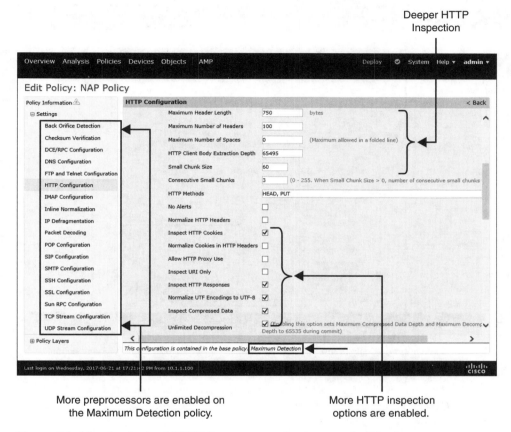

Deeper HTTP Inspection

More preprocessors are enabled on the Maximum Detection policy.

More HTTP inspection options are enabled.

Figure 21-13 *Analysis of HTTP Preprocessor Settings on the Maximum Detection Policy*

Figure 21-14 shows the default configuration settings of the HTTP preprocessor on the Balanced Security and Connectivity policy. If you compare this figure with the previous one, you will find a milder HTTP inspection setting on the Balanced Security and Connectivity policy.

The depth of HTTP inspection is shallow.

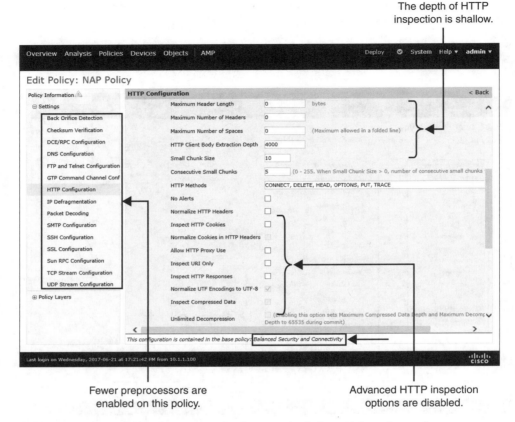

Fewer preprocessors are enabled on this policy.

Advanced HTTP inspection options are disabled.

Figure 21-14 *HTTP Preprocessor Settings on the Balanced Security and Connectivity Policy*

Best Practices for Intrusion Policy Deployment

Note This section discusses various tips for optimal deployment and displays GUI navigations to the related configuration pages. Later in this chapter, you will find detailed configuration steps for each of these items.

Before you deploy an intrusion policy, you should consider the following best practices, in general:

■ To match a packet using five tuples—source port, destination port, source address, destination address, and protocol—you should consider using an access rule, not an intrusion rule. The purpose of a Snort-based intrusion rule is to perform advanced deep packet inspection.

■ Select the **Balanced Security and Connectivity** policy as the default policy when you create the network analysis policy and intrusion policy.

Figure 21-15 shows the selection of Balanced Security and Connectivity as the base policy for both the network analysis policy (top) and intrusion policy (bottom). Also, notice the check boxes for Inline Mode and Drop When Inline; you must select both of them if you want FTD to block an intrusion attempt.

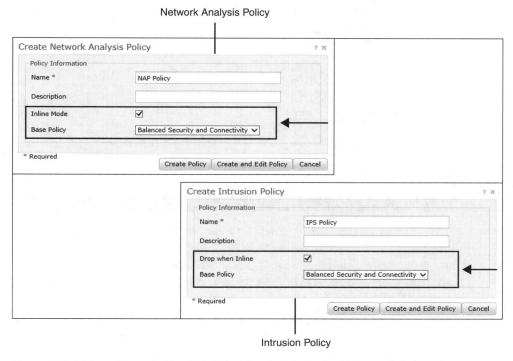

Figure 21-15   *Policy Creation Windows for the Network Analysis Policy and Intrusion Policy*

■ Use the Firepower Recommendations feature within the intrusion policy. This feature can incorporate the network discovery data to determine the intrusion rules that are related to the operating systems, services, and applications running in a network.

■ When you generate Firepower recommendations, define the networks to examine and set Recommendation Threshold (by Rule Overhead) to Medium or Low for optimal system performance.

Figure 21-16 shows the Firepower Recommendations configuration page within the intrusion policy editor. The number of recommended rules can vary based on your settings.

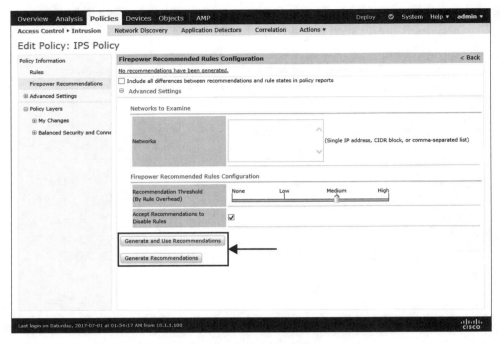

Figure 21-16 *Configuration Page to Generate Firepower Recommended Rules*

■ Enable the Adaptive Profiles and Enable Profile Update features to leverage the service metadata and allow FTD to apply the enabled intrusion rules to the relevant traffic intelligently.

Figure 21-17 shows the advanced settings for an access control policy where you can configure the Adaptive Profiles and Enable Profile Update settings.

Table 21-6 shows the differences between the Firepower Recommendations and Enable Profile Update features. Although both features work together to enable traffic-specific intrusion rules, there are some differences between them.

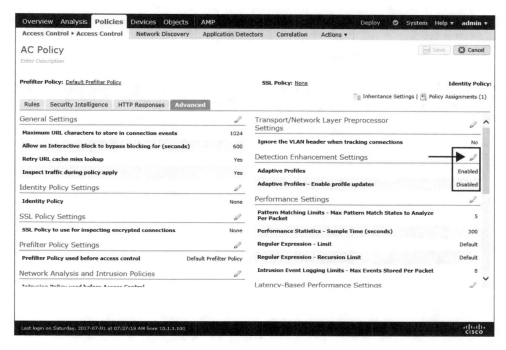

Figure 21-17 *Configuration Page for an Adaptive Profile*

Table 21-6 *Firepower Recommendations Versus Enable Profile Update*

Firepower Recommendation	Enable Profile Update
Recommends enabling and disabling intrusion rules, based on the discovered applications and hosts.	Compares rule metadata with the applications and operating systems of a host and determines whether the FTD device should apply a certain rule to certain traffic from that host.
Can enable a disabled rule if the rule relates to a host and application in the network.	Does not change the state of a disabled rule. Only works on the enabled rules in an intrusion policy.
Configured within an intrusion policy.	Configured within an access control policy.

Tip Enable both features—Enable Profile Update and Firepower Recommendations—at the same time. Doing so enables an FTD device to enable or disable the intrusion rules that are related to the hosts, applications, and services running on a network and then apply the enabled rules to relevant traffic from those hosts.

■ In the network analysis policy, configure the Inline Normalization preprocessor with the Normalize TCP Payload option enabled to ensure consistent retransmission of data (see Figure 21-18).

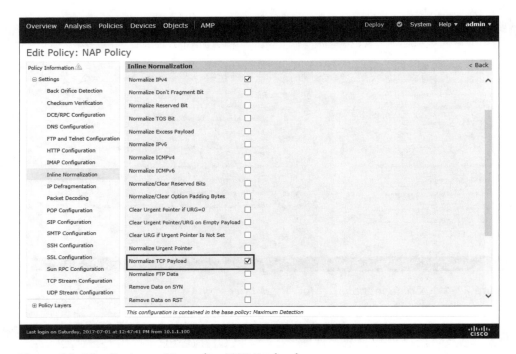

Figure 21-18 *Option to Normalize TCP Payload*

Some of the best practices are applicable to a particular deployment mode, and depend on your traffic handling policy. For example:

■ If you want to prevent cyber attacks by blocking intrusion attempts, you need to deploy FTD device bump in the wire (BITW). The BITW deployment requires an inline interface pair—you include the ingress and egress interfaces to an inline interface pair and then assign the interface pair to an inline set. To learn more about Inline Mode, see Chapter 11, "Blocking Traffic Using Inline Interface Mode."

■ If your goal is to deploy FTD for detection-only purposes—that is, you do not want to block an intrusion attempt in real time—consider deploying an FTD device in Inline Tap Mode instead of in Passive Mode. Doing so enables you to switch to Inline Mode faster, without the need for a cabling change. This is critical in case of an emergency. To learn more, read Chapter 12, "Inspecting Traffic Without Blocking It."

- If you choose to deploy an FTD device in Passive Mode anyway, make sure the Adaptive Profiles option is enabled on the advanced settings access control policy. This option enables an FTD device to adapt intrusion rules dynamically based on the metadata of the service, client application, and host traffic.

- When FTD prompts you to select a firewall mode (during initialization after a reimage), choose Routed Mode. While Transparent Mode can block an intrusion attempt, you could accomplish the same goal—transparency or a bump in the wire—by using Inline Mode, which has less configuration overhead. Using the FTD CLI, you can switch between Routed Mode and Transparent Mode. To learn more about Routed Mode, read Chapter 8, "Firepower Deployment in Routed Mode."

NGIPS Configuration

Configuring an FTD device as a next-generation intrusion prevention system (NGIPS) can involve three different security policies: network analysis policy, intrusion policy, and access control policy. In the following sections, you will learn how to configure all of these policies in order to deploy an FTD device with NGIPS functionality.

Configuring a Network Analysis Policy

To create a network analysis policy (NAP), you need to navigate to the network analysis policy configuration page. However, the FMC does not provide a direct menu to go there. You can navigate to that page in two ways: through the access control policy configuration page or through the intrusion policy configuration page.

Figure 21-19 shows the navigation to the network analysis policy through the intrusion policy page. You will find a similar link on the access control policy page.

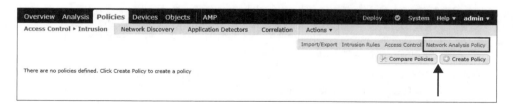

Figure 21-19 *Link to Access the Network Analysis Policy Configuration Page*

Creating a New NAP with Default Settings

Once you are on the network analysis policy configuration page, follow these steps:

Step 1.   Click the **Create Policy** button. The Create Network Analysis Policy window appears (see Figure 21-20).

Step 2.   Give a name to the policy.

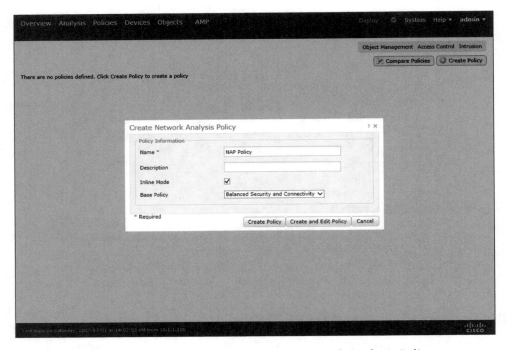

Figure 21-20   *Configuration Window to Create a Network Analysis Policy*

Note   By default, the Inline Mode option is enabled. It allows the preprocessors to normalize traffic flows and drop any packets that contain anomalies.

Step 3.   As the base policy, select **Balanced Security and Connectivity**. This policy provides the best system performance without compromising the detection of the latest and critical vulnerabilities.

Step 4.   Click the **Create Policy** button to create a network analysis policy using the default settings. You will return to the network analysis policy configuration page. The network analysis policy you have just created should appear in the list on this page.

Optionally, if you want to modify the default settings of the network analysis policy, read on; otherwise, skip to the next section, "Configuring an Intrusion Policy".

Modifying the Default Settings of a NAP

FMC enables you to enable or disable the default settings of a network analysis policy. There are two ways to enter the policy editor page. During the network analysis policy creation, you could select the Create and Edit Policy button instead of clicking the Create Policy button. Alternatively, if you already created a network analysis policy, you could find the policy on the network analysis policy configuration page and select the pencil icon next to it. Both methods can take you to the policy editor page right way.

Step 1.   On the network analysis policy editor page, select **Settings** in the panel on the left. A list of preprocessors appears. Figure 21-21 shows the network analysis policy editor page, where you can enable, disable, and modify preprocessor configurations.

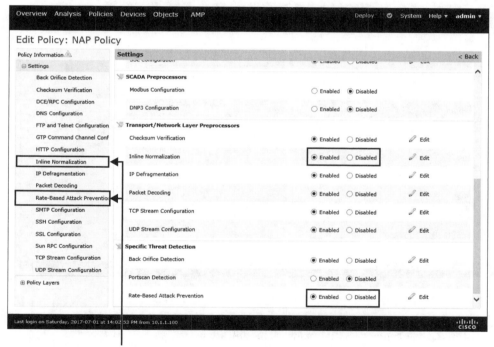

The extra preprocessors appear in this list after you enable them on demand.

Figure 21-21   *Enabling Extra Preprocessors on Top of a Base Policy*

Step 2.   Enable (or disable) any desired preprocessors in addition to the preprocessors enabled (or disabled) by default on the base policy.

> **Tip**   Enable the Inline Normalization preprocessor with the Normalize TCP Payload option to ensure consistent retransmission of data (refer to Figure 21-18).

Figure 21-22 shows the impact of your changes to the network analysis policy. Although Inline Normalization and Rate-Based Attack Prevention preprocessors are disabled on the base policy, your custom configuration overrides the default behavior of the base policy.

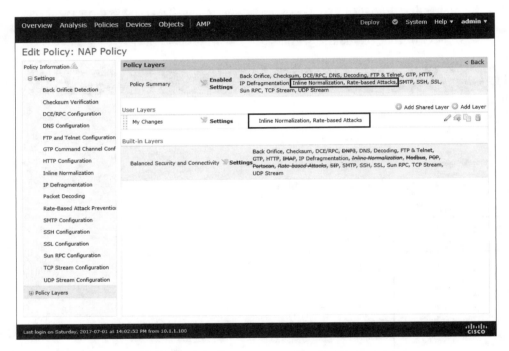

Figure 21-22   *Layered View of the Preprocessor Configurations*

Step 3.   When you are finished with modifications, make sure you save the changes. On the left panel, select the **Policy Information** section, and click the **Commit Changes** button (see Figure 21-23). This button is comparable to a Save button, in that any modification is saved but not deployed on a managed device.

Figure 21-23   *Saving Configuration Changes*

Configuring an Intrusion Policy

Intrusion policy configuration is the key part of an NGIPS deployment. This is where you select a system-provided ruleset and enable any additional intrusion rules.

Creating a Policy with a Default Ruleset

To create an intrusion policy, follow these steps:

Step 1.   Navigate to **Policies > Access Control > Intrusion.** The intrusion policy configuration page appears.

Step 2.   Click the **Create Policy** button. The Create Intrusion Policy window appears (see Figure 21-24).

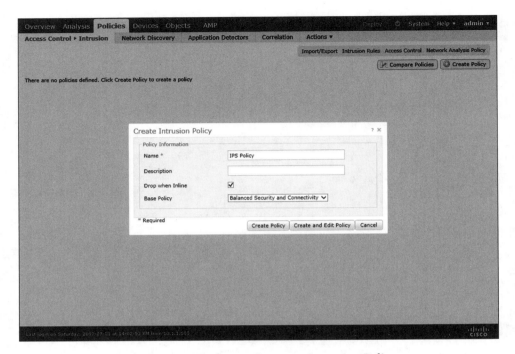

Figure 21-24 *Configuration Window to Create an Intrusion Policy*

Step 3.   Give a name to the policy.

> **Note**   By default, the Drop When Inline option is enabled, which means an FTD device can drop packets when you deploy it in Inline, Routed, or Transparent Mode. This option, however, does not affect the traffic flow if you deploy the FTD device in Inline Tap or Passive Mode.

Step 4.   Select **Balanced Security and Connectivity** as the base policy. This policy provides the best system performance without compromising the detection of the latest and critical vulnerabilities.

Step 5.   Click the **Create Policy** button to create an intrusion policy using the default settings.

Incorporating Firepower Recommendations

By default, the Firepower Recommendations feature is disabled, as it can consume additional resources to analyze the network discovery data and associated vulnerabilities and generate recommendations accordingly. You should leverage the Firepower Recommendations feature, though, because it can suggest enabling or disabling intrusion rules based on the operating systems, services, and applications running in your network.

Tip   Generate and use Firepower Recommendations *after* the majority of your network hosts generate traffic and your FTD discovers them. If you apply recommendations without waiting some time to perform the network discovery, FTD may recommend disabling many intrusion rules, which may not be desired.

To generate and use Firepower Recommendations, follow these steps:

Step 1.   Edit the intrusion policy where you want to enable Firepower Recommendations. If you are currently in the process of creating an intrusion policy, click the **Create and Edit Policy** button to enter the policy editor page right away. If a policy is already created, you can enter the editor page by using the pencil icon, which is next to the name of the intrusion policy (see Figure 21-25).

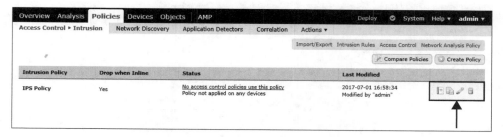

Figure 21-25   *Option to Edit an Intrusion Policy*

Step 2.   On the intrusion policy editor page, select **Firepower Recommendations** from the blue panel on the left. The Firepower Recommended Rule Configuration page appears.

Step 3.   Define the networks to examine and set Recommendation Threshold (by Rule Overhead) to low or medium so that the intrusion rules with higher processing overhead are not considered in the recommended ruleset.

Figure 21-26 shows the configuration of Firepower Recommendations. The configuration in this example analyzes traffic from the 192.168.1.0/24 network and suggests intrusion rules based on the application, services, and operating systems running on the network hosts.

Step 4.   Click the **Generate and Use Recommendations** button. This button appears if the FMC did not generate any recommendation before. If a recommendation has already been generated, you will see different buttons, whose labels are self-explanatory, such as Update Recommendations, Do Not Use Recommendations, and so on.

Figure 21-27 shows the recommendations for 963 rules (20 rules to generate events, 943 rules to drop and generate events). These rules are suggested based on the information on two hosts.

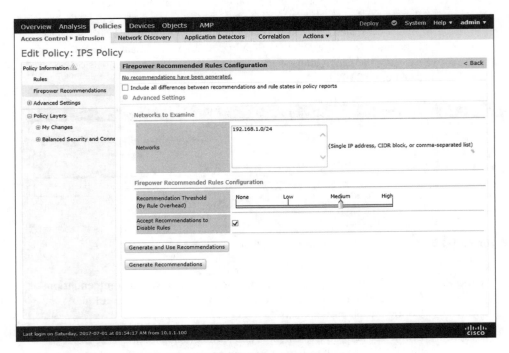

Figure 21-26   *Firepower Recommended Rules Configuration*

963 Rules Are Enabled

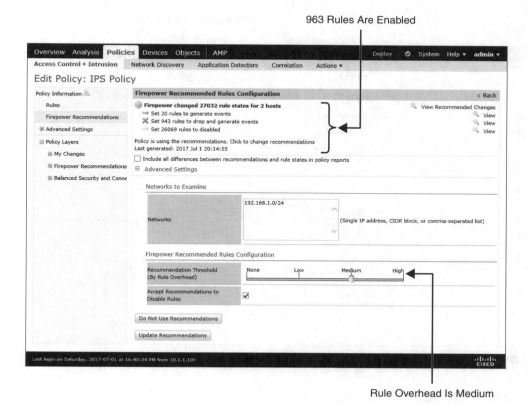

Rule Overhead Is Medium

Figure 21-27   *Firepower Recommended Rules—Rule Overhead Is Medium*

For testing purposes, you can try regenerating recommendations with low rule overhead threshold. You will notice that, for the same network hosts, the number of recommended rules is now significantly lower. Figure 21-28 shows the recommendations for only three rules (two rules to generate events and one rule to drop and generate events). The number of recommended rules for the same two network hosts are significantly lower because the rule processing overhead is set to low.

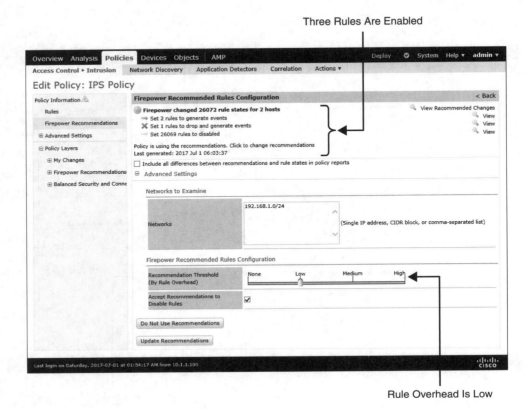

Figure 21-28   *Firepower Recommendations (for Testing Purposes)—Rule Overhead Is Low*

Step 5.   Make sure to save any changes by clicking the **Commit Changes** button on the Policy Information page.

Enabling or Disabling an Intrusion Rule

Optionally, if you want to enable or disable any intrusion rule from the default ruleset, follow these steps:

Step 1.   Edit the intrusion policy where you want to enable or disable an intrusion rule. If you are currently in the process of creating an intrusion policy, click the **Create and Edit Policy** button to enter the policy editor page right away. If a policy has already been created, you can enter the editor page by using the pencil icon, which is next to the name of the intrusion policy.

Step 2.   On the intrusion policy editor page, select **Rules** in the panel on the left. A list of rules appears.

Step 3. When you find a desired rule, select its check box and define the Rule State to enable the rule.

Tip If you manually enable additional intrusion rules (on top of a base policy), and you want FTD to block any matching packets, the state of those rules should be set to Drop and Generate Events.

Figure 21-29 illustrates the steps to find and enable a desired rule using the intrusion policy editor.

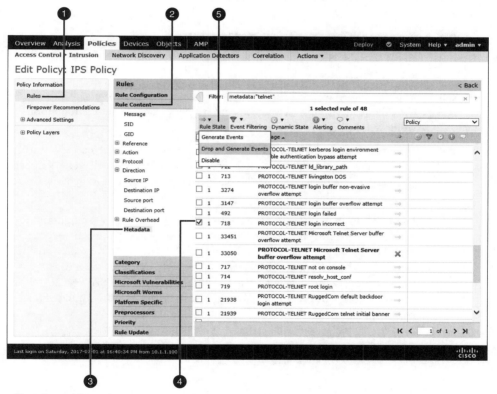

Steps to enable a rule
1. Select **Rules** on the left panel.
2-3. Select the criteria to find the desired rules.
4. Select the desired rules using the check box.
5. Define an action by selecting a rule state.

Figure 21-29 *Enabling an Intrusion Rule*

Step 4. Make sure you save any changes by clicking the **Commit Changes** button on the Policy Information page.

Setting Up a Variable Set

One of the important steps in configuring an intrusion policy is to define the values of a variable set. Because a Firepower system does not make this configuration step mandatory, users may overlook this step.

You must define the $HOME_NET variable based on the network address used in your LAN. If the default value of a variable that represents a specific server is set to any or $HOME_NET, you must change it to a more specific value. Doing so makes a Snort rule more effective and reduces the probability of false positive alerts. Thus, a proper variable setting can improve performance.

To modify the system-provided default set or to add a new variable set, follow these steps:

Step 1.   Navigate to **Objects > Object Management**.

Step 2.   Select **Variable Set** from the menu on the left. The list of available variable sets appears.

Step 3.   You can edit an existing variable set or create a new one. To create a new one, click the **Add Variable Set** button, and the New Variable Set configuration window appears.

Step 4.   Find the variables that need updates. Click a variable's pencil icon to edit the value of the variable. To define a value, you can add a network address directly or select a predefined network object. The system also allows you to create a new network object on the fly.

Figure 21-30 shows how to navigate to the New Variable Set configuration window, where you can customize the default variables. For example, when you click the pencil icon next to the HOME_NET variable, the Edit Variable HOME_NET window, which is a *variable editor*, appears. Figure 21-30 shows the customized values for the HOME_NET, EXTERNAL_NET, and TELNET_SERVERS variables. (You can see the variable editor in the background in Figure 21-31.)

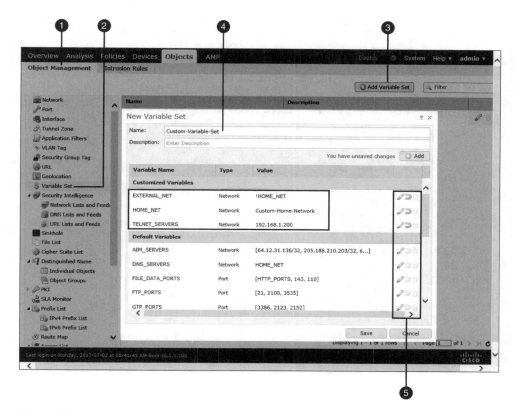

Figure 21-30   *Creating a Custom Variable Set*

Figure 21-31 shows the definition of a new network object, Custom-Home-Network, which will replace the default value of the HOME_NET variable. In the background, you can see the green plus icon on the variable editor that opens the New Network Objects configuration window also shown here.

Step 5.   When the values of the necessary variables are updated with the new network addresses or ports, save the configuration.

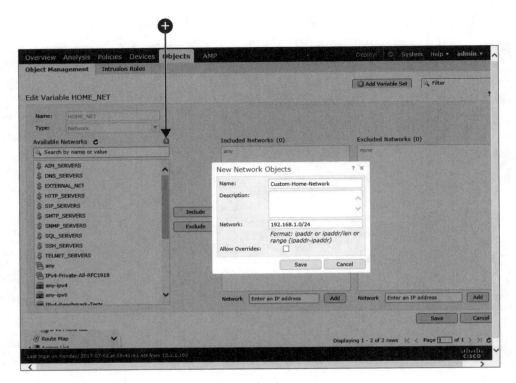

Figure 21-31   *Creating a Custom Network Object*

Configuring an Access Control Policy

In the previous sections of this chapter, you have configured various components to detect anomalies and intrusion attempts. However, they do not begin acting upon traffic until and unless you deploy the necessary policies on an FTD device. On an access control policy, you should configure the following items for the best detection:

■ **Adaptive Profiles:** An access control policy allows you to enable Adaptive Profiles and Enable Profile Updates features, which empower an FTD device to apply the enabled intrusion rules intelligently to the relevant traffic.

Figure 21-32 shows the configuration window for the Adaptive Profiles and Enable Profile Updates features. To find this window, go to the Advanced tab of the access control policy and use the pencil icon next to Detection Enhancement Settings.

■ **Invoking the policies:** An access control policy invokes various Firepower policies that you configure all over the GUI (for example, network analysis policy, intrusion policy).

First, on the Advanced tab, select an intrusion policy that is applied before an access rule is determined for the traffic. Here, you can also select a variable set that is used by the intrusion policy and a network analysis policy that the system uses by default.

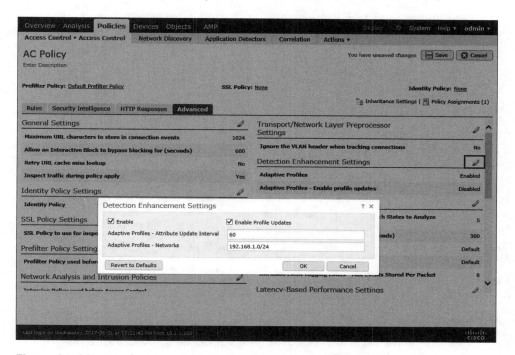

Figure 21-32   *Configuring the Adaptive Profile and Profile Update*

Figure 21-33 shows the selection of an intrusion policy, a variable set, and a network analysis policy with an access control policy.

Then, when you add an access rule, you can invoke an intrusion policy and a variable set for the matching traffic. You can define this on the Inspection tab of the access rule editor.

Figure 21-34 shows the selection of an intrusion policy and a variable set within an access rule. When a packet matches the condition of this access rule, it is subject to the inspection of this intrusion policy and variable set.

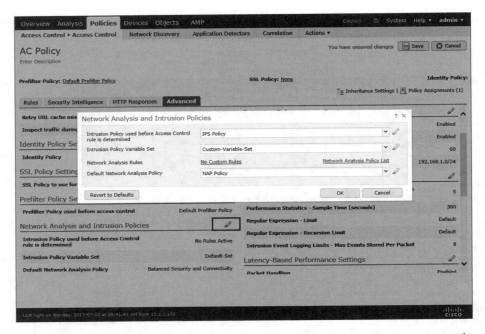

Figure 21-33 *Invoking an Intrusion Policy Before an Access Rule Is Determined*

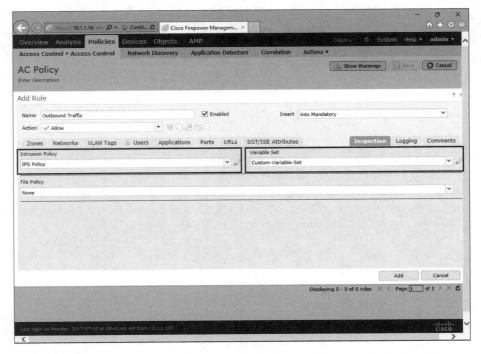

Figure 21-34 *Invoking an Intrusion Policy When It Matches a Rule Condition*

Finally, for any traffic that does not match an access rule condition, you can select an intrusion policy as the default action.

Figure 21-35 shows the selection of a custom intrusion policy as the default action for the traffic that does not match any of the access rule conditions.

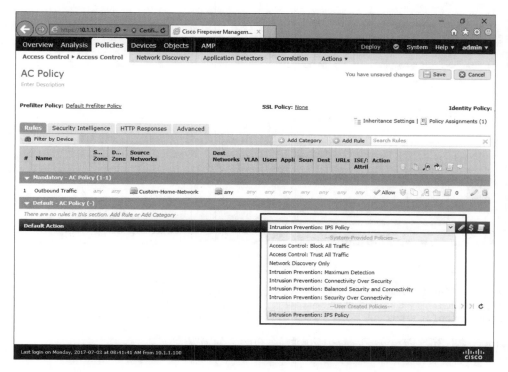

Figure 21-35   *Invoking an Intrusion Policy When Packets Do Not Match Any Access Rules*

Once you have invoked all the necessary policies and configurations in your access control policy, you must click the **Save** button to store the configurations locally. Finally, to activate the new policies, click the **Deploy** button.

Figure 21-36 shows three places where you can connect an intrusion policy with an access control policy. It also clarifies their relationships with traffic flow.

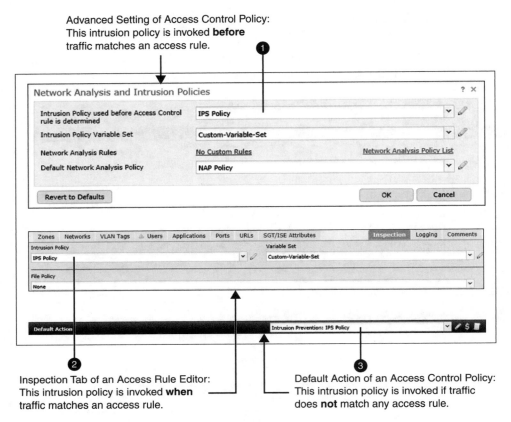

Advanced Setting of Access Control Policy:
This intrusion policy is invoked **before**
traffic matches an access rule.

Inspection Tab of an Access Rule Editor:
This intrusion policy is invoked **when**
traffic matches an access rule.

Default Action of an Access Control Policy:
This intrusion policy is invoked if traffic
does **not** match any access rule.

Figure 21-36   *Various Places to Invoke an Intrusion Policy*

Verification and Troubleshooting Tools

To verify whether an intrusion policy is active, you can run traffic to and from your network host. However, if the traffic does not carry a signature of any vulnerability, FTD does not trigger an intrusion alert for it.

To verify the action of an intrusion policy, this chapter uses a simple Snort rule 1:718. Here is the rule syntax:

```
alert tcp $TELNET_SERVERS 23 -> $EXTERNAL_NET any (msg:"PROTOCOL-TELNET
login incorrect"; flow:to_client,established; content:"Login incorrect";
metadata:ruleset community, service telnet; classtype:bad-unknown; sid:718;
rev:16; )
```

According to the syntax of this rule, when a Telnet server does not authenticate a client and responds to the client with a "Login incorrect" message on its payload (due to an incorrect login credential), an FTD device triggers this rule to prevent any potential brute-force attack. Furthermore, if you define a variable set precisely, this rule is applicable on the Telnet traffic to $EXTERNAL_NET. It should not apply on the Telnet traffic to $HOME_NET.

Figure 21-37 shows the payload of a packet on a packet analyzer. A Telnet server sends this packet when you enter an incorrect credential. Snort rule 1:718 can detect this payload.

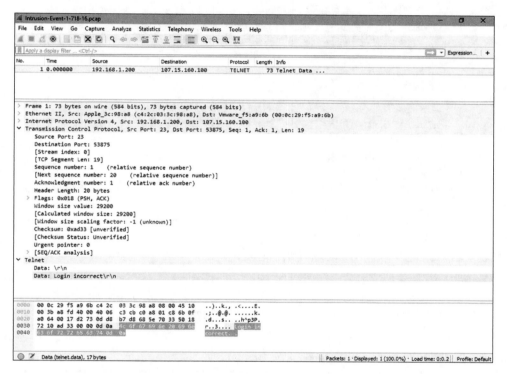

Figure 21-37   *Packet Containing "Login incorrect" on the Payload*

Figure 21-38 shows the lab topology that is used in the configuration examples in this chapter.

If you attempt to connect to your Telnet server from an external network host and enter a valid login credential, you will be able to access the server as usual. However, if you enter an incorrect credential, the server sends the client a "Login incorrect" message in a packet.

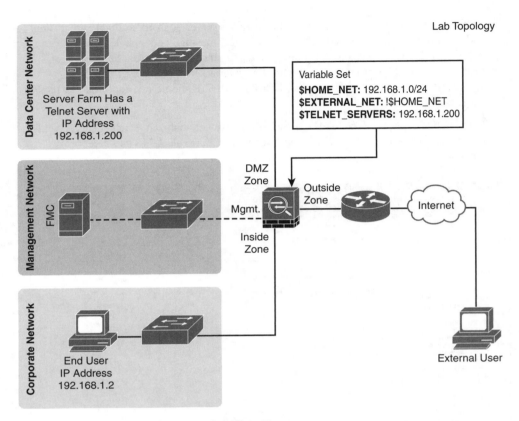

Figure 21-38 *Lab Topology Used in This Chapter*

Example 21-1 shows the messages on the CLI when you attempt to connect to a Telnet server running on a Linux-based system. Note the "Login incorrect" message when the login attempt is unsuccessful.

Example 21-1 *Telnet Server Connection Attempts*

```
! When a login attempt is successful

external-user@Fedora:~$ telnet 192.168.1.200
Trying 192.168.1.200... Open
Connected to 192.168.1.200.

Ubuntu login: internal-user
Password: ********

Welcome to Ubuntu 16.04.2 LTS (GNU/Linux 4.4.0-81-generic x86_64)
```

```
internal-user@Ubuntu:~$


! When a login attempt is unsuccessful

external-user@Fedora:~$ telnet 192.168.1.200
Trying 192.168.1.200... Open
Connected to 192.168.1.200.

Ubuntu login: internal-user
Password: <incorrect_password>

Login incorrect

Ubuntu login:
```

Tip   Some Telnet servers may return a different failure message, such as "Login Failed." To detect this string, a different Snort rule, 1:492, is available.

Depending on the rule state, policy setting, and interface mode, a Firepower system can act differently on the same Telnet traffic, and you may find different types of intrusion events for the same Snort rule. For example, if the interface mode is set to Inline Mode, the intrusion policy is set to Drop When Inline, and the rule state is Drop and Generate Events, then an FTD device can block a matching packet. The FMC displays a "dropped" event (indicated by a dark gray down arrow).

However, if the Drop When Inline option is unchecked in the intrusion policy, or if the interface mode is Inline Tap Mode or Passive Mode, the FMC shows a "would have dropped" event (indicated by a light gray down arrow). To find more scenarios for "would have dropped" events, see Chapter 12.

Figure 21-39 shows three different types of intrusion events triggered by the same Snort rule.

To analyze an intrusion event further, you can click on the down arrow at the beginning of each row. It allows you to drill down into an intrusion event and the associated packet data to determine whether an event is false positive.

Figure 21-40 shows various contextual information about an intrusion event (for example, timestamp, priority, and classification of the event). You can also find the ingress and egress interfaces, source and destination details, and any associated rule and policy references.

Rule State: Drop and Generate Events
Interface Mode: Inline Tap, Passive, or Inline
Mode when the Drop When Inline option is disabled.

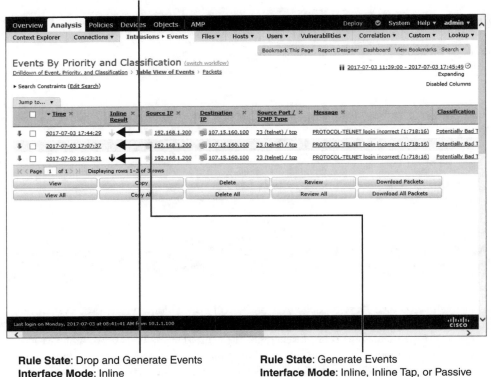

Rule State: Drop and Generate Events   **Rule State**: Generate Events
Interface Mode: Inline   **Interface Mode**: Inline, Inline Tap, or Passive

Figure 21-39   *Snort Rule 1:718 Generating Intrusion Events*

Figure 21-41 shows the packet information associated with an intrusion event. It allows you to compare the rule content with the packet payload on the same page without the need for any additional tool. This page also offers you an option to download any packet for offline analysis on third-party software.

Figure 21-42 shows the option in the Device Management page that enables an FTD device to capture a packet as it matches a Snort rule. You can disable this option if you do not want to store a complete packet due to any privacy or security policy.

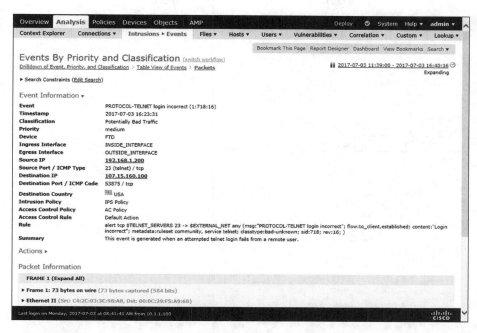

Figure 21-40 *Drill-down into an Intrusion Event—Displaying Event Information*

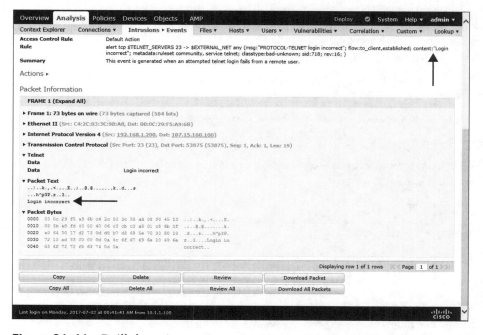

Figure 21-41 *Drill-down into an Intrusion Event—Displaying Packet Information*

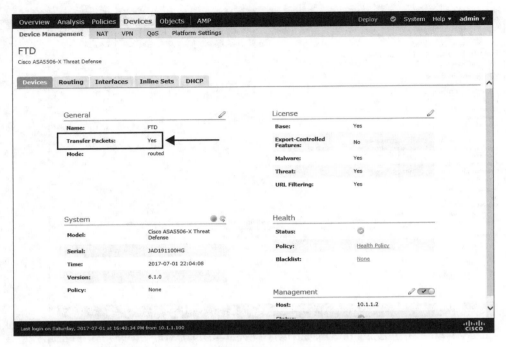

Figure 21-42   *Capturing a Packet That Triggers an Intrusion Event*

By analyzing the tracing data of a packet, you can determine whether a packet is blocked by Snort or any other component of the Firepower System. The process is described in detail in Chapter 10, "Capturing Traffic for Advanced Analysis."

First, run the **capture** tool to begin capturing Telnet packets, making sure to add the **trace** keyword to collect the tracing data:

```
> capture telnet_inside trace interface INSIDE_INTERFACE match tcp any any eq 23
>
```

You can run the **show capture** command any time to see the status of the capture or to view the captured packets:

```
> show capture
capture telnet_inside type raw-data trace interface INSIDE_INTERFACE
[Capturing - 0 bytes]
  match tcp any any eq telnet
>
```

Now, you can attempt to access the Telnet server once again. To reproduce an intrusion event, enter an incorrect credential. The **capture** tool captures all the packets on a Telnet session—including the first three-way handshake, which is completely allowed by the FTD device, per the current intrusion policy.

Example 21-2 shows the first few packets of a Telnet session. Later, it analyzes the tracing data of the first packet. It reveals how an FTD device makes a decision and sends a packet to Snort for deep packet inspection.

Example 21-2 *Capturing Telnet Traffic with Tracing Information*

```
> show capture telnet_inside

119 packets captured

  1: 20:23:21.086802        107.15.160.100.53875 > 192.168.1.200.23: S
1751019501:1751019501(0) win 4128 <mss 1460>
  2: 20:23:21.087229        107.15.160.100.53875 > 192.168.1.200.23: S
1751019501:1751019501(0) win 4128 <mss 1460>
  3: 20:23:21.087565        192.168.1.200.23 > 107.15.160.100.53875: S
232306554:232306554(0) ack 1751019502 win 29200 <mss 1460>
  4: 20:23:21.087702        192.168.1.200.23 > 107.15.160.100.53875: S
232306554:232306554(0) ack 1751019502 win 29200 <mss 1460>
  5: 20:23:21.089717        107.15.160.100.53875 > 192.168.1.200.23: . ack 232306555
win 4128
  6: 20:23:21.089762        107.15.160.100.53875 > 192.168.1.200.23: P
1751019502:1751019514(12) ack 232306555 win 4128
.
.
<Output Omitted for Brevity>


! Now view the tracing data of the first captured packet.

> show capture telnet_inside packet-number 1 trace

119 packets captured

  1: 20:23:21.086802        107.15.160.100.53875 > 192.168.1.200.23: S
1751019501:1751019501(0) win 4128 <mss 1460>
Phase: 1
Type: CAPTURE
Subtype:
Result: ALLOW
Config:
Additional Information:
MAC Access list


Phase: 2
Type: ACCESS-LIST
Subtype:
```

```
Result: ALLOW
Config:
Implicit Rule
Additional Information:
MAC Access list


Phase: 3
Type: NGIPS-MODE
Subtype: ngips-mode
Result: ALLOW
Config:
Additional Information:
The flow ingressed an interface configured for NGIPS mode and NGIPS services will be
  applied


Phase: 4
Type: ACCESS-LIST
Subtype: log
Result: ALLOW
Config:
access-group CSM_FW_ACL_ global
access-list CSM_FW_ACL_ advanced permit ip any any rule-id 268435458
access-list CSM_FW_ACL_ remark rule-id 268435458: ACCESS POLICY: AC Policy -
  Default/1
access-list CSM_FW_ACL_ remark rule-id 268435458: L4 RULE: DEFAULT ACTION RULE
Additional Information:
 This packet will be sent to snort for additional processing where a verdict will be
  reached


Phase: 5
Type: NGIPS-EGRESS-INTERFACE-LOOKUP
Subtype: Resolve Egress Interface
Result: ALLOW
Config:
Additional Information:
Ingress interface OUTSIDE_INTERFACE is in NGIPS inline mode.
Egress interface INSIDE_INTERFACE is determined by inline-set configuration


Phase: 6
Type: FLOW-CREATION
Subtype:
Result: ALLOW
Config:
Additional Information:
New flow created with id 848, packet dispatched to next module
```

```
Phase: 7
Type: EXTERNAL-INSPECT
Subtype:
Result: ALLOW
Config:
Additional Information:
Application: 'SNORT Inspect'

Phase: 8
Type: SNORT
Subtype:
Result: ALLOW
Config:
Additional Information:
Snort Verdict: (pass-packet) allow this packet

Phase: 9
Type: CAPTURE
Subtype:
Result: ALLOW
Config:
Additional Information:
MAC Access list

Result:
input-interface: INSIDE_INTERFACE
input-status: up
input-line-status: up
Action: allow

1 packet shown
>
```

Example 21-3 shows the Snort verdict "drop this packet," which appears in tracing output when a packet matches a Snort rule syntax and the rule state is set to drop and generate the event.

Example 21-3   *Snippet of the Tracing Information When a Packet Is Blocked by Snort*

```
<Output Omitted for Brevity>
.
.
Phase: 7
Type: EXTERNAL-INSPECT
Subtype:
Result: ALLOW
Config:
Additional Information:
Application: 'SNORT Inspect'


Phase: 8
Type: SNORT
Subtype:
Result: DROP
Config:
Additional Information:
Snort Verdict: (block-packet) drop this packet
.
.
<Output Omitted for Brevity>
```

Example 21-4 shows the statistics of a Snort drop. According to this output, Snort requests to drop five frames after an incorrect credential was entered to authenticate a Telnet server.

Example 21-4   *Statistics of a Snort Drop*

```
> show asp drop

Frame drop:
  Snort requested to drop the frame (snort-drop)                    5
  FP L2 rule drop (l2_acl)                                          1


Last clearing: 20:23:14 UTC Jul 3 2017 by enable_1


Flow drop:


Last clearing: 20:23:14 UTC Jul 3 2017 by enable_1
>
```

Summary

This chapter describes one of the most important and widely used features of a Firepower system: the Snort-based next-generation intrusion prevention system (NGIPS). In this chapter, you have learned how to configure an NGIPS, how to apply deploy associated policies, and how to drill down into intrusion events for advanced analysis. Most importantly, this chapter discusses the best practices for generating Firepower recommendations and demonstrates how the recommended ruleset can reduce system overhead by incorporating discovery data.

Quiz

1. Which of the following policy configurations can influence the behavior of the intrusion prevention functionality of an FTD?

    a. Network analysis policy

    b. Intrusion policy

    c. Access control policy

    d. All of the above

2. Which of the following numbering schemes is correct for a Snort rule?

    a. Standard text rule uses GID 1. SID is lower than 1,000,000.

    b. Preprocessor rule can use any GID other than 1 or 3.

    c. Local rule uses SID 1,000,000 or higher.

    d. All of the above.

3. Which of the following base policies enables the largest number of standard text Snort rules by default?

    a. Connectivity over Security

    b. Balanced Security and Connectivity

    c. Security over Connectivity

    d. Maximum Detection

4. Which of the following options is mandatory if you want to drop an intrusion attempt or block a packet that may constitute a potential cyber attack?

    a. The interface set has to be in Inline, Routed, or Transparent Mode.

    b. The intrusion policy must be enabled with the Drop When Inline option.

    c. The rule state must be set to Drop and Generate Events.

    d. All of the above.

Chapter 22

Masquerading the Original IP Address of an Internal Network Host

Any external user, whether an attacker or a legitimate Internet user, should have no visibility into your internal network. You can hide the internal addresses of your network by masquerading them into public addresses. However, assigning a dedicated public address to each of the internal hosts is not a feasible option. You can meet this challenge by enabling the Network Address Translation (NAT) functionality on an FTD device. This chapter demonstrates how to configure NAT and how NAT can masquerade an internal IP address as a public IP address.

> **Note** In this chapter, the terms *translation* and *masquerading* refer to the same operation and are interchangeable. In other words, *translation* of an address and *masquerading* of an address refer to the same technology: NAT.

NAT Essentials

NAT allows FTD to translate an internal IP address into an address from a different subnet. The NAT process is transparent to both internal and external hosts. When NAT is in action, an internal host is unaware that its original IP address is being translated or masqueraded to a public address, while the external host assumes that the public address is the actual address of the internal host.

Figure 22-1 shows that the NAT operations of an FTD device take place on the Firewall engine.

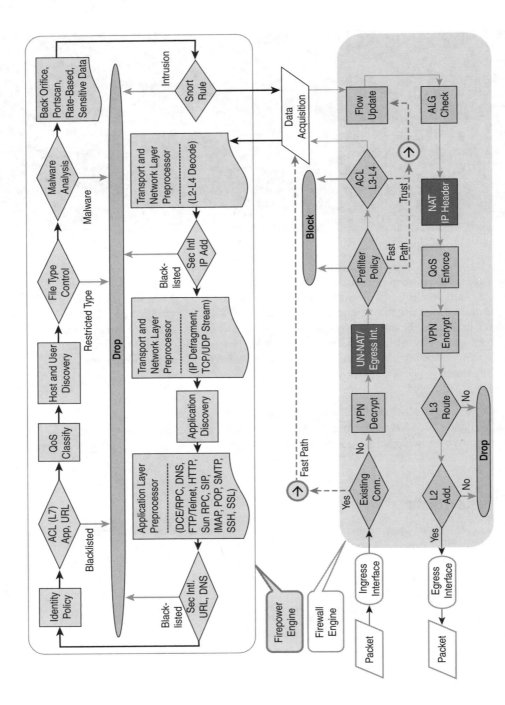

Figure 22-1   *Architectural Overview of an FTD Device, Highlighting the NAT Components*

Another advantage of NAT is the ability to route private traffic to the Internet. Internal hosts of an organization use private IP addresses, as defined in RFC 1918. However, these addresses are not routable to the Internet unless you map or translate them into public addresses. This "limitation" of private address space actually allows different organizations to reuse the same addresses within their internal networks and to maintain them regardless of any changes of their public IP address. Thus, it conserves the use of public IP addresses.

Table 22-1 shows the range of private IP addresses and the number of available hosts in Classes A, B, and C.

Table 22-1 *Private IP Addressing, as Defined in RFC 1918*

Class	Range of Private IP Addresses	Number of Host
Class A	10.0.0.0–10.255.255.255	$2^{24} - 2 = 16,777,214$
Class B	172.16.0.0–172.31.255.255	$2^{20} - 2 = 1,048,574$
Class C	192.168.0.0–192.168.255.255	$2^{16} - 2 = 65,534$

NAT Techniques

NAT allows you to masquerade IP addresses in various scenarios, such as one-to-one, one-to-many, many-to-one, many-to-many, few-to-many, and many-to-few. However, before you enable NAT, you need to answer the following questions:

■ How does an FTD device select a masqueraded or translated address? Is it predefined statically or allocated dynamically?

■ How many external or public addresses are available for selection? One or more?

Your answers to these questions can help you determine the type of translations to enable. You can categorize NAT mainly into three types:

■ **Static NAT:** FTD permanently maps the original IP address with a translated IP address. Because the mapping is permanent, either the internal or an external host is able to initiate a connection.

■ **Dynamic NAT:** Instead of a permanent mapping, FTD selects an IP address from a predefined address pool and translates an original internal address into the selected IP address. The selection of an address is on a first-come, first-served basis.

■ **Port Address Translation (PAT):** If a dynamic address pool has fewer external addresses than there are internal hosts, it is impossible for all the internal hosts to connect to external networks at the same time. To address this issue, FTD can translate both the IP address and port number of a connection (as opposed to just the IP address) and can multiplex over 65,000 connections over a single IP address.

RFC documents describe this feature as Network Address and Port Translation (NAPT), but due to the nature of its operation, this feature is also known as *Port Address Translation (PAT)*, *NAT overload*, and *IP masquerading*. The Firepower System calls it PAT.

Figure 22-2 shows the major differences between NAT and PAT.

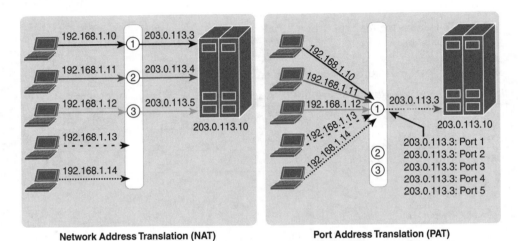

Network Address Translation (NAT)
If the first three hosts are dynamically assigned, the last two hosts must wait until the timeout value expires. But if they are assigned statically, the last two hosts have no chance.

Port Address Translation (PAT)
One address can multiplex more than 65,000 connections over a single IP address before another address is selected from a pool.

Figure 22-2 *NAT Versus PAT*

FTD can use the IP address of the egress interface for PAT operation. This means that when any internal host connects to a resource over the Internet, the source IP address of the connection appears as the egress interface of the FTD device instead of as the original internal host address. However, if the number of concurrent connections exceeds its limit, any additional hosts are unable to connect to the external network. To address this issue, you can combine the PAT functionality with a dynamic address pool. This allows an FTD device to select a new IP address from the pool when the first selection from the pool is no longer available for multiplexing a new connection.

NAT Rule Types

FTD offers two options to configure a NAT rule condition:

- **Auto NAT:** An Auto NAT rule can translate one address—either a source or destination address—in a single rule. This means that to translate both source and destination addresses, two separate Auto NAT rules are necessary.

■ **Manual NAT:** A Manual NAT rule allows the translation of both source and destination addresses within the same rule. A Manual NAT rule may be necessary when you want to make an exception for translation.

Figure 22-3 compares the available translation options in the NAT rule editor. An Auto NAT Rule supports the translation of one address per rule, while a Manual NAT Rule allows you to translate both source and destination addresses in a single rule.

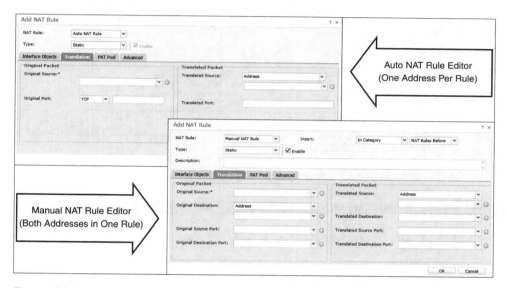

Figure 22-3   *Auto NAT Versus Manual NAT: Comparison of Rule Editor Windows*

A NAT policy editor categorizes NAT rules into three groups: NAT Rules Before, Auto NAT Rules, and NAT Rules After. In the CLI, you can find the rules under Section 1, Section 2, and Section 3, respectively. During evaluation, FTD begins with the rules under Section 1. Until there is a match, FTD continues evaluating the rules in the next sections.

Any rules under the NAT Rules Before and NAT Rules After sections are part of manual NAT policies. Their names and priorities are relative to the Auto NAT Rules, which allow you to translate one type of address at a time. To translate destination addresses, a separate Auto NAT rule is necessary.

Figure 22-4 describes the priority of each section in a NAT policy.

In this chapter, you will learn how to configure Auto NAT rules with both static and dynamic types.

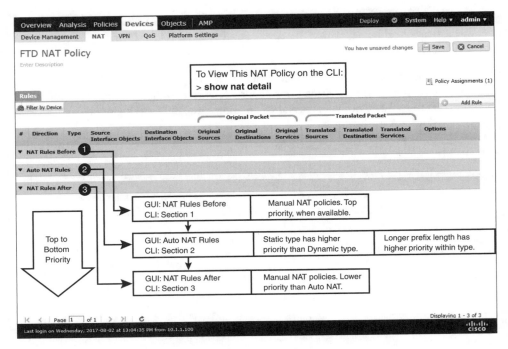

Figure 22-4   *Priorities of Rules on a NAT Policy*

Best Practices for NAT Deployment

Consider the following best practices when you plan to enable NAT on an FTD device:

■ Configuring an Auto NAT rule is simpler than configuring a Manual NAT rule. Cisco recommends that you choose an Auto NAT rule, as you can easily implement most of the common NAT scenarios with it. A Manual NAT rule may be necessary when you want to make an exception for translation.

■ If you modify an existing NAT rule or redeploy a new NAT policy, you may find that the new policy is not in action until the timer for any existing connections expires. To have FTD act on the latest NAT policy immediately, you can clear the current translations by running the command **clear xlate**.

■ The larger the translation table, the higher the processing overhead. If the number of translated connections grows excessively, it can affect the CPU and memory utilization of an FTD device.

■ To improve performance, prefer static NAT to dynamic NAT or PAT.

■ Review the addresses on dynamic and static NAT rules carefully before you apply them. Avoid creating rules with overlapping IP addresses.

■ Ensure that any applications running on a network terminate connections gracefully to prevent an FTD device from handling stale connections.

■ Make sure the idle timeout values for Translation Slot (xlate) and Connection (Conn) are set for optimal performance. You can adjust the timeout values on the Platform Settings page of FTD.

Figure 22-5 shows the timeout values for an FTD. To find this configuration page, go to **Devices > Platform Settings**. You can update an existing policy or create a new one.

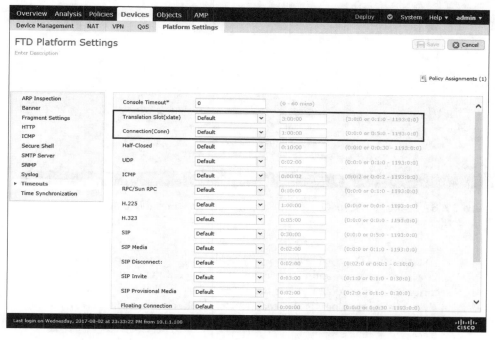

Figure 22-5   *Configuring FTD Timeout Values on the Platform Settings Page*

Fulfilling Prerequisites

Before you add a NAT rule, ensure that you have understood and fulfilled the following items:

■ Any associated interfaces that participate in a NAT configuration have to be in a regular firewall mode. FTD does not support NAT on IPS-only interface types, such as inline, inline-tap, and passive. Figure 22-6 shows the available configuration modes for an FTD physical interface. Select **None** to enable the regular router interface mode, which supports NAT.

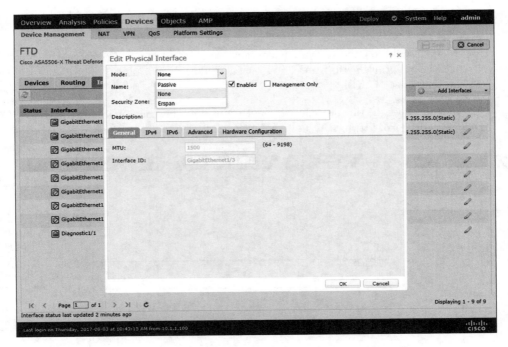

Figure 22-6   *Using the None Option to Turn an Interface into a Regular Firewall Interface*

■ If you use an FTD device in an IPS-only mode, make sure all the associated interfaces where you want to enable NAT are now configured with IP address and security zones. Figure 22-7 shows the allocation of IP addresses and security zones in FTD. The lab topology in this chapter uses three routed interfaces on FTD—GigabitEthernet1/1, GigabitEthernet1/2, and GigabitEthernet1/3.

■ Before you begin the process of adding a NAT rule, define any network objects that may be invoked within a NAT rule. To add a network object, go to the **Objects > Object Management** page and select the **Add Network** menu. Figure 22-8 shows the network objects that are used in the configuration examples in this chapter. You can add any additional objects needed for your own deployment.

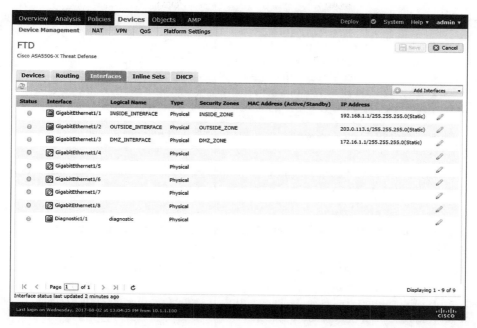

Figure 22-7 *Allocating IP Addresses and Security Zones on FTD Routed Interfaces*

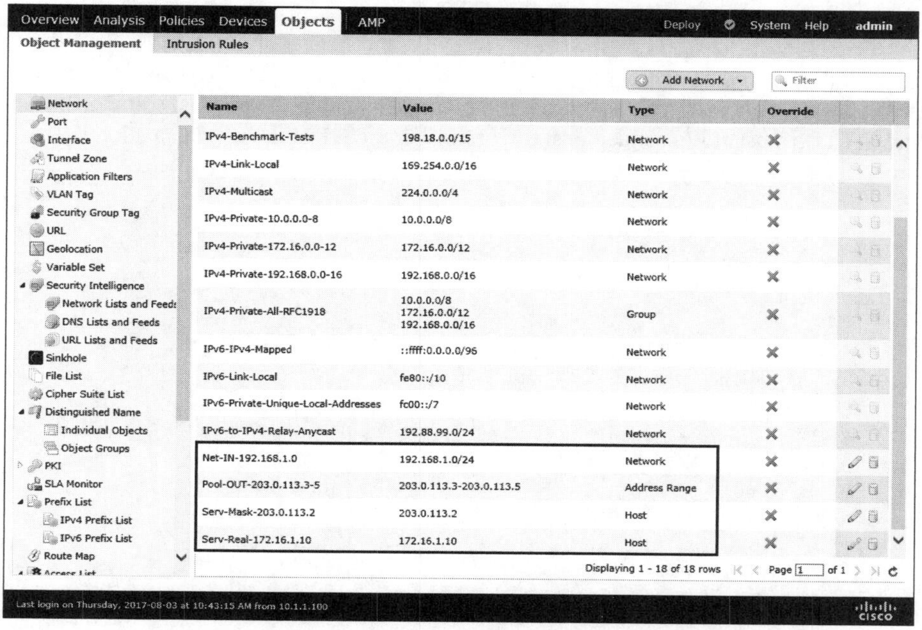

Figure 22-8 *Network Object Configuration Page*

Configuring NAT

FTD enables you to accomplish translation in various ways. You can select any type (static versus dynamic) with any combination of NAT rule (Auto versus Manual). However, Cisco recommends that you use Auto NAT rule, as it is easier to configure and simpler to troubleshoot. In the following sections, you will learn how to configure Auto NAT to masquerade IP addresses in the following real-world deployment scenarios:

- *Masquerading a source address* when an internal host initiates a connection to an external server

- Allowing an external host to connect to an internal host when an external host uses a *masqueraded destination address*

Masquerading a Source Address (Source NAT for Outbound Connection)

When an internal host initiates a connection to the Internet, FTD can translate the internal IP address to a public IP address. In other words, FTD can masquerade the source addresses of outbound connections. This section describes various methods to select a public IP address for an outbound connection.

Note   This section assumes that you have already configured any necessary objects described earlier in this chapter, in the "Fulfilling Prerequisites" section.

Figure 22-9 shows a scenario where an internal host connects to an external host through an FTD device. When an end user initiates a connection using the original source IP address, FTD translates (masquerades) the original source IP address into an address that is predefined in an address pool.

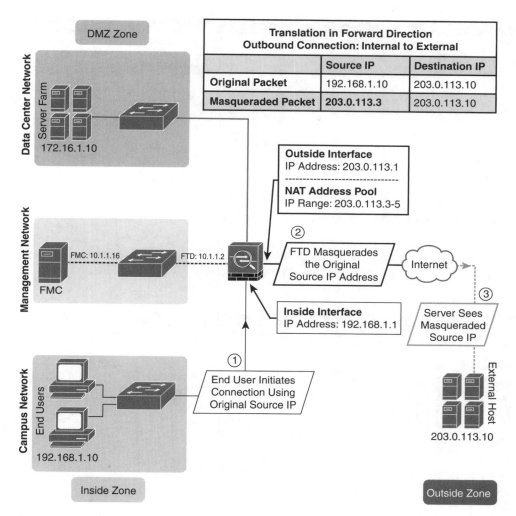

Figure 22-9 *Lab Topology Demonstrating Dynamic NAT for Outbound Traffic*

Configuring a Dynamic NAT Rule

The FMC offers two types of NAT policies—Firepower NAT Policy and Threat Defense NAT Policy. The former is used to enable NAT on classic Firepower hardware, such as 7000 and 8000 Series models. To enable NAT on FTD, you need to deploy Threat Defense NAT Policy on it. To do so, follow these steps:

Step 1. Navigate to **Devices > NAT**. The NAT Policy window appears.

Step 2. To create a new NAT policy for an FTD device, select **Threat Defense NAT Policy** (see Figure 22-10).

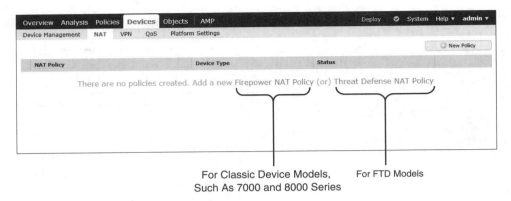

Figure 22-10 *NAT Policy Configuration Options for Different Hardware Models*

Step 3. When the New Policy window appears, give a name to your policy and add your FTD device from the list of available devices to the policy (see Figure 22-11). Click the **Save** button. The NAT policy editor page appears.

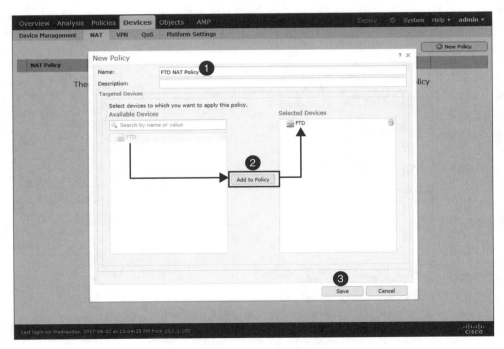

Figure 22-11 *Assigning a NAT Policy to an FTD Device*

Step 4.   On the policy editor page, click the **Add Rule** button to create a NAT rule. The Add NAT Rule window appears.

Step 5.   From the NAT Rule dropdown select **Auto NAT Rule**, and from the Type dropdown select **Dynamic**. Depending on your selections in both of these dropdowns, you will find different configurable options in the Translation tab. For instance, for an Auto NAT Rule with Dynamic type, you need to configure the Original Source and Translated Source.

Step 6.   Use the Original Source dropdown to define the source IP addresses of the packets that you want to masquerade. You can select a network object that you defined in the section "Fulfilling Prerequisites," earlier in this chapter. If you did not create an object earlier, you can create one on the fly by clicking the green plus icon next to a dropdown.

Step 7.   Define a translated address—the address that appears as the source address of a translated packet. You need to select one of the following translation methods on the Translation or PAT Pool tab, depending on the type of NAT (static or dynamic) you want to configure.

   ■ **Destination Interface IP:** This allows an FTD device to use the same IP address as the egress interface of an FTD.

   ■ **Address:** This enables an FTD device to select an address from a predefined address pool.

   Table 22-2 shows a matrix of various Auto NAT rule selections. In this section, you will implement dynamic NAT with an address pool (highlighted row).

Table 22-2   *Auto NAT Rule—Major Configurable Options*

Type	Translation Tab (Translated Source)	Translation Tab (Port Translation)	PAT Pool Tab
Static	Destination Interface IP	Configurable	Not Configurable
Static	Address	Configurable	Not Configurable
Dynamic	Destination Interface IP	Not Configurable	Not Configurable
Dynamic	Address	Not Configurable	Unselected
Dynamic	Address	Not Configurable	Enabled with Address
Dynamic	Address	Not Configurable	Enabled with Destination Interface IP

Figure 22-12 shows the configuration of original and translated addresses in a dynamic Auto NAT rule.

At this point, you could save the configuration and deploy the policy on the FTD device. However, you may want to consider the following optional configurations.

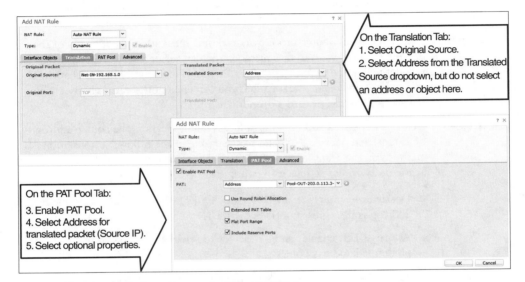

Figure 22-12   *Defining a Dynamic Auto NAT Rule*

Step 8.   On the PAT Pool tab, select **Flat Port Range** and **Include Reserve Ports** to enable an FTD device to use the complete range of port numbers, 1 to 65535, even though the same source port number is unavailable for mapping.

Step 9.   On the Interface Objects tab, select the ingress and egress interfaces for the traffic you want to translate. The Available Interface Objects field shows the associated security zones that you assigned in the Devices > Devices Management page.

When you complete all the steps, click the **OK** button on the NAT rule editor window to create the NAT rule. The browser returns to the NAT policy editor, where you can see the NAT rule you have just created. To activate the policy, first click **Save** to save the policy, and then click **Deploy** to deploy it on your FTD device.

Figure 22-13 shows a dynamic Auto NAT rule that translates the source IP addresses of any hosts from the INSIDE_ZONE to the OUTSIDE_ZONE. The translated packet uses an address from the address pool, Pool-OUT-203.0.113.3-5, as its source IP address.

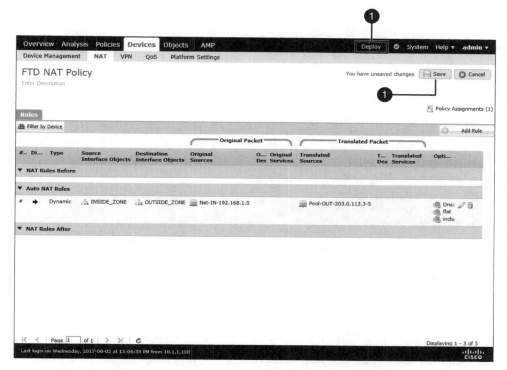

Figure 22-13 *Defining a Dynamic NAT Rule to Translate Outbound Connections*

In the following sections, you will learn how to verify the configuration on the CLI and how to determine whether an FTD device is translating addresses as expected.

Verifying the Configuration

After you deploy a NAT policy, you can run the **show running-config nat** command in the CLI to view the latest NAT configurations and to confirm whether the desired policy is active.

Example 22-1 exhibits the running configurations of NAT and the definitions of any associated objects that are invoked in a NAT rule.

Example 22-1   *Defining a NAT Rule and Any Associated Objects*

```
! To view the NAT configurations:

> show running-config nat
!
object network Net-IN-192.168.1.0
 nat (INSIDE_INTERFACE,OUTSIDE_INTERFACE) dynamic pat-pool Pool-OUT-203.0.113.3-5
  flat include-reserve
>


! To determine the scope of an object:

> show running-config object
object network Net-IN-192.168.1.0
 subnet 192.168.1.0 255.255.255.0
object network Pool-OUT-203.0.113.3-5
 range 203.0.113.3 203.0.113.5
>
```

You can also run the **show nat detail** command to display more detailed information about a NAT policy, such as the priority of a rule (Auto NAT versus Manual NAT) or the type of a rule (static versus dynamic). The output of this command also displays the number of matching connections in both forward and reverse directions, through the translate_hits and untranslate_hits counters, respectively.

Example 22-2 shows an Auto NAT rule (dynamic PAT) for translating traffic from the 192.168.1.0/24 network to the address pool 203.0.113.3 to 203.0.113.5. The zero hit count indicates that the rule has not matched any connections.

Example 22-2   *Output of the* **show nat detail** *Command*

```
> show nat detail
Auto NAT Policies (Section 2)
1 (INSIDE_INTERFACE) to (OUTSIDE_INTERFACE) source dynamic Net-IN-192.168.1.0
  pat-pool Pool-OUT-203.0.113.3-5 flat include-reserve
    translate_hits = 0, untranslate_hits = 0
    Source - Origin: 192.168.1.0/24, Translated (PAT): 203.0.113.3-203.0.113.5
>
```

Examples 22-1 and 22-2 display the source (INSIDE_INTERFACE) and destination (OUTSIDE_INTERFACE) defined in a NAT rule. However, the output in these examples does not show the status, IP address, or name of an interface. You can find them by running other commands, such as **show nameif** and **show interfaces ip brief**.

Example 22-3 shows how to map the physical interfaces with their logical names. It also shows how to verify the IP address and status of an interface.

Example 22-3 *Viewing Various Parameters of FTD Interfaces*

```
! To view the mapping of physical interfaces with their logical names:


> show nameif
Interface               Name                    Security
GigabitEthernet1/1      INSIDE_INTERFACE        0
GigabitEthernet1/2      OUTSIDE_INTERFACE       0
GigabitEthernet1/3      DMZ_INTERFACE           0
Management1/1           diagnostic              0
>


! To view the status and IP addresses of the FTD interfaces:


> show interface ip brief
Interface               IP-Address      OK? Method Status                Protocol
Virtual0                127.1.0.1       YES unset  up                    up
GigabitEthernet1/1      192.168.1.1     YES CONFIG up                    up
GigabitEthernet1/2      203.0.113.1     YES CONFIG up                    up
GigabitEthernet1/3      172.16.1.1      YES CONFIG up                    up
GigabitEthernet1/4      unassigned      YES unset  administratively down down
GigabitEthernet1/5      unassigned      YES unset  administratively down down
.
.
.
<Output omitted for brevity>
```

Verifying the Operation: Inside to Outside

This section describes how to verify the NAT operation on an FTD device. To demonstrate the translation process, this example uses SSH traffic.

Let's initiate a connection from an internal host 192.168.1.10 to an external SSH server 203.0.113.10. If NAT is operational on FTD, the external SSH server sees 203.0.113.3 as the source IP address of the internal host instead of its original source IP address, 192.168.1.10.

Example 22-4 shows an SSH connection between the internal client and the external server. The connection table shows the original IP address (192.168.1.10) of the internal server with a translation (**xlate**) ID. However, you can determine the masqueraded or translated address (203.0.113.3) from the translation table.

Example 22-4 *Connection and Translation Table*

```
> show conn detail
1 in use, 4 most used
Flags: A - awaiting responder ACK to SYN, a - awaiting initiator ACK to SYN,
       b - TCP state-bypass or nailed,
       C - CTIQBE media, c - cluster centralized,
       D - DNS, d - dump, E - outside back connection, e - semi-distributed,
       F - initiator FIN, f - responder FIN,
       G - group, g - MGCP, H - H.323, h - H.225.0, I - initiator data,
       i - incomplete, J - GTP, j - GTP data, K - GTP t3-response
       k - Skinny media, M - SMTP data, m - SIP media, N - inspected by Snort,
   n - GUP
       O - responder data, P - inside back connection,
       q - SQL*Net data, R - initiator acknowledged FIN,
       R - UDP SUNRPC, r - responder acknowledged FIN,
       T - SIP, t - SIP transient, U - up,
       V - VPN orphan, v - M3UA W - WAAS,
       w - secondary domain backup,
       X - inspected by service module,
       x - per session, Y - director stub flow, y - backup stub flow,
       Z - Scansafe redirection, z - forwarding stub flow

TCP OUTSIDE_INTERFACE: 203.0.113.10/22 INSIDE_INTERFACE: 192.168.1.10/41934,
    flags UxIO N, idle 6s, uptime 18s, timeout 1h0m, bytes 6718, xlate id
  0x7f516987ee00


>



> show xlate detail
1 in use, 2 most used
Flags: D - DNS, e - extended, I - identity, i - dynamic, r - portmap,
       s - static, T - twice, N - net-to-net

TCP PAT from INSIDE_INTERFACE:192.168.1.10/41934 to OUTSIDE_INTER-
  FACE:203.0.113.3/41934 flags ri idle 0:00:28 timeout 0:00:30 refcnt 1 xlate id
  0x7f516987ee00
>
```

By looking at the output of the **show nat detail** command, you can determine whether
the traffic matches a particular NAT rule and how many times a rule finds a match.

Example 22-5 confirms that the Auto NAT rule found one matching connection when a host sent traffic from INSIDE_INTERFACE to OUTSIDE_INTERFACE.

Example 22-5   *Matching One Connection in the Forward Direction*

```
> show nat detail

Auto NAT Policies (Section 2)
1 (INSIDE_INTERFACE) to (OUTSIDE_INTERFACE) source dynamic Net-IN-192.168.1.0
  pat-pool Pool-OUT-203.0.113.3-5 flat include-reserve
    translate_hits = 1, untranslate_hits = 0
    Source - Origin: 192.168.1.0/24, Translated (PAT): 203.0.113.3-203.0.113.5
>
```

By capturing the traffic in real time when an address is translated, you can analyze the FTD operation during address translation.

Example 22-6 demonstrates the capture of any SSH traffic on the inside interface. Later, you will analyze the translation of these packets.

Example 22-6   *Capturing SSH Traffic on the FTD Inside Interface*

```
! Begin the capture of SSH traffic on inside interface.

> capture ssh_traffic_inside trace interface INSIDE_INTERFACE match tcp any any
  eq 22


! Verify if the FTD is running a capture for SSH traffic.

> show capture
capture ssh_traffic_inside type raw-data trace interface INSIDE_INTERFACE
  [Capturing - 0 bytes]
  match tcp any any eq ssh
>
```

At this stage, you can initiate an SSH connection from the internal host to the external SSH server. FTD should capture the traffic on the inside interface. You can view the packets in the CLI.

Example 22-7 shows the first few captured packets for an SSH connection. Later, it analyzes the first packet to demonstrate the detailed operation of an address translation.

Example 22-7 *Analyzing Captured Packets*

```
! To view all of the captured packets (press Ctrl+C to exit from a long show):
> show capture ssh_traffic_inside

81 packets captured

   1: 02:59:47.220310        192.168.1.10.41934 > 203.0.113.10.22: S
 1482617093:1482617093(0) win 29200 <mss 1460,sackOK,timestamp 15243390
 0,nop,wscale 7>
   2: 02:59:47.221149        203.0.113.10.22 > 192.168.1.10.41934: S
 1409789153:1409789153(0) ack 1482617094 win 28960 <mss 1380,sackOK,timestamp
 17762742 15243390,nop,wscale 7>
   3: 02:59:47.221256        192.168.1.10.41934 > 203.0.113.10.22: . ack 1409789154
 win 229 <nop,nop,timestamp 15243390 17762742>
   4: 02:59:47.221729        192.168.1.10.41934 > 203.0.113.10.22: P
 1482617094:1482617135(41) ack 1409789154 win 229 <nop,nop,timestamp 15243391
 17762742>
   5: 02:59:47.222186        203.0.113.10.22 > 192.168.1.10.41934: . ack 1482617135
 win 227 <nop,nop,timestamp 17762742 15243391>
.

.

<Output is omitted for brevity>




! To analyze the first captured packet:


> show capture ssh_traffic_inside packet-number 1 trace


81 packets captured


   1: 02:59:47.220310        192.168.1.10.41934 > 203.0.113.10.22: S
 1482617093:1482617093(0) win 29200 <mss 1460,sackOK,timestamp 15243390
 0,nop,wscale 7>
Phase: 1
Type: CAPTURE
Subtype:
Result: ALLOW
Config:
Additional Information:
MAC Access list

Phase: 2
Type: ACCESS-LIST
Subtype:
```

```
Result: ALLOW
Config:
Implicit Rule
Additional Information:
MAC Access list


Phase: 3
Type: ROUTE-LOOKUP
Subtype: Resolve Egress Interface
Result: ALLOW
Config:
Additional Information:
found next-hop 203.0.113.10 using egress ifc  OUTSIDE_INTERFACE


Phase: 4
Type: ACCESS-LIST
Subtype: log
Result: ALLOW
Config:
access-group CSM_FW_ACL_ global
access-list CSM_FW_ACL_ advanced permit ip any any rule-id 268435457
access-list CSM_FW_ACL_ remark rule-id 268435457: ACCESS POLICY: AC Policy -
  Mandatory/1
access-list CSM_FW_ACL_ remark rule-id 268435457: L7 RULE: Traffic Selection
Additional Information:
 This packet will be sent to snort for additional processing where a verdict will be
  reached


Phase: 5
Type: CONN-SETTINGS
Subtype:
Result: ALLOW
Config:
class-map class-default
 match any
policy-map global_policy
 class class-default
  set connection advanced-options UM_STATIC_TCP_MAP
service-policy global_policy global
Additional Information:


Phase: 6
Type: NAT
Subtype:
Result: ALLOW
```

```
Config:
object network Net-IN-192.168.1.0
 nat (INSIDE_INTERFACE,OUTSIDE_INTERFACE) dynamic pat-pool Pool-OUT-203.0.113.3-5
  flat include-reserve
Additional Information:
Dynamic translate 192.168.1.10/41934 to 203.0.113.3/41934


Phase: 7
Type: NAT
Subtype: per-session
Result: ALLOW
Config:
Additional Information:


Phase: 8
Type: IP-OPTIONS
Subtype:
Result: ALLOW
Config:
Additional Information:


Phase: 9
Type: NAT
Subtype: per-session
Result: ALLOW
Config:
Additional Information:


Phase: 10
Type: IP-OPTIONS
Subtype:
Result: ALLOW
Config:
Additional Information:


Phase: 11
Type: FLOW-CREATION
Subtype:
Result: ALLOW
Config:
Additional Information:
New flow created with id 442, packet dispatched to next module


Phase: 12
Type: EXTERNAL-INSPECT
```

```
Subtype:
Result: ALLOW
Config:
Additional Information:
Application: 'SNORT Inspect'


Phase: 13
Type: SNORT
Subtype:
Result: ALLOW
Config:
Additional Information:
Snort Verdict: (pass-packet) allow this packet


Phase: 14
Type: ROUTE-LOOKUP
Subtype: Resolve Egress Interface
Result: ALLOW
Config:
Additional Information:
found next-hop 203.0.113.10 using egress ifc  OUTSIDE_INTERFACE


Phase: 15
Type: ADJACENCY-LOOKUP
Subtype: next-hop and adjacency
Result: ALLOW
Config:
Additional Information:
adjacency Active
next-hop mac address 0023.2472.1d3c hits 139985869104448


Phase: 16
Type: CAPTURE
Subtype:
Result: ALLOW
Config:
Additional Information:
MAC Access list


Result:
input-interface: OUTSIDE_INTERFACE
input-status: up
input-line-status: up
output-interface: OUTSIDE_INTERFACE
```

```
output-status: up
output-line-status: up
Action: allow


1 packet shown
>
```

Verifying the Operation: Outside to Inside

The NAT rule you created earlier evaluates the forward traffic—the traffic that originates from INSIDE_INTERFACE and is destined for OUTSIDE_INTERFACE. However, any traffic in the reverse direction does not match this rule. You can verify this by capturing SSH traffic on OUTSIDE_INTERFACE and by analyzing the trace data.

Example 22-8 shows how to enable the **capture** tool on the outside interface.

Example 22-8 *Capturing SSH Traffic on the FTD OUTSIDE_INTERFACE*

```
! Enable capture on the outside interface:

> capture ssh_traffic_outside trace interface OUTSIDE_INTERFACE match tcp any any
  eq 22


! FTD begins capturing SSH traffic on the outside interface:

> show capture
capture ssh_traffic_inside type raw-data trace interface INSIDE_INTERFACE
  [Capturing - 0 bytes]
  match tcp any any eq ssh
capture ssh_traffic_outside type raw-data trace interface OUTSIDE_INTERFACE
  [Capturing - 0 bytes]
  match tcp any any eq ssh
>
```

Now if you attempt to connect from an external host to an internal host, regardless of the destination IP address you choose—either original or masqueraded—the connection attempt fails.

Example 22-9 shows the failed connection attempts from the external host 203.0.113.10 to the same internal host—through the masqueraded IP address 203.0.113.3 and the original IP address 192.168.1.10.22.

Example 22-9 *Captured Traffic on the FTD OUTSIDE_INTERFACE Shows Only SYN (S) Packets*

```
> show capture ssh_traffic_outside

8 packets captured

   1: 03:56:51.100290     203.0.113.10.48400 > 203.0.113.3.22: S
 3636330443:3636330443(0) win 29200 <mss 1460,sackOK,timestamp 18618684
 0,nop,wscale 7>
   2: 03:56:52.097269     203.0.113.10.48400 > 203.0.113.3.22: S
 3636330443:3636330443(0) win 29200 <mss 1460,sackOK,timestamp 18618934
 0,nop,wscale 7>
   3: 03:56:54.101343     203.0.113.10.48400 > 203.0.113.3.22: S
 3636330443:3636330443(0) win 29200 <mss 1460,sackOK,timestamp 18619435
 0,nop,wscale 7>
   4: 03:56:58.105478     203.0.113.10.48400 > 203.0.113.3.22: S
 3636330443:3636330443(0) win 29200 <mss 1460,sackOK,timestamp 18620436
 0,nop,wscale 7>


   5: 03:57:22.069759     203.0.113.10.53048 > 192.168.1.10.22: S
 1744936567:1744936567(0) win 29200 <mss 1460,sackOK,timestamp 18626426
 0,nop,wscale 7>
   6: 03:57:23.066250     203.0.113.10.53048 > 192.168.1.10.22: S
 1744936567:1744936567(0) win 29200 <mss 1460,sackOK,timestamp 18626676
 0,nop,wscale 7>
   7: 03:57:25.070369     203.0.113.10.53048 > 192.168.1.10.22: S
 1744936567:1744936567(0) win 29200 <mss 1460,sackOK,timestamp 18627177
 0,nop,wscale 7>
   8: 03:57:29.082469     203.0.113.10.53048 > 192.168.1.10.22: S
 1744936567:1744936567(0) win 29200 <mss 1460,sackOK,timestamp 18628180
 0,nop,wscale 7>
8 packets shown
>
```

Example 22-10 analyzes the trace data of the first captured packet, where the external host tries to connect to the internal host using its masqueraded IP address, 203.0.113.3.

Example 22-10 *Trying to Connect to the Masqueraded IP Address of an Internal Host*

```
> show capture ssh_traffic_outside packet-number 1 trace

8 packets captured

   1: 03:56:51.100290     203.0.113.10.48400 > 203.0.113.3.22: S
 3636330443:3636330443(0) win 29200 <mss 1460,sackOK,timestamp 18618684
 0,nop,wscale 7>
Phase: 1
Type: CAPTURE
```

```
Subtype:
Result: ALLOW
Config:
Additional Information:
MAC Access list

Phase: 2
Type: ACCESS-LIST
Subtype:
Result: ALLOW
Config:
Implicit Rule
Additional Information:
MAC Access list

Phase: 3
Type: ROUTE-LOOKUP
Subtype: Resolve Egress Interface
Result: ALLOW
Config:
Additional Information:
found next-hop 203.0.113.3 using egress ifc  OUTSIDE_INTERFACE

Result:
input-interface: OUTSIDE_INTERFACE
input-status: up
input-line-status: up
output-interface: OUTSIDE_INTERFACE
output-status: up
output-line-status: up
Action: drop
Drop-reason: (nat-no-xlate-to-pat-pool) Connection to PAT address without pre-exist-
   ing xlate


1 packet shown
>
```

Example 22-11 analyzes the trace data of the fifth captured packet where the external
host tries to connect to the internal host by using its original IP address, 192.168.1.10.

Example 22-11 *Trying to Connect to the Original IP Address of an Internal Host*

```
> show capture ssh_traffic_outside packet-number 5 trace

8 packets captured

   5: 03:57:22.069759      203.0.113.10.53048 > 192.168.1.10.22: S 1744936567:
  1744936567(0) win 29200 <mss 1460,sackOK,timestamp 18626426 0,nop,wscale 7>
Phase: 1
Type: CAPTURE
Subtype:
Result: ALLOW
Config:
Additional Information:
MAC Access list

Phase: 2
Type: ACCESS-LIST
Subtype:
Result: ALLOW
Config:
Implicit Rule
Additional Information:
MAC Access list

Phase: 3
Type: ROUTE-LOOKUP
Subtype: Resolve Egress Interface
Result: ALLOW
Config:
Additional Information:
found next-hop 192.168.1.10 using egress ifc  INSIDE_INTERFACE

Phase: 4
Type: ACCESS-LIST
Subtype: log
Result: ALLOW
Config:
access-group CSM_FW_ACL_ global
access-list CSM_FW_ACL_ advanced permit ip any any rule-id 268435457
access-list CSM_FW_ACL_ remark rule-id 268435457: ACCESS POLICY: AC Policy -
  Mandatory/1
access-list CSM_FW_ACL_ remark rule-id 268435457: L7 RULE: Traffic Selection
Additional Information:
 This packet will be sent to snort for additional processing where a verdict will be
  reached
```

```
Phase: 5
Type: CONN-SETTINGS
Subtype:
Result: ALLOW
Config:
class-map class-default
 match any
policy-map global_policy
 class class-default
   set connection advanced-options UM_STATIC_TCP_MAP
service-policy global_policy global
Additional Information:

Phase: 6
Type: NAT
Subtype: per-session
Result: ALLOW
Config:
Additional Information:

Phase: 7
Type: IP-OPTIONS
Subtype:
Result: ALLOW
Config:
Additional Information:

Phase: 8
Type: NAT
Subtype: rpf-check
Result: DROP
Config:
object network Net-IN-192.168.1.0
 nat (INSIDE_INTERFACE,OUTSIDE_INTERFACE) dynamic pat-pool Pool-OUT-203.0.113.3-5
   flat include-reserve
Additional Information:

Result:
input-interface: OUTSIDE_INTERFACE
input-status: up
input-line-status: up
output-interface: INSIDE_INTERFACE
output-status: up
```

```
output-line-status: up
Action: drop
Drop-reason: (acl-drop) Flow is denied by configured rule



1 packet shown
>
```

Connecting to a Masqueraded Destination (Destination NAT for Inbound Connection)

When external hosts access any services of your company, they should access through the public IP address of your organization. Any internal addressing scheme must be invisible to the external users. In this section, you will learn how to connect to an internal host by using a masqueraded public IP address.

Figure 22-14 illustrates a scenario where an external host connects to an internal DMZ server of a company. When an external host initiates a connection to a masqueraded public address, FTD translates the address into an internal original address.

Configuring a Static NAT Rule

Because in the previous section you created an Auto NAT rule with dynamic type and analyzed its detailed operation, this section does not duplicate the same procedures for creating a NAT policy from scratch. You can just add a new NAT rule as illustrated in Figure 22-15 and then redeploy the NAT policy. If the policy deployment is successful, FTD should let an external host connect to an internal DMZ server using a masqueraded public IP address. Because the FTD in this case translates a public destination address to an internal address, this translation is known as destination NAT.

Figure 22-15 illustrates a static NAT rule that enables an outside host to connect to a DMZ server (internal IP address 172.16.1.10) via SSH service (internal port 22) without knowing the internal addressing scheme. The outside host can access the DMZ server only if the outside host uses the masqueraded IP address 203.0.113.2 and port 2200 as its destination.

Figure 22-16 shows two rules in a NAT policy—the static Auto NAT rule (bottom) has just been created to translate inbound connections. The dynamic NAT rule (top) was added earlier to translate outbound connections.

After you add a new NAT rule, you must click the **Save** and **Deploy** buttons to enable the new NAT policy on your FTD device.

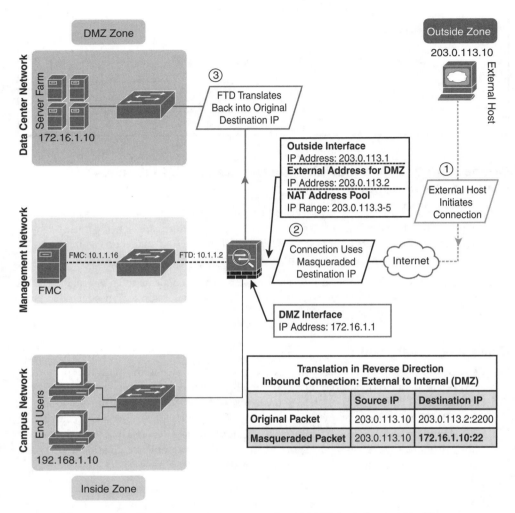

Figure 22-14 *Lab Topology to Demonstrate Static NAT for Inbound Traffic*

Verifying the Operation: Outside to DMZ

This section demonstrates the operation of a static Auto NAT rule on an FTD device. As in the previous exercise, this one also uses SSH service to generate traffic. However, unlike in the previous exercise, the SSH connection is initiated by an external host.

Before you begin, you should clear the NAT counters and any existing translations so that you will be able to notice any new changes quickly:

```
> clear nat counters
> clear xlate
```

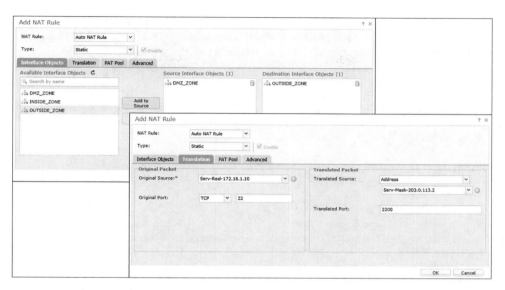

Figure 22-15   *Defining a Static Auto NAT Rule for Inbound Connections*

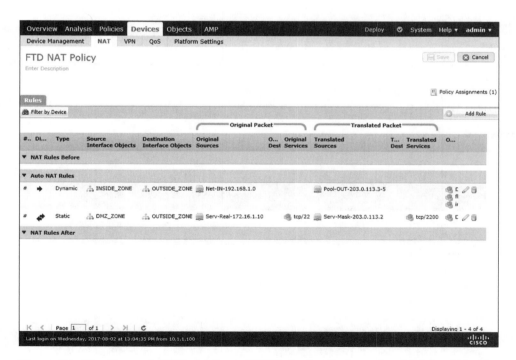

Figure 22-16   *Dynamic NAT and Static NAT Rules for Outbound and Inbound Traffic*

Now you can try to access the internal DMZ server from an external host. Using an SSH client, connect to port 2200 of the translated (masqueraded) IP address 203.0.113.2. You will be connected to the internal DMZ server, although the original IP address of the server is 172.16.1.10, and the server listens to port 22 for SSH connections. This happens due to the static NAT on the FTD device.

Example 22-12 shows confirmation that the inbound SSH traffic matches the first rule on the Auto NAT policy. The untranslate_hits counter confirms the matching of one connection in the reverse direction.

Example 22-12   *Matching a Connection in the Reverse Direction*

```
> show nat detail


Auto NAT Policies (Section 2)
1 (DMZ_INTERFACE) to (OUTSIDE_INTERFACE) source static Serv-Real-172.16.1.10
  Serv-Mask-203.0.113.2  service tcp ssh 2200
    translate_hits = 0, untranslate_hits = 1
    Source - Origin: 172.16.1.10/32, Translated: 203.0.113.2/32
    Service - Protocol: tcp Real: ssh Mapped: 2200
2 (INSIDE_INTERFACE) to (OUTSIDE_INTERFACE) source dynamic Net-IN-192.168.1.0
  pat-pool Pool-OUT-203.0.113.3-5 flat include-reserve
    translate_hits = 0, untranslate_hits = 0
    Source - Origin: 192.168.1.0/24, Translated (PAT): 203.0.113.3-203.0.113.5

>
```

Example 22-13 shows the status of the current translations. The flag confirms a static port translation between an external host and an internal DMZ server.

Example 22-13   *Real-time Translation Status*

```
> show xlate detail
1 in use, 2 most used
Flags: D - DNS, e - extended, I - identity, i - dynamic, r - portmap,
       s - static, T - twice, N - net-to-net
TCP PAT from DMZ_INTERFACE:172.16.1.10 22-22 to OUTSIDE_INTERFACE:203.0.113.2
  2200-2200
    flags sr idle 0:00:54 timeout 0:00:00 refcnt 1 xlate id 0x7f516987ee00


>
```

To better understand the NAT operation, you can capture SSH traffic on an outside interface (on the translated port) and analyze it (see Example 22-14).

Example 22-14   *Capturing SSH Traffic on an Outside Interface (on a Translated Port)*

```
! Enable capture on outside interface:


> capture ssh_traffic_outside_masked trace interface OUTSIDE_INTERFACE match tcp any
  any eq 2200



! Verify that the capture is running:


> show capture
capture ssh_traffic_inside type raw-data trace interface INSIDE_INTERFACE
  [Capturing - 0 bytes]
  match tcp any any eq ssh
capture ssh_traffic_outside type raw-data trace interface OUTSIDE_INTERFACE
  [Capturing - 0 bytes]
  match tcp any any eq ssh
capture ssh_traffic_outside_masked type raw-data trace interface OUTSIDE_INTERFACE
  [Capturing - 0 bytes]
  match tcp any any eq 2200

>



! Now, initiate an SSH connection from the external host to the internal DMZ
  server. Use the masqueraded IP address and port number. It generates the following
  traffic.


> show capture ssh_traffic_outside_masked


59 packets captured


  1: 05:21:23.785436       203.0.113.10.41760 > 203.0.113.2.2200: S
2089153959:2089153959(0) win 29200 <mss 1460,sackOK,timestamp 19887065
0,nop,wscale 7>
  2: 05:21:23.786168       203.0.113.2.2200 > 203.0.113.10.41760: S
29917599:29917599(0) ack 2089153960 win 28960 <mss 1380,sackOK,timestamp 19892875
19887065,nop,wscale 7>
  3: 05:21:23.786336       203.0.113.10.41760 > 203.0.113.2.2200: . ack 29917600
win 229 <nop,nop,timestamp 19887065 19892875>
  4: 05:21:23.786855       203.0.113.10.41760 > 203.0.113.2.2200: P
2089153960:2089154001(41) ack 29917600 win 229 <nop,nop,timestamp 19887066
19892875>
  5: 05:21:23.787312       203.0.113.2.2200 > 203.0.113.10.41760: . ack 2089154001
win 227 <nop,nop,timestamp 19892876 19887066>
.
.
<Output is omitted for brevity>
```

Example 22-15 shows how to analyze the tracing data of a captured packet.
FTD translates and allows the packet as you are connecting through IP address
203.0.113.2 and port 2200.

Example 22-15   *Analyzing a Translated Packet (Where the Packet Matches a Rule)*

```
> show capture ssh_traffic_outside_masked packet-number 1 trace

59 packets captured

  1: 05:21:23.785436        203.0.113.10.41760 > 203.0.113.2.2200: S
 2089153959:2089153959(0) win 29200 <mss 1460,sackOK,timestamp 19887065
 0,nop,wscale 7>
Phase: 1
Type: CAPTURE
Subtype:
Result: ALLOW
Config:
Additional Information:
MAC Access list


Phase: 2
Type: ACCESS-LIST
Subtype:
Result: ALLOW
Config:
Implicit Rule
Additional Information:
MAC Access list


Phase: 3
Type: UN-NAT
Subtype: static
Result: ALLOW
Config:
object network Serv-Real-172.16.1.10
 nat (DMZ_INTERFACE,OUTSIDE_INTERFACE) static Serv-Mask-203.0.113.2 service
  tcp ssh 2200
Additional Information:
NAT divert to egress interface DMZ_INTERFACE
Untranslate 203.0.113.2/2200 to 172.16.1.10/22


Phase: 4
Type: ACCESS-LIST
Subtype: log
```

```
Result: ALLOW
Config:
access-group CSM_FW_ACL_ global
access-list CSM_FW_ACL_ advanced permit ip any any rule-id 268435457
access-list CSM_FW_ACL_ remark rule-id 268435457: ACCESS POLICY: AC
   Policy - Mandatory/1
access-list CSM_FW_ACL_ remark rule-id 268435457: L7 RULE: Traffic Selection
Additional Information:
 This packet will be sent to snort for additional processing where a verdict will be
   reached

Phase: 5
Type: CONN-SETTINGS
Subtype:
Result: ALLOW
Config:
class-map class-default
 match any
policy-map global_policy
 class class-default
   set connection advanced-options UM_STATIC_TCP_MAP
service-policy global_policy global
Additional Information:

Phase: 6
Type: NAT
Subtype: per-session
Result: ALLOW
Config:
Additional Information:

Phase: 7
Type: IP-OPTIONS
Subtype:
Result: ALLOW
Config:
Additional Information:

Phase: 8
Type: NAT
Subtype: rpf-check
Result: ALLOW
Config:
object network Serv-Real-172.16.1.10
```

```
  nat (DMZ_INTERFACE,OUTSIDE_INTERFACE) static Serv-Mask-203.0.113.2 service tcp
  ssh 2200
Additional Information:


Phase: 9
Type: NAT
Subtype: per-session
Result: ALLOW
Config:
Additional Information:


Phase: 10
Type: IP-OPTIONS
Subtype:
Result: ALLOW
Config:
Additional Information:


Phase: 11
Type: FLOW-CREATION
Subtype:
Result: ALLOW
Config:
Additional Information:
New flow created with id 505, packet dispatched to next module


Phase: 12
Type: EXTERNAL-INSPECT
Subtype:
Result: ALLOW
Config:
Additional Information:
Application: 'SNORT Inspect'


Phase: 13
Type: SNORT
Subtype:
Result: ALLOW
Config:
Additional Information:
Snort Verdict: (pass-packet) allow this packet


Phase: 14
Type: ROUTE-LOOKUP
```

```
Subtype: Resolve Egress Interface
Result: ALLOW
Config:
Additional Information:
found next-hop 172.16.1.10 using egress ifc  DMZ_INTERFACE


Phase: 15
Type: ADJACENCY-LOOKUP
Subtype: next-hop and adjacency
Result: ALLOW
Config:
Additional Information:
adjacency Active
next-hop mac address a4ba.db9f.9460 hits 5205


Result:
input-interface: OUTSIDE_INTERFACE
input-status: up
input-line-status: up
output-interface: DMZ_INTERFACE
output-status: up
output-line-status: up
Action: allow



1 packet shown
>
```

Instead of using the translated address, if you attempt to connect using the original IP address, the connection attempt should fail. To verify it, you can use the command shown in Example 22-16, which analyzes the tracing data of a captured packet. FTD captures the packet when an external host attempts to connect to the internal DMZ server using its original IP address, but the attempt fails.

Example 22-16   *Analyzing a Packet (Where the Packet Does Not Match a Rule)*

```
> show capture ssh_traffic_outside packet-number 1 trace

6 packets captured

  1: 05:19:16.438255       203.0.113.10.48556 > 172.16.1.10.22:
 S 1315278899:1315278899(0) win 29200 <mss 1460,sackOK,timestamp 19855229 0,
 nop,wscale 7>
Phase: 1
Type: CAPTURE
```

```
Subtype:
Result: ALLOW
Config:
Additional Information:
MAC Access list


Phase: 2
Type: ACCESS-LIST
Subtype:
Result: ALLOW
Config:
Implicit Rule
Additional Information:
MAC Access list


Phase: 3
Type: ROUTE-LOOKUP
Subtype: Resolve Egress Interface
Result: ALLOW
Config:
Additional Information:
found next-hop 172.16.1.10 using egress ifc   DMZ_INTERFACE


Phase: 4
Type: ACCESS-LIST
Subtype: log
Result: ALLOW
Config:
access-group CSM_FW_ACL_ global
access-list CSM_FW_ACL_ advanced permit ip any any rule-id 268435457
access-list CSM_FW_ACL_ remark rule-id 268435457: ACCESS POLICY: AC
   Policy - Mandatory/1
access-list CSM_FW_ACL_ remark rule-id 268435457: L7 RULE: Traffic Selection
Additional Information:
 This packet will be sent to snort for additional processing where a verdict will be
   reached


Phase: 5
Type: CONN-SETTINGS
Subtype:
Result: ALLOW
Config:
class-map class-default
 match any
```

```
policy-map global_policy
 class class-default
  set connection advanced-options UM_STATIC_TCP_MAP
service-policy global_policy global
Additional Information:


Phase: 6
Type: NAT
Subtype: per-session
Result: ALLOW
Config:
Additional Information:


Phase: 7
Type: IP-OPTIONS
Subtype:
Result: ALLOW
Config:
Additional Information:


Phase: 8
Type: NAT
Subtype: rpf-check
Result: DROP
Config:
object network Serv-Real-172.16.1.10
 nat (DMZ_INTERFACE,OUTSIDE_INTERFACE) static Serv-Mask-203.0.113.2 service tcp
  ssh 2200
Additional Information:


Result:
input-interface: OUTSIDE_INTERFACE
input-status: up
input-line-status: up
output-interface: DMZ_INTERFACE
output-status: up
output-line-status: up
Action: drop
Drop-reason: (acl-drop) Flow is denied by configured rule


1 packet shown
>
```

Summary

This chapter describes various types of NAT on an FTD device. It shows the steps to configure a NAT rule and demonstrates how FTD can leverage NAT technology to masquerade internal IP addresses in a real-world scenario.

Quiz

1. Which NAT technique allows you to translate one external destination IP address to multiple internal hosts?

   a. Static NAT

   b. Dynamic NAT

   c. PAT

   d. All of the above

2. Which NAT section has highest priority during rule evaluation?

   a. NAT Rules Before

   b. Auto NAT Rules

   c. NAT Rules After

   d. All of them have the same priority

3. Which command enables you to determine whether a connection matches a NAT rule and how many times it has matched?

   a. **show nat**

   b. **show nat detail**

   c. **show xlate detail**

   d. **show conn detail**

4. After you deploy a new NAT policy, if a connection still uses a rule from the prior version of the NAT policy, how could you ensure that FTD will use the new policy?

   a. Deploy the NAT policy one more time.

   b. Make the NAT rule more specific.

   c. Clear the current translation table.

   d. All of the above.

Answers to the Review Questions

Chapter 2

1. d
2. b
3. c
4. a
5. a
6. b
7. c
8. d

Chapter 3

1. b
2. d
3. b
4. d
5. b

Chapter 4

1. b
2. d

3. d

4. c

5. b

6. c

7. d

Chapter 5

1. c

2. c

3. d

4. b

5. d

Chapter 6

1. c

2. d

3. d

4. d

5. d

6. c

Chapter 7

1. b

2. c

3. c

4. d

5. c

6. c

Chapter 8

1. c
2. b
3. c
4. d

Chapter 9

1. d
2. c
3. d
4. c

Chapter 10

1. d
2. c
3. a
4. c

Chapter 11

1. d
2. d
3. b
4. c

Chapter 12

1. c
2. b
3. d
4. b

Chapter 13

1. d
2. d
3. d
4. c

Chapter 14

1. d
2. b
3. c
4. d

Chapter 15

1. c
2. d
3. c
4. d

Chapter 16

1. b
2. c
3. c
4. c

Chapter 17

1. d
2. b
3. c
4. b

Chapter 18

1. d
2. c
3. c
4. d

Chapter 19

1. c
2. d
3. c
4. d

Chapter 20

1. d
2. b
3. d
4. c

Chapter 21

1. d
2. d
3. c
4. d

Chapter 22

1. a
2. a
3. b
4. c

Generating and Collecting Troubleshooting Files Using the GUI

The Firepower System allows you to collect copies of various logs and configuration files so that you can investigate any technical issues offline or send them to Cisco for advanced analysis. In this appendix, you will learn the procedures to generate and collect troubleshooting files from the Firepower Management Center (FMC) and Firepower Threat Defense (FTD).

Generating Troubleshooting Files with the GUI

You can use the GUI to generate troubleshooting files from both the FMC and any managed FTD device. Here are the steps to follow:

Step 1. Navigate to **System > Health > Monitor.** The Appliance Status Summary appears, in which you can view the overall health status of all the managed devices as well as the FMC (see Figure B-1).

Step 2. Click on the name of an appliance from which you want to collect troubleshooting files. The Module Status Summary appears.

Tip If you do not see your device in the Appliance Status Summary, expand an arrow key next to the status counts (refer to Figure B-1). This page does not display an appliance if the health status is normal.

Step 3. When you see the buttons Generate Troubleshooting Files and Advanced Troubleshooting next to the appliance name, click the **Generate Troubleshooting Files** button. The Troubleshooting Options window appears (see Figure B-2).

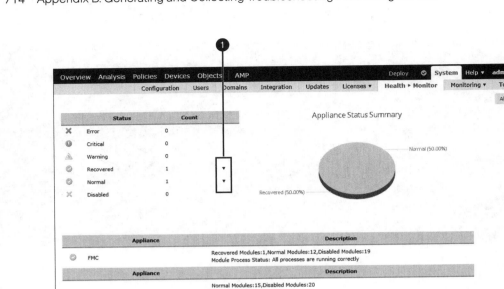

Figure B-1   *Health Monitor Page Showing a Summary of the Appliance Health Status*

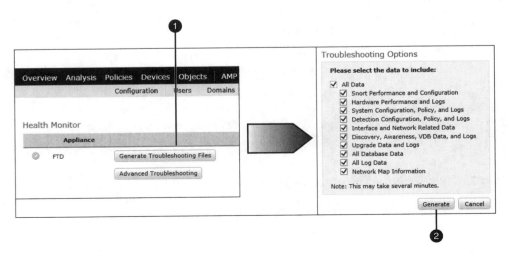

Figure B-2   *Clicking the Generate Troubleshooting Files Button to Get Data Choices*

Step 4. In the Troubleshooting Options window, select the data you want to include in the troubleshooting files. Click the **Generate** button to begin the process. Depending on the volume of events in the database and the sizes of various files, a Firepower system can take several minutes to complete the task.

> **Tip** Selecting the All Data check box allows a Firepower system to include a copy of all of the important configurations and log files in a compressed file (in .tar.gz format). It ensures that any necessary troubleshooting data is not left unidentified during the initial analysis.

Step 5. To view the status in real time, click the health status icon (in the right-top corner), and go to the Tasks tab.

Step 6. When the troubleshooting files are generated, click the **Click to retrieve generated files** download link to begin the download (see Figure B-3).

Click this link to download the files to your desktop.

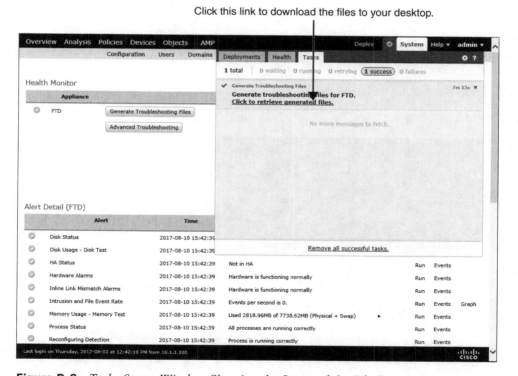

Figure B-3 *Tasks Status Window Showing the Status of the File Generation Process*

Generating and Collecting Troubleshooting Files Using the CLI

Although using the GUI is the preferred method of generating troubleshooting files, in some circumstances, generating the files using the CLI may be the only choice (for example, when the FMC is inaccessible via the GUI or when the registration between the FMC and FTD fails).

The commands to generate troubleshooting files are different at the FMC CLI and at the FTD CLI, as their shells are different. In addition, once the troubleshooting files are generated, there are multiple ways to transfer them from a Firepower system to your desktop. In the following sections, you will learn the available options and see examples.

Generating Troubleshooting Files at the FTD CLI

To generate troubleshooting files on an FTD device using the CLI, run the **system generate-troubleshoot** command at the shell. Use the **all** parameter with the command to include all the data in the .tar.gz file.

Example C-1 demonstrates the use of the **system generate-troubleshoot all** command that creates troubleshooting files at the FTD CLI.

Example C-1 *Generating Troubleshooting Files at the FTD CLI*

```
> system generate-troubleshoot all
Starting /usr/local/sf/bin/sf_troubleshoot.pl...
Please, be patient.  This may take several minutes.
The troubleshoot option code specified is ALL.
getting filenames from [/ngfw/usr/local/sf/etc/db_updates/index]
getting filenames from [/ngfw/usr/local/sf/etc/db_updates/base-6.1.0]
Troubleshooting information successfully created at /ngfw/var/common/
  results-08-10-2017--201713.tar.gz
>
```

Once a .tar.gz file is created, you can view the file status by using the **file list** command.

```
> file list
Aug 10 20:23          73603794  /results-08-10-2017--201713.tar.gz
>
```

Any files you see in the **file list** command output can be copied into your desktop using either of two methods:

■ Using the File Download functionality in the FMC GUI.

■ Using the **file secure-copy** command at the FTD CLI.

Downloading a File by Using the GUI

You can use the FMC GUI to copy a file from FTD. Here are the steps to accomplish that:

Step 1.   Go to **System > Health > Monitor** and select the appliance from which you want to copy the file.

Step 2.   Click the **Advanced Troubleshooting** button. The File Download page appears.

Step 3.   Enter the name of the file you want to download (you do not need to include the full path; just enter the filename). Click the **Download** button.

Step 4.   When the system prompts you to download the file to your desktop, click **Save**.

Figure C-1 shows the steps to download the FTD troubleshooting files in the FMC GUI. Note that only the filename is entered in the form.

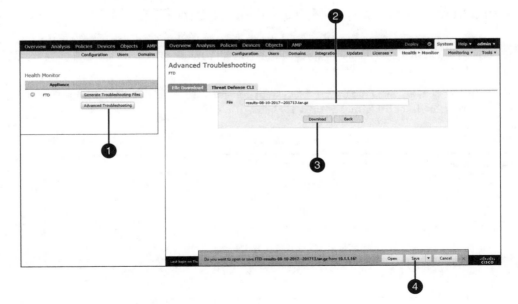

Figure C-1   *Downloading a File from an FTD via FMC*

Copying a File by Using the CLI

You can run the **file secure-copy** command at the FTD CLI to copy the troubleshooting files directly to your desktop. Here is the command syntax:

```
> file secure-copy <remote_IP> <remote_username> <remote_folder> <local_filename_
  on_FTD>
```

And here is an example of using the command:

```
> file secure-copy 10.1.1.100 admin /home/folder results-08-10-2017--201713.tar.gz
```

After you copy a file, you can delete it to free up the disk space. Run the **file delete** command as below:

```
> file delete results-08-10-2017--201713.tar.gz
Really remove file results-08-10-2017--201713.tar.gz?
Please enter 'YES' or 'NO': YES
>
```

Generating Troubleshooting Files at the FMC CLI

To generate troubleshooting files at the FMC CLI, run the **sf_troubleshoot.pl** command with administrative privilege.

Example C-2 shows the use of the **sf_troubleshoot.pl** command, which creates troubleshooting files at the FMC CLI.

Example C-2   *Generating Troubleshooting Files at the FMC CLI*

```
admin@FMC:~$ sudo sf_troubleshoot.pl
Starting /usr/local/sf/bin/sf_troubleshoot.pl...
Please, be patient.  This may take several minutes.
getting filenames from [/usr/local/sf/etc/db_updates/index]
getting filenames from [/usr/local/sf/etc/db_updates/base-6.1.0]
Troubleshooting information successfully created at /var/common/
  results-08-10-2017--184001.tar.gz
admin@FMC:~$
```

Once a .tar.gz file is created, it is stored in the /var/common/ directory. You can view the file status by using the **ls** command.

Example C-3 shows confirmation that the troubleshooting file is generated and stored in the /var/common folder in .tar.gz format.

Example C-3 *Location of the FMC Troubleshooting File*

```
admin@FMC:~$ ls -halp /var/common/
total 115M
drwxrwxr-x  2 admin detection 4.0K Aug 10 18:42 ./
drwxr-xr-x 17 root        4.0K Mar 28  2016 ../
-rw-r--r-- 1 root  root      115M Aug 10 18:42 results-08-10-2017--184001.tar.gz
admin@FMC:~$
```

To copy the file from the FMC CLI to your desktop, you can use the File Download feature on the GUI of the FMC. The processes are identical to the steps you followed for the FTD file transfer in the previous section. Alternatively, you can use the **scp** (Secure Copy over SSH protocol) command at the FMC CLI, which has the following syntax:

```
admin@FMC:~$ sudo scp <local_filename_on_FMC><remote_username>@<remote_IP>:
  <remote_folder>
```

Here is an example of using this command:

```
admin@FMC:~$ sudo scp /var/common/results-08-10-2017--184001.tar.gz
admin@10.1.1.100:/home/folder
```

After you copy a file, you can delete it to free up disk space. To do so, run the **rm** command with administrative privilege:

```
admin@FMC:~$ sudo rm /var/common/results-08-10-2017--184001.tar.gz
Password:
admin@FMC:~$
```

Index

Symbols

A

B

M

W-X-Y-Z

REGISTER YOUR PRODUCT at CiscoPress.com/register
Access Additional Benefits and SAVE 35% on Your Next Purchase

- Download available product updates.
- Access bonus material when applicable.
- Receive exclusive offers on new editions and related products.
  (Just check the box to hear from us when setting up your account.)
- Get a coupon for 35% for your next purchase, valid for 30 days.
  Your code will be available in your Cisco Press cart. (You will also find
  it in the Manage Codes section of your account page.)

Registration benefits vary by product. Benefits will be listed on your account page
under Registered Products.

CiscoPress.com – Learning Solutions for Self-Paced Study, Enterprise, and the Classroom
Cisco Press is the Cisco Systems authorized book publisher of Cisco networking technology,
Cisco certification self-study, and Cisco Networking Academy Program materials.

At **CiscoPress.com** you can
- Shop our books, eBooks, software, and video training.
- Take advantage of our special offers and promotions (ciscopress.com/promotions).
- Sign up for special offers and content newsletters (ciscopress.com/newsletters).
- Read free articles, exam profiles, and blogs by information technology experts.
- Access thousands of free chapters and video lessons.

Connect with Cisco Press – Visit CiscoPress.com/community
Learn about Cisco Press community events and programs.

Cisco Press